S0-BQZ-748

JOURNAL FOR THE STUDY OF THE OLD TESTAMENT
SUPPLEMENT SERIES
170

Editors
David J.A. Clines
Philip R. Davies

Executive Editor
John Jarick

Editorial Board
Richard J. Coggins, Alan Cooper, Tamara C. Eskenazi,
J. Cheryl Exum, John Goldingay, Robert P. Gordon,
Norman K. Gottwald, Andrew D.H. Mayes, Carol Meyers,
Patrick D. Miller

Sheffield Academic Press

Traditional Techniques in Classical Hebrew Verse

Wilfred G.E. Watson

Journal for the Study of the Old Testament
Supplement Series 170

This retrospective is dedicated to Helen and Claire

Copyright © 1994 Sheffield Academic Press

Published by
Sheffield Academic Press Ltd
Mansion House
19 Kingfield Road
Sheffield, S11 9AS
England

Typeset by Sheffield Academic Press
and
Printed on acid-free paper in Great Britain
by Bookcraft
Midsomer Norton, Somerset

British Library Cataloguing in Publication Data

A catalogue record for this book is available
from the British Library

ISBN 1-85075-459-4

CONTENTS

Preface

The articles collected here span several years of study and some of them appeared before the publication of *Classical Hebrew Poetry*. There are several reasons for reprinting them here. It is convenient to have together in one volume studies which are scattered in several periodicals and in various collected works. Also, several articles on a single topic can now be read together. In addition, the present work provides an opportunity for compiling indexes and making corrections and it has been possible to bring these studies up-to-date with more recent interpretations and additional bibliography. As well as reprints of articles already published there are three new studies: on ethnopoetics and Hebrew verse; on parallelism in the Song of Songs and on a metaphor in Jeremiah.

There are now quite a number of treatises and manuals on Hebrew poetry. It would seem, therefore, that there is little need for additional books on the subject. Even so, there is room for more work. The syntax of poetry, in particular, requires further study. There is, of course, M. O'Connor's monumental work, *Hebrew Verse Structure*, which addresses this topic. In addition, two significant studies deserve to be mentioned. They are Greenstein's paper on parallelism in Hebrew (with some reference to Ugaritic) and de Moor's paper on the syntax of Ugaritic verse. Both make important contributions to our understanding of parallelism in terms of the use of ellipsis ('gapping'). Other areas requiring research include the macrostructure of Hebrew (and Ugaritic) verse, the relationship between verse and prose, figurative language, especially imagery, and, in general, overall interpretations of complete compositions.

Among those who suggested this reprint I would like to mention Professor David T. Tsumura and several of the students at Kampen. My thanks go to Sheffield Academic Press, in particular to Professor David J.A. Clines, for accepting this work for publication and to Steve Barganski for his thoughtful editing.

ACKNOWLEDGMENTS

Grateful acknowledgment is made to the publishers for granting permission to reprint the following: 'Introductions to Discourse in Ugaritic Narrative Verse', *AuOr* 1 (1983), pp. 253-61; 'The Ahiqar Sayings: Some Marginal Comments', *AuOr* 2 (1984), pp. 253-61; 'The Hidden Simile in Psalm 133', *Bib* 60 (1979), pp. 108-109; 'The Metaphor in Job 10,17', *Bib* 63 (1982), pp. 255-57; 'Allusion, Irony and Wordplay in Micah 1,7', *Bib* 65 (1984), pp. 103-105; 'Internal Parallelism in Classical Hebrew Verse', *Bib* 66 (1985), pp. 365-84; 'The Structure of 1 Sam 3', *BZ* 28 (published by Verlag Ferdinand Schöningh, 1984), pp. 90-93; 'Further Examples of Semantic-Sonant Chiasmus', *CBQ* 46 (1984), pp. 31-33; 'Splitting Hairs in Babylon and Israel', *IBS* 4 (1982), pp. 193-97; 'Gender-Matched Synonymous Parallelism in the OT', *JBL* 99 (1980), pp. 321-41; 'The Character of Ugaritic Poetry', *JNSL* 11 (1983), pp. 157-69; 'Internal or Half-line Parallelism Once More', *Liber Annuus* 39 (1989), pp. 27-36; 'An Unrecognised Hyperbole in *Krt*', *Or* 48 (Rome: Pontificial Biblical Institute Press, 1979), pp. 112-17; 'Middle-Eastern Forerunners to a Folktale Motif', *Or* 53 (Rome: Pontificial Biblical Institute Press, 1984), pp. 333-36; 'Internal Parallelism in Ugaritic Verse', *SEL* 1 (1984), pp. 53-67; 'Delaying Devices in Ugaritic Verse', in *Cananea Selecta: Festschrift für Oswald Loretz zum 60. Geburtstag* (= *SEL* 5 [1988]) (Verona: Essedue edizioni), pp. 207-18; 'The Word Pair "Eye(s)" // "Heart" Once More', *SEL* 9 (1992), pp. 27-31; 'Quasi-Acrostics in Ugaritic Poetry', *UF* 12 (1980), pp. 445-47; 'Gender-Matched Synonymous Parallelism in Ugaritic Poetry', *UF* 13 (1981), pp. 181-87; 'Reversed Word-Pairs in Ugaritic Poetry', *UF* 13 (1981), pp. 189-92; 'Trends in the Development of Classical Hebrew Poetry: A Comparative Study', *UF* 14 (1982), pp. 265-77; 'Strophic Chiasmus in Ugaritic Poetry', *UF* 15 (1983), pp. 259-70; 'Apostrophe in the Aqhat Poem', *UF* 16 (1984), pp. 323-26; 'Internal Parallelism in Ugaritic Verse: Further Examples', *UF* 17 (1985), pp. 345-56; 'Antithesis in Ugaritic Verse', *UF* 18 (1986), pp. 413-19; 'Internal (Half-Line) Parallelism in Ugaritic Once More', *UF* 20 (1988), pp. 365-74; 'Parallelism with *Qtl* in Ugaritic', *UF* 21 (1989), pp. 435-42; 'Abrupt Speech in Ugaritic Narrative Verse', *UF* 22 (1990), pp. 415-23; 'Tribute to Tyre (Is XXIII 7)', *VT* 26 (1976), pp. 371-74; 'A Note on Staircase Parallelism', *VT* 33 (1983), pp. 510-12; 'Reflexes of Akkadian Incantations in Hosea', *VT* 34 (1984), pp. 242-47; 'Internal or Half-Line Parallelism in Classical Hebrew Again', *VT* 39 (1989), pp. 44-66; 'Problems and Solutions in Hebrew Verse: A Survey of Recent Work', *VT* 43 (1993), pp. 372-84; 'More on Metathetic Parallelism', *WO* 19 (1988), pp. 40-44; 'An Unusual Prostration Formula in Ugaritic Akkadian', *WO* 24 (1993), pp. 39-41;

'The Unnoticed Word-Pair "eye(s)" // "heart"', *ZAW* 101 (1989), pp. 398-408; 'The Hebrew Word-pair *'sp // qbṣ*', *ZAW* 96 (1984), pp. 426-34; 'Chiastic Patterns in Biblical Hebrew Poetry', in J.W. Welch (ed.), *Chiasmus in Antiquity* (Hildesheim: Gerstenberg, 1981), pp. 118-68; 'Poetry, Hebrew', in R.J. Coggins and J.L. Houlden (eds.), *A Dictionary of Biblical Interpretation* (London: SCM Press; Philadelphia: Trinity Press International, 1990), pp. 553-54.

ABBREVIATIONS

AfO	*Archiv für Orientforschung*
AJSLL	*American Journal of Semitic Languages and Literature*
ANLR	*Rendiconti dell' Accademia Nazionale dei Lincei (Roma)*
AnSt	*Anatolian Studies*
AnOr	*Analecta orientalia*
AOAT	Alter Orient und Altes Testament
AOS	American Oriental Series
ARM	Archives Royales de Mari
ArOr	*Archiv orientální*
AuOr	*Aula Orientalis*
BA	*Biblical Archaeologist*
BASOR	*Bulletin of the American Schools of Oriental Research*
BASORSup	*Bulletin of the American Schools of Oriental Research*, Supplements
BBB	Bonner biblische Beiträge
BETL	Bibliotheca ephemeridum theologicarum lovaniensium
BHK	R. Kittel (ed.), *Biblica hebraica*
Bib	*Biblica*
BibOr	Biblica et orientalia
BKAT	Biblischer Kommentar: Altes Testament
BO	*Bibliotheca orientalis*
BSO(A)S	*Bulletin of the School of Oriental (and African) Studies*
BZ	*Biblische Zeitschrift*
BZAW	Beihefte zur ZAW
CAD	*The Assyrian Dictionary of the Oriental Institute of the University of Chicago*
CAT	Commentaire de l'Ancien Testament
CBQ	*Catholic Biblical Quarterly*
CTA	A. Herdner (ed.), *Corpus des tablettes en cunéiformes alphabétiques*
EI	*Eretz Israel*
GKC	*Gesenius' Hebrew Grammar*, ed. E. Kautzsch, trans. A.E. Cowley
HAR	*Hebrew Annual Review*
HAT	Handbuch zum Alten Testament
HR	*History of Religions*

HSM	Harvard Semitic Monographs
HTR	*Harvard Theological Review*
HUCA	*Hebrew Union College Annual*
IBS	*Irish Biblical Studies*
ICC	International Critical Commentary
IDBSup	*IDB*, Supplementary Volume
IEJ	*Israel Exploration Journal*
IJAL	*International Journal of Applied Linguistics*
JANESCU	*Journal of the Ancient Near Eastern Society of Columbia University*
JAOS	*Journal of the American Oriental Society*
JBL	*Journal of Biblical Literature*
JCS	*Journal of Cuneiform Studies*
JEOL	*Jaarbericht...ex oriente lux*
JETS	*Journal of the Evangelical Theological Society*
JJS	*Journal of Jewish Studies*
JNES	*Journal of Near Eastern Studies*
JNSL	*Journal of Northwest Semitic Languages*
JPOS	*Journal of the Palestine Oriental Society*
JQR	*Jewish Quarterly Review*
JSS	*Journal of Semitic Studies*
JTS	*Journal of Theological Studies*
KAI	H. Donner and W. Röllig, *Kanaanäische und aramäische Inschriften*
KAT	Kommentar zum Alten Testament
LA	*Liber Annuus*
MIO	*Mitteilungen des Instituts für Orientforschung*
MVAG	Mitteilungen der Vorderasiatisch-ägyptischen Gesellschaft
NCB	New Century Bible
OLP	*Orientalia Lovaniensia Periodica*
Or	*Orientalia*
OTS	*Oudtestamentische Studiën*
PEQ	*Palestine Exploration Quarterly*
PRU	*Le Palais royal d'Ugarit*
RA	*Revue d'assyriologie et d'archéologie orientale*
RB	*Revue biblique*
RevQ	*Revue de Qumran*
RSP	L. Fisher (ed.), *Ras Shamra Parallels*, I-II; S. Rummel (ed.), *Ras Shamra Parallels*, III
SAOC	Studies in Ancient Oriental Civilizations
SBLDS	SBL Dissertation Series
SBLMS	SBL Monograph Series
ScrB	*Scripture Bulletin*
SEÅ	*Svensk exegetisk årsbok*
SEL	*Studi epigrafici e linguistici sul Vicino Oriente antico*

TGUOS	Transactions of the Glasgow University Oriental Society
UF	*Ugarit-Forschungen*
UT	C.H. Gordon, *Ugaritic Textbook*
VT	*Vetus Testamentum*
VTSup	*Vetus Testamentum*, Supplements
WBC	World Biblical Commentary
WO	*Die Welt des Orients*
ZA	*Zeitschrift für Assyriologie*
ZAW	*Zeitschrift für die alttestamentliche Wissenschaft*
ZDMG	*Zeitschrift der deutschen morgenländischen Gesellschaft*
ZDPV	*Zeitschrift des deutschen Palästina-Vereins*

Chapter 1

INTRODUCTION

1. *Hebrew Poetry*[1]

In some translations of the Bible and even in some printed editions of the Hebrew text there is no indication that much of the OT is in verse. While the Psalms have always been considered to be poetry, as has Proverbs, it is now evident that nearly all the prophetic books are also in verse. This includes most of Isaiah, large sections of Jeremiah and Ezekiel, almost all of Hosea, and so on. Whether or not the non-narrative parts of the OT (that is, excluding the Pentateuch, Joshua to Kings, Chronicles, Ezra–Nehemiah and Esther) are verse has been a matter of debate since at least the first century BC. Now that our models are not classical Greek and Latin verse but the poetic traditions of the ancient Near East, the debate, in essence, has been resolved. Hebrew poetry is very like the poetry of ancient Syria (written in Ugaritic on clay tablets dating to approximately the fourteenth century BC) and not unlike Assyrian and Babylonian verse. The surprising aspect of the OT now is why the narrative sections are not in verse; the bulk of Ugaritic literature, for instance, is narrative verse.

Scholars have isolated several fragments of poetry in the prose books (e.g. Exod. 16.12; Num. 14.2) and there are also complete poems (Gen. 49; Deut. 32 and 33; Judg. 5; etc.). Generally speaking, however, the division between books in verse and books in prose is clear, even allowing for the short passages identified as verse. It follows, therefore, that passages and books in verse cannot be properly understood if they are read simply as prose. 'In interpreting the

1. First published in R.J. Coggins and J.L. Houlden (eds.), *A Dictionary of Biblical Interpretation* (London: SCM Press; Philadelphia: Trinity Press International, 1990), pp. 553-54.

prophetic texts we need to make allowance for the prophets' use of exalted and poetic language...and their use of symbols, metaphors and ambiguous diction'.[2] In other words, too literal an interpretation is misguided; poetry must be read and understood on its own terms.

Here only a brief indication can be given of how recognizing poetic devices and techniques can lead to correct interpretation. Special attention will be paid to recent developments, some still controversial, since they are not all included in the available textbooks. Awareness of such devices, techniques and structural patterns, many of which have come to light from comparison with ancient Near Eastern verse, is significant, but always within the overall evaluation of a poem or segment of verse. While it is now accepted that parallelism is fundamental to Hebrew poetry, the usual classification of parallelism as synonymous, antithetic or synthetic is far from accurate and complete. Here some additional comments will be made on parallelism and other topics and several texts will be discussed by way of illustration.

It is now evident that often synonymous parallelism between consecutive lines in a couplet is really parallelism of greater precision: the B-line specifies the A-line in some way. In Job 7.13 the second line, 'My bed will ease my complaint', is narrower in meaning than the first: 'If I say "My couch will comfort me"'. Similarly, Ezek. 6.6, Ps. 34.13 and so on. In such cases the poet is not merely repeating himself in different words but correcting his focus.

In some parallel word-pairs, such as the numerical pairings 'seven' // 'eight', the focus is on only one of these numbers. In Job 5.19, 'He will deliver you from six troubles/in seven, there shall no evil touch you', 'seven' symbolizes any kind of trouble and the accompanying 'six' is unimportant. The same applies to 'mother' in Prov. 4.3 where matching 'father' (in the first line) is the really significant term.

Another type of parallelism explains the difficult verse Job 38.30. If the final verbs are understood as interchanged then the couplet makes sense: 'Like a stone the waters become hidden/and the surface of the deep is frozen' (contrast RSV). First water freezes, then the surface is obscured from view. This kind of switch, called metathetic parallelism, also explains Ps. 35.7, Mic. 2.1, Isa. 17.5 and so on.

Beside antithetic parallelism (e.g. Prov. 12.10) antithesis is also effective on a large scale. Judg. 5.2-31, which at first reading appears

2. J. Lindblom, *Prophecy in Ancient Israel* (Oxford: Basil Blackwell, 1962), p. 363.

to be an impressionistic composition, is in reality a carefully structured series of antitheses (powerful God/miserable people; the willing and unwilling tribes; curse and blessing; and the final contrast: Jael victorious/Sisera's mother vainly awaiting victory), closed by a summary couplet in antithetic parallelism: 'So perish all your enemies, O Yahweh/but may your friends be like the emergence of the sun at its strongest'. See also Jer. 10.2-16 and Psalm 73.

A recent advance in techniques of interpretation is the discovery of word-pairs common to the OT and to ancient Near Eastern literature. One such is 'to recover' // 'to get up' in Hos. 6.2. There it refers neither to covenant renewal nor to resurrection but to healing, since the same word-pair in Babylonian also denotes healing.

Some poems are set out as acrostics, each of the 22 lines or sets of lines beginning with a different letter of the alphabet. One purpose of such poems was to include everything 'from *aleph* to *taw*' (the first and final letters of the Hebrew alphabet). This is particularly evident in Psalm 119 where the psalmist is demonstrating how he observes God's law in everything he does, in every way and at all times. Another purpose may have been to impose some sort of order on seemingly disparate elements. An additional implication is that acrostic poems (Pss. 9–10; 25; 34; Lam. 1–4 etc.) should be interpreted as complete units and not as mere compilations.

In chiasmus a sequence (ABC...) is followed by the same sequence in reverse (...CBA) focusing attention on the central element. For example, chiastic patterning shows the core of Psalm 26 to be vv. 6-8 which describe the officiant 'going round' Yahweh's altar, which in turn provides the setting (the temple) and the genre (private prayer). Also, it is at the centre of his chiastic prologue (Job 32.6-10) that Elihu makes the crucial observation that wisdom comes from inspiration and is not merely the concomitant of age.

In one form of wordplay the same word is repeated, the second time with a different meaning, for example Job 11.7, 'Can you understand (*mṣ'*) the designs of God/or can you attain (*mṣ'*) the perfection of Shadday?' The second line goes beyond the first: Job cannot even grasp the divine plan let alone reach divine perfection. Elsewhere repetition is not simply monotonous, but highlights the key word of a poem, for instance, 'land' in Jer. 2.6-7.

Nah. 2.14, 'I will burn your chariots in smoke/and the sword will devour your "young lions"', comes in the context of war, and so a literal meaning for 'young lions' must be excluded. The expression is metaphorical for 'warriors' (cf. 2.3). The same applies to 'the beast of the reeds' and 'the herd of bulls with the calves of the peoples' (Ps. 68.31 EVV 30), which evidently refer to Israel's enemies. 'Woe to...the notable men at the head of the nations...they shall now be at the head of those going into exile' (Amos 6.1-7). The ironic aspect of the mock-lamentation—those first in rank will be the first to go into exile—is reinforced by the mention of 'the first-class perfumes' (v. 6) which they used.

Form cannot be dissociated from content, as these examples show, and appreciation of poetic technique can provide crucial clues to the correct interpretation of passages in verse.

2. *Problems and Solutions in Hebrew Verse: A Survey of Recent Work*[3]

2.1. *Introduction: Some General Trends*

Since the publication of *Classical Hebrew Poetry*[4] substantial progress has been made in the study of verse traditions in Hebrew, Akkadian and Ugaritic. Some account of what has been achieved will be presented here.[5]

2.1.1. *Hebrew*. The 1980s saw an upsurge in publications on Hebrew verse, notably general books by Alonso Schökel,[6] Alter,[7] Kugel[8] and O'Connor.[9]

3. First published in *VT* 43/3 (1993), pp. 372-84.

4. W.G.E. Watson, *Classical Hebrew Poetry: A Guide to its Techniques* (JSOTSup, 26; Sheffield: JSOT Press, 1984; 2nd edn, 1986). The second edition incorporated some minor corrections and several additional pages of bibliography. The more significant reviews are L. Alonso Schökel, *Bib* 67 (1986), pp. 120-24; A. Berlin, *JAOS* 106 (1986), pp. 578-80; J. Healey, *ScrB* 17 (1987), pp. 49-50; A. Niccacci, *LA* 35 (1985), pp. 470-73; H. Simian-Yofre, *AuOr* 6 (1988), pp. 285-87; W.J. Urbrock, *JBL* 106 (1987), pp. 328-30; and J. Wansbrough, *BSO(A)S* 50 (1987), pp. 360-61.

5. Versions of this talk were given at a seminar in Kampen, on 24 March 1992 and at the Erasmus Intensive Programme ('The Hebrew Bible: Exegesis and Linguistics') in Leuven, on 4 April 1992.

6. L. Alonso Schökel, *A Manual of Hebrew Poetics* (Subsidia biblica, 11; Rome: Pontificio Istituto Biblico, 1988).

7. R. Alter, *The Art of Biblical Poetry* (New York: Basic Books, 1985).

8. J.L. Kugel, *The Idea of Biblical Poetry: Parallelism and its History* (New

There were also several monographs on more specific topics: colometry,[10] parallelism,[11] antithesis,[12] chiasmus,[13] centripetal and centrifugal structures,[14] the strophe,[15] word-pairs,[16] metre[17] and repetition.[18] In addition there have been collections of articles on Hebrew verse.[19] Furthermore, there has been considerable probing

Haven: Yale University Press, 1981). For a review, see A. Cooper, 'On Reading Biblical Poetry', *Maarav* 4 (1987), pp. 221-41.

9. M. O'Connor, *Hebrew Verse Structure* (Winona Lake, IN: Eisenbrauns, 1981).

10. O. Loretz and I. Kottsieper, *Colometry in Ugaritic and Biblical Poetry: Introduction, Illustrations and Topical Bibliography* (UBL, 9; Altenberge: CIS-Verlag, 1987); W.T.W. Cloete, *Versification and Syntax in Jeremiah 2–25: Syntactical Constraints in Hebrew Colometry* (SBLDS, 117; Atlanta: Scholars Press, 1989); cf. W.T.W. Cloete, 'The Colometry of Hebrew Verse', *JNSL* 15 (1989), pp. 15-29.

11. A. Berlin, *The Dynamics of Biblical Parallelism* (Bloomington: Indiana University Press, 1985); D. Pardee, *Ugaritic and Hebrew Poetic Parallelism: A Trial Cut. (*'nt *I and Proverbs 2)* (VTSup, 39; Leiden: Brill, 1988). A.A. Ranieri, 'Studio grammaticale e semantico del parallelismo in Proverbi I–IX' (Pontificum Athenaeum Antoniarum Sectio Hierosolymitana Facultati Theologiae Studium Biblicum Franciscarum, Thesis ad Doctoratum no. 337, Jerusalem, 1993).

12. J. Krašovec, *Antithetic Structure in Biblical Hebrew Poetry* (VTSup, 35; Leiden: Brill, 1984); J.A. Loader, *Polar Structures in the Book of Qohelet* (BZAW, 152; Berlin: de Gruyter, 1979).

13. J. Welch (ed.), *Chiasmus in Antiquity* (Hildesheim: Gerstenberg, 1981).

14. D. Grossberg, *Centripetal and Centrifugal Structures in Biblical Poetry* (SBLMS, 39; Atlanta: Scholars Press, 1989).

15. P. van der Lugt, *Strofische structuren in de Bijbels-Hebreeuwse poëzie* (Dissertationes Neerlandicae, Series Theologica; Kampen: Kok, 1980).

16. Y. Avishur, *Stylistic Studies of Word-Pairs in Biblical and Ancient Semitic Literature* (AOAT, 210; Neukirchen–Vluyn: Neukirchner Verlag, 1984).

17. H.W.M. van Grol, *De versbouw in het klassieke Hebreeuws: Fundamentele verkenningen deel een: Metriek* (Katholieke Theologische Hogeschool, Amsterdam: private publication, 1986); G. Fecht, *Metrik des Hebräischen und Phönizischen* (Ägypten und Altes Testament, 19; Wiesbaden: Otto Harrassowitz, 1990).

18. E. Zurro, *Procedimientos iterativos en la poesía ugarítica y hebrea* (BibOr, 43; Rome: Biblical Institute Press, 1987).

19. D.J.A. Clines, D.M. Gunn and A.J. Hauser (eds.), *Art and Meaning: Rhetoric in Biblical Literature* (JSOTSup, 19; Sheffield: JSOT Press, 1982); E.R. Follis (ed.), *Directions in Biblical Hebrew Poetry* (JSOTSup, 40; Sheffield: JSOT Press, 1987); W. van der Meer and J.C. de Moor (eds.), *The Structural Analysis of Biblical and Canaanite Poetry* (JSOTSup, 74; Sheffield: JSOT Press, 1988).

into the differentiation between prose and verse.[20] There is, too, a welcome trend for studying poetic texts not only in respect of their smaller component units but also in terms of larger structures.[21]

2.1.2. *Akkadian*. More attention has been focused recently by Akkadian scholars on verse.[22] In a lengthy article Buccellati[23] discusses the differences between European and Mesopotamian verse traditions. Besides the Akkadian metrical system[24] he also deals with discourse analysis, compositional devices and stylistic analysis. He defines the foot, the colon, the verse and the stanza (which he calls a maximal unit), and then applies all this to the first lines of *Enūma eliš*. Significant, too, was the publication of a selection of Assyrian texts, chiefly in verse.[25]

2.1.3. *Ugaritic*. There is now a general tendency to evaluate Ugaritic poetry on its own merits, that is to say, not so much in relation to Hebrew—as exemplified by Aitken's studies on formula, theme and word-pairs.[26] Pardee's re-edition of selected Ugaritic texts

20. W. Koopmans, *Joshua 24 as Poetic Narrative* (JSOTSup, 93; Sheffield: JSOT Press, 1990) and many articles in the journals, e.g. R.D. Haak, '"Poetry" in Habakkuk 1:1–2:4?', *JAOS* 108 (1988), pp. 437-44.

21. See Grossberg, *Centripetal and Centrifugal Structures.*

22. Notably E. Reiner, *Your Thwarts in Pieces, Your Mooring Rope Cut: Poetry from Babylonia and Assyria* (Michigan: Horace H. Rackham School of Graduate Studies at the University of Michigan, 1985) as well as J.M. Sasson (ed.), *Studies in Literature from the Ancient Near East... Samuel Noah Kramer JAOS* 103 [1983], pp. 1-353). Previously, the only monograph on Akkadian verse was K. Hecker's *Das akkadische Epik* (AOATS, 8; Neukirchen–Vluyn: Neukirchner Verlag; Kevelaer: Butzon & Bercker, 1974).

23. G. Buccellati, 'On Poetry—theirs and ours', in T. Abusch, J. Huehnergard and P. Steinkeller (eds.), *Lingering over Words* (HSS, 37; Atlanta: Scholars Press, 1990), pp. 399-427.

24. According to Buccellati ('On Poetry', p. 404), there are metrical and non-metrical words; non-metrical words have no effect on the foot which can comprise one metrical word with or without additional non-metrical words.

25. A. Livingstone, *Court Poetry and Literary Miscellanea* (State Archives of Assyria, 3; Helsinki: Helsinki University Press, 1989).

26. K. Aitken, 'Oral Formulaic Composition and Theme in the Aqhat Narrative', *UF* 21 (1989), pp. 1-16; 'Word Pairs and Tradition in an Ugaritic Tale', *UF* 21 (1989), pp. 17-38; 'Formulaic Patterns for the Passing of Time in Ugaritic Narrative', *UF* 19 (1987), pp. 1-10.

is important because it includes, almost as a matter of course, a presentation and discussion of these texts as verse.[27] The narrative aspects of Ugaritic verse have also been examined.[28]

2.2. *The Methodology of Approach*

One criticism of my *Guide* made by several reviewers was that it does not apply an overall theory.[29] This is largely because scholars themselves have not yet formulated such a theory. In his review, Andersen stated, 'Until a more convincing integrated general theory is worked out which can adequately deal with [metre, stanza and strophe, parallelism] and other phenomena, a satisfactory account of the techniques of Hebrew poetry will be unattainable' ([n. 26], p. 93). Andersen himself would like to see everything come under the umbrella of 'information theory'.[30]

Another comment by reviewers regards the lack of aesthetic awareness: describing and cataloguing the techniques of a poem is not a substitute for aesthetic appreciation. Similarly, some reviews of Pardee's book[31] consider that the whole is lost in the catalogues of minute detail (various types of parallelism, listing of consonant frequencies and so on).[32] Since then there have been studies of individual poems which involve a more holistic approach.[33]

27. D. Pardee, *Les textes para-mythologiques de la 24ᵉ campagne (1961)* (Ras Shamra-Ougarit, 4; Paris: Editions Recherche sur les Civilisations, 1988).

28. T.L. Hettema, '"That it be repeated" A Narrative Analysis of *KTU* 1.23', *JEOL* 31 (1989–90), pp. 77-94.

29. T. Andersen, 'Problems in Analysing Hebrew Poetry', *East Asia Journal of Theology* 4 (1986), pp. 68-94, esp. p. 88; Berlin, review of *Classical Hebrew Poetry*.

30. In this respect the joint article by M.C.A. Korpel and J.C. de Moor, 'Fundamentals of Ugaritic and Hebrew Poetry', *UF* 18 (1986), pp. 173-212, reprinted with minor changes in Korpel and Moor (eds.), *Structural Analysis*, pp. 1-61, is important as a proposal of a large-scale hypothesis.

31. *A Trial Cut* (a comparison between a passage from the Ugaritic Baal Epic and Prov. 2).

32. I can also refer to S. Geller, 'Theory and Method in the Study of Biblical Poetry', *JQR* 73 (1982), pp. 65-77, a review article of Kugel *Biblical Poetry* and O'Connor, *Hebrew Verse Structure*, and to Z. Zevit, 'Roman Jakobson, Psycholinguistics, and Biblical Poetry', *JBL* 109 (1990), pp. 385-401 with the rebuttal by F. Landy, 'In Defense of Jakobson', *JBL* 111 (1992), pp. 105-13.

33. E.g. M.L. Barré, 'Psalm 116: Its Structure and its Enigmas', *JBL* 109 (1990), pp. 61-78. S.A. Geller, 'The Dynamics of Parallel Verse: A Poetic Analysis

It is interesting that recently in linguistics there has been some study of the cohesive character of poetic techniques. Brinton[34] reminds us of the distinction between schemes and tropes. Schemes (e.g., anaphora, anadiplosis [terrace pattern], asyndeton [omitting conjunction between clauses], ellipsis or gapping, hyperbaton [unusual word order] and so on) involve a change in *form* or *arrangement* though the meaning stays the same. Tropes (e.g., metaphor, metonymy, hyperbole, irony and so on) involve a change in *meaning*. Brinton argues that 'schemes function as cohesive devices, while at the same time they often contribute to thematic coherence' (p. 163). 'In schemes of parallelism, the repetition of structures rather than of words will create perceptible bonds between clauses of a text' (p. 171), in other words, one of the functions of parallelism is cohesion. He examines a whole range of such devices and it would be a useful exercise to transpose his findings to Hebrew.

Whereas some reviewers consider that there is too much emphasis on isolating these techniques, scholars like Brinton show how significant recognition of these schemes can be. One scholar who has gone along this road is Grossberg in his book on structural elements in Hebrew verse. As he says, 'I provide a reading that seriously addresses the whole of the relevant texts and not just individual parts like word-pairs or poetic lines'.[35]

2.3. *New or Neglected Topics*

On the other hand, there are some new topics which were not included in my *Guide*. One is 'Half-line or Internal Parallelism' on which I have written several papers (see below). This topic will not be discussed here. (I would now have to re-write much of the *Guide* to take account of half-line parallelism). However, I emphasize its importance for determining whether the basic unit in Hebrew and Ugaritic verse comprises two half-lines or a single half-line.[36]

Another topic is *metathetic parallelism*, a form of synonymous

of Deut 32:6-12', *HTR* 75 (1982), pp. 35-56; A.R. Ceresko, 'Psalm 149: Poetry, Themes (Exodus and Conquest), and Social Function', *Bib* 67 (1986), pp. 177-94 and many others.

34. L.J. Brinton, 'The Iconicity of Rhetorical Figures: "Schemes" as Devices for Textual Cohesion', *Language and Style* 21 (1988), pp. 162-90.

35. Grossberg, *Centripetal*, p. 105.

36. For the half-line as an independent colon see Korpel and de Moor, 'Fundamentals'.

parallelism where the corresponding objects and predicates are transposed. The switch is not actually effected but the sentence is read as if it had been and only then does the couplet become fully intelligible. This type of parallelism was identified by Broznick in Hebrew[37] and I added further texts from Ugaritic and Akkadian.[38] Another example in Hebrew is Isa. 29.10

wy'ṣm 't-'ynykm 't-hnby'ym	For Yahweh has poured into you
w't r'šykm hḥzym ksh	a spirit of deep sleep

Literally: 'and has shut your eyes, the prophets/and your heads, the seers, has hooded'.[39] In fact, 'closing eyes' should correspond to 'seers'—'covering heads' corresponds to 'prophets'. Possibly:

the eyes of the seers (*ḥzh*) are closed—they cannot see the future
the heads of the prophets (*nb'*) covered—they cannot speak.

Note the aspect of poetic justice: professionals are punished in a way which prevents them functioning again. This practice is known from Mesopotamia, for example blinding a diviner.[40]

Similarly, Job 38.10

w'šbr 'lyw ḥqy	When I shattered my bounds upon it,
w'sym bryḥ wdltym	I imposed bolt and doors.

To make sense of this couplet without correcting the text Dhorme suggests that the two verbs should be transposed.[41]

This type of parallelism, in fact, underlies the well-known saying from *Aḥiqar*: (*Aḥiqar* col. XVI 1)

['l th]wy l'rby ym'	[Do not s]how a Bedu the sea
w[l]ṣydny ['rt' zy mdbr]	or [a] Sidonian [the desert roads]
ky '[b]ydthm pry[n]	for their o[cc]upations are differe[nt].

37. N.M. Bronznick, '"Metathetic Parallelism":—An Unrecognized Subtype of Synonymous Parallelism', *HAR* 3 (1979), pp. 25-39.

38. See 'More on Metathetic Parallelism' in Chapter 6.

39. W.H. Irwin, *Isaiah 28–33: Translation with Philological Notes* (BibOr, 30; Rome: Pontifical Biblical Institute, 1977), p. 56.

40. An example of this is discussed by U. Jeyes, *Old Babylonian Extispicy: Omen Texts in the British Museum* (Leiden: Nederlands Instituut, 1989), p. 36; she comments, 'it was in accordance with the thinking of the times to punish a professional so that he forever after should be prevented from functioning in his task'.

41. E. Dhorme, *A Commentary on the Book of Job* (London: Nelson, 1967; ET of *Le livre de Job* [Paris: Gabalda, 1926]), pp. 578-79.

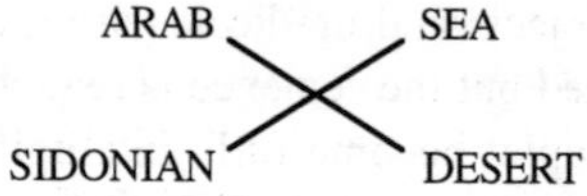

It may explain *KTU* 1.17 ii 8-9

bd(!)ni[l] pnm. tšmḫ.	While Danil's face was happy,
w'l. yṣhl pit	and above his brow gleamed etc.[42]

Margalit points out that *pit* is probably feminine and the two verbs should be interchanged.[43] Accordingly, 'While D.'s face gleamed/and above (his) forehead was happy'. Confirmation comes from Hebrew where, as Margalit mentions, the verb *ṣhl* is used with *pnym* (p. 174 n. 20).

2.3.1. *Clusters*. 'In the "cluster" the Biblical writer draws from the poetical resources available to him a number of word pairs and standard epithets and uses them to construct a complex poetic structure, or to set the background framework of the material that he is presenting.'[44] Greenfield's examples include Hos. 13.12 and Job 26.7-8 where the phrase *ṣrrt ṣpn* is being played with. He also discusses Ps. 21.3-5 in terms of passages from the Ugaritic tale of *Aqht*.

2.3.2. *Parody*. According to Yee,[45] Isaiah 14 is a parody of the dirge form as used in 2 Samuel 1. It is significant that Isaiah 14 is only fully intelligible once the element of parody is recognized. Another such parody, it can be added, is Isa. 23.7-9, a dirge over Tyre. Also, Ezek. 15.1-5 is a parody of Israel as the vinestock, on which Greenberg comments, 'Comparison of the vinestock to Jerusalem [vv. 6ff.]

42. The translation follows E. Verreet, *Modi ugaritici: Eine morpho-syntaktische Abhandlung über das Modalsystem im Ugaritischen* (Orientalia Lovaniensia Analecta, 27; Leuven: Peeters, 1988), p. 242, who shows that here there is a temporal clause. For the use of this couplet in formulaic speech introductions, cf. G. del Olmo Lete, *Anuario de Filología* 2 (1976), pp. 234-36.

43. B. Margalit, *The Ugaritic Poem of Aqht* (BZAW, 182; Berlin: de Gruyter, 1989), p. 174: 'for grammatical reasons we must suppose that in line 9 the (masc.) *pnm* has interchanged with the fem. *pit*'. However his own reconstruction of the whole couplet is hypothetical.

44. J.C. Greenfield, 'The "Cluster" in Biblical Poetry', *Maarav* 5–6 (1990), pp. 159-68.

45. G.A. Yee, 'The Anatomy of Biblical Parody: The Dirge Form in 2 Samuel 1 and Isaiah 14', *CBQ* 50 (1988), pp. 565-86.

is a grotesque distortion of the traditional use of the vine as a figure for Israel'.[46] In fact, as Greenberg remarks, the oracle approaches allegory here.

2.3.3. *Antithesis* is more than antithetic parallelism. Alonso Schökel states, 'In Hebrew poetry...antithesis is one of the most important stylistic techniques'.[47] In fact, he devotes a whole chapter to 'Antithesis and Polarised Expression'. Krašovec went further and wrote a whole book on the topic, while Loader looked at polar structure in the book of Qohelet.[48] Yet there is still room for further study. Examples are Sir. 38.24–39.11, where the life of the scholar is contrasted with a series of craftsmen. The model for this passage, directly or indirectly, was the famous Egyptian *Satire on Trades* (*ANET*, pp. 432-34), another example of sustained antithesis. Other passages are Isa. 31.1-3 ('Woe to those who rely on horses...but do not look to the Holy One of Israel') and 1 Sam. 16.7 'A man looks on the outward appearance, but Yahweh looks on the heart (= mind)'.[49]

2.3.4. *Syntax*, with a few exceptions[50] remains a neglected aspect of Hebrew verse. The verb, in particular, requires investigation.

2.4. *Further Comments on Topics Already Considered*

2.4.1. *Acrostics*. The acrostic has come under scrutiny again. It is shown as being more than merely ornamental.[51] Stol uses the new term 'telestic' to describe a poem where the *ends* of the lines form a pattern, but the telestic is found only in Babylonian. He also shows that the acrostic is not necessarily a construct of wisdom but is used in a variety of genres, for aesthetic reasons and not for ease of memorization. Signals of the acrostic are the alphabetic arrangement and the repetition of stanza-structure, particularly evident in Psalm 119.[52]

46. M. Greenberg, *Ezekiel, 1–20* (AB, 22; Garden City, NY: Doubleday, 1983), p. 268.

47. *Hebrew Poetics*, p. 85.

48. *Polar Structures.*

49. See my review of J. Krašovec, *Antithetic Structure in Biblical Hebrew Poetry*, *CBQ* 50 (1988), p. 504.

50. E.g., M.L. Barré, 'Jonah 2,9 and the Structure of Jonah's Prayer', *Bib* 72 (1991), pp. 237-48.

51. W.M. Stol, 'Babylonian and Biblical Acrostics', *Bib* 69 (1988), pp. 305-323.

52. J.F. Brug, 'Biblical Acrostics and their Relationship to Other Ancient Near

2.4.2. *Functions*. The work of Brinton has already been mentioned. Zurro[53] has catalogued a whole range of repetitions (chiefly short-range repetitions), but has commented only very little on the *function* of repetition. He does mention the following. The intensifying function (by partial repetition of the syntagma when the adjectives are semantically related), for example 'great kings' // 'powerful kings' (Ps. 136.17-18; pp. 151-52); to bring out the contrast (when the adjectives are antonyms), for example 'prudent' // 'disgraceful' (Prov. 10.5; pp. 152-53); for merismus, for example 'the eastern sea' // 'the western sea' (Joel 2.20; Zech. 14.8; pp. 154-55); to express strong hyperbole: *hmwnym hmwnym*, 'ever more multitudes' (Joel 4.14; p. 170); and to connect successive bicola, as in Ps. 121.1-2 '...my help/My help' (p. 172).

2.4.3. *Metre*. This topic is too controversial and too technical to be presented in brief but two recent explanations can be mentioned. According to van Grol[54] the underlying metrical patterns are regular, but are realized on the surface in varying ways. Therefore, the strophe is more important for metre than the verse-line. Fecht gives a detailed list of verse rules for Hebrew[55] and Phoenician[56] cataloguing metrical and non-metrical words, to use Buccellati's terminology; however, we are not told how these rules are derived. As ever, in the absence of actual objective data, there is the danger of circular reasoning. My own view is that metre, if it is present,[57] should be transparent and obvious so that the long and complex rules of Fecht and Margalit seem out of proportion. Van Grol's approach is more

Eastern Acrostics', in W.W. Hallo *et al.* (eds.), *The Bible in the Light of Cuneiform Literature: Scripture in Context III* (Ancient Near Eastern Texts and Studies, 8; Lewiston, NY: Edwin Mellen, 1990), pp. 283-304, rejects 'quasi-acrostics' in Ugaritic. Buccellati ('On Poetry') also mentions acrostics; according to him the acrostic 'provides a compositional frame which should not be underestimated in its literary effect'. Also, D. Pardee, 'Acrostics and Parallelism: The Parallelistic Structure of Psalm 111', *Maarav* 7–8 (1992), pp. 117-38 and H. Quecke, 'Eine koptische alphabetische Akrostichis', *Or* 61 (1992), pp. 1-9.

53. *Procedimientos iterativos.*

54. *De versbouw.*

55. *Metrik*, pp. 47-60.

56. *Metrik*, pp. 183-90.

57. For scepticism on this matter see my *Classical Hebrew Poetry*, pp. 91 and 109.

attractive because it is simpler. In actual fact, Hebrew verse, like Ugaritic and Akkadian poetry, can be appreciated and understood even though we cannot describe metre exactly.

2.4.4. *Prose or Verse*. In his presidential address to the Annual Meeting of the Linguistic Society of America in 1989, W. Bright[58] presented material from American Indian oral poetry and made several points of great significance to our studies. They are as follows. (1) The verse of American Indian oral poetry should not be judged by European traditions. (2) 'Some forms of verbal art use lines which are in part definable in terms of nonphonological criteria...units which one may identify as LINES, and higher-order units which may be called VERSES, can often be defined both by the occurrence of "initial particles"—often translated as English *and then*, *so then*, or the like—and also by internal patterns of morphosyntactic, semantic, and lexical PARALLELISM'.[59] (3) Although the (semantically parallel) COUPLET is general in the verbal art of Meso-America, the single line and the triplet also occur. (4) The formal oratory of Classical Nahuatl comprises a series of embedded parallel lines.

Significant in such texts are (1) the sustained use of parallelism; (2) the use of verse in what is essentially a prose statement; (3) the use of certain couplets with metaphorical function (e.g. 'with one lip, with two lips' = 'speaking indirectly'). Further (4) non-parallel material can be mixed with parallel material—this has implications for our so-called 'synthetic parallelism' in Hebrew, where the second line of a couplet simply continues the first line (i.e., is not parallel to it). This may be a feature of oral verse tradition. Sometimes non-parallel material may break up the parts of a couplet. Compare, for example, 'They have possessions, / those people, / they have property', with Ps. 120.7: 'I am for peace / but when I speak / they are for war'.

Some biblical scholars have made use of the researches of M. Parry and A.B. Lord into Yugoslavian folk poetry. We can now look to Meso-America for comparative material in our attempts to understand Hebrew (and Ugaritic) verse traditions.

58. W. Bright, '"With One Lip, with Two Lips": Parallelism in Nahuatl', *Language* 66 (1990), pp. 437-52.

59. Bright, 'With One Lip', pp. 437-38.

2.4.5. *Alliteration*. The chief exponent of this device is Margalit,[60] but he has been criticized as attaching excessive importance to alliteration and for inaccurate data. In an attempt at obtaining more exact data, Pardee[61] provided an overwhelming and exhaustive set of consonantal counts for sample texts in both Ugaritic and Hebrew.

2.4.6. *Other Topics*. In spite of several studies[62] IMAGERY still requires more extensive treatment. AMBIGUITY has been studied in respect of the psalms[63] and as a form of repetition.[64]

2.4.7. *Word-Pairs*. Compilations of cross-cultural word-pairs in the ancient Near East—principally Avishur's collection of word-pairs but also the listings in *RSP* I-III—have been criticized precisely because they look at word-pairs across languages instead of within a particular language/poem. According to Aitken,[65] word-pairs are a by-product of using formulas and parallelism, and there were no 'dictionaries' of parallel word-pairs. However, data from other areas also need to be considered. In Mesopotamia 'it was usual for almost every type of information to be summarized and recorded by listing pairs of associated items, arranged in columns'.[66] Further, current work on Meso-American languages indicates such a view to be too simplistic. In a recent study Norman[67] has shown that 'in the Quiché-speaking communities[68]...a special form of speech, marked by extensive

60. Full references in my *Classical Hebrew Poetry*, p. 229.

61. *A Trial Cut.*

62. E.g., J. Day, *God's Conflict with the Dragon and the Sea: Echoes of a Canaanite Myth in the Old Testament* (University of Cambridge Oriental Publications, 35; Cambridge: Cambridge University Press, 1985); M.S. Smith, 'The Near Eastern Background of Solar Language for Yahweh', *JBL* 109 (1990), pp. 29-39.

63. P.R. Raabe, 'Deliberate Ambiguity in the Psalter', *JBL* 110 (1991), pp. 213-27.

64. A.R. Ceresko, 'The Function of *Antanaclasis* (*mṣ'* "to find" // *mṣ'* "to reach, overtake, grasp") in Hebrew Poetry, Especially in the Book of Qoheleth', *CBQ* 44 (1982), pp. 551-69.

65. 'Oral Formulaic Composition'.

66. A. Livingstone, *Mystical and Mythological Explanatory Works of Assyrian and Babylonian Scholars* (Oxford: Clarendon Press, 1986), p. 2.

67. W.M. Norman, 'Grammatical Parallelism in Quiché Ritual Language', *Berkeley Linguistics Society* 6 (1980), pp. 378-99.

68. Quiché is a language spoken in Guatemala, in the communities of

use of grammatically parallel couplets, is utilized [for ceremonies]'. Ceremonial speeches of this type were delivered by specialists known as *k'amal b'eh* 'guides' (literally 'bringer of the road') and others who learned their craft from years of apprenticeship with a 'guide'. 'The most striking feature of Quiché ceremonial speech is its couplet structure: lines come in pairs, one word of the second line contrasting with the corresponding word of the first line'. One of its most salient characteristics is that 'the same pairs of lexical items are repeated a number of times throughout the same text', for example PATH // ROAD, BRING // RAISE, WALL // FORTRESS. 'In most cases the relative order of the paired items is invariant.'

Norman also discusses the question: 'what must a *k'amal b'eh* learn...to be able to produce ceremonial rhetoric...?' Part of the answer is that he 'must memorize the stock lexical pairs...' He also notes that the *k'amal b'eh* 'may present couplets in either an expanded or a condensed form, with several intermediate stages between the most expanded and the most condensed style'. The range (from expanded to condensed) is represented by this example (given by Norman):

It echoes in the forbidden TREE,
It echoes in the forbidden VINE.

Its VOICE, its SPEECH, echoes wonderfully in the forbidden TREE, in the forbidden VINE.

It also echoes in the forbidden TREE, the forbidden VINE

2.4.8. *Further Word-Pairs*. Two of the many additional word-pairs can be discussed here.

'*Throne*' // '*footstool*'. It has long been known that both Ugaritic and Hebrew use the pair *ks'* // *hdm*. The correspondence can be shown to be even closer since Hebrew *ks'* // *hdm rgl*, 'throne' // 'footstool' (Isa. 66.1) is matched by Ugaritic *ks'* // *hdm p'nh* in *KTU* 1.161 13-14.[69] Is this lexical borrowing or does it point to a shared tradition of versification?[70]

Santa Caterina Ixtahuacán and Nahualá.

69. Identified in A. Caquot, J.-M. de Tarragon and J.-L. Cunchillos, *Textes ougaritiques* (LAPO, 14; Paris: Cerf, 1989), II, p. 107 n. 328, due to the reading *hdm p'nh* established by P. Bordreuil and D. Pardee, 'Le rituel funéraire ougaritique RS 34.126', *Syria* 59 (1982), p. 125.

70. Note, too, the word-pair common to 'the GODS approached, the STARS were

'Nose' // 'cheek(s)'. In a text listing colourful names for bird-calls[71] comes an intriguing appellation for the cry of the heron: *quddudu appāšu lētāšu dakkā*, 'Its NOSE is bent down, hollow its CHEEKS'. The word-pair in Hebrew also occurs only once, in Job 40.26 (EVV: 41.2) as part of the description of Behemoth (recently equated by J. Day with 'the calf of Ilu, 'Atik'[72]):

htsym 'gmwn b'pw	Can you place a cord through his NOSE,
wbw tqwb lḥyw	or pierce his CHEEK with a hook?

Apart from the word-pair, the only factor common to both texts is that they concern animals. However, it can be noted that a little further on in the same passage, the beast is compared to a bird: Job 40.29a (EVV 41.5a), 'Can you play with him as with a *bird*?'

2.4.9. *Ballast Variant.* Kugel[73] discusses the expression 'ballast variant' only to reject it as incorrect. His example is Prov. 2.16:

To save you from a 'foreign' woman,
from an alien woman who talks smoothly

Kugel explains that ellipsis here (i.e. the omission of 'to save you') (1) *frees space* in the second line for some elaboration of a parallel item in the first line, and (2) *isolates for attention* the expanded topic. 'Since the verb "to save" does double duty for both versets, the poet has space in the second verset to make the dangerous temptress the subject of a brief subordinate clause ["who talks smoothly"].' However, elsewhere the ballast variant is clearly a filler as in Prov. 7.16:

I have decked my couch with coverings,
coloured spreads of Egyptian linen.

where the ellipsis of almost all of the first line allows for a little embroidery in the second.

invited' (D. Edzard, *Hymnen, Beschwörungen und Verwandtes (Aus dem Archiv L. 2769)* [Archivi reali di Ebla, 5; Rome: Missione Archeologica Italiana in Siria dell'Università di Roma 'La Sapienza', 1984], p. 29 = text 6 ix 2b-3) and 'when the STARS of the morning sang together and all the GODS (lit., sons of God) cried out' (Job 38.7) recognized by W.G. Lambert, 'Notes on a Work of the Most Ancient Semitic Literature', *JCS* 41 (1989), pp. 1-33 (20).

71. W.G. Lambert, 'The Sultantepe Tablets (*continued*) IX. The Birdcall Text', *AnSt* 20 (1970), pp. 111-17.

72. 'God's Conflict', pp. 75-84.

73. *The Idea of Biblical Poetry*, pp. 23-26.

2.5. *The Distinctive Character of Hebrew Verse*

I will close by commenting on the features which go to make Hebrew verse unique. It is well known that Hebrew, Ugaritic and, to a lesser extent, Akkadian (Babylonian) and Phoenician verse traditions have many aspects in common: parallelism, a range of versifying techniques, the use of formulas and so on.

In a short article written some years ago I attempted to establish the characteristics of Ugaritic verse.[74] Too many articles (including several by myself) and books (for example Zurro's catalogue of repetition[75]) focus on *similarities*—but it is also important to determine what makes Hebrew verse *different* from Ugaritic, Akkadian or, for that matter, from Egyptian verse. This is a topic requiring careful research. We are hampered to a certain extent because there is less Ugaritic verse than Hebrew, which skews any conclusions we might reach. (And there is even less Phoenician poetry.) For example, there are no alphabetic acrostics in Ugaritic: is this because they were unaware of the technique or is the reason, perhaps, that they preferred not to use it? Or does chance explain the fact that no Ugaritic acrostics have been disovered so far? There are very few short poems in Ugaritic since it is mostly lengthy epic and the range of literary forms is much narrower than in Hebrew. Is this accident or design? Such considerations are significant in evaluating cross-cultural comparisons. Ultimately, we can only use the material we have available, always aware that new discoveries could alter our conclusions.

3. *Ethnopoetics and Hebrew Verse*

3.1. *Introduction*

Just over a year ago, while preparing a talk on Hebrew poetry,[76] I came across an article on parallelism in the periodical *Language*.[77]

74. 'The Character of Ugaritic Poetry', *JNSL* 11 (1983), pp. 157-69, reprinted below.

75. *Procedimientos iterativos*.

76. Unpublished lecture given at 'Prose and Verse' the first Symposium on Relations between Prose and Verse in Ancient Near Eastern Texts, held in the Theologische Universiteit, Kampen, 1–3 June, 1993. The other lectures given then are published in J.C. de Moor and W.G.E. Watson (eds.), *Verse in Ancient Near Eastern Prose* (AOAT, 42; Kevelaer: Butzon & Bercker; Neukirchen–Vluyn: Neukirchener Verlag, 1993).

77. W. Bright, 'With One Lip'.

Since the only other article on the same topic in that periodical had appeared as long ago as 1966[78] this recent article was of particular interest. It was also significant because it dealt with the distinction between verse and prose in American Indian literature[79] and in addition provided supplementary references to other publications in the wider field of ethnopoetics.

Further reading of this material showed that many of the problems we come across in our own field (ancient Near Eastern studies) also occur in the study of American Indian literature, as well as in other literature of the Americas (including Eskimo literature) as we shall see. Of course, this is not a new observation. Several years ago M.P. O'Connor drew a comparison between the discontinuities in these traditions and in Hebrew verse tradition.[80] In his recent book on Hebrew verse, W.T.W. Cloete also described (very briefly) the approach under discussion here.[81] However, in spite of such studies, the topic remains relatively unknown to specialists in our area.[82]

A word about the term 'ethnopoetics' is required. It was first used by Tedlock and Rothenberg[83] and is analogous to such terms as

78. R. Jakobson, 'Grammatical Parallelism and its Russian Facet', *Language* 42 (1966), pp. 399-429.

79. Both William Bright ('With One Lip') and W. Norman ('Grammatical Parallelism in Quiché Ritual Language', *Berkeley Linguistics Society* 6 [1980], pp. 387-99) refer to Ugaritic (and Hebrew) poetry.

80. M. O'Connor, '"I only am Escaped to Tell thee": Native American and Biblical Hebrew Verse', *Religion and Intellectual Life* 3 (1986), pp. 121-32, a review of D. Hymes, *'In Vain I Tried to Tell you': Essays in Native American Ethnopoetics* (Philadelphia: University of Pennsylvania Press, 1981). O'Connor noted that 'the poetic line is at the core of the revisualization involved in the renewed understanding of Biblical Hebrew and Native American verse. The line is the crucial concept in understanding all poetry or verse; indeed, verse may be defined as language material organized in lines' (p. 125).

81. Cloete, *Versification and Syntax*, pp. 52-54, under 3.2.3.

82. But see A. Berlin, 'Ethnopoetry and the Enmerkar Epics', *JAOS* 103 (1983), pp. 17-24; H. Jason, 'The Poor Man of Nippur: An Ethnopoetic Analysis', *JCS* 31 (1979), pp. 189-215.

83. In the periodical *Alcheringa* in 1970; see V. Turner, 'A Review of "Ethnopoetics"', *Boundary* 2/6 (1978), pp. 583-90, reprinted in J. Rothenberg and D. Rothenberg (eds.), *Symposium of the Whole: A Range of Discourse toward an Ethnopoetics* (Berkeley: University of California Press, 1983), pp. 337-42. According to Turner ('Review', p. 341) 'Ethnopoetics... is a liminoid genre in a

'ethnohistory', 'ethnolinguistics', 'ethnomusicology' and the like.[84] It can be roughly paraphrased as the study of 'non-Western verse traditions'. Its two aims are (1) to determine patterns within these traditions and (2) to assist non-native speakers in understanding the literature of these cultures.[85] Hornberger states in this context, 'When we analyze a narrative in terms of its poetic organization, we gain insight into the story told; at the same time it is the story itself which provides the overall organization of the narrative'.[86] However, it is not possible to provide here a detailed description of ethnopoetics in general or even of current approaches to Native American literature, for obvious reasons.

The following general aims of this section can be listed:

1. To draw attention to narrative traditions in other cultures—that is North American Indian and other cultures of the Americas.
2. To show that problems concerning the differentiation between verse and prose also occur there (for example, definition of the line, determining verse structure, the falsifying effects due to translation [literal translations, literary translations] and to the imposition of Western European tradition on these cultures).
3. To describe briefly the various approaches to this literature.

metaphorically liminal phase of history—viewing the world as one vast initiatory seclusion camp'.

84. See Rothenberg and Rothenberg (eds.), *Symposium of the Whole*, p. ix, n. 1: 'The word "ethnopoetics" suggested itself, almost too easily, on the basis of such earlier terms as ethnohistory, ethnomusicology, ethnolinguistics, ethnopharmacology, and so on. As such it refers to a redefinition of poetry in terms of cultural specifics, with an emphasis on those alternative traditions to which the West gave names like "pagan", "gentile", "oral", and "ethnic".'

85. J. Sherzer, 'Modes of Representation and Translation of Native American Discourse: Examples from the San Blas Kuna', in B. Swann (ed.), *On the Translation of Native American Literatures* (Washington: Smithsonian Institution Press, 1992), pp. 426-40 (427), considers the essence of ethnopoetics to comprise the twin tasks of capturing the way a particular culture experiences their own discourse and ways of making this experience meaningful for outsiders. See, too, Bright, 'With One Lip', p. 450: 'An equally important aim of ethnopoetic study is that of making the esthetic values of oral literature more accessible to the literate public in general'.

86. N.H. Hornberger, 'Verse Analysis of "The Condor and the Shepherdess"', in Swann, *Translation*, pp. 441-69 (441).

4. To show that, in particular, parallelism in the form of word-pairs and couplets clearly occurs in certain traditions within Native American literature.
5. To point to further comparative material from living oral traditions.[87]
6. To draw comparisons between ancient Near Eastern texts and North American Indian texts.

It must be emphasized, though, that this is not an exhaustive treatise but only a general introduction.

3.2. *Prose or Verse in North American Indian Texts?*

I can begin with a rather extreme example. It is the first sentence of a legal text (from Papago, Southern Arizona) and according to one scholar it can be read as a poem:[88]

Long ago
when did here make us
our maker
did these two things give us
which are our Indian way
and our language.

According to Bahr, it centres on one line, 'our maker' and there is also (near-) rhyme (lines 2 and 4) and parallelism (lines 2 // 4; 5 // 6). It must be admitted, however, that this is a weak example and shows that not all such literature is verse and that some passages are simply poor verse.

Very much more convincing are the studies by Dell Hymes and an illustration of his approach—division of texts into lines and other structures—can be given. It is significant that his final (or rather latest) result is the outcome of repeatedly re-reading the text.

The following passage is from a Chinookan story involving hunters and a she-bear who attacks them:[89]

87. Cf. M. Parry, *The Making of Homeric Verse* (Oxford: Clarendon Press, 1971); A.B. Lord, *The Singer of Tales* (Cambridge, MA: Harvard University Press, 1960) and in general the bibliography in A.B. Lord, *Epic Singers and Oral Tradition* (Ithaca, NY: Cornell University Press, 1991), pp. 245-57.

88. D. Bahr, 'Translating Papago Legalese', in Swann, *Translation*, pp. 256-75, shows a legal text to be poetry (pp. 257-75, esp. 265-67).

89. Hymes, '*In Vain*', pp. 184-99, a revised form of his 'Verse Analysis of a Wasco Text: Hiram Smith's "At'unaqa"', *IJAL* 46 (1980), pp. 65-77.

The Text as Prose

He tried to do everything to her. Then (*kwapt*) he got afraid. He had two arrows left. (*kwapt*) He took one—I don't know what he put on it—he lit it on this arrow. Then (*kwapt*) he shot the arrow. Then (*kwapt*) it started to burn. (*wit'a* [not translated]) He did the same with the other arrow.

First Analysis as Verse

He tried (in vain) to do everything to her;
then (*kwapt*) he got afraid.
He had two arrows left,
he took one.
I don't know what he put on it—he lit it on this arrow. Then (*kwapt*) he shot the arrow.
Then (*kwapt*) it started to burn.
(*wit'a* [not translated]) He did the same with the other arrow.

Second Analysis as Verse

He tried to do everything to her.
Then (*kwapt*) he got afraid.
Only two arrows left,
then (*kwapt*) he took one.

I don't know what he put on it, he lit it on this arrow,
then (*kwapt*) he shot the arrow.
Then (*kwapt*) it started to burn.

Third Analysis as Verse

He tried to do everything to her,
then (*kwapt*) he got afraid:
< > only two arrows left.

Then (*kwapt*) he took one,
he lit I don't know what,
he put <> it <> on this arrow,
then (*kwapt*) he shot the (arrow),
then (*kwapt*) it started to burn.

(NEW VERSE)
Again (*wit'a*) he did the same with one (arrow) etc.

This illustrates: (1) how what appears to be prose can be set out as verse—a crucial particle (*wit'a*, 'again') remains untranslated in the prose version and even in the first version as verse; it marks a new verse in the final version; (2) how the final (or latest) version is arrived at by repeated attempts at analysis; (3) how particles, especially line-initial particles (such as *kwapt*, 'then'; *wit'a*, 'again') help to structure the lines and verses; (4) how parallelism of verbs is significant ('he took', 'he lit', 'he put', 'he shot', 'it started to burn'); (5) how (as Hymes repeatedly insists) one cannot simply apply an analytical technique mechanically—it has to be thought through, taking account of content as well as of structural markers.

3.3. *Two Approaches*

Broadly speaking, there have been two basic approaches to Native American Indian discourse. (1) The oral approach entails the examination of expressive features (especially pauses) in *performance*, and is based on live recordings. The main proponent is Tedlock. (2) The other approach is principally an examination of grammatical devices which mark lines and groups of lines and is based on transcripts (transliterations) and translations. The principal practitioner is Hymes. These approaches have been criticized as tending to re-write or re-cast all American Indian literature as verse. Some scholars reject both approaches, others see them as complementary.

According to two scholars, Mattina[90] and Krupat, neither approach is correct since both Tedlock and Hymes argue that North American Indian texts should be transcribed as verse for different reasons. Tedlock's transcriptions reflect performance: he applies oral poetics and in effect writes 'scores', based on tape recordings. Hymes's studies are based on rhetorical organization of the text: 'text reconstructions that mirror some intuited underlying structure'.[91] Using the grammar of narrative he 'recasts paper transcriptions from a paragraph format into a verse format'.[92] Mattina argues that neither Tedlock nor Hymes have the final say in how these texts should be presented (especially as Hymes's criteria are rather loose): 'Not all of North American Indian narrative is verse'.[93] Similarly, A. Krupat states that presenting these texts as verse in a sequence of lines is only one of the various options available.[94]

90. A. Mattina, 'North American Indian Mythography: Editing Texts for the Printed Page', in A. Krupat and B. Swann (eds.), *Recovering the Word: Essays on Native American Literature* (Berkeley: University of California Press, 1987), pp. 129-48.

91. Mattina, 'Indian Mythography', p. 129.

92. Mattina, 'Indian Mythography', p. 133.

93. Mattina, 'Indian Mythography', p. 137.

94. One of these options would be to translate these texts in a particular way.

> Their [Hymes's and Tedlock's] insistence on the presentation of Native performance, regardless of whether these are sung, chanted, or narrated, in lines and stanzas, as 'poetry' on the page, that is, rather than in sentences and paragraphs of a prose page format, has increasingly been called into question for making a necessity of what is perhaps better considered an option.[95]

The general consensus, however, is that the two approaches complement each other.[96] For example, Virginia Hymes has successfuly used a combination of both analytical techniques. She remarks,

> the difference it makes to have access to tapes is not crucial to the discovery of the major structural organization of the narrative in most cases... most narrators use more than one linguistic device to signal a new unit (verse, stanza, scene) of the narrative and to give cohesion to the lines in a verse, the verses in a stanza, and so on.[97]

Several observations are valid here, I think. First, neither approach can exclude the other—they do indeed appear to be complementary and, as far as is possible in such matters, objective. More significant, though, is the fact that for some traditions no live recording of actual performance is possible. To a certain extent scholars have to rely on transcriptions and translations made after the Conquest where the living tradition for such texts has died out.[98] It is also the case that each tradition, each language, each composer or performer is different. Even when line-initial particles are used, *how* they are used varies from one poet to the next, so there are no hard and fast rules.

3.4. *The Combined Approach*

Many of the following definitions, used in the study of Native American Indian texts, coincide with those used by scholars in our own field; the others are easily identified.[99]

95. A. Krupat, 'On the Translation of Native American Song and Story: A Theorized History', in Swann, *Translation*, pp. 3-32 (18).

96. W. Bright, 'Poetic Structure in Oral Narrative', in D. Tannen (ed.), *Advances in Discourse Processes: Exploring Orality and Literacy* (Norwood, NJ: Ablex, 1982), pp. 171-84; V. Hymes, 'Warm Springs Sahaptin Narrative Analysis', in J. Sherzer and A.C. Woodbury (eds.), *Native American Discourse: Poetics and Rhetoric* (Cambridge: Cambridge University Press, 1987), pp. 62-102.

97. Hymes, 'Warm Springs', p. 65.

98. The same applies, of course, to ancient Near Eastern texts.

99. For similar terminology for Ugaritic and Hebrew, cf. M.C.A. Korpel and

Line: generally, one line one verb—but there are exceptions.[100] This is the most significant component of North American Indian verse.
Verse: groups of lines (i.e. a strophe).
Versicle: short groups of lines within a verse (a sub-stanza).
Stanza: groups of verses, often with some overall rhetorical form.

Longer segments have no fixed labels; terms such as 'scenes', 'acts' or even 'parts' are used, corresponding to ancient Near Eastern cantos, canticles and so on. Also significant are structure, 'the form of repetition and variation, of constants and contrasts, in verbal organization'[101] and the numerical component, that is sequences of 5 and 4.[102]

3.4.1. *The Line*. According to Sherzer[103] there is no clear-cut distinction between written and oral discourse, 'rather, it is necessary to recognize poetic structures and processes in a wide range of forms of Kuna discourse, from everyday and informal to ritual and formal'. The line is 'in several ways the basic poetic unit of Kuna discourse'.[104]

These lines are marked in four ways: (1) *grammatically*, by initial and final words, particles, affixes

Well (*tek*) thus (*inso*) indeed (*taykeluti*) one level down indeed (*taylekuti*) the prophet descended.
Truly don't you hear it is said (*pittosursokeye*)

(2) *by parallelism*, 'Especially in more formal and ritual styles, lines are marked by extensive syntactic and semantic parallelism. This

J.C. de Moor, 'Fundamentals of Ugaritic and Hebrew Poetry', *UF* 18 (1986), pp. 173-212; reprinted in W. van der Meer and J.C. de Moor, *The Structural Analysis of Biblical and Canaanite Poetry* (JSOTSup, 74; Sheffield: JSOT Press, 1988), pp. 1-61.

100. For an example of one verb per line in Hebrew 'prose', cf. M. O'Connor, *Religion and Intellectual Life* 3 (1986), pp. 127-28 (Jer. 22.10).

101. Hymes, '*In Vain*', p. 42.

102. Hymes has shown that 3 and 5 in Chinookan correspond to 2 and in Tonkawa; cf. V. Hymes, 'Tonkawa Poetics: John Rush Buffalo's "Coyote and Eagle's Daughter"', in Sherzer and Woodbury (eds.), *Native American Discourse*, p. 22.

103. J. Sherzer, 'Poetic Structuring of Kuna Discourse: The Line', *Language in Society* 11 (1982), pp. 371-90 (Reprinted in Sherzer and Woodbury [eds.], *Native American Discourse*, pp. 103-39).

104. Sherzer, 'Poetic Restructuring', p. 372; The term 'Kuna' refers to the Kuna Indians of Panama.

parallelism is organized in terms of line structure and in turn contributes to this structure', for example

It is dusk.
It has become night.
It is getting darker

(3) *by intonation patterns*, including pause, pitch, tempo and 'coughs', for example

The basil plant in the golden box is moving/(PAUSE)
in the golden box is moving//
(COUGH)
The basil plant in the golden box is swinging from side to side/(PAUSE)
In the golden box is swinging from side to side//
(COUGH).

(4) and according to *audience response*,[105] for example

At the level of the golden dirt, it is said/
the dirt people come to life, I utter//
(RESPONSE): Indeed.

He suggests that the line may be a universal unit of oral discourse.

3.4.2. *Parallelism.* The importance of parallelism can be illustrated by looking at various devices used to achieve parallelism in Sahaptin narrative tradition.[106] They are (1) *sets of three or five*

kútas kwná wínana	And we went there,
kútas wínana áu	and we went then,
kútas áu panaitíya	and we then climbed.[107]

In fact, this is a form of the 'tendency to fill out a pattern of three verbs in parallel construction, even if one of the three is merely a repetition'.[108] Sets of five are also common. (2) *Variation of verb-form with the same stem:* (a) forms with different person

You are burning,
Burn, *they* burned

105. In Sherzer's terminology, 'a coparticipant dialogic interactional structure'.
106. Hymes, 'Warm Springs', pp. 63-76.
107. Hymes, 'Warm Springs', p. 71.
108. Hymes, 'Warm Springs', p. 71.

(b) forms with different meanings

> Now then she packed them now, (*pákwnaitiya*)
> she packed them uphill now (*pákwtltxa*)

The root of both forms is *kw-*. (3) *Use of particles*

> *áu* Now then
> *kú* and, but, so
> *áuku* so then, etc.

There is a whole set of particles which are used to create parallel lines.[109] In effect this is a form of anaphoric repetition.

Parallelism in the form of couplets also pervades the work known as 'Popol Vuh' ('Council Book') in Quiché Maya. The first passage comes from a speech in which the gods, creators of the human race, call upon older gods (diviners and artisans) for assistance:

> Fulfil your names:
> Hunahpu Possum,
> Hunahpu Coyote,
>
> bearer twice over,
> begetter twice over,
>
> great peccary,
> great tapir,
>
> lapidary,
> jeweller,
>
> sawyer,
> carpenter,
>
> maker of green plates,
> maker of green bowls,
>
> incense maker,
> master craftsman,
>
> grandmother of day,
> grandmother of light.

However, the structure reflected in performance is to some extent different from analysis based on literary criteria:

109. Hymes, 'Warm Springs', p. 77, gives a selective list.

Fulfil your names—
Hunahpu Possum,
Hunahpu Coyote,
bearer twice over, begetter twice over,
great peccary, great tapir,
lapidary, jeweller, sawyer, carpenter, maker of green plates, maker of green bowls, incense maker, master craftsman,
grandmother of day, grandmother of light.

Some of the couplets on the written page are performed as single lines with inner parallelism ('bearer…', 'great…', 'grandmother…') or simply as a list ('lapidary…').

Prayer to ancestors on behalf of clients:

Pardon my sins all mums:
all six generations,
all six jarsful,

all mothers,
all fathers,

all workers,
all servers,

all mixers,
all pointers,

all counters of seeds,
all readers of cards,

who received,
who entered,

this work,
this service,

before the mums,
before the dads.

Again, this set of couplets can be set out in echelon formation as follows:

all counters of seeds,
all readers of cards, who received,
who entered this work,
this service before the mums,
before the dads.

Quiché narrative tends to be prose rather than verse even though it includes some parallel elements.[110]

3.5. *Features Common to both Traditions*

Both in North American Indian and ancient Near Eastern verse oral tradition seems to have preceded and then co-existed with written tradition. In present-day North American Indian tradition, techniques of oral composition and performance can be recorded, providing us with some idea of what oral tradition may have been like in the ancient Near East.

The distinction between prose and verse is not self-evident and requires study. However, rather more texts in both traditions are in verse than previously thought.[111]

Correct (literal rather than literary or versifying) translation reveals the patterns of verse in the text. It is of particular importance to provide exactly the same equivalent for any repeated word and not to mask such repetition by using synonyms. This has been noted for Ugaritic and Hebrew by Zurro.[112]

North American Indian verse is not metrical. As is now recognized, much (if not all) ancient Near Eastern verse also lacks strict metre. Accordingly, the expression 'measured verse', used by Hymes of Native American Indian verse, is probably preferable to 'metrical verse'. Unlike European verse, rhyme is not generally important either.

The most significant component of verse is the line. In fact, verse has been defined as 'language in lines'.[113] Therefore, it is very important in both traditions to determine where lines begin and end (colometry). It also seems to be the case that long and short lines can co-exist within a narrative poem.

110. D. Tedlock, 'Hearing a Voice in an Ancient Text: Quiché Poetics in Performance', in Sherzer and Woodbury (eds.), *Native American Discourse*, pp. 140-75 (154).

111. For examples in the Qumran documents, see F. García Martínez, *Textos de Qumrán* (Madrid: Editorial Trotta, 1992), pp. 50-51, 61-66 and *passim*.

112. E. Zurro, *Procedimientos iterativos en la poesia ugarítica y hebrea* (BibOr, 43; Rome: Biblical Institute Press, 1987).

113. See, for example, Hymes, '*In Vain*', p. 340, with additional references.

Segmentation of verse into lines, verses (or strophes), stanzas and so on is determined by special particles, by parallelism and by content.[114] Certain patterns, such as the echelon formation, emerge as common to both traditions.[115]

Other features that require to be taken into account are: (1) particles of undetermined meaning, for example, the final *-m* in certain Ugaritic texts[116] or *'hy* in Hos. 13.10 and 14.14; (2) lengthened vowels[117] when used in oral performance can indicate that a woman is speaking. This occurs in some ancient Near Eastern text traditions, for example Akkadian poetry, as noted by Reiner:

> The poem exhibits a spelling peculiarity in that some words contain an extra vowel sign that is motivated neither by the cuneiform writing conventions nor by grammatical reasons... This spelling pattern is certain to have a function, even if we do not know what it is. It has been suggested that such extra-long vowels add to the elegiac tone; other explanations are possible. The spelling perhaps endeavors to render a linguistic feature signalling, for example, that the speaker is a woman...[118]

(3) Introductions to speech may or may not be part of verse—this has been discussed elsewhere;[119] (4) word-pairs, now known to occur in a wide variety of languages;[120] (5) chiasmus is an occasional feature of North American Indian verse.[121]

114. See Hymes, 'Warm Springs', pp. 69-79 for fuller discussion.

115. For the echelon formation in Sumerian, cf. H.L.J. Vanstiphout, '"Verse Language" in Standard Sumerian Literature' in Moor and Watson, *Verse*, pp. 305-29, esp. 320-21. Hymes, 'Use All there is to Use', in Swann, *Translation*, p. 100 calls this feature a 'step by step run'. Similar patterns occur in Hebrew, e.g. Cant. 2.15; 8.4, 14.

116. Especially in *KTU* 1.12, 1.23 and RIH 78/20. Final *-m* is used some 18 times in *KTU* 1.23.

117. E.g. 'Your children b-u-u-urn' (*luuuutmas*).

118. Reiner, *Your Thwarts in Pieces*, p. 90.

119. See especially S.A. Meier, *Speaking of Speaking: Marking Direct Discourse in the Hebrew Bible* (VTSup, 46; Leiden: Brill, 1992).

120. Norman, 'Grammatical Parallelism', p. 397 concludes, 'Quiché ritual language is basically a lexical pair system like Aztec or Hebrew, with a few additional rules'.

121. D. Hymes, 'Use All there is to Use', in Swann, *Translation*, pp. 83-124 (96).

3.6. *Conclusion*

From the brief and partial survey provided here it is evident that many of the problems which arise in the study of ancient Near Eastern texts also confront scholars who study texts from the Americas, many of which have ancient tradition behind them. One of the most difficult problems is the differentiation between prose and verse which has been the focus of attention in Native American narrative. We can learn from the approaches developed to analyse these texts. In addition, many of these 'texts' are still being performed today. This enables us to study living oral tradition and extrapolate the findings, with the requisite adaptations, for application to ancient Near Eastern texts which unfortunately, but by nature of the case, are only known to us in written form.[122] We cannot expect all the answers to come from a sister discipline, of course, but we may find that the right questions are being asked and so improve our own understanding of ancient Near Eastern texts.

4. *A Review of Kugel's* The Idea of Biblical Poetry[123]

When asked to write a review of Kugel's book for *JSOT* I was somewhat hesitant at first. I had already written a full critique for *Biblica*, which has since appeared[124] and at the time felt that any gaps would be filled by my own book. On the other hand it seemed a good opportunity to explore in depth some aspects of Kugel's approach, indeed, some aspects of Hebrew poetry, which could only be touched on in a normal review. At the same time, I thought, here was a chance to update what I had previously written. Accordingly, I accepted the invitation to contribute to the discussion.

Oversimplifying a great deal and omitting the historical element, Kugel's *Idea* can be reduced to the following principal topics:

1. Parallelism
2. Metre
3. Prose or poetry.

122. With the exception of biblical Hebrew to some extent.
123. First published in *JSOT* 28 (1984), pp. 89-98.
124. *Bib* 64 (1983), pp. 134-36.

My own remarks, therefore, will comprise three main paragraphs which take up each of these points in turn. A final section will examine some other aspects not already mentioned, including the topic of expansion.

Before beginning, though, I will briefly summarize my own book review in *Biblica*. There I make the point that Kugel does not examine parallelism at the theoretical level.[125] I also observe that little account is taken of ancient Near Eastern poetry, though to be fair he does include detailed discussion of some aspects of Ugaritic verse (repetition, staircase parallelism).[126] In general, too, I consider Kugel's approach to be stimulatingly oblique and thought provoking.

We begin, then, with the subject of *parallelism*; after all, the subtitle is 'Parallelism and its History'. Fundamentally, it must be remembered, the notion of 'parallelism' is based on an analogy drawn from mathematical theory and applied to poetic structure. It is a useful guide to classification but must not be idealized into an entity in its own right (if I may mix metaphors).[127] Translated into simple terms, parallelism implies that in general Hebrew/Ugaritic/Akkadian verse is composed in couplets with the second line corresponding more or less closely to the first. This sets up the poles or extremes. If line B is identical with line A, then we have pure repetition. When line A and line B are totally dissimilar in every respect then we can dub the resulting couplet 'structurally parallel'. In between these two extremes there is a whole range of types. Table 1 (see following page) provides one possible classification which is neither obligatory nor exhaustive.

With such variety it is evident that the term 'parallelism' is a useful catch-all. Or, to put it differently, the term is hard to define in any accurate way. Even so, it remains a convenient descriptive label. Kugel's own definition, I would like to argue, is instead rather narrow. He is aware of the many different types, of course, and even lists some under the heading of 'differentiation'[128] though without any grouping into categories.

125. For a detailed discussion, see the opening to ch. 6 of my book *Classical Hebrew Poetry*.

126. Kugel, *Idea*, pp. 27-28 and 38-40.

127. See n. 125 and the references given in *Bib* 64 (1983), p. 136.

128. Kugel, *Idea*, pp. 16-23.

structural	*grammatical*[129]
alternating	abstract // concrete
chiastic	active // passive
conjunctive	gender
disjunctive	numerical
distant	singular // plural
horizontal	*yqṭl // qṭl*[130]
internal	noun // verb
partial	*syntactic*[131]
repetitive	
staircase	*semantic*
vertical	antithetic
	epithetic
other	numerical
emblematic	synonymous
impressionistic	

Table 1. *Types of parallelism*

a	*qṭl // yqṭl*
b	chiasmus
c	singular // plural
d	m. // f.
e	suffix // article
f	different grammatical person
g	suffix // Ø
h	prep. A // prep. B
i	ellipsis of 'particle' in one line
j	'all' // Ø

Table 2. *Types of parallelism*

These types belong to a grammatical parallelism, in fact. Some, of course, such as g and j, can be reversed, as Kugel remarks. Other

129. All these sequences can be inverted.

130. An example in prose(?) is 1 Sam. 15.33.

131. Of significance here are T. Collins, *Line-Forms in Hebrew Poetry: A Grammatical Approach to the Stylistic Study of the Hebrew Prophets* (Studia Pohl, Series Major 7; Rome: Pontifical Biblical Institute, 1978), reviewed by me in *Bib* 61 (1980), pp. 581-83, and M. O'Connor, *Hebrew Verse Structure* (Winona Lake, IN: Eisenbrauns, 1980), reviewed in *Bib* 64 (1983), pp. 131-34.

classifications are available.[132] Kugel, however, prefers to restrict parallelism to one type only: 'A, and what's more, B'.[133] Now I heartily concur that quite often this is the case: that line B does not simply reiterate line A in different words. There are quite a few couplets, in fact, where line B completes/rounds off/adds to line A. What cannot be correct, though, is the reduction of *all* parallelism to such terms. Several years ago, in a paper overlooked by the author, Haran explored precisely this aspect of Hebrew poetry, particularly in the domain of numerical parallelism.[134] Therefore, while Kugel's reminder that very often line B completes line A is useful and positive, it is by no means the whole story.

In any couplet comprising lines A and B the following possibilities emerge:

1. A and B are interchangeable.
2. A is important; B is added (for 'parallelism').
3. B is more significant than A.
4. A plus B comprise a unit.

Kugel himself has provided ample illustration of set 3, and Haran, too, considered this set. We now need some examples for sets 1, 2 and 4. Interchangeability is illustrated by Job 10.4

> Do you have eyes of flesh?
> Do you see as a mortal sees?

Further examples for set 1 include Hos. 10.2b, 8b, 11.11a, 12.11b-12c, most of Psalm 33 and so on. Also, *CTA* 16 vi 11-12, a couplet in Ugaritic:

npšh llḥm tptḥ	His throat she opened for food,
brlth lṯrm	his gullet for a meal.

132. For example: P.D. Long, 'Principles of Ancient Near Eastern *Parallelismus Membrorum* Applied to the Interpretation of the Poem and some Related Passages of Hesiod's *Theogony*' (PhD thesis, Pittsburgh, 1979), pp. 60-61. There he lists 'nine characteristics of parallelistic poetry' under the headings 'structural symmetry' and 'balance of corresponding words'.

133. Kugel, *Idea*, p. 42 and *passim.*

134. M. Haran, 'The Graded Numerical Sequence and the Phenomenon of "Automatism" in Biblical Poetry', in *Congress Volume Uppsala 1971* (VTSup, 22; Leiden: Brill, 1972), pp. 238-67.

Couplets where the first line overshadows the second (set 2) include Hos. 11.26, Pss. 18.25, 20.10, Job 36.24, 38.26, 27 and so on. Examples occur in Ugaritic, too, notably *CTA* 17 v 26b-28a:

bd dnil ytnn qšt	In Daniel's hand he placed the Bow,
lbrkh y'db qṣ't	on his knees he sets the arrows,

where the all-important component is the bow, to which arrows are a mere accompaniment.[135] An additional argument in favour of the first three sets (A = B; A > B and B < A) is the use of gender-matching within couplets.[136] Set 4 is equivalent to merismus[137] and a fifth set, not listed, would comprise couplets where A and B are merely in structural parallelism. A good illustration of this last set (with some overlap of set 1) also comes from Ugaritic. In three passages the couplet

yprq lṣb wyṣḥq	He uncreased his frown and laughed.
p'n lhdm yṯpd	His feet he placed on the footstool.

occurs, as part of formulaic response to glad tidings, but in one of these passages the sequence is inverted completely.[138]

One last point in connection with parallelism: although a high proportion of Hebrew poetry is in couplets (and this applies in differing degrees to other ancient Semitic poetry) there is also extensive use of the monocolon,[139] not to mention tricola, quatrains and longer sequences. A full account of this poetry, therefore, must take these strophic patterns into consideration as well.

The second topic is *metre* and here, as Kugel acknowledges, he is dependent on the writings of I. Baroway,[140] though unaware,

135. Also *CTA* 2 iv 28b-29a; 5 vi 23-24; etc.

136. See Chapter 4.

137. J. Krašovec, *Der Merismus im biblisch-Hebräischen und Nordwestsemitischen* (BibOr 33; Rome: Biblical Institute Press, 1977); 'Merism-Polar Expressions in Biblical Hebrew', *Bib* 64 (1983), pp. 231-39, with bibliography, p. 232 n. 1.

138. Full details are provided by G. del Olmo Lete, 'Notas de semántica ugaritica II', *Anuario de filologia* 2 (1976), pp. 227-51, esp. 232-36.

139. In general, B. Margalit, *A Matter of 'Life' and 'Death': A Study of the Baal-Mot Epic (CTA 4-5-6)* (AOAT, 206: Kevelaer: Butzon & Bercker; Neukirchen–Vluyn: Neukirchener Verlag, 1980), pp. 33, 59, 68 etc. See the comments by D. Pardee 'Ugaritic', *AfO* 28 (1981–82), p. 268.

140. Kugel, *Idea*, p. 235 n. 73.

apparently, of Cobb's researches.[141] Kugel argues that there is no metre in Hebrew poetry, a conclusion he shares with O'Connor, though they have little else in common.[142] Undeniably the problem of metre in (ancient) Hebrew poetry has taxed the ingenuity of scholars for generations and if this view is correct then time and ink have been expended in quantity for little purpose. In his review of the book J. Barr made the observation that since metre palpably does not translate but parallelism does, there would be little difference between the Hebrew original and even the best rendering should Kugel prove correct. It can equally be argued, in agreement with Kugel, that since almost all the features of Hebrew poetry can be transferred to the target language (parallelism, figurative language, structural patterns and so on) then it does not really matter whether Hebrew is metrical or not. However, there is some loss: phonological features cannot be reproduced in translation (and this would include wordplay); when they can it is usually at the expense of other components. Accordingly, the oral/aural/metrical element must be present to some extent. For apposite comments on the distinction between prose and poetry in this regard see below.

Elsewhere I argue that Hebrew poetry uses a metrical system based on stress.[143] This is because (1) stress is phonemic in Hebrew; (2) silent stress is present in some couplets;[144] and (3) unusual word order can be exploited, as in the broken construct chain, to produce a determined metrical pattern. If one accepts the Masoretic pointing as at least indicative of ancient pronunciation and intonation patterns, then it too can be invoked as favouring a stress-based metre in classical Hebrew.[145]

Since there is not even agreement concerning metre in English poetry, it is small wonder that a consensus is lacking for ancient

141. W.H. Cobb, *A Criticism of Systems of Hebrew Metre* (Oxford: Clarendon Press, 1905).

142. For Kugel's view of O'Connor, cf. *Idea*, pp. 315-23.

143. In ch. 5 of *Classical Hebrew Poetry*.

144. Notably the so-called 'pivot pattern', more accurately labelled 'pivot-patterned couplet with silent stress' on which see, provisionally, 'The Pivot Pattern in Hebrew, Ugaritic and Akkadian Poetry', *ZAW* 88 (1976), pp. 239-53.

145. J. Kuryłowicz, *Studies in Semitic Grammar and Metrics* (Prace Jezykoznawe, 67, Warsaw: Polska Akademia Nauk, 1972), pp. 158-87; E.J. Revell, 'Pausal Forms in Biblical Hebrew: Their Function, Origin and Significance', *JSS* 25 (1980), pp. 165-79.

Semitic verse. For example, scholars cannot decide whether Ugaritic poetry is metrical or not; and if it is, what system was followed.[146] For Akkadian, too, we still await a generally acceptable theory.[147]

A profitable line of enquiry might be the study of cadence patterns in *both* prose and poetry which, in turn, might lead us to a closer understanding of Hebrew prosody.[148] Ultimately, perhaps, we may have to concur with Youmans who concluded that 'the boundary between metrical and unmetrical lines is "fuzzy" rather than exact'.[149]

The differentiation between prose and poetry has long been a problem in the study of biblical Hebrew. The extremes are easy enough to determine. Psalms, Proverbs, Job, Song of Songs, Lamentations and most of the prophetic writings are clearly poetry. The rest, however, is not prose since there are sections of poetry in Genesis, Exodus, Numbers, Deuteronomy, Judges, 1–2 Samuel and so on, and there are also borderline texts such as Qoheleth. All this is rehearsing what is well known and takes in such mixtures as Ezekiel, Jeremiah and Jonah. I agree with Kugel that one should not necessarily turn all 'prose' into poetry, but there is a clear difference between recognition

146. Consult B. Margalit, 'Introduction to Ugaritic Prosody', *UF* 7 (1975), pp. 289-313; D. Pardee, 'Ugaritic and Hebrew Metrics', in D. Young (ed.), *Ugarit in Retrospect: Fifty Years of Ugarit and Ugaritic* (Winona Lake, IN: Eisenbrauns, 1981), pp. 113-30.

147. W. von Soden, 'Untersuchungen zur babylonischen Metrik, Teil I', *ZA* 71 (1982), pp. 161-204.

148. So J. Wansbrough, 'Hebrew Verse: Scansion and Parallax', *BSO(A)S* 45 (1982), pp. 5-12, esp. his comment 'as in composition (writing) so in analysis (reading), cadence may affect the number as well as the choice of words/syllable between pauses' (p. 12). Note, too, his paper 'Hebrew Verse: Apostrophe and Epanalepsis', *BSO(A)S* 45 (1982), pp. 425-33. Also rewarding would be a comparison between metrically equivalent lines with and without an additional/inserted word. See, for Akkadian, K. Hecker, *Untersuchungen zur akkadischen Epik* (Neukirchen–Vluyn: Neukirchener Verlag, 1974), pp. 143, 116. Relevant, too, are some of the comments in R. Jakobsen and J. Lotz, 'Axioms of a Versification System—Exemplified by the Mordvinian Folksong', in *Roman Jakobsen. Selected Writings. V. On Verse, its Masters and Explorers* (The Hague: Mouton, 1979), pp. 160-66, esp. Rule II-301: 'A word-constant (refrain) may be inserted in homogeneous verses without constituting a part of a segment [i.e. part of a phrase] or being counted as a segment (it may be placed at the beginning or at the end of the verse or between two segments)' (p. 164).

149. G. Youmans, 'Generative Tests for Generative Meter', *Language* 59 (1983), pp. 67-92 (quote is from p. 91).

and reconstruction which cannot be ignored.

To bring in an element of objectivity it is useful to turn to non-Hebrew literature here. In Ugaritic, to begin with a familiar corpus of texts, there is no doubt concerning the distinction between tablets in prose and tablets in poetry: the matter is decided by literary form. All letters, treaties, administration texts, rations lists, prescriptions for sick horses and so forth are in prose. 'Literary' texts—myths, epics, legends—are in verse. The distinction is also marked by a definite difference in language.[150] The problem, therefore, hardly arises.[151] Even more interesting are the Punic texts read as prose and therefore misunderstood until Krahmalkov identified them as verse.[152] The message, then, is not that modern interpreters are imposing modern categories on ancient texts (so Kugel); rather, such texts can only be correctly understood if they are first classified as either prose or poetry. The writers of Ras Shamra knew well enough whether to use prose or poetry once the genre of composition had been determined by or for them.

I will end this section by quoting from Polivanov whose work, written in 1930, was not published for 44 years.[153] In his paper 'The General Phonetic Principle of any Poetic Technique'[154] he discusses the distinction between poetry and prose. He comments,

> We relegate to poetry any piece whose verbal material reveals organization according to some phonetic (i.e. phonic) aspect or other (despite and independently of its organization by meaning); prose, on the contrary, is everything where this phonetic (phonic) organization is *lacking*.[155]

He concludes,

> By way of generalization of all the various systems of poetic technique (or versification), one main principle may be pointed out according to which

150. On which cf. M. Liverani, 'Elementi innovativi nell' ugaritico non letterario', *ANLR* 8/19 (1964), pp. 173-91.

151. However, cf. F.M. Cross, 'Prose and Poetry in the Mythic and Epic Texts from Ugarit', *HTR* 67 (1974), pp. 1-15. The whole question could be turned on its head by asking why it is that narrative sections of the Hebrew Bible are in prose?

152. 'Two Neo-Punic Poems in Rhymed Verse', *Rivista di studi fenici* 3 (1975), pp. 169-205.

153. E.D. Polivanov, *Selected Works: Articles on General Linguistics* (Janua linguarum, series major, 72; The Hague: Mouton, 1974).

154. Polivanov, *Selected Works*, pp. 350-67.

155. Polivanov, *Selected Works*, pp. 350-51, following V. Tomaševskij. He distinguishes between facultative (occasional) devices and canonized devices.

> the language material is organized in a poetic work. This is the *principle of repetition* of phonetic images.[156]

It remains to be seen what relevance these comments have for the topic in question.

Before going on to discuss some points of detail, I think it worthwhile mentioning a topic which has come to the fore recently in the study of ancient poetry, namely, expansion (and its counterpart, contraction). Ancient poets of the traditions under examination had a tendency to expand single lines into couplets or longer sequences. The implication is that single lines were significant or carried the message and any lines added to such cores were of lesser importance. The practice is attested in the tablets of the *Epic of Gilgamesh*, as Jeffrey Tigay has shown.[157] In Tablet X, for example, the single line

> If it is possible, the sea will I cross.

of the Babylonian edition becomes

> If it is possible, the sea I will cross.
> If it is not possible, over the steppe will I range.

in the late standard version.[158] Expansion of a similar order has been documented for Ugaritic[159] and biblical Hebrew.[160] An additional example from Ugaritic is expansion of the stock phrase

> *mdl 'r ṣmd pḥl* — Saddle an ass, yoke a donkey.[161]

156. Polivanov, *Selected Works*, pp. 358-59.

157. J.H. Tigay, *The Evolution of the Gilgamesh Epic* (Philadelphia: University of Pennsylvania Press, 1982), p. 61.

158. Tigay, *Evolution*, p. 61 n. 15 (end, on p. 62); text, p. 96. Other examples he mentions are Gilg. P i 10 and 30, monostichs expanded to quatrains in the later edition (Gilg. I v 31-34 and vi 9-12); also, Gilg. P v 10, 11, 13 and Gilg. II ii 38-41.

159. By J.C. de Moor, 'The Art of Versification in Ugarit and Israel', I, in Y. Avishur and J. Blau (eds.), *Studies in Bible and the Ancient Near East Presented to S.E. Loewenstamm on his Seventieth Birthday* (Jerusalem: E. Rubinstein's Publishing House, 1978), pp. 119-39; II: *UF* 10 (1978), pp. 187-217; III: *UF* 12 (1980), pp. 311-15.

160. Besides de Moor's papers (n. 159): S.E. Loewenstamm, 'The Address "Listen" in the Ugaritic Epic and the Bible', in G. Rendsburg *et al.* (eds.), *The Bible World: Essays in Honor of Cyrus H. Gordon* (New York: Ktav and the Institute of Hebrew Culture and Education of New York University, 1980), pp. 123-31.

161. *CTA* 4 iv 9; 19 ii 52-53.

This component of a command to prepare to mount becomes, in execution:

bkm tmdln 'r	At once she saddled an ass,
bkm tṣmd pḥl	at once she yoked a donkey.[162]

The single line (with, it must be admitted, latent parallelism) has been expanded into a genuine couplet.[163] An example from Hebrew is Hab. 2.14 expanded from Isa. 11.9. The converse of expansion is, of course, contraction and it occurs in Akkadian,[164] Ugaritic and Hebrew verse.[165] Both tendencies suggest parallelism to be a secondary feature based on the single line and to which the strophe can revert with no loss of meaning.

At the close I realize that I have not touched on many topics, for example, whether Hebrew poetry was oral in origin (which Kugel denies) or the subject of word-pairs (which he plays down). This is partly because my own views have been set out elsewhere and partly because I wanted to concentrate on key issues. Whatever our disagreements, it is undeniable that James Kugel's book has stimulated welcome discussion of thorny problems in Hebrew poetry which, in the long run, we can only hope will produce acceptable solutions.

162. *CTA* 19 ii 57-58.

163. Less clear is the expansion of *tgly wtbu* of *CTA* 16 vi 4 into couplets (1 iii 13; 4 iv 23 and 3E 15).

164. Tigay, *Evolution*, p. 62, to which should be added Gilg. P ii 24-26 (a quatrain) contracted to one line in Gilg. I iv 40.

165. See the papers by de Moor in n. 159.

Chapter 2

CONVENTIONS OF STYLE

1. *The Character of Ugaritic Poetry*[1]

1.1. *Introduction*

Shortly before beginning preparation for this paper I received through the post a slim volume of papers on Ugaritic topics.[2] Included was a study of an incantation against impotence, the fourth attempt at translating a difficult Ugaritic text from Ras Ibn Hani, and each was different from the last.[3] The text, as it happens, is in verse, and it occurred to me that it would be a great help in deciding who is correct, or rather which parts of the four translations are correct, if we could apply what one might term the rules of Ugaritic poetry. In other words, if we really could compile the norms of Ugaritic versification we would then be able to see which translations took these norms into account with a corresponding chance of being accurate. As yet such a rule-book does not exist; the present contribution is a preliminary to its compilation.

1.2. *Poetic Material in Ugaritic*

We can begin by taking a look—a general look—at the kind of poetry used in Ras Shamra, Ras Ibn Hani and so on, in other words, at Ugaritic verse. The texts themselves are well known, of course, and therefore quickly listed. They comprise:

1. First published in *JNSL* 11 (1983), pp. 157-69.

2. S. Ribichini and P. Xella (eds.), *Materiali lessicali ed epigrafici* (Rome: Consiglio Nazionale delle Ricerche, 1982), I, pp. 9-55.

3. The text is RIH 78/20; see now D. Fleming, 'The Voice of the Ugaritic Incantation Priest (RIH 78/20)', *UF* 23 (1991), pp. 141-54.

1. The Ba'alu Cycle (incomplete), *KTU* 1.3-1.6
2. The Aqhatu Tale (with no ending extant), *KTU* 1.17-1.19
3. The Legend of Kirta (practically complete), *KTU* 1.14-1.16
4. Mythological fragments, *KTU* 1.12, 1.13, 1.20-1.22, etc.
5. A Wedding Poem, *KTU* 1.24
6. Incantations, *KTU* 1.82, 1.96, 1.100, 1.107, RIH 78/20
7. Prayers, *KTU* 1.119
8. Rituals, *KTU* 1.41, 1.43, 1.87, etc.
9. Other texts

Broadly speaking, these poems can be divided into two categories: (a) narrative verse; (b) religious verse, where (a) comprises the first four items on the list and category (b) the remainder, with the label 'religious' as a convenient catch-all. There is evidently some overlap. The narrative verse is also 'religious' since the gods are involved, but the underlying thrust is of a story which is told. In fact, the gods feature very little in either *Kirta* or *Aqhatu*.[4] Most striking about these two categories is that there is no secular or profane verse; there are no proverbs, no snatches of song, laments or the like. Any that can be so labelled have already been incorporated within the larger compositions, a fact so far unnoticed.[5] There are exceptions, though, as will be seen.

Again, if we consider the whole corpus of Ugaritic texts we see that there are two main types: (1) prose texts; (2) poetic texts.[6]

Under 'poetic texts' come the two categories already mentioned. The prose texts comprise economic and administrative documents, letters, lists, contracts, extracts from veterinary manuals and so on. Accordingly, the overall picture is:

4. On myth cf. G.S. Kirk, *Myth: Its Meaning and Functions in Ancient and Other Cultures* (Sather Classical Lectures, 40; Cambridge: Cambridge University Press; Berkeley: University of California Press, 1971), esp. pp. 8-19.

5. For Mesopotamian literature, see J.H. Tigay, *The Evolution of the Gilgamesh Epic* (Philadelphia: University of Pennsylvania Press, 1982), pp. 161-77.

6. More specific classification is set out in *KTU*, pp. xi-xii (4.1.3). Note that some of these classifications are not necessarily appropriate; see, for example, G.N. Knoppers, 'Treaty, Tribute List of Diplomatic Letter: *KTU* 3.1 Reexamined', *BASOR* 289 (1993), pp. 81-94; J. Sanmartín, 'El *ordo* litúrgico KTU 4.14', *AuOr* 8 (1990), pp. 89-99.

(1) prose
(2) poetry
  (a) narrative verse
  (b) religious verse

The language used in each type overlaps but does not exactly coincide, and to a large extent vocabularies and grammars are distinct.[7]

It was B. Margalit who uncovered what he terms 'the most striking inter-connection between the prose and poetry of Ugarit to be found in the entire corpus of Ugaritic literature'.[8] The reference is to the blessing which the goddess 'Anatu gives to the sun-goddess Shapshu:

an. lan yšpš	From strength to strength, O Shapshu,
an. lan. il. yǵ[	from strength to strength may Ilu guar[d you;]
tǵrk. [	may the gods keep you [safe].[9]

As Margalit was the first to notice, this blessing reformulates the stock greeting formula used in letters:

yšlm lk ilm	May the gods keep you safe,
tǵrk tšlmk	may they guard you and keep you safe.[10]

In spite of what was said earlier, this is a couplet in prose, a couplet which the poet of the Ba'alu text converted into 'staircase parallelism', using wordplay into the bargain.[11] Parenthetically, 'Anatu's words

7. S.B. Parker, 'Studies in the Grammar of the Ugaritic Prose Texts' (unpublished dissertation, The Johns Hopkins University, 1967).

8. B. Margalit, *A Matter of 'Life' and 'Death': A Study of the Baal-Mot Epic (CTA 4-5-6)* (AOAT, 206; Kevelaer: Butzon & Bercker; Neukirchen–Vluyn: Neukirchener Verlag, 1980), pp. 174.

9. *KTU* 1.6 iv 22-24. Note that others translate differently, though in general the sense remains the same. 'Where (and) whither (you go), o Shapash, where (and) whither (you go), may El protect [you], may [ ] protect you!', J.C.L. Gibson, *Canaanite Myths and Legends* (Edinburgh: T. & T. Clark, 1978), p. 78; similarly, del Olmo Lete, *Mitos y leyendas*, p. 230. 'Whatever the outcome, o Shapshu, whatever the outcome, may Ilu protect you, may [the gods] protect you in p[eace]!', J.C. de Moor, *An Anthology of Religious Texts from Ugarit* (Nisaba, 16; Leiden: Brill, 1987), p. 93.

10. For variants, occurrences and discussion, cf. O. Kaiser, 'Zum Formular der in Ugarit gefundenen Briefe', *ZDPV* 86 (1970), pp. 10-23 as well as A.L. Kristensen, 'Ugaritic Epistolary Formulas: A Comparative Study of the Ugaritic Epistolary Formulas in the Context of the Contemporary Akkadian Formulas in the Letters from Ugarit and Amarna', *UF* 9 (1977), pp. 143-58, esp. 157.

11. Margalit, *A Matter*, p. 174.

provide us with the content of the blessing asked for in the Aqhatu Tale,[12] and we now know that blessings on travellers were incorporated into the *Epic of Gilgamesh* in much the same way, though their content was different. One such runs,

> May Shamash open for you the barred path,
> keep the road in order for your treading,
> the open country in order for your foot.[13]

Another link between poetic and prose texts is once again provided by the letters. A well-attested formula used in letters from Ugarit, El Amarna and elsewhere is the equivalent of a very elaborate 'your humble servant', except that it comes before the main message rather than after it.[14] It is worded as follows:

> At a respectful distance I fall at my lord's feet,
> seven times (on my belly) and
> seven times (on my back).

Several passages in the mythological texts portray a sequence of actions adopted when someone delivers a message: arrival at abode, entry, worship, physical prostration, utterance of message. For example, 'Anatu's visit to Ilu is described as follows:

tgly. d̠d il. w. tbu	She appeared in the encampment of Ilu,
qrš mlk. ab. šnm.	and entered the camp of the King, the Father of Years.
lp'n il. thbr. wtql	At the feet of Ilu she bowed and fell down,
tšt̩ḥwy. wtkbdnh	prostrated herself and honoured him.
tšu. gh. wtṣḥ	She raised her voice and called out:[15]

and then comes her message. The sequence, only implicit in the letters, is spelled out in detail in the narrative texts.[16]

12. *KTU* 1.19 iv 32-33: 'Bless me so that I may go blessed, reassure me so that I may go reassured'.

13. Tigay, *Evolution*, pp. 169-70 (his translation).

14. S.E. Loewenstamm, 'Prostration from afar in Ugaritic, Accadian and Hebrew', *BASOR* 188 (1967), pp. 41-43.

15. *KTU* 1.6 i 34-39, as translated by de Moor, *Anthology*, p. 84. For the difficult words *d̠d* and *qr*, see F. Renfroe, *Arabic-Ugaritic Lexical Studies* (ALASP, 5; Münster: Ugarit-Verlag, 1992), pp. 97-100.

16. For religious elements in the letters, cf. J.-L. Cunchillos, *Estudios de epistolografía ugarítica* (Fuentes de la ciencia bíblica, 3; Valencia: Institución San Jerónimo, 1989), pp. 195-234.

By contrast, the difference between prose and poetry is evident from the example quoted where 'seven' is parallel, as it were, to 'seven'. Another example, from a Namburbi (or apotropaic) ritual, describes how a man, anxious to avert the evil portended by a howling dog, has to immerse himself in the river 'seven times facing upstream, seven times facing downstream'.[17] This is never the case in Ugaritic poetry where numerical parallelism follows the pattern n // n + 1 (where 'n' stands for an integer) as in

'mk. šb't ġlmk	(Take) with you your seven lads,
ṯmn. ḫnzrk	your eight 'boars'.[18]

1.3. *Survey of Studies on Ugaritic Poetry*

Ever since the Ugaritic texts were first discovered (in 1929), deciphered and translated they have been compared with (ancient) Hebrew literature. This is particularly true of their common poetic tradition. So much store has been set on parallels and similarities, in fact, that differences have tended to be submerged. It is true to say that very few studies have been made of the Ugaritic character of Ugaritic poetry. Little has been done to show how it is differentiated from Hebrew or Akkadian verse.

To list all the studies on Ugaritic poetry would take some time and would serve little purpose in this context. I would like, instead, to look first at the early stages in the history of research and then survey those studies exclusively on Ugaritic poetry.

One of the earliest modern scholars to consider Ugaritic poetry (in connection with Hebrew tradition, it must be admitted) was Umberto Cassuto.[19] He commented on the 'phenomenon' (his term) that Hebrew literature shows 'no signs of experimental groping or of searching for techniques'; instead 'they are perfected and polished writings which bear witness to the existence of an artistic tradition which had evolved

17. Text in R. Caplice, *The Akkadian Namburbi Texts: An Introduction* (Sources and Monographs Sources from the Ancient Near East, 1.1; Los Angeles: Undena Publications, 1974), pp. 16-17. See W.G.E. Watson, 'Number Parallelism in Mesopotamian Texts', *Maarav* 7 (1991), pp. 241-52.

18. *KTU* 1.5 v 8-9, on which cf. N. Wyatt, 'Ba'al's Boars', *UF* 19 (1987), pp. 391-98.

19. This is not to ignore the pioneering work of H.L. Ginsberg, notably his *The Legend of King Keret, a Canaanite Epic of the Bronze Age* (BASORSup, 2-3; New Haven: ASOR, 1946) and many other studies.

in the course of many centuries'.[20] He concluded that Israel took over Canaanite tradition. The corollary, not stated by Cassuto, is that Ugaritic verse-making had itself evolved over many years, perhaps centuries, since on the clay tablets there is no evidence of trial and error. We can assume, therefore, that Ugaritic tradition had already evolved in either oral or literary form. Other important scholars are Cyrus Gordon who examined 'syntax and poetic structure' in his comprehensive grammar,[21] and William Foxwell Albright.[22]

Without in any way being exhaustive, a summary of recent study can touch on the following aspects: metre, word-pairs, strophe and stanza, and parallelism. These will be considered briefly. In 1950 Young more or less established that there was no regular metre in Ugaritic verse.[23] Since then various scholars have wrestled with the problem and names that spring to mind are Margalit[24] (one of the few to study Ugaritic metre in its own right, as did Young), de Moor[25] and Pardee.[26] From such studies it seems that some form of free rhythm was used to the accompaniment of music.

Parallel word-pairs have been the subject of intensive study but nearly always in the context of word-pairs common to Ugaritic and Hebrew.[27] An inner-Ugaritic word-pair found in the Kirta Legend has

20. U. Cassuto, *The Goddess Anath: Canaanite Epics of the Patriarchal Age. Texts, Hebrew Translation, Commentary and Introduction* (Jerusalem: Magnes, 1971; ET of Hebrew edition, 1951), p. 18.

21. Latest edition: C.H. Gordon, *Ugaritic Textbook* (AnOr, 38; Rome: Pontifical Biblical Institute, 1965), ch. 13.

22. W.F. Albright, *Yahweh and the Gods of Canaan* (London: Athlone Press, 1968), pp. 4-25.

23. G.D. Young, 'Ugaritic Prosody', *JNES* 9 (1950), pp. 124-33.

24. B. Margalit, '*Studia Ugaritica* I: "Introduction to Ugaritic Prosody"', *UF* 7 (1975), pp. 289-341.

25. J.C. de Moor, 'The Art of Versification in Ugarit and Israel. I: The Rhythmical Structure', in Y. Avishur and J. Blau (eds.), *Studies in Bible and the Ancient Near East Presented to S.E. Loewenstamm on his Seventieth Birthday* (Jerusalem: E. Rubinstein's Publishing House, 1978), pp. 119-39.

26. D. Pardee, 'Ugaritic and Hebrew Metrics', in D. Young (ed.), *Ugarit in Retrospect* (Winona Lake, IN: Eisenbrauns, 1981), pp. 113-30.

27. *RSP* I-III. Exceptional in this respect are the following: K. Aitken, 'Formulaic Patterns for the Passing of Time in Ugaritic Narrative', *UF* 19 (1987), pp. 1-10; 'Oral Formulaic Composition and Theme in the Aqhat Narrative', *UF* 21 (1989), pp. 1-16; 'Word Pairs and Tradition in an Ugaritic Tale', *UF* 21 (1989), pp. 17-38.

therefore gone unnoticed. In the course of a dream or vision in which the hero is informed of future events, his enemy is quoted as saying:

> DEPART (*ng*), O King, from my house,
> BE FAR (*rḥq l*), Kirta, from my courts!

When the event actually takes place, though, the message (from King Pabil) is slightly different:

> BE FAR (*rḥq l*), O King, from my house,
> DEPART (*ng*), Kirta, from my courts![28]

Evidently, the initial words have been switched round. Trivial though it is, since no change in meaning is involved, such free variation is indicative of oral poetic technique, inviting us to look for other examples of the same type.

Among others, de Moor and Margalit have worked on the difficult topics of strophe and stanza, attempting to establish how poems should be segmented.[29] Sauren and Kestemont's joint paper on the same subject has been rather neglected, largely because it assumed too rigid a framework right at the outset, but it remains valuable.[30] Further research is needed and conclusions are, as yet, premature.

By far the greatest proportion of research has been devoted to parallelism in all its forms, particularly staircase parallelism (discussed later). In conclusion, it is clear that by concentrating on comparison between Hebrew and Ugaritic and by confining themselves to well-worn topics, students of Ugaritic poetry have provided an uneven, indeed an inaccurate picture. We still lack in-depth analysis of many aspects of Ugaritic versification.

1.4. *The Oral Poet in Ugarit: Verse and Music*

The Ugaritic tablets provide us with some information on what we can anachronistically call the 'troubadours'. The third tablet of the 'Ba'alu Cycle' begins with a banquet at which there was singing:

28. *KTU* 1.14 iii 27-29 // vi 14-15; the sequence in vv. 44-45 is uncertain.

29. J.C. de Moor, 'The Art of Versification in Ugarit and Israel. II: The Formal Structure', *UF* 10 (1978), pp. 187-217. B. Margalit, 'Alliteration in Ugaritic Poetry: Its Rôle in Composition and Analysis', *UF* 11 (1979), pp. 537-57; 'Alliteration in Ugaritic Poetry: Its Role in Composition and Analysis (Part II)', *JNSL* 8 (1980), pp. 57-80, 62-64.

30. H. Sauren and G. Kestemont, 'Keret, roi de Ḫubur', *UF* 3 (1971), pp. 181-221.

qm. ybd. wyšr	Up he got, intoned and sang;
mṣltm. bd. n'm	the cymbals were in the hands of the minstrel,
yšr. ǵzr. ṭb. ql	sing did the dulcet-voiced lad
'l. b'l. bṣrrt ṣpn.	in the presence of Ba'alu in the recesses of Zaphunu.[31]

At another banquet Rapi'u is described as one

dyšr. wyḏmr	who sings and makes music
bknr. w ṯlb	with lyre and flute
btp. wmṣltm.	with tambourine and cymbals
bmrqdm. dšn	with ivory castanets
bḫbr. kṯr. ṭbm	among the boon companions of Kutharu.[32]

Not unexpectedly, then, it appears that singers used musical instruments to accompany their songs, improvised to suit the occasion. More evocative is the text (of which two versions have been found) which describes the goddess 'Anatu applying cosmetic after a careful toilette. Then,

tiḫd knrh bydh	She takes her lyre in her hand
tšt rimt lirth	she places the bull-headed(?) harp on her breast,
tšr dd aliyn b'l	and sings of her love for Mightiest Ba'alu.[33]

In another passage two messengers come to Danel with word that his son, Aqhatu, is dead. As they approach in mourning garb they sing dolefully and, it would seem, use mime to convey their message from a distance, though Danel's daughter, Pughatu, is the first to see them. Presumably they are preparing Danel for the worst:

hlm. ṯ[nm q]dqd.	Twice they hit each other over the head,
ṯlṯid. 'l. ud[n]	three times on the ear.[34]

If correctly interpreted the passage describes the two lads miming what happened to Aqhatu.[35] Such evidence, combined with traces of

31. *KTU* 1.3 i 18-21.

32. *KTU* 1.108: 3-5; for text and translation, see D. Pardee, *Les textes paramythologiques de la 24ᵉ campagne (1961)* (Ras Shamra-Ougarit, 4; Paris: Editions Recherche sur les Civilisations, 1988), pp. 76-78, 81 and 97-101.

33. Composite (and slightly simplified) text from *KTU* 1.3 iii 4-6 and 1.101: 17'-18'; for text, translation and discussion see Pardee, *Les textes*, pp. 121-25, 150-52.

34. *KTU* 1.19 ii 29-30.

35. So Gibson, *Canaanite Myths*, p. 116 n. 3; similarly, de Moor, *Anthology*,

oral poetic technique in the poems, points to a degree of live improvisation at some stage in the creation of these works.

1.5. *Poetic Technique*

Of the many poetic devices and techniques used in Ugaritic poetry only a few can be considered here. They are parallelism, expansion and contraction, and chiasmus.

Parallelism in all its forms is well represented in Ugaritic verse. Synonymous, antithetic, chiastic, number and congruent (or 'gender-matching') parallelism all occur. An example of synonymous parallelism is:

bm nšq whr	On kissing there was conception,
bḥbq ḥmḥmt	on embracing there was orgasm.[36]

According to de Moor, a 'fundamental law of West-Semitic versification is that within certain limits, every structural unit could be elaborated or condensed, expanded or contracted'.[37] As an example of such expansion and contraction he cites the following variants which all fill the same 'metrical' slot:

ylkm. qr. mym	Woe to you, 'Water Fountain';
ylk. mrrt. tǵll. bnr	Woe to you, 'Tree Growing Deep in Tilth';
ylk. qrt. ablm	Woe to you, 'City of Mourners'.[38]

The place names (which I have attempted to translate) are obviously of differing lengths, which suggests a degree of freedom with regard to length of line.[39]

Chiastic patterning is by no means exclusive to the poetry I am describing; it is found in most ancient literature to a greater or lesser degree.[40] However, in some texts from Ras Shamra it is used in a special way, namely, to show two or more individuals acting as one.

p. 253 and n. 198 and, in general, B. Margalit, 'The Messengers of Woe to Dan'el: A Reconstruction and Interpretation of *KTU* 1.19: II: 27-48', *UF* 15 (1983), pp. 105-17. However, cf. del Olmo Lete, *Mitos y leyendas*, p. 391.

36. *KTU* 1.23: 51 // 56.

37. J.C. de Moor, 'The Art of Versification. I', p. 127.

38. De Moor, 'The Art of Versification. I', p. 125. On the enigmatic name *mrrt tǵll bnr*, see B. Margalit, *The Ugaritic Poem of AQHT: Text, Translation, Commentary* (BZAW, 182; Berlin: de Gruyter, 1989), pp. 413-15, 418-22.

39. See, similarly, Margalit, '*Studia Ugaritica* I', pp. 295-96.

40. J.W. Welch, *Chiasmus in Antiquity* (Hildesheim: Gerstenberg, 1981).

For instance, the artisan god 'Sir Adroit-and-Cunning', as Gaster neatly translates,[41] is seen approaching Danel:

hlk kṯr ky'n	The coming of Kutharu he surely saw,
wy'n tdrq ḫss	he saw the rapid advance of Hasisu.[42]

By crossing over the components of the couplet chiastically the deity is depicted not as two separate beings but as one.

1.6. *Imagery*

Imagery lifts technique to a higher and more immediately appealing plane. We can all appreciate parallelism, chiastic patterns and so on, but imagery infuses life into dry words, particularly if the imagery is apt. A crude taxonomy can divide figurative language into similes, metaphors, personification and just plain imagery. In this section I will look briefly at the last topic and indicate how imaginative the Ugaritic poets could be. In one text, wine is described in the following terms:

hn. ym. yṣq. yn. ṯmk	Look! For one day he poured wine of Thamuka,
mrṯ. yn. srnm.	must-wine, fit for rulers,
yn. bld ǵll.	wine with no after-thirst,
yn. išryt.	wine of happiness,
'nq. smd lbnn	the purple necklace of the Lebanon,
ṭṣ. mrṯ. yḫrṯ. il	must-dew grown by a god.[43]

This mini-poem (in de Moor's rendering)[44] to the virtues of wine is a gem and the imagery, especially of the final couplet, is masterly.[45]

1.7. *Problems*

The Ugaritic texts still present many unsolved problems of which I shall concentrate on only three aspects. They are stichometry,

41. T.H. Gaster, *Thespis: Myth, Legend and Custom in the Old Testament* (New York: Henry Schuman, 1950), p. 187.

42. *KTU* 1.17 v 10-11 and par.

43. *KTU* 1.22 i 17-20; text as in W.T. Pitard, 'A New Edition of the "Rapi'uma" Texts: *KTU* 1.20-22', *BASOR* 285 (1992), pp. 33-77, 56-63.

44. Translation: de Moor, *Anthology*, p. 272; cf. del Olmo Lete, *Mitos y leyendas*, p. 424. For some difficult terms, cf. Renfroe, *Lexical Studies*, pp. 90 (*bld*), 107 (*ll*).

45. For another example, cf. W.G.E. Watson, 'Imagery in a Ugaritic Incantation', *UF* 24 (1992), pp. 367-68.

translation and metre. By stichometry is meant arranging the lines of a poem in the correct way so that each line of verse is separate and does not run on; in a word, layout. It might be imagined that on his clay tablet a scribe would begin each new line of verse on a new line, but that was not always the case. The scribes did so for a lot of the time, but just as often they would ignore layout and write line 2 on the same line as line 1, without using 'carriage return' as it were, and carry on in that way, just fitting the words into the space available. This may have been due to laziness, lack of skill, difference in convention, dictation[46] or to other factors. Apparently there were aids for the scribes built into the text. For example, consecutive lines tended to begin with the same letter for runs of two, three or even as many as eight lines. Yet, in spite of almost every line in the 'Incantation against the Evil Eye'[47] beginning with *'n*, 'eye', the copyist perversely acted as if the last few lines began with *l*, 'to'. The result is aesthetically pleasing but belies the underlying reality which is that the ancient scribe ignored lineation. It is occasionally difficult to translate precisely because we are unsure of the lineation, a difficulty compounded when different scholars have differing views.

This brings us to our second, related hurdle, translation problems. In some cases we simply do not know what certain words mean and cognate Semitic languages are not always helpful. There are also certain repeated passages which defy exact interpretation.[48] On the whole, though, there is general agreement on translating the poetic texts of Ugarit and in general we are able to appreciate them from the aspect of style with some confidence.

As mentioned, of all the problems inherent in ancient Semitic verse, metre is the most intractable. I think we have to admit that we can only guess at what the metre of Ugaritic poetry was (if it ever existed) and hope that by dint of deeper study and further discoveries our understanding will improve. Lack of regular metre may be an indication of oral composition to the accompaniment of music (as suggested above).

46. W.J. Horwitz, 'Our Ugaritic Mythological Texts: Copied or Dictated?', *UF* 9 (1977), pp. 123-30, esp. 128-30; 'The Ugaritic Scribe', *UF* 11 (1979), pp. 389-94.

47. Cf. G. del Olmo Lete, 'Un conjuro ugarítico contra el "mal ojo" (*KTU* 1.96)', *Anuari de filología* 15 (1992), pp. 7-16.

48. Notably *KTU* 1.3 iii 14-17 and par.

1.8. *Distinctive Features*

We now come to what I consider to be the nub of this paper: What makes Ugaritic poetry different from other poetry? What are its distinctive features? Not easy questions to answer because Ugaritic shares so many other features with ancient Semitic poetry in general. Staircase parallelism has already been mentioned, for many scholars the outstanding contribution of Ugaritic to poetic tradition. Alliteration also was developed into a refined technique, as Margalit has shown. Another aspect is the narrative nature of Ugaritic verse. These features can be looked at one by one.

One of the better examples of staircase parallelism describes the lesser god Athtaru coming down off his, or rather Ba‘alu's throne. Having tried it for size he realizes it is too big for him:

yrd. ‘ṯtr. ‘rẓ	Descend did Athtaru the ‘terrible’,
yrd lkḥṯ. aliyn. b‘l	descend did he from the throne of Mightiest Ba‘alu,
wymlk. barṣ. il. klh	and rule the earth of Ilu, all of it.[49]

The mimesis of descent here is superb. There is an unusually high density of staircase parallelism in Ugaritic. If we very roughly estimate the number of verse lines in the corpus to be between 4000 and 4500, then, taking repetition into account there are about 1500 strophes. Of these, some 40 exhibit staircase parallelism. Or, moving away from dry figures, the Tale of Aqhatu, for example, uses the pattern four times in the first 16 lines. On top of high density, then, there is a tendency to cluster, a sign perhaps of oral composition. Unique to Ugaritic is the combination of staircase parallelism (epanalepsis) and the terrace pattern (anadiplosis), a combination which is found at least five times. For example:

wyšu. ‘nh. aliyn. b‘l
wyšu. ‘nh.wy‘n
wy‘n. btlt. ‘nt
n‘mt. bn. aḫt. b‘l

Lift up his eyes did Mightiest Ba‘alu,
lift up his eyes *and see*
and see the Virgin ‘Anatu,
the prettiest among Ba‘alu's sisters[50]

49. *KTU* 1.6 i 63-65.

50. *KTU* 1.10 ii 13-16; also *ibid.* lines 21-23 and 26-28. See, too, *KTU* 1.3

The result is an interlocked quatrain which here has the effect of slowing down the action and delaying the identity of the person Ba'alu has noticed. So fixed was the pattern in Ugaritic that few deviations can be detected. One example is

aṯt [*.tqḥ*]. *ykrt*	The wife you take, O Kirta,
aṯt tqḥ. btk[.]	the wife you take into your house,
[*ǵ*]*lmt. tšʿrb ḥẓrk*	[the w]ench you introduce into your court[51]

where the first word of line 3 should have been a repeat of *aṯt* had the standard sequence been followed. Instead it has been changed to *ǵlmt*. Another instance, possibly, is

mlkn. aliyn. bʿl.	Our king is Mightiest Baʿalu!
ṯpṭn in. dʿlnh.	Our *ruler*, above whom there is none![52]

Margalit has presented evidence to suggest that the requirement of alliteration in Ugaritic poetry tended to determine choice of words. He has even gone so far as to suggest it to be a distinctive feature of Northwest Semitic poetry, or at least of Ugaritic and Hebrew verse. The corollary is that recognition of alliterative sets will indicate structural units, particularly the strophe.[53] Certainly, alliteration and alliterative patterning seem to have dictated the selection of some words and the avoidance of others in many texts, though the requirement of alliteration cannot be pressed too hard.[54] One of his many examples (with alliterating letters in capitals) shows that the choice of *tbṯḫ*, 'couch' (probably a loanword from Akkadian) over commoner *mt* or *ʿrš* (both meaning 'bed') was due to the underlying alliterative pattern.

Yṣq ḪYm wTBṯḪ	He poured a canopy and a couch,
kT il dT rBT	a huge twenty-thousand shekel pedestal[55]

However, we also have to reckon with another factor: the intentional selection of a rare word. Rather than use common terms, the poet shows his mastery of language and his learning by inserting a

v 19-21 and 1.161: 20-22.

51. *KTU* 1.15 ii 21-23.

52. *KTU* 1.3 v 32-33. It is possible that *ṯpṭ* may mean 'judge' here.

53. See above, n. 30.

54. See especially D. Pardee, *Ugaritic and Hebrew Poetic Parallelism: A Trial Cut* ('nt *I and Proverbs 2)* (VTSup, 39; Leiden: Brill, 1988).

55. *KTU* 1.4 i 29-30.

technical word or, as here, a loanword into his strophe. Thus there are two concomitant or even competing elements: (1) alliteration and (2) lexicon or use of a 'poetic' word. One or other could dominate, though in our example both were of equal importance.

Two more features can be looked at: they are narrative and repetition and they are related. As already mentioned, Ugaritic poetry is largely narrative. It generally tells a story and so is very much closer to Mesopotamian models such as the *Epic of Gilgamesh* or the *Legend of Adapa* than it is to Hebrew tradition where narrative is in prose.[56] Ugaritic narrative poetry tends to be repetitive. Whole sections are repeated word for word: foretelling dreams and their enactments; command and fulfilment; plans and their execution. There is, besides, a fondness for stereotyped passages. For instance, there is a stock reaction when someone is given bad news: she (or he) stamps her feet, contorts her spine, sweats, convulses her vertebrae and the small of her back.[57] The implication (once again) is that we are dealing with oral poetry.

As Ruth Finnegan observes,

> The emphasis on repetition in oral literature makes sense in practice... Oral poetry is necessarily ephemeral. Once said, it cannot, for that performance anyway, be recaptured. Repetition has real point in such circumstances: it makes it easier for the audience to grasp what has been said and gives the singer/speaker confidence that it has understood the message he is trying to communicate.[58]

1.9. *Folktale Elements*

The story-poems of Ras Shamra use many folktale motifs. Magic clubs are named and can dance away from hands, people can fly and so on. Of these, one stands out as very familiar to us in the guise of 'seven league boots'. Several times gods and goddesses travel

balp d rbt kmn	over a thousand fields, ten thousand hectares

56. However, see the various contributions on Hebrew narrative verse in J.C. de Moor and W.G.E. Watson (eds.), *Verse in Ancient Near Eastern Prose* (AOAT, 42: Kevelaer: Batzon & Bercker; Neukirchen–Vluyn: Neukirchener Verlag, 1993.

57. For some of these details, cf. J.C. de Moor, 'The Anatomy of the Back', *UF* 12 (1980), pp. 425-26.

58. R. Finnegan, *Oral Poetry: Its Nature, Significance and Social Context* (Cambridge: Cambridge University Press, 1976), pp. 129. See also Z. Zevit, 'Cognitive Theory and the Memorability of Biblical Poetry', *Maarav* 8 (1992), pp. 199-212.

to arrive at their destinations almost immediately. This corresponds, even in its use of number parallelism, to a similar repeated formula in the *Epic of Gilgamesh*:

> At twenty leagues they broke off a morsel,
> at thirty leagues they prepared for the night.

Sometimes the explanatory couplet is added:

> Fifty leagues they travelled in one day,
> a journey of a month and fifteen days.[59]

The mathematical precision of Babylonia is not matched by the text from ancient Syria, but each tradition in its own way provided a forerunner to the magic boots of fairytale.

1.10. *Conclusions*

I began by asking what is specifically Ugaritic in Ugaritic poetry and ended up discussing techniques of oral composition. There are indications that such techniques were used in Ugaritic. However, we cannot simply say, 'There is evidence for techniques of oral improvisation in the Ugaritic poems, narrative and otherwise, and therefore it was an oral poetry'. For one thing, that poetry only exists in written form on clay tablets. True, these writings could be the record, from dictation or from memory, of a dead or dying tradition of improvising poets. However, there is also the possibility that writing poets took over or, if you prefer, continued traditions of oral composition, or even that they interacted with a living tradition of bards.[60] We can only guess.

To return to our original quest, if there is a specific contribution made by Ugaritic to a poetic tradition (aside from such patterns as staircase parallelism, certain forms of chiasmus and so on) it seems to lie in injecting originality into a well-worn, stereotyped body of versification. Or, to change the metaphor, it is an attempt at breaking out of a set mould. The single copies of Ugaritic tablets that have been found are, perhaps, the work of a single school which re-worked stock and static verse and made it sparkle with new life.[61]

59. Gilg. IV i 1-5, etc.

60. See the comments in Gibson, *Canaanite Myths*, p. 6 n. 4.

61. For discussion of some of the duplicates that have been found, cf. Pardee, *Les textes*, pp. 152-54.

2. *Middle-Eastern Forerunners to a Folk-tale Motif*[62]

We are all familiar with the folk-tale or fairy-tale motif of magical transportation, particularly in the guise of 'seven league boots'.[63] The same motif seems to be attested in Ugaritic poetry and in the *Epic of Gilgamesh*, as I hope to show in this note written in memory of Mitchell Dahood, enthusiastic teacher and friend.

In the Ugaritic Baal Cycle, the representation of moving extraordinarily fast is conveyed by a fixed formula, usually in combination with other stock expressions. The formula is none other than

(1)	*balp šd rbt kmn*	By the thousand *šiddu*, ten thousand *kumānu*.[64]

which occurs no less than six times.[65] Most often it follows the introductory line

62. First published in *Or* 53.2 (Rome: Pontifical Biblical Institute Press, 1984), pp. 333-36.

63. See S. Thompson, *Motif-Index of Folk-Literature: A Classification of Narrative Elements in Folktales, Ballads, Myths, Fables, Mediaeval Romances, Exempla, Fabliaux, Jest-Books, and Local Legends* (Bloomington: Indiana University Press, 1955), II, pp. 374-78, under D2120, 'magic transportation', D2122.2, 'hundred-league stride', D2122, 'journey with magic speed'; pp. 257-64, under D1521.1 'seven-league boots'. Also, G. Jobes, *Dictionary of Mythology, Folklore and Symbols* (New York: Scarecrow Press, 1962), p. 1424.

64. On the identity of *kmn* (*kumānu*) and *šd* (*šiddu*), see S.E. Loewenstamm, 'Notes on the Alalakh Tablets', *IEJ* 6 (1956), pp. 220-21; M. Dietrich and O. Loretz 'Die soziale Struktur von Alalaḫ und Ugarit (V). Die Weingärten des Gebietes von Alalaḫ im 15. Jahrhundert', *UF* 1 (1969), pp. 37-64, 61-62. Cf., too, M. Liverani, 'The *kumānu* Measure as $\frac{1}{4}$ of 1 *ikū*', *Assur* 1/1 (1974), p. 11. Since the *iku* could denote length as well as area (cf. *CAD*, I/J, p. 69) *kmn* = *šd* may also refer to distance. The use of the same formula in *KTU* 1.4 v 56-57 *alp šd aḫd bt rbt kmn hkl*, 'Let (Baal's) house occupy a thousand *š*., ten thousand *k*. his palace', simply alludes to enormous size. Similar is the description of Huwawa's forest which is said to stretch for ten thousand *bēru* in all directions (Gilg. Y iii 107). Note, too, line 43 of the Shamash Hymn, 'To regions (*šiddu*) far off, unknown, and unnumbered 'miles' (*bīru*)' (W.G. Lambert, *Babylonian Wisdom Literature* [Oxford: Clarendon Press, 1960], p. 128 l. 43) which describes the daily circuit of the sun.

65. See, in general, M. Dietrich and O. Loretz, 'Anats grosse Sprünge. Zu *KTU* 1.3 IV 31-40 et par.', *UF* 12 (1980), pp. 383-89. References are provided, p. 384 and n. 13.

(2)	*idk lytn (/ttn) pnm (‘m)*	Thereupon he (/she) set face (toward) (personal/place-name).[66]

Marvellous though it is, an approach of this kind is sometimes perceived prior to arrival, as in *KTU* 1.3 iv 39-40:

(3)	*hlk. aẖth. b‘l. y‘n.*	His sister's coming did Baal perceive,
	tdrq. bnt(!). *abh.*	the onrush of his father's daughter,[67]

which suggests, possibly, a cloud of dust thrown up by the swift approach of the newcomer. In *KTU* 1.3 iv 31-40 these standard expressions are combined with two additional formulae, which are novel.

(4)	[33]*atm. bštm. wan. šnt*	You in two years, but I in (the space of) sleep!
	[34]*b*(!)*ġr. lrḥq. ilm.*	From my mountain to an enormous distance,
	inbb [35]*lrḥq. ilnym.*	from Inbb to a fantastic distance.
(5)	*ṯn. mṯpdm* [36]*ṯḥt. ‘nt. arṣ.*	Two launchings—the earth's furrows below;
	ṯlṯ. mtḥ. ġyrm	three—the breadth of the lowlands (below).

The problems of these lines have largely been resolved,[68] except for the first four words of (4). These are usually rendered, ‘You delay, but I am away’,[69] but Dahood, in one of his papers, proposed instead, ‘You in two years, but I in one’.[70] I have gone one step further in my translation (above), understanding *šnt* to mean ‘sleep’ as elsewhere in Ugaritic.[71] The implication is that Anath travelled a two-year journey in the space of a single night. Evidence for nocturnal travel comes

66. For the Akkadian reflex *pāni nadānu*, ‘to get ready for travel’, cf. *AHw*, p. 702b under 3cγ.

67. I agree with Dietrich and Loretz (see n. 64) that the ‘seeing formula’ is separate from the ‘travel formula’, but they slur over the difficulties in *KTU* 1.17 v 9-11.

68. See n. 65.

69. For example, A. Caquot, M. Sznycer and A. Herdner, *Textes ougaritiques. I. Mythes et légendes* (LAPO, 7; Paris: Cerf, 1974), p. 171; but del Olmo Lete, *Mitos y leyendas*, p. 187: ‘vosotros podéis ir despacio, pero yo he de dejar’.

70. M.J. Dahood, review of Gibson, *Canaanite Myth*, *Bib* 62 (1981), pp. 274-77.

71. *KTU* 1.14 i 33 and 1.19 iii 45.

from *KTU* 1.4 iv 31-34. There, Athirat is greeted on arrival by El with the words:

(6)	[31]*ik. mġyt. rbt. aṯr[t. y]m*	How has Lady Athirat of the sea arrived?
	[32]*ik. atwt. qnyt. i[lm]*	How has the creatress of the gods come?
	[33]*rġb. rġbt. wtġt*[ ]	Are you very hungry, having journeyed afar?
	[34]*hm. ġmu. ġmit. w'*s[*t*]	Or are you very thirsty, having travelled all night?[72]

Additional evidence is supplied by descriptions of Qdš-wamrr lighting the way ahead for a traveller on a donkey.[73]

The Ugaritic expressions (1), (4) and (5) evoke a corresponding, but more complex, formula used in the *Epic of Gilgamesh*. The formula, used several times (with variations) to mark the hero's journeys, is worded in its most complete form as follows:

(7)	*ana 20 bēr iksupū kusāpa*	At 20 'leagues' they broke off a morsel,
	ana 30 bēr iškunū nubatta	at 30 (further) 'leagues' they prepared for the night.
	50 bēr illikū kal ūmi	50 'leagues' they travelled in the whole day,
	mālak arḫi u šapatti	a journey of a month and 15 days.
	ina šalši ūmi iṯḫû ana GN	On the third day they approached GN.
	maḫar [d]*Šamaš uḫarrû būra*	Before Shamash they dug a well.[74]

The first point to notice is the unmistakable numerical parallelism in the form 'twenty // thirty'.[75] The incredible speed of travel is the next feature; a six-week journey is compressed into a single day. Lastly, on nearing their goal Gilgamesh and Enkidu dig a well. Without pushing

72. For *ik*, 'how?', in this passage, cf. C.H. Gordon, 'Ugaritic ik "How?"', *Newsletter for Ugaritic Studies* 26 (1981), pp. 9-10. For the translation of lines 33-34, cf. G.R. Driver, *Canaanite Myths and Legends* (Old Testament Studies, 3; Edinburgh: T. & T. Clark, 1955), p. 97; and Gibson, *Canaanite Myths*, p. 59.

73. See W.G.E. Watson, 'Parallels to Some Passages in Ugaritic', *UF* 10 (1978), pp. 397-402, 397-99 for texts and discussion. In the *Epic of Gilgamesh*, however, night travel is explicitly excluded.

74. For text, translation and parallel passages, see, conveniently, J.H. Tigay, *The Evolution of the Gilgamesh Epic* (Philadelphia: University of Pennsylvania Press, 1982), p. 8.

75. The numbers are added to make '50' in the third line.

the comparison too far, an ever-present danger in studies of this kind, it is indisputable that in the *Epic of Gilgamesh* and in the Ugaritic texts quoted above, magical transportation is expressed in similar ways. Both traditions use numerical parallelism, and, in particular, the '2 // 3' of (5) corresponds to the '20 // 30' of (7). Number parallelism is also present in (1) and (4). In both traditions, too, travel over very long distances is compressed in terms of time. Finally, a ritual component appears in both sets of texts.[76] There is no need to imply dependency either way.[77] It seems more likely that the common factor is psychological. In helping their listeners to visualize incredible speed of travel the storytellers of old resorted to concrete imagery. A formula such as 'hundred-league sandals' had more impact than any piling up of abstract superlatives and in this respect the tales of the ancient Near and Middle East were no different from their more recent counterparts.[78]

3. *The Aḥiqar Sayings: Some Marginal Comments*[79]

James Lindenberger's new edition of the *Proverbs of Aḥiqar*[80] is very welcome. Apart from its intrinsic merit as a critical edition of these important sayings, based on actual study of the original papyrus (from Elephantine) his study is of significance at other levels. He has confirmed the current consensus that the original language of both the

76. For the *Epic of Gilgamesh*, cf. Tigay, *Evolution*, p. 81, nn. 31 and 152. The obscure Ugaritic ritual is *KTU* 1.3 iv 27-31 (and par.).

77. D. Freedman, 'Counting Formulae in the Akkadian Epics', *JANESCU* 3 (1971), pp. 65-81 concludes that the source for the Akkadian passages he discusses is Ugaritic.

78. The horse listed by Gilgamesh as one of Ishtar's discarded lovers was able to gallop for seven 'miles' by her decree (Gilg. VI 55; cf. *CAD*, B, p. 209).

79. First published in *AuOr* 2 (1984), pp. 253-61.

80. J.M. Lindenberger, *The Aramaic Proverbs of Aḥiqar* (The Johns Hopkins Near Eastern Studies: Baltimore: The Johns Hopkins University Press, 1983). I have also consulted his 1974 doctoral thesis with the same title (Ann Arbor, Michigan, 1982; No. 77-16, p. 567). These works will be referred to as Lindenberger, *Proverbs* and 'Proverbs'. Appendix A of the original thesis has now appeared as 'The Gods of Aḥiqar', *UF* 14 (1982), pp. 105-18. Both his thesis and his paper in *UF* 14 were invaluable for my own preparation of a course in wisdom texts given in the Department of Religious Studies, University of Newcastle upon Tyne. Since then I have been able to consult his book.

story and the proverbs is Aramaic, not Akkadian.[81] This in turn means that *Aḥiqar* can now be considered as Aramaic literature, a welcome addition to the small but growing corpus of extant Aramaic poetry.[82] Lindenberger has commented on poetic aspects of these sayings[83] arguing that while some are definitely verse, others are prosaic, with various grades between the extremes.[84] Finally, he has provided evidence for an origin in northern Syria, which again fills a gap in the known wisdom traditions of that area, quite apart from any comparisons that can be drawn with Ugaritic and Hebrew literature.

My comments here do not constitute a critical review, rather they are intended as an acceptance of Lindberger's invitation for renewed study of these interesting sayings. I will point to some unnoticed parallels in ancient Near Eastern literature and concentrate on poetic aspects, in line with Lindenberger's own remarks. First I will comment on individual sayings, in sequence, then I will make some observations on versification and lastly, draw some tentative conclusions. Some lesser comments will be reserved to footnotes.[85] Throughout, I reproduce Lindenberger's translation.

81. In addition, Lindenberger has shown that E.Y. Kutscher and J.C. Greenfield were correct in asserting that the Sayings and the frame narrative are in different dialects of Aramaic. Details are provided in *Proverbs*, pp. 379-404 (= Appendix A; 'Proverbs', pp. 488-518 = Appendix B).

82. For a brief bibliography, see my *Classical Hebrew Poetry: A Guide to its Techniques* (Sheffield: JSOT Press, 1984), p. 5 n. 2. In addition, R.C. Steiner and C.F. Nims, 'A Polemical Poem from the Aramaic Text in Demotic Script', *JNES* 43 (1984), pp. 89-114, and S.P. Vleeming and J.W. Wesselius, 'An Aramaic Hymn from the Fourth Century BC', *BO* 391 (1982), pp. 502-509. Also, J.C. VanderKam, 'The Poetry of IQApGen, XX, 2-8a', *RevQ* 10 (1979–81), pp. 57-66; he shows that these lines comprise a nine-stanza poem which exhibits repetition, parallelism, chiasmus, rhyme, assonance, alliteration, paronomasia, envelope figure (*inclusio*) and a degree of metrical patterning. Cf., too, J.C. Greenfield, 'Early Aramaic Poetry', *JANESCU* 11 (1979), pp. 49-51.

83. Lindenberger, *Proverbs*, pp. 23-24 ('Proverbs', pp. 18-20) and *passim*.

84. Lindenberger, *Proverbs*, p. 23 ('Proverbs', p. 19). For Hebrew, see J.L. Kugel, *The Idea of Biblical Poetry: Parallelism and its History* (New Haven: Yale University Press, 1981), pp. 59-95.

85. Saying 1, 'What is stronger (louder?) than a braying ass?', evokes a couplet from the Babylonian Flood Story: 'The flood bellows like a bull/Like a howling vulture the wind sounds' (*Atr.* III iii 15-16, as restored and translated by J.G. Westenholz, review of B. Lewis, *The Sargon Legend*, *JNES* 43 [1984], p. 76).

Saying 5

> A blow for a serving-boy, a rebuke for a slave-girl,
> and for all your servants discipline!

The internal parallelism[86] of the first line—*mh'h l'lm // k'*[*y'*] *lḥnt*—shows that, like Sayings 29 and 30, this saying is a couplet, not a tricolon as set out by Lindenberger.[87]

Saying 9

> The lion catches the scent(?) of the stag in (his)
> hidden den(?) and he...
> and sheds its blood and eats its flesh.
> Just so is the concourse of men(?).

Such sapiential reflections occur in the OT (Job 39.5-6) and the *Legend of Sargon* (in broken context)[88] as J. Westenholz has observed.[89] On the 'third' line Lindenberger comments, 'The symmetry of *wdmh y'šd // wbśrh y'kl* leads one to suspect that the entire saying (except perhaps the final clause) is couched in quasi-poetic form'[90] and recovery of the word-pair *bśr // dm* in a recently edited Aramaic poem[91] lends support to his argument.

Saying 12

> There are two things which are good,
> and a third which is pleasing to Šamaš (etc.)

86. On internal parallelism, see Chapter 3.

87. Lindenberger, *Proverbs*, p. 53 ('Proverbs', p. 74).

88. For example, 'The wolf did not escape the blood' (col. ii 13); text and translation in B. Lewis, *The Sargon Legend: A Study of the Akkadian Text and the Tale of the Hero who was Exposed at Birth* (ASOR Dissertation Series, 4; Cambridge, MA: American Schools of Oriental Research, 1980), p. 29.

89. J.G. Westenholz, review of Lewis, *The Sargon Legend*, p. 77.

90. The wording has been altered slightly to 'Note the quasi-poetic symmetry of *wdmh y'šd // wbśrh y'kl*' in Lindenberger, *Proverbs*, p. 61 (my quote is from 'Proverbs', p. 92).

91. Steiner and Nims, 'Polemical Poem', p. 95 lines 6-7: 'Let us eat meat (*bśr*) and become fat; Let us cause blood (*dm*) to flow and drink to saturation'; see their comments, pp. 101-102. Lindenberger, 'Proverbs', p. 19 discussed the word-pair, but the Aramaic poem in Demotic script had not then been edited.

The function of many such numerical sayings[92] is delayed explanation: one does not know what the last item will be until it comes, as a climax.[93]

Saying 13

> Her kingdom is eternal

This extract from the six-line description of Wisdom personified which comprises Saying 13—with the restoration [*ḥk*]*mt*[*h*] proposed by Lindenberger[94]—accords well with the alliterative Ugaritic passage which he quotes[95] and evokes the expression *mlk ʿlmk*, 'your perpetual rule' (*KTU* 1.2 iv 10).[96]

Saying 20

> When a royal word is commanded you,
> it is a burning fire (etc.)

Similar imagery may underlie the description of *Yammu*'s twin messengers delivering his message to El (*KTU* 1.2 i 32-33):

išt. ištm. yitmr.	(like) a fire, (like) two fires they appeared,
ḥrb. lṭšt [*lš*]*nhm.*	a whetted sword their tongue.

More apposite is the passage from the (Middle Assyrian) *Fable of the Fox*, where Fox accuses Wolf of spreading false reports:

92. See now H.-P. Rüger, 'Die gestaffelter Zahlensprüche des Alten Testaments und aram. Achikar 92', *VT* 31 (1981), pp. 229-34.

93. See, too, Sayings 22, 29 and 30. For examples in Hebrew, cf. M.J. Dahood, *Psalms III* (Garden City, NY: Doubleday, 1970), pp. 51, 52, 56, 57, 115, 128, 201, 232, 245 and 260; also, N. Airoldi, 'Esodo 22, 28a: Esplicitazione ritardata', *Bib* 54 (1973), pp. 63-64. W.G. Lambert discusses this feature in 'A Neo-Babylonian Tammuz Lament', *JAOS* 103 (1983), p. 214 apropos a Neo-Babylonian lament.

94. Lindenberger, *Proverbs*, pp. 68-69 ('Proverbs', pp. 117-18), correcting Grelot.

95. Lindenberger, *Proverbs* p. 283 n. 129 ('Proverbs', p. 122, n. 22); the passage is *tḥmk il ḥkmk ʿm ʿlm*, 'Wise is your decree, O El; your wisdom is to eternity' (*KTU* 1.4 iv 41-42). See now M. Dietrich and O. Loretz, 'Die Weisheit des ugaritischen Gottes El im Kontext der altorientalischen Weisheit', *UF* 24 (1992), pp. 31-38.

96. See, too, my comments in 'Reversed Rootplay in Ps 145', *Bib* 62 (1981), pp. 101-102, and reference there to Dan. 3.33 and 4.31.

You, Wolf, are an image of 'filth'
an evildoer, who cuts his friend's throat.
why do you spread flames to the (?) of the (?) reed-thicket?
(Why do you) send up smoke from the dried up forest?
set on fire... the bitumen pits?[97]

Saying 22

I have tasted even the bitter medlar,
and have eaten endives(?),
but there is nothing more bitter than poverty.

As in Sayings 12 (see above) 21, 29 and 30, the 'bite' of the proverb is reserved to the end, another example, therefore, of delayed explanation. The term *mrrt* has been discussed extensively[98] while *ḥsyn* may have its analogue in Ugaritic[99] in spite of Lindenberger's hesitation.[100]

Saying 25

A king is like the Merciful
even his voice is haughty
Who is there who could stand him
except one with whom El is?

Lindenberger comments that the adjective *rḥmn* ('merciful') 'is an epithet of El, who is mentioned by name in the last clause of the saying'.[101] An addition to the material he has collected in support of

97. Text and translation: Lambert, *Babylonian Wisdom Literature*, pp. 194-95 lines 13-18. The word *ṭapiltu* (lit. 'filth') means 'backbiting' (so Lambert, *Babylonian Wisdom Literature*, p. 195, see his note, p. 313); cf. 'Schmähung', *AHw*, p. 1380. On the Aramaic verb used in Saying 20, see now P. Grelot, 'On the Roots *'bq/'bṣ* in Ancient Aramaic and Ugaritic', *JSS* 1 (1956), pp. 202-205, and his 'Complementary Note on the Semitic Root *'bq/'bṣ*', *JSS* 2 (1957), p. 195 where he discusses *'b'* in 1QApGen 20.8-9, the 'missing link' in the development *'bq→'b'→'b'*.

98. Especially, D. Pardee, 'The Semitic Root *mrr* and the Etymology of Ugaritic *mr(r) // brk*', *UF* 10 (1978), pp. 249-88.

99. H.A. Hoffner, 'Hittite and Ugaritic Words for "Lettuce"', *JCS* 25 (1973), p. 234; however, cf. M. Dietrich and O. Loretz, 'Ug. *ḪS/ŚWN* "Thymian"(?)', *UF* 10 (1978), p. 431.

100. Lindenberger, *Proverbs*, p. 243 n. 253 ('Proverbs', p. 188 n. 12). On *ḥdh* + *lbb* in Saying 24, see my comments, 'Hebrew "Is he happy"—an Idiom Identified', *VT* 31 (1981), pp. 92-95.

101. Lindenberger, *Proverbs*, p. 93 ('Proverbs', p. 194).

his view[102] comes from the Assyrian–Aramaic bilingual inscription from Tell Fekheriye.[103] Line 5 of the Aramaic version refers to Adad as *'lh rḥmn*, 'merciful god', which corresponds to DINGIR LID^ú^ = *ilu rēmē'u* of line 6 in the Assyrian text.[104] The evidence is oblique, since *'lh* means 'god', not 'El'. However, in the first and last lines of Saying 13 there may be the 'break-up' of *b'l šmyn*[105] (and break-up is a poetic device attested elsewhere in Aramaic verse[106]) so that here too we may possibly have the break-up of **'l rḥmyn*.

Saying 34

> There is no lion in the sea
> therefore the sea-snake(?) is called *labbu*.[107]

102. Notably in 'The Gods of Aḥiqar', *UF* 14 (1982), pp. 105-18, 107-11.

103. A. Abou-Assaf, P. Bordreuil and A.R. Millard, *La Statue de Tell Fekherye et son inscription bilingue assyro-araméenne* (Etudes assyriologiques, 7; Paris: Editions Recherche sur les civilisations, 1982). See also, A.R. Millard and P. Bordreuil, 'A Statue from Syria with Assyrian and Aramaic Inscriptions', *BA* 45 (1982), pp. 135-41, with bibliography, and J.C. Greenfield and A. Schaffer, 'Notes on the Akkadian-Aramaic Bilingual Statue from Tell Fekherye', *Iraq* 45 (1983), pp. 109-16. And now T. Muraoka, 'The Tell Fekherye Bilingual Inscription and Early Aramaic', *Abr-Nahrain* 22 (1983-84), pp. 79-117, again with bibliography.

104. Abou-Assaf, Bordreuil and Millard, *La Statue*, pp. 18 and 30; Greenfield and Shaffer, 'Notes', p. 114 comment that *rēmē'û*, with syncopated sonants, looks like a spoken form.

105. Lindenberger, 'The Gods of Aḥiqar', p. 115. M. O'Connor, *Hebrew Verse Structure* (Winona Lake, IN: Eisenbrauns, 1980), pp. 112-13, 371-77 uses the term 'binomination' when this device involves proper (and geographic) names. See A. Berlin's comments, 'Parallel Word Pairs: A Linguistic Explanation', *UF* 15 (1983), pp. 7-16 (14).

106. Steiner and Nims, 'Polemical Poem', pp. 104-105 suggest that in line 12 of the poem the phrase *'ny w'mr*, 'he speaks up and says', has been broken up over parallel lines.

107. To Lindenberger's comment that '*l* / *r* is not a normal variant in northwest Semitic cognates', *Proverbs*, p. 102 ('Proverbs', p. 218), with respect to Saying 32 can be added the following: Inner-Aramaic *'rh ('rw* / *hlw*; Aramaic *'rh('rw)* / Ug. *hl* (Akk. *allu*)—discussed by J. Ribera i Florit, 'Evolución morfológica y semántica de las partículas *k'n y 'ry* en los diversos estadios del arameo', *AuOr* 1 (1983), pp. 227-33, 231. Ug. *prsḥ* / Akk. *naparsuḫu* / *napalsuḫu* (see W.G.E. Watson, 'Lexical Notes', *Newsletter for Ugaritic Studies* 28 [1982], p. 9). A. Fitzgerald, 'The Interchange of L, N, and R, in Biblical Hebrew', *JBL* 97 (1978), pp. 481-88 and the interesting fluctuation between *l* and *r* in 'Eblaite', on which cf. L. Cagni

Similar pairing of 'lions' and sea-creatures is apparent in a mythological text from Ras Shamra (*KTU* 1.5 i 14-16 // 1.133:2-5).

pnpš npš lbim thw	My appetite is the appetite of lions of the steppe,
hm brlt anḫr bym	or/and the voracity(?) of dolphins in the sea.[108]

In the Aramaic proverb there is a pun on Akkadian *labbu* = 'lion' (poetic synonym for *nēšu*) and mythological sea-dragon, and as Lindenberger shows, a cognate of this word in its second meaning is Ugaritic *ltn*.[109] The word-pair *thw* // *ym* has a reflex in Saying 110, discussed below.

Saying 40

Hear, o my son:
Harvest any harvest,
and do any job (etc.)

Lindenberger points out, 'this is the earliest occurrence in Aram of the vocative particle *yā*' and mentions that it is found, too, in Ugaritic as well as Arabic, Mandaic and Syriac.[110] He also discusses the idiom *'bd kl 'bydh*[111] and it may perhaps occur in another Aramaic papyrus from Elephantine if the restoration *'bydh '*[*l t'bdw*] is correct.[112]

(ed.), *La lingua di Ebla: Atti del convegno internazionale (Napoli, 21-23 aprile 1980)* (Seminario di Studi Asiatici, Series Minor, 14; Naples: Istituto Universitario Orientale, 1981), pp. 19 and 32 (Gelb); p. 260 (Pettinato) etc.

108. For full details and bibliography for this much discussed passage, see del Olmo Lete, *Mitos y leyendas*, p. 214 and *Interpretación de la mitología cananea. Estudios de semántica Ugaritica* (Valencia: Institución San Jerónimo, 1984), pp. 65-67.

109. The etymology of *labbu* proposed (from *lawûm*, 'to encircle') and mention of the Ug. cognate *ltn* in particular are interesting. J.A. Emerton, 'Leviathan and the *ltn*: the vocalization of the Ugaritic word for dragon', *VT* 32 (1982), p. 326 suggests the spelling to be *lītānu*—a proposal confirmed by S.V. Udd, 'More on the Vocalization of *ltn*', *VT* 33 (1983), pp. 509-10.

110. Lindenberger, *Proverbs*, p. 121 ('Proverbs', p. 267); he adds that it may also occur in Punic and the Deir Alla Inscriptions.

111. Lindenberger, *Proverbs*, p. 121 ('Proverbs', p. 267).

112. 'Do no work'; text and translation: P. Grelot, 'Sur le "papyrus pascal" d'Eléphantine', in A. Caquot and M. Delcor (eds.), *Mélanges bibliques et orientaux en l'honneur de M. Henri Cazelles* (AOAT, 212; Kevelaer: Butzon & Bercker; Neukirchen–Vluyn: Neukirchener Verlag, 1981), pp. 163-72, line 6.

Saying 44

For,
a man's charm is his truthfulness,
his repulsion is the lying of lips

The chiasmus here in the form *ḥn-gbr hymnwth* // *śn'th kbdt-śpwth* reinforces the antithetic parallelism.[113] Similar vocabulary is used in the Aramaic 'Polemical Poem'[114] and in Prov. 10.18a.[115]

Saying 46

The liar should have is throat (lit. neck) cut (etc.).

To the data from Mesopotamia collected by Lindenberger on this topic[116] should be added the epithet used of the god Nabu: *pārim napištu raggu*, 'who cuts the throat of the wicked'[117] as well as the description of Wolf as one 'who cuts his friend's throat' by slander (cited above in connection with Saying 20).[118]

Sayings 50-52

My distress is my own fault,
in whose sight can I be vindicated?
My own son spied out my house,
and uttered slander to strangers.
He was a false witness against me,
who, then, will declare me innocent?
That which poisoned me came from my house;
against whom can I struggle?

113. On chiastic parallelism in Aramaic prose, see B. Porten, 'Structure and Chiasm in Aramaic Contracts and Letters', in J.W. Welch (ed.), *Chiasmus in Antiquity* (Hildesheim: Gerstenberg, 1981), pp. 169-82.

114. The expression *l'-trtyn bpymy*, 'no duplicity/slander (is) in my mouth', occurs twice (lines 3 and 9); text and translation: Steiner and Nims, 'Polemical Poem', p. 95; discussion, pp. 97-98.

115. The word-pair 'first' // 'last' of Saying 45 is discussed in n. 143.

116. Lindenberger, *Proverbs*, pp. 130, 256 n. 395, p. 257 n. 397 ('Proverbs', p. 291). See, too, Prov. 21.23.

117. Cited in another connection by W.G. Lambert, 'A Neo-Babylonian Tammuz Lament', *JAOS* 103 (1983), p. 213.

118. The expression 'in his father's name or in his mother's name' of Saying 49 is another example of internal parallelism, though the Saying itself is prosaic.

This proverb stands out as an eight-line stanza of 'four poetic bicola'.[119] It is interesting, too, that the theme of this mini-poem is akin to the theme of the Babylonian 'Poem of the Righteous Sufferer' in *Ludlul* I 77-97. In these lines the Sufferer complains that everyone, including close friends and even his family shun him and defame him.[120]

The Aramaic 'Polemical Poem' includes the same motif, even to the extent of equating slander with venom, as in *Aḥiqar*.[121]

Saying 53

Do not reveal your secrets before your friends,
in case your name should be diminished before them.

There would appear to be wordplay in the form of paronomasia[122] here between the verbs *gly*, 'to reveal' and *qll*, 'to lower, diminish'. The couplet is also marked by partial chiasmus[123] and the repetitive word-pair *qdm* // *qdm*.[124]

Saying 66

May El twist the mouth of the treacherous,
and tear out (his) tongue.

119. Lindenberger, *Proverbs*, p. 136 (contrast his 'Proverbs' where he treated these Sayings individually).

120. Text and translation in Lambert, *Babylonian Wisdom Literature*, pp. 34-35. Also, E. Leichty, in M. de J. Ellis (ed.), *Essays on the Ancient Near East in Memory of Jacob Joel Finkelstein* (Memoirs of the Connecticut Academy of Arts and Sciences, 19 [December 1977]: Hamden, CT: Hamden Books for the Connecticut Academy of Arts and Sciences, 1977), p. 145.

121. The couplet closing Stanza 2, *ḥmh bpmhn / mrrh mn-tḥt lšnhn*, 'Venom is in their mouth; poison under their tongue!'—Steiner and Nims, 'Polemical Poem', p. 95, lines 11-12—contrasts with 'No slander (is) in my mouth' of lines 3 and 9 (cited in footnote 112).

122. To cite T. Todorov's definitions in *Théories du symbole* (Paris: Seuil, 1973), pp. 309-10: 'occurrence unique du même, *syllepse*'; 'occurrence multiple du même, *antanaclase*'; 'occurrence multiple du semblable, *paronomase*'; 'occurrence unique du semblable, *contamination* (mot-valise) / *calembours*'.

123. In the form NP_2 V M // V NP_2 M.

124. In Saying 59 the fourfold repetition of *'l* contributes to the overall quasi-acrostic effect.

Comparable is Ps. 12.4: 'May Yahweh cut off all smooth lips, (every) tongue which utters great words'.[125] A similar, but again not identical threat concludes a royal grant from Ras Shamra, written in Akkadian. Tabiyanu and his sons used a copy of the royal seal to dispossess Kalbeya and his sons. The document sets matters to rights and ends: 'If, in the future, Tabiyanu and his sons [should undertake?] any proceedings against Kalbeya (or) his sons, their tongue will be cut off'.[126]

Saying 75

> [The city] of the wicked will be swept away in the day of storm,
> and into ruin will its gates fall (etc.)
> for the spoil of the wicked shall perish.

The first two lines of this tricolon are in chiastic parallelism but more interesting is the word-pair 'city // gates'. The same word-pair is attested in a Babylonian proverb:

ālu ša kakkâšu lā dannū	A city whose weapons are not powerful:
nakru ina pān abullišu ul ippaṭṭar	the enemy does not depart from before its gate.[127]

The word-pair also occurs, reversed, in Isa. 14.31:

hylyly š'r z'qy-'yr	Wail, O gate! Cry, O city!

These texts[128] suggest that Lindenberger's restoration of *qryt* in the Aramaic proverb is probably correct.[129]

Saying 77

> If a wicked man grasps the fringe of your garment,
> leave it in his hand (etc.)

125. If correct, the rendering 'every tone that speaks distortions' proposed by M.J. Dahood, *Psalms I* (Garden City, NY: Doubleday, 1968), p. 73 would be apposite but his version is very conjectural. P.C. Craigie, *Psalms 1–50* (WBC, 19; Waco, TX: Word Books, 1983), pp. 135-36 is more cautious.

126 Text in *PRU*, III, p. 98: 34 (= RS 16.249: 34).

127. Text in Lambert, *Babylonian Wisdom Literature*, p. 245: iv 56; his translation: 'The enemy does not depart from before the gate of a city whose weapons are not powerful' (p. 250); similarly, *CAD*, A/1, p. 85.

128. To which, perhaps, Ps. 122.2b-3a can be added.

129. Lindenberger, *Proverbs*, p. 171 ('Proverbs', p. 387) following Halévy.

In Ugaritic and Hebrew the idiom 'to seize the hem (of a garment)' means to beg someone for something,[130] and if the same idiom is present here then the proverb may have to be re-interpreted, though no ready explanation springs to mind.

Saying 106

> A man said one day to the wild ass:
> 'Let me ride on you and I will provide for you'
> The wild ass replied:
> 'Yours be your care and your fodder.
> As for me, let me not see your riding!'

In fact, the man's offer is couched in a line with (weak) inner parallelism:

> *['rkb] 'lyk w'n[h] 'sblnk.*

The animal's reply, then, uses the core words of this line (*rkb*, *sbl*) in inverted sequence, expanding the line to a couplet, a technique known in other verse traditions:[131]

> *[lk yhw]y sbwlyk wkstk*
> *w'nh rkbyk l' 'ḥzh.*

Saying 107

> Between skin and my sandal may no pebble get into my foot.

It has gone unnoticed that this obscure saying may be compared with the Old Babylonian omen concerning King Amar-Su'en, who died *ina nišik šēnim*, 'from the bite of a shoe'.[132] Perhaps the proverb is an illustration of dire consequences resulting from what would appear to be only a minor cause.

130. As shown by, E.L. Greenstein, '"To Grasp the Hem" in Ugaritic Literature', *VT* 32 (1982), pp. 217-18.

131. See Chapter 3 for Ugaritic examples.

132. *YOS* 10 p. 18: rev. 61 and p. 25: obv. 32; p. 26: ii 53; see the very brief discussions of this text by J. Cooper, 'Apodotic Death and the Historicity of "Historical" Omens', in B. Alster (ed.), *Death in Mesopotamia: Papers read at the XXVIe Rencontre assyriologique internationale* (Mesopotamia, Copenhagen Studies in Assyriology, 8; Copenhagen: Akademisk Forlag, 1980), pp. 99-105, and by U. Jeyes, 'Death and Divination in the Old Babylonian Period', in Alster (ed.), *Death in Mesopotamia*, pp. 107-21 n. 55, with references. The similarity may simply be superficial, of course.

Saying 110

Do not show an Arab the sea
or a Sidonian the steppe,
for their occupations are different.

This proverb uses two parallel phrases (or inner parallelism) in combination with a word-pair which make it somewhat less prosaic in character. In fact, it cannot be ruled out that the last line is a later explanatory gloss. The word-pair, *ym'* // *b*[*r'*] may correspond to Ugaritic *thw*, 'waste' // *ym*, 'sea' in *KTU* 5 i 14-16 cited in full above, under Saying 34, though, as is evident, the ordering of the components is inverted.

The comments collected above show that the Aramaic *Proverbs of Aḥiqar* exhibit quite a number of poetic devices and techniques. These include the following (with references to the proverbs/sayings in brackets): alliteration (2, 3, 16, 17, 18, 20, 25, 33, 40, 107), assonance (26), break-up of a stereotype phrase (13, 25), chiastic parallelism (10, 44, 60, 68, 75, 106), delayed explanation (12, 22, 29, 30), hendiadys (40, 50, 52),[133] internal parallelism (5, 9, 29, 30, 49, 68, 106, 110), multiple rhetorical questions (50-52), tricola (18, 21, 22, 23, 26, 33, 41, 44, 45, 47, 67, 68, 70, 73, 75, 76, 110 etc.), word-play (11, 27, 41, 53, 73, 106). The list, of course, is incomplete even if Lindenberger's own remarks are added to it. There is evidently room for further research, for example, on the use of *kl*, 'all' as in Saying 74:

[*ṣ*?]*dyq 'n*[*š*]*' b'drh*	[The u]pright: a ma[n] to his aid!
kl ntḥwhy hwyn	All who clash with him are laid low

This illustrates the general tendency for *kl* to occur in the first or last line of a strophe or stanza.[134] Envelope figure, too, occurs (e.g. *mlt mlk*, 'the royal command', in Saying 20) while another feature that requires fuller study is the use of word-pairs.[135] Lindenberger has

133. Mentioned by Lindenberger, 'Proverbs', pp. 267, 316.

134. See, too, Sayings 14b and 15; also, VanderKam, 'Poetry of IQApGen, XX, 2-8a', p. 63. Relevant, too, is H. Ringgren, 'The omitting of *kol* in Hebrew parallelism', *VT* 32 (1982), pp. 99-103.

135. Berlin, 'Parallel Word Pairs' concludes that 'the linguistic rules underlying word associations also seem to fit when applied to word pairs, and in many cases provide better explanations for certain pairs than were heretofore available. Moreover, the theory of word associations is a "unified theory"... (it) shows that the

commented on this[136] and as an aid to later research I have added to his list, inserting repetitive pairs as significant, too.

’b // ’m	‘father’ // ‘mother’ (49)[137]
’mn // kdb	‘truth’ // ‘lying’ (44)
’rb // ’rb	‘treachery’ // ‘treachery’ (16)
’šd // ’kl	‘shed (blood)’ // ‘eat’ (9)
dm // bśr	‘blood’ // ‘flesh’ (9)
ḥl’ // mlḥ	‘sand’ // ‘salt’ (29)
ḥly // mr(r)	‘sweet’ // ‘bitter’ (59)[138]
ṭb // tbyr	‘good’ // ‘broken’ (27)
ywm // [*ly*]*lh*	‘day’ // ‘night’ (14a)
ym’ // b[*r’*]	‘the sea’ // ‘the steppe’ (110)
lḥm // [*ḫmr*(?)]	‘bread’ // ‘[‘wine’(?)] (91)[139]
mdd // lbb	‘character’ // ‘heart’ (68)
mwbl’ // ṭ‘wn	‘burden’ // ‘be laden’ (10)
mḥ’ // šbq	‘beat’ // ‘leave (alone)’ (4)
m(w)t // ḥyh	‘die’ // ‘live’ (4)
nś // ṭ‘n	‘lift’ // ‘load’ (10, 29)
nś’ // nsb	‘lift’ // ‘carry’ (30)
‘bd // ’mh	‘slave’ // ‘maid’ (6)[140]
‘yn // lbb	‘eye(s)’ // ‘heart’ (76)[141]
pm // lbb	‘mouth’ // ‘heart’ (15)
pm // lšn	‘mouth’ // ‘tongue’ (66)[142]
pm // mlḥm	‘mouth’ // ‘battle’ (16)

pairing of *yqtl* - *qtl* forms and the break-up of idioms are of the same nature as the pairing of synonyms and antonyms, etc.... (and) poetic pairings are the same as those in prose’. However, she does not take into account the factor of density. Y. Avishur, *Stylistic Studies of Word-Pairs in Biblical and Ancient Semitic Literatures* (AOAT, 210; Kevelaer: Butzon & Bercker; Neukirchen–Vluyn: Neukirchener Verlag, 1984), brought to my attention by J. Healey, is unavailable to me.

136. Lindenberger, *Proverbs*, p. 24 (‘Proverbs’, pp. 10-20) lists *dm // bśr*; *nś’ // ṭ‘n*; *pm // lbb*; *pm // lšn*; *šmr // nṭr* and *trtyn // tlt’* (‘two’ // ‘three’).

137. On *’kl + šb‘* in Sayings 40 and 42, see Lindenberger, *Proverbs*, p. 121 (‘Proverbs’, p. 267).

138. The same antonymic pairings recur in Saying 90 (‘Hunger makes the bitter sweet...’) and in the ‘Polemical Poem’, lines 10-12a; see the comments of Steiner and Nims, ‘Polemical Poem’, p. 103.

139. For a similar pair in Ug., see *KTU* 1.23: 6 *lḥm blḥm ay // šty bḫmr yn ay*, ‘Eat of any food, drink of intoxicating wine’.

140. Cf. *‘lym // lḥnt* in Saying 5.

141. Cf. Prov. 23.33.

142. The same word-pair recurs at least three times in the ‘Polemical Poem’.

qdmn // 'ḥrn	'first' // 'last' (45)[143]
qdm // qdm	'before' // 'before' (53)[144]
qṣr // 'bd	'harvest' // 'work' (40, 40)
qrb // rḥq	'near' // 'far' (96)
[qryt] // tr'	['city'] // 'gate(s)' (75)
qšt // ḥṯ	'bow' // 'arrow' (39, 41, 93)
rm // špl	'exalted' // 'humbled' (60)[145]
śgy' // z'r	'multitude' // 'meagre number' (24)
šm // šm	'name' // 'name' (49)[146]
šmr // nṭr	'protect' // 'guard' (69)
špyr // ṭb	'good, fine' // 'happy' (68)
špyr // rḥym	'good' // 'pleasing' (12)
tbn // prn	'straw' // 'bran' (30)[147]

Certain impressions can be gained even from this incomplete list, notably the high number of sets beginning with *q-* or the fact that *nś'* and *pm* are probably 'A-words', but such impressions will need refinement.

Of particular interest is the 'asterisk'[148] which the scribe of the Elephantine papyrus used 'to separate the end of one saying from the initial word of another beginning on the same line'.[149] Each of the proverbs, then, can be considered a self-contained poem or at least a stanza (or strophe) and the asterisk (really the letter *aleph* according to Lindenberger) is of great significance in determining the beginnings and ends of such units. Comparable, though by no means identical, is the red dot used in certain Egyptian texts to mark off the ends of lines.[150]

143. Comparable pairings are used in Isa. 9.11; 41.4b; 44.6; 48.12 and Job 18.20.

144. Cf. *'l // 'l*, 'in (her) presence' // 'in (her) presence' in *KTU* 1.15 iv 17-18. Also, the repeated 'parallelism' of *qdm* in Sfire i A 7-12.

145. Cf. *rm // špl* in *KTU* 1.23:32.

146. The same pair is used in *KTU* 1.2 iv 11-12 and 18-19.

147. Comparable is *ḥšš // qš*, 'chaff' // 'stubble' in Isa. 33.10; cf. too Jer. 23.28 and Job 41.19-21. To the list of word-pairs can be added the triple set *'yn // 'dn // pm*, 'eyes' // 'ear' // 'mouth' in Saying 67; cf. Ps. 115.5-6 and J. Khanijan, 'Wisdom', in *RSP* II no. 42 (p. 396).

148. Lindenberger, *Proverbs*, pp. 305-309 (= Appendix B; 'Proverbs', pp. 537-42 = Appendix D).

149. Lindenberger, *Proverbs*, p. 305 ('Proverbs', p. 537).

150. J.L. Foster, 'Thought Couplets in Khety's Hymn to the Inundation', *JNES* 34 (1975), pp. 1-29 and 'Sinuhe: The Ancient Egyptian Genre of Narrative Verse',

The preliminary findings represented by the observations set out above show that the *Proverbs of Aḥiqar* belong to the mainstream of ancient Semitic versification and that more can be learned of their specific character by inner-Aramaic comparisons and by turning to ancient Near Eastern poetry generally. Lindenberger has established the text and set the ball rolling but there is still plenty of scope for further study.

4. *Trends in the Development of Classical Hebrew Poetry*[151]

4.1. *Introductory*

4.1.1. *Introduction*. Recently, several important books and quite a few papers have been published on the subject of classical Hebrew poetry. They include Collins's *Line-Forms in Hebrew Poetry*,[152] which provides an objective yardstick for measuring syntactical patterns in poetry, and O'Connor's *Hebrew Verse Structure*[153] which runs to over 600 pages and is linguistically very deep. A book of the same length as O'Connor's is Van der Lugt's work on strophic structure, in Dutch, which I have not yet seen.[154]

Somewhat earlier came Geller's work on parallelism[155] and Stuart's brief book on metre.[156] Besides these, there have also been at least two significant doctoral dissertations: Sappan on features of syntax in Hebrew poetry[157] and Cooper's 'Biblical Poetics: A Linguistic Approach'.[158] All these works, plus a spate of papers there is no time

JNES 39 (1980), pp. 89-117. Also, V.L. Davis, review of Y. Koenig, *Le papyrus Boulaq 6: Transcription, traduction et commentaire*, *JAOS* 104 (1984), p. 359.

151. First published in *UF* 14 (1982), pp. 265-77.

152. T. Collins, *Line-Forms in Hebrew Poetry* (Studia Pohl, Series Major, 7; Rome: Biblical Institute Press, 1978). See my review, *Bib* 61 (1980), pp. 581-83.

153. My paper was written as a result of reading O'Connor's stimulating book (esp. p. 28).

154. P. van der Lugt, *Strofische structuren in de bijbels-hebreeuwse poëzie* (Dissertationes Neerlandicae Series Theologica; Kampen: Kok, 1980).

155. S.A. Geller, *Parallelism in Early Biblical Poetry* (Harvard Semitic Monographs 20; Missoula, MT: Scholars Press, 1979).

156. D. Stuart, *Studies in Early Hebrew Meter* (HSM, 13; Missoula, MT: Scholars Press, 1976).

157. R. Sappan, 'The Typical Features of the Syntax of Biblical Poetry in its Classical Period' (thesis, Hebrew University, Jerusalem, 1974).

158. A.M. Cooper, 'Biblical Poetics: A Linguistic Approach' (thesis, Yale

to list here, show that there has been a revival in the study of Hebrew poetry. Such an upsurge of interest is only to be welcomed.

Yet, in spite of such extensive writings, little progress can be charted concerning our knowledge of the *development* of Hebrew poetry. Or, to put it more bluntly, we are still very much in the dark as to how to date this or that particular poem. Dates for the book of Job, for example, range from before the exile to as late as 300 BC. The topic of this paper, then, is *stylistic dating*: how we can date a poem or poetic work by scrutinizing its style, techniques, form and so on. As its title indicates, comparisons with extra-biblical literature will be a contributive factor.[159]

The outline of the paper is as follows: after further comments on style and dating and a brief mention of some general principles comes a lengthy section on general trends. Section 4.3 deals with the history of single devices, the next section with a variety of topics and lastly come the conclusions.

4.1.2. *Style and Dating*. Very few attempts have been made at mapping out a relative chronology for classical Hebrew poetry on the basis of poetic technique. Isolated instances include brief references to the development of metre (itself a conjectural topic),[160] discussion of staircase parallelism (the so-called expanded colon) by Loewenstamm,[161] an examination of the history of a formula, again by Loewenstamm[162] and some remarks on line-forms (Collins).[163]

University, 1976). See, too, J.L. Kugel, *The Idea of Biblical Poetry: Parallelism and its History* (New Haven: Yale University Press, 1981).

159. This paper was read at the Summer meeting of SOTS, St John's College, Cambridge on 23 July 1981. My reason for publication in *UF* is provided by O'Connor, *Hebrew Verse Structure*, p. 25: 'The consensus that pre-exilic Hebrew and Ugaritic verse are similar leads to an important clue for further exploration. Insofar as the verse works in the same way in the two corpora, a description of Hebrew verse will have to describe Ugaritic verse.'

160. B. Margalit, 'Introduction to Ugaritic Prosody', *UF* 7 (1975), pp. 289-313, 300 n. 16, and 298 n. 15; also S. Segert, 'Versbau und Sprachbau in der althebräischen Poesie', *MIO* 15 (1969), pp. 312-21.

161. S.E. Loewenstamm, 'The Expanded Colon in Ugaritic and Biblical Verse', *JSS* 14 (1969), pp. 176-96, esp. 195-96 where he mentions that in Hebrew verse the poets tended to go beyond the 'rigid formal rules' of Ugaritic epic.

162. S.E. Loewenstamm, 'The Address "Listen" in the Ugaritic Epic and the Bible', in G. Rendsburg *et al.* (eds)., *The Bible World: Essays in Honor of Cyrus*

The subject has been touched on by Revell in his discussion of parallel couplets.[164] None of these has been full-scale in any way, they are rather in the nature of soundings. The close to a more widely based study was by Albright.[165]

The normal approach in studies of Hebrew poetry is to accept the dates currently proposed for various books of the OT, and work from there. So, for example, Sappan in his 1974 thesis and O'Connor in his book (where he follows Freedman). In view of the sudden revival of interest in Hebrew poetry already referred to, it seems appropriate to re-examine stylistic criteria for dating Hebrew poetry. Such a study, I hope, will complement the work of David Robertson who used grammatical criteria to establish the chronology of early Hebrew poetry.[166]

4.1.3. *Some Principles*. In an attempt at reaching a degree of objectivity I have used the following guidelines. My main concern is with form and technique, not with content and still less with historical indicators. I have tried not to be influenced by currently accepted dating, although I cannot entirely prescind from such dates as have been assigned. Having no particular axe to grind—I am not concerned to date this or that psalm to before or after the exile—I will follow the chronology suggested by stylistic analysis as far as possible.

4.2. *General Trends*

By comparing the Dead Sea Scrolls with earlier Hebrew poetry and taking the poetic traditions of Ugarit, Mesopotamia and Phoenicia into consideration, at least four general forms of development can be outlined. They are: the origins of the acrostic, expansion of various

H. Gordon (New York: Ktav and The Institute of Hebrew Culture and Education of New York University, 1980), pp. 123-31. Loewenstamm, 'The Expanded Colon'.

163. Collins, *Line-Forms*, pp. 65, 192, 281 etc.

164. E.J. Revell, 'Pausal Forms and the Structure of Biblical Poetry', *VT* 31 (1981), pp. 186-99, esp. 196-97.

165. W.F. Albright, *Yahweh and the Gods of Canaan* (London: Athlone Press, 1968), pp. 1-46.

166. D.A. Robertson, *Linguistic Evidence in Dating Early Hebrew Poetry* (Missoula, MT: University of Montana, 1972). See also R.S. Sirat, 'Brèves remarques sur l'évolution de la langue poétique en hébreu', *Revue de l'Ecole Nationale des Langues Orientales* 5 (1968), pp. 37-48, and W.J. Adams, Jr, and L.L. Adams, 'Language Drift and the Dating of Biblical Passages', *Hebrew Studies* 18 (1977), pp. 160-64. These last two are unavailable to me.

kinds, types of inversion, and the increasing use of rhyme. These will be looked at in turn.

4.2.1. *From Anaphora to Acrostic.* It is fairly safe to assume that before poetry was composed in writing, and even before it was copied down or adapted in written forms, bards composed 'live'. Unquestionably, they used stock formulas, fixed word-pairs, conventional imagery and so on, but there was a great deal of improvisation. The trouble is, though, that our records of such poetry are only in written form and we are reduced to extrapolating from written documents to oral composition.[167] Help is to hand, though, from the peculiar literary form known as the alphabetic acrostic. If we take the two extremes of Ugarit (as early) and Qumran (as late), it is quite obvious that while the Ras Shamra texts yield no alphabetic acrostics, this form was quite a favourite at Qumran. Of the extra-biblical compositions found in cave 11, no less than 3 out of the 9 are in acrostic form (if we include Sir. 51).[168] This provides corroborative evidence for the 'oral poetry as early' theory since acrostics can only be appreciated in written form. Accordingly, the Hebrew acrostics (Pss. 24, 111 etc.; Prov. 31; Lam. 1–4) would appear to be late compositions.

The picture is not so simple, however. To begin with, acrostics are well known in Mesopotamian tradition (even though they are not alphabetic acrostics, of course) and probably this tradition is earlier than some at least of the Hebrew poems referred to. Secondly, quasi-acrostics are to be found in the Ugaritic poems, even if alphabetic acrostics are not.[169]

A quasi-acrostic is a series of lines each beginning with the same letter, and such sequences developed from anaphora. Anaphora is the technical term for repetition of the same word at line-initial:

hlh tšpl	See, she moved down,
hlh trm	See, she moved up,
hlh tṣḥ ad ad	See, she cried 'Father, father';
hlh tṣḥ um um	See, she cried, 'Mother, mother'.
	(*KTU* 1.23:32-33)

167. Even here, though, thanks to Krahmalkov's study (n. 183, below) we can distinguish between writing down for sight-reading and writing down for reading out loud.

168. Ps. 155; The 'Apostrophe to Zion' (4Q88 col. xxii); Sir. 51.

169. For details, see Chapter 10, esp. 'Anaphoric Alliteration in Ugaritic Verse'.

The next step was to vary the first word in the second line, without changing the initial letter as in

ks qdš ltphnh aṯt	A holy cup which woman should not see
krpn lt'n aṯrt	a beaker a goddess should not look at.
	(*KTU* 1.3:13-15)

It was only when oral poetry was being copied down (or adapted to writing) that such patterns became evident to the eye. This probably resulted in sets of lines each beginning with a different letter of the alphabet. The development, then, was anaphora, quasi-acrostics, true (alphabetic) acrostics. A further stage was, perhaps, the use of 22-line stanzas as standard units.

Poems of 22 lines (and with multiples of 22 lines) were obviously modelled on alphabetic acrostics, without the restrictive feature of alphabet sequence. Lamentations 5 consists of 22 couplets and is evidently a freer form of the acrostics in chs. 1–4. Therefore, the 22-verse nonacrostic is later than the true alphabetic acrostic. Examples are Psalm 38, Isa. 10.27-34, Psalm 94, Sir. 6.18-37 and so on. Num. 23.18-24 (oracle of Balaam) also follows this model, suggesting that it may belong to a late stage in the development of Hebrew poetry.

In true acrostics the alphabet used can vary: certain letters can be omitted or transposed. Professor William Johnstone has argued that *pe* replaced *waw* at some stage in the Hebrew alphabet.[170] Since Sirach 51 has a *waw* verse and an extra *pe* verse at the end, while Psalms 25 and 34 do not have the *waw* verse (but do have the extra *pe* verse) then the acrostic in Sirach 51 may mark a transitional stage and perhaps it is older than the two psalms.

In summary form, then, the line of development can be reconstructed as follows. First came anaphora (repetition of the same word at the beginning of each line), this lead to line-initial alliteration, which in extended form became the quasi-acrostic (a series of lines starting with the same letter). Subsequently, attempts were made to use all the letters of the alphabet as line-initial consonants, resulting in alphabetic acrostics. Imitations of the acrostic pattern resulted in compositions of 22 lines, and then in poems or stanzas with multiples

170. W. Johnstone, 'Cursive Phoenician and the Archaic Greek Alphabet', *Kadmos* 17 (1978), pp. 151-66, esp. 166 n. 40.

of 22. There were, of course, mixed forms: Prov. 23.29-35 is a 22-line poem of which the first eight begin with *lamedh*.

4.2.2. *Expansion and Reduction*. The general tendency is for units within poetry to be expanded as time goes on. Expansion can be simply inserting words within existing lines of verse, or more drastically, by increasing single lines to couplets, couplets to tricola and so on. An example of expansion by the *addition of extra words* is Ezek. 12.2 which changes Jer. 5.21

'ynym lhm wl' yr'w	who have eyes but cannot see,
'znym lhm wl' yšm'w	who have ears but cannot hear

to

'šr 'ynym lhm lr'wt wl' r'w	who have eyes to see, but will not see
'znym lhm lšm' wl' šm'w	ears to hear but will not hear

This[171] and other examples such as Isa. 59.7 and Prov. 1.16 could be dismissed as instances of glossing or of later interpretation, but cases where the single line becomes a couplet, the couplet a longer strophic form, indicate the general tendency. The bicolon

twrt ḥkm mqwr ḥyym	A wise man's teaching is a fountain of life
lswr mmqšy mwt	to escape the snares of death

in Prov. 13.14 is evidently a monocolon in origin.[172] The couplet

hrw 'ml	(all) conceive mischief
whwlyd 'wn	and give birth to nothing

of Isa. 59.4 becomes a tricolon in Ps. 7.15

hnh yḥbl 'wn	See, he has birth-pangs for nothing,
whrh 'ml	is pregnant with mischief
wyld šqr	and gives birth to treachery

and also in Job 15.35

hrh 'ml	Pregnant with mischief,
wyld 'wn	he gives birth to nothing
wbṭnm tkyn mrmh	their womb nurtures evil.

171. In fact, an extra line is added into the bargain.

172. Cf. W. McKane, *Proverbs: A New Approach* (London: SCM Press, 1970), pp. 1-3, following J. Schmidt.

How, though, can we differentiate between the techniques of reduction and expansion? It is equally possible to consider long passage A an expansion of short passage B, and to label passage B a reduction of its lengthier counterpart. Given two near-parallel texts, one shorter than the other, how can we determine which came first? A degree of control is available from the Ugaritic poetic texts. It is reasonable to suppose that such compositions were written out from beginning to end, so that passages coming in tablet 1 or column 1 are earlier than those in tablet 4 or column 4. Lines 2-3 of the 'Serpent text', *KTU* 1.100,

'm il mbk nhrm	towards El at the source of the rivers,
b'dt thmtm	at the confluence of the deeps

are reduced in line 9 to a single stichos:

'm b'l mrym ṣpn	towards Baal in the heights of Zaphon

and similarly in the following nine stanzas. This is simply due to the fact that the first occurrence in the opening stanza is stylistically different from all the others. Another possible example is

šm' laliyn b'l	Listen, O Mightiest Baal,
bn lrkb 'rpt	understand, O Cloudrider

in column 5 lines 59-60 of *KTU* 1.4. This is shortened to

šm' m' laliyn b'l	Listen, please, O Mightiest Baal

in column 6 line 4 of the same tablet. However, both De Moor and Loewenstamm[173] have shown that we are dealing with expansion here, since this monocolon is more frequent whereas the couplet occurs only once. There are other examples, which can be explained by scribal omission, but the indications are that there was very little in the way of expansion or reduction in Ugaritic verse—though the topics need to be studied.

The evidence in Hebrew is somewhat mixed. Genuine cases of reduction include Job 13.27:

wtsm bsd rgly	Put my feet in fetters,
wtšmwr kl 'rḥwty	to mark all my paths,
'l šršy rgly ttḥqh	make prints on the soles of my feet

173. De Moor, 'The Art of Versification. II', p. 199; for Loewenstamm, see n. 162, above.

becoming (33.11):

ysm bsd rgly	He puts my feet in fetters,
yšmr kl 'rḥty	marks my every path

and the parallels to Isa. 12.4.[174]

The evidence from the Dead Sea Scrolls is also mixed. Whereas the quatrain of Isa. 59.3 becomes a tricolon in the Isaiah Scroll, that is reduction, the opposite also occurs. Gevirtz has shown how what looks like an unbalanced line in Gen. 49.8 as handed down to us in MT is preserved in better form in col. 12 of the War Scroll.[175] In general, though, the tendency at Qumran and elsewhere is to expand; apart from additional refrains (to be discussed later), a striking example is Ps. 135.6 of the Psalms Scroll (11QPs) where 4 lines lacking in MT are inserted within a parallel couplet:

'šr ḥpṣ yhwh 'śh bšmym wb'rṣ	Whatever he wishes Yahweh does in the sky and on land,
l'śwt y'śh	he surely acts;
'yn kyh	none is like Yah,
'yn kyhwh	none is like Yahweh,
w'yn šy'śh kmlk 'lwhym	and none who acts like the king of gods,
bymym wbkwl thwmwt	in the seas and in all the deeps.

Among the many forms of expansion which could be discussed we will look at the simile and rhetorical questions.

The development of the simile can be traced as follows. First came the simple simile, on its own:

> I eat ashes like bread. (Ps. 102.10)

Then came paired similes, due to the influence of parallelism in Hebrew:

> I am like a moth to Ephraim,
> and like dry rot to the houses of Judah. (Hos. 5.12)

A further stage was the expansion of such sets to similes in series—from three (2 Sam. 23.4; Joel 2.5l; Job 7.1-2) up to eleven (Sir. 50.5-10).

174. Ps. 105.1 and 1 Chron. 16.8.

175. S. Gevirtz, 'Adumbrations of Dan in Jacob's Blessing on Judah', *ZAW* 93 (1981), pp. 21-37, esp. 22-24.

The simile itself also seems to have undergone changes. The cumulative simile uses the particle k^e, k^e, *kēn* as in Ps. 103.15

> Man, like grass his days
> like a wild weed,
> so he flourishes

a pattern already found in Ugaritic. It seems to have originated in the two-pronged explicit simile of the type

> As a lily among brambles
> so is my love among maidens (Cant. 2.2.)

However, although the cumulative simile is found in Ugaritic (KTU 1.6 ii 28-30),

klb arḫ l‘glh	Like the heart of a cow for her calf,
klb ṯat límrh	like the heart of a ewe for her lamb
km lb ‘nt aṯr b‘l	so is the heart of ‘Anat toward Baal

the explicit simile is not. In fact, in Hebrew such similes only occur in the Song of Songs and Isaiah 25, suggesting a rather more complex line of development than has been outlined here.

The rhetorical question is largely an evocative way of stating a denial, of presenting a firm ‘No’. Its origins lie in oral composition and oral delivery:

> Listen, you elders
> hear me, all you living in the land:
> Has the like of this happened in your days?
> or in your fathers’ days?

Joel’s prophecy begins in this way and he obviously expects a negative answer. Yet Joel is a *writing* prophet and he is here only reproducing the speech patterns of oral poets. It is significant that the rhetorical question is a firm favourite in wisdom literature, particularly in the form of questions in series. Especially is this true of the book of Job: no other book uses this device so untiringly, nor do rhetorical questions in series crop up so often as in Job. The commonest number is four in a row (6.5-6 etc.), though sets of six, eight, nine, eleven and even sixteen (in 40.24-31) can be found. I would suggest that this is a late development when literary texts were imbued with an oral flavour. This explains why rhetorical questions occur so frequently in Job: since the whole book is cast in the form of a set of speeches the constant rhetorical questions make the written word into spoken verse.

4.2.3. *Inversion*. Inversion implies a later development: a form or device widely used by poets has been turned on its head for a particular reason, or simply for respite from monotony. It is a secondary technique based on earlier techniques. Established gender patterns, for instance, can be reversed to form other patterns such as chiasmus, as I have shown elsewhere. I am not claiming that such inversions were exclusive to Hebrew poetry of a later date, many inverted forms were already common in Ugaritic and Akkadian verse. What does seem to be true, though, is that the general trend is for such inversions to become more frequent and, in the case of word-pairs, to be used more loosely.[176] Here we will have space to look at only two types: inverted staircase parallelism and the reversed blazon.

In staircase parallelism (found only in Ugaritic and Hebrew but not in Akkadian) the vocative normally comes *after* an opening imperative:

šwby btwlt yśr'l	Return, O Virgin Israel
šby 'l 'ryk 'lh	return to these your cities (Jer. 31.21)

In what appears to be an *inverted* form of this structure the vocative can come in the second line, for instance, Ps. 96.1-2:

šyrw lyhwh šyr ḥdš	Sing to Yahweh a new song,
šyrw lyhwh kl h'rṣ	sing to Yahweh all the earth.

This aspect has not so far been considered in studies of the parallels in Ps. 98.1 and 1 Chron. 16.23-24.[177] Another example is Ps. 135.1:

hllw 't šm yhwh	Praise the name of Yahweh,
hllw 'bdy yhwh	praise, O servants of Yahweh

which discounts Dahood's rendering of the second line as 'Praise the works of Yahweh'.[178]

Certain poems are evidently based on a catalogue of parts of the body and were originally descriptions of divine statues. The god Ninurta, for example, is described in one passage on the basis of the set: head, face, cheeks, hair, hands, chest, body, right foot, left

176. See Chapter 6.

177. De Moor, 'The Art of Versification. II', p. 207.

178. Dahood, *Psalms*, III, pp. 257-59. As he himself notes, 11QPs[a] both inverts and expands these two lines, indicating inverted staircase parallelism to be rare and liable to be misunderstood.

foot.[179] Later, such descriptions were used as the basis of love poems to women and sometimes for men. Generally speaking, such catalogue poems run *downwards*, from head to toe. Examples such as Prov. 6.17 and Dan. 2.32-33, as well as the many poems in Song of Songs, could be multiplied. It is curious that the top-to-toe sequence obtains even in quasi-poetic parts of the decalogue, notably in

eye for eye
tooth for tooth
hand for hand
foot for foot (Deut. 19.21 and par.)[180]

Upward sequences are unusual; the best example is Cant. 7.2-10 where items come in the following order: feet, thighs, navel(?), belly, breasts, neck, eyes, nose, head, hair.

Even more interesting are poems where the head-to-foot order is then inverted once more. Curiously, such double sequences are to be found in the Ugaritic texts. In an obscure text (*KTU* 1.101) there is reference to Baal's head, forehead, legs, horns and again head. Again, in a description of mourning rites the catalogue is: head, crown, skin, sideburns and beard, collar-bone, chest, torso, voice. It is difficult to decide whether texts such as Cant. 5.11-16 (head, locks, eyes, cheeks, lips, arms, body, legs, speech), Pss. 115.5-7 and 135.16-17 are based on ancient models or whether they should be classed as later variations of a standard pattern.

4.2.4. *The Move towards Rhyme*. End-rhyme is not an obligatory feature of Hebrew verse, yet even though never as common as in European poetry, it does occur and at times is even exploited. If we begin at the late end of the spectrum, with Neo-Punic poetry and Qumran verse, and work backwards in time, it may be possible to trace the progressive use of rhyme. However, there are many gaps, we are uncertain about pronunciation, and as O'Connor points out, we may be dealing with branching traditions.[181]

179. Cf. F. Köcher, 'Der babylonische Göttertypentext', *MIO* 1 (1953), pp. 57-107, and M.H. Pope and J.H. Tigay, 'A Description of Baal', *UF* 3 (1971), pp. 119-20.

180. For discussion of the parallels, see A.D.H. Mayes, *Deuteronomy* (NCB; London: Oliphants, 1979), pp. 290-91.

181. O'Connor, *Hebrew Verse Structure*, p. 26.

Krahmalkov recognized that two Neo-Punic inscriptions from Mactar dating to before 164 BC are in fact poems.[182] The most striking component of these two short compositions is the obligatory end-rhyme. Every line in the first text (A) ends in *-ot*. In the second, (B), the rhyme scheme is *-ut*/ *-im*/ *-o*/ and again *-ut*. Now, although these two poems comprise all that survives of what must have been a flourishing literary tradition, it is fairly clear that the roots of this tradition lie back in Ugaritic and Hebrew patterns of composition. They are an extension and a later development of that same tradition.[183] The innovatory feature is persistent end-rhyme.

If we turn to the Qumran compositions, we have to agree with Thiering's conclusion: one of the novel elements in the Hodayoth (1QH) and similar poems is the deliberate and sustained use of rhyme. Examples are 1QS xi 1-3, 4b-5a and the high proportion of complex rhyme in the 'Plea for Deliverance'.[184]

At the other end of the scale, we can point to the Akkadian tradition where, as Kinnier Wilson has shown, end-rhyme is deliberately avoided in some texts by the use of 'desonance'.[185]

What is the picture in classical Hebrew? One of the longest sets is Job 10.8-12 with ten consecutive lines ending in *-î*. More common are shorter sequences of from 3 to 5 lines. The lengthy pattern of end-rhyme in Sir. 44.1-15[186] is already overlapping the same time slot as Neo-Punic and Qumran.

The trend here, then, can be reconstructed as going from non-rhyme to consistent end-rhyme. Further analysis is required before more specific conclusions can be reached.

182. C.R. Krahmalkov, 'Two Neo-Punic Poems in Rhymed Verse', *RSF* 3 (1975), pp. 169-205.

183. 'Punic verse is deeply rooted in Canaanite prosody and exhibits numerous features common to Ugaritic and Hebrew', Krahmalkov, 'Two Neo-Punic Poems', p. 175. To the features he lists can be added gender-matched parallelism as in Mactar B iii 12.

184. B. Thiering, 'The Poetic Forms of the Hodayot', *JSS* 8 (1963), pp. 189-209, esp. 205.

185. J.V. Kinnier Wilson, '"Desonance" in Akkadian', *JSS* 13 (1968), pp. 93-103; also J.V. Kinnier Wilson, 'Two Medical Texts from Nimrud', *Iraq* 18 (1956), pp. 130-46, 146. I owe these references to a personal letter (17 April 1969) from the late Jean Nougayrol.

186. P.W. Skehan, 'Strophic Patterns in the Book of Job', *CBQ* 23 (1961), pp. 125-42, 133 n. 20.

4.3. *The History of Single Devices*

To complement the rather general outline of the previous section it will be helpful to try and trace the history of individual poetic devices. In effect this means closer scrutiny of a limited number of techniques and will, to a great degree, be speculative and hypothetical. Our attention will be given mostly to a single word-pair, but some idea of what is involved can be gained from examining briefly some other devices.

4.3.1. *A Formula*. The first of these is the formula for 'listen' in Ugaritic and Hebrew. Loewenstamm[187] (as already mentioned) has shown how in Ugaritic the formula LISTEN + VOCATIVE (e.g. 'listen O Lady Huraya') was occasionally expanded into a bicolon:

> Listen, O Mightiest Baal,
> understand, O Cloudrider

but never into a tricolon. In Hebrew, too, the single line became a couplet (Judg. 5.3; Isa. 49.1 etc.) or even a double couplet (Isa. 28.33; 37.17). Once at least the monocolon has been extended to a tricolon:

> Hear this, O priests!
> Pay attention, House of Israel!
> Royal House: give ear! (Hos. 5.1)

We can therefore deduce that the process of expansion was more developed in classical Hebrew—with Ugaritic as its model, perhaps—and incidentally, that the tricolon is not of itself an indication of antiquity. This second point is confirmed by the Neo-Punic poems which have a three-line strophic structure throughout.[188]

4.3.2. *Refrain*. The refrain is well attested in Hebrew (Pss. 67, 99 etc.) but is used much less frequently in the Ugaritic texts (although this may be due to the scarcity of liturgical poems so far discovered). It is very much commoner in Akkadian, particularly in the form of an antiphonal response after each line. Looking at the Qumran texts, particularly at the Psalms Scroll from Cave 11, we are struck by the number of refrains and antiphons that have been added into the biblical text. For example 11QPs 145 adds the recurrent refrain

187. See n. 162, above.
188. Cf. Krahmalkov, 'Two Neo-Punic Poems', pp. 174-75.

> *brwk yhwh wbrwk šmw l'lm w'd*
> Blessed by Yahweh and blessed be his Name for evermore.

Such additions can be ascribed to adaptation for liturgical use, yet they show how use of the refrain was increasing. Other factors include a possible influence of Mesopotamian tradition and the general move towards expansion, illustrating yet again that there are no facile answers.

4.3.3. *A Word-Pair.* We come now to the history of a word-pair (see Table 1). It has long been recognized that Amos 2.9 and Isa. 37.31 (= 2 Kgs 19.30) are almost identical in wording with part of the curse on the 6th century Eshmunazor inscription:

> May he not have
> root below
> or fruit above
> or beauty among the living under the sun.

The parallel pair *šoreš* // *p^erî*, 'root // fruit' is common to all these texts and most probably the Hebrew couplets derive from the Phoenician.[189] As can be seen from the table, the same word-pair was used in several other Hebrew passages (Isa. 14.29 etc.). It is interesting to note (as I have pointed out elsewhere)[190] that a possible forerunner to the word-pair occurs in the Neo-Babylonian *Epic of Erra* (IV 125):

> The root of the tree I want to cut
> so its fruit may not prosper.

189. See H.L. Ginsberg, '"Roots Below and Fruit Above" and Related Matters', in D.W. Thomas and W.D. McHardy (eds.), *Hebrew and Semitic Studies presented to Godfrey Rolles Driver in celebration of his seventieth birthday, 20 August 1962* (Oxford: Clarendon Press, 1963), pp. 72-76; also, J. Becker, 'Wurzel und Wurzelspross. Ein Beitrag zur hebräischen Lexicographie', *BZ* 20 (1976), pp. 22-44 and Y. Avishur, 'Studies of Stylistic Features Common to the Phoenician Inscriptions and the Bible', *UF* 8 (1976), pp. 5-6.

190. W.G.E. Watson, 'Puzzling Passages in the Tale of Aqhat', *UF* 8 (1976), pp. 374-75, cf. O. Loretz, *Die Psalmen. Teil II* (AOAT, 207/2; Neukirchen–Vluyn: Neukirchener Verlag, 1979), pp. 479-82.

CROWN // ROOT	ROOT // SHOOT	ROOT // FRUIT
Sumerian (?) pa.zu an.šè úr.zu ki.šè pa.zu an.šè giš.búr.búr.ru úr.zu ki.šè te.me.en.sig$_7$.ga (*Šurpu* IX)		
	Babylonian (1500?) *šuršūšu qaqqaru lā išabbatū* *ziqpūšu lā illâma* *šamša lā immarū* *šuršūšu â iṣbatū eṣenṣēru* *ziqpūšu ai ilput šamê libbīja* (*Šurpu* V/VI)	
		Neo-Babylonian (9th C) *ša iṣṣi šurussu lipparima* *lā išammuḫa per 'šu* (*Erra* IV)
Ugaritic (pre 1400) *šršk barṣ al yp'* *riš ǵly bd ns'k* (1 *Aqht*)		Phoenician (6th C) *'l ykn lm* *šrš l mṭ* *wpr lm'l* *wt'r bḥym tḥt šmš* (*KAI* 14)
		Hebrew *šrš // pry* (Isa. 14.29; Ezek. 17.9; Hos. 9.16; Amos 2.9; Isa. 37.31; cf. Mal. 3.19; Ps. 52.7; Isa. 53.2; Jer. 12.2)
	Hebrew *šrš // prḥ* (Sir. 40.15; Isa. 5.24; 27.6; Hos. 14.6; Job 14.8; 15.29-30)	
	Aramaic (2nd C) (Dan. 4.12)	

Table 1

Things are not that simple, though, since there is a third line in the Phoenician text:

> nor beauty among the living under the sun

and the question arises: where did that line come from? The middle column of the table sets out two verses from the *Šurpu* incantations.[191] The first of these runs:

> Like this onion he peels and throws into the fire
> —the fire consumes it utterly—
> whose roots will not take hold in the soil
> whose shoots will not sprout
> and will not see the sun.

The final line is remarkably like the final line in Eshmunazor's curse. Though Hebrew poetic tradition continued to be dependent on Phoenician—witness 'he had no beauty' in Isa. 53.2—yet some lingering elements of the *Šurpu* incantations must have remained since in Mal. 3.19 the 'root // fruit' pair is mentioned in connection with universal burning on the day of the Lord; Isa. 5.24 is similar, also Job 15.29-30.

The Ugaritic passage is problematic and may have a Sumerian antecedent in yet another passage from *Šurpu*

> Above your crown,
> below, your root;
> above, your crown gives life upwards,
> below, your root cleanses downwards.

In any event it is obviously a gross oversimplification to maintain that the Ugaritic and Hebrew poets shared a common tradition of parallel pairs; the complex history set out above (which does not take word-pair inversion into account so as not to confuse matters further) shows how little we yet know.

191. These incantations, incidentally, contain a high number of poetic elements and could probably be classed as poetry—see already E. Sievers, 'Beiträge zur babylonischen Metrik', *ZA* 38 (1929), pp. 1-38, 36 (on *Šurpu* II 73-86). Further features include envelope figure (VIII 1 and 90), sorites (VII 84-87), mirror chiasmus (II 98-99), gender parallelism (II 34, contrast 32), triple synonyms (II 46.59–61.119; IV 22; V 160-61; VII 80-81; VIII 4.47), personification (V 191), the refrain in III and IV, the use of vertical parallelism in III and the widespread use of similes in series.

4.4. *Other Topics*

I could go on to consider a whole range of other topics, and point, in particular, to cases where ancient poetic techniques were misunderstood later (gender parallelism, staircase parallelism and so on) but I will discuss briefly only two subjects. They are allusion and imagery.

4.4.1. *Allusion*. One way of establishing relative chronology for Hebrew literature is to determine inner-biblical allusions and set them out in tabular form. Some work in this area has been carried out by David Gunn (on allusions to the Flood in Deutero-Isaiah)[192] and there is room for further study. An example is Mic. 7.3 where the best of the judges and princes are compared to briers and thorn hedges. This is evidently an allusion to Jotham's tree fable in Judges 9. Caution is needed, though, since the topos may have been commonplace in ancient Near Eastern literature, so such comparisons are indicative rather than conclusive. More telling is Nah. 3.18:

npšw ʿmk ʿl hhrym	Your troops expire upon the mountains,
wʾyn mqbṣ	with none to gather them up.

It is a description of the Assyrian army lying dead and, what is worse, unburied on the mountains. Not only that, Nahum is also making mocking allusion to the Song of Songs where the male lover is described as

mdlg ʿl hhrym	jump-dancing over the mountains,
mqpṣ ʿl hgbʿwt	leap-dancing over the hills (Cant. 2.8)

(following Gruber's paper on dance)[193]—in other words, very much alive. Clearly the Nahum passage is later than Song of Songs.[194]

4.4.2. *Imagery*. Even a study of imagery in Hebrew poetry can be revealing. When old and time-worn imagery is dusted off and given a new twist, then we are dealing with a later rather than an earlier stage. In Joel 1.6-7 the stock image of devouring locusts is combined with the equally well-worn metaphor of devouring lions to become:

192. D.M. Gunn, 'Deutero-Isaiah and the Flood', *JBL* 94 (1975) pp. 493-508.

193. M.I. Gruber, 'Ten Dance-Derived Expressions in the Hebrew Bible', *Bib* 62 (1982), pp. 328-46.

194. On the Nahum passage, see K. Cathcart, *Nahum in the Light of Northwest Semitic* (BibOr, 26; Rome: Biblical Institute Press, 1973), p. 149.

Their teeth are lions' teeth
their jaws a lioness's
making havoc of my vines,
defoliating my figs.

Again, the much-used figure 'numberless as sea-sand' is altered by Job (6.1-2) to great effect:

Could my anguish but be weighed
my misery heaped on the balance,
it would be heavier than the sands of the sea.

4.5. *Conclusion*

We are still very far from assigning absolute dates to every poem and it seems unlikely that we ever shall. I think the handbooks tend to be optimistic in this regard. We can map general trends—towards expansion, towards rhyme and so on—and we can reconstruct the history of certain poetic techniques as I have attempted to show. On these topics the contribution of ancient Near Eastern texts (from Mesopotamia to Qumran) has yet to be fully exploited. No single person can hope to span such a variety of fields and we can look forward to a continuing effort of cooperation between scholars in recovering the history of classical Hebrew poetry.[195]

195. After completing this paper I came across J.C. Greenfield, 'Early Aramaic Poetry', *JANESCU* 11 (1979, pub. 1981), pp. 45-51. In his survey he touches on points mentioned by me, notably the trend towards *expansion* (p. 48) and the *blazon*, in 1QApGen 20 (pp. 49-50) where the top-to-toe sequence is classical, it may be added. Without pre-empting Greenfield's projected study (p. 46 n. 12) it should be pointed out that the most frequent poetic device in the Aḥiqar Proverbs is gender-matched parallelism (lines 98, 100, 103-104, 105-106, 118-20, 132, 134, 169-70; cf. 83, 92, 95, 127) a fact to be reckoned with in tracing the development of ancient Semitic verse.

Chapter 3

HALF-LINE (INTERNAL) PARALLELISM

1. *Ugaritic Verse*[1]

1.1. *Description and Definition*

As is well known, the commonest form of parallelism in Ugaritic verse (as in many ancient Semitic verse traditions) is the couplet, where line B is parallel in some way to line A.[2] With internal parallelism (here abbreviated to IP), however, this feature applies to a single verse line. IP, therefore, is a descriptive term for a line of verse where the second half is parallel to the first half. Parallelism occurs *within* the verse line.

An example is the following passage from the Baal Cycle where dew is described in various ways, beginning with

(1) *KTU* 1.3 ii 39
ṭl. šmm. šmn. 'arṣ — Sky-dew; terrestrial oil.[3]

We can determine the length of the verse line by comparing it with the lines which follow:

ṭl šmm. šmn. 'arṣ.
rbb [*r*]*kb* '*rpt.*
ṭl. šmm. tskh
[*r*]*bb. nskh. kbkbm*

The alternation of *ṭl* and *rbb* (which are components of a word-pair, discussed below) and the prevailing length of line combine to show that the first of the set is a single line, not two separate lines, which exhibits IP.

1. First published in *SEL* 1 (1984), pp. 53-67.
2. For parallelism in Ugaritic, see S.B. Parker, 'Parallelism and Prosody in Ugaritic Narrative Verse', *UF* 6 (1974), pp. 283-94, largely a discussion of *Keret*.
3. Also cf. 1.19 i 44 and contrast 1.6 iii 6.

To my knowledge the topic of IP has not been studied in depth as an aspect of ancient Semitic verse.[4] However, John Foster has discussed IP in ancient Egyptian verse[5] though he prefers to use the expression 'two-element lines' which he defines as 'those which...seem to be divided into two clauses or employ paired epithets'.[6] I would place rather more emphasis on the component of parallelism. A fuller impression of IP, particularly in Ugaritic, will emerge from the illustrations provided in section 1.3, below.

1.2. *Layout*

The present paper will examine the occurrences of IP in Ugaritic verse against the wider background of related poetic traditions (excluding Hebrew). First, the texts will be set out following the sequence of *KTU*. Then, after an assessment of distribution, come descriptions of the structure and functions of IP in Ugaritic. Next, a brief look at this feature in other (ancient) literature. After some observations of IP in relation to verse components come the final conclusions.

1.3. *Ugaritic Examples*

The texts will be numbered sequentially for ease of reference; example (1) has already been set out, above. Notes on grammatical structure will be provided[7] but textual and philological comment kept to a minimum.

(2) *KTU* 1.3 iii 22-23 (and par.)
rgm 'ṣ wlḫšt 'abn Word of tree and whisper of stone.

4. However, cf. K. Hecker, *Untersuchungen zur akkadischen Epik* (AOAT, 8; Kevelaer: Butzon & Bercker; Neukirchen–Vluyn: Neukirchener Verlag, 1974), pp. 130-31.

5. J.L. Foster, 'Thought Couplets in Khety's Hymn to the Inundation', *JNES* 34 (1975), pp. 1-29, and 'Sinuhe: The Ancient Egyptian Genre of Narrative Verse', *JNES* 39 (1980), pp. 89-117. Incidentally, he reminded us of the distinction between verse and poetry in his second paper (p. 103) which is why I prefer to use 'verse' instead of 'poetry' in my title. In Foster's own words: 'poetry is verse of high quality' (p. 102) whereas the distinction operative here is that between prose and verse (which Foster explains very clearly).

6. Foster, 'Sinuhe', p. 105.

7. Broadly following T. Collins, *Line-forms in Hebrew Poetry: A Grammatical Approach to the Stylistic Study of the Hebrew Prophets* (Studia Pohl, Series Major, 7; Rome: Pontifical Biblical Institute, 1978), pp. 22-70.

The nominal construction in each half is identical: noun in construct + noun.

(3) *KTU* 1.3 iv 33
'atm. bštm. w'an.šnt

It is difficult to know how this line should be translated. Elsewhere I propose 'You in two years, but I in (the space of) sleep'.[8] De Moor suggested 'You depart but I too am leaving'.[9] Whatever the actual meaning the two-part structure of the line is clear.

(4) *KTU* 1.3 iv 38[10]

b'alp šd rbt kmn	By the thousands *š*., the myriad *k*.

The line is formulaic, nominal in construction, and can be expanded to a full couplet.[11]

(5) *KTU* 1.3 vi 7-9

[']br. gbl. 'br q'l	Cross crests, cross peaks,
'br. 'iht np. šmm.	cross the region of celestial summits.

IP is present in the first line with the pattern V M // V M. Here I follow del Olmo Lete in taking the nouns as common nouns[12] though they are usually understood as place names.[13]

(6) *KTU* 1.4 i 25-26

yṣq. ksp. yšlḥ. ḫrṣ	He smelted silver; he cast gold.

8. See Chapter 2, 'Middle-Eastern Forerunners to a Folktale Motif'.

9. J.C. de Moor: 'Donkey-Packs and Geology', *UF* 13 (1981), p. 303; cf. 'Contributions to the Ugaritic Lexicon', *UF* 11 (1979), p. 647 n. 54.

10. For reference later the parallel texts have been identified as follows: 4a: 1.3 iv 38; 4b: 1.3 vi 17-18; 4c: 1.4 v 24; 4d: 1.4 viii 24-26; 4e: 1.17 v 9-10; 4f: 1.18 i 21-22.

11. In 1.4 v 56-57.

12. G. del Olmo Lete, *Mitos y leyendas de Canaan según la tradición de Ugarit* (Fuentes de la Ciencia Bíblica, 1; Madrid: Ediciones Cristiandad, 1981), p. 192 and entries in glossary. So already A. Caquot, M. Sznycer and A. Herdner, *Texte ougaritiques*. I. *Mythes et légendes* (LAPO, 7; Paris: Cerf, 1974), pp. 177-78: 'Passe par la montagne, passe par la hauteur, passe par les plages du zénith'.

13. So J.C.L. Gibson, *Canaanite Myths and Legends* (Edinburgh: T. & T. Clark, 1978), p. 54; J.C. de Moor, *The Seasonal Pattern in the Ugaritic Myth of Ba'lu according to the Version of Ilimilku* (AOAT, 16; Kevelaer: Butzon & Bercker; Neukirchen–Vluyn: Neukirchener Verlag, 1971), p. 51, n. 52; cf. E. Lipiński, 'Recherches ougaritiques', *Syria* 50 (1973), pp. 35-37. Another example of IP may be 1.3 vi 19-20 (// 1.4 iv 26, etc.).

The line which can be analysed as V NP_2 // V NP_2, initiates a set of *yṣq* repeated four times in as many lines.[14]

(7)	*KTU* 1.4 iii 18-20	
	dbḥ bṯt. wdbḥ} {dnt	a sacrifice of shame and a sacrifice
	wdbḥ. tdmm 'amht	and a sacrifice of debauching maids.

The third *dbḥ* in the first line is evidently a mistake;[15] the structure is nominal throughout.[16]

(8)	*KTU* 1.4 iv 4-5 (// 1.19 ii 3-4)	
	mdl 'r ṣmd pḥl	Harness an ass; saddle a donkey.

The formula, expanded to a couplet in 1.19 ii 8-9 (see below) uses V NP_2 in both halves.[17]

(9), (10)	*KTU* 1.5 ii 2-6	
		(If Mot sets[?])
	[špt l'a] rṣ. špt. lmm	a lip to the earth and a lip to the sky,
	[ ] *lšn. lkbkbm.*	(and extends?) his tongue to the stars,
	y'rb b'l. bkbdh	Baal will enter his insides,
	bph. yrd kḥrr. zt.	falling into his mouth like a dry olive,
	ybl. 'arṣ. wpr 'ṣm.	produce of the earth and fruit of the trees.

Both stichometry and translation are debatable, partly because of the gaps in the text. I follow del Olmo Lete[18] and, with reserve, Margalit.[19] IP occurs at both the beginning and end of this stanza, a pattern matched by examples (22) and (23) below.

(11)	*KTU* 1.6 vi 17 = 18-19 = 20	
	mt 'z b'l 'z	Mot was strong; Baal was strong.

14. Contrast *UT* §13.112 (p. 134). Other examples, perhaps, are 1.4 i 33-34; ii 24-26, 26-28.

15. I.e. dittography; see the standard works, e.g. *KTU* p. 16 (footnote).

16. On the meaning of *dnt*, see G. del Olmo Lete, 'Notes on Ugaritic Semantics IV', *UF* 10 (1978), pp. 45-46 and *Mitos y leyendas*, pp. 198, 538. On *tdmm*, see my remarks in 'Parallels to some Passages in Ugaritic', *UF* 10 (1978), p. 401. For the rhetorical device used here (priamel), see W.H. Race, *The Classical Priamel from Homer to Boethius* (Leiden: Brill, 1982), esp. pp. 7-17.

17. IP may be present, too, in 1.4 v 20-21.

18. Del Olmo Lete, *Mitos y leyendas*, p. 216.

19. B. Margalit, *A Matter of 'Life' and 'Death': A Study of the Baal-Mot Epic (CTA 4-5-6)* (AOAT, 206; Kevelaer: Butzon & Bercker; Neukirchen–Vluyn: Neukirchener Verlag, 1980), pp. 107-13 with very different stichometry.

The refrain occurs three times; the fourth time there is a variation (next example).[20]

(12) *KTU* 1.6 vi 21-22
mt. ql. b'l. ql. Mot fell; Baal fell.

As noted, this is a climactic variant to (11). The following word (*'ln*) does not belong here[21] but to the next stanza.[22] The NP_1 V // NP_1 V pattern here suggest that the same analysis applies to (11) and therefore *'z* is a verb, not an adjective.

(13) *KTU* 1.10 ii 29
tr. blkt. wtr. bḫl She fled running and she fled leaping.

Whatever the meaning here[23] there can be no doubt that IP is used, since the first half of the line (*tr blkt*) repeats the second half of the preceding line.

(14) *KTU* 1.16 i 12-13
ybky wyšnn. He wept and ground his teeth.

This and the parallel *tbky. wtšnn.* (ii 35) comprise the only use of IP in *Keret*. The structure is V // V as in example (19).

(15) *KTU* 1.18 i 24
'at. 'aḫ. w'an. 'a[ḫtk] You are my 'brother' and I am your 'sister'.

This is similar to example (3).[24]

(16) *KTU* 1.19 i 44
bl. ṭl. bl rbb No dew, no rain.

20. Again, Margalit, *'Life' and 'Death'*, pp. 187-90, has different stichometry.

21. So, incorrectly, del Olmo Lete, *Mitos y leyendas*, p. 233.

22. 'Above the Sun etc.'; cf. Margalit, *'Life' and 'Death'*, pp. 190, 192 and independently, J.C. de Moor, 'Rāpi'ūma–Rephaim', *ZAW* 88 (1976), p. 344. P. Xella, *I Testi rituali di Ugarit*. I. *Testi* (Pubblicazioni del Centro di Studio per le civiltà fenicia e punica, 21; Studi Semitici, 54; Rome: Consiglio Nazionale delle Ricerche, 1981), p. 282 (cf. p. 286): 'da lontano'.

23. For a survey of opinions cf. del Olmo Lete, *Mitos y leyendas*, p. 470 and glossary (p. 594) under *ntr*.

24. The 'parallel' in Akk. epic, 'You must be my husband, I your wife', (text: *Gilg. nin.* vi 9 = *Nergal and Ereškigal* aA 82, cited by Hecker, *Epik*, p. 131 n. 1) also exhibits IP.

Example (1) is related; the construction is also nominal.

(17) *KTU* 1.19 iii 4-5 = 19 = 33-34
hm 'iṯ šmt hm 'iṯ 'ẓm If there is fat, if there is bone.

Although very long the verse line matches the one immediately before it. The climax refrain in the set (line 39) is a shortened variant: *'iṯ šmt 'itṯ 'ẓm*.

(18) *KTU* 1.19 iii 11 = 25
'in šmt 'in 'ẓm There is no fat, there is no bone.

This example, also a refrain, is a negative form of the previous set (example 17).

(19) *KTU* 1.19 iii 5 = 20 = 34
'abky w'aqbrnh I shall weep and I shall bury him.

Yet another refrain, interspersed with the refrains of (17) and (18), which could also be understood as hendiadys. The parallel passage *tbkynh wtqbrnh*, 'she buried him whilst weeping' (1.6 i 16-17) is even clearer in this regard because there the suffix is repeated. Line-form analysis in all cases is VV (with inclusion of suffixes).

(20) *KTU* 1.23:7
šlm. mlk. šlm. mlkt. Well-being to the king! Well-being to the queen!

The stichometry is unclear; that adopted here is suggested by the similar passage in 1.161:32-34.[25]

(21) *KTU* 1.23:32
hlh. tšpl. hlh. trm. See! One goes up. See! One goes down.

The lengths of the next two lines in this list of actions confirm the presence of IP here.[26]

(22) and (23) *KTU* 1.23:61-63
špt l'arṣ. špt lšmm. One lip to the ground, one lip to the sky
wy'rb. bphm. and into their mouth went
'ṣr. šmm wdg bym. birds of the sky and fish from the sea.

This double example is very like (9) and (10) in structure and wording.

25. See Xella, *Testi rituali*, p. 283 for translation.

26. In the same text problematic *'agzr ym bn ym* (lines 23, 58-59 and 61) may also constitute IP.

(24) *KTU* 1.24:20-21
'alp. ksp. wrbt. ḫrṣ — A thousand (units) of silver,
ten thousand of gold.

Similar, of course and also nominal is example (4).

(25) *KTU* 1.24:38-39
'ar yrḫ. wyrḫ y'ark — Light may Y. give;
may Y. give light to you.

Elsewhere I have argued that this is a couplet (V NP_1 // NP_1 V-np_2)[27] but I now prefer to consider it a single line with IP. The chiasmus is noteworthy (see comments below).

(26) *KTU* 1.161:21-22
'arṣ rd. w.špl. 'pr. — To the underworld descend
and collapse in the dust.

Exactly as in example (13) the initial half-line is a verbatim repetition of the half-line immediately before. Another rare example of chiasmus (M V // V M).[28]

1.4. *Distribution*

Distribution of IP over the main literary texts in Ugaritic is as follows:

Baal Cycle:	12 examples (1, 2, 3, 4, 5, 6, 7, 8, 9, 10, 11, 12) of which 3 (1, 4, 8) are formulaic.[29]
Keret:	1 only (14).
Aqhat:	6 examples (15, 16, 17, 18, 19) one of which (8) is formulaic.
Šḥr wŠlm:	4 (20, 21, 22, 23).[30]
Others:	*KTU* 1.10:1 (example 13); *KTU* 1.24:2 (examples 24, 25); *KTU* 1.161:1 (example 26).

Some of these examples recur in different compositions (e.g. 8), others are repeated within the same composition (e.g. 17, 18, 19). The *Legend of Keret* is remarkable in only providing one example of IP, a

27. See Chapter 7, 'Strophic Chiasmus in Ugaritic Poetry'.

28. Xella, *Testi rituali*, p. 283 translates 'discendi nell'aldilà e sprofonda nella polvere'.

29. Plus other dubious examples (nn. 13, 14, 16 and 46) and section 7.4.

30. See also n. 26.

feature comparable to the relative rarity of strophic chiasmus in the same work.[31]

1.5. *Structure and Functions*

1.5.1. *Structure*. Not surprisingly the grammatical parallelism in each half of a verse line with IP tends to be similar and even identical, as in example (6) where the pattern is V NP_2 // V NP_2. This applies even with nominal clauses. Antithetic parallelism is rare, attested only in (3) and (21). Similarly, chiastic parallelism occurs only twice (25 and 26). Commonly, each half of a verse line with IP begins with the same letter (alliteration), as in 3, 9, 13, 14, 15, 20, 22, 23. Word-pairs, too, often form the basis for the pattern under discussion.

Here is a sample list, in alphabetic order:

'alp // rbt	(4, 24)
'arṣ // 'pr	(26)
'arṣ // šmm	(9, 22; reversed in 1)[32]
ṭl // rbb	(1, 16)
ksp // ḫrṣ	(6)
'ṣ // 'abn	(2)
šd // kmn	(4)
šmt // 'ẓm	(17, 18) etc.

Note, too, the formulas in (4) and (8).

IP often occurs in lists, perhaps to break the monotony (cf. 1, 2, 5, 6, 7, 16, 24). Some one-line passages can be expanded into couplets. Example (8), *mdl 'r ṣmd pḥl*, becomes *bkm tmdln 'r // bkm tṣmd pḥl* in 1.19 ii 8-9. Similarly, example (1) is expanded in (16) and 1.4 v 56-57 develops example (4). There is no clustering and also no use of wordplay (see below).

1.5.2. *Functions*. The following structural functions can be noted.

Refrain:	examples (11, 12, 17 and 18).[33]
Envelope figure (inclusio):	in (9-10) and (22-23).

31. As shown in section 1.3.2 of Chapter 7, 'Strophic Chiasmus in Ugaritic Poetry'.

32. On reversed word-pairs, see Chapter 6, 'Reversed Word-Pairs in Ugaritic Poetry'.

33. See already *UT* §13.114.

To open a strophe or longer sequence:	IP is used to open a couplet (1, 5, 19) a tricolon (4d)[34] and a lengthier section (2, 6, 7, 9, 21, 22).
To close a section:	IP is closural to a couplet (3, 4e), a tricolon (4a, b, c), a quatrain (4f) and the longer sections in (10, 11, 12 and 23).

1.6. *IP in other Verse Traditions*

IP within the verse-line is not confined to Ugaritic, of course. Mention has already been made of its recognition in Akkadian and ancient Egyptian verse. Aramaic, too, supplies material in the form of a double example from the Carpentras Stele (lines 2-3):

mnd'm b'yš l' 'bdt wkrṣy 'yš l' 'mrt tmh
qdm 'wsry brykh hwy mn qdm 'wsry myn qḥy
She did not evil at all, nor calumny against any man did she utter up there.
Before Osiris be (you) blessed; from Osiris receive water.[35]

There is a case, too, in Neo-Punic[36] and no doubt more will come to light from these traditions, meagre as they are in verse passages. As for Akkadian, Hecker has already provided some data.[37] Curiously, the few additional texts I have looked at show a marked contrast with the features outlined above for Ugaritic verse.

Specific to Akkadian are clustering,[38] frequent use of chiasmus,[39] a

34. See n. 10.

35. Text and translation follow J.C.L. Gibson, *Textbook of Syrian Semitic Inscriptions*. II. *Aramaic Inscriptions* (Oxford: Oxford University Press, 1975), pp. 120-22.

36. *s*]*r tyl' hkyrt r'qm by'tn š'bt*, '(When) he hanged the rebel / cut off the seditionists—our terror came to an end' (Mactar A I 2) as translated by C.R. Krahmalkov, 'Two Neo-Punic Poems in Rhymed Verse', *RSF* 3 (1975), pp. 177-78, who comments, 'the members of the hemistich exhibit a functional parallelism that facilitates the reconstruction' (p. 180).

37. See n. 4.

38. Couplets: *Atr*. III i 22-23; *Gilg*. XI 21-22; *Erra* I 109-113, 115; IV 71-72, 73-74 (cf. V 57-58); Theodicy 76-77, 292-293; Great Šamaš Hymn 145. Sets of three: *Ludlul* IV 37-39; Theodicy 27-29. Note 14 consecutive lines in *Erra* IId 4-12a. However, there is *no* clustering in *Ee*.

39. *Erra* I 144; IIc 13, 17; IV 93, 123; V 14, 57-59; *Atr*. I iv 171; v 243; vi 289; *Ludlul* III 12; IV 39; Theodicy 76-77, 292; Great Šamaš Hymn 151; *Ee* III 9 (= 134); IV 102.

degree of wordplay[40] and the use of IP as a 'call to attention'.[41] Common to both traditions is initial alliteration, particularly to begin each half of a line,[42] expansion into couplet from one-line IP[43] and the rarity of antithetic parallelism.[44] Of course, my own examination has been restricted to relatively few of the more readily accessible Akkadian texts, so this impression may not be representative. Even so it is worth investigating whether the features of clustering, chiasmus and wordplay are in fact peculiar to Akkadian versification, since aside from two instances of chiasmus they are not found in Ugaritic in conjunction with IP.

1.7. *IP as a Structural Component in Verse*

Here, three aspects of the verse-line will be discussed in the light of the above findings. The are caesura, the verse-line itself and the 'half-colon'. An example will be examined in depth by way of illustration.

1.7.1. *Caesura.* Recognition of IP is tantamount to recognition of both caesura and end-stopping. Caesura is a break or juncture within the line. While it can sometimes be difficult to pinpoint caesura, with IP there can be no doubts at all. For instance, in example (21) *hlh tšpl hlh trm*, there is a self-evident pause after the second word, or technically, there is caesura.

1.7.2. *Verse-line.* Since the second half of a line with IP is modelled on the first half it is equally easy to determine where the verse-line ends (end-stopping). More important is a second corollary which is that two 'halves' of a line with IP combine to make up a single verse-line and the lengths of neighbouring lines can also be checked. In (17), while it might be possible to read the six words as two lines, *hm 'iṯ šmt* / *hm 'iṯ 'ẓm*, the parallel in (19) as well as the lengths of associated lines (e.g. 1.19 iii 3-4: *'ibq' kbdthm w'aḥd*, numbering 14 letters) are indications to the contrary.

40. *Erra* IIc 13; *Ludlul* III 12; Theodicy 292.

41. *Erra* V 27; *Gilg.* XI 21-22; Theodicy 25-26.

42. *Atr.* I v 243; S iv 59; *Ludlul* IV 94; Theodicy 135; Great Šamaš Hymn 180; Lambert, *Babylonian Wisdom Literature*, p. 102 line 61.

43. E.g. *Atr.* I v 240-241 from I i 2.

44. *Erra* V 58; Great Šamaš Hymn 180.

1.7.3. *The 'Half-Colon'*. As has been seen (example 26) the half-line or half-colon is a structural element which can be used to form a full verse-line. While this is transparently obvious in verses with IP it is also noticeable elsewhere, particularly with repetitive patterns such as the terrace pattern (anadiplosis).[45]

1.7.4. *A Dubious Example*. To demonstrate the difficulties involved in recognizing IP we can look at a disputed example. The passage in question is 1.2 iv 22-23 (// 25-26):

yprṣḥ ym (w)yql l'arṣ Y. collapsed (and) he fell to earth.

It comes in the section 1.2 iv 11-26 (set out in full, Table 1) which divides naturally into two parts: 11-18a and 18bcd-26. Each part comprises the naming of a weapon and the assignment of its task (command). In part I the task is carried out to no avail:

'z ym lmk
ltnǵṣn pnth lydlp tmnh[46] (lines 17-18a)

In part II a similar command is also fulfilled, this time effectively:

yprṣḥ ym yql l'arṣ
tnǵṣn pnth wydlp tmnh (lines 25b-26)

The first line here, which corresponds to *'z ym lymk* in part I, occurs at the close of the command in part II as well (lines 22b-23). Accordingly, there are strong indicators of IP in our example:

a. its correspondence to *'z ym lymk*, a single line;
b. its parallelism with *tnǵṣn pnth wydlp tmnh*;
c. its occurrence within a set of longer lines.

Against is the possibility that both *yprṣḥ*... and *(l)tnǵṣn*... could equally well be full couplets rather than single lines with IP Also, the resultant clustering would be rare in Ugaritic. The example, therefore, remains uncertain.[47]

45. As in 1.17 vi 35b-36a and often in 1.10.

46. For this difficult line cf. J.C. de Moor, 'The Anatomy of the Back', *UF* 12 (1980), pp. 425-26.

47. Also difficult is *mlkt*.[ ]*hm. lmlkt* (1.2 iii 22). Gibson, *Canaanite Myths*, p. 38 restores *mlkt 'an lmlkt 'an*, translating 'Am [I indeed] king or am I not king?', which would certainly be IP. For other opinions, see del Olmo Lete, *Mitos y leyendas*, p. 168.

	Command	Fulfilment
I	*kṯr ṣmdm ynḥt*	
	wyp‘r šmthm	
	šmk ’at ygrš	
	ygrš grš ym	
	grš ym lks ’ih	
	nhr lkḥṯ drkth	
	trtqṣ bd b‘l	*yrtqṣ ṣmd bd b‘l*
	km nšr b’uṣb‘th	*km nšr b’uṣb‘th*
	hlm ktp zbl ym	*ylm ktp zbl ym*
	bn ydm tpṭ nhr	*bn ydm tpṭ nhr*
		‘z ym lymk
		ltnǵṣn pnth lydlp tmnh
II	*kṯr ṣmdm ynḥt*	
	wyp‘r šmthm	
	šmk ’at ’aymr	
	’aymr mr ym	
	mr ym lks’ih	
	nhr lkḥṯ drkth	
	trtqṣ bd b‘l	*wyrtqṣ ṣmd bd b‘l*
	km nšr b’uṣb‘th	*km nšr b’uṣb‘th*
	hlm qdqd zbl ym	*ylm qdqd zbl ym*
	bn ‘nm tpṭ nhr	*bn ‘nm tpṭ nhr*
	yprṣḥ ym wyql l’arṣ	*yprṣḥ ym yql l’arṣ*
		tnǵṣn pnth wydlp tmnh

Table 1. *KTU* 1.2 iv 11-26

1.8. *Conclusions*

If parallelism can be considered as corresponding to end-rhyme in European poetry then IP amounts to a kind of internal rhyme. Enough examples have been set out—discounting those that are uncertain—to establish the presence of IP in Ugaritic verse. The distribution table shows that there is a marked preference for the form in the Baal Cycle, the *Aqhat Tale* and 1.24, which contrasts with its almost complete absence from *Keret* as well as from the more recently discovered texts of *Ugaritica* V. This may be due to developments within the poetic tradition or may be due to stylistic preference.[48] We

48. In the Babylonian Theodicy it would seem that IP is set largely in the mouth

cannot say. Of special interest in determining the specific character of Ugaritic poetry has been the difference in usage shown to exist between Ugaritic and Akkadian versification.[49] This has yet to be tested by further examples from Assyro-Babylonian verse not to mention corresponding patterns in classical Hebrew poetry. While recognition of internal parallelism can be of assistance in determining stichometry, there are ambiguous cases where other factors need to be considered, as has been shown. Finally, the relationship between this form and metre needs to be explored.[50] The survey provided here is merely the beginning of further research into one aspect of verse structure in Ugaritic literary texts.

2. *Ugaritic Verse: Further Examples*[51]

2.1.1. *Introduction*

Since my first study on IP[52] I have identified several further examples in Ugaritic verse which are presented here. As before, the sequence will follow that of *KTU* in the main, and the examples are numbered for ease of reference. For each text there will be brief discussion of salient points. Next, inner-line features (lines with IP) of these passages are described. After a short paragraph on clustering (of lines with IP), IP in other verse traditions is examined briefly. Problems connected with IP in Ugaritic are then discussed and finally a table of occurrence is provided.

of the 'Sufferer' (lines 25-26, 27-29, 76-77, 135, 292-93). However, the 'Friend' appears to use this form of parallelism in stanza XX (lines 214, 218, 219) and since there are several gaps in the text as a whole (see Lambert, *Babylonian Wisdom Literature*, pp. 63-91, 302-10, 345) any definite conclusions are precluded. It is worth mentioning, too, that there is only one example in the 'Dialogue of Pessimism', i.e. line 78.

49. See Chapter 2, 'The Character of Ugaritic Poetry'.

50. A significant paper on Ugaritic metre is J. Wansbrough, 'Metra ugaritica: pro et contra', *BSOAS* 46 (1983), pp. 221-34.

51. First published in *UF* 17 (1985), pp. 345-56.

52. 'Internal Parallelism in Ugaritic Verse', *SEL* 1 (1984), pp. 53-67 (Chapter 3, 'Ugaritic Verse'). This topic is discussed briefly by Y. Avishur, *Stylistic Studies of Word-Pairs in Biblical and Ancient Semitic Languages* (AOAT, 210: Kevelaer: Butzon & Bercker; Neukirchen–Vluyn: Neukirchener Verlag, 1984), pp. 53-63, though he prefers the description 'intra-colon parallelism'. See, too, S. Segert, 'Parallelism in Ugaritic Poetry', *JAOS* 103 (1983), pp. 295-306, 298, 299.

The aims of the present paper are as follows: to present new examples in Ugaritic verse and describe the features of IP in Ugaritic; to re-open the discussion of line-length, lineation, end-stopping, caesura, monocola and of parallelism in general; to correct my own presentation of Ugaritic (and Hebrew) verse in my *Classical Hebrew Poetry*.

2.2. *Passages*

(1) *KTU* 1.6 vi 48-50

(a) *'dk. ilm. hn. mtm 'dk.*	To you (come) the gods, yes to the dead.
(b) *kṯrm. ḥbrk wḫss. d'tk*	Kothar is your spell-caster, and Hasis your 'knower'.

These lines, which belong to the final section of Tablet 6 in the Baal Cycle,[53] are difficult in respect of both stichometry and meaning. If correct, the version proposed here, dependent in part on recent studies by Day[54] and Smith,[55] assumes IP in both (a) and (b).

The intrusive *hn* can be matched by patterns of IP in Hebrew verse (e.g. *gm* in Judg. 5.4; *'p* in Ps. 74.16).[56] A certain degree of alliterative rootplay (*'dk/d'tk*) is evident as is the break-up of *kṯr-w-ḫss* to form a word-pair.[57]

(2) *KTU* 1.6 vi 55-58

(a) *rb khnm rb. nqdm*	Chief of the Priests, Chief of the Shepherds,
(b) *ṯ'y. nqmd. mlk ugrt*	Inspector of Niqmaddu, King of Ugarit,

53. For the tablet sequence cf. del Olmo Lete, *Mitos y leyendas*, pp. 81-95 and J.C.L. Gibson, 'The Theology of the Ugaritic Baal Cycle', *Or* 53 (1984), pp. 204-206, 255-61.

54. J. Day, *God's Conflict with the Dragon and the Sea: Echoes of a Canaanite Myth in the Old Testament* (University of Cambridge Oriental Publications, 35; Cambridge: Cambridge University Press, 1985), p. 45.

55. M.S. Smith, 'The Magic of Kothar, the Ugaritic Craftsman God, in *KTU* 1.6 VI 49-50', *RB* 91 (1984), pp. 377-80. B.A. Levine and J.-M. de Tarragon, 'Dead Kings and Rephaim: The Patrons of the Ugaritic Dynasty', *JAOS* 104 (1984), pp. 649-659, 657, prefer 'Near you—gods! Behold, the dead—near you! Kothar—your close friend! And Ḫasis—your intimate!', and see p. 657 n. 34.

56. See Chapter 3, 'Classical Hebrew Verse'. New examples include Mal. 1.6, Ps. 125.5 and 1 Chron. 12.19. Also, 2 Sam. 23.5d.

57. On the meaning of *kṯr*, see now I.J. Gelb, '*Šîbût kušurrā'im*, "Witnesses of Indemnity"', *JNES* 43 (1984), pp. 263-76, esp. 276. The word-pair *ḥbr // d't* recurs in *ygrš. ḥrn. ḥbrm. wǵlm. d'tm.* 'May Horon drive away the companions, may the Youth (drive away) the friends' (RIH 78/20:9-10).

(b) *ṯ'y. nqmd. mlk ugrt* Inspector of Niqmaddu, King of Ugarit,

The closing lines of colophon to Tablet 6 comprise yet another much discussed text. The version adopted here is that of Astour[58] and Del Olmo Lete.[59] Line (b) may also be internally parallel. Word-repetition as here (of *rb*) is a common feature of such lines.

(3) *KTU* 1.14 iv 38-39
aṯrt. ṣrm wilt. ṣdynm Asherah of the Tyrians and the goddess of the Sidonians.

Strictly speaking, this formulaic expression is part of longer verse lines both times it occurs—as *i iṯt. aṯrt. ṣrm wilt. ṣdynm* (here) and as *ym[ġy.] lqdš aṯ[r]t* [.] *ṣrm. wlilt ṣd*[y]*nm* (lines 35-36).

(4) *KTU* 1.14 iii 4-5, 30; iv 47-48; v 41-42; vi 11-12
udm rbt wudm ṯrrt Greater Udum and Lesser Udum

Again, this is a formulaic expression in inner-line parallelism which is part of a larger segment of verse.[60] It is noteworthy that in the two passages where *udm ytnt il wušn ab adm* ('Udum, El's present and the Father of Mankind's gift') does not immediately follow, a line in IP comes next (see the next example and comments on clustering, below).

(5) *KTU* 1.14 iii 6-7 (command; iv 49-50: fulfilment)
gr.nn 'rm šrn pdrm Attack his cities, besiege his villages.

The word-pair *'r(m) // pdr(m)*, used elsewhere over two parallel lines (1.4 vii 7-8.9-10; 1.16 vi 6-8 and perhaps v 47-48) occurs here within a single line.[61]

58. M.C. Astour, 'Place Names', in *RSP* II, pp. 291-93.

59. Cf. del Olmo Lete, *Mitos y leyendas*, p. 235, though in a personal communication G. del Olmo Lete said that he had now changed his mind slightly with respect to his previous translation since in the following line *yrgb b'l* was a personal name attested elsewhere.

60. For the translation, see J. Sapin, 'Quelques systèmes socio-politiques en Syrie au 2e millenaire avant J.-C. et leur évolution historique d'après des documents religieux (légendes, rituels, sanctuaires)', *UF* 15 (1983), pp. 157-90, 160 n. 17. I. Kottsieper, 'KTU 1.100—Versuch einer Deutung. (Eine weitere Eule nach Athen getragen)', *UF* 16 (1984), pp. 97-110, 105 and 107 prefers 'regenreich' and 'wasserreich' for the corresponding formula in *KTU* 1.100:63, 64 (my example 18 below).

61. If J.W. Wesselius, 'Three Difficult Passages in Ugaritic Literary Texts' *UF* 15 (1983), pp. 312-14 is correct, *KTU* 1.14 ii 32-34 would be a double example of IP, but his proposal is unconvincing because it does not tackle the

(6) *KTU* 1.17 vi 44-45

ašqlk. tṭt [p'ny	I'll trample you underfoot
(l)ḥ]tk. n'mn. 'mq. nšm	O handsome scion, wisest of mortals.

If Margalit's restoration and translation are correct (as reproduced here)[62] this would be a rare example of IP in the second line of a couplet.

(7) *KTU* 1.19 iv 5-6

'wrt. yštk. b'l.	May Baal blind you
lht w'lmh. l'nt. pdr. dr	from now to eternity, from this moment to generations.

The refrain *'nt brḥp'lmh / 'nt pdrdr* of 1.19 iii 48 and 56, cast in the form of a couplet, has been reduced here to a single line with IP. Both halves of the line begin with *l* (quasi-acrostic) and this is another example of IP in the second line of a couplet (see example 6).

(8) *KTU* 1.19 iv 13-14

lymm. lyrḫm lyrḫm. lšnt	From days to months, from months to years.

Also recurring in 1.6 v 7, this formulaic expression may be an expansion (by anadiplosis or use of the terrace pattern) of *lymm lyrḫm* (1.6 ii 27).

(9) *KTU* 1.23:16

tlkm. rḥmy. tṣd [aṯrt]	R. went and A. hunted.

The restoration, first proposed by Gaster, has been accepted by Del Olmo Lete[63] and would appear to be confirmed by line 24b of the same text:

ynqm. bap ẓd.	Who suck the teats of the breasts
aṯrt. [wrḥmy]	of Asherah and Raḥmay

In view of the cyclic nature of such an argument, though, this second text (with IP in the second line) has not been set out as a separate example.[64]

62. B. Margalit, 'A Restoration Proposal in AQHT (*CTA / KTU* 1.17: VI:45)', *RB* 90 (1983), pp. 360-64.

63. See del Olmo Lete, *Mitos y leyendas*, p. 442 for details. On the relationship between Asherah and Rḥmy in this text, see J. Day 'Asherah in the Hebrew Bible and North-West Semitic Literature', *JBL* 105 (1986), pp. 385-408 where he suggests that Rḥmy may be a separate goddess.

64. Another example may be *KTU* 1.23:14 *gd. bḥlb. annḫ bḫmat*, 'coriander(?)

(10) *KTU* 1.93:2-3

bpy. t'lgt. blšn[*y*] *ġr*	In/From my mouth stammering, in/from my tongue??

The text is difficult; de Moor renders lines 1-3, 'Cow! Remove the word spoken in negligence, the stammering from my mouth, the negligence from my tongue!', understanding *ġr* to mean 'negligence, inadvertence' (Arabic *ġirrah*).[65] Margalit, instead, suggests: 'A cow cried out from the mountain: "In my mouth (there's) a thickness. On my tongue, a ridge;" etc.'[66] which is more plausible. Until we can be sure of the exact meaning of *ġr*, though, the translation will remain uncertain, though the presence of nominal IP is undeniable.

(11) RIH 78/20:3-4

(a) *kqṭr. urbtm. kbṯn. 'mdm*	Like smoke through a hole, like a snake at the base of a wall,
(b) *ky'lm. ẓrh. klbim. skh*	like mountain-goats to the summit, like lions to the thicket.

A comprehensive study of this text is Caquot's[67] whose version is used here. The set of four similes—a common feature in Akkadian incantations, incidentally[68]—forms a couplet, with IP in each line.

(12) RIH 78/20:5-6a

(a) *ḫṭ. nqh. uqrb. ḫṭ*	Stick, get up! And come near, Stick!
(b) *tḫṭa. lgbk wtrš'. ltmntk.*	May you suffer on your back, may you become puny in form.

in milk, mint in butter' (Cacquot *et al.*, *Textes ougaritiques*, p. 371; Gibson, *Canaanite Myths*, p. 123 and n. 11) or, less probably, 'un cabrito en leche, una cria en manteca' (del Olmo Lete, *Mitos y leyendas*, p. 441). Problems of text, stichometry and translation remain. On *annḫ*, cf. *CAD*, A/2, p. 111 under *ananiḫu* (also *naniḫu* and *nanaḫu*), and *AHw*, p. 50; the Akk. word is listed with *urnû*, 'mint' (*AHw*, p. 1432) in lexical texts.

65. J.C. de Moor 'Contributions to the Ugaritic Lexicon', *UF* 11 (1979), pp. 639-54, 648-49.

66. B. Margalit, 'KTU 1.93 (= PRU V:124): The Prayer of a Sick Cow', *SEL* 1 (1984), pp. 89-101.

67. A. Caquot, 'Une nouvelle interpretation de la tablette ougaritique de Ras Ibn Hani 78/20', *Or* 53 (1984), pp. 163-76. K. Aartun ('Neue Beiträge zum ugaritischen Lexikon I', *UF* 16 [1984], pp. 1-52, 5) now translates the first line '(sie sollen hinausgehen) wie die giftige Schlange zum Schlupfwinkel hin, wie die Viper zur Bleibe(stelle) hin'.

68. F. Saracino, 'Appunti in margine a RIH 78/20', *SEL* 1 (1984), pp. 69-83, 71, refers to the similar set in *KTU* 1.18 iv 24-26.

If correctly understood by Caquot, there is chiasmus in the first line (NP_1 V // V NP_1)[69] followed by the pattern V M // V M. The repetitive word-pair *ḫṭ* // *ḫṭ* of the first line is also found in 1.23:8-9.[70] Taken together, examples (11) and (12) comprise a cluster of four lines in IP.

(13) RIH 78/20:7-8

b mrmt b miyt. bẓlm. bqdš	In the high places, in the watered places, in darkness, in the sanctuary(?).

Again I follow Caquot, though de Moor has the same translation (with *b* understood as 'from' rather than as 'in').[71] It would seem that the author of this composition had a preference for lines with IP.

(14) *KTU* 1.133:18-19

babn. '{.}z. wrgbt. zbl	among the stones, the Strong One, among the clumps, the Prince

The description is of the god Mot rejoicing. I have followed Xella's reading and rendering here[72] but the text remains difficult. There are other examples which will be discussed below.

2.3. *Inner-Line Features of IP*

Under four headings (phonological aspects, structural aspects, semantic aspects and style) some of the inner-line features of lines with IP in Ugaritic will now be described,[73] with references to the examples already set out.

69. The chiasmus is recognized by Saracino, 'Appunti', p. 72.

70. Note the apostrophe here; for further examples, see my 'Apostrophe in the Aqhat Poem', *UF* 16 (1984), pp. 323-26. The second line may perhaps be compared with the expression 'helpless on your back' common to Isa. 14.12 and Gilg. XI 6, as shown by R.C. van Leeuwen, '*Ḥôlēš 'al gwym* and Gilgamesh XI.6', *JBL* 99 (1980), pp. 173-84.

71. J.C. de Moor 'An Incantation against Evil Spirits (Ras Ibn Hani 78/20)', *UF* 12 (1980), pp. 429-32, 429. Aartun ('Neue Beiträge', pp. 1-2) now suggests 'du sollst trinken vom geklärten (Wein) ohne Trockenheit d.h. vom süssen Liebesgetränk auf der "Erhebung" in der Natur'.

72. Xella, *Testi rituali*, p. 46.

73. For corresponding features in Hebrew verse, see my paper, cited in n. 56.

2.3.1. *Phonological Aspects*. In so far as it can be singled out, alliteration[74] is present in (1), (5), (6), (8), (14) and (15).[75] Quasi-acrostic elements (each half-line beginning with the same letter)[76] occur in (7), (8), (9), (10), (12), (13) and (16).[77] Internal end-rhyme, an established feature of IP in Hebrew,[78] seems to be present in (1b), (2a), (3), (4), (5), (10), (11b) and (16) (for example [6] *grnn ʿrm / šrn pdrm*[79]). Chiastic rhyme may be identifiable in (1a): *ʿdk ilm hn mtm ʿdk*, as *ilm–mtm*. Example (1) exhibits wordplay, perhaps, but *figura etymologica* or turn[80] is not used.

2.3.2. *Structural Aspects*. Chiastic parallelism is clear only in (12a)[81] (antithetic parallelism is discussed in the next paragraph). In general, IP comes in the first line of a couplet or longer strophic unit, but in (6), (7) and perhaps (10) it is present in the second line.[82] Gender-matched synonymous parallelism[83] occurs in (3).

74. See the comments by G. del Olmo Lete, 'David's Farewell Oracle (2 Samuel XXIII 1-7): A Literary Analysis', *VT* 34 (1984), pp. 414-87. Also, M. O'Connor, 'The Rhetoric of the Kilamuwa Inscription', *BASOR* 226 (1977), pp. 15-29, 16-17 and, at the theoretical level, M. Shapiro, *Asymmetry: An Inquiry into the Linguistic Structures of Poetry* (Amsterdam: North-Holland, 1976), pp. 135-203.

75. To complete the picture references to examples from my previous paper (n. 52 above) will be provided for each of the features listed. These examples, numbered *in italics* to differentiate them from those presented here, are as follows: (*1*) *KTU* 1.3 ii 39; (*2*) 1.3 iii 22-23; (*3*) 1.3 iv 33; (*4*) 1.3 iv 38; (*5*) 1.3 vi 7-9; (*6*) 1.4 i 25-26; (*7*) 1.4 iii 18-20; (*8*) 1.4 iv 4-5 = 1.19 ii 3-4; (*9*) and (*10*) 1.5 ii 2-6; (*11*) 1.6 vi 17 (etc.); (*12*) 1.6 vi 21-22; (*13*) 1.10 ii 29; (*14*) 1.16 i 12-13; (*15*) 1.18 i 24; (*16*) 1.19 i 44; (*17*) 1.19 iii 4-5 (etc.); (*18*) 1.19 iii 11 (etc.); (*19*) 1.19 iii 5 (etc.); (*20*) 1.23:7; (*21*) 1.23:32; (*22*) and (*23*) 1.23:61-63; (*24*) 1.24:20-21; (*25*) 1.24:38-39; (*26*) 1.161:21-22. Examples with alliteration: (*15*), (*25*) and (*26*).

76. For the phenomenon see Chapter 10, 'Anaphoric Alliteration in Ugaritic Verse'.

77. Also, (*3*), (*6*), (*13*), (*15*), (*19*), (*20*), (*21*), (*22*), (*25*).

78. See below, 'Classical Hebrew Verse', pp. 149-66.

79. Also (*5*) and (*7*).

80. For the terminology, cf. my *Classical Hebrew Poetry: A Guide to its Techniques* (Sheffield: JSOT Press, 1984), p. 239.

81. Cf. (8); also, (*25*) and (*26*).

82. Also (*1*), (*3*), (*11*), (*12*), (*13*), (*14*), (*15*), (*24*), (*25*). It occurs in the third line in (*4*) and (*17*).

83. See Chapter 4, 'Ugaritic Poetry'.

2.3.3. *Semantic Aspects*. Repetition, in effect a weak form of parallelism, is a common feature of lines in IP: (1a), (2a), (4), (7), (8), (10), (11), (12a) and (13).[84] More remarkable are two examples of antithetic parallelism since it is so rare in IP in Ugaritic.[85] They can be set out here.

(15) *KTU* 1.2 iv 32 (// 34)
ym. lmt. b'lm yml[k] Yam is truly dead! Baal shall be king!

Like its equivalent in line 34 (*ym. lmt*[. *b'lm. ymlk.*]—a refrain?) this line,[86] which opens a couplet, exhibits strong antithesis. The other example is

(16) *KTU* 1.4 vii 43
umlk. ubl. mlk (Will) either a king or a non-king.

Again there is antithesis in connection with kingship (possibly mere coincidence), this time in a nominal phrase.[87] As has been pointed out, the line corresponds to Phoenician *kl mmlkt wkl 'dm.*[88]

Not unexpectedly, word-pairs figure prominently in lines with IP; some of them can be listed here: *adn // b'l* (2c);[89] *hlk // ṣ(w)d* (9);[90] *ḥbr // d't(yd')* (1);[91] *ym // b'l* (15);[92] *ym // yrḫ* (8);[93] *yrḫ // šnt* (8); *'lm // drdr* (7);[94] *'r // pdr* (5);[95] *p // lšn* (10); *rbt // ṯrrt* (4);[96] *ṣr // ṣdyn* (3). Formulas or formulaic phrases do not occur.[97]

84. And (*5*), (*7*), (*9*), (*11*), (*12*), (*13*), (*16*), (*17*), (*18*), (*20*), (*21*), (*22*).

85. I.e. (15), (16).

86. Only (*3*) and (*21*).

87. See, too, *KTU* 1.2 iii 22; also, RS 16.353:20 (= *PRU* III 114; 20) 'If T. should say to the King of Ugarit *ma ul bēlni attami ma šarru šanu bēlni*, "You are not our ruler; another king is our ruler"', and Dan. 2.21.

88. Gibson, *Canaanite Myths*, p. 65 n. 14. The phrase occurs in *KAI* 7:4.6-7, 10-11 and *KAI* 10:11.

89. *RSP* I, p. 148; II, p. 36; cf. Avishur, *Word-Pairs*, pp. 222, 384 on *mlk // 'dn.*

90. See Avishur, *Word-Pairs*, p. 331.

91. Avishur, *Word-Pairs*, pp. 523-24, 538. Note, in addition, *ḥbrm // d'tm* RIH 78/20:9-10.

92. Cf. *KTU* 1.2 i 36-37 and iv 27.

93. Cf. *b. ym. ḫdṯ // b. yrḫ pgrm* in *KTU* 4.172 and 4.336:1-2.

94. Avishur, *Word-Pairs*, pp. 7-8, 18, 42, 301, 440, 551-54, 577.

95. As in *KTU* 1.4 vii 7-8, 9-10. Cf. Judg. 11.36.

96. G. del Olmo Lete, 'Algunos pares ugarítico-hebreos preteridos', *AuOr* 2 (1984), pp. 11-22, 20 cites Ps. 56.3, Jer. 13.9-10 and Lam. 1.1 as Hebrew equivalents of this pair.

97. Previously, (*4*) and (*8*).

2.3.4. *Style.* Figurative language is represented by the simile (11) and the use of imagery (10).[98] Personification as apostrophe (11)[99] and hyperbole, too (7)[100] can be registered.

2.4. *Clustering*

Unlike Hebrew and Akkadian verse,[101] clustering of lines with IP is not a common component of Ugaritic poetic texts. Clusters of two and four have been set out above (examples 1 and 11 + 12 respectively).[102] Accordingly it is difficult to determine whether or not clustering of lines with IP is present in

(17) *KTU* 1.6 ii 31-35[103]

bḥrb tbq'nn bḥ̱tr. tdrynn.	With a threshing sledge she split him; with a pitchfork she winnowed him.
bišt. tšrpnn brḥm. tṯḥnn. *bšd tdr'. nn.*	With fire she burnt him, with mill-stones she ground him; in the field she scattered him.

The arguments concerning the presence or otherwise of IP here can be listed. Arguments for:

1. the length of framing lines (*tiḫd b n ilm mt*; *širh ltikl 'ṣrm*) is similar;
2. the length of lines in the 'parallel' passages *KTU* 1.6 v 11-19 (*'lk b'lm pht qlt*, etc.) for seven or eight lines;[104]
3. the presence of such features as the quasi-acrostic (every half-line has the sequence *b- t-*) and end-rhyme (*-nn*) throughout.

98. Also (*9*) and (*10*); (*22*) and (*23*) (hyperbolic imagery).

99. Personification: (2).

100. Example (*7*) and those in n. 98.

101. See my comments in the papers cited, nn. 52 and 56. Also, the table provided in the next section.

102. Also (*18*) + (*19*).

103. I follow J.F. Healey, 'Burning the Corn: New Light on the Killing of Mōtu', *Or* 52 (1983), pp. 248-51, incorporating some of the suggestions he relegated to footnotes in my translation.

104. *bḥ̱tr.* / *'lk. pht. bq'.* may have to be supplied in lines 13-14; see del Olmo Lete, *Mitos y leyendas*, p. 231 for details. Note, too, *Ugaritica* V, text 162 (= RS 25.460) lines 34'-37' (pp. 268 and 269).

Arguments against:

1. such clustering is rare in Ugaritic;
2. the resultant lines seem to be very long, in spite of arguments 1 and 2 under 'arguments for';
3. the third and final line would be extremely long (although lines of '$1\frac{1}{2}$' units are attested in other verse traditions).[105]

In sum, there seem to be strong pointers towards the presence of IP here, but the question remains open.

2.5. *IP in other Verse Traditions*

Elsewhere I have presented the data for IP in classical Hebrew.[106] Here I will list texts in Aramaic and Akkadian which feature lines with IP. Since the main thrust of this paper concerns Ugaritic, however, discussion will be brief.

Aramaic Texts

KAI 215.11	
bḥkmth. wbṣdqh	because of his wisdom and because of his uprightness[107]
KAI 216.10-11	
b'ly. ksp. wb'ly. zhb.	owners of silver and owners of gold.
Proverbs of Aḥiqar	Sayings 5, 9, 29, 30, 49, 68, 106, 107, 110[108]
Aramaic Incantation Bowls[109]	
14.5-6	
l' ḥbr' bymm' wl' ṣwt' blylh	no company by day and no society by night

105. Note the prose introduction in *KTU* 5.9:2-6 *ilm tǵrk. tšlmk t'zzk. alp ymm wrbt. šnt b'd 'lm*, 'May the gods guard you, keep you safe (and) strengthen you for a thousand days, ten thousand years, through eternity' which seems to comprise two lines each '$1\frac{1}{2}$' units in length.

106. See n. 54. For Sumerian, cf. A. Berlin, 'Shared Rhetorical Features in Biblical and Sumerian Literature', *JANESCU* 10 (1978), pp. 35-42, 39.

107. Gibson, *Textbook*, II, p. 61 dates Panammu to 780–743 BC. Both *KAI* 215 and 216 are by this king.

108. For details, see Chapter 2, 'The Aḥiqar Sayings: Some Marginal Comments'.

109. Conveniently collected in C. Isbell, *Corpus of the Aramaic Incantation Bowls* (SBLDS, 17; Missoula, MT: Scholars Press, 1975); I have used his text numbering. J. Naveh and S. Shaked, *Amulets and Magic Bowls: Aramaic Incantations of Late Antiquity* (Jerusalem: Magnes Press; Leiden: Brill, 1985) is now available.

Aramaic Texts (continued)

21.15	
b'ysryn b'r'h wḥytmyn bsmy'	by bonds on earth and by seals in heaven
60.4	
hpyk' 'r'h hpyk' šmy'	Overturned is the earth, overturned is heaven
70.6	
bḥrb kpyph bql' psyṭh	with a sword is she conquered, with a rope is she flayed;
bql' psyṭh bḥrb kpyph	with a rope is she flayed, with a sword is she conquered
35.5	
l' bymh wl' blylh	either during the day or during the night
A Tale of Two Brothers[110]	
col. XVII 4-5	
bṣn bnn'wh ṭyn-hw	Nineveh is a swamp, mud is she!
col. XVII 9-10[111]	
ywmn dlhww šnn dl' pḳ/kw	(Then came) days which had not been, years which had not been spent/turned
col. XIX 14	
ky-šm' lmly wttb l'mrn	Do listen to my words and pay attention to my speech[112]
col. XX 16-17	
lṭpsr dlḥm wmlk qrb dṭ'nykn wḥnkyk	war-scribe and battle adviser for your swordsmen and for your soldiers

Dan. 2.21; 4.16; 5.10; 6.19-28[113]

In these passages, alliteration (especially in the form of the quasi-acrostic), end-rhyme, repetition and word-pairs feature prominently. As in Ugaritic, though, there is no clustering beyond sets of two. Next, passages in Akkadian (Assyro-Babylonian) texts where IP is

110. R.C. Steiner and C.F. Nims, 'Ashurbanipal and Shamash-Shum-Ukin: A Tale of two Brothers from the Aramaic Text in Demotic Script. Part I', *RB* 92 (1985), pp. 60-81.

111. Used as an (opening) refrain here and in col. XVII 13-14; XVIII 1.

112. Also a refrain, with variations, in col. XIX 7-8; XX 6-7 and XXI 6.

113. Recognized by J.C. Greenfield, 'Early Aramaic Poetry', *JANESCU* 11 (1979), pp. 45-51, on p. 47.

used are listed, in alphabetic sequence for convenience. This complements and extends my earlier list[114] and uses more or less standard abbreviations.

Akkadian Texts

AnOr 12 (1959), pp. 282-301	lines 23, 24, 25, 29, 32, 33, 43, 51, 55[115]
Anzû(SB)	I iii 8, 16, 25, 37, 50, 71, 79, 92[116]
Atr.	I i 2, 4; iii 150; iv 24, 171; v 243; vi 289; III i 22-24; 35; iv 24; S iii 9b-10; iv 59
BWL	86.274; 102.61; 104.127-28, 131; 128.50; 148.78
Descent of Ištar *(Nin)*	17-18, 31, 33, 77, 87, 96, 101, 128-29[117]
Ee	I 6, 13, 38, 50, 95; III 9, 134; IV 9, 91, 102, 106; VI 106, 122, 131; VII 83, 151
Erra	I 33bc, 106, 144; IIb 20; IIc 13, 17; IV 32, 93, 123; V 5, 14, 17, 57b, 58
Gilg	I i 5; vi 1, vi 2, 22; X iii 44; XI 21-22, 180
Gilg. Meissner fragment	iii 11
Gilg. (Nin)	VI 9[118]
Great Prayer to Ištar	lines 21 and 1, 6, 12, 29, 39, 40[119]
Great Šamaš Hymn	lines 33, 39, 145, 151, 176-77, 180[120]
Hymn to Gula[121]	lines 2, 11, (13), 31, 32, 35, 47, 48, 54, 62, 63, 65, 74, 75, 103, 106, 154, (177), 190-91, 193-94

114. See nn. 1, 23 and 38-44.

115. A.L. Oppenheim, 'A New Prayer to the "Gods of Night"', *AnOr* 12 (1959), pp. 282-301; also M.-J. Seux, *Hymnes et Prières aux dieux de Babylonie et d'Assyrie* (Paris: Cerf, 1976), pp. 246-48.

116. Following W.W. Hallo and W.L. Moran, 'The First Tablet of the SB Recension of the Anzû Myth', *JCS* 31 (1979), pp. 65-115.

117. Occasionally, one line in the Nineveh (*Nin.*) recension corresponds to two in the Assyrian recension.

118. For text and translation, see, conveniently, J.H. Tigay, *The Evolution of the Gilgamesh Epic* (Philadelphia: University of Pennsylvania Press, 1982), at the appropriate passages.

119. Text and translation: E. Reiner and H.G. Güterbock, 'The Great Prayer to Ishtar and its Two Versions from Boğazköy', *JCS* 21 (1967), pp. 255-66.

120. Edition in Lambert, *Babylonian Wisdom Literature*, pp. 121-38, 318-23; cf. Seux, *Hymnes*, pp. 51-66.

121. Text and translation: W.G. Lambert, 'The Gula Hymn of Bulluṭsa-rabi', *Or* 36 (1967), pp. 105-32, pls. VIII-XXIII; cf. M.L. Barré, 'Bulluṭsa-rabi's Hymn to Gula and Hosea 6:1-2', *Or* 50 (1981), pp. 241-45.

Akkadian Texts (continued)

Hymn to the Queen of Nippur[122]	II 14, 17-18; III 38, 53; IV 23, (28), 31, (33), 35, 36 = 38
Ludlul	I 105; II 13, 16, 24, 60, 86-87, 101, 111[123] 114; III 12; IV(?) 94
Maqlû	I 12, 14, 31, 34, 50, 61, 63-64, 116; II 100-101, 132, 203-204; IV 140; VII 31; VIII 57
šu.íl.lá to *Ištar*[124]	lines 1, 9, 16, 17, rev. 20, 21, 22, 23[125]

The commonest components in these examples are alliteration (quasi-acrostic), end-rhyme (and end-assonance), chiasmus particularly, repetition and use of word-pairs. Antithetic parallelism is quite rare. The most noticeable feature, though, is clustering of lines with IP in sets of three and more, as the table shows (with examples provided):

sets of 3	*AGH* 14.3-5[126]
	BWL 58.37-39 (*Ludlul* IV[?])
	Great Prayer to Ištar 15-17
sets of 3	Hymn to Gula 150-52
	Maqlû I 97-99
	V 166-68
	TCS 2 no. 14.1-3[127]
sets of 4	*AnOr* 12, 283.35-38
	Maqlû II 93-96

122. Text and translation: W.G. Lambert, 'The Hymn to the Queen of Nippur', in G. van Driel, T.J.H. Krispijn, M. Stol and K.R. Veenhof (eds.), *Zikir šumim* (Leiden: Brill, 1982), pp. 173-218.

123. Text and translation: D. Wiseman, 'A New Text of the Babylonian Poem of the Righteous Sufferer', *AnSt* 30 (1977), pp. 101-107, 106.

124. S.D. Sperling, 'A šu-íl-lá to Ištar (Ebeling, Handerhebung 60)', *WO* 12 (1981), pp. 8-20 refers to the internal parallelism of line 21 (p. 18) but fails to distinguish between synonymous parallelism within a line and across two lines (p. 20).

125. Other texts include VAT 17107 rev. 12 and 18 (edited by W.G. Lambert, 'Divine Love Lyrics from the Reign of Abi-ešuḫ', *MIO* 12 (1966–67), pp. 41-56, 54, 56; EA 169:7-10l Sargon Legend 2 (cf. 6), 14 (cf. 24).

126. Cited (in translation) in Lambert, *Babylonian Wisdom Literature*, p. 19. *AGH* = E. Ebeling, *Die akkadische Gebetsserie 'Handerhebung'* (Berlin: de Gruyter, 1953).

127. R.D. Biggs, ŠÀ.ZI.GA *Ancient Mesopotamian Potency Incantations* (TCS, 2; Locust Valley, NY: Augustin, 1967), pp. 32-33; he cites the parallel in Atr. II i 14-17; see W.G. Lambert and A.R. Millard, *Atra-ḫasīs: The Babylonian Legend of the Flood* (Oxford: Clarendon Press, 1969), p. 156, *Atr.* 156.

sets of 5	*Erra* I 109-13
	IV 131-35
	BWL, pp. 178-79
	lines 27-31
sets of 6	*Gilg.* V iv 15-20
sets of 7	*Maqlû* II 38-49
sets of 14	*Erra* IId 4-12a

2.6. *Discussion*

In the previous section I discussed the problems of caesura, the verse-line, metre[128] and the half-colon or half-line in connection with IP in Ugaritic.[129] Here I will confine myself to remarks on the half-line, as illustrated by the new material studied in the last few pages. The line with IP emerges as a unit which tends to have independent existence, comprising two halves (two half-lines) in the form of a miniature couplet. If we compare

KTU 1.4 i 25-26
yṣq. ksp. yšlḥ. ḫrṣ He smelted silver; he cast gold.[130]

with

KTU 1.4 vii 38-39
ib. hd(!). lm. tḫš Foes of Haddu, why are you scared?
lm. tḫš. nṯq. dmrn Why are you scared of D.'s weapon?[131]

it is immediately apparent that the phrase *lm tḫš* (a) is used twice in succession[132] and (b) corresponds metrically (prosodically) to *ib hd(!)* and to *nṯq dmrn*. In other words, half-lines correspond to half-lines, whether in parallelism or not. Turning to a much-debated example from Old Babylonian (*Atr.* III i 22-24) we find the same equivalence.

128. See pp. 104-16. On metre (or its lack) in Ugaritic, see Z. Zevit, 'Nondistinctive Stress, Syllabic Constraints and *Wortmetrik* in Ugaritic Poetry', *UF* 15 (1983), pp. 291-98.

129. See pp. 104-16.

130. Cited as example (6) p. 106, above.

131. For the textual problems here, cf. del Olmo Lete, *Mitos y leyendas*, p. 209.

132. What I have termed the 'terrace pattern', following Austerlitz; cf. my *Classical Hebrew Poetry*, pp. 208-13. S. Segert, 'Parallelism in Ugaritic Poetry', *JAOS* 103 (1983), p. 303 prefers 'chain', but makes no reference either to me or to Austerlitz.

(a) *ub/pud/t būta*	(b) *bini eleppa*	
	(c) *mak(k)zūra s/ṣ/zerma*	(d) *napišta bulliṭ*
Flee (your) house;	build a boat;	
	a ship design;	save life![133]

Half-line (b) (if Hoffner is correct) is parallel to half-line (c) even though they belong to different lines. In any case, the couplet clearly comprises four half-lines. We can widen the discussion slightly to include Ugaritic couplets of the abc // b'c' type.[134] For example,

KTU 1.14 iii 7-9 // iv 51-52.v 1-2[135]

s't bšdm ḥṭbt	Swept[136] from the fields will be the (wood) collectors,
wbgrnt ḥpšt	and from the threshing floors, the (straw) gatherers;
s't bnpk šibt	Swept from the spring will be the water-drawers,
wbmqr mmlat	and from the well the (pitcher) fillers.

Here, two sets of lines with inner parallelism (*bšdm ḥṭbt // bgrnt hpšt* and *bnpk šibt // b mqr mmlat*) have each been prefaced by *s't*. Instead of abc // b'c', the pattern is better represented by x(ab // a'b'), with augmentation rather than ellipsis. This passage and the formulaic phrase *udm rbt wudm ṯrrt* which is preceded in turn by *al tṣr*, *ymǵy* and *wtmǵy* (example 4 above) point to the use of lines with IP as longer equivalents of formulaic word-pairs. Another, new, example is

(18) *KTU* 1.100:63-64

tk aršḫ. rbt waršḫ. ṯrrt.	towards *greater A. and Lesser U.*

133. Following H.A. Hoffner, Jr, 'Enki's Command to Atrahasis', in B.L. Eichler (ed.), *Kramer Anniversary Volume: Cuneiform Studies in Honor of Samuel Noah Kramer* (AOAT, 25; Kevelaer: Butzon & Bercker: Neukirchen–Vluyn: Neukirchener Verlag, 1976), pp. 241-45.

134. See my discussion in *Classical Hebrew Poetry*, pp. 174-77; add *KTU* 1.16 vi 17-18 // 20-21 and 30-31 // 43-44. Also 1.14 ii 48-50 // iv 27-28; RIH 78/20:9-10.

135. See del Olmo Lete, *Mitos y leyendas*, p. 295 for details.

136. This is the generally accepted rendering, following J.C. Greenfield, 'Some Glosses on the Keret Epic', *EI* 9 (1969), pp. 60-65, 63. Also possible as cognates to Ug. *s't* might be Akk. *se'û*, 'to oppress' (*AHw*, p. 1038b, where Syr. *s'ā*, 'to attack' and Ethiop. *š'j*, 'to winnow' are cited) and, less plausibly, Akk. *sâ'u*(*sā'?*), 'to cry out in pain' (*AHw*, p. 1033b).

where *tk* is followed by a standard expansion of *rbt // ṯrrt* (cf. *udm rbt wudm ṯrrt*).[137] If not an abc // b'c' couplet, then it is a line with IP to which a preposition has been tacked on.

2.7. *Occurrence*

Before setting out the table of occurrence some additional but dubious examples need to be set out for the sake of completeness.

(19) *KTU* 1.2 i 23-24 // 25 // 27-28 // 29[138]
lẓr brkthm wlkḥṯ zblhm on top of their knees and on their princely seats

(20) *KTU* 1.3 i 12
bk rb ʻẓm. ri a large beaker, looking enormous

These two examples illustrate two common failings of other possible texts: either the resulting line seems too long (as in example 19) or the parallelism is too loose (example 20). To these categories respectively belong *KTU* 1.100:65-67 (*ʻrʻrm ynʻrnh ssnm ysynh / ʻdtm yʻdynh ybltm yblnh*); 1.108:6-7 (*bʻlt. mlk. bʻlt. drkt*); 1.108:22-23 (*bḏmrh. bl*[*anh*]. *bḥtkh. bnmrth.*) and 1.2 i 13 (// 19) (*tbʻ. ǵlm*[*m. al. ṯṯb*]).

The table previously given for occurrences of IP in Ugaritic verse[139] must now be extended to include the new examples discussed above.

IP in Ugaritic Texts

Baal Cycle	22
Krt Text	4
Aqhat	9
Šḥr-w-Šlm	8
Others	7
RIH 78/20	5

As noted in my previous paper, some examples recur in different compositions and some are repeated in the same text. The Baal Cycle (*KTU* 1.1-6, etc.) is remarkable in providing the highest number of

137. See J.C. Greenfield, 'The Epithets *rbt // ṯrrt* in the Krt Epic', in E.W. Conrad and E.G. Newing (eds.), *Perspectives on Language and Text: Essays and Poems in Honor of Francis I. Andersen's Sixtieth Birthday* (Winona Lake: Eisenbrauns, 1987), pp. 35-37.

138. Note the change of pronominal suffix (*-km* for *-hm*) and the lengthened second preposition (*ln*) in the parallel passages.

139. See n. 52.

examples, though the Ras Ibn Hani incantation and *Šḥr-w-Šlm* (*KTU* 1.23) show high density since they are both very short compositions.

A number of topics remain to be examined and they can be listed here as requiring future study. One is the different sequences of strophic patterns used in Ugaritic (couplets, tricola and so on) which also incorporate one or more lines with IP. Another topic is the possibility that the tricolon or three-line strophe[140] developed from three sets of half-line units ($1\frac{1}{2}$-unit lines). Lastly, there are the extremes of two or three non-parallel lines forming couplets and tricola with 'structural' or 'synthetic' parallelism on the one hand and the $1\frac{1}{2}$-unit lines already mentioned on the other, which involve the very nature of parallelism itself and comprise a topic involving the forms discussed in the present paper.[141]

3. *Ugaritic Once More*[142]

3.1. *Preliminary Remarks*

After writing two articles on internal (or half-line) parallelism in Ugaritic verse,[143] I was surprised to be able to pick out several more

140. I retain 'strophe' (and 'strophic') in spite of S. Segert, review of Watson, *Classical Hebrew Poetry*, *CBQ* 46 (1984), pp. 336-38, who comments, 'This term has to be respectfully and firmly rejected as both Greek and modern uses of the term "strophe" point to a unit combining lower units commonly called "verse"'.

141. Examples of IP in *Etana*, now conveniently available as J.V. Kinnier Wilson, *The Legend of Etana: A New Edition* (Warminster: Aris & Phillips, 1985), include OV I/C 5.9 = 11(.42), 44; MAV I/A 12; I/C 3(?), 6(?); LV II 5, 50, 64-65 (.74), 76, 90, 134 (140, 142-43, 147-48); IV/B 10, 11. For the term *ṣullupu*, 'in Halbzeilen eingeteilt' (which may or may not be relevant), cf. H. Hunger, *Babylonische und assyrische Kolophone* (AOAT, 2; Kevelaer: Butzon & Bercker; Neukirchen–Vluyn: Neukirchener Verlag, 1968), pp. 6 n. 1, 7, 53 (= Nr 136:2) and 172-73 (index). For unrecognized examples of IP in Egyptian, see I. Shirun, 'Parallelismus membrorum und Vers', in J. Assmann, E. Feucht, R. Grieshammer (eds.), *Fragen an die altägyptische Literatur: Studien zum Gedenken an E. Otto* (Wiesbaden: Otto Harrassowitz, 1977), pp. 463-92. Additional note: In a letter, A. Berlin drew my attention to her book *Enmerkar and Ensuḫkešdanna: A Sumerian Narrative Poem* (Occasional Publications of the Babylonian Fund, 2; Philadelphia: University of Pennsylvania, University Museum, 1979). I have now been able to consult this work, and in ch. 2 ('Poetic Structure and Technique') p. 20 (and p. 22) she refers to IP (also p. 72 on line 77).

142. First published in *UF* 20 (1988), pp. 365-74.

examples; they will be presented here. Perhaps it was not too much of a surprise since, after completing what I had thought to be a full study of the same type of parallelism in classical Hebrew[144] even more examples came to light. These are published elsewhere.[145] The fact of the matter is that internal or half-line parallelism has gone virtually unnoticed. The result is that it tends to be disregarded or obscured in the presentation of texts with or without accompanying translation. What at first sight seemed to be an isolated phenomenon now appears to be a well-used pattern in some traditions of ancient Near Eastern poetry and it merits extensive analysis. Some of the preliminary findings are provided here.

Once the new examples have been set out in full it will be easier to discuss their features and matters of theory. Unfortunately, some of the texts involved are very difficult and this in turn means that not all the examples can be considered as certain.

3.2. *Passages with IP*

With these provisos, then, the following passages can be added to those previously listed and discussed. The examples are numbered for easy reference.

(1) *KTU* 1.3 iii 46-47

imtḫṣ ksp itrṯ. ḫrṣ	I have smitten for silver, I have (re-)possessed the gold.

143. See above, 'Ugaritic Verse' and 'Ugaritic Verse: Further Examples'. For a different view on the length of a colon in Ugaritic, cf. M.C.A. Korpel and J.C. de Moor, 'Fundamentals of Ugaritic and Hebrew Poetry', *UF* 18 (1986), pp. 173-212, esp. 175 n. 8. On the term 'colon', see O. Loretz and I. Kottsieper, *Colometry in Ugaritic and Biblical Poetry: Introduction, Illustrations and Topical Bibliography* (UBL, 5; Altenberge: CIS-Verlag, 1987), p. 24, and H. van Grol, *De veersbouw in het klassieke Hebreeuws*. I. *Metriek* (Amsterdam: Katholieke Theologische Hogeschool, 1986), pp. 17-18.

144. See below, 'Classical Hebrew Verse'.

145. See below, 'Classical Hebrew Again'. Add Gen. 7.23; 16.7; 26.5; Deut. 1.33 (combined with the AXB pattern, on which cf. D. Tsumura, 'Literary Insertion (AXB Pattern) in Biblical Hebrew', *VT* 33 [1983], p. 479); 25.1 (cf. Prov. 17.15); 28.65; 1 Sam. 4.20; 2 Sam. 2.7; Isa. 66.6; Jer. 32.19; 50.41; Ezek. 8.2; 11.3; 13.15; 16.36; Job 28.27; Qoh. 12.13 and Sir. 4.1.

Although it would appear that the sentence begun in this line continues in the next,[146] this example has been included because of the clear VO // VO structure.

(2) *KTU* 1.12 ii 52-53

bskn. sknm. b'dn 'dnm	In front of the highest rank, in front of the crack troops.

As elsewhere the pattern is clear even though the translation is disputed.[147] Commonly, this line is considered as referring to time (as do lines 44b-45), for example, 'In his utmost jeopardy, in his most critical hour'.[148] Alternatively, the line describes the persons of rank before whom Baal fell (similarly, lines 50-51), the interpretation adopted here.[149]

(3) *KTU* 1.12 ii 56-57

ittk. lawl išttk. lm. ttkn	be induced to poor out, so that there will be stability.[150]

Once again a very difficult line. If del Olmo Lete's rendering is correct, 'He ceded supremacy to him. He gave up being established to him',[151] then half-line parallelism is present.

(4) *KTU* 1.16 i 25-26

wy'ny krt ṯ'	And Kirta the Magnificent(?) replied
bn.	'My son,

146. Following J.C. de Moor, *An Anthology of Religious Texts from Ugarit* (Nisaba, 16; Leiden: Brill, 1987), p. 12 ('I shall battle for the silver, (and) gain possession of the gold'), though for him these are two lines. Contrast D. Pardee, 'Will the Dragon Never be Muzzled?', *UF* 16 (1984), pp. 251-55, esp. 252 and 253. He comments, 'The quantitative analysis certainly favours taking *'imtḫṣ ksp 'itrṯ ḫrṣ* as a line-segment, rather than as an independent bicolon (*sic*). If I link it with the following lines, rather than with the preceding ones, it is because I agree with Dietrich and Loretz that these words appear to introduce the following statements'. In Hebrew, too, IP can open a sentence continued in the next line, as in Ps. 20.8.

147. E.g. *KTU* 1.6 vi 48-50; 1.93.2-3.

148. J. Gray, 'Ba'al's Atonement', *UF* 3 (1971), p. 66. Similarly, de Moor, *Anthology*, p. 134.

149. Del Olmo Lete, *Mitos y leyendas*, p. 485; see there for other possible renderings. On *skn*, cf. H.M. Kümmel, 'Ugaritica-Hethitica', *UF* 1 (1969), p. 160 and *CAD*, S, p. 76 (under *sākinu*).

150. So de Moor, *Anthology*, p. 134.

151. Del Olmo Lete, *Mitos y leyendas*, p. 485.

al. tbkn. al tdm. ly.	do not weep for me. Do not wail for me.
al tkl. bn qr. ʿnk.	Do not use up your eye's water source,
mḫ. rišk udmʿt	your brain marrow (with) tears'.[152]

The line with inner parallelism is *al tbkn // al tdm ly*; the extrametrical character of *bn* was almost recognized by Parker who brackets it off as having no parallel word in the line.[153] It is, in fact, a clear case of anacrusis (see below).

(5) *KTU* 1.19 ii 43-44 (and par.)

[šṣat] btlt. ʿnt.	Drive out did Virgin Anath
kr[ḥ. npšh] kiṯl. brlth	like wind his breath, like spitttle his inwards(?).

The line *krḥ npšh kiṯl brlth* is formulaic, and reappears, slightly expanded, in 1.18 iv 24-26 // 36-37.

(6) *KTU* 1.20 i 6-7

[iln]ym. tlḥm [wrp]ʿum. tštyn	May the gods eat. May the rpum drink.[154]

(7) *KTU* 1.20 ii 2-4

[mrkbt] asr sswm tṣmd	They tied up [the chariots], harnessed the horses,
dg[lm. tšu]	[raised] the ban[ners[.
	They mounted their chariots,
	ca[me to their city].[155]

152. Beside the standard translations, cf. M.I. Gruber, *Aspects of Nonverbal Communication in the Ancient Near East* (Studia Pohl, 12/1; Rome: Biblical Institute Press, 1980), pp. 394-95, with parallels; J. van der Westhuizen, 'A Proposed Possible Solution to *KTU* 1.14 ii 7 Based on Babylonian and Biblical Evidence', *UF* 17 (1985), pp. 357-70, 366 and in particular, P. Xella, 'Eblaita *mu-ḫu* SAG ed ugaritico *mḫ riš*', *SEL* 1 (1984), pp. 27-33, who has shown that the correction to *my* is unnecessary.

153. S.B. Parker, 'Parallelism and Prosody in Ugaritic Narrative Verse', *UF* 6 (1974), pp. 283-94. Another possible example may be *KTU* 1.17 vi 30-31a.

154. Following K. Spronk, *Beatific Afterlife in Ancient Israel and in the Ancient Near East* (AOAT, 219; Kevelaer: Butzon & Bercker; Neukirchen–Vluyn: Neukirchener Verlag, 1986), p. 164; contrast del Olmo Lete, *Mitos y leyendas*, p. 417. I translate *ilnm* 'gods' rather than 'ghosts' (so Spronk) in view of Phoen. *alonim*—see G. del Olmo Lete, 'Fenicio y Ugarítico: correlación lingüística', *AuOr* 4 (1986), p. 41.

155. Again following Spronk, *Afterlife*, p. 165; for different restorations, cf. del Olmo Lete, *Mitos y leyendas*, p. 418. The term *ʿr* (last word of example) is more

(8)	*KTU* 1.22 i 8-9	
	ṯm. ṯmq. rpu. b‘l.	There rose up Baal Rapiu,
	mhr b‘l wmhr. ‘nt	the warriors of Baal and the warriors of Anat.[156]

The nominal phrase with half-line parallelism, *mhr b‘l wmhr ‘nt*, recurs in *KTU* 1.22 ii 7-8.[157]

(9)	*KTU* 1.100:1	
	um pḥl pḥlt	The stallion's mother, Mare
	bt. ‘n. bt. abn	daughter of spring, daughter of stone,
	bt šmm wthm	daughter of sky and deep.[158]

Here, it is the second line which has half-line parallelism.

An additional example may be 1.16 ii 26-36; however the tablet is damaged here.

(10)	*KTU* 1.16 ii 26-36		
	a	*tṣr. q[l. rm]*	She shrieked with a loud voice,
	b	*tṣr. trm. tnq[th]*	she shrieked, she raised her cry.
		—three couplets—	—three couplets—
	i	*t[bk/ṣr q]l trm*	She wept/shrieked, she raised her voice,
	j	*tṣr trm tnqt*	she shrieked, she raised her cry,
	k	*tbky. wtšnn[.]*	she wept and ground her teeth,
	l	*ttn gh. bky*	she let out her voice in weeping.

likely to mean 'city' (so del Olmo Lete) than 'stallion' (Spronk). The similarity to Jer. 46.3ff., which also uses half-lines, is striking.

156. So Spronk, *Afterlife*, p. 171 who follows de Moor (references Spronk, *Afterlife*, p. 171 n. 5). In view of the expansion to *ṯm yṯmqn mhr b‘l / rpu b‘l wmhr ‘nt* in *KTU* 1.22 ii 6-8, *ṯmq* must be a verb (so de Moor) whatever its meaning, not a noun. On the *mhrm*, cf. J.-L. Cunchillos, 'Le dieu Mut. guerrier de El', *Syria* 62 (1985), pp. 205-18; also J. Zorn, 'LU.*pa-ma-ḫa-a* in EA 162:74 and the Role of the *mhr* in Egypt and Ugarit', *JNES* 50 (1991), pp. 129-38

157. Note, in addition, *w.l.tikl wltš*[*t*], 'and it/she did not eat and did not drink', *KTU* 1.88:3.

158. On this text, see most recently M. Dietrich and O. Loretz, 'Die akkadische Tierbezeichnungen *immeru*, *puḫadu* and *puḫalu* im Ugaritischen und Hebräischen', *UF* 17 (1985), pp. 99-103, and F. Renfroe, 'Arabic Evidence for Ugaritic *pḥl* "Stallion"', *UF* 17 (1985), pp. 410-11. Other examples may be *ḥrn ḥbrm. wġlm. d‘tm* (RIH 78/20:9-10), on which cf. M. Dijkstra, 'Once Again: The Closing Lines of the Ba‘al Cycle (*KTU* 1.6. VI. 42ff.)', *UF* 17 (1985), pp. 147-52, 150, and *b‘l ṣdq skn. bt mlk. tġr mlk. bny* (*KTU* 7.63:4-7). See also *yḥ. wlymt KTU* 6.30 (cited by Xella, *Testi rituali*, in his dedication).

I have accepted, in part, the translations and restorations of de Moor and Spronk but propose slightly different stichometry in i.[159] IP is present in lines b, i, j and k—with half-line parallelism clearest in k.

3.3. *Inner-Line Features*

As in my second article[160] some of the salient features of these examples will be set out under appropriate headings.

3.3.1. *Phonology*. Alliteration in the form of the 'quasi-acrostic' is used in examples (1), (2), (3) and (4). End-rhyme is apparent in (1) and (9). With vocalization, these examples most probably read as follows:

(1) *'imtaḫiṣ kaspa 'itariṯ ḫarūṣa*[161]

(9) *bittu 'êni bittu abni*
bittu šamêma watihāmi[162]

Assonance occurs in (1) and perhaps (2).

3.3.2. *Structure*. The only examples to occur in the second line of a strophe are (8) and (9).

3.3.3. *Semantics*. Repetition is used in (2) [*skn, 'dn*], (3) [*l*] and (8) [*mhr*]. Anaphoric repetition is noticeable in (6) [*k-*] and (8) [*mhr*] but more noteworthy is the pattern

A - - - - A - - - - -
A - - - - - - - - - - - -

in both (4) and (9):

(4) *al tbkn al tdm ly*
al tkl bn qr 'nk (etc.)

159. J.C. de Moor and K. Spronk, 'Problematical Passages in the Legend of Kirtu (I)', *UF* 14 (1982), pp. 153-71. Note that lines i to l are an expansion of the first two lines, a and b, and together with them form an inclusio.

160. See above, 'Ugaritic Verse: Further Examples'.

161. Following D. Pardee, 'Will the Dragon Never be Muzzled?', *UF* 16 (1984), pp. 251-55.

162. So D. Pardee, 'A Philological and Prosodic Analysis of the Ugaritic Serpent Incantation *UT* 607', *JANESCU* 10 (1978), pp. 73-108, p. 74.

(9) *bt ʿn bt abn*
bt šmm wthm

This pattern, common enough in Hebrew and Akkadian[163] is found only twice elsewhere in Ugaritic (*KTU* 1.3 vi 7-9; 1.4 iii 8-10).[164] See below for repetition in (11) [*šlm*].

The following word-pairs can be listed: *asr // ṣmd* (6); *ilnym // rpum* (6); *bky // dm* (4); *bʿl // ʿnt* (8); *ksp // ḫrṣ* (1); *lḥm // šty* (6); *npš // brlt* (5); *ʿly // atw* (7); *skn // ʿdn* (2); *ʿn // abn* (9); *rḥ // iṯl* (5); *rkb(mrkbt) // ssw* (7) and // *ʿr* (7).

Formulas or set phrases are *krḥ npšh kiṯl brlth* (etc.) (5) and *mhr bʿl mhr ʿnt* in (7) and its parallel.

3.3.4. *Rhetorical functions*. Lines with IP are often used to open a segment of verse: (1), (2), (4) and (9). For a closing passage see example (11) below.

3.3.5. *Other features*. Enjambment is discernible in (1) and (5),[165] anacrusis in (4) [*bn*]. (2), (5), (8) and (9) are nominal phrases. Examples (3), (4) and (6) each comprise two short sentences.[166]

163. See below, 'Classical Hebrew Verse', §4.3.

164. Possibly, too, in 1.4 vi 33-34.

165. According to W. von Soden, 'Untersuchungen zur babylonischen Metrik. Teil I', *ZA* 71 (1982), pp. 161-204, 177, enjambment does not occur in classical Babylonian poetry. He also states that, with a few isolated exceptions, it is absent from Ugaritic and Hebrew verse (p. 177 n. 18). However, several examples of enjambment have been identified in Ugaritic. They include *KTU* 1.3 i 10-15 and iii 46-49 (Pardee, 'Will the Dragon?', p. 255); 1.16 i 44-45 (de Moor and Spronk, 'Legend of Kirtu', p. 184: 'The bicolon furnishes us with an exceptionally clear example of enjambment in Ugaritic poetry') and 1.14 vi 36-37 (etc.), 1.19 i 38-40; iv 58-59; 1.23.62-63 (all cited by Segert, 'Parallelism', pp. 300-301. Also, 1.6 i 56-57 (Watson, *Classical Hebrew Poetry*, p. 335). See, in general, Watson, *Classical Hebrew Poetry*, pp. 332-36, with bibliography; also S.A. Geller, *Parallelism in Early Hebrew Poetry* (HSM, 20; Missoula, MT: Scholars Press, 1979), pp. 6 and 379. For Akkadian, cf. L. Cagni, *Epopea di Erra* (Rome: Istituto di Studi del Vicino Oriente dell'Università, 1969), p. 143 (citing *Erra* I 13-14, 41-44, 55-56, 79-80, etc.) and C. Walker, 'The Myth of Girra and Elamatum', *AnSt* 33 (1983), pp. 145-52, 147 (on the Myth of Girra and Elamatum, lines 36-38).

166. Contrast S. Segert, *A Basic Grammar of the Ugaritic Language with Selected Texts and Glossary* (Berkeley: University of California Press, 1984), p. 109: 'Two short sentences within one colon are rare' (he cites *KTU* 1.6 vi 17, 18-19).

3.4. *Clustering*

As has already been noted[167] the use of lines with internal (half-line) parallelism in sets is rare in Ugaritic. The only passage of those set out here where there is a cluster is example (6) and even there both restoration and stichometry are a matter for dispute. An additional example, already referred to previously but not set out or discussed[168] is:

(10) *KTU* 1.161:31-34

šlm.		Hail!
šlm. ʿmr[pi]	*w.šlm. bt(!)h.*	Hail, Ammurapi! And hail to his household!
šlm. [ṯ]ryl	*šlm. bth.*	Hail, Tharyelli! Hail to her household!
šlm. ugrt	*šlm. ṯǵrh*	Hail, Ugarit! Hail to her gates![169]

Evidently this is not high quality poetry; it is verse, and not very good verse at that. Even so, it exhibits two of the features associated with lines using internal (half-line) parallelism, which are anacrusis (the initial *šlm*) and anaphoric repetition (of *šlm*). In addition, these three lines comprise the concluding section to the whole liturgy and so constitute a self-contained unit in a structurally significant position.[170]

Another set, this time of only two lines, may be

(11) *KTU* 1.10 iii 29-31

wtʿl. bkm. barr	She then(?) climbed upon Arru,
bm. arr. wbṣpn	upon Arru and upon Ṣapunu
bnʿm. bǵr. tliyt	upon the nice place, upon the triumphal hill.

The second line of this tricolon exhibits half-line parallelism; the third is internally parallel and is probably intended to match the middle line. The four-fold initial *b-* is, of course, an established component of

167. Above, p. 124.

168. Above, p. 114.

169. Text established by P. Bordreuil and D. Pardee, 'Le rituel funéraire ougaritique RS 34.126', *Syria* 59 (1982), pp. 121-28. Translation: B.A. Levine and J.M. de Tarragon, 'Dead Kings and the Rephaim: The Patrons of the Ugaritic Dynasty', *JAOS* 104 (1984), pp. 649-59, p. 651; discussed p. 658; however, they set out this passage as seven lines and not as above. See, too, G. del Olmo Lete, 'Los nombres "divinos" de los reyes de Ugarit', *AuOr* 5 (1987), pp. 39-69, 55-56.

170. See Levine and de Tarragon's remarks, 'Dead Kings', p. 658 on this closing 'salutation'.

internal (half-line) parallelism. The place names involved have been discussed recently.[171]

3.5. *Occurrence and Distribution*

Once again the table of occurrence and distribution needs to be emended.[172]

Baal (and Anath) Cycle	26(+ 9)[173]
	2(+ 2)[174]
	3(+ 1)[175]
Kirta Legend	8(+ 7)[176]
Aqhat Tale	11(+ 3)[177]
Rephaim texts	2(+ 3)[178]
Gracious Gods	5(+ 3)[179]
Nikkal's Wedding	1(+ 1)[180]

171. P. Bordreuil, 'Arrou, Gourou et Sapanou: Circonscriptions administratives et géographie mythique du royaume d'Ougarit', *Syria* 61 (1984), pp. 1-10. For the translation, cf. p. 10 and del Olmo Lete, *Mitos y leyendas*, pp. 473-74 and contrast de Moor, *Anthology*, p. 115 and n. 35.

172. Above, pp. 110 and 131.

173. 1.2 i (13.20), 23-24 (etc.); (iii 22); iv 32 // 34; 1.3 (i 12); ii 39; iii 22-23 (and par.); 46-47; iv 22-23 // 25-26, 33, 38; vi 7-9 (19-20); 1.4 i 25-26, (33-34); iii 18-20; iv 4-5 (26 [etc.]); v 20-21; vii 43; 1.5 ii 2.6; 1.6 i 16-17; ii (31-35); vi 17 = 18-19 = 20, 21-22, 48-50, 55-58. Also, 1.4 vi 13-14 (if Margalit, *'Life' and 'Death'*, pp. 47 and 49, is correct). 33.

174. 1.10 ii 29. (30a); iii 30.

175. 1.12 i (36-37); ii 52-53, 56-57.

176. 1.14 i (43-52, etc.); ii (32-34); iii 4-5 (and par.), 6-7 (and par.); iv 38-39; 1.15 iv 10-11; v 14-15; 1.16 i 12-13, 25-26; ii 26-36. Additional, but uncertain examples may be 1.14 ii 1-3 (and par.—a cluster of two?); 1.15 iv 10-11 and v 14-15, for which cf. De Moor and Spronk, 'Legend of Kirtu', pp. 158-60, 178 and 179 respectively. Note, too, *aṯr ṯn ṯn hlk* (1.14 ii 41-42 // iv 19-20), if translated 'Two marched, two walked' (so M.J. Dahood, 'Ugaritic-Hebrew Parallel Pairs', in *RSP*, II, p. 9) would be in half-line parallelism; however, the stichometry is uncertain (cf. del Olmo Lete, *Mitos y leyendas*, pp. 294, 298 and 519—according to him, *aṯr* belongs to the previous line).

177. 1.17 vi (30-31a), 44-45; 1.18 i 24; iv 24-26 // 36-37; 1.19 i 44; ii 3-4, 38-39 // 43-44; iii 4-5 = 19 = 33-34, 5 = 20 = 34, 11 = 25; iv 5-6 (and par.), 13-14. Possibly 1.17 vi 6 and 1.18 i 31-32 as well.

178. 1.20 i (6-7); ii 2-4; 1.21 (ii 5-6 = VV); 1.22 i 2; i 8-9 = ii 7-8.

179. 1.23:7, (14), 16, 32, (51), (58-69 // 61), 61-63.

180. 1.24:20-21 (Delete 38-39); cf. del Olmo Lete, *Mitos y leyendas*, p. 460; however, cf. de Moor, *Anthology*, p. 145.

Miscellaneous	5(+ 2)[181]
Serpent texts	3(+ 1)[182]
Rephaim ritual	4[183]
Incantation	5(+ 1)[184]

Note: As far as possible, repeated and parallel passages have only been counted once. The numbers preceded by the plus sign in parentheses denote uncertain examples.

As expected there is a high number of examples in the Baal and *Aqhat* texts. Now that more examples have been recognized in the *Kirta* story it appears much less anomalous than my previous studies indicated, though many of the occurrences are dubious.

The high density in ritual texts (*KTU* 1.161; RIH 78/20) remains unexplained.

As in my earlier articles on this topic, I append, in a footnote, a list of Akkadian (Assyro-Babylonian) passages for comparative purposes.[185] By way of illustration, some of these passages will be set out, with brief comment where appropriate.[186]

181. (1.88:3); 1.93:2-3; 1.124:14-15; 1.133:18-19; 1.151:11-12 (cf. D. Pardee, 'More on the Preposition in Ugaritic', *UF* 11 (1979), pp. 685-92, 689 and n. 25; 5.9:2-6; (7.63).

182. 1.100:1.63-64, (65-67); 1.108:6-7, 22-23.

183. 1.161: 21-22, 31-34.

184. RIH 78/20: 3-4, 5-6a, 7-8, (9-10).

185. J.G. Westenholz, 'Heroes of Akkad', *JAOS* 103 (1983), pp. 327-36, 334-35; F. Köcher, *Die babylonisch-assyrische Medizin in Texten und Untersuchungen* (Berlin: de Gruyter, 1963–64), p. 234, lines a, d, h(a), o, u, [a'], b'; p. 248 col. iii line 12; *Ee* I 8; IV 63–64; *Gilg*. VII iv 46; VIII ii 14; XI 25; *Gilg. M(eissner fragment)* II 8; III 11; *Gilg. P* iii 31 (with chiasmus); Descent of Ištar 16-17, rev. 20-21, 36a, 37b; J. Black, 'Babylonian Ballads: A New Genre', *JAOS* 103 (1983), p. 31 lines 17, 19; *Maqlû* II 160, 192-93, 198, 203-204, 209, 210-12; III 127; V 166-68; Great Šamaš Hymn 120; V. Scheil, 'Textes funéraires', *RA* 13 (1916), pp. 165-74, 169; cf. M. Held, 'Pits and Pitfalls in Akkadian and Biblical Hebrew', *JANESCU* 5 (1973), pp. 173-90.

186. For the half-line in Akkadian/Babylonian verse, cf. Westenholz, 'Heroes of Akkad', pp. 334-35 ('The normal Old Babylonian poetic style has basically a simple structure: the basic unit is the line which is a unit of sense and is usually divisible into four metric units or two half-lines'); also, W. von Soden, 'Untersuchungen zur babylonischen Metrik. Teil II', *ZA* 74 (1984), pp. 213-34, 213-15 (on Ee) and J.V. Kinnier Wilson, *The Legend of Etana: A New Edition* (Warminster: Aris & Phillips, 1985), p. 8 ('balanced imperative clauses'). Also, E. Reiner, *Your Thwarts in Pieces, Your Mooring Ropes Cut: Poetry from Babylonia and Assyria*

Adapa A 9

ebbu ellam qāti pasīšu mušte''u parṣi	Chaste, with pure hands; anointing-priest, ritualist(?)

Picchioni notes that the line is composed of two hemistichs each of which exhibits IP.[187]

Ee I 8

šuma lā zukkuru šīmāte lā šīmū	(when) no (god) had been given a name, no destinies had been established

This line, omitted from my previous list,[188] has been studied recently by von Soden.[189]

Gilg. XI 25

muššir mešrê še'i napšāti	Abandon wealth; seek life.

As in the previous example, the alliterative -*š*- is self-evident.[190]

Great Šamaš Hymn 120

urappaš kimta mešrâ iraššì	(The just creditor) will enlarge (his) family, he will acquire riches.

Note the chiasmus.[191]

In addition to these single lines with half-line parallelism, I have identified another cluster (of six lines) in the incantation-prayer to *Madānu* lines 20-25:[192]

(Michigan: Horace H. Rackham School of Graduate Studies at the University of Michigan, 1985), p. 91 (on K 890:2-3a, 6).

187. Text: S.A. Picchioni, *Il poemetto di Adapa* (Budapest: G. Komoroczy, 1981), p. 112; he translated (p. 113): 'Illibato, di mano pura, sacro untore, osservante del rito' and comments (p. 128): 'I versi sembrano però suddivisi in due emistichi... composti da attributi analoghi e paralleli'.

188. Above, n. 141.

189. Von Soden, 'Untersuchungen', p. 219 and n. 13.

190. See J.H. Tigay, *The Evolution of the Gilgamesh Epic* (Philadelphia: University of Pennsylvania Press, 1982), p. 292 for comparison with *Gilg.* XI 26 and (OB)Atr. III 23-24.

191. Lambert, *Babylonian Wisdom Literature*, p. 132 line 120; CAD, M/1, p. 385; Seux, *Hymnes*, p. 59; Reiner, *Poems*, pp. 75-76.

192. Text and translation: W. Mayer, *Untersuchungen zur Formensprache der babylonischen 'Gebetsbeschwörungen'* (Studia Pohl, Series Major, 5; Rome: Biblical Institute Press, 1976), pp. 459-65, esp. 462-64. For line 24, cf. *AHw*, p. 1319a; for line 25, *CAD*, N/1, p. 104 ('I will make known your deeds, I will praise your name'). The strong assonance is noteworthy.

[ib]bi šumī šūrik ūmēj[a]
[su]pūrī ruppiš lim'id lillidī
ukkiš murṣī qibi balāṭī
annī lippaṭir littābil adīrī
limmaši gillatī supuḫ tānīḫtī
lušāpi narbîka lutta''id zikirka

Name(?) my name! Lengthen my days!
Enlarge my sheepfold! Let my (animals') young be many!
Drive away my illness! Pronounce me healthy!
May my sin be absolved. Removed be my fear.
Forgotten be my misdeed. Do away with my weariness.
I will proclaim your greatness. I will keep on praising your name.

The only other six-line cluster is *Gilg.* V iv 15-20.[193]

Phrases with internal (half-line) parallelism also occur in prose letters[194] and on seals.[195]

3.6. *Conclusions*

Now that over 60 examples have come to light in Ugaritic verse (without counting the additional score or so of debatable passages), internal parallelism—or half-line parallelism[196]—must be considered an established component of Ugaritic versification and not an isolated phenomenon. In fact, Ugaritic shares this feature with other ancient Semitic verse traditions (Akkadian, Hebrew, Aramaic). In addition, most of the elements associated with this kind of line in Hebrew and Akkadian are found in Ugaritic too, but there is a lesser degree of

193. Cf. 2.5 above and n. 238 below. The clustering in DT 71:5-8, 10-13 is difficult to establish as there are gaps in the text.

194. ARM VIII 13; rev. 11'; ARM X 4:38-39 (cf. A. Finet, 'Un cas de clédomancie à Mari', in G. van Driel, T.J.H. Krispijn, M. Stol and K.R. Veenhof [eds.], *Zikir šumim* [Leiden: Brill, 1982], p. 50); 53:10; ARM XIV 61:12; 102; edge 27; 110: rev. 16 (= core of report); EA 287:26; ND 2715:7; VAB 4 280 vii 55; YOS 2 41:12-13.

195. H. Limet, *Les légendes des sceaux cassites* (Brussels: Palais des académies, 1971), 7.9, 7.21, 9.7 (lines 3 and 6-7) etc. Also A.J. Ferrara, 'A Kassite Cylinder Seal from the Arabian Gulf', *BASOR* 225 (1977), p. 69 (set of three lines in IP).

196. So D. Pardee, 'Ugaritic and Hebrew Poetry: Parallelism' (Communication prepared for the First International Symposium on the Antiquities of Palestine, Aleppo 1980) now published in D. Pardee, *Ugaritic and Hebrew Poetic Parallelism: A Trial Cut* ('nt *I and Proverbs 2)* (VTSup, 39: Leiden: Brill, 1982), p. 50.

clustering. These findings may possibly have implications for the determination of metre in Ugaritic.[197]

4. *Classical Hebrew Verse*[198]

Elsewhere I have examined the characteristics and distribution of IP in Ugaritic verse.[199] Here I will describe IP in classical Hebrew verse since there is no comprehensive study of the topic and it is not included in my *Classical Hebrew Poetry*.[200] I have not included every phrase with IP in my survey, nor have I considered occurrence and distribution since otherwise this paper would be too long.[201] First

197. The following extra examples of internal parallelism have been identified: *KTU* 1.4 i 33: *kh*ṯ. *il. n*ḫ*t. b*ẓ*r* (note A - - A' - - A" - - - pattern with next line); 1.4 vi 13-14: [*wql*ṣ. *y*] *ql*ṣ*n wp*ṯ*m* [*ywp*ṯ*n*] (so Margalit, AOAT 206, 47.49, contrast del Olmo Lete, *Mitos y leyendas*, p. 205); 1.17 vi 6; 1.18 i 31-32; 1.22 i 2; 1.151: 11-12: *wl.b'l ql* š*r. l. 'nt* (translation: D. Pardee, 'More on the Preposition in Ugaritic', *UF* 11 [1979], p. 689 and n. 25).

198. First published in *Bib* 66 (1985), pp. 365-84.

199. See above, 'Ugaritic Verse'. This form of parallelism is mentioned by S. Segert, 'Parallelism in Ugaritic Poetry', *JAOS* 103 (1983), pp. 295-306 under 4.1.2 (p. 299), 4.1.4 (p. 300) and p. 298. IP is also found in Aramaic verse; examples include Aḥiqar, Proverbs 5, 9, 20, 29, 30, 49, 68, 106 and 110; *KAI* 215:11 (Panammu) and 216: 10-11 (Barrakkab 1); also Dan. 2.21; 6.28. J.C. Greenfield, 'Early Aramaic Poetry', *JANESCU* 11 (1979), pp. 45-51 makes oblique reference to IP. Additional examples occur in magical texts, e.g. C. Isbell, *Corpus of the Aramaic Incantation Bowls* (Missoula, MT: Scholars Press, 1975), Texts 14:5-6; 21:15; 35:5; 60:3-5 and 70:6. A double example occurs in the Mandaic text cited by J.C. Greenfield, 'A Mandaic Miscellany', *JAOS* 104 (1984), pp. 81-85, 82 lines 2-3. Also, the whole of the Tell Siran Bottle inscription, in Ammonite, may be in IP, but translation is problematic and even the reading (especially of the last word) is unsure. Cf. most recently H.O. Thompson, 'The Tell Siran Bottle Inscription: An Additional Note', *BASOR* 249 (1983), pp. 87-89, with bibliography. Note that J.C. de Moor, 'The Poetry of the Book of Ruth (Part I)', *Or* 53 (1984), pp. 262-83, uses the term to denote 'the delicate semantic, formal, syntactical or stylistic balance between the cola forming a verse' (p. 264).

200. Dennis Pardee, 'Ugaritic and Hebrew Poetry', discusses IP under the heading 'half-line parallelism'. He refers to L.I. Newman, 'Parallelism in Amos', in L.I. Newman and W. Popper, *Studies in Biblical Parallelism* (Berkeley: University of California Press, 1918), pp. 155-58 who used the term 'reduplication or internal synonymity', citing Amos 5.12, 15a, 7.14 and 8.5b.

201. A preliminary count yields the following occurrences of IP: Deut. 32 (3); Judg. 5 (2); 2 Sam. 1 (2); Isa. 1–12 (23); 13–23 (12); 24–27 (6); 28–33 (17);

comes a description of IP in terms of line-forms. Next, different features of Hebrew verse will be shown to occur in combination with IP. The third section deals with the phenomenon of clustering and then comes a section on patterns. The last section looks at some aspects of style.

4.1. *IP and Line-Forms*

Line-form analysis of Hebrew verse was pioneered by T. Collins[202] and the patterns adopted here depend in large measure on his work, though he made no mention of IP.[203] Here are listed the different syntactic patterns which obtain in verse lines with IP, using the sequence given in Collins's book.[204] For each pattern a single instance will be provided with additional texts having the same pattern listed for reference. It will become evident that IP works at the level of syntax besides being semantic in character. In addition, the analysis of each 'half' of a line will be seen to match, with due allowance for chiastic inversions.

4.1.1. *NP_1V // NP_1V*

yhwh ntn wyhwh lqb	Y. gives and Y. takes away (Job 1.21).

Other examples: Judg. 5.4; Isa. 46.4b; 54.10.

4.1.2. *V NP_1 // NP_1 V*

ky	For
kšlh yrwšlm wyhwdh npl	stumble did Jerusalem and Judah fell (Isa. 3.8).

40–66 (40); Jeremiah (40); Ezekiel (5); Hosea (7); Joel (4); Amos (4); Obadiah (1); Nahum (6); Habakkuk (1); Zephaniah (2); Psalms (42); Job (3); Proverbs (24); Canticles (12); Qoheleth (2); Lamentations (4); Sirach (17). Ps. 46 and 68 exhibit high density. Examples from the Dead Sea Scrolls: 1QH 2.21; 7.18-19; 1QS 10.8; 11QPs[a] 19 (Plea for Deliverance). 4-5 = 10-11 (refrain); 11QPs[a] 28.7, 9 (= Ps. 151A.4, 5); also Pss. 154.5; 155.18.

202. *Line-forms*, reviewed in *Bib* 61 (1980), pp. 581-83.

203. Apart from the indirect reference, Collins, *Line-forms*, p. 229.

204. Briefly, sentences are broken down into their components; NP_1 denotes the subject (pronoun, noun, nominal phrase or clause); NP_2 denotes the object; V is the verb and M stands for modifier (adverb, prepositional phrase, etc.). The pronominal suffix is denoted by -np_2.

Isa. 26.19 is the only other example.

4.1.3. *V NP_1 // V NP_1*

ygl y'qb yšmḥ yśr'l	May Jacob exult, may Israel rejoice (Ps. 14.7).

Other examples: Judg. 5.3; Isa. 1.2; 14.31; 24.23; 29.20; 31.3; 46.1; 49.13; Pss. 16.9; 46.7a; 104.8a; Cant. 4.16; Qoh. 1.5a.[205]

4.1.4. *V M // V M*

y'lw šmym yrdw thwmwt	They lurched skywards, plumbed the abyss (Ps. 107.26).

Other examples: Isa. 28.9b; 30.11a; 33.15; 48.20; 65.19; Pss. 15.2; 46.11b and possibly Prov. 10.9.

4.1.5. *M V // M V*
This is the previous pattern reversed:

mnšrym qlw m'rywt gbrw	They were swifter than eagles, stronger than lions (2 Sam. 1.23).

Other examples: Isa. 1.9b; 33.18; 55.12 (cf. 28.7) and Jer. 20.6.

4.1.6. *NP_1 V-np_2 // NP_1 V-np_2*

my r'nw wmy ywd'nw	'Who sees us?' and 'Who knows us?' (Isa. 29.15b).

The other example is Ezek. 31.4b.

4.1.7. *V-np_2 NP_1 // NP_1 V-np_2*

'zbny yhwh w'dny škḥny	Abandon me did Y., my Lord has forgotten me (Isa. 49.14).[206]

4.1.8. *V NP_2 // V NP_2*

hrp m'p w'zb ḥmh	Desist from anger and give up wrath (Ps. 37.8).

205. Cf. Lam. 4.18, a sequence of '$1\frac{1}{2}$' (discussed below).
206. Also, perhaps, Isa. 27.11.

Other examples: Isa. 9.2; 10.6; 12.4b; 16.3; 28.29; 52.7; 56.1; Jer. 13.1; 17.10; 51.11, 12b; Ezek. 26.12; Hos. 8.13; 13.15; Joel 1.14 = 2.15; Amos 4.1b; 5.15; Nah. 2.10; Zeph. 2.3; Pss. 7.15; 9.6a; 26.11b; 37.37; 89.14b; 96.2a; 105.2; Sir. 7.31a.[207]

4.1.9. *V NP₂ // NP₂ V*

yšsw btyhm wnšyhm tšglnh	Their houses will be ransacked, and ravished will be their wives (Isa. 13.16).

Other examples: Isa. 28.25; 54.2b; Jer. 20.8 and Ezek. 19.7.

4.1.10. *NP₂ V // V NP₂*

The lone example is Ps. 46.10b:[208]

qšt yšbr wqṣṣ ḥnyt	He breaks a bow, a spear he snaps.

4.1.11. *NP₂ V // NP₂ V*

'lyk t'kl wpryk tšrš	They'll consume your leaves, uproot your fruit (Sir. 6.2).

Other examples: Isa. 4.1b; 14.20 and Hos. 8.7a.

4.1.12. *V-np₂ M // V-np₂ M*

hšby 'ny bmrwrym hrwny l'nh	He has sated me with bitterness, he has filled me with wormwood (Lam. 3.15).

Other examples: Isa. 63.3b; Hos. 11.8a and Cant. 2.5a.

4.1.13. *V-np₂ M // M V-np₂*

y'šhw bmqṣ'wt wbmḥwgh yt'rhw	He fashions it with planes, and with a compass marks it (Isa. 44.13d).

207. An additional text may be Cant. 5.7 (V-np2 // V-np2); on Isa. 47.2-3 see under 4.3.4.

208. In *JNES* 43 (1974), p. 113 R.C. Steiner and C.F. Nims correct their previous study, 'A Paganized Version of Psalm 20.2-6 from the Aramaic Text in Demotic Script', *JAOS* 103 (1983), pp. 261-74, and show that the Aramaic Text (P. Amherst Egyptian 63, Col XI: 16), *'lh bqšt 'lh bḥnt*, corresponds in structure to Ps. 20.8 but uses the rare word-pair, *qšt // ḥnyt* of Ps. 46.10b. These three passages and the variant refrains of the Aramaic 'Polemical Poem' discussed by the same authors (R.C. Steiner and C.F. Nims, 'A Polemical Poem from the Aramaic Text in Demotic Script', *JNES* 43 [1974], pp. 89-114) are all in IP.

The other passage, also a chiastic form of 1.12, is Isa. 22.19.

4.1.14. *M V-np2 // M V-np2*

The sole example is Isa. 60.10b:

ky	For,
bqṣpy hkytyk wbrṣwny rḥmtyk	in my anger I struck you and in my mercy had compassion on you.[209]

4.1.15. *V // V*

wštw wl'w	They shall drink and swallow (Obad. 16).[210]

A common pattern: Isa. 1.16; 7.7; 8.9; 11.9;[211] 23.4; 40.21, 24;[212] 42.2, 4; 44.8; 65.25b; Jer. 4.8, 11b; 8.2, 9; 14.3; 46.4; 48.40; 49.8; 50.11; Pss. 27.2d;[213] 48.6b; 106.6; Job 3.26;[214] Cant. 2.7 = 3.5; 8.4; Sir. 42.21.[215]

4.1.16. *Nominal Patterns*

The high number of examples in this category is an indication that further sub-grouping is required, though for present purposes the catch-all term 'nominal', borrowed from Collins, will suffice.

hm't bqr wḥlb ṣ'n	Cow butter and sheep fat (Deut. 32.14).

Other examples: Deut. 32.24, 25; 2 Sam. 1.22; 1 Kgs 18.26; Isa. 1.26b; 2.20; 3.1; 5.20, 29a; 7.7; 8.13b, 20; 9.5c, 13; 22.2b; 24.13; 28.2, 5, 11a;[216] 33.16c; 34.6, 11; 41.14, 29; 42.6; 43.28; 44.6, 22; 45.13, 14;

209. The same theme is developed in Ludlul I, often in lines with IP. For the text, see now W.L. Moran, 'Notes on the Hymn to Marduk in *Ludlul bēl nēmeqi*', *JAOS* 103 (1983), pp. 255-60.

210. The two verbs constitute hendiadys.

211. VV-M according to Collins, *Line-forms*, p. 221.

212. Collins, *Line-forms*, p. 221: VMV. On *'p bl*, cf. J. Wansbrough, 'Rhetorica Semitica', *BSO(A)S* 46 (1983), pp. 531-33, 533 n. 20 ('neither... nor... nor...').

213. Cf. Jer. 46.6 and Ps. 26.11b.

214. Really a set of VV // VV; see under 4.2.

215. Collins, *Line-forms*, pp. 219-23 discusses the phenomenon of doubled verbs. For Aramaic, cf. Greenfield, 'Early Aramaic Poetry', pp. 47-48.

216. Isa. 28.11a could also be analysed as MM, i.e. as modifiers of the following verb.

48.1d; 57.8b; 62.6c; 65.19c; 66.12; Jer. 1.18; 4.18a; 5.11c; 7.17; 14.18c; 15.11; 16.21; 17.20,[217] 25; 19.3; 22.18; 31.23; 47.3; 49.31; 50.44; Ezek. 29.5;[218] Hos. 2.21b; 4.9a; Amos 4.13; 9.7d; Nah. 1.14; Hab. 2.17; Zeph. 2.9; Pss. 8.9;[219] 19.4; 20.8; 22.7; 49.3; 60.9 (= 108.9); 68.6a, 8, 26a, 28b; 74.16; 78.12b; 89.12; 107.3bc; 113.6b; 119.127b; Job 4.10; Prov. 3.2, 22; 6.10 (= 24.33); 17a, 19b, 23; 7.12a; 10.26; 20.1; 25.3, 19, 26a; 26.1, 3,[220] 21; 27.3,[221] 4, 21a; 28.15; 30.31a; 31.30a; Cant. 1.5cd; 2.1; 4.8d, 12, 14; 7.7; Lam. 1.22; 4.13; Sir. 6.12; 41.14; 43.17a; 44.6; 45.12.[222]

From the foregoing it is evident that the standard line-forms of two-line parallelism are used in lines with IP. It is also clear that nominal patterns (4.1.16) are preferred (over 100 texts are listed). Next come the V // V type (4.1.15, some 30 examples), then V NP_2 // V NP_2 (4.1.8) and V NP_1 // V NP_1 (4.1.3).[223]

4.2. *Inner-Line Features of IP*

Certain features of Hebrew verse occur in lines with IP to a degree which marks them off as independent units. These features will be described under three headings, corresponding to patterns of sound, structure and meaning, followed by a short discussion.

4.2.1. *Phonological Aspects of IP*

Assonance is represented by Jer. 51.12b:

hqymw šmrym hkynw h'rbym Get up blockades, set up ambuscades.[224]

217. For the reading, with omission of *yšby* following the Greek, cf. J.G. Janzen, *Studies in the Text of Jeremiah* (HSM, 6; Cambridge, MA: Harvard University Press, 1973), p. 40.

218. The phrase follows the verbal IP expression 'you shall not be gathered nor shall you be buried', and both examples are part of longer lines.

219. Corresponding to Ugaritic *'ṣr šmm // wdg hym*, 'birds of the sky and fish from the sea' (*CTA* 23:61-62), also in IP.

220. The IP pattern in Prov. 26.3 is the same as in *Aḥiqar*, Proverb 5.

221. Again there is a structural parallel in *Aḥiqar* (Proverb 29; cf. 30).

222. The only case of *semantic* IP is Ps. 39.10.

223. In Ugaritic, too, the nominal line-form is commonest, though V // V is rare.

224. As J. Bright, *Jeremiah* (AB, 21; Garden City, NY: Doubleday, 1965), p. 356 points out, men were stationed 'to block possible sorties'; accordingly, he translates *šomᵉrîm* not 'watchmen' but 'road blocks'.

See, too, Isa. 22.2; 29.15b; 31.3; 48.8; Jer. 15.13; 51.11; Ezek. 26.12; Joel 1.14; Amos 4.1; Ps. 15.2; note Cant. 6.10, with an *a* sound throughout.

Alliteration is exploited in Judg. 5.3, Isa. 1.2, 26b, 21.2b, 56.1, Pss. 14.7, 78.12b, Cant. 4.14 and elsewhere. More significant is alliteration in the form of the quasi-acrostic, by which is meant the use of the same letter (or letter cluster) to begin each half of the line.[225] In Ps. 104.8a, for example, the letter is *yodh*:

y'lw hrym yrdw bq'wt	Mountains rose up, valleys sank down.

Other examples, with the operative letter (-cluster) in brackets are: Deut. 32.14c (*ḥ*); 2 Sam. 1.22, 23c (both *m*); Isa. 8.20 (*l*); 28.11 (*b*); 44.22 (*k*); 54.10 (*h*); 60.10b (*b*); Ezek. 29.5 (*l*); Joel 1.14 (*q*); Pss. 46.10 (*q*); 48.6b (*n*); 104.8a (*y*); 106.6b (*h*); 107.26 (*y*); Cant. 4.8 (*m*); 7.7 (*m*); Lam. 3.15 (*h*). Very frequently, too, the second word of the second half begins with the same letter (-cluster) as its counterpart in the first: Isa. 5.29a (*l š*); 9.2 (*h h*); 24.13 (*h b*); 55.12 (*t b*); 63.3 (*b w'*); 66.12 (*š k*); Hos. 2.21b (*b b*); Pss. 14.7 (*y y*); 89.14b (*y t*); 107.3bc (*wm t*); Prov. 10.26 (*l k*). In many texts this results from word repetition: Deut. 32.25b; Isa. 7.7; 8.13; 11.9; 40.21, 24a; 44.8; 48.1; 65.19c, 25b; Jer. 4.11; 5.11; 14.18c; 50.11; Pss. 20.8; 46.11; 74.16; Prov. 7.12a; 23.29a;[226] Cant. 2.7; Sir. 6.12 and 42.21.

Internal end-rhyme is exemplified by Isa. 28.29b (-*â*):

hply' 'ṣh hgdyl twšyh	He is wonderful in counsel, he excels in wisdom.

Other examples, classed by sound:

-â	Isa. 8.20; 16.3a; 24.23; Jer. 15.11
-tā	Isa. 14.20b
-ām	Hos. 8.13; Ps. 22.7
-î	Isa. 23.4; 63.3; Jer. 50.11; Ps. 16.9; Prov. 31.2
-îm	Judg. 5.3; 2 Sam. 1.22; Isa. 25.6; Ps. 68.26a; Prov. 3.2; Cant. 5.16

225. See my discussion in Chapter 10, 'Anaphoric Alliteration in Ugaritic Verse'.

226. My discussion of this text in *Classical Hebrew Poetry*, pp. 20-30, esp. 21-25, should be corrected accordingly.

-ô	Hos. 13.15
-ôy	Prov. 23.29a
-ôn	Isa. 46.6
-ôt	Prov. 6.10
-û	2 Sam. 1.23; Isa. 1.16; 11.9; 28.7; 40.21, 24; 44.8; 65.25b; Jer. 4.8; 8.2, 9; 14.3; 46.6; 48.20; 49.8; Obad. 16; Hos. 8.7a
-hû	Ezek. 31.4a

Feminine end-rhyme occurs as follows: *-êhā* Lam. 4.13; *-êkā* Isa. 44.22; *-ênu* Lam. 4.18; *-inû* Isa. 1.9b; *-ôhû* Isa. 34.11; *-ûnî* Cant. 5.7 and *-nāyim* Prov. 10.26.

Other phonological features are less significant. Anacrusis is common, as in Prov. 3.2:

ky	For,
'rk ymym wšnwt ḥyym	length of days and years of life...

Also Isa. 3.8 (*ky*); 4.1 (*l'mr*); 9.5a (*ky*); 14.20b (*ky*); 28.1 (*hwy*); 29.20 (*ky*) 41.29 (*hn*); 54.10 (*ky*); 55.12 (*ky*); Jer. 14.18c (*ky*); 40.44c (*ky*); Hos. 8.7 (*ky*), 13 (*'th*); 11.8 (*'yk*); Pss. 7.15 (*hnh*); 16.9 (*lkn*); Prov. 6.23 (*ky*); Cant. 2.1 (*'ny*); Lam. 1.22 (*ky*).

Figura etymologica or 'turn'[227] occurs in Isa. 10.6, 21.2b, 24.16 and Jer. 5.11b. Onomatopoeia is rare: Isa. 29.6, Prov. 23.32 and Sir. 43.17a.

4.2.2. *Structural Features of IP*

Chiastic parallelism is relatively common; examples are listed above under 4.1.2, 4.1.5, 4.1.7, 4.1.9, 4.1.10 and 4.1.13. Nominal chiasmus is present in Isa. 28.11, 25, 41.29, 43.28, Prov. 3.22; 6.23 and Lam. 1.22:

ky	For,
rbwt 'nḥty wlby dwy	many are my sighs and my heart is sick.[228]

227. See *Classical Hebrew Poetry*, p. 239 for this term.

228. On the meaning of *lb* here, see R. Lauha, *Psychopsysischer Sprachgebrauch im Alten Testament: Eine strukturalsemantische Analyse von* לב, נפש *und* רוח. I. *Emotionen* (Annales Academiae Scientiarum Fennicae, Dissertationes Humanarum Litterarum, 35; Helsinki: Academia Scientiarum Fennica, 1983), pp. 103-104.

IP as the second line in a couplet: the norm is for IP to come as the initial line of a couplet.[229] Accordingly, Jer. 5.11b is unusual:

ky	For,
bgwd bgdw by	truly treacherous to me are
byt yśr'l wbyt yhwdh	*the House of Israel and the House of Judah.*

Isa. 1.26b, 8.13b, 28.29, Jer. 4.8, 8.9 Pss. 26.11b, 48.6b and Cant. 4.12 also share this feature. Even more remarkable, then, is Ps. 68.28b, with IP in the third line.

4.2.3. *Semantic Aspects*

Repetition occurs very often and the result is akin to the quasi-acrostic (see above) with each half of the line beginning or ending with the same word. Initial (anaphoric) repetition:

bqšw-ṣdq bqšw ʿnwh	Look for justice, look for humility (Zeph. 2.3)

Final repetition (epistrophe):

šyrw-lw zmrw-lw	Sing to him, chant to him (Ps. 105.2)

Also: Isa. 2.20; 4.4d; 24.16; 28.10, 13; 33.18; 42.2; 44.6; 48.8; Jer. 20.6; 50.44; Mic. 7.12; Pss. 49.3; 68.28b; Prov. 6.10 (= 24.33) and Qoh. 1.5a. Other examples are listed under 4.4.3.

Antithetic parallelism is exceptional since usually the first half of a verse line with IP is synonymous with the second.

krb rḥmyw kn twkḥtw	Great as is his mercy so is his reproof (Sir. 16.12).

Likewise: Isa. 5.20; 60.10b; Amos 5.15; Pss. 104.8a; 107.26; Job 1.21; Prov. 25.3. Qoh. 3.2-8 is discussed below.

Much as is the case with Ugaritic verse[230] word-pairs are used extensively in Hebrew IP, perhaps to bond the two halves of the line together. Occasionally, twin sets are used, as in Amos 5.15 where 'hate' // 'love' and 'evil' // 'good' are combined:

śn'w-rʿ w'hbw ṭwb	Hate evil and love good.

229. This certainly applies to Ugaritic.
230. See above, 'Ugaritic Verse'.

Also note the following:

Deut.	32.14a	'butter' // 'fat'
		'cattle' // 'flocks'
2 Sam.	1.22	'blood' // 'fat'[231]
Isa.	1.2	'listen' // 'give ear'
		'sky' // 'earth'
	1.9b	'Sodom' // 'Gomorrah'
	1.26b	'city' // 'town'
	2.20	'silver' // 'gold'
	3.8	'stumble' // 'fall'
		'Jerusalem' // 'Judah'
	10.6	'spoil' // 'plunder'
	14.31	'gate' // 'city'[232]
	23.4	'have birth pangs' // 'give birth'
	28.11	'lips' // 'tongue'
	33.16	'bread' // 'water'
	34.6	(as 2 Sam. 1.22)
	34.11	'chaos' // 'void'
	41.14	'Jacob' // 'Israel'
	42.6	'people' // 'nations'
	44.6	'first' // 'last'
	48.8	'hear' // 'know'
	49.13	'rejoice' // 'exult'
		'sky' // 'earth'
	54.10	'mountains' // 'hills'
	56.1	'justice' // 'uprightness'
	65.19a	'be happy' // 'exult'
Jer.	5.11b	'Israel' // 'Judah'[233]
Ezek.	26.12	(as Isa. 10.6)
	29.5d	'gather' // 'collect'[234]
	29.5e	'earth' // 'sky'
	31.4a	'waters' // 'deeps'[235]
Hos.	8.13	'iniquity' // 'sin'

231. Corresponding to Akkadian *lipû // dāmu*, 'fat' // 'blood' in Lambert, *Babylonian Wisdom Literature*, p. 240: obv. II 9-10 (translation, p. 247) in a different context.

232. This inverts the sequence of *qryt // t'ryh* in Aḥiqar, Proverb 75 and of *ālu // abullu* in Lambert, *Babylonian Wisdom Literature*, p. 245: rev. IV lines 53-57. The pair 'city' // 'town' is used in Isa. 22.2 (also in combination with IP).

233. The 'family' word-pairs in Jer. 22.18 are unclear.

234. See my discussion in Chapter 6, 'The Hebrew Word-Pair *'sp // qbṣ*'.

235. The pair *rwmm // gdl* (cf. Isa. 1.2) may also be present.

Joel	1.14 = 2.15	'sanctify' // 'call'[236]
Amos	4.1b	'poor' // 'orphans'
Nah.	2.10	'silver' // 'gold'
Pss.	8.9	'sky' // 'sea'
	14.7	'Jacob' // 'Israel'
		'exult' // 'rejoice'
	16.9	'rejoice' // 'exult'
	37.8a	'anger' // 'wrath'
	68.5a	'sing' // 'chant'
	68.6a	'orphans' // 'widows'
	89.12	'sky' // 'earth'
	89.14b	'hand' // 'right hand'
	96.11a	(as Isa. 49.13)
	104.8a	'go up' // 'descend'
		'mountains' // 'valleys'
	105.2	(as Ps. 68.5a)
	107.26	'go up' // 'descend
		'sky' // 'deeps'
Prov.	3.2	'days' // 'years'
	6.17a	'eyes' // 'tongue'
	6.19b	'witness' // 'testifier'
	25.13	(as Ps. 89.12)
Cant.	4.16	'north' // 'south'
Lam.	3.15	'bitterness' // 'wormwood'[237]

All these features—the matching half-line assonance, the quasi-acrostic, internal end-rhymes, chiastic and antithetic parallelism, the forms of repetition and the word-pairs—indicate that the Hebrew poets considered such lines as comprising two matching halves, as scaled down equivalents of the couplet. Even the examples of onomatopoeia are islands of sense-loaded sound. This amply confirms the impression already gained from examination of the line-forms used with IP (above, section 4.1).

236. Cf. Mic. 3.5 and Joel 4.9 for this word-pair, inverted.

237. While re-writing this article, Avishur, *Word-Pairs* came to hand. He discusses word-pairs used in what he terms 'intra-colon parallelism' (i.e. IP) and in addition to the texts I list mentions Isa. 2.9; 28.29; 40.7-8; Pss. 32.11; 145.8; Prov. 12.1; 13.3; 14.5, 29; Job 7.12; Sir. 35.24; 43.9 and others (pp. 53-63 and elsewhere). His encyclopaedic work should be used to complement my own study, but his distinction between 'intra-colon parallelism' and 'verses wherein each colon comprises two words (or two beats), and they are verses unto themselves' (for which he cites Gen. 49.7; Isa. 63.3 etc.), p. 57 n. 1, is not clear to me.

4.3. *Clustering*

Perhaps the most remarkable characteristic of IP in Hebrew verse is its occurrence in clusters, a feature common in Akkadian verse tradition but not in Ugaritic.[238] In Hebrew, runs of two three, four and five can be identified and some runs are longer. Clusters of '1½' will be examined later.

4.3.1. *Sets of Two*

One of the clearest is Isa. 5.27a:

'yn-'yp w'yn-kwšl bw	None is weary; none of them stumbles;
l' ynwm wl' yyšn	no-one slumbers; no-one sleeps.

Also, Isa. 19.2;[239] 21.2b; 25.6; 30.5; 45.7; 64.3b-4a; 64.7;[240] Jer. 44.6; 51.12; Nah. 2.2bc; Pss. 68.16; 81.3; Prov. 23.29a; Cant. 5.16 and Sir. 7.31b.[241]

4.3.2. *Sets of Three*

whyh	Alike shall be
k'm kkhn k'bd k'dnyw	people and priest, a slave and his master
kšpḥh kgbrth kqwnh kmwkr	a maid and her mistress, buyer and seller,
kmlwh klwh knš' k'šr nš' bw	lender and borrower, creditor and debtor.

In Isa. 24.2 the poet was unable to find a one-word antonym for 'creditor', which accounts for the clumsy last line. In addition, the structural pattern is in tension with the semantic parallelism since '(alike shall be) people...mistress' is a sub-unit (all terms of social class) and the rest of the strophe (denoting members of the commercial world) is another.[242] The result is a combination of /1½ + 1½/

238. Akkadian examples of clustering are Lambert, *Babylonian Wisdom Literature*, 58:37-39; 114:51-52; L. Cagni, *L'Epopea di Erra* (Rome: Istituto di Studi del Vicino Oriente dell'Università, 1969), p. 68 (= I 109-113); 100.102 (= IIId 4-10) and 118 (= IV 131-135). Also, *Gilg.* V iv 15-20 and *Maqlû* II 38-49, 93-96; V 166-68.

239. For an Akkadian parallel also in IP, cf. *Classical Hebrew Poetry*, p. 352.

240. Isa. 64.7 (with anacrusis of the first two words) is a completely nominal short poem: 'However, Yahweh / you are our father / we are the clay; / you are our potter / and all of us your handiwork'.

241. Clusters of two with intrusive lines: Isa. 2.10 (cf. 19); 16.3; 25.4-5 and 30.20, 21.

242. For such tension, cf. Collins, *Line-forms*, pp. 231-32. Isa. 21.7 may be another set of three.

instead of an expected /1 + 1 + 1/. The quasi-acrostic based on initial *kaph* is striking. Another set of three is Jer. 7.34, though there are extraneous elements:

whšbty	I will banish
m'ry yhwdh wmḥṣwt yršlm	from the cities of Judah and from the streets of Jerusalem,
qwl ššwn wqwl šmḥh	the voice of mirth and the voice of merriment,
qwl ḥtn wqwl klh	the voice of groom and the voice of bride (for the land will become a ruin).

Curiously, although the core ('the voice of mirth...the voice of bride') is common to Jer. 16.9, 25.10 and 33.10-11, each time it is extended in different ways to form a set of three lines with IP. In our passage the formula 'in the cities of Judah and in the streets of Jerusalem' (Jer. 7.17; 11.6; 33.10; 44.6, 17, 21) has been added in adapted form (by a change of preposition) which indicates clustering to be an accepted technique in composing poetry.[243]

4.3.3. *Set of Four*

The only set to occur, Jer. 1.10, follows an introductory couplet: 'See! I have placed my words in your mouth / Look! I have appointed you overseer this very day':

'l-hgwym w'l-hmmlkwt	over nations and over king(dom)s,
lntwš wlntws	to uproot and to pull down,
lh'byd wlhrws	to destroy and to tear down,
lbnwt wlnṭw'	to rebuild and to plant.

This is a fully expanded form of a formulaic set found several times in Jeremiah;[244] word-pairs are used and the passage evokes Qoh. 3.2-8.

4.3.4. *Sets of Five*

qḥy rḥym wṭḥny	Take twin millstones and grind meal;
gly ṣmtk hśpy-šbl	take off your veil; remove your robe.
gly-šwq 'bry nhrwt	Bare your thighs—cross rivers,
tgl 'rwtk gm tr'h ḥrptk	reveal your 'nudity', show your 'shame', even.
nqm 'qḥ wl' 'pg' 'dm	I will take vengeance; no-one will I spare.

243. One could speculate that the core couplet is itself an expansion with antithesis of 'the sound of weeping and the sound of distress' (Isa. 65.19).

244. For details cf. Janzen, *Text of Jeremiah*, p. 35.

The pattern in Isa. 47.2-3 is not entirely consistent since the first and central lines are forms of progressive parallelism. The persistent V NP_2 // V NP_2 line-form, though—changed to a closing chiastic NP_2 V // V NP_2 sequence only at the end—and the overall structure indicate that we are dealing with a set of five lines in IP.[245] The other set is Sir. 36.6-7.[246]

4.3.5. *Other Sets*

Clustering of lines with IP is very noticeable in the short book of Nahum, and Assyrian influence cannot be excluded. Nah. 3.1-3a begins with anacrusis and a monocolon. After three complete lines with IP comes a half-line, then the run is resumed for another three lines. The cumulative effect is a vivid picture of mounting battle and the inevitable piles of victims. Since Nah. 3.1-4 is a unit, it is quite probable that a less strict form of IP has been used throughout, including vv. 1a and 4.[247] Other complex sets are Nah. 3.14-15 and Joel 1.10-12.[248]

By far the longest set is Qoh. 3.2-8[249] which has fifteen in a row. However, as Wright has shown,[250] the poem (which perhaps existed independently of the book) comprises two sets of six lines marked off by refrains of a sort, plus a closing couplet. No-one, it would seem, has remarked on the IP and it is even more curious that such a long sequence uses antithetic parallelism in so sustained a manner since the preferred type with IP is synonymous. It is too long to set out here

245. The alliterative envelope figure *qḥy... qmḥ—nqm 'qḥ* also marks off these lines as a unit.

246. F. Vattioni, *Ecclesiastico: Testo ebraico con apparato critico e versioni greca, latina e siriaca* (Pubblicazioni del Seminario di Semitistica, Testi, I; Naples: Istituto Orientale di Napoli, 1968), p. 189 cites the marginal variant to v. 6, also apparently in IP.

247. For translation, see K.J. Cathcart, *Nahum in the Light of Northwest Semitic* (BibOr, 26; Rome: Biblical Institute Press, 1968), pp. 115 and 126-28.

248. Clustering is recognized by E.D. Mallon, 'A Stylistic Analysis of Joel 1:10-12', *CBQ* 45 (1983), pp. 537-48.

249. Cf. A.G. Wright, '"For Everything there is a Season": The Structure and Meaning of the Fourteen Opposites (Ecclesiastes 3,2-8)', in A. Caquot and M. Delcor (eds.), *Mélanges bibliques et orientaux en l'honneur de M. Henri Cazelles* (AOAT, 212; Kevelaer: Butzon & Bercker; Neukirchen–Vluyn: Neukirchener Verlag, 1981), pp. 321-28.

250. Wright, 'Structure', p. 326.

and v. 5 is problematic[251] but the quasi-acrostic effect produced by anaphoric repetition of *'t* is a clear characteristic of IP (see above, 4.2.3).

4.4. *Structural Patterning in IP*

4.4.1. *Introduction*

Lines with IP fall into certain patterns, most of which involve a degree of word repetition. These patterns are set out here, with one example for each and a list of additional examples, as before. The letters 'A, B, C' stand for single words. Similar or analogous patterns using IP in other verse traditions are cited in the footnotes. Before going on to the patterns, some remarks on the components of the line may be helpful.

4.4.2. *Components of the Line*

There is some evidence for lines comprising one word (outside of anacrusis [cf. 4.2.1]), for example, *wy'mrw*, 'they say' and *hpkkm*, 'your perversity!' in Isa. 29.15b-16a.[252] More often, though, two (repeated) words can comprise a half-line (examples under 4.4.3). As in Ugaritic verse[253] the half-line or half-colon is one of the building

251. Possibly Qoh. 3.5 may be translated 'a time to expose sons and a time to accumulate sons'; cf. Ezek. 22.21. This would entail understanding *'bn* as a form of *bn*, 'son' (i.e. with prothetic *aleph*) and *hašlîk* in the sense of 'to expose', a meaning proposed by M. Cogan, 'A Technical Term for Exposure', *JNES* 27 (1968), pp. 133-35 (though he does not mention our text). See, in general, D.B. Redford, 'The Literary Motif of the Exposed Child', *Numen* 14 (1967), pp. 209-28, with bibliography p. 221 n. 9. However, O. Loretz, 'Poetry and Prose in the Book of Qoheleth (1:1-3:22; 7:23–8:1; 9:6-10; 12:8-14)', in J.C. de Moor and W.G.E. Watson (eds.), *Verse in Ancient New Eastern Prose* (AOAT, 42; Kevelaer: Butzon & Bercker; Neukirchen–Vluyn: Neukirchener Verlag, 1993), p. 176 n. 50, rejects this suggestion.

252. Following W.H. Irwin, *Isaiah 28–33: Translation with Philological Notes* (BibOr, 30; Rome: Biblical Institute Press, 1977), p. 60. J.C. de Moor, 'The Art of Versification in Ugarit and Israel. I: The Rhythmical Structure', in Y. Avishur and J. Blau (eds.), *Studies in the Bible and the Ancient Near East Presented to S.E. Loewenstamm on his Seventieth Birthday* (Jerusalem: E. Rubinstein's Publishing House, 1978), pp. 119-39 concludes, 'In Ugaritic and Hebrew poetry the smallest structural unit was not the syllable, but the word or cluster of words bearing a main stress', i.e., the foot, and he cites Mic. 1.10-11 as including a one-foot stichos (p. 139 and n. 45).

253. See above, 'Ugaritic Verse' (§7.3).

blocks of Hebrew versification. Culley and Pardee have discussed the topic briefly[254] and it requires more extensive coverage than can be provided here. Examples in Hebrew include Pss. 26.11b, 113.6b, Job 8.15 and the many occurrences in 'identity' proverbs such as Prov. 10.1ab, 5ab, 8a, 9, 10a, 11, 20a, but also elsewhere, for example Hos. 4.9a.[255] The half-line is significant because lines with IP generally comprise two consecutive half-lines. Sometimes there are sets of three as in Prov. 31.2:

mh-bry wmh-br-bṭny wmh br-ndry	What my son? And what, son of my womb? And what, son of my vows?

Similar are Isa. 1.8, 21.5a, 49.7, Jer. 1.18, 18.18, Hos. 9.16, Nah. 3.15, Pss. 7.15, 37.27, 65.8 and Job 3.26. Such lines correspond to a pattern found in Akkadian incantations, for example,

išāt mūtu išāt šipṭu išātu kāsistum	Fire of death, fire of judgment, consuming fire[256]

and would appear to be longer than normal expansions of a line with IP, modelled, perhaps, on threefold repetitions of the type

erṣetum erṣetum erṣetumma	Netherworld! Netherworld! Netherworld![257]

A Hebrew example is Jer. 7.4 (cf. Isa. 6.3).

In some texts the 'overhanging unit' which results from using three half-lines in a row is matched so as to produce what appear to be two parallel lines. In Job 3.26, for instance, the pattern is $1\frac{1}{2} + \frac{1}{2}$ with the last two words extraneous to the overall parallelism:

254. R.C. Culley, *Oral Formulaic Language in the Biblical Psalms* (Near and Middle East Series, 4; Toronto: University of Toronto Press, 1967), p. 31 comments that 'there are instances in which a colon is composed of two short formulas, each half a colon long' and 'in a number of cases the position in which free substitution of formulas takes place occupies half a colon, the remaining half of the colon being constant'; see his examples 17 (p. 43), 20 (p. 45), 23 (p. 47), 30 (p. 50), 37 (p. 53), 38 (p. 53), 58 (p. 64), 109 (p. 76) and 147 (p. 84). Pardee, 'Parallelism', also discusses half-line parallelism.

255. An initial component of Isa. 24.2 (also in IP).

256. Text and translation, W.G. Lambert, 'Fire Incantations', *AfO* 23 (1970), pp. 39-45, Section II: 7 (p. 40).

257. *Maqlû* I 37.

l' šlwty wl' šqṭy	I have no peace, I have no quiet,
wl'-nḥty wyb' rgz	I have no rest—but disturbance comes.

In Isa. 1.8 the extraneous element comes at the beginning, instead, while in Isa. 33.10 there is an intrusive phrase halfway through the first line.[258] It may be conjectured that such non-standard $1\frac{1}{2}$-unit lines were tolerated in early poetry but tended to be 'squared off' in verse of a later period.

4.4.3. *Structural Patterns of IP*

Preliminary classification of some of the patterns used in lines with IP results in the following list.

A -, A -	*'lh brkb w'lh bswsym*	Some in chariots and some in horses (Ps. 20.8)

Also Deut. 32.25b; 1 Kgs 18.26; Isa. 7.7; 8.13b; 11.9; 29.15b; 42.4; 44.6, 8; 45.13; 48.1; 62.6b; 65.19, 25b; Jer. 4.11; 5.11b; 14.18; 15.11, 13; 16.21; 49.31; 50.11a; Ezek. 20.4; Zeph. 2.3; Nah. 2.10; Pss. 46.11; 60.9 (= 108.9); Job 1.21; Prov. 7.12a; Cant. 2.7; 3.5; 5.16; 8.4.[259] This pattern, perhaps, is modelled on immediate word repetition (AA) as in Judg. 5.12, Ezek. 22.2, Zeph. 1.2 and Job 19.21.[260] See AABB, below. The pattern AA/BB/CC occurs in Isa. 28.10, 13.

A-, A -	*m'ṭ šnwt m'ṭ tnwmwt*	A little nap, a little sleep,
A - - - -	*m'ṭ ḥbq ydym lškb*	a little lie-down with folded arms (Prov. 6.10 = 24.33).

Also Isa. 33.18; 40.24; 42.2; 46.4b; 48.8; Jer. 50.44; Sir. 42.21.[261] Note the additional A-line in Isa. 40.21 and the extra B-line in Isa. 23.4.

258. Note that in Isa. 33.10 the $1\frac{1}{2}$ unit is followed by a (separate) line in IP.

259. For the same pattern in Akkadian, cf. *Atr.* III iv 24 and *Maqlû* VIII 90-92. A common pattern is AA followed by one or more A-, A- lines, e.g. *Maqlû* III 158-59; VI 26-27; W. von Soden 'Duplikate aus Niniveh', *JNES* 33 (1974), pp. 339-41, 341-42, lines 1-4.

260. Compare Ugaritic *lk lk*, 'Go, go!' (*CTA* 1 iii 17; 3 iv 76); *'ad 'ad*, 'Father, father!' (*CTA* 23:32.43) and *'um 'um*, 'Mother, mother!' (*CTA* 23:33).

261. Similarly, *Maqlû* I 42-43 and VIII 57-58.

AB	*hylyly wz'qy*	Wail and cry (Jer. 48.20)
AABB	*wym mym whrh hr*	And (to) sea from sea, to mountain (from) mountain (Mic. 7.12).[262]
ABAB	*ht'zrw wḥtw ht'zrw wḥtw*	Equip yourselves but be dismayed, equip yourselves but be dismayed (Isa. 8.9c).[263]
A -, B -	*hylyly š'r z'qy-'yr*	Wail, O Gate! Cry, O City! (Isa. 14.31).
A -, A -	*qnh ḥkmh qnh bynh*	Acquire wisdom. Acquire insight.
B -, B -	*'l-tškḥ w'l-tṭ m'mry py*	Do not forget. Do not turn from my utterances (Prov. 4.5).

4.5. *IP and Poetic Style*

4.5.1. *Figurative Language*

Figurative language is represented chiefly by the simile, probably more because IP often entailed repetition of the comparative particle than for any other reason. For example,

htkbd kylq htkbdy k'rbh	Multiply like the young locust, multiply like the locust (Nah. 3.15b).

Other examples: Isa. 1.8, 9; 5.29a; 28.2; 44.22; 66.12; Hos. 4.9a; 11.8; Prov. 10.26; 23.32; 25.19; 26.1; 27.21a; 28.15; Cant. 1.5cd; Sir. 16.12. Texts combining *imagery* and IP include 2 Sam. 1.22, 23; Isa. 28.9; 30.20; 33.10; 34.6, 11; 41.4; Jer. 17.10; Hos. 8.7a; 9.16; Ps. 7.15; Prov. 6.21; Cant. 2.1 and 4.12. Personification (including apostrophe) occurs in Isa. 1.26b; 3.8; 14.31; 22.2; 49.13; Jer. 48.20; Pss. 68.16 and 96.11a.

262. Cf. W. Rudolph, *Micha—Nahum—Habakuk—Zephanja* (KAT, 13/3; Gütersloh: Gerd Mohn, 1975), p. 129 n. h for this consonantal redivision and rendering. The AABB pattern is common in incantations, e.g. *Maqlû* IV 1; R.D. Biggs, ŠÀ-ZI-GA. *Ancient Mesopotamian Potency Incantations* (Texts from Cuneiform Sources, 2; Locust Valley, NY: Augustin, 1967), p. 22 (= Text 6:1); also 19 (3:20), 21 (4:15), 50 (35:4') and the incipits in the catalogue 12-13 (col. i 2.19.20; col. ii 15). Also, Gilg. XI 21-22.

263. Cf. *Maqlû* V 89.

4.5.2. *Rhetorical Functions*

IP can be used to open a segment of verse:

šm'w šmym wh'zyny 'rṣ	Listen, O Heavens! Give ear, O Earth! (Isa. 1.2).

Isa. 33.15, 40.21, 24, 44.6, 45.14, 46.1 and 48.20 also use IP in this way. IP is closural in 2 Sam. 1.22a:[264]

mdm ḥllym mḥlb gbwrym	(but) by the blood of the slain, by the fat of warriors.

Also, Isa. 13.16b; 22.19; 41.29; 43.28; 45.13; Ps. 14.7b; Job 3.26 and Lam. 1.22. It is used as a refrain in Ps. 39.10, Cant. 2.7 (and par.) and perhaps Isa. 40.7-8. IP is used to effect in proverbial sayings:

šwṭ lsws mtg lḥmwr *wšbṭ lgw ksylym*	A whip for the horse, a bridle for the ass and a stick for the back of fools (Prov. 26.3).

and other texts in Proverbs; also Ps. 37.27, 31 and Qoh. 3.2-8.

5. *Classical Hebrew Again*[265]

5.1. *Introductory*

The usual form of parallelism in Hebrew verse is the couplet where the second line of the couplet is parallel to the first. In 'internal parallelism' (here abbreviated to IP) the same feature occurs within a single verse line. In such lines, accordingly, the first half of the line has a parallel in the second. This characteristic is reflected in the alternative label 'half-line parallelism'. Although I have already written three articles on IP,[266] there are several reasons for yet another. To begin with, quite a number of new examples have been identified and these need to be set out. Many of these examples are interesting in

264. For this line as a closing refrain, see my comments in 'Chiastic Patterns in Biblical Hebrew Poetry', in Chapter 7. For lack of space, the line-forms, inner-line features and stylistic aspects of the cluster (section 3) have not been set out, apart from a few remarks.

265. First published in *VT* 29/1 (1989), pp. 44-66.

266. The line with IP has its nearest equivalent in 'Leonine Verse' (which has internal rhyme), a term defined in M. Drabble (ed.), *The Oxford Companion to English Literature* (London: Guild Publishing, 1985), p. 564.

themselves. In addition, examples have been found in books of the OT previously unrepresented. IP in the form of two half-lines is as important an element in Hebrew poetry as it is in some other ancient Semitic verse traditions (Ugaritic, Akkadian) though here I will limit myself to classical Hebrew, and needs to be examined in respect of its implications for metre, lineation and the differentiation between prose and poetry.

5.2. *List of Passages*

The sequence followed will be that of the Hebrew Bible with the addition of Ben Sira. Only a selection of passages can be set out and discussed.

Genesis

2.23;[267] 7.4, 12; 8.2, 22; 11.1, 6; 13.10; 15.17; 16.12b; 17.20; 19.4; 24.35; 25.34; 29.17; 30.42; 31.36, 43a; 32.12; 39.10; 41.3, 4, 19, 44; 43.33; 49.3,[268] 19. The core of 8.22 is an enumeration.

'd kl-ymy h'rṣ	During all Earth's days
zr' wqṣyr wqr wḥm	seeding, harvest, cold, heat,
wqyṣ wḥrp wywm wlylh	summer, winter, day and night
l' yšbtw	shall not end.[269]

Exodus

4.10; 6.9; 9.31; 15.11.

nwr' thlt 'śh pl'	Awe-inspiring, Wonder-worker.
	(15.11; see below, 5.3.7)

Leviticus

5.4; 6.13; 12.45; 27.30 (cf. 2.10, 28; 10.10; 19.26, 35, 36). Most of these are phrases used in long sentences.

Numbers

5.22 (// 27); 10.35 (cf. Ps. 68.2); 14.8; 15.16; 17.27; 20.20; 21.5a; 23.24; 24.6, 9; 33.55 (cf. 15.39; 21.17b; 18b).

267. Discussed in Chapter 6, 'Some Additional Wordpairs'.

268. S. Gevirtz, 'The Reprimand of Reuben', *JNES* 30 (1971), pp. 87-98. Is this an expansion of *kḥy wr'šyt 'wny* in the same verse?

269. G. Del Olmo Lete, 'Algunos pares ugarítico-hebreos preteridos', *AuOr* 2 (1984), pp. 11-22, 14. See, in addition W. Brueggemann, 'Kingship and Chaos. (A Study of Tenth Century Theology)', *CBQ* 33 (1971), pp. 317-22.

mbrkyk brwk w'rryk 'rwr	Blessed be anyone blessing you, cursed be anyone cursing you. (24.9)

Deuteronomy

26.8; 28.3-6 (// 16-19); 29.22; 30.15; 32.14c, 24, 25b (cf. 12.15; 28.4-5; 32.29).

Joshua

10.13; 14.11; 23.13 (// Num. 33.55).

wydm hšmš wyrḥ 'md	The sun stood still, stay did the moon[270] (10.13)

Judges

5.3, 4, 21, 25[271] (cf. 4.7; 9.28; 14.16; 16.28, 29).

nḥl qyšwn grpm *nḥl qdwmym nḥl qyšwn*	Wadi Kishon swept them away, the onrushing wadi, Wadi Kishon.[272] (5.21)

The quasi-acrostic component[273] comes in both elements of the couplet: *n- q- // n- q- // n- q-*.

1 Samuel

2.30c; 12.4; 16.12, 18; 17.44, 46; 20.1; 24.15; 25.3, 6, 9, 25; 26.12; 30.8 (cf. 13).

2 Samuel

1.21, 21,[274] 22, 23; 3.29b, 31a; 12.3; 15.21; 16.7;[275] 22.1; 23.5d.

270. J. Sanmartín Ascaso, *Las guerras de Josúe: Estudio de semiótica narrativa* (Valencia: Institución San Jerónimo, 1982), p. 159 n. 457, considers this phrase to be a secondary gloss, in prose, inserted in place of a lost or deleted line originally parallel to *'d yqm gwy 'ybyw*.

271. Discussed by A. Berlin, *The Dynamics of Biblical Parallelism* (Bloomington: Indiana University Press, 1985), pp. 12-13.

272. Contrast M. O'Connor, *Hebrew Verse Structure* (Winona Lake, IN: Eisenbrauns, 1980), p. 226: 'Wadi Qishon is an ancient wadi'.

273. Explained in my *Classical Hebrew Poetry*, pp. 195-96; below, Chapter 10, 'Anaphoric Alliteration in Ugaritic Verse'. It is the use of the same letter to begin lines, half-lines or corresponding sub-sections of half-lines.

274. Contrast P. Kyle McCarter, Jr, *II Samuel* (Garden City, NY: Doubleday, 1984), pp. 66, 71, and W.H. Shea, 'Chiasmus and the Structure of David's

qr'w bgdykm wḥgrw śqym	Rip your clothes, wear sacking
wspdw lpny 'bnr	and beat the breast in front of Abiner.[276] (3.31a)

None of the passages in 1 or 2 Samuel is pure verse.

1 Kings
3.22, 26; 8.57c; 18.26; 19.6; 20.8, 25; 22.4 (cf. 3.24; 5.13a, 18c).

2 Kings
3.7; 4.26, 30, 31; 5.26; 7.6; 14.26; 18.12 (cf. 3.14; 5.7; 6.27; 7.4).

Isaiah
1.2, 4a, 7, 8, 9b, 16 (etc.), 23, 26b; 2.10, 20; 3.1, 8; 4.1; 5.15, 20, 27, 29a; 6.7b, 10a; 7.7, 11; 8.1, 9, 13b, 20; 9.2, 9, 11, 13; 10.6; 11.9; 12.4b; 13.16; 14.4, 5, 20b, 31; 16.2, 3a, 3c; 19.2; 21.2b, 5, 7; 22.2, 12-13, 19; 23.4; 24.2, 13, 16, 23; 25.4-5, 6; 26.19; 28.2, 5, 9, 11, 16, 19, 25; 29.9a, 15b, 20; 30.5, 11a, 20-1, 27; 31.3; 33.8, 10, 15, 16, 18, 20, 22; 34.6, 11; 37.22; 40.7, 8, 10 (= 52.11), 21, 24; 41.14, 26, 29; 42.2, 4, 6; 43.24b, 28; 44.6, 8, 13d, 22; 45.7, 13, 14; 46.1, 4b, 11b, 13; 47.2-3; 48.2, 8, 20; 49.7, 13, 14; 52.7; 53.3; 54.2, 10; 55.12; 56.1; 57.8b, 14a; 58.9b, 13-14; 60.10b, 19; 62.6b, 11; 63.3; 64.7; 65.3b-4a, 19a, 19c; 66.3, 12; (cf. 9.5a; 14.15; 28.7; 32.18b; 41.10; 57.19b; 65.22b).

'rm mqdm wplštym m'ḥr	Aramaeans from the east and Philistines from the west. (9.11)
šlḥ 'ṣb' wdbr 'wn	to point the finger and utter slander. (58.9b)

Jeremiah
1.10, 18; 2.19; 3.23, 24; 4.5a, 8, 11, 18a; 5.11b, 21b; 7.12, 17 (etc.), 34; 8.2, 20; 9.24, 25; 12.7, 8, 13, 14; 14.2, 3, 18; 15.10, 11, 13; 16.9, 21; 17.8, 10, 20, 25; 18.7, 18; 19.3; 20.6, 8; 21.6; 22.18, 23a; 25.10; 30.12-13; 31.9, 12, 27, 28; 32.21, 31; 33.10-11; 44.6, 12; 46.14, 18b;

Lament', *JBL* 105 (1986), pp. 13-25, esp. p. 15.

275. The phrase is discussed in detail by McCarter, *II Samuel*, p. 373.

276. See McCarter, *II Samuel*, pp. 105, 110, 119, on this passage. For the gestures, cf. M.I. Gruber, *Aspects of Nonverbal Communication in the Ancient Near East* (Rome: Biblical Institute Press, 1980), II, p. 447.

47.3, 7; 48.8b, 15, 21, 28a, 32; 49.4 (= 20), 15, 31, 35b, 44; 51.11, 12, 26, 30 (cf. 6.14b [= 8.11]), 18, 23; 8.9; 12.6; 13.11, 25, 27; 30.24; 31.19; 46.6; 48.20; 49.8, 30; 50.2, 11).

hgydw byhwdh wbyršlym hšmy'w	Proclaim in Judah and in Jerusalem declare. (4.5a)
yšbty blbnwn mqnnty b'rzym	Dweller in Lebanon, Nester in the cedars. (22.23a)

Ezekiel

2.5, 7; 3.11; 6.4, 6, 11; 7.6, 10, 12; 12.24; 13.6, 8, 9; 16.3, 44; 17.1, 3, 8, 17, 23; 18.9; 19.7, 14; 21.17; 23.34; 24.8; 25.6, 10; 26.12; 27.27; 28.12; 29.5, 18c, 19; 30.4, 14; 31.3, 4a; 37.11; 48.21-24a; 50.2 (cf. 21.14; 28.4a).

hkh bkpk wrq' brglk	clap your hand and stamp your foot.[277] (6.11)

Hosea

2.1b, 7, 11,[278] 21b; 3.4; 4.2, 3b, 9a, 13c; 6.1, 10b; 7.11b; 8.7a, 13; 9.6, 7b, 14b, 16; 10.4a, 11b, 13a;[279] 11.8; 12.2a; 13.10, 15; 14.5a, 16 (cf. 5.11a).

Joel

1.10-12,[280] 14 (= 2.15), 17; 2.9, 12, 13, 14, 20, 21,[281] 25; 3.2; 4.1, 6, 9.

w'lh b'šw wt'l ṣḥntw	his stink will go up and his stench will go up. (2.20)

277. Avishur, *Word-Pairs*, p. 83, notes that the word pair *kp // rgl* is rare and that *yd // rgl* is commoner, as in Ezek. 15.6 (also IP, incidentally).

278. The pattern is unnoticed by F.I. Andersen and D.N. Freedman, *Hosea* (Garden City, NY: Doubleday, 1980), pp. 132, 240-41.

279. 'Verse 13a has the same feature [as in v. 12a] of short lines. Each line has the same syntax (verb and object), with the same sequence in the first and third, which again achieves symmetry. In the second line the sequence is inverted', Andersen and Freedman, *Hosea*, p. 563.

280. The poem, already mentioned above is discussed in detail by Andersen and Freedman, *Hosea*, pp. 339-40, without recognition of the half-line components.

281. Note the expansion in Joel 2.21. The two verbs occur in exactly the same sequence in the Ammonite Tell Siran Bottle Inscription as *ygl wyśmḥ*.

Amos

2.9; 4.1b, 9, 13; 5.15; 8.5; 9.7, 11 (cf. 2.2; 8.11).

lhqṭyn 'yph wlhgdyl šql	lessening the ephah, increasing the shekel. (8.5)

Most other examples in Amos are poor.[282]

Jonah

2.1

šlšh ymym wšlšh lylwt	three days and three nights.[283]

Micah

1.6; 2.12; 3.2, 7; 4.2, 6; 6.8; 7.1, 4, 9, 19a (cf. 1.8, 16; 2.10; 3.10; 7.15).

wbšw hḥzym wḥprw hqsmym	The seers shall be disgraced and the diviners put to shame (3.7, RSV).

Nahum

1.14; 2.2, 10; 3.1-3a, 8, 14-15. None new.

Habakkuk

1.3, 15, 16; 2.2,[284] 17.

lmh	Why
tr'ny 'wn w'ml tbyṭ	do you make me see wrongs and look at trouble? (1.3)

Zephaniah

1.13, 18; 2.3, 6,[285] 9c, 14; 3.6, 12, 14, 19 (cf. 3.4).

whyh	Become
ḥylm lmšsh wbtyhm lšmmh	spoil will their wealth, waste their houses. (1.13)

282. Note, too, Obad. 16 (verb, verb).

283. Contrast D.L. Christensen, 'The Song of Jonah: A Metrical Analysis', *JBL* 104 (1985), pp. 54-75, for whom this is a bicolon.

284. For the meaning of this verse, cf. D.T. Tsumura, 'Hab. 2.2 in the Light of Akkadian Legal Practice', *ZAW* 94 (1982), pp. 294-95.

285. Text and translation: J.S. Kselman, 'A Note on Jer 49.20 and Ze 2.6-7', *CBQ* 32 (1970), pp. 579-81 and n. 13.

Zechariah
2.6; 10.4; 12.1.

nṭh šmym wysd 'rṣ	Who stretched out the sky, set foundations to the earth,
wysr rwḥ 'dm bqrbw	and formed man's inner spirit. (12.1)

Malachi
1.4;[286] 3.2, 3, 4, 7 (cf. 3.5). All previously unrecognized.

kymy 'wlm wkšnym qdmnywt	as in past days, as in former years. (3.4)

Psalms
2.2; 4.3;[287] 7.15;[288] 8.9; 9.6a; 10.17; 12.5, 6; 14.7; 15.2; 16.9; 17.3a, 6b, 13; 18.1, 47; 19.4; 20.8; 22.7, 25; 24.4; 26.11b; 27.2d, 7, 9c, 12b; 29.9; 30.6; 32.1a; 34.15a (= 37.27a); 37.8a, 27, 37; 38.11a, 19; 39.10; 44.4; 45.8; 46.7, 10b, 11;[289] 48.3, 6b, 9a; 49.3; 53.7 (= 14.7); 55.7b, 8b, 14; 59.13; 60.9; 62.4; 65.8, 11; 66.4; 68.2, 5a, 6a, 8, 16, 26a, 28b; 71.24; 74.2,[290] 16; 75.8;[291] 76.3; 78.12, 20a, 36; 81.3, 9; 82.5; 83.2b; 84.4; 85.9b; 88.7b;[292] 89.12, 14b; 90.7; 92.4; 96.2a, 11a; 100.4; 101.5; 102.27; 103.8; 104.8a, 20; 105.2; 106.6, 31, 48; 107.3bc, 26, 37; 108.9; 109.28; 113.6b; 115.1 (// 138.2); 119.113, 127b; 120.2-3; 121.4; 122.7; 123.4; 125.5-6; 126.5; 128.2b; 130.5-6; 133.1; 135.6; 136.12; 137.2; 139.12; 140.13; 144.14; 145.8; 148.8-10 (cf. 27.6c,

286. For a possible example in Mal. 1.6 (with verb ellipsis), cf. A. Berlin 'Shared Rhetorical Features in Biblical and Sumerian Literature', *JANESCU* 10 (1978), pp. 35-42, 40.

287. For different stichometry, cf. P.C. Craigie, *Psalms 1–50* (Waco, TX: Word Books, 1983), p. 78.

288. According to J.T. Willis, 'The Juxtaposition of Synonymous and Chiastic Parallelism in Tricola in Old Testament Hebrew Psalm Poetry', *VT* 29 (1979), pp. 465-80, 468, this is a tricolon.

289. Ps. 46.11 has been compared with Isa. 33.10 by M. Weiss, 'Wege der neuen Dichtungswissenschaft in ihrer Anwendung auf die Psalmenforschung: (Methodologische Bemerkungen, dargelegt am Beispiel von Psalm XLVI)', *Bib* 42 (1961), pp. 255-302.

290. The line with IP occurs within a longer verse, examined by P. Auffret, 'Essai sur la structure littéraire du Psaume LXXIV', *VT* 33 (1983), pp. 129-48, 131, though he did not recognize the half-lines.

291. Avishur, *Word-pairs*, p. 554, recognized 'intra-colon' parallelism here.

292. For the stichometry, cf. O. Loretz, *Ḫabiru—Hebräer* (Berlin: de Gruyter, 1984), p. 255.

10a, 14; 35.4; 45.4; 57.8; 86.15; 103.20; 104.9; 119.15; 120.7; 121.5, 6, 8; 124.5; 141.5; 144.2).

ḥy yhwh wbrwk ṣwry	Yahweh lives! Blessed be my Rock (18.47)
zh yšpyl wzh yrym	one he promotes, another he demotes (75.8)

Job

1.1, 21; 2.2, 11; 3.26; 4.10; 7.12; 9.4a; 10.10; 14.1b; 15.29, 35; 17.11; 18.19; 20.8, 13; 26.7; 29.25; 30.8, 20, 26; 33.9, 15; 37.13; 38.3b (// 40.7b // 42.4b); 39.21; 42.6 (cf. 19.14).

hrh ʿml wyld ʾwn	Pregnant with mischief they give birth to evil.[293] (15.35)

Proverbs

3.2, 7b; 4.5, 7; 5.19a; 6.10 (= 24.33), 12a, 13, 14, 17a, 19b, 23; 7.7, 12a; 9.2; 10.9, 26; 14.5b; 16.24; 17.3 (= 27.21), 15; 19.20, 26; 20.1, 10, 12; 21.4, 6b, 9 (// 25.24), 30; 22.8; 23.23, 29a, 32; 25.3, 12, 19, 26a; 26.1, 3, 10, 21; 27.3, 4, 21a, 27; 28.15; 30.4, 31a; 31.2, 30a[294] (cf. 18.22; 23.9).

šmʿ ʿṣh wqbl mwsr	Listen to advice and accept instruction (19.20, RSV).

Song of Songs

1.5cd; 2.1, 5, 7 (etc.); 4.8, 12, 14, 16; 5.7, 16; 6.10; 7.7 (cf. 2.8). None new.

Qoheleth

1.2, 4, 5a, 6, 9-10, 18; 2.25; 3.2-8, 11, 17; 5.2; 6.4; 7.12a; 8.16; 9.1, 2, 10; 12.1, 5, 14.

dwr hlk wdwr bʾ	a generation goes, a generation comes. (1.4)

293. M.H. Pope, *Job* (Garden City, NY: Doubleday, 1965), p. 113, compares Ps. 7.14, adding ‘Apparently it was a proverbial expression’.

294. Other possible examples in Proverbs are 1.18, 2.4, 3.7a, 22, 6.32a, 8.2a, 3a, 14, 14.29. See also n. 329 (below).

Lamentations
1.4, 5, 22; 3.15; 4.13, 18 (cf. 1.12; 3.49). None of these examples is clear.

Esther
2.7; 3.2, 7; 7.16; 9.13 (and par.) (cf. 3.13).

Daniel
11.20.[295]

Nehemiah
1.6, 10; 8.10.

1 Chronicles
12.15b, 19,[296] 41a; 28.9, 20b; 29.2, 5.

lm'h hqṭn whgdwl l'lp	the smallest (a match) for a hundred, for a thousand the biggest.[297] (12.15b)

2 Chronicles
2.3, 13, 14, (EVV, 4, 14, 15); 19.7b; 32.7 (cf. 36.17b).

Ben Sira
6.2, 11-13; 7.21, 31; 10.10b, 22; 11.7, 14; 12.5, 7, 18a; 12.24; 14.4, 5, 18b; 16.12, 16a, 22; 25.22; 30.23; 35.10b; 36.6-7; 37.18; 38.22b; 39.15; 41.14; 42.11c, 21; 43.9, 17a; 44.6; 45.4, 12; 46.13, 19; 47.23; 49.7, 15; 50.27; 51.5 (cf. 3.11; 6.27; 10.2; 14.16a; 26.3; 32.8, 23; 33.12, 14a, 20; 43.6; 51.25).

r'š yny' whnyp yd<y>w	His head he will nod and rub his hands. (12.18a)

5.3. *Features*
Following the plan of my previous article[298] I will first provide examples for inner-line features of the additional texts with half-line

295. See Gruber, *Aspects*, p. 485, for discussion of this phrase.
296. See J.M. Myers, *I Chronicles* (Garden City, NY: Doubleday, 1965), pp. 93, 97, and, with a Ugaritic parallel, B.A. Levine and J.-M. de Tarragon, 'Dead Kings and Rephaim: The Patrons of the Ugaritic Dynasty', *JAOS* 104 (1984), pp. 649-59, 658-59.
297. The succint combination of numerical and chiastic parallelism is noteworthy.
298. See above, 'Classical Hebrew Verse'.

parallelism presented in this article. Certain features will be taken as read since they occur so frequently (assonance, alliteration in the form of the quasi-acrostic, repetition and word-pairs) and will not need documentation unless of exceptional interest. Then I will list new passages where clustering occurs. Next come accounts of structural patterns and rhetorical features. The last paragraph deals with compression.

5.3.1. *Phonological Aspects*. Assonance is evident in Gen. 16.12b, 1 Sam. 30.8, 2 Kgs 14.26, Zech. 2.6, Pss. 32.1a, 75.8b and so on. Alliteration within an acrostic can be seen in the following:

t'wt 'nwym šm't yhwh	You have heard the desire of the afflicted, Yahweh.
tkyn lbm tqšb 'znk	You will strengthen their heart; you will turn your ear. (Ps. 10.17)

Psalms 9–10 form an alphabetic acrostic and in the closing *taw*-strophe the use of initial *taw* is extended beyond the first line to both halves of the second (in the translation the pattern *T*- - - - - // *T*- - - // *T*- - - is reflected in the use of 'you'). See also Ps. 24.15 (= 37.27a) and contrast 119.15. Sometimes only the *second* components of each half-line begin with the same letter (or cluster) as in

hr ṣywn yrkty ṣpwn	Mount Zion, the recesses of Zaphon. (Ps. 48.3)

Also Gen. 11.1 ('), 6 ('); Lev. 19.26 (*l*); 1 Kgs 20.8 (*t*), 25 (*k*); Isa. 9.11 (*m*); Jer. 12.7 ('); 22.23 (*b*); Hos. 6.1 (*wy*); Mic. 3.7 (*h*); Mal. 3.7 ('); Ps. 119.15 ('); Job 2.11 (*h*); 14.7 (*y*); Prov. 6.13 (*b*); 17.3 (= 27.21) (*l*), 19.26 ('); Neh. 8.10 (*m*); Sir. 7.21 (*m*); 12.18a (*y*); 42.11e ('),[299] 13 (also '). This is a feature of some Babylonian verse.[300]

299. For the text, cf. B. Jongeling, 'Un passage difficile dans le siracide de Masada (Col IV, 22a = Sir. 42.11e)', in W.C. Delsman, *et al.* (eds.), *Von Kanaan bis Kerala: Festschrift für J.P.M. van der Ploeg*... (Kevelaer: Butzon & Bercker; Neukirchen–Vluyn: Neukirchener Verlag, 1982), pp. 303-10.

300. The poems have been edited by J.A. Black, 'Babylonian Ballads: A New Genre', *JAOS* 103 (1983), pp. 25-34, with corrections by W.G. Lambert, '*šiā'lu* "to rejoice"', *RA* 77 (1983), pp. 190-91, though this feature (lines 1b-3b, 4b-5b, 6b-7b, 13b-14b, 16b-17b, 23b-28b) has gone unnoticed.

End-rhyme occurs in: Gen. 31.36; 39.10; 1 Kgs 8.57c; Isa. 1.23; 7.11; 33.20; 40.10 (= 62.11); Jer. 12.14; 32.31; 50.15, 35b; Hos. 7.11b; Mic. 3.7; 4.6; 7.9a; Zeph. 1.18; Zech. 2.6; Pss. 17.6b; 29.9; 48.3; 59.13; 66.4; 71.24; 82.5; 119.13; 123.4; 136.12; 138.2; 139.12; Prov. 20.9; 30.4; Job 10.10; Qoh. 9.1; Neh. 8.10; 1 Chron. 12.19; Sir. 25.22, 45.4 and so on.

A sound-pair is defined by Berlin as 'the repetition in parallel words or lines of the same or similar consonants in any order with close proximity'.[301] Since a line with IP behaves like a couplet it can also contain a sound-pair. Examples are few:

hgydw bmṣrym whšmy'w bmgdwl	Give out in Egypt and announce it in Migdol. (Jer. 46.14)

The words *hGyDw* and *mGDwl* are related only by similarity of sound. A better illustration is

yerā' 'et-yhwh wᵉsûr mērā'	REVERE Yahweh and turn from EVIL. (Prov. 3.7b)

Similarly, Hos. 9.14b (*MŠkyl—ŠdyM*);[302] cf. Ezek. 19.4, below (5.3.2).

Sound-pairs which are also word-pairs[303] include Gen. 15.17 (*'šn* // *'š*); Jer. 8.20 (*qṣyr* // *qyṣ*); Hos. 9.6 (*qbṣ* // *qbr*); Hab. 1.15 (*ḥkh* // *ḥrm*—contrast *ḥrm* // *mkmrt* in 1.16); Pss. 38.19 (*'gyd* // *'d'g*), 122.7 (*šlwm* // *šlwh*)[304]; Job 42.6 (see below); Lam. 1.49 (*'yny—m'yn*). Strictly speaking, word-pairs belong in a semantic category but some are mentioned here because of their connection with sound-pairs (see 5.3.3).

'ylt 'hbym wy'ly-ḥn	A lovely DEER, a graceful DOE. (Prov. 5.19a)

The sound + word-pair *'ylt—y'lt* involves repetition of the letters *y*, *l* and *t* which may explain the use of rare *y'lh* here. See also Sir. 14.18b:

'ḥd gw' w'ḥd gmwl	one is BLIGHTED, another BLOOMS.

301. *Dynamics*, p. 104.
302. Perhaps also Mal. 1.6, Pss. 122.4, 124.5.
303. Berlin, *Dynamics*, pp. 106-108.
304. Discussed by Berlin, *Dynamics*, p. 107.

5.3.2. *Structural Features*. Chiastic patterns obtain in

qṣ b' b' hqṣ	An end comes, comes the end.[305] (Ezek. 7.6)
qynh hy' wthy qynh	This is a dirge and a dirge it becomes.[306] (Ezek. 19.14)

Both these comprise 'mirror chiasmus'.[307]

hn hkh-ṣwr	When he struck a rock
wyzwbw mym wnḥlym yšṭpw	water gushed and gullies overflowed.
	(Ps. 78.20a)

The chiasmus here is phonological (*-îm -û // -û -îm*), grammatical (V S // S V) and semantic (there is weak onomatopoeia too). Also, Gen. 16.12b; Isa. 6.7b; 44.13d;[308] Jer. 4.5a; 14.2; 44.12; Hos. 4.13c; Amos 9.11; Hab. 1.3, 15; Zeph. 3.19; Pss. 38.11a, 19; 76.3; 90.7; 119.15; 124.5; 141.5; Job 19.14; 26.7; Prov. 17.15; Sir. 12.18a; 14.5a.

IP occurs in the second line in Gen. 16.12b; 1 Sam. 16.12b; 17.44b; Isa. 6.10; 58.9b; Jer. 5.21b; Pss. 66.4b; 140.13b; 145.8b; Job 14.1b; Prov. 3.7b; 14.5b; 16.24; 21.6b, 9 (// 25.24); 36.10b; Sir. 6.16b; 11.7b; 13.24; 35.10b; 38.22b; 49.15; 50.27.

'd 'mwnym l' ykzb	A truthful witness does not lie
wypyḥ kzbym 'd šqr	but a lying testifier is a false witness.
	(Prov. 14.5b)

In some of these passages the second line glosses (or is parallel to) the last word or words of the first line, for example:

'm tsyr mtwkk mwṭh	If you remove from your midst injustice:
šlḥ 'ṣb' wdbr 'wn	pointing the finger, speaker slander.
	(Isa. 58.9b)

Also Ps. 66.4b; Prov. 16.24b; 2 Chron. 19.7b (previous examples: Jer. 4.8; Ps. 48.6b). Note the enjambment in Ps. 140.13 (previously: Jer. 15.11b).

305. The chiasmus is noted by M. Greenberg, *Ezekiel 1–20* (Garden City, NY: Doubleday, 1983), pp. 145-47. The next line comprises two non-parallel half-lines.

306. So Greenberg, *Ezekiel*, p. 354.

307. See *Classical Hebrew Poetry*, p. 203. For apposite comments on the possible danger of over-labelling, see L. Alonso Schökel's review, *Bib* 67 (1986), p. 122. Another example of mirror chiasmus is Prov. 17.15.

308. Cf. Collins, *Line-forms*, p. 123.

IP comes in the third line in Ps. 115.1:

l' lnw yhwh l' lnw	Not to us, Yahweh, not to us,
ky-lšmk tn kbwd	but to your own name give honour
'l hsdk w'l 'mtk	because of your kindness and fidelity.[309]

5.3.3. *Semantic Features.* Antithetic parallelism occurs in: Num. 24.9; Judg. 5.25; Jer. 12.13; 48.28a; Hos. 6.1; Mal. 1.4; Pss. 34.15; 45.8; 75.8 (cited above); 102.27; 109.28; 119.113; 126.5; Qoh. 1.4; 5.2; 6.4; Sir. 10.10b; 12.7; 14.4, 5a.[310]

Of these the most interesting is Ps. 45.8a:

'hbt ṣdq wtśn' rš'	You loved uprightness and hated wickedness,

that is [+ love] + [+ good] // [– love] + [– good].[311]

Word-pairs, of course, are used in almost all the texts. Of interest and importance are the following: Isa. 9.11; 53.13; 60.6; Jer. 32.31; 48.8b; 50.35b; Ezek. 6.11; 28.12; Hos. 7.11b; Mal. 3.4; Pss. 101.5; 107.37; Job 15.35; Prov. 6.12a; 20.12; 21.4; Qoh. 9.1; Sir. 30.23. See also above (5.3.1)

Lines which use or amount to formulas are: Gen. 29.17 (// 39.6; 1 Sam. 16.12; 25.3; Esther 2.7);[312] Num. 10.35 (// Ps. 68.2); 14.18; 1 Sam. 34.15; Jer. 51.26 (combines Isa. 28.16 and 1.7, both examples of IP), 19.25; Joel 2.13; Mic. 3.2; Pss. 103.8; 121.5; 136.12; 138.2 (= 115.1); Job 38.3b, and so on. See below.

Positive-negative parallelism occurs in Prov. 23.23 and Job 20.13, and hendiadys in Jer. 5.30 and Ps. 85.9b (cf. 2 Sam. 16.7).

5.3.4. *Clustering.* As I established in a previous article,[313] sustained sequences of lines with IP occur in classical Hebrew verse as well as in Akkadian though not in Ugaritic. Here additional examples (for Hebrew) are listed according to the number of full lines per cluster.

309. Previous example: Ps. 68.28b.

310. Already noted by J. Krašovec, *Antithetic Structure in Biblical Hebrew Poetry* (VTSup, 35; Leiden: Brill, 1984), pp. 124-27: Num. 24.9; Jer. 12.13a; Pss. 102.27-28; 109.28; 119.113; Qoh. 1.4.

311. Cf. *šarru kīma* [d][š]*amaš mīšara irām* [ragga izîr], 'Like Shamash, the king loves righteousness [and hates evil]'; Lambert, *Babylonian Wisdom Literature* , p. 223: 5, translation, p. 234.

312. Avishur, *Word-pairs*, pp. 215, 219, 644, 730.

313. See above, 'Classical Hebrew Verse'.

One and a half	Gen. 17.20; 31.43a; 1 Sam. 26.12; 1 Kgs 18.29; 22.4; 2 Kgs 3.7; 4.26; Hos. 2.7; 10.4a, 11b; 14.1b; Joel 2.9, 12; Ps. 37.27; Job 1.1; 2.11; 17.11; Prov. 9.2; 21.30; Qoh. 9.6; 12.1; Lam. 3.49.
Two	Gen. 24.35; Deut. 26.8; 28.3-6 (// 16-19); 1 Sam. 25.25; 2 Sam. 3.29b; 1 Kgs 5.13a; Isa. 9.9; 33.22; Jer. 3.24; 31.28; Ezek. 31.3; Hos. 11.8; Ps. 65.11; Job 30.26; 42.6; Ezra 1.4; Sir. 12.7 (cf. Num. 24.6; 1 Sam. 15.3; 2 Kgs 6.27; Ps. 48.9a; Job 33.9).
Two and a half	Jer. 9.25; 18.7; 32.21; 51.30; 1 Chron. 29.2; 2 Chron. 2.13.
Three	1 Sam. 16.18; Hos. 3.4;[314] 9.6; Sir. 6.11-13.
Four	Isa. 66.3.
Five and a half	Jer. 48.21-24a; 50.2.
Mixed	Ezek. 7.10-12; Ps. 148.8-10; Sir. 11.14.

5.3.5. *Structural Patterning*. The main type is

A - - - - A - - - -
A - - - - - - - - - - -

as in Deut. 29.22; 1 Sam. 12.4; 20.1; Isa. 41.26; Amos 8.5; Zeph. 3.12; Pss. 92.4; 144.14; Job 18.19; 37.13.

'm-lšbṭ 'm-l'rṣw	Whether for a correction, whether for his grace,
'm lḥsd ymṣ'hw	(or) whether for kindness—it reaches him.[315] (Job 37.13)

The pattern is extended in Zech. 10.4, inverted in Judg. 5.21; 1 Sam. 25.6 and Ps. 10.17.

5.3.6. *Rhetorical Functions*.

As an opening line:	Isa. 37.22; 57.14a; Jer. 4.5a; 46.14; 48.28a; 50.4; Ezek. 30.4; Hos. 14.5a; Joel 4.1; Zeph. 3.14; Pss. 12.5-6; 18.47; 24.4; 29.9; 32.1a; 82.5; 133.1; Sir. 11.7b; 16.22.

314. 'The six items are grouped in three pairs'; Andersen and Freedman, *Hosea*, p. 305.

315. The meaning 'his favour' proposed for *'rṣw* (root *rṣh*, with prosthetic *aleph*) by M.J. Dahood, has been accepted by Pope, *Job*, pp. 243-44, and L.L. Grabbe, *Comparative Philology and the Text of Job* (SBLDS, 34; Missoula, MT: Scholars Press, 1977), pp. 117-19.

To close:	Num. 29.9; Isa. 41.10; Jer. 13.11; 22.23; Ezek. 3.11; 19.24; 23.34; Pss. 2.2; 4.3; 34.15; 66.4; 122.4; 139.12; Job 42.6;[316] Qoh. 12.4; Sir. 39.15; 46.19 (cf. 50.27).
As a delaying device:	Ezek. 25.10; Hos. 4.3b; Prov. 17.3 (= 27.21); 19.26; 21.4; Sir. 25.22; 37.18.

5.3.7. *Compression*. Into a line with IP can be packed the equivalent of a couplet, which may explain why this type of parallelism is used in sayings and proverbs. For example, Jer. 8.20:

'br qṣyr klh qyṣ	Past is the harvest, gone the summer heat,
w'nḥnw lw' nwš'nw	but we are not yet rescued.

Such couplets could also be considered tricola—with the equivalent of three lines packed into two—or they may be the forerunners of true tricola with three full lines.[317] Of particular interest is the artificial proper name used in Isa. 8.1, 3:

mhr šll ḥš bz	Speedy for spoil, precipitate for plunder,

with the two halves in parallel.[318] The word-pair *šll // bz* recurs in Isa. 10.6 and Ezek. 29.19. Also, the collocation of *mhr* and *ḥyš* (Isa. 5.19) is here 'broken up' over two half-lines. With four words the whole horror of war is evoked and such compression is a strong feature of lines with IP.

O'Connor has commented on the constraints shared by proper names and verse in Hebrew. In fact, he cites Isa. 8.3 (only), but does not remark on the features described here.[319] Another, even more artificial name occurs in Isa. 9.5 (also cited by O'Connor) and it, too, may be a double instance of IP. This aspect is also to the fore in Exod. 15.11 and implicit in my rendering above (5.2).

316. On this verse, cf. W. Morrow, 'Consolation Rejection and Repentance in Job 42.6', *JBL* 105 (1986), pp. 211-25.

317. In fact, R. Yaron, 'The Climactic Tricolon', *JJS* 37 (1986), pp. 153-59, considers Prov. 10.26, 17.3, 15, 20.12, 25.3, 27.3 and 31.30a to be sets of three lines, not two.

318. Literally, 'Hastening for booty, rushing for plunder'. For philological discussion, cf. H. Wildberger, *Jesaja 1–12* (Neukirchen–Vluyn: Neukirchener Verlag, 1972), pp. 312-13. According to him both *ḥāš* and *mahēr* (for *m^{e}mahēr*) are most probably participles. He translates 'Eilbeute—Raschraub' and my own version is an attempt at alliteration.

319. *Hebrew Verse Structure*, pp. 160-61, §1.7.3.

5.4. *Occurrence and Distribution*

With no claim for precision, the figures that emerge overall (counting in all the passages listed above in 2, but disregarding dubious examples and not counting single lines within clusters) are as follows:

Genesis	27	Jonah	1
Exodus	4	Micah	11
Leviticus	4	Nahum	6
Numbers	11	Habakkuk	5
Deuteronomy	7	Zephaniah	10
Joshua	3	Zechariah	3
Judges 5	4	Malachi	5
1 Samuel	14	Psalms	119
2 Samuel	11	Job	27
1 Kings	8	Proverbs	51
2 Kings	8	Song of Songs	12
Isaiah 1–39	80	Qoheleth	20
40–55	35	Lamentations	6
56–66	16	Esther	5
Jeremiah	72	Daniel	1
Ezekiel	40	Nehemiah	3
Hosea	27	1 Chronicles	7
Joel	14	2 Chronicles	5
Amos	8	Ben Sira	40

Some of these books were unrepresented in my previous article (i.e., Genesis, Exodus, Leviticus, Numbers, Joshua, 2 Samuel, 1 and 2 Kings, Jonah, Micah, Zechariah, Malachi, Esther, Daniel, Nehemiah, 1 and 2 Chronicles), while to others (Nahum, Song of Songs) there have been no additions. Not unexpectedly, there are relatively few in the prose books, though Genesis and Qoheleth have quite a few examples. The figure for 2 Samuel is partly skewed by the poems incorporated there, the totals for Isaiah, Ezekiel, Hosea, Joel, Zephaniah, Malachi, Psalms and Ben Sira are large and Nahum is rich in clusters. High density of lines with IP is also evident in 2 Sam. 1.21 (see below), Jer. 31.1; and Psalms 26, 45, 48, 55, 68 and 78. The impressions conveyed by these numbers is that lines with IP are far from rare and occur in almost every book.

5.5. *IP and the Formula*

In view of the widespread use of lines with IP or, more accurately, half-line parallelism in Hebrew verse documented above (as well as in other verse traditions), it seems worth looking a little more closely at the function of such half-lines in the process of versification as far as we can reconstruct it. If, for instance, we take 'David's Lament over Saul and Jonathan' (2 Sam. 1.19-27) apart and pick out the half-lines (or their equivalents) it contains and arrange them in groups, the result is as follows.

1. noun in bound form + noun: *'ḥy yhwntn*; *bnwt h'rlym*; *bnwt yśr'l*; *bnwt plštym*; *hṣby yśr'l*; *ḥrb š'wl*; *kly mlḥmh*; *mgn gbrym*; *mgn š'wl*; *(w)śdy trwmt*; *'dy zhb*; *qšt yhwntn*.
2. as 1, with preposition: *bḥwṣwt 'šqlwn*; *btwk hmlḥmh*; *hry bglb'*; *m'hbt nšym*; *mdm ḥllym*; *mḥlb gbwrym*.
3. negative + noun: *'l ṭl*; *'l mṭr*.
4. negative + verb: *'l tbśrw*; *l' hprdw*; *pn-t'lznh*; *pn-tśmḥnh*.
5. adverb + verb: *m'rywt gbrw*; *mnšrym qlw*.
6. adjective + preposition + suffix: *ṣr-ly*.
7. verb + preposition + suffix: *n'mt-ly*.

These phrases account for nearly half the total words of the poem (50/100);[320] therefore it seems more than likely that one of the 'building blocks' used by the poet was the half-line.

Another example is Psalm 101, recently analysed from a different viewpoint by J.S. Kselman.[321] Of its 81 words, 42 make up half-lines, though the poem itself is not a cluster of half-lines. These too can be classified under a number of syntactical headings.

1. noun in bound state + noun: *p'ly 'wn*; *rš'y 'rṣ*.
2. as 1, with preposition: *bdrk tmym*; *bqrb byty* (twice); *btm-lbby*; *lngd 'yny* (also twice).
3. co-ordinated nouns: *ḥsd-wmšpṭ*.
4. noun + adjective: *gbh-'ynym*; *lbb 'qš*; *rḥb lbb*.
5. verb / noun: *dbr-bly'l*; *dbr šqrym*; *'śh-sṭym*; *'śh rmyh*.
6. verb + prepositional phrase: *'wtw 'ṣmyt*; *yswr mmny*.
7. negative + verb: *l'-'šyt*; *l'-ykwn*; *l'-yšb*.

The repetition of two of the phrases (vv. 2a, 7a and 3a, 7b) is significant not only in determining the overall structure, as already

320. On the 'vertical parallelism' in 2 Sam. 1.23, cf. *Classical Hebrew Poetry*, p. 170.

321. 'Psalm 101: Royal Confession and Divine Oracle', *JSOT* 33 (1985), pp. 45-62.

recognized,[322] but also because it indicates these phrases to be self-contained units. Additional proof comes from Kselman's article in which he showed (in a quite different context) that many of the half-lines units are identical with or correspond to half-line units in other sections of Hebrew poetry (Job, Proverbs, other Psalms).

Phrases of this type correspond to the 'paired expressions' or 'expression pairs' collected by Avishur in his study of word-pairs.[323] Many of these expressions consist of paired nouns connected by *waw*. This is not the place for a systematic presentation of 'expression pairs', but two further examples provide an indication of the material yet to be studied. One is Psalm 27, which contains seven such expressions (*'by w'my*; *'wry wyš'y*; *'šyrh w'zmrh*; *ḥzq wy'mṣ*; *ḥnny w'nny*; *kšlw wnplw*; *ṣry w'yby*) as well as some half-lines (vv. 4, 9, 12, 12). The other is Lamentations 1–5, with over 40 groups of two near-synonyms connected by *waw*, for example *btwlty wbḥwry*, 'my lasses and lads' (Lam. 1.18c).[324] Similar groupings elsewhere have also been identified by other scholars.[325] Particularly significant is H. Weippert's study of the speech passages in prose of Jeremiah.[326] In it she identified several formulas which, in fact, correspond in length to twin half-lines. Examples are *byd ḥzqh wb(')zr(w)' nṭwyh*, 'with powerful hand and extended arm';[327] *l'wp hšmym wlbhmt h' rṣ*, 'for the birds of the air and beasts of the land';[328] and *l'lh wlšmh wlśrqh*

322. H. Kenik, 'Code of Conduct for a King', *JBL* 95 (1976), pp. 391-403.

323. *Word-Pairs*, pp. 318-21, 607-25, 769, following U. Cassuto.

324. Also Lam. 1.7, 12, 18, 19; 2.2, 5, 6 (×2), 8, 9 (×2), 11, 12, 14 (×2), 18, 20, 21 (×2), 22 (×2); 3.2 (×2), 4, 5, 8, 18, 19 (×2), 38, 47 (×2), 50, 63; 4.12, 21 (×2); 5.1 (without *waw*: 2.16, 19; note the repetitions in 1.16 and 4.15). Avishur's assertion (*Word-pairs*, p. 624) that 'the Book of Lamentations is fundamentally composed of verses rooted in expression pairs similar to those of the El Amarna letters' is a little sweeping but has a core of truth in it.

325. O'Connor, *Hebrew Verse Structure*, pp. 380-81; B. Margalit, 'Studia Ugaritica I: Introduction to Ugaritic Prosody', *UF* 7 (1975), pp. 289-313, esp. p. 294.

326. *Die Prosareden des Jeremiabuches* (BZAW, 132; Berlin: de Gruyter, 1973), esp. pp. 107-27.

327. Deut. 4.34; 5.15; 7.19; 11.2; 26.8; 1 Kgs 8.42; Jer. 32.21; Ezek. 20.33, 34; Ps. 136.12; 2 Chron. 6.32; and with reversal of attributes, Jer. 21.5. See Weippert, *Prosareden*, p. 76 and n. 217.

328. Jer. 7.33; 15.3; 16.4 etc. This formula and its variants are set out in tabular form by Weippert, *Prosareden*, p. 185; see also pp. 184 and 186. To the texts cited by her add Dan. 2.38 (see next note).

wlḥrph, 'to (be) a curse, a terror, a hissing and a byword'.[329]

It would seem, then, that the expression pair, in whatever guise, is equivalent to the (twin) half-line, and each is used as an inseparable component of verse. This amounts to saying that the half-line corresponds to the formula of oral-formulaic theory. In essence, this is not a new suggestion since R.C. Culley put forward much the same proposal several years ago.[330] However, my approach is different from his. He was looking at Hebrew verse for the equivalent of the formula established by M. Parry and others and he isolated segments of verse-lines which seemed to fit metrical slots. Some of these segments are, in fact, half-lines.[331] I have been examining symmetrical parallelism within the line, concluding that half-lines tend to be metrically interchangeable. In effect this means that Culley's definition of the formula must now be extended to include half-lines (the 'half colon' in his terminology).[332] This does not account for lines which cannot be split into half-lines, or are longer than two half-lines (perhaps even incorporating half-lines, as in Ps. 66.4 and elsewhere) or even shorter.

5.6. *Stichometry*

The isolation of lines with inner (half-line) parallelism is bound up with determining the lineation of a poem or segment of verse.

329. Jer. 29.8, etc., as tabulated by Weippert, *Prosareden*, p. 188. For the 'build/plant—destroy' formula (with half-line parallelism) in Jer. 18.7, 9, 21.28, see Weippert, *Prosareden*, p. 194. IP formulas in Aramaic are also collected by P.W. Coxon, 'The "List" Genre and Narrative Style in the Court Tales of Daniel', *JSOT* 35 (1986), pp. 95-121; texts include sets of one and a half in Dan. 2.38, 47, and sets of two (according to Coxon, 'The "List" Genre', p. 100, a 'fourfold list') in 2.2, 27, 3.21, 4.4 and 5.11.

330. *Oral Formulaic Language in the Biblical Psalms* (Toronto: University of Toronto Press, 1967). He concludes (p. 118), 'If the investigation of the preceding chapters is correct, it appears that the major device in Hebrew oral composition was the formula'.

331. Examples are *'rk 'pym wrb ḥsd* (Num. 14.18, Exod. 34.6; Joel 2.13; Jon. 4.2; Pss. 86.15; 103.8; 145.8), Culley, *Oral Formulaic Language*, pp. 62-63 (§55); *swr mr' w'śh ṭwb* (Pss. 34.15; 37.27), Culley, *Oral Formulaic Language*, p. 84, (§144); *šyrw lw zmrw lw* (Ps. 105.2), Culley, *Oral Formulaic Language*, pp. 59-60 (§51, where the variants are listed) and *'šyrh w'zmrh* (Pss. 27.6; 57.8), Culley, *Oral Formulaic Language*, p. 75 (§102).

332. The coincidence of line and formula(ic phrase) is discussed by Culley, *Oral Formulaic Language*, p. 29.

Occasionally, recognition of such lines can help solve problems of tricky stichometry. An example is Mic. 7.1:

a	*'lly ly ky hyyty*	Woe is me! For I am
b	*k'spy-qyṣ k'llwt bṣyr*	like (after) the summer harvest, the grapes (already) gleaned.
c	*'yn- škwl l'kwl*	There is no cluster to eat,
d	*bkwrh 'wth npšy*	or ripe fig which my appetite craves.

Line b matches lines c and its parallel d in length, which may indicate the layout as above.[333] Another difficult passage is Ps. 10.17, set out above (5.3.1). 2 Kgs 5.26, Pss. 59.13, 62.4, 88.7, 130.5-6, 135.6, Prov. 6.12-14, 7.7 and other passages also present problems of this nature which may be resolved by identifying lines with IP.

5.7. *Closing Comments*

My evaluation of the material presented here clearly needs refinement. Aspects of metre have only been touched on (chiefly with reference to the formula), but the line with IP is evidently on a par with the acrostic as a means of defining metrical patterns. The contribution that 'expressions pairs' or the twin half-line formula can make to the thorny problem of determining whether a passage is prose, poetry or 'high-flown' prose[334] has yet to be assessed. These problems must be held over for another occasion.

6. *Classical Hebrew Once More*[335]

There are two reasons for this article. One is to present even more examples of half-line parallelism. The other is to discuss aspects of theory in the light of recent studies on Hebrew and Ugaritic verse.[336]

333. For different lineation, cf. R. Vuilleumier and C.-A. Keller, *Michée Nahoum Habacuc Sophonie* (Neuchâtel: Delachaux et Niestlé, 1971), p. 78, and W. Rudolph, *Micha—Nahum—Habakuk—Zephanja* (Gütersloh: Mohr, 1975), pp. 120-21. For an explanation of *'lly*, cf. Watson, *Classical Hebrew Poetry*, p. 310.

334. My approximate rendering of 'Kunstprosa', on which see Weippert, *Prosareden*, pp. 76-81, esp. p. 80. Whether or not one can speak of 'Entmetrisierung' in several stages (p. 78) remains to be determined.

335. First published in *LA* 39 (1989), pp. 27-36.

336. M.C.A. Korpel and J.C. de Moor, 'Fundamentals of Ugaritic and Hebrew Poetry', *UF* 18 (1986), pp. 173-212, reprinted in W. van der Meer and J.C. de Moor (eds.), *The Structural Analysis of Biblical and Canaanite Poetry* (JSOTSup, 74; Sheffield: JSOT Press, 1984), pp. 1-61; O. Loretz and I. Kottsieper,

6.1. *Additional Hebrew Examples*

The following additional passages in Hebrew can be listed. A few examples are set out by way of illustration.

Gen. 12.12b; 20.5; 24.53; 26.5, 14; 28.20d; 31.36, 39, 43; 32.4; 50.9.[337]

w'mrw 'štw z't	They (the Egyptians) will say: 'That's his wife'.
whrgw 'ty w'tk yḥyw	Me they will kill but let you live.[338] (12.12)

Exod. 4.10, 11; 6.6; 8.1, 9; 12.32; 18.21; 19.6, 13; 20.17, 24; 22.23 (EV 24); 34.6-7; 35.31.

whyw	then shall be
nšykm 'lmnwt wbnykm ytmym	your women widows and your children fatherless.[339] (22.23)

This line of verse closes a prosaic threat and uses a stock word-pair.

Lev. 3.1, 17; (15.22); (5.7; 8.17; 10.10?, 15; 15.22; 19.11, 18, 26b, 30; 22.24; 26.16; 27.10, 14 [cf. 33]).

Num. 33.55 (// Josh. 23.13).

Deut. 4.34; 10.20; 12.29; 28.20, (61), 65.

Josh. 1.6, 9; (10.25); 7.24; 8.1 (// 10.25); 10.12-13; 12.8; 20.6; 22.5 (// 23.14), 8, 22, 26 (// 28); 23.7; 24.12, 19.

l' bḥrbk wl' bqštk	neither by your sword nor by your bow.[340] (24.12)

Judg. 11.19; 14.16; 17.10 (// 18.19); 18.7 (// 27).[341]

Colometry in Ugaritic and Biblical Poetry (UBL, 5; Altenberge: CIS-Verlag, 1987); L. Alonso Schökel, *A Manual of Hebrew Poetics* (Subsidia biblica, 11; Rome: Pontificio Istituto Biblico, 1988).

337. Also, perhaps, Gen. 7.23 and 16.7.

338. See A. Niccacci, *Sintassi del verbo ebraico nella prosa biblica classica* (Jerusalem: Franciscan Printing Press, 1986), §11, p. 20 for the tense shift (w^{e}QATAL to WAW-X-YIQTOL) within this line. Note the chiasmus.

339. Curiously omitted by Avishur, *Word-Pairs*, pp. 373-74.

340. Described by Avishur, *Word-Pairs*, p. 258, as 'in syndetic combination'.

341. Also, Judg. 1.15c and 11.22b.

rq-śn'tny wl'-'hbtny	You only hate me and do not love me! (14.16)

Here the (inverted) word-pair *'hb // śn'* is used.

1 Sam. 8.12; 15.29;[342] 17.46; 25.3, 16.[343]

2 Sam. 20.20; 22.47 (// Ps. 18.47); 24.17 (contrast 1 Chron. 21.7).[344]

1 Kgs 1.35; 2.4; 3.22, 22, 23, 23; 4.16a // 17; 5.5 (EV 4.25), 13b (EV 4.33); 8.23, 25, 42, 48; 9.8; 18.27,[345] 29b (cf. 26); 20.31 (cf. 32).[346]

2 Kgs 2.2 (// 4 // 6), 19; 4.10, 23; 6.10, 27; 11.12; 14.16; 17.36; 19.21 (// Isa. 37.22), 26 (// Isa. 37.27); 22.36; 23.3, 25.[347]

Isa. 7.15, 16;[348] 26.6; 32.2;[349] 58.13; 66.6.

Jer. 11.6, 12; 13.11b, 14; 18.7, 9; 14.10 (see below); 20.4b; 21.4; 23.29 (// 30.23); 31.27; 32.4, 11, 17, 19, 32, 39, 41, 44 (cf. 33.13!); 33.15; 34.4-5; 50.41.[350]

Ezek. 1.18; 3.5 // 6.7; 4.10; 8.2; 11.3, 7; 16.7, 10, 16, 36; 18.21; 21.31; 22.27; 24.8, 16; 31.3-4a; cf. 35.5b, 6; 44.7 // 9.

Hos. 1.2;[351] 3.2; 9.9b; (cf. 8.13!, discussed below); 12.5.

Amos 3.12.

342. Cf. Jer. 4.28 and Alonso Schökel, *Hebrew Poetics*, pp. 131-32.

343. Also 1 Sam. 4.20 and 8.12.

344. Also 2 Sam. 2.7 and 3.31.

345. For the meaning of the expression, cf. G.A. Rendsburg, 'The Mock of Baal in 1 Kings 18:27', *CBQ* 50 (1988), pp. 414-17.

346. Also 2.33; 3.8, 13; 6.18b, 38; 8.35, 37, 38, 59; 10.5, 6b, 25; 14.18a; 15.19; 17.10; 18.38; 20.5, 43 (// 21.4); 21.19; 22.27.

347. Also 2 Kgs 2.11, 16; 3.4; 4.14b; 5.7; 7.10b; 8.5; 10.18; 16.5; 17.4, 13, 34, 37; 18.8b; 19.1b; 20.1; 23.5.

348. Alonso Schökel, *Hebrew Poetics*, p. 43 (see discussion below).

349. Cf. Watson, *Classical Hebrew Poetry*, p. 259 and contrast E. Zurro, review of O. Loretz, *Der Prolog des Jesaja Buches (1,1–2,5): Ugaritologische und kolometrische Studien zum Jesaja-Buch*, *AuOr* 5 (1987), pp. 316-19.

350. Also Jer. 33.4, 5, 6, 10, 12, 18; 34.17, 20; 35.8b, 13; 36.30; 41.5; 42.10 (// 44.12); 44.9b, 17 (// 21).

351. On the ellipsis of the verb *yld* here, cf. Alonso Schökel, *Hebrew Poetics*, pp. 166-67. Note, incidentally, that in his review of my book of Hebrew poetry in *UF* 19 (1987), pp. 467-68, O. Loretz gives the correct stichometry for Hos. 4.1.

Jon. 4.2.[352]

Hag. 1.6a.

Zach. 4.6; 5.4c, 9; 7.6; 8.13, 18, 19, 22; 14.7, 9.

Pss. 116.8;[353] 118.17a (cf. Ezek. 18.21).

Job 28.27.

Prov. 21.30.

Ruth 2.23; 3.10.

Cant. 8.10.

Qoh. 12.13.

Est. 9.31.

Neh. 2.19; 4.11; 9.17.

Dan. 1.10; 9.5, 7, 19, 19, 23, 24b; 11.17, 33; 12.4a, 4b (for passages in Aramaic see below).

2 Chron. 25.14; 32.7; 36.17b.

Sir. 46.5b.[354]

Comments on Occurrence. Half-line parallelism is now attested in Haggai, Ruth and Nehemiah (previously unrecognized). Significant additions are to occurrences in Exodus (+ 14), Leviticus (+ 13), Joshua (+ 14), 1 and 2 Kings (+ 17 and + 15), Zachariah (+ 6) and especially Daniel (+ 11). The total for Jeremiah is now close on 100. The occurrences in prose are particularly noteworthy (see below) and there is no doubt that further examples remain to be identified.

6.2. *Examples in Ugaritic*

Four more passages in Ugaritic can be added to previous lists.[355] They are *KTU* 1.1 v. 27; 1.82 rev. 43; 2.17:1-3; 3.9 r. 15-16.

352. For the presence of sarcasm, cf. Alonso Schökel, *Hebrew Poetics*, p. 164.
353. Cf. Alonso Schökel, *Hebrew Poetics*, p. 38.
354. Also Sir. 4.1; 39.15.
355. Sections 1.4, 2.7 and 3.5.

1.1 v. 27	*ltzd. ltptq* How you covet it! How you want to take it over![356]
1.82 r. 43	*k'ṣm. lttn. kabnm tiggn* if the trees do not give (sound), if the stones do not murmur![357]
2.17: 1-3	*lyblt. ḫbṯm ap ksphm lyblt* I have not brought the freebooters: I have not even brought their wages.[358]
3.9 r. 15-16	*tn ksp ṯql d'mnk* 'Give the money, weigh out what you have'.[359]

For the word-pair *ytn // šql* cf. Job 28.15.[360] Of course, these last two passages in Ugaritic are prose (see below).

6.3. *Indications that the Half-Line is a Unit*

Korpel and de Moor do not consider the half-line or hemistich to be a building block in poetry 'because many cola cannot be divided into two whereas others should clearly be divided into three if we are to adopt this principle'.[361] They further maintain that a line such as *mdl. 'r. ṣmd. pḥl* (*KTU* 1.4 iv 9 etc.) is really a bicolon which 'was written on one line [on the tablet] to save space'.[362] In general, they print lines

356. De Moor, *Anthology*, p. 28. A. Caquot, 'Un receuil ougaritique de formules magiques: KTU 1.82', *SEL* 5 (1988), pp. 31-43, 43 translates 'car les arbres ne regardent (?) pas, car les pierres ne murmurent pas'.

357. De Moor, *Anthology*, p. 181.

358. Cf. *UT* §13.50 for the chiastic structure here. For recent translations, cf. M. Dietrich and O. Loretz, 'Philologische und inhaltliche Probleme im Schreiben *KTU* 2.17', *UF* 14 (1982), pp. 83-88, 86, and M. Dijkstra, 'Marginalia to the Ugaritic Letters in *KTU* (I)', *UF* 19 (1987), pp. 37-48, 38-39.

359. E.D. Mallon, 'The Ugaritic Verb in Letters and Administrative Documents' (dissertation, Catholic University of America, 1982), p. 73.

360. This word-pair is not listed in *RSP* I, II or III or by Avishur, *Word-Pairs*. Yet another example in prose, which must be fortuitous, is *KTU* 1.112:3-4 *wṯq[l] ksp. wṣ' rgbt.*, 'and a shekel of silver and a dish of reverance'—note the expression *ṣ' rgb[t]* (?) in line 25; on *rgbt*, see G. del Olmo Lete, 'Ritual regio ugarítico de evocación/adivinición (KTU 1.112)', *AuOr* 2 (1984), pp. 197-206, 200 n. 12 and to the cognates cited there add (EA) Akkadian *ragabu* for which see *AHw*, p. 941b and C. Grave, 'Northwest Semitic *ṣapanu* in a Break-up of an Egyptian Stereotype Phrase in *EA* 147', *Or* 53 (1984), pp. 161-82, 180 and n. 112 (on EA 147:13-15).

361. Korpel and de Moor, 'Fundamentals', p. 175 n. 8.

362. Korpel and de Moor, 'Fundamentals', p. 175.

with double half-line (internal) parallelism as two lines[363] but there is one exception. For them *KTU* 1.6 vi 16-20 is a set of eight lines not twelve:

> *yt'n. kgmrm*
> *mt. 'z. b'l.* (etc.)

They comment, 'The strong internal parallelism and the total absence of markers of separation render any subdivision artificial. It is a strophe of four verses.'[364]

There are, in fact, strong indications that the half-line is a unit which always occurs combined with another unit (usually, but not always, another half-line) to form a line. Although it is modular it rarely occurs alone; an example in Ugaritic may be the second colon in *KTU* 1.24: 27-28

aqrbk abh. b'[l]	I will bring you in contact with her father Ba'lu,
yǵtr. 'ṯtr[t?]	he will entreat 'Athtar(t?).[365]

In Hebrew there is the recurrent refrain *hllw yh*,[366] an independent half-line. These indicators are as follows.

6.3.1. *Expansion*. With the addition of a half-line the two-phrase set *w'yn qwl w'yn 'nh* of 1 Kgs 18.26 becomes *w'yn-qwl w'yn-'nh w'yn qšb*, 'but no sound, no reply, no heed', in v. 29, the climax of the episode. The same type of expansion (1 to 1½) occurs in Jer. 33.10b (contrast 10a) and 2 Kgs 23.25 (see under 'formula').

Other '1½' long lines are: Gen. 26.14; 31.43; Exod. 4.10, 11; 8.1, 9; Deut. 28.65; 1 Sam. 8.12; 2 Kgs 17.36; 23.25; Jer. 33.18; Dan. 9.24b.

6.3.2. *Interchangeability (Inversion) within Formulaic Lines*. In the prose narrative 1 Kgs 3.16-28 Solomon suggests settling the dispute of the two courtesans by cutting the surviving child in half. The key sentence of the narrative recurs three times in the form

363. Korpel and de Moor, 'Fundamentals', pp. 179, 188, 192 and 197.

364. Korpel and de Moor, 'Fundamentals', p. 198. For a translation of this passage, see now M. Dietrich and O. Loretz, 'Ringen und laufen als Sport in Ugarit (*KTU* 1.6 VI 16B-22A)', *UF* 19 (1987), pp. 19-21.

365. De Moor, *Anthology*, p. 144 for translation of the first line.

366. Pss. 104.35, 45; 106.1, 48; 111.1; 112.1; 113.1; 115.18; 116.19; 117.2; 135.1, 21; 146.1, 10; 147.1, 20; 148.1, 14; 149.1, 9; 150.1, 6.

bny ḥḥy wbnk hmt	It is my son who is alive but your son is dead

(v. 22a, spoken by the second woman and v. 23ab, spoken by Solomon) and once (v. 22b used by the first woman) in the inverted form

bnk hmt wbny ḥḥy

Each time it is preceded by different phrases (*l' ky*, three times; *zh-*, once) but remains an independent statement. The only alteration is the inversion of the two component clauses, *bny ḥḥy* and *bnk hmt* in v. 22b, within the statement. This is very significant because it indicates each half-line clause to be a separate unit.[367]

Similar inversion of half-lines within a line occurs in Akkadian, too. The expression

attā lū mutīma anāku lū aššatka	You be my husband and I'll be your wife

common to the *Epic of Gilgamesh* and *Nergal and Ereshkigal* corresponds to

attā lū aššatu anāku lū mutka

in *Ardat-lili*.[368] In fact, there were separate formulas for each of the two participants: in the wedding ceremony husband and wife each said the appropriate formula.[369]

6.3.3. *The A- A- // A— Pattern (see below)*. The two half-line (A-A-) correspond in length to the full line (A—).

6.3.4. *Modular Use of the Half-Line*. In Isa. 22.3

kl qṣynyk	*nddw yḥd*	*mrḥwq brḥw*
kl nmṣ'yk	*'srw yḥdw*	*mqšt 'srw*
All your leaders	ran away together	to a distance did flee
All those in you	were captured together	without a bow were captured

367. Other double half-line expressions used in this episode are *gm ly gm lk* (v. 26) and the tellingly mimetic *'t ḥḥṣy l'ḥt w't ḥḥṣy l'ḥt* (v. 25).

368. Texts: T. Abusch, 'Ishtar's Proposal and Gilgamesh's Refusal: An Interpretation of *The Gilgamesh Epic*, Tablet 6, Lines 1-79', *HR* 26 (1986), pp. 143-87, 149 and n. 12.

369. Abusch, 'Ishtar's Proposal', pp. 143-87, with references; the expression is negated in divorce.

there are three components in each line: *kl qṣynk* (corresponding to *kl nmṣ'yk*); *nddw yḥd* (// *'srw yḥdw*) and *mrḥwq brḥw* (// *mqšt 'srw*). In other words, these phrases are metrically equivalent. See below on 1 Kgs 3.16-28.

Additional evidence is available from Ugaritic. In the well-known tricolon

ht ibk b'lm
ht ibk tmḫṣ
ht tṣmt ṣrtk

the last two lines are formed by repetition of the initial *ht* and the splitting up of the (unattested) single line *ibk tmḫṣ / tṣmt ṣrtk* which is clearly chiastic[370]

ht ibk tmḫṣ
ht tṣmt ṣrtk

On the other hand, though, it is also possible for the half-line to occur alone, as for example in Gen. 20.6

(I know that) you did this in integrity of heart
(*btm-lbbk*)

The phrase used in v. 5 is *btm-lbby wbnqyn kpy*, 'in the integrity of my heart and the innocence of my hands'.[371] The half-line and double half-line phrases are interchangeable. Similar is the contraction of *bzrw' nṭwyh wbšpṭym gdlym* of Exod. 6.6 *bšpṭym gdlym* in 7.5. These are not expansions since the abbreviated form comes later in the narrative.

In conclusion it is clear that while the half-line can occasionally occur on its own in both Ugaritic and Hebrew this only happens when there is no parallel half-line. (This in turn gives rise to sets of $1\frac{1}{2}$, $2\frac{1}{2}$ etc.) When there is an even number of half-lines (2, 4, 6, etc.) the result is a 'tidy' set of full lines (1, 2, 3, etc.). These verse traditions only tolerate an independent half-line if it cannot be matched.

In some ways, in fact, the isolated line with inner parallelism comes

370. D.T. Tsumura, 'The Literary Structure of Psalm 46.2-8', *Annual of the Japanese Biblical Institute* 6 (1980), pp. 29-55, 31. Note M.C. Astour's comment, 'Remarks on KTU 1.96', *SEL* 5 (1988), pp. 1-24, 16: 'After all, pairs of words connected by status constructus... were counted as metric units in Ugaritic prosody'.

371. The word pair denotes cultic purity.

close to what Alonso Schökel has termed the 'rhythmic cell'.[372] According to Alonso Schökel, the rhythm of Isa. 7.14-16 is 2 + 2 throughout, with a final 2 + 2 + 3 identified by recognition of the rhythmic cell in vv. 14 and 15 (*mā'ôs bārā' ûbāḥôr baṭṭôb*).[373]

6.4. *Characteristics*

The following patterns occur: A- A- // A—

l' tgnb wl' tkḥšw	You must not steal; you must not cheat;
wl' tšqrw 'yšb'mytw	you must not swindle a fellow-man.
	(Lev. 19.11)
	Then the slayer may go again
'l - 'yrw w'l-bytw	to his town and to his house
'l-h'yr 'šr-ns mšm	to the town from which he fled.
	(Josh. 20.6)

Also Jer. 13.14 and Dan. 9.19.[374] The pattern is inverted in Lev. 19.26b and 1 Kgs 3.13.

Enumeration.[375]

Itemization is a common form of half-line parallelism: Gen. 26.5; Exod. 20. 17, 24; 35.31; Lev. 8.17; 10.10; Josh. 7.24; 12.8; 22.8; 23.7; 1 Kgs 2.22; 5.13b; 8.37b-38a; 18.38; 20.5; 2 Kgs 4.10; 17.34; Jer. 13.11b; 32.32; 35.8b; 42.18 (etc.); Zach. 8.19; Dan. 11.33; 2 Chron. 36.17b and so on.

Sets of two: (some are already entered under 'lists') Exod. 18.21; 20.24; Lev. 8.17; 10.10; Josh. 23.7; 1 Kgs 5.13b; Jer. 32.32; Ezek. 16.10; Zach. 8.19.

Set of three: Jer. 32.44 (// 33.13).

Clusters: Jer. 33.10; 44.17; Ezek. 31.3-4a; Zech. 7.6.

Formulas and formulaic phrases: Jer. 11.6, 12; Gen. 24.53; 1 Kgs 10.25; 2 Kgs 2.2, 4, 6; 12.14; Dan. 9.7. Variations on *byd ḥzqh wbzrw' nṭwyh* (Deut. 4.34) occur in Exod. 6.6, 2 Kgs 17.36, Jer. 21.5, 32.17 and elsewhere.[376] The phrase *bkl lb wbkl npš*,

372. L. Alonso Schökel, *Hebrew Poetics*, p. 42; *Estudios de poética hebrea* (Barcelona: Juan Flors, 1963), p. 169.

373. Alonso Schökel, *Hebrew Poetics*, p. 43.

374. Cf. Isa. 66.6.

375. Here I accept L. Alonso Schökel's comment—in his review of my book of Hebrew poetry, *Bib* 67 (1968), pp. 121-22—that 'numeration' is preferable to the term 'list'.

376. Cf. F.I. Andersen and D.N. Freedman, *Hosea* (AB 24; Garden City, NY:

2 Kgs 23.3 is found with different suffixes in Josh. 22.5, 23.14, 1 Kgs 2.4, 8.48 and Jer. 32.41.[377] In 2 Kgs 23.25 it is extended to

bkl lbbw wbkl npšw wbkl m'dw

The distinction between prose and poetry is evident from two sets of passages:

wtdbr bpyk wbydk ml't	you spoke with your mouth and with your hand fulfilled (1 Kgs 8.24)

is much more succinct than:

'šr dbr bpyw 't dwd 'by wbydw ml'	who with his hand had fulfilled what he promised with his mouth to David my father (1 Kgs 8.15)

Jer. 36.30 is closer to verse

	And his corpse shall be cast out
lḥrb bywm wlqrḥ blylh	to heat by day and to frost by night;

than is Gen. 31.40 'By day heat consumed me and cold at night and sleep fled from my eyes'.[378]

It is significant that of the four additional examples in Ugaritic, two are in prose texts (*KTU* 2.17:1-3 and 3.9 r. 15-16) an indication that the examples from Hebrew prose have been correctly identified.

Anacrusis is a common component of lines with half-line parallelism and is very clear from the parallel passages Hos. 8.13b (quoted in Jer. 14.10) and 9.9b. Hos. 8.13b has already been listed;[379]

'th	Now
yzkr 'wnm wypqd ḥṭ'tm	he will remember their sin, and will punish their fault.

Hos. 9.9b is identical apart from lack of the initial *'th*. Accordingly, *'th* does not belong to the pattern of the line which has independent status.

Finally, antithesis can be mentioned, even though it is rare: Gen. 12.12; 1 Kgs 2.33; 3.22a, b, 23a, b; Hag. 1.6a.

Doubleday, 1980), pp. 510-11, 518; A.D.H. Mayes, *Deuteronomy* (NCB; London: Oliphants, 1979), p. 158.

377. Cf. Avishur, *Word-pairs*, pp. 218, 568-69, though he does not cite either 2 Kgs 23.3 or Jer. 32.41.

378. Similarly, contrast Prov. 17.15 (verse) with Deut. 25.1 (prose). See now my 'Half-Line Parallelism as Indicative of Verse in Hebrew Prose', in de Moor and Watson, *Verse in Ancient Near Eastern Prose*, pp. 331-44.

379. Above, p. 147 n. 208.

The following examples of IP in Aramaic can be added to those already recognized:[380] Dan. 2.38, 47; 4.9, 27; 5.3b, 4b, 18; 6.9; 7.10, 23; Ezra 4.12; *Gen. Apoc.* xix 14-15; xxii 10-11, 12-13; *KAI* 215:10.23; Bowl 13.18.[381] New passages with IP in Phoenician and Punic are: *KAI* 4:6-7;[382] 24:11-12;[383] 26 A I 19; A III 8-9;[384] 74:10.[385]

6.5. *Conclusions*

In summary form the following holds true of internal or half-line parallelism. Now that even more occurrences have been identified and the distribution covers virtually all the books of the Hebrew Bible there can be no doubt at all that this type of parallelism is an established part of Hebrew versification. Further, the half-line does occur alone but only when it cannot form part of a full line. In addition, it is very interesting that double half-line parallelism is also found in prose (both in Hebrew and in Ugaritic). Can it be that such lines belong to natural speech rhythms?[386]

380. §2.5.

381. J. Naveh and S. Shaked, *Amulets and Magic Bowls: Aramaic Incantations of Late Antiquity* (Jerusalem: Magnes; Leiden: Brill, 1985), pp. 202-203.

382. Avishur, *Word-pairs*, pp. 216, 546.

383. Avishur, *Word-pairs*, pp. 216, 591.

384. Avishur, *Word-pairs*, p. 217.

385. Cf. Avishur, *Word-pairs*, p. 449. Note the following example in Mishnaic Hebrew *hy ḥsyd hy ʿnw*, 'Alas, O pious one; alas, O weak one' (*b. Sanh.* 11a, cited by Greenberg, *Ezekiel*, p. 67).

386. For the same phenomenon in modern Arabic it is worth consulting M.A.F. Yassin, 'Spoken Arabic Proverbs', *BSOAS* 51 (1988), pp. 59-68. For Ugaritic, see the comments by M. Dietrich and O. Loretz, *Die Keilalphabete: Die phönizisch-kanaanäischen und altarabischen Alphabete in Ugarit* (ALASP, 1; Münster: UGARIT-Verlag, 1988), pp. 196-97: 'Exkurs II—Sprechzäsuren bei der Rezitation des Alphabets'.

A recently recognized example of half-line parallelism in Assyrian is *i-ri-šu ma-al-ka-ni* / *i-t[al-la]-lu na-at-ba-ka-ni*, 'The water channels rejoice, the gullies cry out with joy' (Banquet Stele of Aššurnaṣirpal II 10) for which cf. J.V. Kinnier Wilson, 'Lines 40-52 of the Banquet Stele of Aššurnaṣirpal II', *Iraq* 50 (1988), pp. 79-82, 80-81. See E. Revell, 'Pausal Forms and the Structure of Biblical Poetry', *VT* 31 (1981), pp. 186-99, esp. on 'unbalanced distichs' (p. 190). His examples are Pss. 31.3; 40.3; 78.20; Prov. 30.14; Isa. 11.13; 45.12; Jer. 8.23 etc. p. 190 and n. 19. He also refers to extra-biblical texts, e.g. *Atra-ḫasis* I 1-2, 3-4 etc. and 11QPs^a 151.6; 151.4 (pp. 193-96).

Chapter 4

GENDER-MATCHED PARALLELISM

1. *Ugaritic Poetry*[1]

The poetic device of gender-matched synonymous parallelism[2] was first identified in Ugaritic[3] and then found to occur in classical Hebrew poetry and elsewhere. In this paper occurrences of GMS in Ugaritic poetry will be looked at, and from the data some conclusions will be drawn. Two basic problems bedevil discussion of possible examples in Ugaritic: uncertainty of interpretation and our partial ignorance of noun gender. The result is that some of the examples given may not be incontrovertible; they are included for the sake of completeness, several appearing only in footnotes. For ease of reference the texts will be presented in the sequence used by *KTU*. The principal examples will be numbered sequentially to facilitate cross-references.

(1) *KTU* 1.2 i 25-26

aḥd ilm t'ny	One of the gods answered
lḥt mlak ym	the tablets (f.) of Yam's messengers (m.),
t'dt tpṭ nh[*r*]	the embassy (f.) of Judge Nahar (m.).[4]

Though strictly speaking the gender of two nouns linked by the construct state is that of the first,[5] the evident symmetry of gender (f.-m. // f.-m.) is intentional as shown by the choice of *t'dt*, corresponding to

1. First published in *UF* 13 (1981), pp. 181-87.
2. Here abbreviated to GMS.
3. By U. Cassuto, *The Goddess Anath* (Jerusalem: Magnes, 1971), pp. 44-46.
4. On *t'dt* cf. J.C.L. Gibson, *Canaanite Myths and Legends* (Edinburgh: T. & T. Clark, 1978), p. 159.
5. For details, see M.H. Ibrahim, *Grammatical Gender: Its Origin and Development* (The Hague: Mouton, 1973), pp. 59 and 96.

lḥt (both f.). GMS is merely ornamental in function.[6]

(2) *KTU* 1.3 ii 9-11

tḥth kkdrt ri[*š*]	Under her (roll) heads (m.) like balls (f.),
'lh kirbym kp	above her (fly) hands (f.) like locusts (m.)
kqṣm ǵrmn kp mhr	like destructive grasshoppers (m.) warriors' hands (f.).

The use of mis-matching gender in each line serves to reinforce the set of three similes.[7]

(3) *KTU* 1.3 ii 25-27

tǵdd kbdh bṣḥq	With laughter (m.) does her liver (f.). swell,
ymlu lbh bšmḫt	with happiness (f.) is her heart (m.) full,
kbd 'nt tšyt	Anath's liver (f.) (is full) with victory (f.).

Another three-line strophe using GMS; see example 2. The chiastic gender pattern of the first two lines is, in effect, merismus, as the verb *mlu* indicates. For the final line see the comment on example 6.

(4) *KTU* 1.3 iii 14-17 etc.
qryy barṣ mlḥmt
št b'prm ddym

The translation of this repeated passage is disputed; Gray proposed 'I am averse to strife on earth; scatter love-tokens on the ground...'[8] It is possible that both nouns in the first line are feminine and those in the second, masculine, but until a consensus is reached on what the quatrain refers to, little can be decided concerning its poetic structure.[9]

(5) *KTU* 1.3 iii 22-25

rgm 'ṣ	A tree's tale (m.-m.)
wlḫšt abn	and a stone's sussuration (f.-f.).

The remarks on example 1 apply here, too, only the genders in each line now match. It may be no accident that Jer. 2.27, besides personifying these objects as here, also makes explicit reference to their

6. *KTU* 1.2 iv 20-21 may be other examples of GMS.

7. Following the translation by J. Gray, 'The Blood Bath of the Goddess Anat in the Ras Shamra Texts', *UF* 11 (1979), pp. 315-24, 317.

8. Gray, 'The Blood Bath', p. 321.

9. This stereotyped quatrain always occurs as part of a command (or its fulfilment) to travel in haste and seems to be an extended metaphor of some kind.

genders. GMS improves parallelism within the couplet.[10]

(6)	*KTU* 1.4 v 61-62 (etc.)	
	bl ašt urbt bbhtm	I will surely put an aperture (f.) in the mansion (m.),
	ḥln bqrb hklm	a window (f.) within the palace (m.).

However this couplet is translated[11] the gender patterns seem to have been used merely for the sake of parallelism. Even when in vii 17-19 the word-pairs are deliberately reversed[12] the pattern remains unaltered, but an additional one-gender line is added, *wy[p]tḥ bdqt ʻrpt*, 'and let him open up a rift (f.) in the clouds (f.)',[13] which effectively rounds off the strophe[14] at what is evidently its last occurrence.

(7)	*KTU* 1.5 vi 17-21		
	ǵr babn ydy	I	His skin (m.) with a stone (f.) he scraped,
	psltm byʻr		his braids (f.) with a razor (m.),
	yhdy lḥm wdqn		he shaved sideburns (m.) and beard (m)
	yṯlṯ qn ḏrʻh	II	He tri-ploughed his humeral bone,
	yḥrṯ kgn aplb		his chest (m.) he harrowed like a garden (f.),
	kʻmq yṯlṯ bmt		like a valley (m.) his back (f.) he tri-ploughed.

10. See also *KTU* 1.3 iii 42-43 *klbt ilm išt*, 'Fire, the divine Bitch'—where the operative nouns are feminine; contrast 'fire, hound of the gods' in W. Beyerlin (ed.), *Near Eastern Religious Texts relating to the Old Testament* (trans. J. Bowden; OTL; London: SCM Press; Philadelphia: Westminster Press, 1978), p. 198. The GMS in *KTU* 1.4 iv 14-15 (cf. 19 ii 10-11) was one of the first examples which Cassuto noticed. There may also be an example of the device in *KTU* 1.4 iv 59-61, but the gender of *ulṯ* (and its meaning) is uncertain.

11. B. Margalit, *A Matter of 'Life' and 'Death': A Study of the Baal-Mot Epic* (*CTA* 4-5-6) (AOAT, 206: Kevelaer: Butzon & Bercker; Neukirchen–Vluyn: Neukirchener Verlag, 1980), pp. 45-50 defends the view that Baal wants windows in the palace, against the advice of his architect.

12. The reversal and its function were first noticed by S. Gevirtz, *Patterns in the Early Poetry of Israel* (SAOC, 32: Chicago: University of Chicago Press, 1963), pp. 39-40.

13. 'Let a rift be opened' (Gibson, *Canaanite Myths*, p. 64) cannot be correct since there is no concord between *yptḥ* and *bdqt*; the same applies to *ḥln yptḥ*.

14. See, in general, B.H. Smith, *Poetic Closure: A Study of how Poems End* (Chicago: University of Chicago Press, 1968). Other examples of GMS: *KTU* 1.4 vi 17-21 and 1.5 i 16-17.

There is some difference of opinion over exact meanings and stichometry here,[15] but it can be argued that stanza I refers to shaving and haircutting, and stanza II to body gashing. This seems to be borne out by the complex chiastic gender pattern which can be set out as follows:

I	m. + f.
	f. + m.

II	----
	f. + m.
	m. + f.

Here the rites of mourning, which effectively reverse one's normal appearance, are mimicked by the use of inverted gender-matching. The passage is so tightly constructed that it has been transferred without change to portray actions carried out by Anath, even though she has no beard—an indication of origins in oral poetry.[16]

(8)	*KTU* 1.12 i 9-11	
	kbdn il abn	Our, liver O El our father,
	kbd kištikln	our liver (f.) they consume like fire (f.),
	ṯdn km mrm tqrṣn	our breast (m.) they gnaw like worms (m.).

Once again gender-matching is used to reinforce a set of similes. The meaning of the couplet is by no means certain;[17] some scholars consider *iš* to mean 'mole'[18] which would spoil the symmetry of

15. Contrast J.C de Moor, *The Seasonal Pattern in the Ugaritic Myth of Ba'lu according to the Version of Ilimilku* (AOAT, 16; Kevelaer: Butzon & Bercker; Neukirchen–Vluyn: Neukirchener Verlag, 1971), p. 193, A. Caquot, M. Sznycer and A. Herdner (eds.), *Texte ougaritiques*. I. *Mythes et légendes* (LAPO, 7; Paris: Cerf, 1974), p. 25; Gibson, *Canaanite Myths*, p. 73; Margalit, *'Life' and 'Death'*, p. 129.

16. For contradictions of this kind having their origin in oral poetry, cf. R. Culley, *Oral Formulaic Language in the Biblical Psalms* (Toronto: University of Toronto Press, 1967), p. 97, and R.G. Boling, 'Synonymous Parallelism in the Psalms', *JSS* 5 (1960), pp. 221-55, 121, who cites Ps. 84.9. Further examples: *KTU* 1.6 ii 6-9, 16-18 and 35-37.

17. See, particularly, N. Wyatt, 'Atonement Theology in Ugarit and Israel', *UF* 8 (1976), pp. 415-30, p. 416 who translates: 'They (= the two goddesses) are destroying us, El our father, (Our) liver like a fluke they are devouring, our vitals like worms they gnaw'.

18. Following H.L. Ginsberg, 'Ba'lu and his Brethren', *JPOS* 16 (1936), pp. 139-49, 140.

gender. The rendering adopted, in fact, finds support from Isa. 66.24 where *twlʿh*, ‘worm’, is parallel to *ʾš*, ‘fire’, in a similar context.

(9)	*KTU* 1.13: 13-14	
	kbkbm ṯm tpl klbnt	Stars (m.) fall there like white petals (f.),
	[ṣ]rḫm kyrkt ʿṯqbm	comets (m.) like winglets of ashes (f.).

The pairing of nouns with opposite genders in each line favours de Moor's restoration and translation reproduced here[19] (similes yet again).

(10)	*KTU* 1.14 i 16-21	
	mṯlṯt kṯrm	She who was the third to bear, died in childbirth (m.),
	mrbʿt zblnm	the fourth (f.) in illness (m.).
	mḫmšt ršp	The fifth (f.) was gathered in by Rašp (m.),
	mṯdṯt ǵlm ym	the sixth (f.) by the satellites of Yam (m.).
	mšbʿthn bšlḥ ttpl	His seventh wife fell by a javelin (m.).

In each line a feminine noun is coupled with a masculine noun in mimesis of the destructive effect each agent had on Keret's wives.[20]

(11)	*KTU* 1.14 ii 27-29	
	ʿdb akl lqryt	Let (Krt) prepare corn (m.) from the granary (f.),
	ḥṭt lbt ḫbr	grain (f.) from the cellar (m.).

This translation follows Albright[21] who failed to note the gender-pattern expressing merismus: all available food was to be made ready.[22]

19. J.C. de Moor, ‘Contributions to the Ugaritic Lexicon’, *UF* 11 (1979), pp. 639-54, 650; another example may be *KTU* 1.13: 26-30, but the text is very difficult—see the convincing proposal put forward by J. Sanmartín, ‘Semantisches über *'MR* “Sehen” und *'MR* “Sagen” im Ugaritischen’, *UF* 5 (1973), pp. 263-70, 268-69, and cf. M. Dietrich and O. Loretz, ‘GZR, “Abschneiden, Abkneifen” im Ugar., und Hebr.’, *UF* 9 (1977), pp. 51-56, 53. Translated ‘Là tomberont comme des briques... comme (*dans*) *une fosse* (tomberont) les *forts*’ in Caquot *et al.* (eds.), *Textes ougaritiques*, II, p. 24.

20. For the translation, cf. de Moor, *Contributions*, p. 644.

21. W.F. Albright, ‘Some Canaanite-Phoenician Sources of Hebrew Wisdom’, in *Wisdom in Israel and in the Ancient Near East* (VTSup, 3; Leiden: Brill, 1955), pp. 10-12. For an alternative version (which does not affect the gender pattern) cf. Gibson, *Canaanite Myths*, p. 84.

22. Other examples are *KTU* 1.14 ii 48-50 and (already noted by Cassuto) *KTU* 1.15 iii 23-25.

(12) *KTU* 1.16 i 34-35

al tšt bšdm mmh	She should give her cry (m.) in the fields (m.),
bsmkt ṣat npšh	in the grass-covered places (f.) her throat's utterance (f.).

Whatever the meaning of *smkt*—possibly a cognate of Akk. *samāku*, 'to cover'[23]—its gender is feminine. The principal purpose of GMS in the couplet is to achieve better parallelism.

(13) *KTU* 1.16 iii 10-11

n'm lḥṭt b'n	Sweet (m.) to the wheat (f.) in the furrow (f.),
bm nrt ksmm	in the tilth (f.) like perfume (m.),
'l tlm k'ṭrṭrt	on the ridge (m.) like fragrant herbs (f.).

The careful combinations of noun gender (again giving bite to a pair of similes) lend support to this recently proposed translation.[24]

(14) *KTU* 1.16 rev. iv 4-5, 6-8, 10-12

In these passages *ilš* is termed *ngr il* and *ngr bt b'l*, while his wife is referred to as *ngrt ilht* ('the female n. of the goddesses'). Whether *ngr* means 'steward', 'herald'[25] or even 'carpenter'[26] it is evident that the *ngr* looked after the gods and the *ngrt* attended to the goddesses. The *kṯrm* and *kṯrt* also had sex-related roles.[27]

(15) *KTU* 1.17 v 26-28

bd dnil ytnn qšt	In Danel's hand (f.) he set the bow (f.)
lbrkh y'db qṣ't	on his knees (f.) he left arrows (f.).

Although both giver (Kothar-and-Hasis) and recipient(s) are male, the poet has evidently used a set of nouns which are all feminine—perhaps because the principal gift (the Bow) is also of that gender. Other

23. See *AHw*, p. 1017. Gibson prefers 'heights' (citing Arabic *samku*)—Gibson, *Canaanite Myths*, p. 153 and in support of his view Judg. 11.37-38 could be quoted.

24. M. Dietrich and O. Loretz, 'Ein ug. Fruchtbarkeitsritus (KTU 1.16 III 1-11)', *UF* 10 (1978), pp. 424-25, and, independently, de Moor, 'Contributions', p. 646.

25. Akk. *nāgiru* (*AHw*, p. 711) from the root *nagāru*, 'to announce' (*AHw*, p. 710).

26. Akk. *nagāru*, from Sumerian nagar (*AHw*, p. 710). For full discussion, see Caquot *et al.* (eds.), *Textes ougaritiques*, p. 562, n. t.

27. See, besides, *KTU* 1.16 v 44-46; vi 6-7.

expressions could have been used, such as **ldnil ytn qšt* and **lmt hrnmy ytn qṣʿt*, suggesting that his (or her) choice of words was intentional.[28]

(16) *KTU* 1.19 iii 7 (etc.)

bph rgm lyṣa	Scarce had his word (m.) from his mouth (m.) gone out
bšpth hwth	from his lips (f.), his word (f.).

The second line simply echoes the first, but to offset this expletive (or filler) effect the poet combines GMS with final silent stress[29] and achieves a masterly couplet which is repeated several times.[30]

(17) *KTU* 1.19 iv 9-12

ʿrb b <bth b> kyt	The weepers (f.) entered his house (m.),
bhklh mšspdt	the lamenters (f.) his palace (m.),
bḥẓrh pẓġm ġr	the skin-gashers (m.) his court (f.).

The comments on mourning mimicry in example 7 apply here as well.[31]

(18) *KTU* 1.93:1-3

bpy tʿlgt	(Cow! Remove...) the stammering (f.) from my mouth (m.),
blšn [*y*]*ġr*	the negligence (m.) from my tongue (f.).

The view has been put forward by de Moor (whose translation is used here) that these are the opening lines of a prayer to Anat, and the comparative material he cites from Mesopotamia certainly favours his classification.[32] The two lines set out above suggest merismus lies behind the chiastic gender pattern. It is interesting that these lines are framed by single-gender lines (*td rgm bġr*, 'remove the word [m.] spoken in negligence [m.]'—*ṯyb b<n>pšy k*[*nt*], 'restore true words

28. Similarly in *KTU* 1.17 iv 41-42, all the nouns are f. Further texts: *KTU* 1.17 v 22-25 and 1.19 i 6-7 (on which cf. B. Margalit, 'Alliteration in Ugaritic Poetry: Its Role in Composition and Analysis', *UF* 11 [1979], p. 556). *KTU* 1.19 ii 10-11 has already been commented on by Cassuto.

29. So creating suspense.

30. For the meaning 'scarce, scarcely' of the negative here compare the use of *lā* in EA 82:16, as explained by W.F. Albright and W.L. Moran, 'A Re-Interpretation of an Amarna Letter from Byblos (*EA* 82)', *JCS* 2 (1949), p. 240.

31. Also *KTU* 1.24: 31 and 45-47.

32. De Moor, 'Contributions', pp. 648-49; the author was kind enough to send me an offprint.

[f.] to my throat [f.]'), respectively masculine and feminine. The final extant line uses mismatch of gender to express reversal of state: *ḥkr* [*li*]*šry*[*t yṯb*], 'may my distress (m.) turn into happiness (f.)'.

(19)	*KTU* 1.96:4	
	tspi širh lbl ḥrb	She eats his 'flesh' (m.) without a knife (f.),
	tšt dmh lbl ks	she quaffs his 'blood' (m.) without a cup (f.).[33]
(20)	*KTU* 1.100:2-3	
	'm il mbk nhrm	To El at the source (m.) of the twin rivers (m.),
	b'dt thmtm	at the confluence (f.) of the double deeps (f.).

Perhaps the choice of words in this much-studied text[34] was dictated by the need to improve on the stock couplet *'m il mbk nhrm // qrb apq thmtm* (*KTU* 1.4 iv 21-22 and 6 i 33-34). The genders in each line correspond.[35]

The following patterns or types occur. Straightforward patterns are: m. + m. // f. + f., examples 12, 16; f. + f. // m. + m., examples 4, 8; m. - m. // f. - f.,[36] examples 5, 20 and f. - f. // m. - m., example 1. Reversed patterns include m. + f. // m. + f., examples 9, 19, 17; f. + m. // f. + m., examples 6, 10. Chiastic gender patterns: m. + f. // f. + m. examples 7 (stanza I), 11 and 18; f. + m. // m. + f., example 7 (stanza II); other chiastic patterns are not represented. At least three tricola-patterns occur (examples 2, 3 and 13) and one single gender (f.) text: example 15.

Gender-matched parallelism in all its forms is used in the following ways: to express merismus, examples 3, 11; to improve parallelism, examples 5, 6, 12, 16 and 20; to portray destruction (8, 10) and inversion of state (7, 17) and to reinforce similes, examples 2, 8, 9 and 13. Sex-related functions are represented by 14 and 19.

33. 'She' is the Evil Eye.

34. For bibliography, cf. W. Johnstone, 'The Sun and the Serpent: The Interpretation of the Ugaritic Text RS 24.244', *TGUOS* 26 (1978, pub. 1979), pp. 44-62, esp. 57, and D. Pardee, *Les textes paramythologiques de la 24e campagne (1961)* (Ras Shamra-Ougarit, 4; Mémoire, 77: Paris; Editions Recherche sur les Civilisations, 1988), p. 194.

35. In *KTU* 1.4 ii 21-26 m. and f. genders alternate in consecutive lines, so there is gender parallelism but not congruent parallelism.

36. The first of two nouns in sets marked by / - / is in the construct state.

In comparison with classical Hebrew poetry, which provides over two hundred examples of GMS, the number of instances in Ugaritic verse is meagre. This is in proportion with the poetic corpus for each language, but that is not the whole story; differences remain. Compared to Hebrew, Ugaritic has more examples of tricola and of GMS in combination with similes, while on the other hand, the relatively large number of GMS quatrains of classical Hebrew is totally unrepresented in Ugaritic. Without going into more detail it seems evident that the device of GMS was much more developed in Hebrew and the implication is that its origins lie, partially at least, in the poetic traditions of ancient Ugarit.

In the closing paragraph it is worth mentioning, even if briefly, a topic not unrelated to the main theme of this section, namely, gender congruence in proper names. It has now been fairly well established that there is congruence of gender between a name-bearer and his/her name as regards both predicate and deity in verbal theophoric names.[37] For example, a man will have a name combining a masculine verbal form and a male deity's name—with corresponding changes for a woman—according to the formulae:

(a) MALE: $PN_m = DN_m + V_m$
(b) FEMALE: $PN_f = DN_f + V_f$

As Edzard has shown, exceptions merely prove the rule, the name-form then being treated as a unit, no account being taken of its component parts. The formulae, then, are:

(c) MALE $PN_m = (DN_{m/f} + V_{m/f})_m$
(d) FEMALE: $PN_f = (DN_{m/f} + V_{m/f})_f$

even though there may not be gender agreement within the parentheses. Illustration is provided by the Ugaritic texts. Normally, full congruence is operative[38] as in formulae (a) and (b). Exceptions: formulae (c) and (d) include *il-ʿnt*,[39] *ili-šala*, *il-špš/ili šapaš*,[40] *špš-mlk*,

37. D.O. Edzard, 'Das Genuskongruenz im akkadischen theophoren Personennamen', *ZA* 21 (1963), pp. 112-30; P. Fronzaroli, 'The Concord in Gender in Eblaite Personal Names', *UF* 11 (1979), pp. 275-82.

38. F. Grøndahl, *Die Personennamen der Texte aus Ugarit* (Studia Pohl, 1; Rome: Pontifical Biblical Institute, 1967), p. 46 (§75) and pp. 55-56 (§§92-93).

39. Cf. *Ištar-il*, cited by Edzard, 'Genuskongruenz', p. 114.

40. Cf. *šapaš-šumu-na*, Grøndahl, *Personennamen*, p. 194.

adanu-ummu, *'ṯtr-um* and *hy-abn*.[41] Also the female PNs *bin-ḫattiya(ma)*, *bin-quṭubuya* and *bin-šipṭe*. Further exceptions are *bn-ḥṣqt/ḫaṣiqatanu* and the feminine names *adada* (= Hadad), *pi-zibli*, *pi-ṣidqi* as well as the masculine name *dmty*.[42]

Elsewhere I hope to examine GMS in Akkadian (Assyro-Babylonian) verse.[43] Meanwhile, this collection of examples in Ugaritic will provide material for proper evaluation of the occurrences themselves, their poetic function and their significance within the broader traditions of Semitic versification.

2. *The Old Testament*[44]

With a few exceptions such as BDB, noun gender is not immediately obvious in the lemmata of classical Hebrew dictionaries,[45] and there is

41. These last three names are verbless; the final one means 'She (the goddess X) is our father'.

42. For text-references to these names, cf. Grøndahl, *Personennamen* and R. Whitaker, *A Concordance of the Ugaritic Literature* (Cambridge, MA: Harvard University Press, 1971).

43. To the Phoenician examples mentioned below, p. 203 n. 51, two more can be added, *t'bt 'strt*, 'taboo (f.) to Astarte (f.)' (*KAI* 13 = Tabnit:6) and *'nk mnty km glt*, 'Your eye (f.), O M. (f.) is like a sphere (f.)' (Arslan Tash 2:6-7, as translated by Y. Avishur, 'The Second Amulet Incantation from Arslan-Tash', *UF* 10 [1978] p. 36—a rendering supported, in fact, by *KTU* 1.14 vi 29-30 which Avishur does not mention.

An example from Aramaic comes from the *Targum Yerushalmi* to Gen. 49.26a, which reads (in translation): 'May the blessings of your father be added to the blessings / wherewith Abraham and Isaac, who are like mountains (*ṭwwry'*, m.) blessed you, / and to the blessings of the four mothers who are like hills (*glymt'*, f.) / Sarah and Rebekkah, Rachel and Leah'.

G. Rendsburg, 'Janus Parallelism in Gen. 49.26', *JBL* 99 (1980), pp. 292-93, 292, whose translation is cited, comments, 'The patriarchs Abraham and Isaac are equated with *ṭwwry'*, "mountains", and the four matriarchs are equated with *glymt'*, "hills"'—but fails to note the congruent parallelism which, as in Ugaritic, reinforces the similes. Another Aram. example is Dan. 3.33.

44. First published in *JBL* 99/3 (1980), pp. 321-41.

45. The same observations apply to both *AHw* and *CAD* for Akkadian, and to J. Aistleitner, *Wörterbuch der ugaritischen Sprache* (ed. O. Eissfeldt; Berlin: Akademie Verlag, 1963) for Ugaritic. The standard works on noun gender in Hebrew are K. Albrecht, 'Das Geschlecht der hebräischen Hauptwörter', *ZAW* 15 (1895), pp. 313-25, and *ZAW* 16 (1896), pp. 41-121; and H. Rosenberg, 'Zum Geschlecht der hebräischen Hauptwörter', *ZAW* 25 (1905), pp. 325-29.

correspondingly little attention paid to the topic of gender in standard Hebrew grammars. In fact, it is no novel observation that gender does not play an important role in Hebrew, for which several reasons can be given. For a start, the article has a fixed form irrespective of gender, which is in marked contrast to the gender-related definite and indefinite articles of languages such as French, German and Italian. Also, many verb-forms are genderless; *qāṭ*^{e}*lû*, for example, can mean both 'they (f.) killed' and 'they (m.) killed', the determining factor being context. Also, the use of adjectives in Hebrew is very restricted, as the tendency is to substitute nouns in the bound form (construct state) even when pure adjectives are available[46] obviating the need for concord. All the same, gender is more than marginally significant (as I hope to show), and while there has been some sporadic theorizing,[47] Ibrahim is correct when he observes,

> Gender in the Semitic languages has not been explored to the same degree as it has been in the Indo-European family. The study of Semitic gender, therefore, is still at a primitive stage compared with Indo-European studies. This is not an isolated phenomenon, but reflects the backwardness of Semitic linguistics in general.[48]

The poetic feature which is the subject of this section[49] was discovered some decades ago (see below) but has remained almost unnoticed and unremarked on. As it consists chiefly of the use of nouns of matching gender within a colon, I have labelled it with the expression 'gender-

46. For a discussion of the distinction between 'noun' and 'adjective' in Hebrew, cf. D.J. Kamhi, 'The Term *tōar* in Hebrew and its Status as a Grammatical Category', *BSO(A)S* 34 (1971), pp. 256-72. Among examples of the construct state being used even where a pure adjective is available, he cites (p. 272) Judg. 9.51; 2 Kgs 3.19 and Prov. 20.15.

47. To cite some relevant studies: I.J. Gelb, *Sequential Reconstruction of Proto-Akkadian* (Chicago: University of Chicago Press, 1969), esp. pp. 31-47; G. Janssens, 'The Feminine Ending—*(a)t* in Semitic', *OLP* 6/7 (1975/76), pp. 277-84; A. van Selms, 'Some Reflections on the Formation of the Feminine in Semitic Languages', in H. Goedicke (ed.), *Near Eastern Studies in Honor of W.F. Albright* (Baltimore: The Johns Hopkins University Press, 1971), pp. 421-31.

48. M.H. Ibrahim, *Grammatical Gender: Its Origin and Development* (The Hague: Mouton, 1973), p. 39. Ibrahim's survey is excellent and some of his insights have been incorporated here. Particularly useful is his bibliography, pp. 105-109.

49. This section is a modified form of a short paper first read at the Sixth International Congress on Biblical Studies, Oxford, April 1978. I am indebted to Dr John F.A. Sawyer for critical comment.

matched synonyms' or, since the norm in Hebrew poetry is synonymous parallelism,[50] more descriptively as 'gender-matched synonymous parallelism' (GMS). Before proceeding to outline the contents of this section it is perhaps useful to provide a single clear illustration of the device in question; Ps. 31.11 will suit:

ky klw bygwn ḥyy	For, spent by worry (m.) is my life (m.)
wšnwty b' nḥh	my years (f.) by groaning (f.).

In the first colon a masculine noun (*yāgôn*) is used in connection with *ḥayyîm* (here with possessive suffix) which is also masculine; while in the parallel colon both nouns (*šāna*, *anḥâ*) are feminine. As will be seen, the gender pattern exhibited here is only one of several available to the ancient poets.

The plan of this section is as follows. After describing how GMS was first recognized, examples will be given of the different forms it takes in Hebrew poetry. The various functions of the device will then be outlined and its relationship to other poetic devices evaluated. Next, the implications of recognizing this formal pattern will be set out. A few examples will also be given for extra-biblical Hebrew and for Ugaritic and Akkadian. After a few observations on theory, this section will close with tables of the various types of gender-pattern to be found in Hebrew, full references being given for each.

The device of matching synonyms with gender was first recognized in Ugaritic by Cassuto.[51] Sensitive to the techniques of Ugaritic poetry, he noticed that in several passages the gender of the nouns involved corresponded to the sex of the person under discussion. For example, in the *Legend of Keret*, the term 'sons' is used with reference to King Keret in the first line of a couplet, while the parallel line speaks of

50. Bearing in mind, however, the criticism of the concept 'parallelism' set out by M.Z. Kaddari, 'A Semantic Approach to Biblical Parallelism', *JJS* 24 (1973), pp. 167-75, and especially by M. Shapiro, *Asymmetry: An Inquiry into the Linguistic Structure of Poetry* (Amsterdam: North-Holland, 1976).

51. U. Cassuto, *The Goddess Anath: Canaanite Epics of the Patriarchal Age* (Jerusalem: Magnes, 1971 [1951]), pp. 44-46; he refers to M. Lidzbarski, *Handbuch der nordsemitischen Epigraphik, nebst ausgewählten Inschriften* (Weimar: Felber, 1898), II, p. 151: 'Auf den cyprischen Inschriften steht für Statue *sml*, wenn sie eine männlich, *smlt* wenn sie eine weiblich Person darstellt'; see also pp. 160-61 and 358.

'daughters' in relation to Huray, his wife. The text is *CTA* 15 iii 23-24:[52]

bn krt kmhm tdr	Keret's sons: they were as she had pledged,
ap bnt ḥry kmhm	Huray's daughters, even were like them.

Cassuto commented, 'The ancient Canaanites were accustomed to employ synonyms according to sex; when they spoke of a male they used a masculine term, and when they referred to a female they used a feminine synonym'.[53] Once he had discovered this poetic device in Ugaritic (and he mentioned three other texts),[54] Cassuto could then discuss several passages in Hebrew where the same device is used.[55] It is important to note, however, that it was Ugaritic usage which alerted him in the first instance. Since Cassuto wrote in Hebrew not many scholars were acquainted with his work so that his insights have largely remained dormant. John Gray was one of the few to adopt Cassuto's proposition,[56] another scholar being Tsevat.[57] In support of his new translation of Gen. 49.15 Gevirtz, too, discussed the device adding further OT examples.[58]

To provide some idea of the various patterns into which gender-matching can fall, a whole range of examples will now be set out. After they have been looked at it will be possible to draw up a typology of verse-patterns based on gender (see below). To begin with, then, come the most straightforward couplets, which use masculine nouns in the first colon and feminine nouns in the second, parallel

52. The exact meaning of *kmhm* is disputed, but this does not affect the parallelism. Cf. Caquot *et al.* (eds.), *Textes ougaritiques*, p. 541 n. r for details.

53. Cassuto, *Goddess Anath*, p. 44.

54. *CTA* 4 iv 14-15; vi 47-54 and 19 ii 19-20.

55. Num. 21.29; Deut. 21.10-11; Isa. 3.1, 8; Jer. 48.46; Nah. 2.13; Ps. 144.12 and Prov. 1.8. See also U. Cassuto, *Biblical and Oriental Studies*. II. *Bible and Ancient Oriental Texts* (Jerusalem: Magnes, 1975), pp. 66-68.

56. J. Gray, *The KRT Text in the Literature of Ras Shamra* (Leiden: Brill, 1964), p. 61; review of A.S. Kapelrud, *Baal in the Ras Shamra Texts*, *JNES* 13 (1954), p. 204.

57. M. Tsevat, 'Alalakhiana', *HUCA* 29 (1958), pp. 109-34, 111 n. 4.

58. S. Gevirtz, *EI* 12 (1975), p. 111*; besides Gen. 31.52, Isa. 28.17, Joel 4.3 and Prov. 18.7 he discussed the gender discrepancy of noun and adjective in Gen. 32.8-9, 1 Sam. 10.3 and 1 Chron. 2.48, noting, 'The whole subject is worthy of thorough treatment'. His remark spurred me to publish my collected examples, and I am grateful to him for an exchange of letters on the subject.

colon. The example already given (Ps. 31.11) is in this form, and another is Isa. 3.24:[59]

tḥt bśm mq yhyh	Instead of perfume (m.), putrefaction (m.) there'll be,
wtḥt ḥqwrh nqph	and instead of a belt (f.), bonds (f.)

with the pattern m. + m. // f. + f. The reverse of this pattern occurs but in far fewer passages, for instance Ps. 85.12:

'mt m'rṣ tṣmḥ	Fidelity (f.) from the earth (f.) will spring up,
wṣdq mšmym nšqp	and justice (m.) from the sky (m.) will peer down.

Occasionally, each pair of nouns involved is in a construct relationship, the first set being masculine and the second feminine. So, in Joel 1.6

šnyw šny 'ryh	His teeth are lion's teeth (m.)
wmtl'wt lby' lw	his jaws (f.) a lioness's,

both nouns in the expression *šny 'ryh* are masculine, while in the corresponding phrase *mtl'wt lby'* the nouns are feminine.

Gender parallelism can be extended beyond the simple couplet, though as the number of cola gets larger, the patterns tend to become more and more complex. An elementary form is clear in part of a catalogue poem in an oracle against Egypt (Isa. 19.2):

wnlḥmw	Embattled will be
'yš b' ḥyw	a man and his brother,
w'yšbr'hw	a man and his neighbour (m.),
'yr b'yr	city (f.) with city (f.),
mmlkh bmmlkh	kingdom (f.) with kingdom (f.).

Other, more complicated patterns are listed in the final section, under typology. Finally, certain texts use one gender only, to great effect, either in single lines or within couplets. All the nouns in the following bicolon, for example, are masculine:

hyš lmṭr 'b	Has the rain a father?
'w my-hwlyd 'gly-ṭl	Or: Who sired the dew-drops? (Job 38.28)

59. L. Alonso Schökel, *Estudios de poética hebrea* (Barcelona: Juan Flors, 1963), p. 95 notes: 'el cambio operado par Yave está sèñalado par una disposición quiástica', which corroborates my analysis.

Curiously, though, all-feminine lines and couplets are much commoner, one text from many being Prov. 23.27:[60]

ky šwḥh ʿmqh zwnh	For, a deep pit (f.) is the whore,
wbʾr ṣrh nkryh	and a narrow well (f.) the Bohemian (f.).

We now come to a deliberate variation on the poetic device so far illustrated and discussed; instead of a noun corresponding in gender with its 'companion noun' (so to speak), a noun of the *opposite* gender is chosen.[61] The first to notice this variant was Gevirtz,[62] but to his examples many more can now be added. In Isa. 41.2 each line contains a masculine noun followed by a feminine noun:

ytn kʿpr ḥrbw	(Who) makes (them) like dust (m.) with his sword (f.),
kqš ndp qštw	like chaff (m.), drives (them) with his bow (f.)?

Sometimes the feminine nouns come first as in another couplet from the same prophet:

ʾṣq rwḥy ʿl zrʿk	I will pour out my spirit (f.) on your seed (m.)
wbrkty ʿl ṣʾṣʾyk	and my blessing (f.) on your offspring (m.) (Isa. 44.3b)

The use of this pattern with synonyms paired in sets of opposite gender permits the poet to exploit chiasmus. Such gender chiasmus is apparent in Joel 4.3:[63]

60. The same use of feminine nouns only is found in the parallel text: *sinništu būrtu būrtu šuttatu ḫirītum*, 'Woman is a pitfall, a pitfall, a hole, a ditch', for which cf. W.G. Lambert, *Babylonian Wisdom Literature* (Oxford: Clarendon Press, 1960), pp. 146-47, lines 51-52.

61. Comparable to the phenomenon of polarity in the numbers between three and ten, on which see R. Hetzron, 'Agaw Numerals and Incongruence in Semitic', *JSS* 12 (1967), pp. 169-97. Other studies include G.R. Driver, 'Gender in Hebrew Numerals', *JSS* 1 (1948–49), pp. 90-104; R. Hetzron, 'Innovations in the Semitic Numeral System', *JSS* 22 (1977), pp. 167-201, which should be read together with the critique by M. Powell, 'Notes on Akkadian Numbers and Number Syntax', *JSS* 24 (1979), pp. 13-18.

62. See n. 58. Comparable is the device of inverting the traditional sequence of word-pairs in order to express the reversal of existing conditions, a technique commented on by S. Gevirtz, *Patterns in the Early Poetry of Israel* (Chicago: University of Chicago Press, 1963), pp. 36-40, esp. p. 40, and by Y. Avishur, 'Pairs of Synonymous Words in the Construct State (and in Appositional Hendiadys) in Biblical Hebrew', *Semitics* 2 (1971–72), pp. 17-81, esp., p. 42 n. 122.

63. The same device would seem to be operative in the parallel Phoenician text

wytnw hyld bzwnh	They bartered a boy for a whore,
whyldh mkrw byyn wyštw	a girl they swapped for wine (m.) and imbibed.

The pattern is as follows:

m. (*yld*)	f. (*zwnh*)
f. (*yldh*)	m. (*yyn*).

The inverse of this pattern is also to be found; Prov. 20.29[64] is an example:

tp'rt bḥwrym kḥm	Young men's glory (f.) is their strength (m.),
whdr zqnym śybh	but old men's splendour (m.), their greyness (f.);

schematically:

f. (*tp'rt*)	m. (*kḥ*)
m. (*hdr*)	f. (*śybh*)

As with the patterns using straightforward gender-matched synonyms, bound forms are also used in the inverted patterns. This is evident in the example just given (Prov. 20.29) and in Job 29.13:

brkt 'bd 'ly tbw	The dying man's blessing (f.) came before me,
wlb 'lmnh 'rnyn	and the widow's heart (m.) I made sing,

where the two nouns in each line are in the bound state. There is, then, a whole range of different patterns involving gender, and for convenience a table will be drawn up at the end of this section, setting out the typology of gender-matched synonymous (and antithetic) parallelism, with corresponding references to OT texts.

Having isolated and described the poetic device of matching nouns and genders (as well as its reversed form), the next step is to determine its functions; in other words, to account for the device in any particular text.[65] For several reasons, however, the following considerations are

KAI 24:8 *'lmt ytn bš // wgbr bswt*, 'A girl one bartered for a sheep (m.), a lad for a mantle (f.)'.

64. Sets such as *tp'rt bḥwrym* can be represented schematically as (N_1N_2)genitive, where 'N' stands for a noun. 'In such constructions N_1 is the gender carrier in the sense that other elements in the sentences have to agree with it, and not with N_2', Ibrahim, *Grammatical Gender*, p. 59 (also p. 96).

65. Or, to put it another way, 'the crucial question is what effects patterning can have' since 'poetic effects constitute the data to be explained', J. Culler, *Structuralist*

only of a tentative character and are by no means to be taken as hard and fast rules. To begin with, the notion of function in Hebrew poetry is novel and has hardly been explored.[66] Then, since the gender of many nouns cannot be determined, not a few texts which probably exhibit the pattern in question have had to be left out, so that the list of functions actually drawn up is incomplete and may have to be extended and modified. A final reason: where two or more poetic devices co-exist it can be difficult to assign to each its appropriate function.[67]

With such provisos in mind, the picture that emerges can be sketched out for the two main classes of gender-matched synonyms (i.e. for both the normal and the reversed forms). The main function, it would seem, is to present a global picture[68] as in Jer. 46.12:

šm' gwym qlwnk	The nations (m.) have heard your cry (m.),
wṣwḥtk ml'h h'rṣ	and the earth (f.) is filled by your shout (f.)

which implies that everyone was aware of Judah's plight. (Other texts include Num. 21.29; Jer. 13.27; Joel 2.16; Nah. 2.13; Hab. 2.5; 3.3; Pss. 31.11; 32.2; 57.5-6; 123.2; 147.15; Job 5.20; 8.2; 24.7; Lam. 1.20.)[69] Merismus is operative, too, when there is a mismatch of gender, a case in point being Isa. 41.4:

'd yšym b'rṣ mšpṭ	Until he has set justice (m.) in the land (f.),
wltwrwtw 'yym yyḥlw	and the coastlands (m.) attend on his law (f.).

(Similarly, Jer. 14.8; 16.3; Pss. 98.5-6; 135.6; Prov. 22.17.)[70] Gender-matching can also be used to heighten antithesis or express contrast as illustrated by Prov. 14.13:

Poetics: Structuralism, Linguistics and the Study of Literature (London: Routledge & Kegan Paul, 1975) states, pp. 71 and 74; see also p. 95.

66. See F.I. Andersen, *The Sentence in Biblical Hebrew* (The Hague: Mouton, 1974), pp. 121-24, and A.R. Ceresko, 'The Function of Chiasmus in Hebrew Poetry', *CBQ* 40 (1978), pp. 1-10 for the application of function.

67. Generally speaking, coexistent devices, such as chiasmus and gender-matched parallelism, combine to reinforce the same poetic effect, but this is not always the case.

68. I.e., Merismus, on which see conveniently J. Krašovec, *Der Merismus im biblisch-Hebräischen und Nordwestsemitischen* (BibOr, 33; Rome: Biblical Institute Press, 1977).

69. Anticipating a later paragraph, this function is also evident in Ugaritic, e.g. *CTA* 6 ii 35-37 (set out below).

70. Less certain are Deut. 32.14 and Isa. 3.1.

gm-bṣḥq yk'b-lb	Even in laughter (m.) a heart (m.) may grieve
w'ḥryt h śmḥh twgh	and the end of joy (f.) be sorrow (f.).

(Also, Isa. 3.24a; 5.7; 28.17; Prov. 15.6, 13.) With reversal of gender concord the contrast is even stronger, as in Prov. 15.8:

zbḥ rš'ym tw'bt yhwh	Bad men's sacrifice (m.) is Yahweh's abomination (f.),
wtplt yšrym rṣwnw	but upright men's prayer (f.) is His delight (m.).

(Likewise: Ps. 73.7; Prov. 10.15; 20.29; 29.3.) Another function for both types of gender pattern is the expression of harmony, for example, Ps. 122.7:

yhy šlwm bḥylk	Let there be peace (m.) within your ramparts (m.),
šlwh b'rmnwtyk	tranquillity (f.) within your fortress (f.).

(Of this type too are Ps. 128.3 and Sir. 3.29; with reversal of gender: Isa. 11.4; 28.15; 42.4; 62.1b; Pss. 25.13; 37.30; Prov. 3.16, 22; 8.20.) Occasionally, the poet has chosen synonyms of one or other gender to achieve better parallelism. An instance is Sir. 3.29:

lb ḥkm ybyn mšly ḥkmym	A wise mind (m.) will understand wise proverbs (m.),
w'zn mqšbt lḥkmh tśmḥ	and an attentive ear (f.) rejoices in wisdom (f.).

(To which can be added Joel 1.6; Pss. 18.7b; 76.3; 125.3; Job 10.12; 28.2; 30.18; 33.3; 42.24; Lam. 5.3 and Sir. 31.1.) The effect is produced even when nouns of opposite gender occur in each line; besides Prov. 30.19b, Cant. 7.8 can be quoted:

z't qwmtk dmth ltmr	Your very stature (f.) is like a palm tree (m.),
wšdyk l'šklwt	and your breasts (m.) like (its) clusters (f.).

Gender-matched synonymous parallelism is sometimes used for emphatic denial or affirmation (Ps. 88.13 and Gen. 49.6a; Isa. 54.10; Prov. 20.3 and Sir. 32.20). Inevitability can also be expressed, as in Sir. 42.13:[71]

ky mbgd yṣ' 'š	For, out of clothes (m.) comes a moth (m.),
wm'šh r't 'šh	and from a woman, a woman's wickedness (f.).

71. For a recent discussion of this text, cf. H. Tawil, 'A Curse Concerning Crop-Consuming Insects in the Sefire Treaty and in Akkadian: A New Interpretation', *BASOR* 225 (1977), pp. 59-62, esp. p. 62 for 'moth' in Hebrew.

Exactly the reverse is true when the genders are switched; in Job 18.10, for example, unexpectedness is emphasized:[72]

tmwn b'rṣ ḥblw	Hidden in the ground (f.) is a rope (m.) for him,
wmlkdtw 'ly ntyb	and a trap (f.) for him is on the path (m.),

(Other texts are Deut. 32.14, Prov. 5.5, 18.7 and 26.13.) A variety of other functions can be assigned, none with so many examples as in the foregoing. Job 20.24 expresses poetic justice, as does Ps. 59.13 where the genders are inverted. Abundance is implied by such couplets as Pss. 72.3 (cited below), 89.2, 128.3 and 144.12—all with straightforward gender patterns. Peculiar to inversion of gender-matching are three special and related functions, namely, to denote the abnormal or unusual, to depict destruction of various sorts, and to portray the reversal of normal or existing conditions. They will be dealt with in turn. Evidently Isa. 43.16 describes an unusual event which the reversed gender sequences only serve to emphasize:

hnwtn bym drk	Who sets a road (f.) in the sea (m.),
wbmym 'zym ntybh	in the mighty waters (m.) a path (f.).

(Also Isa. 28.8; 29.4; 41.2; 44.4b; 56.5; 60.17b; Ezek. 11.18-20; Joel 4.3, 10; Pss. 104.2;[73] 105.27; Job 11.14; Prov. 5.16; 26.13.)[74] Destruction is denoted in Isa. 41.2, Job 18.15 and the following text:[75]

whb'rty b'šn rkbh	I will burn your chariots (f.) in smoke (m.),
wkpyryk t'kl ḥrb	and the sword (f.) will devour your young lions (m.) (Nah. 2.14).

Thirdly, inversion of gender-matching aptly serves to portray inversion of state, as for example in Ps. 44.14:

tśymnw ḥrph lšknynw	You have made us a taunt (f.) to our co-citizens (m.),
l'g wqls lsbybwtynw	derision (m.) and scorn (m.) to our neighbourhood (f.).

72. The suffixes are, of course, dative.

73. Courtesy P. Auffret.

74. See also Ruth 1.8-9 where the use of a masculine term (*ḥesed*, 'kindness') in connection with the maternal home contrasts with feminine *m*^e^*nûḥâ*, 'residence', which refers to the home of Ruth's future husband, presumably to mark off a reversal: from now on Ruth was to begin a new life. The passage is prose.

75. For translation, see K.J. Cathcart, *Nahum in the Light of Northwest Semitic* (BibOr, 26; Rome: Biblical Institute Press, 1973), p. 79.

(Further texts: Isa. 28.8; 44.3b; 60.17c; Joel 4.10; Job 11.14; 29.13; Prov. 3.8; Sir. 6.29.)

Assuming that the poetic device here termed 'gender-matched synonymous parallelism' has been shown to exist in both its normal and inverted forms, the question then arises: Were all the occurrences that have been identified used intentionally by the poets or are some merely fortuitous? Cassuto expressed his doubts regarding Ps. 144.12 and Prov. 1.8[76] and other texts may be equally dubious. In fact, the problem concerns not only the technique under consideration here, but the method as a whole of analysing Hebrew poetry which is implied. How much did the poets really intend, how much is actually present, and to what extent are scholars reading such devices into the text?[77]

Accordingly, in an attempt at reaching some degree of objectivity, certain criteria can be proposed. First, where both masculine and feminine forms of the same noun exist, it must be shown that the appropriate gender has been deliberately selected. For example, in the taunt-song of Isa. 23.15 the feminine form *šîrâ* is used in the expression *kšrt hznh*, 'like a harlot's song', since it matches the sex of the lady concerned, although the masculine form *šîr* would have made no difference to the meaning. The converse applies to Ps. 98.1, where the masculine form is used relative to Yahweh.[78] This criterion discounts Isa. 5.1 where *šîrâ* does not match *kerem*, 'vineyard' (m.) in gender.[79] In much the same way, where a range of synonyms is available, it must be evident that one fitting the gender pattern has been chosen, as in Isa. 65.18c:

ky hnny bwr'	For look: I am creating
't yrwšlym gylh	Jerusalem (f.): happiness (f.);
w'mh mśwś	and her people (m.): joy (m.),

76. Cassuto, *Goddess Anath*, p. 46 n. 38.

77. For similar strictures on Roman Jakobson's method of analysing poetry, consult Culler, *Structuralist Poetics*, pp. 55-74. See, too, J.S. Kselman, 'Semantic-Sonant Chiasmus in Biblical Poetry', *Bib* 58 (1977), pp. 219-23, 220.

78. At least twice *kerem* is feminine (Isa. 27.2, 3) but this cannot be the case here in view of the masculine verbs and suffixes.

79. Other examples are the use of *n*^{e}*tîbâ*, 'path' (f.) not *nātîb*, also 'path' (m.) in Isa. 43.16 and the gender-matching of *šebî*, 'captivity' (m.) and 'sons' in parallelism with the synonym *šibyâ* coupled with 'daughters' in Jer. 48.46.

where *śimḥâ* could have been used instead of *māśôś*, both words meaning 'joy'.[80]

Occasionally there is a passage which is closely parallel to the text in question, and then the presence or otherwise of the purported gender pattern can be checked; this is our third criterion. The most well-known of such sets is Isa. 2.4[81] and Joel 4.10. The first text reads:

wkttw ḥrbwtm l'tym	They'll beat their swords (f.) into plowshares (m.),
wḥnytwtyhm lmzmrwt	their spears (f.) into pruning-knives (f.),

where only one of the nouns ('plowshares') is masculine, and no obvious pattern emerges.[82] Instead, in Joel 4.10,

ktw 'tykm lḥrbwt	Beat your plowshares (m.) into swords (f.),
wmzmrtykm lrmḥym	and your pruning knives (f.) into *lances* (m.)

romaḥ, 'lance',[83] replaces *ḥ^anît*, 'spear' (f.), since its gender is masculine and creates the pattern m. + f. // f. + m., expressing the reversal of existing conditions: peace is to become war. The contrast between the next two quasi-parallel passages is even more striking; they are Ps. 98.9b:

yšpṭ-tbl bṣdq	He will judge the world (f.) with justice (m.),
w'mym bmyšrym	and the people (m.) with uprightness (m.).

The other, Ps. 96.13b, differs in the last word to create the reverse (chiastic) pattern f. + m. // m. + f.:

yšpṭ-tbl bṣdq	He will judge the world (f.) with justice (m.),
w'mym b'mwntw	and the peoples (m.) with his *truth* (f.).[84]

80. See also Gen. 49.6a where *lēb*, 'heart' (m.) could have been *kābēd*, 'liver' (f.) with no change in meaning.

81. With the almost identical text Mic. 4.3.

82. Instead, both Isa. 2.4 and Mic. 4.3 employ onomatopoeia.

83. W. Whallon, 'Formulaic Poetry in the Old Testament', *Comparative Literature* 15 (1963), p. 3 is ill-advised to posit 'an Aramaic scribe' for the change of vocabulary in Joel, especially since the Ugaritic cognate *mrḥ*, 'lance' is well attested. In a private discussion, Dr John Sawyer considered Joel to have preserved an ancient text more faithfully than either Isaiah or Micah.

84. Except that created by a combination of assonance (*tebel–ṣedeq* and *'ammîm–mêšārîm*) and parallelism between singular nouns in the first colon and plural nouns in the second.

Two further passages which are also almost identical are Isa. 28.15 and 28.18. A difficult expression occurs in each, and in both cases the context suggests the meaning to be 'pact'. The two texts will first be set out and then commented on.

krtnw bryt 't mwt	We will cut a covenant (f.) with Death (m.),
w'm š'wl 'śynw ḥzh	and with Sheol (f.) we will 'press the breast' (m.).
wkpr brytkm 't mwt	Cancelled will be your covenant (f.) with Death (m.),
wḥzwtkm 't š'wl l' tqwm	and your pact (f.) with Sheol (f.) will not stand.

In Isa. 28.15, MT *ḥōzeh* 'seer' (which makes no sense at all), should be repointed to *ḥāzê*, 'breast'. The expression *'āsa ḥāzê* corresponds to the Akkadian idiom *ṣibit tulê*, 'making a pact', literally, 'touching the breast' which describes the ratifying gesture made by both parties.[85] The word *ḥāzût* in Isa. 28.18 also means 'pact',[86] its gender breaking the pattern that is so evident in v. 15.[87] Other sets are Job 11.8 (contrast Prov. 9.18), 24.7 (compare 31.19), Prov. 26.13 (as against 22.13) and Lam. 1.20 (contrast Deut. 32.25).[88] The criterion of parallel passages overlaps somewhat the cases where a gender pattern has been intentionally flouted. Many texts which would be expected to exhibit gender-matched parallelism do not, for example, Isa. 61.10c. A poet can, in fact, achieve a special effect by disturbing the gender pattern he has established, often in the last line or final word. This is known as 'defeated expectancy' or foregrounding.[89] In Jer. 31.22b,

85. As explained by me in my review of W.H. Irwin, *Isaiah 28–33: Translation with Philological Notes*, *Bib* 59 (1978), pp. 132-33. For the idiom see *CAD*, Ṣ, pp. 165-66.

86. So M. Weinfeld, 'Covenant Terminology in the Ancient Near East and its Influences on the West', *JAOS* 93 (1973), pp. 190-99, 196 n. 87.

87. The poet chose precisely these two words (*ḥāzê*, *ḥāzût*) because they sounded similar, had the same meaning, but were of opposite gender.

88. In this connection two variants of a Hebrew expression meaning 'stubborn, determined', can be mentioned: *qᵉšê lēb* (lit. 'hard of heart', both m.) in Ezek. 3.7, referring to the 'House of Israel' and *qᵉšat rûaḥ* (lit. 'hard of spirit', both f.) in respect of Hannah in 1 Sam. 1.15. It seems as if the appropriate form of the idiom was selected in each case as regards gender, a point unnoticed by G.W. Ahlström, '1 Sam. 1:15', *Bib* 60 (1979), p. 254.

89. Also termed 'disautomatization' or 'actualization'. For the concept see J. Mukařovský, 'Standard Language and Poetic Language', in P. Garvin (ed.), *A Prague School Reader on Esthetics, Literary Structure and Style* (Georgetown: Georgetown University, 1964), pp. 17-30.

for instance, all the significant nouns are feminine except the last, so that form and content marry:

ky br' yhwh ḥdšh b'rṣ	For Yahweh has created a novelty (f.) on earth (f.):
nqbh tswbb gbr	a female protects a male!

Other passages using this effect are Isa. 60.4, Prov. 23.29 and 30.14.[90]

A final criterion is stylistic preference: when five examples turn up in as short a book as Joel (1.6; 2.1, 16; 4.3, 10) it can safely be argued that this is not due to chance. Similarly, some thirty occurrences can be numbered in Proverbs and in Job, indicative that even more remain to be identified.[91] On the other hand, the paucity of examples in Ezekiel puts the onus of proof on those wishing to identify more. In this context it is worth mentioning that density in the Song of Songs is particularly high, which is not totally unexpected.

The relationship of gender-matched synonymous parallelism to other poetic techniques and devices can be explored only briefly here. Two main topics will be considered: parallel pairs and chiasmus. Since many word-pairs in Hebrew use a masculine noun in parallel with a feminine noun (and, of course, the other way round), there will be some overlapping of such word-pairs and gender-matched synonyms.[92] An example is the use of *'ṣ*, 'tree' (m.) // *'bn*, 'stone' (f.) in Isa. 60.17b where gender-matched parallelism is also exploited. It is unnecessary to go through every word-pair, but I think it valuable to test the relationship between our poetic device and one specific word-pair. The set I have selected for this purpose is *hr*, 'mountain' (m.) // *gb'h*, 'hill' (f.) which occurs 31 times: not so often as to be unwieldy, but a high enough frequency for a representative sample.[93] Of these,

90. Akin is Amos 8.9-10 where in each line a feminine noun intrudes on the prevailing gender which is masculine to form the pattern m. + m. f. + m. // m. + m. m. + f. // m. + m. f. + m.

91. Note, too, clustering in texts such as Isa. 11.2, 4, 5; Prov. 30.3, 4, 15a, 19b, 21-31.

92. As pointed out to me by Dr Adele Berlin, in a letter; cf. R.G. Boling's reference to the 'high preponderance of feminine forms employed in second position *metri causa*' when discussing parallel pairs in his review of R.C. Culley, *Oral Formulaic Language in the Biblical Psalms*, *JSS* 14 (1969), p. 122.

93. Three times in reverse sequence (Jer. 3.23; 17.2-3; Ezek. 6.13). The occurrences have been listed and discussed by Gevirtz, *Patterns*, pp. 56-57 and 56 nn. 20-22.

five show simple parallelism of the m. // f. type,[94] 23 can be discounted,[95] leaving three which qualify: Isa. 54.10, Ps. 72.6 and Cant. 4.6. They will be looked at in turn. First to be noted is Isa. 54.10:[96]

ky hhrym ymwsw	For the mountains (m.) may vanish,
whgb 'wt tmwṭnh	and the hills (m.) may shake,
wḥsdy m 'tk l'-ymwš	but my love (m.) will never vanish,
wbryt šlwmy l' tmwṭ	nor my peace-covenant (f.) be shaken.

The (m.-f.) gender sequence of the first two lines is matched by that of the last two with which they are parallel.[97] Then comes Ps. 72.3 which requires no comment:[98]

yś'w hrym šlwm l'm	May the mountains (m.) bring peace (m.) to the people,
whgb'wt bsdqh	and the hills (f.), justice (f.).

Cant. 4.6 uses two nouns in the bound state in each line, with both nouns masculine in the first colon, and both feminine in the second:[99]

'lk ly 'l hr hmwr	I will go to the mount (m.) of myrrh (m.),
w'l gb't hlbwnh	and to the hill (f.) of frankincense (f.).

The use of a masculine-feminine word-pair, then, does not automatically imply gender-matched parallelism; in fact, when it suits, one member of a standard word-pair can be changed to create such parallelism, as already seen in Isa. 65.18c (quoted above). This suggests, perhaps, that our device is higher in rank than word-pairs.

The overlay of gender-patterns with chiasmus in all its forms has

94. Isa. 2.14; 30.25; Nah. 1.5; Prov. 8.25; Cant. 2.8.

95. Gen. 49.26 (cf. LXX); Deut. 33.15; Isa. 2.2; 10.32; 30.17; 31.4; 40.12; 41.15; 65.7; Jer. 4.24; 16.16; 50.6; Ezek. 34.6; 35.8; Hos. 4.13; 10.8; Joel 4.18; Amos 9.13; Mic. 4.1; 6.1; Hab. 3.6; Ps. 114.4, 6.

96. I have used the passive in the last line for smoothness of translation; cf. NEB.

97. For a different version, see M.J. Dahood, review of J.M. Allegro, *Discoveries in the Judaean Desert of Jordan*. V. *Qumrân Cave 4. I (4Q158–4Q180)*, *Bib* 50 (1969), pp. 270-72, 271-72: 'But my love which I repeat to you a hundred times shall never depart, and the covenant which I fulfil shall not waver'.

98. The word *'m* in the first line is also masculine, which explains why it is omitted from the second.

99. For the construction used here, see T. Muraoka, 'On the so-called *dativus ethicus* in Hebrew', *JTS* 29 (1978), pp. 495-98, who describes the idiomatic preposition as 'centripetal', p. 497.

been examined elsewhere;[100] whole range of texts could be listed (for example: Isa. 33.6; Job 31.10; Prov. 10.12, 15; 30.3). In Prov. 3.16, to take one text, there is chiasmus both of the nouns used and of their respective genders:

'rk ymym bymynh	Length of days (m.) in her right (f.),
bśm 'wlh 'šr wkbwd	in her left (f.), riches (m.) and honour (m.).

Of particular interest is the use of our device in an ABA' chiastic tri-colon,[101] Job 6.4:

ky ḥṣy šdy 'mdy	For the Almighty's arrows (m.) are toward me (m.);
'šr ḥmtm šwth rwḥy	their poison (f.) my spirit (f.) drinks;
b'wty 'lwh y'rkwny	Eloah's terrors (m.) are arrayed against me (m.).

Here, in the central (B) colon, the poet has replaced the masculine suffixes of the two outer lines (A, A') by the feminine noun *rûaḥ*, in order to match the gender of *ḥēmâ*. Finally, the chiastic assonance of Prov. 10.12 is noteworthy, since it is combined with reversal of gender matching:[102]

śn'h t'rr mdnym w'wl	Hatred (f.) stirs up malicious quarrels (m.),
kl pš'ym tksh 'hbh	all offences (m.) are covered by love (f.).

The vocalic sequence *mᵉdānîm wᵉ'ôl* of the first line is inverted in the second (*kol pᵉšā'îm*) just as the gender sequence f. + m. becomes m. + f. The overall effect is to bring out the deep contrast between 'hate' and 'love'. Chiasmus and gender-matched parallelism, therefore, often coincide and reinforce the effect each produces.

Of the many implications which result from recognition of gender-matched synonymous parallelism, I will touch on only two aspects: textual criticism and determining gender. A few examples will be enough to show how relevant gender patterns can be to establishing the correct text. In Isa. 34.13 the word *ḥāṣîr*, 'grass' (m.) is usually emended to *ḥāṣēr*, 'habitat' (f.) to suit the context:[103]

100. See Chapter 7 'Chiastic Patterns in Biblical Hebrew Poetry'.

101. Which also exhibits end-rhyme (in *-i*); for this type of tri-colon see the study mentioned in the previous footnote.

102. For a translation, see M.J. Dahood, 'Una coppia di termini ugaritici e Prov 10, 12', *BeO* 15 (1973), pp. 253-54.

103. E.g., E.J. Kissane, *The Book of Isaiah* (Dublin: Browne & Nolan, 1960), I, p. 377, following LXX *aulē strouthōn* 'court for ostriches'.

whyth nwh tnym	It will be a haunt (m.) for jackals (m.),
ḥṣr lbnwt y'nh	a habitat (f.) of ostriches (f.).

The resulting m. + m. // f. + f. pattern corroborates the emendation proposed.[104] Another illustration is Ps. 91.7 which can be shown to require no textual change:

ypl mṣdk 'lp	Should there fall a thousand (m.) at your side (m.),
wrbbh mymynk	ten thousand (f.) at your right (f.)

Altering *mṣdk* to *mydk*, 'at your hand' (f.), as has been suggested[105] would destroy the evident gender pattern. Lastly, Van Dijk's correction of MT *bm dbry* to *bammidbār* in Ps. 105.27[106] improves not only the sense, but the gender pattern as well:

śmw bmdbr 'twtyw	They brought over the Desert (m.) his signs (f.),
wmptym b'rṣḥm	and his wonders (m.) over the land (f.) of Ham.

(Other examples: Isa. 5.29; 11.4 and Job 11.8.)[107] Gender-matched parallelism can sometimes provide corroborative evidence for determining noun gender. The gender of *tappûaḥ*, 'apple(-tree)', is probably masculine as in late Hebrew and as the plural forms (both absolute and construct) seem to indicate. An additional pointer is Cant. 2.3:

ktpwḥ b 'ṣy hy'r	Like an apple-tree in the trees of the forest (m.),
kn dwdy byn hbnym	so is my beloved (m.) among the boys,

where all the nouns are evidently masculine if gender-matching applies.[108] Similarly, *nešeq*, 'weapon', is also masculine in view of

104. Unnoticed by J. Muilenberg, 'The Literary Character of Isaiah 34', *JBL* 59 (1940), pp. 339-65.

105. By Gevirtz, *Patterns*, p. 16 n. 3, following Cassuto.

106. H.J. van Dijk, 'A Neglected Connotation of Three Hebrew Verbs', *VT* 18 (1968), pp. 16-30, p. 28.

107. In Isa. 5.29 the *kethib* (*wišᵉ'ag*) and not the *qere* (*yiš'ag*) is to be followed—against H. Wildberger, *Jesaja*. I. *Jesaja 1–12* (BKAT, 10/1; Neukirchen–Vluyn: Neukirchener Verlag, 1972), p. 207. The emendation of *'ereṣ*, 'land' (f.) to *'ārîṣ*, 'fierce' (m.) in Isa. 11.4 would ruin the f. + m. // f. + m. pattern. Job 11.8 need not be emended to conform with Prov. 9.18. Gender parallelism also confirms the text of Sir. 6.18 as reconstructed by P.W. Skehan, 'The Acrostic Poem in Sirach 51:13-30', *HTR* 64 (1971), pp. 387-400, 399 on the basis of the Greek version.

108. This noun is also incorporated into the gender-patterns of Cant. 7.9 as well as Joel 1.12.

Job 20.24 (gender pattern: m. + m. // f. + f.), and additional support can be given to McKay's argument that *šaḥar*, 'dawn', is a suppressed feminine form in Hebrew.[109] In particular instances, too, it can be established whether a noun of common gender is considered as masculine or feminine. In Ps. 34.14, for example, *lāšôn*, 'tongue', is masculine:

nṣwr lšnk mr'	Guard your tongue from evil (m.)
wšptyk mdbr mrmh	and your lips (f.) from speaking deceit (f.)

but feminine in Ps. 126.2:

'z yml' śḥwq pynw	Then filled was our mouth (m.) with laughter (m.),
wlšwnnw rnh	and our tongue (f.) with hurrahs (f.).

Similarly, *derek*, 'way', is normally feminine, but in Isa. 40.3 and Ps. 67.3 it is masculine. It is evident, then, that very often words were chosen more for their gender than for their exact meaning. As a footnote to this section, then, I would like to point out that it is not always advisable to draw theological conclusions on the basis of a particular word, differentiating, for example, between *ṣedeq* and *ṣᵉdēqâ*, both basically meaning 'justice'. They can have different connotations,[110] but there are texts (e.g. Ps. 72.3) where choice has been dictated by poetic convention.

Although the main subject of this paper is treated with respect to OT Hebrew, a few words are in order on the occurrence in extra-biblical texts since, as has been said, the device was first recognized in Ugaritic. Accordingly, selected passages from the Qumran texts, the Talmud, Ugaritic poetry and Akkadian verse will be examined briefly here. A good example from the Dead Sea Scrolls is 11QPs[a] 19.9-10:

lmwt hyyty bḥṭ'y	Near death (m.) was I for my sins (m.),
w'wwnwty lš'wl mkrwny	and my iniquities (f.) had sold me to Sheol (f.),

109. As argued by J.W. McKay, 'Helel and the Dawn-Goddess. A Re-examination of the Myth in Isaiah XIV 12-15', *VT* 20 (1979), pp. 451-64, esp. p. 459 on Cant. 6.10.

110. As set out by K. Koch 'צדק *ṣdq* gemeinschaftstren/heilvoll sein', in E. Jenni (ed.), *Theologisches Handwörterbuch zum Alten Testament* (Munich: Kaiser Verlag; Zürich: Theologischer Verlag, 1976), II, cols., 507-30; and J.J. Scullion, '*ṣedeq-ṣedaqah* in Isaiah cc. 40–66 with Special Reference to the Continuity in Meaning between Second and Third Isaiah', *UF* 3 (1971), pp. 335-48.

And from the Hodayoth (1QH 2.28b):[111]

w'ny bmws lby kmym	And I, when my heart (m.) melts like water (m.),
wtḥzy npšy bbrytk	my soul (f.) holds fast to your covenant (f.).

One example from the Talmud can be cited: *M. Qaṭ.* 25b:[112]

śmḥh ltwgh nhpnh	Joy (f.) to weariness (f.) was turned,
śśwn wygwn ndbqw	gladness (m.) and sadness (m.) were united.

Even modern Hebrew poetry is not without examples of the device.[113] To the texts in Ugaritic already mentioned above quite a few more could be added, but this is not the place, and two passages will be enough by way of illustration.

hn bpy sprhn	See, in my mouth (m.) is their number (m.),
bšpty mnthn	on my lips (f.) their enumeration (f.).[114]
	(*CTA* 24.45-47)
širh ltikl 'ṣrm	His remains (m.) the birds (f.) do eat,
mnth ltkly nprm	his limbs (f.) the sparrows (m.) do consume.[115]
	(*CTA* 6 ii 35-37)

From the many instances in Akkadian,[116] I will mention only one:[117]

ina āli ardatu zamārša šani	In the city the woman's song (m.) is changed;
ina āli eṭlu nissassu šanāt	in the city the man's lament (f.) is changed.

111. Other passages include 1QH 3.23; 4.17-18; 7.14-15; 9.16-17; 1QS 10.26-11.1; 11.4-5, 12, 13.

112. Cited in another connection by G.B. Gray, *The Forms of Hebrew Poetry* (London: Hodder & Stoughton, 1915), p. 30 n. 1.

113. See S. Burnshaw, T. Carmi and E. Spicehandler (eds.), *The Modern Hebrew Poem itself* (New York: Schocken Books, 1966), p. 20 (stanzas I-IV); p. 48 line 2; p. 50 (stanzas I-II); p. 79 lines 6-9; p. 84 (stanza I); p. 160 lines 3-4; p. 172 line 7; p. 186 line 8; though the editors have not noticed this use of gender.

114. For the translation, see my remarks in 'Ugarit and the OT: Further Parallels', *Or* 45 (1976), p. 438.

115. Also *CTA* 3B ii 9-10, 25-26; 4 v 123-24; 5 vi 17-18; 6 ii 7-8; 17 vi 15-16; 19 iv 170-73.

116. To cite only those most easily available: Lambert, *Babylonian Wisdom Literature*, p. 38 lines 12-13; p. 46 lines 117-18; W.G. Lambert and A.R. Millard, *Atra-ḫasīs: The Babylonian Story of the Flood* (Oxford: Clarendon Press, 1969), p. 112 (= S v 18b-21), and L. Cagni, *L'epopea di Erra* (Studi Semitici, 34; Rome: Università di Roma, 1969), p. 88 (= IIc 33-34).

117. G. Reisner (ed.), *Sumerisch-babylonische Hymnen nach Thontafeln griechischer Zeit* (Mitteilungen aus den orientalischen Sammlungen, 10; Berlin: W. Spemann, 1896), p. 112 rev. 12-13—cited in *CAD*, E, p. 410.

The genders of *zamāru*, 'song', and *nissatu*, 'lament', are apparent from the verb forms.

In this closing section I will deal with some points which have only been referred to briefly and make some general observations on the significance of gender for understanding and appreciating Hebrew, particularly Hebrew poetry. Repeating what has already been said in the opening paragraph, it is evident that the topic of gender is by no means a central issue in current research, and yet it is undeniably important. One example will be enough to show this. In the well-known tree fable of Judg. 9.8-15 four trees are mentioned (though strictly speaking, the last one is a bush): *zayit*, 'olive tree (m.), *tᵉ'ēnâ*, 'fig tree' (f.), *gepen*, 'vine' (f.) and *'āṭād*, 'boxthorn' (m.). However the fable is to be understood, it seems clear that the genders of these plants play their part and have to be accounted for.[118]

Gender parallelism, as the passage just referred to shows, is by no means confined to poetry. Like parallelism itself, gender-matched synonyms are also to be found in prose. In Deut. 22.5, to take only one example, the choice of synonyms is evidently deliberate:[119]

l' yhyh kly-gbr 'l- 'šh	A man's gear (m.) should not be on a woman,
wl'-ylbš gbr śmlt 'šh	and a man should not dress in a woman's garment (f.).

(Other prose texts already cited are Deut. 21.10-11 and Ruth 1.8-9.)[120] In Deut. 23.19 our device is not used, in spite of its evident aptness ('a harlot's hire or a male prostitute's price') showing that, in poetry, it was not adopted automatically in every possible passage.

To be aware of gender in Hebrew is generally of value; for example, it can help distinguish homonyms such as *šēn*, 'tooth' (f.), and *šēn*, 'prong' (m.; 1 Sam. 2.13).[121] It is also not without relevance to figurative language. Ibrahim has shown that in Arabic 'the use of

118. For further details see the study cited in n. 100.

119. For some Mesopotamian parallels, cf. W.H.P. Römer, 'Randbemerkungen zur Travestie von Deut. 22,5', in M.S.H.G. Heerma van Voss *et al.* (eds.), *Travels in the World of the Old Testament* (Assen: Van Gorcum, 1974), pp. 217-22.

120. For a full list see 2.7 below.

121. See S.R. Driver, *Notes on the Hebrew Text and the Topography of the Books of Samuel* (Oxford; Clarendon Press, 1913), p. 30 who cautiously comments, 'to be sure, in 14,5 *šn* in the *metaph.* sense of a *pointed rock* is masc.; whether it was also in that of the tooth of a prong, is more than we can say'.

gender in metaphor depends, above all, on grammatical gender'.[122] This is particularly evident in metaphorical compounds, on which he states,[123]

> Whether the metaphorical compound should have a masculine or a feminine word as its first element (and it is the first element which determines the gender of the whole compound) depends entirely on the grammatical gender of the referent, i.e., the gender of the noun to which the compound refers.

What he means, in effect, is that compounds formed with, say, the word *ben*, 'son (of)', and its plural, are masculine in gender and have masculine referents.[124] This explains such expressions as *b*^{e}*nê 'ašpāto*, 'sons of his quiver' (Lam. 3.13), and *ben qāšet*, 'son of a bow' (Job 41.20), for although both times the second word is feminine, the compounds are two different ways of denoting 'arrow(s)', which in Hebrew is masculine (*ḥēṣ*). Accordingly, the meaning 'sparks' is quite in order for disputed *b*^{e}*nê rešep* (Job 5.7) since both the nouns with this meaning—*nîṣôṣ* and *kîdôd*—are also masculine.[125] Therefore gender can be basically significant in understanding Hebrew which is itself the first step in interpreting Hebrew poetry.

Well aware of the main conclusions reached by Ibrahim regarding gender and its origins,[126] I would like to add some closing remarks at an extra-linguistic level with regard to the relationship between sex-related roles and gender, especially in poetry. In the ancient world it was customary for deities to be offered sacrificial animals of the appropriate sex: males to gods and females to goddesses.[127] Applying

122. Ibrahim, *Grammatical Gender*, p. 95.

123. Ibrahim, *Grammatical Gender*, p. 96; see, also, p. 59.

124. The same applies to compounds formed with *'ab*, 'father (of)' while the reverse is true of constructions using *'ēm*, 'mother (of)' and *bat*, 'daughter (of)', for which see the dictionaries. Hence, the conclusions of A. Fitzgerald, 'The Mythological Background for the Presentation of Jerusalem as a Queen and False Worship as Adultery in the Old Testament', *CBQ* 34 (1972), pp. 403-16 on *bt*, *btlt*, *'m* and *qdšt* may have to be modified.

125. Note, too, 'Has the rain a father?' (Job 38.28) cited above.

126. Namely, that 'gender in its origin was an accident of linguistic history, and that as a grammatical category gender owes its emergence and existence to various linguistic (and no extralinguistic) forces', Ibrahim, *Grammatical Gender*, p. 50.

127. For ancient Anatolia, see O.R. Gurney, *Some Aspects of Hittite Religion* (Oxford: Oxford University Press, 1977), p. 48, and for ancient Urartu, cf. D. Frankel, *The Ancient Kingdom of Urartu* (London: British Museum, 1979), p. 29.

this knowledge to a difficult passage in Ugaritic (*CTA* 4 vi 47-52), where gods and goddesses are mentioned alternately as recipients of offerings, may resolve a dilemma. One interpretation is to see the 'rams' (*krm*), 'oxen' (*alpm*) and 'seats' (*kḥtm*) as designating the gods, and the 'ewes' (*ḫprt*), 'cows' (*arḫt*) and 'thrones' (*ksat*) as referring to the various female deities. It seems more likely that it is the unnamed gods (*ilm*) who are given rams, oxen and seats, since these are masculine nouns, while the ewes, cows and thrones (all feminine) are offered to the equally nameless goddesses (*ilht*).[128] In the same way, the sex of servants corresponded to that of their owners,[129] and this is reflected unmistakably in Isa. 24.2:[130]

k'bd k'dny	Alike are slave and master,
ksphh kgbrth	alike are maid and mistress,

where economy of expression could scarcely by surpassed.

In this concluding section I have tried to classify the patterns into which gender-matched synonymous (and antithetic) parallelism appears to fall. It must be emphasized that I make no claim to be definitive and hope that further study will refine the broad divisions given here. For each type I will give a schematic pattern, an example and a list of occurrences.

2.1. *Straightforward Patterns*

m. + *m.* // *f.* + *f.* For example Isa. 49.22:

whby' bnyk bḥṣn	They shall bring your sons in their embrace (m.),
wbnwtyk 'l ktp tnś'nh	and your daughters shall be carried out on their shoulder (f.).

(Gen. 49.11; Num. 21.29; 2 Sam. 22.7b; Isa. 3.24a; 5.7; 24.2; 28.17; 34.13; 40.3; 59.9b; 60.10; Jer. 46.12; 48.46; Joel 2.16; Nah. 2.13;

128. For the two possible versions, cf. J.C.L. Gibson, *Canaanite Myths and Legends* (Edinburgh: T. & T. Clark, 1978), pp. 63-64 and 63 n. 4.

129. 'Traditionally, male and female servants were paired with masters of the same sex', P. Albenda, 'Landscape Bas-Reliefs in the *Bīt-Ḫilāni* of Ashurbanipal', *BASOR* 24 (1976), pp. 49-72, p. 67.

130. The same may apply to Prov. 9.4; see M.J. Dahood, *Proverbs and Northwest Semitic Philology* (Rome: Biblical Institute Press, 1963), pp. 16-17 who comments that it would be against 'the Semitic sense of propriety' for 'female servants to invite male guests' to a banquet.

Hab. 3.3; Pss. [18.7b]; 31.11; 32.2; 33.7; 34.14; 61.7; 72.3; 73.9; 78.33; 88.13; 89.2; 91.7; 100.5; 119.55; 122.7; 123.2; 126.2; 144.12; Job 5.20; 8.2; 10.12; 28.2; 30.18; 41.24; Prov. 5.10; 14.13; 15.6, 13; Lam. 1.15bc; 5.3; Sir. 3.29; 31.1; 42.13.)

f. + f. // m. + m. For example Jer. 48.38:

'l kl ydym gdrt	On every pair of hands (f.) a slash (f.),
w'l kl mtnym śp	and on every pair of hips (m.), sackcloth (m.).

(Isa. 5.29; 65.18c; Jer. 13.27; 48.37; Hab. 2.5; Pss. 57.5; 85.12; 147.15; Lam. 1.2.)

m. – m. // f. – f. (The first noun in each line being in the construct state), for example Isa. 18.6:

y'zbw yḥdw	Together shall they be abandoned
l'yṭ hrym	to the mountain (m.)—vultures (m.),
wlbhmt h'rṣ	and to the beasts (f.) of the earth (f.).

(Deut. 33.29; Isa. 54.2; Jer. 16.4; Hos. 7.1; Joel 1.6; Pss. 18.16; 109.14; Job 20.24; 31.16; Prov. 1.8; 7.21; Cant. 4.6; 6.31; Sir. 6.31.)

f. – f. // m. – m. (The previous pattern reversed) is extremely rare. Besides Deut. 33.14 there is Ps. 107.16:

ky šbr dltwt nḥšt	For he shatters the bronze (f.) doors (f.),
wbryḥy brzl gd'	and splits the iron (m.) bars (m.)

2.2. *Reversed Patterns*

m. + f. // m. + f. For example Prov. 3.22:

wyhyw ḥyym lnpšk	They will be life (m.) to your soul (f.),
wḥn lgrgtyk	and adornment (m.) for your neck (f.).

(Gen. 49.6a, 17a; Isa. 41.2; 43.16; Joel 2.1; Nah. 2.14; Pss. 104.2ab; 105.27; 135.6; Job 11.14; 18.15; Prov. 22.17; 26.13.)

f. + m. // f. + m. For example Isa. 62.1b:

'd yṣ' kngh ṣdqh	Till her vindication (m.) emerges like brightness (f.),
wyšw 'th klpyd yb'r	and like a torch (m.) her victory (f.) burns.

(Isa. 28.15; 42.4; 44.3b; Ps. 57.6, 12 [= 108.6]; Job 5.9; 18.10; Prov. 5.5; 29.3; Sir. 6.29.)

2.3. *Chiastic Gender Patterns*
m. + *f.* // *f.* + *m.* For example Ps. 37.30:

py ṣdyq yhgh ḥkmh	A just man's mouth (m.) utters wisdom (f.),
wlšwnw tdbr mšpṭ	and his tongue (f.) speaks justice (m.).

(Isa. 33.6; 60.17b; Joel 4.3, 10; Pss. 73.7; 98.5-6; Prov. 3.16; 10.15; 15.8; Lam. 3.47.)

f. + *m.* // *m.* + *f.* For example Isa. 66.3:

hywḥl 'rṣ bywm 'ḥd	Is a land (f.) born in one day (m.)?
'm ywld gwy p'm 'ḥt	Can a nation (m.) be brought forth in one moment (f.)?

(Gen. 49.15; Isa. 1.27; 5.28b; 29.4; 60.17c; Pss. 25.13; 36.7; 44.14; 67.3; 128.3; Job 16.18; Prov. 3.8; 10.12; 20.29; 30.4, 19b; Cant. 7.7; Lam. 2.2.)

m. – *f.* // *f.* – *m.* (Each initial noun in the construct state) occurs only once, in Prov. 8.20:

b'rḥ-ṣdqh 'hlk	On the road (m.) of uprightness (f.) will I walk,
btwk ntybwt-mšpṭ	upon paths (f.) of justice (m.).

f. – *m.* // *m.* – *f.* (The reverse of the preceding pattern), for example Ps. 59.13:

ḥṭ't pymw	For slip (f.) of mouth (m.),
dbr śptymw	for word (m.) of lips (f.)
wylkdw bg 'wnm	let them be trapped by their pride.

(Deut. 32.14; Isa. 24.18; Ps. 102.7; Job 29.13.)

There are several couplets of mixed pattern[131] and only one tricolon (Job 6.4) which has already been set out in full. Gender-matched parallelism can also extend to the quatrain and beyond.

2.4. *Quatrains*
There is no standard pattern, so the texts will simply be listed with the corresponding gender sequences after each one.

131. Mic. 6.7; Zech. 9.10b; Pss. 13.3; 37.19; 141.3; Job 6.12; 11.8; 38.33.

Isa.	19.2	m. + m. // m. + m. // f. + f. // f. + f.
	41.19	m. + f. + f. // m. + m. + m. // f. + m. + m. // f.
Jer.	14.18	m. // f. // f. // m.
	16.3	m. + f. // f. // m. + f.
	16.9	m. // f. // m. // f.
Hos.	9.10	m. + m. + m. // f. + f. + f. // m. // f.
Joel	1.12	f. // f. // m. + m. + m. // m. + m.
Mic.	7.6	m. + m. // f. + f. // f. + f. // m. + m. + m.
Prov.	8.30b-31b	m. + m. + m. // f. + f. // f. + f. + f. // m. + m. + m.
	18.6-7	f. + m. // m. + f. // m. + f. + m. // f. + m. + f.
	23.15-16	m. // m. // f. // f.
Sir.	44.13-14	m. + m. // f. // f. + m. // m. + f.

2.5. *Longer Sequences*

Again, no fixed patterns, so enumeration will suffice (Judg. 9.8-15; Ezek. 11.18-20;[132] Job 1.3; Prov. 16.1-3; 30.21-23).

2.6. *Single Gender Passages*

Certain texts use only masculine nouns (Isa. 1.18; Hos. 14.6; Mal. 3.24; Ps. 104.19; Job 5.5; 38.28; Prov. 29.29-31) or all feminine (Judg. 5.26; Isa. 11.2; 23.15; Ezek. 16.44; Amos 4.2b; Hab. 3.8; Ps. 119.28a; Prov. 5.4; 22.14; 23.27; Lam. 2.11; 3.51; Sir. 44.16b).

2.7. *Prose Passages*

Gender-matched parallelism is also used in texts classified as prose (Gen. 1.2; 11.1, 3, 6; 12.16; 31.52; 40.9b-11, 16b-17; Exod. 2.1-10;[133] 21.23-25; Lev. 5.6; 18.22; Deut. 4.18; 7.13; 21.10-11; 22.5; Josh. 11.6; 1 Sam. 1.15; 1 Kgs 2.6; 5.12; 17.14; 19.11-12; Ezek. 3.7; Ruth 1.8-9; 2.21-22), though some, such as Deut. 22.5 are closer to poetry.

132. Poetic text as reconstructed by W.H. Brownlee, 'The Aftermath of the Fall of Judah according to Ezekiel', *JBL* (1970), pp. 393-404, esp. 398-99.

133. I.M. Kikawada, 'Some Proposals for the Definition of Rhetorical Criticism', *Semitics* 5 (1977), pp. 67-92 points out that Exod. 2.1-10 'is very rich in female terms' with 'eight different nouns used to denote female' and 'only four for males', leading to the climax, when Moses is named by his adoptive mother, an Egyptian (pp. 78-79).

3. *A Re-appraisal, with Particular Reference to the Song of Songs*

3.1. *Introduction*

Over the years I have collected a great many examples of 'gender-matched parallelism' (a device first recognized by Cassuto)[134] not only in Hebrew but in other languages as well. Here this particular type of parallelism will be appraised and then some additional examples will be presented, mostly from the Song of Songs. At the close, further material will be provided from ancient Near Eastern texts.

3.2. *Notes on Theory*

In her book on parallelism, Berlin discusses 'gender-matched parallelism' under the general heading of 'morphologic parallelism' with the sub-heading 'Morphologic pairs from the same word class, sub-section 4: contrast in gender'.[135] She states,

> There may be incidental morphologic parallelism when a masculine noun is paired with a feminine noun, as in the common pair *hrym // gb'wt*, 'mountains (m.) // hills (f.)'. The real contrast, however, comes when the same noun (or same root) appears in two different genders'.

Then come several examples previously proposed by Cassuto.[136] However, instead of agreeing with him that such sets were chosen in order to match genders within each line, Berlin suggests that the pairs were chosen for *morphological* reasons.[137] Further on she discusses gender-matched parallelism in Pss. 126.2, 144.12 and Prov. 1.8 and asks the question: 'Does the morphologic parallelism in these verses belong to the poetic function, or is it a random happening of no poetic significance(?)'. Her answer is that they have no poetic significance

134. For references see above p. 192, n. 3. Note also M.G. Slonim, 'The Substitution of the Masculine for the Feminine Hebrew Pronominal Suffixes to express Reverence', *JQR* 29 (1938–39), pp. 397-403. On gender, see D.A. Zubin and K.-M. Koepcke, 'Gender: A Less than Arbitrary Grammatical Category', in R.A. Hendrick, C.S. Masek and M.F. Miller (eds.), *Papers from the Seventeenth Regional Meeting Chicago Linguistic Society* (Chicago: Chicago Linguistic Society, 1981), pp. 439-449.

135. A. Berlin, *The Dynamics of Biblical Parallelism* (Bloomington: Indiana University Press, 1985), pp. 41-44.

136. Jer. 48.46 (cf. Deut. 21.10-11); Nah. 2.13b; Isa. 3.1.

137. Her examples (*Dynamics*, pp. 42-43) are Isa. 52.2 (*šby* and *šbyh*, 'captive'); Jer. 23.19 (*s'rt* and *s'r*, 'storm') as well as Ezek. 25.13, 15.

since such gender contrasts are concomitant with parallel word-pairs, which in turn depend on lexical association. According to Berlin, only in Isa. 3.8a is a morphological contrast operative:

ky kšlh yrwšlm	For Jerusalem has stumbled (f.);
wyhwdh npl	And Judah has fallen (m.).

'The presence of this alternation in gender heightens the effect of the parallelism.'[138]

In a recent article on Hebrew poetry,[139] Andersen is critical of the functions assigned to gender-matched parallelism[140] commenting,

> Such a diversity induces scepticism as to whether these are functions of the form per se. Except for the last item (to improve parallelism) it is clear that all these functions are achieved by the semantic relationships of the particular words involved in each case, and that the gender-matched neither adds to nor subtracts from the effect. Only the aesthetic function of improving the parallelism is a realistic candidate for a real function.[141]

My allocation of functions was intended to be experimental and required correction. In fact, Andersen was one of the few reviewers to discuss the aspect of function and his critique is both constructive and welcome.[142] In view of his remarks, though, I leave it to others to determine the specific functions of gender-matched parallelism generally and in the passages discussed below.[143]

138. Berlin, *Dynamics*, p. 44. Note that this is *not* an example of gender-matched parallelism. Another example is Prov. 6.16 where 'Yahweh', m., is parallel to 'his self', f., (*napšô*), as noticed (without reference to the genders) by E. Greenstein, 'How Does Parallelism Mean?', in *A Sense of Text: The Art of Language in the Study of Biblical Literature* (JQRSupplement 1982; Winona Lake, IN: Eisenbrauns, 1983), pp. 41-70 (p. 49).

139. T.D. Andersen, 'Problems in Analysing Hebrew Poetry', *East Asia Journal of Theology* 4 (1986), pp. 68-94.

140. Watson, *Classical Hebrew Poetry*, p. 125.

141. Andersen, 'Problems', p. 93; see also p. 77: 'It is doubtful that such patterns are significant because they are likely to occur fairly frequently in any case just by random combination'.

142. Andersen, 'Problems', pp. 92-93. It can be noted that this type of parallelism also occurs in prose texts, for example, *yš'lw 'yš m't r'hw w'šh m't r'wth kly-ksp wkly zhb*, 'A man from his neighbour (m.) and a woman from her neighbour (f.) should demand silver ornaments and gold ornaments' (Exod. 11.2).

143. Other scholars who discuss or refer to this form of parallelism are: J. Kim, *The Structure of the Samson Cycle* (Kampen: Kok, 1993), p. 190 (Judg. 13.7); D.L. Petersen and K.H. Richards, *Interpreting Hebrew Poetry* (Minneapolis:

3.3. *The Song of Songs*

In previous listings of gender-matched synonymous parallelism,[144] many occurrences in the Song of Songs were omitted since I had intended to make a full-scale study of this feature in that book.[145] That study is now complete and the principal results will be set out here in abbreviated form.

Since the Song of Songs is a composition dealing with the relationship between a man and a woman (however that relationship was understood in later tradition)[146] it would seem quite natural that gender polarity would be reflected in the poetic style used.[147] It remains to be seen, though, whether such is the case.

The primary indication of the significance of grammatical gender comes from the use of the feminine form *šwšnh* (probably to be translated 'lotus')[148] used for the woman.[149] This is reinforced by the

Fortress Press, 1992), p. 33; M.I. Gruber, 'The Motherhood of God in Second Isaiah', *RB* 90 (1983), pp. 351-59 (on Isa. 42.13-14; 45.10 and Ps. 123.2); B.K. Waltke and M. O'Connor, *An Introduction to Biblical Hebrew Syntax* (Winona Lake, IN: Eisenbrauns, 1990), p. 106 §6.4.3 on gender doublets; p. 106 n. 39 and p. 109 n. 45; E. Zurro, *Procedimientos iterativos en la poesía ugarítica y hebrea* (BibOr, 43; Rome: Biblical Institute Press, 1987), p. 42 n. 240. On gender, see M. Ben-Asher, 'The Gender of Nouns in Biblical Hebrew', *Semitics* 6 (1978), pp. 1-14. The comments by T. Booij, review of my *Classical Hebrew Poetry*, *BO* 45 (1988), pp. 390-91 are also useful.

144. Add Ezek. 11.3; Prov. 30.21-23; Qoh. 2.13; 4.6; 10.13.

145. In fact, Cant. 2.3, 4.6, 7.7 and 7.8 were quoted in my earlier article and there is also a reference to 7.9.

146. See the very extensive survey in M. Pope, *Song of Songs* (AB, 7C; Garden City, NY: Doubleday, 1977), pp. 89-229. Note, in addition, F. Dünzl, *Braut und Bräutigam* (Tübingen: Mohr, 1993).

147. See the brief remarks by M. Falk, *Love Lyrics from the Bible: A Translation and Literary Study of the Song of Songs* (Sheffield: Almond Press, 1982), p. 74 and n. 4.

148. On the meaning of this term, see R. Gordis, *The Song of Songs* (New York: Jewish Theological Seminary of America, 1961), p. 81 ('probably a red or dark purple flower'); F. Landy, *Paradoxes of Paradise: Identity and Difference in the Song of Songs* (Sheffield: Almond Press, 1983), p. 301 n. 17; Pope, *Song*, p. 368; R.J. Tournay, *Quand Dieu parle aux hommes le langage de l'amour: Etudes sur le Cantique des Cantiques* (Paris: Gabalda, 1982), p. 42; G. Garbini, *Cantico dei cantici: Testo, traduzione, note e commento* (Biblica, Testi e studi, 2; Brescia: Paideia, 1992), p. 197, etc.

149. The m. sing. form *šwšn* occurs only in 1 Kgs 7.19, 22, 26 (// 2 Chron 4.5 f. form) and in Ps. 60.1. In Hos. 14.6 *yprḥ kšwšnh* said of Israel, there is no match

equally feminine noun *hṣblt*[150] in the first colon:

'ny hbṣlt hšrn	I am a crocus (f.) of the plain,
šwšnt h'mqm	a lotus (f.) of the valleys (2.1-2).

It must be stressed that in this couplet there is no gender-matched parallelism. The passage, though, does explain the contrast of genders exploited in 2.2-3[151] where first the woman is described with (predominantly) feminine terms and then, in the second couplet, exclusively masculine terms are used for the male lover:

kšwšnh byn hḥwḥym	Like a lotus (f.) among thorns (m.),
kn r'ty byn hbnwt	so is my beloved (f). among the lasses (f.);
ktpwḥ b'ṣy hy'r	like an apple-tree (m.)[152] in the trees (m.) of the forest,
kn dwdy byn hbnym	so is my beloved (m.) among the lads (m.).[153]

Again, the feminine form of *sws*, 'horse', occurs only in the Song of Songs:[154]

lssty brkby pr'h dmytyk r'yty	To a mare (f.) in Pharaoh's chariots have I compared you, my love (1.9).

Landy comments, 'The sex of the horse in our verse may primarily have been suggested by the sex of the Beloved, to whom the verse is addressed'.[155]

of genders; nor in the simile in 2 Chron. 4.5. Note that the gender of a noun is the gender of its form in the singular.

150. For discussion of the word *hbṣlt*, see Pope, *Song*, pp. 367-68; Garbini, *Cantico*, pp. 196-97; Gordis, *Song*, p. 80; it may mean the narcissus, a pale lilac-coloured flower, the saffron or the rose.

151. However, the pattern is partially incomplete, since otherwise the expected gender of the second noun in line 1 would be f. Even so, the patterning applies in three lines out of four.

152. For the 'apple tree' (*ḫašḫur*) as denoting the male lover in Sumerian love poetry, cf. B. Alster, 'Marriage and Love in the Sumerian Love Songs. With some Notes on the Manchester Tammuz', in M.E. Cohen, D.C. Snell and D.B. Weisberg (eds.), *The Tablet and the Scroll: Near Eastern Studies in Honor of William W. Hallo* (Bethesda, MD: CDL Press, 1993), pp. 15-27, 20.

153. The next couplet also uses only m. nouns (*l*, *pry* and even *k*).

154. Garbini, *Cantico*, pp. 191-92 corrects to *swswt* and renders the line: 'Alle cavalle aggiogate ai carri del faraone ti paragono, amica mia'. Note that *sswt* occurs in Ugaritic (*KTU* 6.63:3).

155. Landy, *Paradoxes*, pp. 176-77.

Similarly, masculine terms are used to describe the male lover:

ṣrwr hmr dwdy ly byn šdy ylyn	a bundle (m.) of myrrh (m.) is my beloved to me, spending the night between my breasts,
'škl hkpr dwdy ly	a cluster (m.) of henna (m.) is my beloved to me, etc. (1.13-14).

Also significant are the apt comparisons to trees used for each of the lovers. The man (or rather, his height) is compared with that of cedars:

mr'hw klbnwn bwr k'rzym	His appearance (m.) is like Lebanon, choice as cedars (m.) (5.15).

The woman is likened to a palm-tree, of feminine gender in Hebrew:

qwmtk dmth ltm	Your stature (f.) is like the palm-tree (f.) (7.8).

It is probably no accident, then, that *mr'h* is used for the man (even though a word for 'height' would have been preferable) in 5.15 whereas in 7.8 the corresponding word is *qwmh*.[156]

There is an occasional match of gender elsewhere, for example:

my z't 'lh mn-hmdbr ktymrwt 'šn	Who is this (f.) coming up from the desert like columns (f.) of smoke[157] etc. (3.6).

Here the rare word *tîmārâ* (elsewhere only Joel 3.3) is used as a synonym of *'ammud* which is much commoner but masculine in gender.[158]

And in the refrain

hšb'ty 'tkm bnwt yrwšlm	I adjure you, daughters of Jerusalem,
bṣb'wt 'w b'ylwt hśdh	by the gazelles (f.) or by the hinds (f.) of the field (2.7 = 3.5),

the unusual feminine form *ṣb'yh* (elsewhere only 4.5 and 7.4) occurs, coupled with *'ylh* (f.) in connection with 'the daughters of Jerusalem'.

156. For an echo of these passages in the Genesis Apocryphon, see below.

157. From the Vetus Latina, Garbini (*Cantico*, pp. 60-61, 212) reconstructs *kzymwrt hgpn*, 'like a vine-shoot'; this makes no difference as the two terms are also f.

158. See Pope, *Song*, p. 426.

In the Waṣfs, too, such matches also occur, but never systematically.[159] These matches can be set out for each Waṣf, for both masculine and feminine forms, as follows.[160]

3.3.1. *First Waṣf (1.9-10)*
(a) masculine

n'ww lḥyyk btrym	adorned are your cheeks (m.) with bangles (m.),
ṣw'rk bḥrwzym	your neck (m.) with beads (m.) (1.10);[161]

(b) feminine. See 1.9 cited above.

3.3.2. *Second Waṣf (4.1-7)*
(a) masculine

s'rk k'dr h'zym, *šglšw mhr gl'd*	your hair (m.) is like a flock (m.) of goats (m.) flowing in waves from (Mount) Gilead (4.1);[162]

159. It is well known that the sequence of body parts in such compositions is generally listed from the head downwards (cf. my, *Classical Hebrew Poetry*, pp. 353-55). This is confirmed by the progression 'crown of head', 'ears', 'shoulders', 'chest', 'waist', 'vulva', 'thighs' (with only 'wrists' and 'breasts' out of sequence) used in an Old Babylonian love poem found at Kish and edited by J. G. Westenholz, 'A Forgotten Love Song', in F. Rochberg-Halton (ed.), *Language, Literature, and History...Presented to E. Reiner* (AOS, 67; New Haven, CT: American Oriental Society, 1987), pp. 415-25. Similar sequences occur in the Qumran horoscopes (4Q186); translations: G. Vermes, *The Dead Sea Scrolls* (Harmondsworth: Penguin Books, 1987), pp. 306-307; F. García Martínez, *Textos de Qumrán* (Madrid: Editorial Trebolla, 1992), p. 471. For a Ugaritic parallel see L.R. Fisher in *RSP*, II, pp. 134-38 and the comments of A. Cooper in *JAOS* 111 (1991), p. 835.

160. For the significance of the imagery in the Waṣfs, see R.N. Soulen, 'The *Waṣfs* of the Song of Songs and Hermeneutic', *JBL* 86 (1967), pp. 183-90. He argues that the imagery is 'a means of arousing emotions consonant with those experienced by the suitor as he beholds his beloved's attributes (or so the maiden as she speaks of her beloved in 5.10-16)', p. 189.

161. Garbini, *Cantico*, pp. 191-93: 'sono belli i tuoi fianchi /quando ancheggi nella danza/ e il tuo collo nei fili di perle'. The translation of the last word, the *hapax legomenon aruzîm*, is a guess but I suggest that it may be explained by Akk. (*ḫ*)*urīzu* which denotes a stone (*AHw*, p. 1431a).

162. For the translation, cf. S.S. Tuell, 'A Riddle Resolved by an Enigma: Hebrew GLŠ and Ugaritic *glṯ*', *JBL* 112 (1993), pp. 99-121.

kmgdl dwyd ṣw'rk,	like a tower (m.) of David is your neck (m.) (4.4; similarly 7.5);
šny šdyk kšny 'prym t'my ṣbyh hrw'ym bšwšnym,	your two breasts (m.) are like two fawns (m.), twins of a gazelle, browsing (m.) among the lotuses (c.) (4.5).

(b) feminine

'ynyk ywnym,	your (f.) eyes (f.) are doves (f.) (4.1);[163]
kplḥ hrmwn rqtk,	like the cleft (f.)[164] of a pomegranate is your temple (f.) (4.3 = 6.7).[165]

Also, although in 4.2 the direct object of comparison for the teeth is *'dr*, 'flock (of)', which is masculine, the clustering of feminine forms, most only found here and in all probability neologisms,[166] indicates an intentional focus on the feminine:

šnyk k'dr hqbwṣwt š'lw mn-hrḥṣh	Your teeth (f.) are like a flock (m.) of ewes who have come up from the washing (f.),
šklm mt'ymwt wšklh 'yn bhm	all of them twinning and a bereft one (f.) is not among them.

Thus, apart from 4.3 ('thread', m. and 'lips', f.) GMS is used throughout.

3.3.3. *Third Waṣf (5.10-16)*
(a) masculine

r'šw ktm pz	his head (m.) is finest gold (m.) (5.11);[167]

and possibly

ydw glyl zhb	his member (m.) is a gold case (m.) (5.14a).[168]

163. Both *'yn* and *ywnh* have a plur. ending in *-îm* although both words are f.
164. For the gender see BDB, p. 812.
165. Garbini, *Cantico*, p. 222, has a very different meaning and suppresses 6.7 as dittography (p. 69).
166. These are *qṣwbwt*, *rḥṣh* and *mt'ymwt*; see Garbini, *Cantico*, p. 218.
167. Philological details in Pope, *Song*, pp. 534-35.
168. If Garbini (*Cantico*, pp. 89-90, 158-59 and 242) is correct in altering the plural forms to the singular here.

(b) feminine

ʿynyw kywnym,	his eyes (f.) are like doves (f.) (5.12) (see above ([4.1]);
lḥyw kʿrwgt hbśm mgdlwt mrqḥym,	his cheeks (f.) are like beds (f.) of spices strong with aromatics (5.13a).[169]

and possibly

śptwtyw šwšnym nṭpwt mwr ʿbr	His lips[170] (f.) are lotuses (f.),[171] dripping (f.) liquid myrrh (m.) (5.13b).

3.3.4. *Fourth Waṣf (6.4-7)*

(a) masculine

šʿrk kʿdr hʿzym.	your hair (m.) is like a flock (m.) of goats (m.) (6.5)—see above in the Second Waṣf.

(b) feminine

yph ʾt rʿty ktrṣh	You are beautiful (f.) my darling (f.) as Tirzah (f.),
nʾwh kyrwšlm	lovely (f.) as Jerusalem (f.),
ʾymh kndglwt	terrible (f.) as trophies (f.) (6.4).[172]
yph klbnh	beautiful (f.) as the moon (f.),
brh kḥmh	bright (f.) as the sun (f.),
ʾymh kndglwt	terrible (f.) as trophies (f.) (6.10)

Note that instead of *yareaḥ* or *keseʾ*, both masculine, a feminine word for 'moon' has been used; similarly, *labana* has been preferred to

169. For the imagery, cf. 'my bed of incense is *ballukku*-perfumed' in an Old Babylonian love poem; see Westenholz, 'A Forgotten Love Song', p. 423 col. i 8'. Garbini (*Cantico*, p. 243) suggests instead, 'I suoi glutei sono come aiuole di balsamo/ dove crescono piante di aromi'.

170. Garbini, *Cantico*, pp. 241-42 reads *ptym* which he translates 'testicles'.

171. It is more than likely that though the plural form looks m., the gender of *wnym* is f. In Sir. 50.8 *kwn ʿl ybly mym*, 'like a lotus by running waters', the m. form of the word is used in respect of Simeon. In fact, in the series of six paired similes (50.6-10) all the nouns used for comparison are m. except in v. 7 (both *m* and *qt* are f.).

172. See Pope, *Song*, pp. 558-63, and Gordis, *Song*, pp. 93-94 for the strange comparison with a city (Tirzah) and the possible meanings of *nidgalôt*. Here, the only issue is the gender of these two words, and both are f. Instead of 'Tirzah' Garbini (*Cantico*, p. 216) very plausibly suggests 'grazia' (root *rṣh*).

šemeš (m.), 'sun', as McKay has noted.[173] This is proved by *'l tr'wny š'ny šḥšḥrt ššzptny hšmš*, 'Do not stare (f.pl.) at me that I am black, that the sun (f.) has tanned(?) me' 1.6[174] where the gender of *šemeš* is appropriate.

3.3.5. *Fifth Waṣf (7.1-7)*
(a) masculine forms

ḥmwqy yrkyk kmw ḥl'ym	The curves (m.) of your thighs (f.) are like ornaments (m.) (7.2).
šrrk 'gn hshr,	Your vulva[175] (m.) is like a rounded bowl (m.)... (7.3).
šny šdyk kšny 'prym t'my ṣbyh	Your two breasts (m.) are like two fawns (m.), twins of a gazelle, (7.4) (formulaic; see above)
ṣwrk kmgdl hšn,	your neck (m.) is like a tower (m.) of ivory (7.5)
'pk kmgdl hlbnwn,	your nose (m.) is like a tower (m.) of Lebanon. (7.5)
šdyk k'šklwt hgpn	your breasts (m.) like clusters (m.) of the vine,
wryḥ 'pk ktpwḥym	and the scent (m.) of your nipple (m.) like apples (m.)
wḥkk kyyn hṭwb.	and your palate (m.) like sweet wine (m.) (7.9).

See also

wšdyk l'šklwt	and your breasts (m.) like [ellipsis of *dmh*] its clusters (m.) (7.8).

(b) feminine forms

bṭnk 'rmt ḥṭym,	your belly (f.) is like a heap (f.) of wheat... (7.3)
'ynyk brkwt bḥšbwn,	your eyes (f.) are like pools (f.) in Heshbon... (7.5)

173. J.W. McKay, 'Helel and the Dawn Goddess', *VT* 20 (1970), pp. 451-64, 459.

174. See the commentaries.

175. So Pope, *Song*, p. 617; 'navel' is just as likely, though.

There is one deviation: 'hairs' (f.) and 'purple' (m.) (7.6).[176] Of the Waṣfs, three use gender-matched parallelism almost invariably: the first, second and fifth.

Further, in 3.6 sixty mighty *men* surround Solomon's litter whereas in 6.8-9 sixty *queens*, eighty *concubines* and innumerable *maidens* accompany the woman who is unique to her *mother* and her *progenitress* and *girls* and *concubines* praise her.[177] Many *hapax legomena* in the Song of Songs are feminine forms of masculine words[178] and, as has been seen, in most cases the feminine form is exploited. Exceptions are *'bqh* (3.6), *ḥtwnh* (3.11), *gdyh* (1.8) and *šḥrḥwrt* (1.6).

3.4. *Ancient Near Eastern Examples*

It is accepted that gender-matched parallelism is used in ancient Near Eastern verse to some extent.[179] In Akkadian this is apparent from such passages as:

> I will change the heart of mankind so that
> father will not listen to son,
> daughter will speak hateful things to mother[180]

176. The same pattern emerges in Sir. 50.

177. For these comments, see J.C. Exum, 'A Literary and Structural Analysis of the Song of Songs', *ZAW* 85 (1973), pp. 47-79, 66, though there is no explicit reference to the type of parallelism considered here. Garbini, *Cantico*, p. 247 understands *brh* to mean 'daughter' in 6.9; he translates 'la figlia per chi l'ha partorita'.

178. Garbini, *Cantico*, p. 298 provides a list; to the forms can be added *ḥllt* in 2.5 (for MT *ḥwlt*) and as proposed by Garbini, *Cantico*, pp. 45 and 201. A m. form of a f. word is *ṣpḥ* in 7.5 (for MT *ṣwph*), on which cf. Garbini, *Cantico*, pp. 106 and 257.

179. E.g., J.H. Tigay, *The Evolution of the Gilgamesh Epic* (Philadelphia: University of Pennsylvania Press, 1982), p. 265, note to ii 16: 'Relating sons to fathers and daughters to mothers is a standard device in ancient Near Eastern literature (see *Erra* IIc, 33-34; III, 9-10; cf. *Atr.* S, v, 18-21 = vi, 7-10; for west-Semitic examples, see Ruth 1.8; Song of Songs 3.4; 8.2; Gen 24.28; *Keret* B (= *UT*, no. 128; *ANET*, p. 146b), iii, 23-24'. Also, 'There seems to be no direct evidence that carnelian stands for a female and lapis lazuli for a male child. But the gender of the Akkadian *sāmtu* and *uqnû* do suggest this distribution': W. Farber, *JNES* 43 (1984), p. 312 n. 6. Comparable is 7 *mārēšu ana pān Adad lišrupu* 7 *mārātēšu ana Ištar ḫarimatu luramme*, 'May he burn his seven sons before Adad, may he release his seven daughters to Ishtar as prostitutes' (B. Meissner, *Die Keilschrifttexte auf den steinernen Orthostaten und Statuen aus dem Tell Ḫalâf* [AfO Beiheft, 1; Graz: 1933], p. 73 no. 8.7).

180. *Erra Epic* III A 9-10; similarly, IIc 33-34 (see previous note).

and

> who estranged son (from father),
> who estranged father (from) son,
> who estranged daughter (from) mother,
> who estranged mother (from) daughter,
> who estranged daughter-in-law (from) mother-in-law,
> who estranged brother from brother,
> who estranged friend (m.) from friend (m.),
> who estranged companion (m.) from companion (m.).[181]

That the poets used grammatical gender to advantage is indicated by several passages where the feminine noun is specified as 'daughter': 'The Bow (*qaštu*) he kissed: "This is truly my Daughter"';[182] *kibrītu elletu mārat šamê rabûti anāku*, 'I am pure sulphur, daughter of great Anu';[183] and *ḫarrānu mārat ilāni rabûti*, 'the road, daughter of the great gods';[184] *īumm šamutu šimān*, 'my mother is a rain (f.) at the right season'.[185] Also, in explaining the imagery of an Assyrian elegy, Reiner comments, 'the metaphor of the boat, a word of feminine gender in Akkadian, identifies the person addressed as a woman'.[186] The same procedure is illustrated by a couplet:

ūlidka ṣēru kīma abīka	the steppe (m.) sired you as if he were your father,
ukannīka qerbet kīma ummīka	the field (f.) cared for you as if she were your mother.[187]

181. *Šurpu* II 20-28; E. Reiner, *Šurpu: A Collection of Sumerian and Akkadian Incantations* (AfO Beiheft, 11; Graz: E. Weidner, 1958; repr.; Osnabrück: Biblio Verlag, 1970), p. 13; the same pattern may occur in line 19.

182. *Ee* VI 87.

183. *Maqlû* VI 73; also IX 108.

184. *Šurpu* V-VI 191. Text: Reiner, *Šurpu*, p. 35; for the gender of *ḫarranu* cf. *AHw*, p. 326b (m. but later f.).

185. *Ugaritica* V, p. 169 line 33.

186. E. Reiner, *Your Thwarts in Pieces Your Mooring Rope Cut: Poetry from Babylonia and Assyria* (Michigan: Horace H. Rackham School of Graduate Studies at the University of Michigan, 1985), p. 91 (on K 890 line 1). Similarly, *ša kīma narkabti eleppa rakbū kūm sīsê ṣandū parrisāni*, '(kings) who ride a boat (f.) instead of a chariot (f.), instead of horses (m.) harness oarsmen (m.)' (R. Borger, *Die Inschriften Esarhaddons, Königs von Assyrien* [AfO Beiheft, 9; Graz: Ernst Weidner, 1956], p. 57 col. iv line 83).

187. E. von Weiher, *Spätbabylonische Texte aus Uruk* (Berlin: Mann, 1983), II, p. 21 lines 18-19; near-parallel: H. Zimmern, *Beiträge zur Kenntnis der*

Here are some more examples of gender-matched, first from incantations:

ana ilišu arnušu ana ištaršu gillassu	his sin (m.) is against his god (m.), his misdeed (f.) against his goddess.[188]
pûša lu lipu lišanša lu ṭabtu	may her mouth (m.) be tallow (m.), her tongue (f.) salt (f.).[189]

There is also at least one occurrence in a Ugaritic incantation

n. bṯy lbṯy. ṯṯb.	May the eye of the enchanter return to the enchanter,
ʻn.[bṯt] lbṯt. ṯ[ṯb]	may the eye of the enchantress return to the enchantress.[190]

From the Akkadian literary texts:

liššur eqlu išpikišu	let the fields (m.) fall short in its/their yield (m.),
liteddil irtaša nisaba	(the goddess) Nissaba close up her breast (f.).[191]
mala kappa niṭil ineka ul imṣû šamāmu	the heavens (m.) do not amount to the bowl (m.) into which you gaze,

Babylonischen Religion (Assyriologische Bibliothek, 12; Leipzig: J.C. Hinrichs'sche, 1901), No. 100:15 (cited in *CAD*, Q, p. 212b).

188. *Šurpu* II 34; Reiner, *Šurpu*, p. 14; this echoes line 33: 'He scorned the god, despised the goddess'. Contrast line 32, where there is no match in gender.

189. *Maqlû* I 31; for the gender of *ṭabtu* cf. *atti ṭabtu*, 'you (f.) (are) salt', *Maqlû* VI 111, etc. Comparable is BM 122691 obv. 15'-16': *īnīša mulli<a> ṭabtam piša mullia digima*[*m*], Fill her eyes (f.) with salt (f.), fill her mouth (m.) with ashes' (W. Farber, 'Zur älteren akkadischen Beschwörungsliteratur', *ZA* 71 [1981], pp. 51-72, 63-64; the gender of the last word, for which cf. *AHw*, pp. 169 and 1550b, is probably m.). Other examples of gender-matched are *Maqlû* I 36b-37; III 50-51, 63-64; V 12 and VII 168. Also, as part of a curse from a treaty: *qīru kupru lu mākalākunu šināt imēri lu mašqītkunu*, 'May asphalt and dry asphalt (m.) be your food (m.)! May donkey urine (f.) be your drink (f.)!' (Text and translation: K. Watanabe, *Die* adê-*Vereidigung anläßlich der Thronfolgeregelung Asarhaddons* (Baghdader Mitteilungen Beiheft, 3; Berlin: Mann, 1987), pp. 166-67, lines 490-91.

190. *KTU* 1.96:11-12; cf. G. del Olmo Lete, 'Un conjuro ugarítico contra el "mal ojo" (KTU 1.96)', *Anuari de filologia* 15 (1992), pp. 7-16.

191. Text: Lambert and Millard, *Atraḫasis*, pp. 72-73 = *Atr.* II i 18-19; pp. 108-109 = *Atr.* S iv 46-47 // S v 5-6 *line'i* (for *liteddil*); also pp. 110-11 = *Atr.* S iv 56-57.

mala makālti bārûti ul imṣâ gimiršina mātāti	all the lands (f.) do not amount to the saucer (f.) of the seer.[192]
šetka qerbetu rapa[štum]	(Oh Shamash), your net (f.) is the wide earth (f.),
gišpirraka [šamau ruqu]tu	your trap (m.) the distant sky (m.)[193]
išmema ḫādûa immeru pānūšu	He who gloats over me heard, his face (m.) lit up,
ḫādīti ubassiru kabattaša ipperdu	they informed her who gloats over me, and her mood (f.) brightened[194]

This type of parallelism is also found in the texts from Qumran, for instance:

bmws lby kmym	when my heart (m.) liquified like water (m.),
wtḥzq npšy bbrytk	you strengthened my soul (f.) in your covenant (f.) (1QH 10.28).[195]

An example in Aramaic comes from the 'Genesis Apocryphon':

> Abraham, dreamt a dream, on the night of my entry into Egypt. And in my dream I saw a cedar and a palm-tree. 15 [. . .] Some men arrived attempting to cut and uproot the cedar, leaving the palm-tree alone. 16 But the palm-tree shouted and said: Do not hew down the cedar because both of us are of the same family. And the cedar was saved thanks to the palm-tree 17 and was not hewn down.

Sarai then interprets the dream as men threatening Abraham's life on account of her and so Abraham asks her to pretend that she is his sister, not his wife.[196]

It is significant that here the terms for 'cedar' and 'palm-tree', *'rz* and *tmrh* are masculine and feminine respectively. Fitzmyer comments, 'It is not impossible that Ct 5.15 (where the youth is compared

192. *Shamash Hymn* 154-155; Lambert, *Babylonian Wisdom Literature*, p. 134.

193. Text and translation: J.V. Kinnier Wilson, *The Legend of Etana: A New Edition* (Warminster: Aris & Phillips, 1985), pp. 36-37 (= OV I/C 47-48) parallel: pp. 94-95 (LV II 68-69); cf. *CAD*, Q, p. 213b. See, similarly, the Babylonian Theodicy 60 and 62 (Lambert, *Babylonian Wisdom Literature*, pp. 74-75) and *Erra* V 33-34.

194. *Ludlul* II 117-118, translation: J.S. Cooper, 'The Conclusion of Ludlul II', *JCS* 27 (1975), pp. 248-50; cf. *CAD*, N/1, p. 23. Another example is *Gilg*. I ii 49-50.

195. See above, 'The Old Testament', for other examples.

196. Genesis Apocryphon col. xix 14-17; translation: F. García Martínez, *Textos de Qumrán* (Madrid: Editorial Trotta, 1992), pp. 280-82.

to a cedar) and 7.7-8 (where the girl is compared to a palm) may (also) have influenced this passage'.[197] In this connection it is worth pointing out that in Judges 9 the genders of the trees are also significant.[198]

3.5. *Conclusion*

Parallelism based on the match of gender evidently occurs in the Song of Songs in much the same way as it is to be found generally in Hebrew and in ancient Near Eastern texts. That is to say, although relatively frequent,[199] its use is not systematic. It is used principally to reinforce similes, especially in the Waṣfs and occasionally to focus on one or other of the protagonists. To some extent masculine terms are used for the male and feminine terms for the female, but on the whole such usage is subordinate to higher-level patterns.[200]

197. J.A. Fitzmyer, *The Genesis Apocryphon of Qumran Cave 1: A Commentary* (BibOr, 18A; Rome: Pontifical Biblical Institute, 1971), p. 111. He notes that rabbinical literature connects Ps. 92.13 with the story of Abram and Sarai (Gen. 12.17).

198. See Chapter 7, 'Chiastic Patterns in Biblical Hebrew Poetry'; also J.C. de Moor, *The Rise of Yahwism: The Roots of Israelite Monotheism* (BETL, 9; Leuven: Uitgeverij Peeters, 1990), p. 189 n. 365.

199. A very approximate count indicates some 40 times over about 180 lines of text.

200. Note also A. Brenner (ed.), *A Feminist Companion to The Song of Songs* (The Feminist Companion to the Bible, 1; Sheffield: JSOT Press, 1993); C. Meyers, 'Gender Imagery in the Song of Songs', *HAR* 10 (1986), pp. 209-23.

Chapter 5

Other Types of Parallelism

1. *Parallelism with Qtl in Ugaritic*[1]

1.1. *Need for Study*

Study of parallelism between different forms of the verb in the Ugaritic poetic texts has been partial as the brief outline provided in the next paragraph shows. While it is generally accepted that in these texts the *yqtl* or prefix form of the verb is commoner, with *qtl* forms correspondingly less frequent, and while it is also accepted opinion that *qtl* was used more in the non-literary texts,[2] very little is known about the co-occurrence of either or both forms in parallel lines. For instance, Segert completely ignores this aspect in his grammar.[3]

In a verse tradition dominated by parallelism it is evidently of significance to determine the combinations of *yqtl* and *qtl* forms attested within couplets and other strophic units. In his review of my book[4] Niccacci commented that I should have provided more information on *yqtl // qtl* and *qtl // yqtl* in Hebrew poetry.[5] I agree, and in response to his request I have conducted a preliminary study on this topic in Ugaritic verse. The results are presented here. Since the *yqtl* form is

1. First published in *UF* 21 (1989), pp. 435-42.

2. See M. Liverani, 'Elementi innovativi nell'ugaritico non letterario', *ANLR* 8.19 (1964), pp. 173-91 and the conclusions drawn by Fenton and Verreet (see below).

3. S. Segert, *A Basic Grammar of the Ugaritic Language with Selected Texts and Glossary* (Berkeley: University of California Press, 1984), no. 64.22-23 (p. 89).

4. W.G.E. Watson, *Classical Hebrew Poetry: A Guide to its Techniques* (JSOTSSup, 26; Sheffield: JSOT Press, 1986).

5. A. Niccacci, review of *Classical Hebrew Poetry*, *LA* 35 (1985), p. 473. Some time ago, B. Margalit pointed out to me (oral communication) that parallelism between non-identical verbs had not been studied.

so frequent in Ugaritic verse this survey is limited to finite, affixing verbal forms (*qtl* or *qatala*). Imperatives and the difficult non-inflected *qtl* form which may or may not correspond to the absolute infinitive[6] are therefore excluded.

1.2. *Survey*

Our survey begins with Cassuto who noted that it is 'normal poetic usage' in Ugaritic for *qtl* and *yqtl* forms of the same verb to occur in consecutive lines.[7] In correcting Goetze,[8] Brockelmann[9] showed that Ugaritic *qtl* denotes a perfect (his best example is 1.4 ii 21-24) and added 'in reports, also, the perfect can alternate with the imperfect'.[10]

In his series of workbooks for students, culminating in the *Ugaritic Textbook* (1965), C.H. Gordon mentions the verb sequences *yqtl // qtl* and *qtl // yqtl* with several examples. He notes, too, that 'there is a tendency to use the same verbal forms in parallel constructions' but gives no explanation for such usage.[11]

6. For the best explanation of this form (uninflected *qtl*) in Ugaritic, see E.D. Mallon, 'The Ugaritic Verb in the Letters and Administrative Documents' (unpublished thesis, Washington, 1982), pp. 105-27.

7. U. Cassuto, *The Goddess Anath: Canaanite Epics of the Patriarchal Age. Texts, Hebrew Translation, Commentary and Introduction* (ET; Jerusalem: Magnes, 1971 [1951]), pp. 46-47 cites 1.4 iii 14-16; vi 36-38; 1.19 iii 8-9. See also U. Cassuto, 'Il palazzo di Baal nella tavola II AB di Ras Shamra', *Or* NS 7 (1938), pp. 288-89.

8. C. Brockelman, 'Zur Syntax der Sprache von Ugarit', *Or* 10 (1941), pp. 223-40, 227-31, esp. 228-30.

9. A. Goetze, 'The Tenses of Ugaritic', *JAOS* 58 (1938), pp. 266-309, esp. 268-84. Other studies are E. Hammershaimb, *Das Verbum im Dialekt von Ras Schamra. Eine morphologische und syntaktische Untersuchung des Verbums in den alphabetischen Keilschrifttexten aus dem alten Ugarit* (Copenhagen: Ejnar Munksgaard, 1941), and J. Aistleitner, *Untersuchungen zur Grammatik des Ugaritischen* (Berichte über die Verhandlungen der Sächsischen Akademie der Wissenschaft zu Leipzig, 100/6; Berlin: Akademie Verlag, 1954). As Mallon remarks ('Ugaritic Verb', p. 39) the studies by Goetze, Hammershaimb and Aistleitner are now chiefly of historical value only.

10. Brockelmann 'Syntax der Sprache'. His examples are 1.1 ii 18 (// 1.3 iv 33); 1.2 iv 7-8; 1.4 i 23-28 and v 26-27.

11. *UT* §13.58. Not all his examples are correct; note his explanation of the *yqtl* form *ištbm* (if that is the correct reading; see D. Pardee, 'Will the Dragon Never be Muzzled?', *UF* 16 [1984], pp. 251-55) in *KTU* 1.3 iii 40 as due to 'the general avoidance of *qatala* forms in Gt'.

As the title of his paper shows, Held set out a series of couplets in Ugaritic where *yqtl* was used in the first line, *qtl* in the second (and the other way round, too).[12] Though restricted to forms of the same verb (verbal root), his study provided a useful starting point for later work.[13] Held also looked at parallelism between passive and active forms of the same verb.[14]

In his description of the Ugaritic verb Delekat[15] assigned four functions to the suffix conjugation (*qatala*):

1. to narrate events or describe states prior to the enacted event (or state)—the pluperfect;
2. to describe a circumstance which has come about due to an event which has occurred recently;[16]
3. to portray the rapid succession or overlapping of events;
4. to shorten narrative.

Fenton's unpublished thesis on the Ugaritic verb[17] is not directly concerned with parallelism between *qtl* and *yqtl* forms, though he does discuss this aspect. His study on parallel passages[18] can be summarized in the following table:

Command	Fulfilment
tqtl	narr. *yqtl*
impv. *qtl*	narr. *qtl*
juss. *yqtl*	narr. *yqtl*

12. M. Held, 'The *yqtl-qtl* (*qtl-yqtl*) Sequence of Identical Verbs in Biblical Hebrew and Ugaritic', in M. Ben Horin *et al.* (eds.), *Studies in Honor of Abraham A. Neuman* (Leiden: Brill, 1962), pp. 281-90.

13. S. Gevirtz, 'Evidence of Conjugational Variation in the Parallelization of Selfsame Verbs in the Amarna Letters', *JNES* 32 (1973), pp. 99-104. See also S. Gevirtz, 'On Canaanite Rhetoric: The Evidence of the Amarna Letters from Tyre', *Or* NS 42 (1973), pp. 162-77, 169-70.

14. M. Held, 'The Action-Result (Factitive-Passive) Sequence of Identical Verbs in Biblical Hebrew and Ugaritic', *JBL* 84 (1965), pp. 272-82.

15. L. Delekat, 'Zum ugaritischen Verbum', *UF* 4 (1972), pp. 11-26.

16. 'Das *qatala* wird verwendet um einen Zustand zu schildern, der durch ein kurz zurückliegendes Ereignis eingetreten ist', Delekat, 'Zum ugaritischen Verbum', p. 11.

17. T.L. Fenton, 'The Ugaritic Verbal System' (unpublished thesis, Oxford, 1963).

18. T.L. Fenton, 'Command and Fulfilment in Ugaritic—*'tqtl : yqtl'* and *'qtl : qtl''*, *JSS* 14 (1969), pp. 34-38.

In other words, when a command is given in the prefix conjugation its performance is narrated by a narrative *yqtl*—and similarly for the other two sets.

Fenton also shows that

> whereas *yqtl* forms are often accompanied by such emphatic adverbs as *k*, *apn(k)*, *apnk*, *aphn*(+ *k*), *idk*(+ *l* or *al* emphatic), *hlm*/*k*/*n*, *bkm*, this is not the case with *qtl* forms (though the latter may be preceded by the emphatic *l*). The evidence would indicate that *qtl* had an emphasis which *yqtl* lacked.

He proposes the formula: '*qtl* formation = *yqtl* formation + emphatic element(s)'.[19]

In a later study, having noted that '[t]he most obvious and pervasive feature of verbal usage in the Ugaritic literary texts is that the form *yqtl* and not *qtl* is the normal narrative tense, that is, the form used to report past acts',[20] he adds, 'in Ugaritic poetry *yqtl* is the "omni-temporal" form with *qtl* occasionally replacing it as the narrative form'.[21] He then goes on to specify 'four circumstances where *qtl* replaces *yqtl* as the narrative form'. They are:

1. when a verb from the same root is used in parallel lines (as seen by Cassuto and Held; see above);
2. in reporting the fulfilment of a command in the imperative (*qtl*) form (see above);
3. 'in conversations, that is, when the "characters" of the poems address each other, they refer, to or inform of, past events in the *qtl* form';
4. 'when a significant stage in the narrative is reached, when there is a change of subject matter, or when the narrative turns to a "character" who has not been the focus of attention in the preceding lines, the first verb or verbs of the new episode may be in the *qtl* form before the narrative reverts to *yqtl*'.

In other words, unlike the free use of *yqtl*, *qtl* 'is restricted to certain circumstances'.[22] Co-occurrence (of *qtl* and *yqtl*) is not discussed.

19. Fenton, 'Command and Fulfilment', p. 37.

20. T.L. Fenton, 'The Hebrew "Tenses" in the Light of Ugaritic', in *Proceedings of the Fifth World Congress of Jewish Studies* (Jerusalem: World Union of Jewish Studies, 1969), IV, pp. 31-39; the quote is from p. 32.

21. Fenton, 'The Hebrew "Tenses"', p. 34.

22. All quoted passages from Fenton, 'The Hebrew "Tenses"', p. 35.

Robertson[23] set out the distribution of prefix and suffix conjugations in five narrative passages[24] also without considering the co-occurrence of these forms within strophes. He concluded as follows:

> Ugaritic seems to have a past narrative suff[ix] conj[ugation] resembling the Hebrew suff[ix] conj[ugation] and a past narrative pref[ix] conj[ugation] resembling the Akkadian preterit tense, and to all appearances there is no syntactical difference between them. Reinforcing this impression of syntactical equivalence is that a narrative can be related with the pref[ix] conj[ugation] predominant (as in [*CTA*] 3 ii [= *KTU* 1.3 ii]) or with the suff[ix] conj[ugation] predominant (as in [*CTA*] 4 vi 38-59 [= *KTU* 1.4 vi 38-59]) or with neither predominant (as in [*CTA*] 14 iii 156-211 [= *KTU* 1.14 iii 52–iv 48]).

He then added, 'The parallelism of suff[ix] and pref[ix] conjugations provides further reinforcement' and cites three narrative passages: 1.4 v 20-21, 1.4 v 25-26 and 1.4 vi 36-37. He also showed that *yqtl* forms preceded by *w* (*wyqtl*) are equivalent both to other *yqtl* forms and to *qtl* forms.[25]

Segert's exposition of verb forms in Ugaritic[26] can be tabulated as follows (the table is mine):

	Prose	*Poetry*
	(temporal)	(aspectual)
yqtl	non-past actions	cursive/dependent
qtl	active: past actions	constative aspect
	stative: result of past action	independent actions

> In poetry the function of the perfect and imperfect can be characterized by the notion of aspect. Aspect is by definition subjective, i.e., it expresses the subjective attitude of the speaker to an action or state. The constative aspect[27] is indicated by the perfect... The cursive aspect is expressed by the imperfect. The speaker follows the action in its course, taking its circumstances into consideration. Actions dependent on other actions and those conditioned by circumstances may be indicated by the imperfect.

23. D.A. Robertson, *Linguistic Evidence in Dating Early Hebrew Poetry* (SBLDS, 3; Missoula, MT: University of Montana, 1972), pp. 9-17.

24. *KTU* 1.3 ii 1-41 and 1.4 iv 8-20; v 20-26 + 35-50; vi 36 + 38-59.

25. Robertson, *Linguistic Evidence*, pp. 14-16.

26. Segert, *A Basic Grammar*, no. 64.2 (pp. 88-90).

27. The term 'constative' indicates that an action has occurred without stressing when it began or ended; cf. *OECD Supplement* (Oxford: Oxford University Press, 1972), I, p. 616. 'On dit d'une phrase qu'elle est *constative* quand elle décrit seulement l'événement (par opposition à performative)', J. Dubois *et al.*, *Dictionnaire de la linguistique* (Paris: Larousse, 1973).

> [In prose]...the perfects and imperfects have temporal character. The tenses expressed by the perfect and imperfect indicate the relation of the action or state to the basic level of time, the present. The perfect of active verbs expresses actions... in the past.[28]

However, in a review article of the *Grammar* Rainey criticized Segert's exposition of the verb.[29] Other studies on the verb in Ugaritic have also appeared[30] though they do not address the aspect of parallelism under discussion here.

1.3. *Narrative or Discourse?*

Before listing the passages where *qtl* is parallel to *qtl* or *yqtl*—in varying combinations—it is important to note the distinction between narrative and discourse. This distinction has been largely ignored, though it does feature prominently in Fenton's thesis and some of his published work[31] and is most evident where a 'command' passage (discourse) has its parallel in a 'fulfilment' passage (narrative). Talstra describes the difference well:

> The discursive verbal forms can be found in utterances concerning the speaker and the listener, e.g. in a dialogue, a sermon, a prayer. They refer to what is present or actual in the situation of communication.
>
> The narrative verbal forms are used in utterances concerning persons or actions not present or actual in the situation, i.e. when 'I' tell 'you' about a 'him, her, it'.[32]

This distinction has been observed in the following list of passages for *qtl* // *qtl* or *yqtl* forms. Occasionally, scholars differ in assigning passages to one or other of these categories but I list such passages (for example 1.114:17-18) only once. There are also some divergences of

28. Segert, *A Basic Grammar*, no. 64.21 (p. 88); see also no. 64.22-23 (p. 89).

29. A.F. Rainey, 'A New Grammar of Ugaritic', *Or* 56 (1987), pp. 391-402, 396-98. For example, 'We flatly reject Segert's assertion (64.21) that the prefix and suffix conjugation patterns have aspectual functions in poetry. He has had to admit that they function as tenses in prose' (p. 397).

30. Besides the references in n. 6, see E. Verreet, 'Beobachtungen zum ugaritischen Verbalsystem', *UF* 18 (1986), pp. 363-86; also, 'Beobachtungen zum ugaritischen Verbalsystem II', *UF* 17 (1985), pp. 319-44; 'Der Gebrauch des Perfekts *qtl* in den ugaritischen Nebensätzen', *OLP* 17 (1986), pp. 71-83.

31. See nn. 17, 18 and 20.

32. E. Talstra , 'Text Grammar and Hebrew Bible. I: Elements of a Theory', *BO* 35 (1978), pp. 169-74, p. 170.

opinion concerning stichometry, but discussion has been reserved to footnotes. Speech which is in effect a narrative, relating an event for example, as in 1.19 iv 50-52, has been classed as speech (discourse) because it is spoken.[33]

1.4. *List of Passages*

	Narrative	*Discourse*
Couplets		
qtl // qtl	1.3 i 2-4	1.1 iii 18 (// 1.3 iv 33)
	1.3 ii 11-13	1.2 iii 22
	1.4 iii 23-24	1.2 iv 7-8
	1.4 vi 40-41	1.4 ii 21-24[34]
	1.4 vii 7-8 (cf. 9-10)	1.4 iii 30-32 (in 28-32)
	1.5 ii 6-7	1.4 iv 31-32, 33-34[35]
	1.6 vi 17 = 18-19 = 20	1.6 i 41-43[36]
	1.6 vi 21-22	1.13 r. 24-25[37]
	1.10 iii 7-8	1.16 i 39-41
	1.12 ii 50-51	1.16 ii 19-20//22-23 (cf. 24)[38]
	1.13 r. 24-25	1.17 i 39-42
	1.14 i 6-8 (pass.)	1.19 ii 15-16 (pass.)
	1.14 iv 49-50[39]	1.19 iv 29-30
	1.16 vi 13-14	1.19 iv 51-52[40]
	1.17 v 31-33 (id. verb)	1.161:2-3//9-10
	1.19 iii 22-23[41]	
	1.22 i 12-13[42]	
	1.114:1-2	

33. A. Niccacci, *Sintassi del verbo ebraico nella prosa biblica classica* (Jerusalem: Franciscan Printing Press, 1986), no. 74.

34. Cf. 1.3 iii 36.

35. Cf. 1.5 ii 25-28

36. Parallel: 1.6 iii 1.

37. Also, perhaps, 1.15 ii 25-28.

38. Cf. 1.16 vi 35-36 // 50-52.

39. Report in discourse. For 1.82 9, cf. J.C. de Moor and K. Spronk, 'More on Demons in Ugarit (*KTU* 1.82)', *UF* 16 (1984), pp. 241-42.

40. Cf. 1.15 ii 9-10.

41. Possibly // 8-9 // 36.

42. Unless a quatrain: *qtl // qtl* // 0 // 0.

	Narrative	*Discourse*
qtl // 0	1.2 iv 6-7 (and par.)	1.2 i 40-41
	1.4 ii 3-4	1.2 i 45-46
	1.3 ii 19-20[43]	1.4 iii 17-18
	1.4 i 23-24 (nom.)[44]	1.4 v 27-29 (pass.?)
	1.4 ii 8-9	1.4 vi 36-38 (etc.)
	1.4 v 36-37	1.5 i 6-8
	1.4 vii 9-10 (cf. 7-8)	1.5 vi 23-24//1.6 i 6-7
	1.14 iv 17-18	1.6 iii 20-21 (nom.)[45]
	1.14 iv 19-20	1.10 ii 6-7[46]
	1.16 iii 12-13(+)	1.16 ii 46-47[47]
	1.18 iv 33-34	1.17 ii 14-15 (pass.)
	1.18 iv 34-35	1.100:75-76
qtl // *yqtl*	1.4 v 25-26 (2 × *yqtl*)	1.2 iv 32//34
	1.4 vii 21-22 (2 × *yqtl*)	1.14 ii 43-45[48]
	1.20 ii 3	1.114:17-18[49]
	1.22 ii 22	
	1.100:67-68[50]	
yqtl // *qtl*	1.4 vi 38-40	1.4 v 26-27
	1.24:30-31	1.19 iii 8-9
Tricola		
qtl // *qtl* // *qtl*	1.5 vi 11-14[51]	
	1.6 iii 13-16	
	1.17 i 13-15	
qtl // *qtl* // 0	1.3 iv 40-42	1.19 ii 31-33 (pass.)
		1.19 iv 29-31 (contrast 22-24)
qtl // 0 // *qtl*	1.4 v 38-40	
qtl // 0 // 0	1.14 v 3-5	1.114:21-22
	1.18 iv 36-37	
qtl // *yqtl* // *yqtl*		1.16 vi 32-34//44-48[52]

43. Contrast 1.3 ii 29-30: *yqtl* // 0.
44. Cf. 1.14 i 35-37.
45. Cf. 1.6 i 41-43.
46. Cf. 1.10 iii 13-14.
47. Unless 1.16 ii 44-47 = *yqtl* // 0 // *qtl* // 0 (a quatrain).
48. Fulfilment: 1.14 iv 21 (*ysgr*).
49. Cf. 1.15 iii 28-29.
50. Cf. 1.3 ii 3-5 (parallelism?).
51. Also 1.1 iv 2-4.
52. Note the extra line in execution.

	Narrative	Discourse
qtl // yqtl // 0	1.12 ii 53-55	
	1.19 iv 22-24	
yqtl // 0 // qtl		1.4 v 15-17[53]
Quatrains (cf. Clusters)		
yqtl // 0 // 0 // qtl	1.4 iv 16-19	
Clusters of *qtl*		
	1.4 iv 9-12	1.3 iii 38-46
	1.4 vi 40-54	1.4 iv 31-34
	1.12 ii 31-36[54]	1.5 vi 3-10
	1.14 iii 55-59	1.18 iv 33-37 (see below)
	1.19 ii 28-30	
Sequences[55]		
qtl + qtl		1.4 v 3
qtl + yqtl + yqtl	1.3 i 4-5	
	1.3 i 8-9	
	1.3 i 18	
	1.17 i 3-4 (and par.)[56]	

In general there seems to be no great difference between narrative and discourse in the occurrence of the various patterns. It is noticeable that 0 // *qtl* is found only once in narrative and that quatrains are rare (once only, it seems). The sequence *yqtl // qtl* is commoner than *qtl // yqtl*.[57]

1.5. *Word Order*

The significant aspect of word order has not been evaluated here. The conclusion reached by Wilson in his sample analysis of *KTU* 1.14 i 7–vi 41, that 'word and sentence order remains completely unaffected by the type of verbal form present in it'[58] takes no account of parallelism between verbal forms or of the difference between narrative and

53. And 1.4 v 31-33.

54. Also 1.12 ii 42-47.

55. For such sequences, cf. *UT* §§9.4 and 13.58.

56. Is 1.5 ii 20-21 (N) *qtl // qtl*? *yqtl*?

57. As already asserted by Held, 'The *yqtl-qtl* (*qtl-yqtl*) Sequence', p. 281 n. 2 when the verbal root is identical.

58. G.H. Wilson, 'A Study of Word Order and Sentence Structure in the *Krt* Text', *JSS* 27 (1982), pp. 17-32, 21.

discourse and needs to be tested further. For example, in contrast to Hebrew, where *qtl* is the common initial form in discourse but never in narrative[59] almost the reverse is true of Ugaritic. There *qtl* is normally non-initial in discourse (exceptions: 1.2 iii 22; 1.4 iii 14-16, 30-32; 1.5 vi 3-10; 1.16 ii 46-47; vi 32-34; 1.18 iv 33-37; 1.19 iv 29-31; 1.82:9; 1.100:75-76) but can often open a narrative passage (1.3 ii 11-14; 1.4 ii 3-11; iv 9-12; v 35-37; vi 40-54, etc.).

This survey shows the distribution of *qtl* verb forms vis à vis the *yqtl* forms in Ugaritic, in both narrative and discourse and provides data for further study in terms of stylistic analysis in general and poetic parallelism in particular.[60]

2. *More on Metathetic Parallelism*[61]

The type of parallelism considered briefly here is 'Metathetic Parallelism', first identified by N. Bronznick in several Hebrew texts.[62] It is a form of synonymous parallelism where the corresponding objects and predicates are transposed. For example, in Ps. 35.7

ky	For
ḥnm ṭmnw ly šḥt	secretly they hid a pit for me,
rštm ḥnm ḥprw lnpšy	their net they secretly dug for my person

it is evident that the terms *šaḥat*, 'pit', and *rešet*, 'net', only make sense if they are interchanged (nets are not dug; cf. v. 8 'let the net which they hid ensnare them'). The switch is not actually effected but the sentence is read as if it had been and only then does the couplet become intelligible. This type of implied transposition within a line or couplet Bronznick aptly named metathetic parallelism.[63] The present

59. Niccacci, *Sintassi*, no. 17, etc.

60. I hope to discuss the functions of *qtl* in parallel with *yqtl* elsewhere. For example, in 1.4 iv 16-19 *tbʿ* (*qtl*) appears to express contrast. Similarly, 1.2 iv 32 (// 34). For the present cf. L. Delekat, 'Zum ugaritischen Verbum', *UF* 4 (1972), pp. 11-26, 12.

61. First published in *WO* 19 (1988), pp. 40-44.

62. N.M. Bronznick, '"Metathetic Parallelism":—An Unrecognized Subtype of Synonymous Parallelism', *HAR* 3 (1979), pp. 25-39.

63. The examples discussed by Bronznick are Isa. 17.5; 22.3; 29.3, 5; 49.25; 54.14; 55.5; Amos 6.11; 8.12; Mic. 2.1; Pss. 25.14; 50.19; 90.9; 105.18; Prov. 18.15; Job 13.25; 30.17; 38.30. In a footnote ('"Metathetic Parallelism"', p. 36 n. 3) Broznick refers to Jer. 8.15; Amos 5.21; Pss. 23.5; 56.13; 74.19;

note provides further confirmation for his proposal.

We can begin with a simple form of such implied metathesis in Hos. 13.12b, an example not mentioned by Bronznick:

zbḥy 'dm 'glym yšqwn	sacrificing men, they kiss calves.

P. Mosca would see this line as ironic: 'These people have everything backwards. Instead of kissing human beings and sacrificing calves, the fools have reversed the process!'[64]

Another additional example, this time of metathetic parallelism, is Hab. 3.8b:

ky trkb 'l-swsyk	when you mounted your horses,
mrkbtyk yšw'h	your chariots of victory.

In his recent study of Habakkuk 3, Hiebert comments,

> P. Humbert, suggesting that it is customary for the warrior in the ancient Near East to mount his chariot rather than the horses that draw it, reverses the order of the parallel pair *swsyk/mrkbtyk*. He has some support for his position in that Barb (i.e. Codex Barberini) appears to reflect this same reversal. But all other versions support the MT. The usual sequence of the parallel pair *swsym/mrkbh* in biblical poetry favours the order here... as does the meter... It is best to understand this bicolon as containing 'imagistic parallelism'... in which the poet does not seek to refer to two separate acts but a single act described with two related images.[65]

Job 6.11 and 13.26. Not all these are convincing. He also gives an example from an Amidah prayer.

64. P. Mosca, 'Child Sacrifice in Canaanite and Israelite Religion: A Study in *mulk* and *mlk*' (unpublished dissertation, Harvard University, 1975), p. 258 n. 155 (unavailable to me but cited by G.C. Heider, *The Cult of Molek: A Reassessment* [JSOTSup, 43; Sheffield: JSOT Press, 1985], p. 312 n. 617). A.R.W. Green, *The Role of Human Sacrifice in the Ancient Near East* (ASOR Dissertation Series, 1: Missoula, MT: Scholars Press, 1975), pp. 172-73 discusses the problems of Hos. 13.2 and, though he can provide no solution, concludes, 'there is no doubt that Hosea is talking about something terrible and sacrilegious in the first crisis of the north Kingdom. Within this context human sacrifice may well have been intended.' (I owe this last reference to Professor W. Röllig.) For yet another solution, cf. F.I. Andersen and D.N. Freedman, *Hosea* (AB, 24: Garden City, NY: Doubleday, 1980), p. 632. Another example may be Job 16.6.

65. T. Hiebert, *God of my Victory: The Ancient Hymn in Habakkuk 3* (HSM, 38; Atlanta: Scholars Press, 1986), p. 24 n. 32.

It is possible, instead, that Humbert's suggestion of reversing the components of the word-pair is correct if understood as a form of metathetic parallelism.

Although Bronznick only discussed Hebrew passages, metathetic parallelism is also found in texts outside Hebrew. One occurrence is in an Akkadian šu.íl.lá prayer:[66]

napluski tašmû qibītki nūru	Your glance is favourable hearing, your word, light.

In his study of this poem, Sperling commented, 'the poet has effected a chiastic transfer of properties between the faculties of seeing and hearing'.[67] He added, 'A lesser poet would have preferred "Your glance is light, Your word is light"'.[68] In fact, this is an example of metathetic parallelism (although Sperling did not use that description) and the line is intended to be understood as

Your glance is light, your word is favourable hearing.

It would seem that this sequence was adopted so that the first part of the line (especially *tašmû*) could be linked with the end of the preceding line (rev. 20): *kî ṭābu suppûki kî qerub nešmûki* (variant: *šemûki*), 'How sweet are prayers to you! How near is your favour!'[69]

Another, less certain example—less certain because it occurs on a seal, a material on which mistakes were common—is:

66. Discussed most recently by S.D. Sperling, '"A šu-íl-lá to Ištar" Ebeling, Handerhebung 60', *WO* 12 (1981), pp. 8-20.

67. Sperling, 'A šu-íl-lá to Ištar', p. 18.

68. Sperling, 'A šu-íl-lá to Ištar', p. 20.

69. Such linking occurs elsewhere and may explain the curious word order in the *Descent of Ištar* (Bab.) 2-3:

^{d}Ištar mārat ^{d}Sîn uzunša [*iškun*]	'Ištar, Sin's daughter, set her mind,
iškunma mārat ^{d}Sîn uzu[*nša*]	yes, set Sin's daughter her mind'.

E. Reiner (*Your Thwarts in Pieces, Your Mooring Rope Cut: Poetry from Babylonia and Assyria* [Michigan: Horace H. Rackham School of Graduate Studies at the University of Michigan, 1985], pp. 31-32) comments, 'In other poems, such pairs of lines are usually built on the same pattern, and in fact are identical but for the fact that the second of the pair adds the hero's name... Here this poetic convention is reversed... The inversion, by placing the verb first, also gives syntactic prominence to the predicate which in the first line stands... at the end of the sentence', but makes no reference to the linkage so effected.

dumu.giš $\frac{2}{3}$.dingir $\frac{1}{3}$.àm	son of two-thirds man and one-third god.[70]

This would appear to invert the well-known description of Gilgamesh (as in *Gilg.* I ii 1 and elsewhere):

šittinšu ilu-ma šullultašu amēlūtu	he was one-third god and two-thirds man.

Most probably, however, the inscription on the seal is incorrect.

An intermediate stage is represented by a line from an Old Babylonian prayer studied by B. Groneberg.[71]

burmi-īnīja dimātum	The iris of my eyes weeps,
izannun parsāt	the tears are flowing.[72]

Groneberg comments, 'I suppose that the verb *izannun* refers to *burmīnīja* and *parsāt* to *dimātum*'.[73] This can be represented schematically as:

burmi-īnīja	*dimātum*	*izannun*	*parsāt*
a	a'	b	b'

where the metathesis aa' // bb' marks the transition between parallelism of the type ab // a'b' (alternating parallelism)[74] and true metathetic parallelism, ab' // a'b.

A related form is the chiastic patterning in BAM No. 214 II 10-11:

70. H. Limet, *Les légendes des sceaux cassites* (Brussels: Palais des académies, 1971), pp. 108-109.

71. B. Groneberg, 'Eine Einführungsszene in der altbabylonischen Literatur: Bemerkungen zum persönlichen Gott', in K. Hecker and W. Sommerfeld (eds.), *Keilschriftliche Literaturen: Ausgewählte Vorträge der XXXII. Rencontre Assyriologique Internationale. Münster, 8.–12.7.1985* (Berlin: Reimer Verlag, 1986), pp. 93-108. The text is IM 58424.

72. IM 58424: 18. According to Groneberg, *Einführungsszene*, p. 102, *burmīnīja* is a sandhi spelling of *burmi-īnīja*.

73. Groneberg, *Einführungsszene*, p. 102.

74. For a possible origin in alternating parallelism, cf. Bronznick, '"Metathetic Parallelism"', p. 37. On alternating parallelism, cf. J.T. Willis, 'Alternating (ABA'B') Parallelism in the Old Testament Psalms and Prophetic Literature', in E.R. Follis (ed.), *Directions in Biblical Hebrew Poetry* (JSOTSup, 40; Sheffield: JSOT Press, 1987), pp. 49-76, and E. Zurro, *Procedimientos iterativos en la poesía ugarítica y hebrea* (Rome: Biblical Institute Press, 1987), pp. 218-39.

ᵈšamaš dayyān šamê u erṣetim dayyān mīti u balāṭi attāma
O Shamash, the judge of the heavens and the netherworld, the judge of the dead and the living are you.[75]

The expected sequence to match *šamê u erṣetim* would be *balāṭi u mīti*. Finally, the strange Babylonian extispicy BRM 4 12:26 may be yet another illustration of metathetic parallelism:

ašar (KI) *mūti* (BAD) *iballuṭ ašar balāṭi imât*
(if it is in) the area of death, he will get well, (if in) the area of life, he will die.[76]

The Ugaritic texts provide us with a particularly clear example. It is the formulaic phrase

rgm ʿṣ wlḫšt abn (*KTU* 1.3 iii 22-23 and par.)

conventionally translated 'a tale of trees and a whisper of stones'.[77] In point of fact, the imagery here is of the wind rustling the leaves of the tress and making them whisper.[78] In addition, Ugaritic *rgm* is

75. Text: T. Abusch, '*alaktu* and *halakhah* Oracular Decision. Divine Revelation', *HTR* 80 (1987), pp. 15-42, 27.

76. Parallel: K 9513 (unpublished), cf. R. Borger, *Handbuch der Keilschrift-literatur* (3 vols.; Berlin: de Gruyter, 1967–75), II, p. 34. For the translation, see *CAD*, M/2, p. 317b. Another example of metathetic parallelism is:

aṣaḫu ṣuḫu ajari pān-ia kuzub īnī-ia
the laugh that I laugh is the rosette of my eyes, the voluptuousness of my face.

though the literal translation is 'the laugh that I laugh is the rosette of my *face*, the voluptuousness of my *eyes*' (Text: E. von Weiher, *Spätbabylonische Texte aus Uruk. Teil II* (Berlin: Mann, 1983), p. 127 line 37, translation, p. 128.

77. So J.C.L. Gibson, *Canaanite Myths and Legends* (Edinburgh: T. & T. Clark, 1956), p. 49. Here *ʿṣ* and *ʾbn* are probably collective nouns. Similarly, 'Es un asunto de madera y una charla de piedra', G. del Olmo Lete, *Mitos y leyendas de Canaan según la tradición de Ugarit* (Fuentes de la Ciencia Bíblica, 1; Madrid: Ediciones Cristiandad, 1981, p. 184; 'la parola dell'albero e il mormorio della pietra', P. Xella, *Gli antenati di Dio* (Verona: Essedue edizioni, 1982), p. 101; also M.A. Korpel and J.C. de Moor, 'Fundamentals of Ugaritic and Hebrew Poetry', *UF* 18 (1986), pp. 173-212, 205.

78. According to Gibson, *Canaanite Myths*, p. 49 n. 4, this line refers 'simply to the action of the wind, picturesquely represented as the conversation of the various natural phenomena'. Comparable is *KTU* 1.82:43 *kʿṣm. lttn. kabnm. th(!)ggn*, 'if the trees do not murmur, if the stones make no sound'. The subject of the verb *hgg* is 'trees' and of *ytn* (with ellipsis of *ql*) is 'stones' (metathetic parallelism). Contrast J.C. de Moor, *An Anthology of Religious Texts from Ugarit* (Leiden: Brill, 1987), p. 181 ('if the trees do not give [sound], if the stones do not murmur') and his

equivalent to Akkadian *rigmu*, which denotes a loud voice (*AHw*, pp. 982-83a). If the components of this line are actually in metathetic parallelism (as **lḫšt ʿṣ wrgm abn*) then the more natural and expected translation would be:

a whisper of trees and the noise of stones.

It is possible that *rgm* was placed first in the line in order to match the two neighbouring lines both of which also begin with *rgm*: *rgm iṯ ly wargmk* (lines 20d-21) and *rgm ltdʿ nšm* (line 27).[79]

Less certain is *KTU* 1.6 v 17-19, where Mot says to Baal,

ʿlk. pht. ǵly--bšdm.	On your account I experienced sinking (?) in the fields,
ʿlk. pht drʿ. bym	on your account I experienced sowing in the sea,

which corresponds to the single line (*KTU* 1.6 ii 34-35):

bšd tdrʿ.nn	In a field she (Anath) scattered him (Mot).

This is an indication, perhaps, that in the couplet too, *drʿ*, 'sowing' of the second line really refers to *bšdm*, 'in the fields', of the first, so that *ǵly*. (whatever it may mean) is connected with *bym*, 'in the sea' of the second line.[80]

Bronznick concluded his note by discussing possible functions of metathetic parallelism. He listed three: (1) it enables the poet 'to arrange for the concluding words of the first stich to be read together with the opening words of the second stich as a unit'; (2) the B-word of a word-pair can come in the A word position; and (3) it is used for the purpose of foreshadowing, i.e. proleptically. Whichever function is foremost, the overall effect of metathetic parallelism, according to Bronznick, is to interlock the components of a couplet.[81] The

comment, p. 180 n. 40. He comments, p. 129, 'In Z.37 möchte ich *pānī*(IGI)-*iá* und *īnī*(IGI^2)-*iá* miteinander vertauschen: Rosette meiner Augen—Fülle meines Gesichts'.

79. Note the anacrusis of *dm*; according to Korpel and de Moor, 'Fundamentals', p. 205, *rgm. ʿṣ* etc. begins a new strophe.

80. On *ǵly*, see now G.A. Rendsburg, *JAOS* 107 (1987), p. 627 (according to him it denotes a downward movement) and on the whole passage, J.F. Healey, 'Burning the Corn: new light on the killing of Mōtu', *Or* 52 (1983), pp. 248-51.

81. Bronznick, '"Metathetic Parallelism"', pp. 37-38. On anadiplosis, reversal and interlocking, cf. Watson, *Classical Hebrew Poetry*, pp. 208-13, 356-59 and 273 respectively.

functions of metathetic parallelism in the Akkadian and Ugaritic passages presented here have been discussed above.

The examples of metathesis from Hebrew and Akkadian given here as well as the additional examples of metathetic parallelism in languages other than Hebrew show that this form of parallelism must now be accepted as a genuine sub-type of synonymous parallelism. There is no doubt that future research will extend the range of instances.

3. *An Unusual Prostration Formula in Ugaritic Akkadian*[82]

It is common knowledge that the 'prostration formula' used in letters from Ugarit (both syllabic and alphabetic), El Amarna and elsewhere contains one of the following two numerical sets: (1) 2 times 7 times; (2) 7 times (and) 7 times.[83] It is also generally agreed that both types of expression denote a total of fourteen times (2×7 or $7 + 7$).[84]

Now a completely new version of this formula occurs in a recently published Akkadian letter from Ugarit. It is RS 25.138[85] lines 4-5: [*am-qut*] *a-na ul-tu rugiš* gìr.meš gašan-*ia* 3-*šú* 9-*šú*, literally, '[I fall] at—at a (respectful) distance—the feet of my mistress, three times nine times'.[86] The whole formula is marked off by ruled lines on the tablet.

82. First published in *WO* 24 (1993), pp. 39-41.

83. A.L. Kristensen, 'Ugaritic Epistolary Formulas: A Comparative Study of the Ugaritic Epistolary Formulas in the Context of the Contemporary Akkadian Formulas in the Letters from Ugarit and El Amarna', *UF* 9 (1977), pp. 143-58. See also J. Cunchillos, 'Correspondance', in *Textes ougaritiques* (Paris: Cerf, 1989), II, pp. 449-50. Three other examples occur in the collection edited by D. Arnaud, *Textes syriens de l'âge du bronze récent, avec une contribution d'Hatice Gonnet: Sceaux hiéroglyphiques anatoliens de Syrie* (Aula Orientalis Supplementa, 1; Sabadell: Editorial Ausa, 1991), pp. 148 (letter 94:5-7), 149 (letter 96:5-6) and 219 (107:5-6). In the last letter, which most probably was removed from Ras Shamra, the expression *ištu rūqiš* is not used in the prostration formula. See also n. 98.

84. See, for example, *CAD*, S, p. 204 meaning (a), under *sebîšu*. However, see my final paragraph.

85. S. Lackenbacher, 'Trois lettres d'Ugarit', in H. Behrens, D. Loding and M.T. Roth (eds.), DUMU-E$_2$-DUB-BA-A. *Studies in Honor of Åke Sjöberg* (Occasional Publications of the Samuel Noah Kramer Fund; Philadelphia: University Museum, 1989), pp. 317-20, 318.

86. '[Je m'effondre] aux pieds de ma maîtresse, de loin, trois fois, neuf fois', Lackenbacher, 'Trois lettres', p. 319.

The formula is novel for two main reasons: (1) the numbers involved and (2) the word order. These will be considered in turn.

1. The use of the numbers three and nine is unusual in several ways. The form 'three times, nine times' is unattested elsewhere. The number sequence '3', '9' is otherwise unknown. The use of '9' in number parallelism is very rare.[87] Multiplication is used in parallelism of this kind, but not with the factor '3'.[88] An example in a literary text is:

> *1 me'at ina irti in-da-qut-sú 2 me'at ina na*-x[x x] *ba n*[*u* x]
> One hundred (times) she fell on her breast to him; two hundred (times)...[89]

2. The word order here differs from the sequence of the corresponding formula used in Ugaritic Akkadian which in turn diverges from that used in Ugaritic.[90] The order in Ugaritic Akkadian is (1) 'at', (2) 'the feet of', (3) 'my lady', (4) 'at a distance', (5) '14 times', (6) 'I fall', (e.g. *ana šepe beliya ištu ruqiš 2-šú 7-šú amqut*)[91]. In Ugaritic the corresponding sequence is (1), (2), (3), (5), (4), (6) (e.g. *lp'n adty šb'd wšb'id mrḥqtm qlt*),[92] where the only difference

87. Sir. 25.7; cf. Y. Avishur, '*tqbwlwt hmsprym bmqr' wbsprwt hmyt l hmzrh hqdmwn*' ['Number Parallelism in the Bible and in Ancient Near Eastern Literature'] [in Hebrew] in *Proceedings of the Seventh World Congress of Jewish Studies* (Jerusalem: Magnes, 1981), pp. 2-9, esp. 4-6; as he comments, the pair '8 // 9' does not occur. A possible example is 1 Kgs 18.19 where the pair '400' // '450' could be analysed as 8(× 50) // 9(× 50).

88. See W.G.E. Watson, 'Number Parallelism in Mesopotamian Texts', in R.J. Ratner, L.M. Barth, M.L. Gevirtz and B. Zuckerman (eds.), *Let your Colleagues Praise You: Studies in Memory of Stanley Gevirtz* = *Maarav* 7 (1991), pp. 241-52, esp. 239. If multiplication is involved the number of prostrations would be 27. Is this an approximation to twice the standard number 14?

89. BM 47749:3'. Text and translation: I.L. Finkel, 'The Dream of Kurigalzu and the Tablet of Sins', *AnSt* 33 (1983), pp. 75-80, 78.

90. For discussion of sequence, cf. Kristensen, 'Ugaritic Epistolary Formulas', p. 149.

91. J. Nougayrol *et al.*, *Ugaritica V* (BAH, 80; MRS, 16; Paris: Imprimerie Nationale/Librairie Orientaliste Paul Geuthner, 1968), p. 118 lines 4-5 (= RS 20.16:4-5); *Ugaritica V*, p. 129 lines 5-6 (= RS 20.219:5-6); *PRU*, IV, 221 (RS 17.383) 4-5; 226 (RS 17.391) 4-5; 226 (RS 17.393) 5-6; 223 (RS 17.422) 5-7 and 218 (RS 17.425) 6-7. There are no occurrences in *PRU*, III or *PRU*, VI.

92. Fuller details, see Kristensen, 'Ugaritic Epistolary Formulas', pp. 147-50 and 157. Other texts include *KTU* 2.11:5-7; 2.12:6-11; 2.24:5-7; 2.40:5-8; 2.42:4-5; 2.64:6-8 (text damaged); 2.68:4-7; 2.70:8-10.

is the switch between positions (5) and (6). Here, the sequence is (6), (1), (4), (2), (3), (5). It is particularly noteworthy that whereas in both Ugaritic and Ugaritic Akkadian letters the verb comes at the end, in RS 25.138 it opens the formula. Unfortunately, the initial *am-qut* is illegible on the copy[93] and has been restored. The restoration seems certain since there appears to be no room at the end of line 5 for these two signs and any other restoration at the beginning of line 4 would be unlikely. Also unique is the splitting up of the formula 'at the feet of' by the insertion of 'at a distance' after the first word.

Although in origin it is probable that the prostration was actually performed—seven times on one's belly, the same amount of times on one's back[94]—clearly the present formula is a purely rhetorical embellishment to the salutation portions of letters because the two types of abasement are unequal in number. The question then arises why this form of number parallelism should have been used in the prostration formula of RS 25.138 in which, according to the editor, 'a woman dependent on the queen of Ugarit sends her various products and asks her for others apparently on the occasion of (her?) sons'.[95] It is perhaps significant that the woman is named Alluwa, which is a Hurrian name.[96] Also, in a Hittite ritual to chthonic deities in which nine sheep, nine loaves and nine libation jugs are used, the plea 'Render it (the ritual) nine times favourable!' occurs.[97] There is a possibility, then, that the letter in question is a translation of a non-Semitic original which may have been Hurrian or even Hittite.[98]

93. Lackenbacher, 'Trois lettres', p. 320.

94. For the evidence, from the Amarna Letters and an Egyptian tomb relief, cf. Kristensen, 'Ugaritic Epistolary Formulas', p. 149.

95. Lackenbacher, 'Trois lettres', p. 317.

96. See *ilwn*, *KTU* 4.83: 4 and *i-lu-wa*, *PRU*, IV, 234 (RS 17.112) [5].9.13.15.

97. The text is cited by G. Beckman, 'Proverbs and Proverbial Allusions in Hittite', *JNES* 45 (1986), pp. 19-30, 25 and n. 39. Note also that in the *Ritual of Tunnawi* ii 65-67, the 'attendant woman' uses *nine* combs in a body-cleansing ritual. Cf. H.G. Güterbock, 'A Hurro-Hittite Hymn to Ishtar', *JAOS* 103 (1983), pp. 155-64, 159 under (7) for a brief description of these lines.

98. Of the other two letters from the 25th campaign published by Lackenbacher ('Trois lettres', pp. 317-20), RS 25.461 has the 'twice times seven times' prostration formula in the standard sequence: *a-na* gìr.meš-*ia* 2-*šú* 7-*šú* *am-qut* (without *ištu rūqiš*). The same applies to the formula in a letter from Emar, *ana* gìr.meš en-*ia* 2-*šú* 7-*šú* *aq-qá-ra-ar* (Msk 7451:4-5), with an additional variation in the final verb ('I have rolled over').

In addition there is the following passage in the Hurrian Song of Ullikummi:[99]

> [When] we come before the gate of the house of Ea, we will bow [FIVE times] at Ea's door and [again] FIVE times at Ea's inner door(?). [When] we come [before] Ea, we will bow FIFTEEN times before Ea.

Evidently, as in the Ugaritic letter discussed above, a gesture of deference is repeated three times and the final '15' equals 3 × 5 bows.

A similar act is recorded in 1 Sam. 20.41 where David 'fell on his face to the ground and did obeisance THREE times' (*wypl l'pyw 'rh wytw l p'mym*), presumably in front of Jonathan, whom he then greeted effusively. Yet another repeated act of greeting comes again from the Song of Ullikummi:

> 'When Tasmisu [heard] these words, he ran forth [from...], he [kissed(?)] him on the knees THREE times; he kissed him on the ankles(?) FOUR times'.[100]

Although these numbers are in parallelism, they do add up to seven, a number which appears in the salutation formulae discussed above. This in turn suggests that the sequence 'two times, seven times' (see above) may also be understood as an addition, providing a further instance of the use of 'nine' in letter formulae.

4. *A Note on Staircase Parallelism*[101]

Staircase parallelism is a well-known and well-attested poetic pattern in Hebrew and Ugaritic poetry.[102] Curiously, it appears to occur in prose too as this brief note will attempt to demonstrate. Before that is done, though, it has to be pointed out that the staircase pattern does not occur in Akkadian verse, in spite of one or two approximations. The most convincing belongs to a ritual where milk is addressed:[103]

99. Tablet 3 §49: A col. ii lines 17-26, with restorations from lines 27-32. Translation: H.A. Hoffner, Jr, *Hittite Myths* (SBL Writings from the Ancient World; Atlanta: Scholars Press, 1990), p. 58.

100. *Song of Ullikummi*, Tablet 3, §52 (A ii 7-12); translation: Hoffner, *Hittite Myths*, p. 58.

101. First published in *VT* 33/4 (1983), pp. 510-12.

102. For collected examples, discussion and bibliography, see chapter 6, section 5 in my *Classical Hebrew Poetry*.

103. On apostrophe, see my comments in Chapter 10, 'Apostrophe in the Aqhat Poem'.

šizbi enzī arqāti ša ina tarbaṣi elli ša rē'î Dumuzi i''aldu	O Milk of yellow goat(s), born in the pure fold of Shepherd Dumuzi,
šizbi enzi rē'û ina qātēšu ellēti liddinka	O Milk of a goat, may the Shepherd give you with his pure hands![104]

There are other examples[105] but none as clear as this, and it is probable, therefore, that the pattern is primarily West Semitic in character.[106]

The Hebrew texts to be considered were collected and examined in a different context by H.-W. Jüngling;[107] they are Judg. 4.18, 19.23, 2 Sam. 13.12, 25 and 2 Kgs 4.16. The first passage is Judg. 4.18, where Jael says to Sisera,

swrh 'dny	Turn aside, sir,
swrh'ly	turn aside to me,
'l-tyr'	don't be afraid!

Strictly speaking, there is no parallelism, but in view of the other passages cited below the lay-out proposed seems valid. The example in Judg. 19.23 is not so clear; it runs:

'l-'ḥy	Do not, my brothers,
'l-tr'w n' 'ḥry 'šr-b' h'yš hzzh 'l-byty	do not commit evil, since this man has come into my house!
'l t'św 't-hnnblh hzz't	Do not do this senseless thing.

104. Text and translation as in W. Farber, *Beschwörungsrituale an Ištar und Dumuzi* (Wiesbaden: Steiner, 1977), pp. 68-69, lines 55-56.

105. These include *Descent of Ishtar* lines 3-6: 'Sin's daughter directed her attention *to the* dark *house*, (the Queen of) Irkalla's residence/*to the house* which those entering do not leave/to the road whose course does not turn back', and two examples from letters. The first is from EA 287:32: 'See this land of Jerusalem; neither my father nor my mother (but) the arm of a strong kind *did give, did give* to me'; translation by H. Cazelles, 'De l'idéologie royal orientale', *JANESCU* 5 (1973), pp. 59-73, 66. The second is from an Old Babylonian letter: '*Until you buy for me*, either in two or three days time, *until you buy for me* and can give him...'; for text and translation, see J.V. Kinnier Wilson, '"Desonance" in Akkadian', *JSS* 13 (1968), pp. 93-103, 101.

106. Repetitive parallelism is a different matter; compare Judg. 5.12 with the opening lines of a hymn to Tishpak: 'Steward of Tiamat, fierce warrior, arise! Tishpak, steward of Tiamat, fierce one, arise!'; text and translation as in A. Westenholz, *AfO* 25 (1974–77), p. 102.

107. H.-W. Jüngling, *Richter 19—Ein Plädoyer für das Königtum* (AnBib, 84; Rome: Biblical Institute Press, 1981), pp. 156 and 211-14.

There is a degree of parallelism and the triple anaphoric repetition of *'al* to mark these lines as poetry, an effect offset by the extreme length of the second line. 2 Sam. 13.12 is similar in form and content:

'l-'ḥy	Do not, my brother,
'l-t'nnny	do not force me,
ky l'-y'śh kn byśr'l	for such was never done in Israel.
'l-t'śh 't-hnnblh hzz't	Do not do this senseless thing.

In v. 25 of the same chapter, King David's words to Absalom are:

'l-bny	No, my son,
'l-n' nlk kllnw	not all of us should go,
wl' nkbd 'lyk	in case we burden you.[108]

This is a polite way of declining an invitation,[109] which indicates that the pattern adopted is not of itself tantamount to a strong prohibition. Finally comes 2 Kgs 4.16:

'l-'dny 'yš h'lhym	Do not, sir, man of God,
'l-tkzzb bšpḥtk	do not delude your maidservant.

The expression 'man of God' is omitted in Codex Vaticanus of the LXX, which would fit the pattern set by all the other passages quoted.[110]

All these texts are in direct speech and therefore probably reflect colloquial language, though due allowance must be made for literary style. Although four of the five passages are negative in character, Judg. 4.18 is not, which points to a more general underlying formula than that posited by Jüngling (p. 212), namely, the repetitive form found also in poetry as staircase parallelism. The implication seems to be that the origin of this form of parallelism lies in actual speech. A high proportion of recognized instances of staircase parallelism in

108. For a discussion of *nā'* in this passage, see Jüngling, *Richter 19*, pp. 213-14. The same pattern may underlie v. 16 as reconstructed by H.W. Hertzberg, *Die Samuelbücher* (ATD, 10; Göttingen: Vandenhoeck & Ruprecht, 2nd edn, 1960), p. 258 n. 6, ET *I & II Samuel* (OTL; London: SCM Press, 1964), p. 321 n. d, but this is pure conjecture.

109. So Hertzberg, *Die Samuelbücher*, p. 263; ET, p. 327.

110. The rendering 'you are a man of God and would not lie, etc.' in J. Robinson, *The Second Book of Kings* (The Cambridge Bible Commentary on the NEB; Cambridge; Cambridge University Press, 1976), p. 40, is therefore to be excluded.

verse is couched in direct speech (Pss. 92.10; 94.3; Cant. 4.1, 8, 9, 10, etc.), which also points in the same direction. It is perhaps only an accident that so few instances survive in OT Hebrew prose. Perhaps more remain to be identified by discerning readers.[111]

111. Unless, of course, passages with staircase parallelism are to be classified as poetry.

Chapter 6

WORD-PAIRS

1. *Reversed Word-Pairs in Ugaritic Poetry*[1]

It is well known that the normal or commoner A-B sequence of parallel word-pairs in Ugaritic poetry can occasionally be inverted (as B-A) and that such inversions are comparatively rare.[2] Yet, even though almost all the reversed word-pairs discussed here had previously been identified, they have not been studied as a group.

Related to straightforward B-A inversion is the use of an A-word in second position but in parallel with yet another word (C, D, E etc.). These two possibilities can be set out as follows:

A-B	*becomes*	B-A
A-C, D, E	*becomes*	C, D, E-A

An example of the second type is *lḥm // ṯrm* ('to eat // to dine')[3] and *lḥm // šty* ('to eat // to drink')[4] and the reversed pair *bly // lḥm*, ('to consume // to eat')[5] with the A-word *lḥm* in second place. There are many variations of such pairs, with intermediate stages[6] but the present note will concentrate on inversions of the first type.[7]

1. First published in *UF* 13 (1981), pp. 189-92.

2. Contrasting strongly with Hebrew poetry. See, for instance, R.G. Boling, '"Synonymous" Parallelism in the Psalms', *JSS* 5 (1960), pp. 221-55, 224; P.C. Craigie, 'A Note on "Fixed Pairs" in Ugaritic and Early Hebrew Poetry', *JTS* 22 (1971), pp. 140-43 (but see below); S. Gevirtz, 'The Ugaritic Parallel to Jeremiah 8:23', *JNES* 20 (1961), pp. 41-46, but contrast M.J. Dahood, 'Ugaritic-Hebrew Parallel Pairs', in *RSP* I, pp. 77-78.

3. *KTU* 1.18 iv 18-19 etc.

4. Very common, e.g. *KTU* 1.4 iv 35-36.

5. *KTU* 1.5 i 18-20.

6. For example, note the set *mrṣ // zbl*; *mrṣ // dw(y)* and *dw(y) // zbl* discussed by M. Held, 'The Root *ZBL / SBL* in Akkadian, Ugaritic and Biblical Hebrew', *JAOS* 88 (1968), pp. 90-96, 93. See, too, P.B. Yoder, 'A-B Pairs and Oral Composition in Hebrew Poetry', *VT* 21 (1971), pp. 470-89.

1.1. *urbt // ḥln*

The classic instance of word-pair inversion in Ugaritic poetry comes from the 'Palace of Baal' episode in the Baal Cycle. There, in the debate over whether the palace should have windows or not, the sequence *ḥln // urbt*, 'casement // window' is used, an A-B word-pair. However, when Baal finally makes his decision he inverts the sequence (as *urbt // ḥln*), a stylistic device long since pointed out by Gevirtz.[8] The function of inverting the sequence, as Gevirtz notes, is to show that Baal changed his mind.

1.2. *ytm // almnt*

Another example is the word-pair *almnt // ytm*, 'widow // orphan (or: fatherless)'.[9] This is the sequence in *KTU* 1.17 v 8:

ydn dn almnt	He judged the WIDOW's cause,
ytpṭ ṯpṭ ytm	he tried the ORPHAN's case

which describes justice being done. In sharp contrast, the order is reversed when Yaṣṣubu accuses his father, Keret, of neglecting the needy (*KTU* 1.16 vi 48-50):

lpnk ltšlḥm ytm	You do not feed the ORPHAN in front of you,
b'd kslk almnt	(nor) the WIDOW behind your back.

The picture in Hebrew is more complex.[10]

7. For full references to the Ugaritic texts cf. RSP I and II.

8. S. Gevirtz, *Patterns in the Early Poetry of Israel* (SAOC, 32; Chicago: University of Chicago Press, 1963), pp. 39-40. Compare B. Margalit, *A Matter of 'Life' and 'Death': A Study of the Baal-Mot Epic (CTA 4-5-6)* (AOAT, 206; Kevelaer: Butzon & Bercker; Neukirchen–Vluyn: Neukirchener Verlag, 1980), pp. 45-50.

9. The inverted sequence is noted by Dahood, 'Ugaritic-Hebrew', p. 216 no. 262 (p. 216—with bibliography; add Y. Avishur, 'Word Pairs Common to Phoenician and Biblical Hebrew', *UF* 7 [1975], pp. 13-48, 31-32 and 31 n. 50) but no comment has been made on the *reason* for inversion.

10. The sequence 'widow // orphan' (Isa. 10.2; Ps. 94.6; Job 22.9) is always in a negative context. The inversion is positive in Jer. 49.11, Ps. 68.6, Sir. 4.10, 35.14—but curiously negative in Ps. 109.9 and Job 24.3.

1.3. *lb // kbd*

In Ugaritic *kbd* is definitely an A-word as the pairs *kbd // irt*, 'liver // chest'[11] and *kbd // p*, 'liver // mouth'[12] indicate. However, the pair *kbd // lb* occurs once only, in *KTU* 1.3 ii 25-26, the well-known passage of Anath's exultant combat:

tǵdd kbdh bṣhq	Her LIVER swelled with laughter,
ymlu lbh bšmḫt	her HEART filled with joy

Dahood argues that these two lines form a tricolon with the next line (*kbd 'nt tšyt*, 'Anath's liver, with victory') to produce the chiastic (ABA) set *kbd // lb // kbd*.[13] It would appear that to depict exactly the opposite emotion (sorrow), inversion is effectively used in *KTU* 1.19 i 34-35:

tbky pǵt bm lb	Weep does Pughatu in/from her HEART,
tdm' bm kbd	shed tears from/in her LIVER

when Aqhat's sister bewails his death. Curiously, though, this same inverted sequence (*lb // kbd*) is used in *KTU* 1.12 i 12-13 even though El is in joyful vein:

il yẓḥq bm lb	El laughed in his HEART
wgmḏ bm kbd	and was convulsed with mirth in his LIVER.[14]

Here content (joy), which would require the normal sequence *kbd // lb*, has been overridden by stylistic considerations, so that the word-pair ties in with corresponding nouns in the preceding lines to form the chiastic set *kbd* (f.) // *ṯd* (m., 'breast') // *lb* (m.) // *kbd* (f.):[15] only the inverse sequence is known in Hebrew, in a context of joy (Ps. 16.9).

11. *KTU* 1.18 i 18-19, but note that the sequence could be construed (with line 17) as *lb // kbd // irt*.

12. *KTU* 1.5 ii 3-4.

13. M.J. Dahood, 'Ugaritic-Hebrew Syntax and Style', *UF* 1 (1969), pp. 15-36, 27, reiterated in RSP I, p. 78.

14. Translation: J. Gray, 'Ba'al's Atonement', *UF* 3 (1971), pp. 61-70, 62. See, too, S.E. Loewenstamm, 'Grenzgebiete ugaritischer Sprach- und Stilvergleichung: Hebräisch des Zweiten Tempels, Mittelhebräisch, Griechisch', *UF* 3 (1971), pp. 93-100, 94 who comments explicitly on sequence reversal, and his remarks in 'Ugarit and the Bible, I', *Bib* 56 (1975), pp. 103-19, 110.

15. Ignoring the repetition of *kbd* in the very first line (staircase parallelism).

1.4. *ḥrb // išt*

Less certain is the pair in *KTU* 1.2 i 32:

išt ištm yitmr	(Like) a FIRE, two fires, they appeared,
ḥrb lṭšt [lš]nhm	(like) a sharpened SWORD was their tongue[16]

Evidently a literal meaning is not intended: the word-pair simply heightens the imagery.[17] This set and the pair *išt // pḥm*, 'fire // coals'[18] indicate *išt* to be an A-word. Reversal of order in *KTU* 1.6 v 12-14 apparently connotes destruction:[19]

‘lk pht dry bḥrb	On your account I have experienced splitting by a SWORD,
‘lk pht šrp bišt	on your account I have experienced burning by FIRE.

1.5. *arṣ // šmm*

Since both are A-words the components of this pair seem to be interchangeable. Compare *KTU* 1.5 ii 2 etc. (and 1.23:61-62)

špt larṣ	a lip to earth
špt lšmm	a lip to the sky

with *KTU* 1.3 ii 39 (= iv 43)

ṭl šmm	sky-dew,
šmn arṣ	earth-oil.

1.6. *ḫrṣ // ksp*

In *KTU* 1.43 (= CTA 33) 11-15 the inverse of the normal sequence occurs twice in succession, as Craigie was the first to point out:

ṯql ḫrṣ lšpš wyrḫ lgṯr
ṯql ksp ṭb ap wnpš
l‘nth ṯql ḫrṣ lšpš [w y]rḫlgṯr
ṯn [ṯql ksp] ṭb ap wnpš

16. Following J.C.L. Gibson, *Canaanite Myths and Legends* (Edinburgh: T. & T. Clark, 1978), p. 42.

17. In Hebrew the sequence 'fire // sword' connotes destruction (Isa. 66.16; Nah. 3.15—on the second text, see K.J. Cathcart, 'More Philological Studies in Nahum', *JNSL* 7 [1979], pp. 1-12, 11).

18. *KTU* 1.4 ii 8-9; 1.23:41, 44-45, 47-48.

19. The connection of this passage with Ezek. 5.1-5 is explored below, p. 403, n. 52.

The meaning is obscure[20] and it is doubtful whether this text can be aligned with the others so far discussed; nonetheless, the reversal is certainly worth further study.

In *KTU* 1.10 i 4-5 *kkbm* // *šmm* ('stars // sky') inverts the usual order (e.g. *KTU* 1.3 ii 40-41) but the context is too damaged for confident discussion. Another possible example is the reversal of *ṣḥq* // *šmḫ* ('laughter // joy') in *KTU* 1.6 iii 14-16—so Loewenstamm[21]—but as a line intervenes between the two parallel words, the example is not so clear-cut. In fact, several other passages seem to invert word-pairs but there is usually a complicating factor.[22]

This survey (which is not exhaustive, but does attempt to deal with the principal examples) leads to the following tentative conclusions. It can be confirmed that word-pair reversal is not nearly so common in Ugaritic poetry as it is in Hebrew tradition.[23] Nonetheless, some Ugaritic reversed parallel word-pairs are rare or even unknown in Hebrew. Further, in Ugaritic poetry inversion was, generally speaking, for a specific reason (chiefly in mimesis of inversion of state, but once or twice at least, for stylistic reasons). Hebrew, on the other hand, was much looser in this respect. The implication, therefore, is that there was a certain loss of continuity between the two traditions, resulting in imitation of form but lack of understanding as regards function.[24]

20. P.C. Craigie, 'A Note on "Fixed Pairs" in Ugaritic and Hebrew Poetry', *JTS* 22 (1971), pp. 140-43, 141 translates the first couplet(?): 'A shekel of gold for Sun-and-Moon as a *gṯr*-offering; a shekel of good silver as a body-and-soul offering', following Gordon. However, see A. van Selms, *Marriage and Family Life in Ugaritic Literature* (London: Luzac & Co, 1954), p. 129 n. 2; and P. Xella, 'Sacrifici umani ad Ugarit? Il problema di *NPŠ*', *Religioni e Civiltà* NS 2 (1976), pp. 355-85 (unseen by me).

21. Loewenstamm, 'Grenzgebiete', p. 94. Note that the reversed pair *'*pr* // *arṣ* posited by Craigie, 'A Note on "Fixed Pairs"', p. 142 n. 1, is invalid.

22. For example the reversal of *rgm* // *ṯny* in *KTU* 1.4 i 19-20 etc. which is related to *amr* // *ṯny* (1.2 i 31-32). Another set to be rejected is **škr* // *yn* (so Gevirtz, *Patterns*, p. 39) in view of *KTU* 1.114:3-4.16 (see K.J. Cathcart and W.G.E. Watson, 'Weathering a Wake: A Cure for a Carousal', *Proceedings of the Irish Biblical Association* 4 [1980], pp. 35-58, 48). On *dbr* // *šd* cf. RSP I, pp. 164 (and 348) and 78.

23. For Phoenician see Avishur, 'Word Pairs', pp. 13-47; for Akkadian pairs, J.C. de Moor and P. van der Lugt, 'The Spectre of Pan-Ugaritism', *BO* 31 (1974), pp. 3-26.

24. Recent comparisons between the two traditions include P.C. Craigie, 'The

2. *Some Additional Word-Pairs*[25]

2.1. *Introductory Remarks*

The study of word-pairs continues apace. Recently, certain landmarks have been set; these include the appearance of *RSP III*, with its chapters on word-pairs, the listings by Avishur of word-pairs in different Semitic languages[26] and, at the theoretical level, Berlin's appraisal of word-pairs in terms of linguistic theory.[27] All these have been discussed and reviewed elsewhere so that there is no need for more than a reminder here. However, particular mention must be made of Peter Craigie who, in a number of studies,[28] evaluated the phenomenon of word-pairs with special reference to the writings of M. Dahood. Craigie wanted to determine the degree to which word-pairs were peculiar to Ugaritic and Hebrew Poetry. He showed, in fact, that while Ugaritic and Hebrew did have a number of word-pairs in common (which was to be expected in any case because they are cognate languages), they also shared word-pairs with poetry in other language traditions.[29] In addition, several isolated studies have been made,

Problem of Parallel Word Pairs in Ugaritic and Hebrew Poetry', *Semitics* 5 (1977), pp. 48-58; 'Parallel Word Pairs in the Song of Deborah', *JETS* 20 (1971), pp. 15-22.

25. First published in L. Eslinger and G. Taylor (eds.), *Ascribe to the Lord: Biblical and other Studies in Memory of Peter C. Craigie* (JSOTSup, 67; Sheffield: JSOT Press, 1988), pp. 179-201.

26. Y. Avishur, *Stylistic Studies of Word-Pairs in Biblical and Ancient Semitic Literatures* (AOAT, 210; Neukirchen–Vluyn: Neukirchener Verlag, 1984) with extensive bibliography.

27. A. Berlin, 'Parallel Word Pairs: A Linguistic Explanation', *UF* 15 (1983), pp. 7-16; *idem*, *The Dynamics of Biblical Parallelism* (Bloomington: Indiana University Press, 1985), pp. 64-72.

28. Craigie, 'A Note on "Fixed Pairs"', pp. 140-43; *idem*, 'Word Pairs in the Song of Deborah', pp. 15-22; *idem*, 'Parallel Word Pairs in Ugaritic Poetry: A Critical Evaluation of their Relevance for Ps 29', *UF* 11 (1979), pp. 135-40; *idem*, 'The Problem of Parallel Word Pairs in Ugaritic and Hebrew Poetry', *Semitics* 5 (1979), pp. 48-58.

29. For example: 'From this type of data [i.e. same semantic word pair in Akkadian, Arabic and Egyptian], it might be assumed that in the poetry of any language in which parallelism is employed, parallel word pairs will appear, and that a degree of commonality in human experience, and therefore in human poetry, will contribute to *common* parallel word pairs in the poetry of various languages. If this argument is correct, then one is left with the strong possibility that common parallel word pairs arise independently in various languages and the prior question pertains to

which again need not be listed here.[30]

In this section I wish to set out further examples of word-pairs common to two or more ancient Semitic (Near Eastern) languages as a sort of supplement to Avishur's valuable encyclopaedic work. These word-pairs have been collected over the years and though some are less certain than others they have all been included as material for better evaluation.

Professor Berlin has shown that in essence word-pairs are simply a form of word association.[31] To use her own explanation, 'It is not word-pairs that create parallelism. It is parallelism that activates word-pairs'.[32] Previously, Craigie had already expressed the same opinion: 'Once thought parallelism is chosen as the mode for poetic expression, *inevitably* common parallel word-pairs must be employed'.[33] Identifying word-pairs is not only important for the better understanding of verse, it also provides us with better insight into the languages concerned, an insight all the more valuable, I may add, since these languages are now dead.[34] Berlin adds, 'Not only should we continue to collect them [i.e. word-pairs], but we should document their frequencies and patterns to the extent that textual remains permit'.[35] Prompted by her comment, my main intention has been to provide material for further study. I have made no more than passing reference to the different categories of word-pair established by Berlin—lexical, grammatical, semantic and so on—though, as she has shown, these classifications are extremely important.

the origin of parallelism as such: once parallelism is employed, common parallel word pairs are to be expected' (P.C. Craigie, 'Ugarit and the Bible', in D. Young [ed.], *Ugarit in Retrospect* [Winona Lake, IN: Eisenbrauns, 1981], pp. 105-106).

30. See the bibliography in W.G.E. Watson, *Classical Hebrew Poetry: A Guide to its Techniques* (JSOTSup 26; Sheffield: JSOT Press, 1984), pp. 143-44 (2nd edn, 1986, p. 457).

31. Berlin, 'Word Pairs'; *idem*, *Dynamics*. See, previously, S. Geller, *Parallelism in Early Hebrew Poetry* (HSS, 20; Missoula, MT: Scholars Press, 1979), pp. 31-41. On word association, see S.J. Lieberman, *The Sumerian Loanwords in Old-Babylonian Akkadian* (HSS, 22; Missoula, MT: Scholars Press, 1977), pp. 49-54, 559-65.

32. Berlin, 'Word Pairs', p. 16 (= *Dynamics*, p. 79).

33. Craigie, 'Word Pairs in the Song of Deborah', p. 22.

34. On the distinction between dead and living languages, see Lieberman, *Loanwords*, pp. 18-21, esp. 20 n. 50.

35. Berlin, 'Word Pairs', p. 16 (= *Dynamics*, p. 79).

Since several languages are involved (Akkadian [Assyro-Babylonian, etc.], Aramaic, Hebrew and Ugaritic) it has seemed simpler to list the word-pairs in translation in the alphabetic order of the first component.

2.2. *List of Word-Pairs*

2.2.1. *Arrow // Slingstone*. The comparison between Ugaritic *qšt wql'*[36] and what appear to be the same terms in Job 41.20 made in *RSP I*[37] was strongly criticized by reviewers.[38] They pointed out that the Ugaritic terms occur only in administrative texts, so that there is no question of a poetic word-pair and that, in any case, Ugaritic *ql'* means 'shield' whereas the Hebrew term *ql'* (used in the Job passage) means 'sling'. In truth, matters are rather more complex than would appear at first sight.

Before turning to the text from Job we must first re-examine the Ugaritic word *ql'*. In a recent study Eichler[39] agrees that Ugaritic *ql'* with the equivalent *kabābu*, 'shield', in the total(s) of certain Ugaritic texts does not mean 'shield'—as argued by Landsberger[40] and Grafman[41] independently. However, the term (*ql'*) is not a loan from Egyptian, even though this is the common opinion. Instead, the reverse holds true: Egyptian *qr'w* (Coptic *gl*) is borrowed from Semitic, and besides is not the normal word for 'shield' in Egyptian.[42]

36. Occurrences: *KTU* 4.63 (*passim*); 4.76:9; 4.205:10; 4.453:3; 4.624 (*passim*). On *KTU* 4.63, cf. M. Dietrich and O. Loretz, 'Die Ba'al-Titel *b'l arṣ* und *aliy qrdm*', *UF* 12 (1980), p. 391.

37. Dahood, 'Ugaritic-Hebrew', p. 334 no. 507.

38. E.g. S.E. Loewenstamm, 'Ugarit and the Bible', *Bib* 56 (1975), p. 111; P. van der Lugt and J.C. de Moor, 'The Spectre of Pan-Ugaritism', *BO* 31 (1974), p. 21.

39. B.L. Eichler, 'Of Slings and Shields, Throw-Sticks and Javelins', *JAOS* 103 (1983), pp. 95-102, esp. 95-96.

40. B. Landsberger, 'Akkadisch *aspu* = "Schleuder", *assukku* = "Schleuderstein"', *AfO* 18 (1957–58), p. 379 n. 8. See also his 'Nachtrag zu *aspu* = "Schleuderstein"', *AfO* 19 (1959–60), p. 66.

41. R. Grafman, apud A.F. Rainey, 'The Military Personnel of Ugarit', *JNES* 24 (1965), p. 22 n. 97.

42. So Eichler, 'Slings and Shields', p. 96 n. 11. In Middle Egyptian the term for 'shield' is *i'km* (as listed in D. Shennum, *English–Egyptian Index of Faulkner's Concise Dictionary of Middle Egyptian* [Aids and Research Tools in Ancient Near Eastern Studies, 1: Malibu: Undena Publications, 1977], p. 138).

On the other hand, Hebrew *qela'* definitely means 'sling' (1 Sam. 17.50, etc.). Eichler argues that the common denominator is the verb *ql'*, 'to twist, plait'; it describes both the plaiting together of materials to make a protective cover (Ugaritic *ql'*, 'shield'; Hebrew *qela'*, 'curtain' as in Exod. 27.9, etc. [plur. only]) and the twisting of a sling in the act of flinging slingstones (as in Judg. 20.16).[43] If he is correct, then the suggested comparison is not so far-fetched after all.

This leads us to inspect Job 41.20:

l'-ybryḥnw bn-qšt	An ARROW cannot make him flee,
lqšnhpkw-lw 'bny-ql'	as chaff are SLINGSTONES deflected by him.

To be accurate, the word-pair here is not *qšt* // *ql'* but *bn-qšt*, 'son of a bow' [i.e. an arrow] // *'bny-ql'*. 'slingstones', a point unnoticed by reviewers. The alliteration, of course, is marked.[44]

A better parallel occurs in *KTU* 1.14 iii 12-14:[45]

ḥṣk.al.tš'l qrth	Do not loose your ARROW(S) at the city,
abn.ydk mšdpt	(nor) your SLINGSTONES.[46]

43. Again, following Eichler, 'Slings and Shields', p. 96 n. 11.

44. A combination of lexical word-pair and sound pairing is involved. Relevant are stanzas 12 and 13 of Eleazar ben Kallib's poem 'The Battle between Behemoth and Leviathan' (available in T. Carmi [ed.], *The Penguin Book of Hebrew Verse* [Harmondsworth: Allen Lane and Penguin Books, 1981], pp. 227-32):

> They shoot ARROWS (*ḥiṣṣê qešet*) at him,
> but no ARROWS (*ben-qešet*) can put him to flight,
> bronze to him is rotten wood.
>
> They SLING STONES at him (*wîqalle'û bô ᵃbānîm*) huge as rocks,
> but SLINGSTONES (*'abnê qela'*) turn to chaff on him.
> Then, seized with rage, he rears about to slaughter them.
> (Carmi's translation, p. 230; my emphasis and lineation).

45. See already M.H. Lichtenstein, 'The Poetry of Poetic Justice: A Comparative Study in Biblical Imagery', *JANESCU* 5 (1973), p. 261 who also refers to 1 Chron. 12.2 and 2 Chron. 26.15.

46. The term *mšdpt* could have one of the following meanings.

a. 'thrown' (Š of *ndp*)—F. Rosenthal, 'Die Parallelstellen in den Texten von Ugarit', *Or* 8 (1939), p. 222, followed by G.R. Driver, *Canaanite Myths and Legends* (Old Testament Studies, 3; Edinburgh: T. & T. Clark, 1978), p. 157 and n. 18; A. Caquot, M. Sznycer and A. Herdner, *Textes ougaritiques*. I. *Mythes et légendes* (Paris: Cerf, 1974), pp. 522 n. p and 594. G. del Olmo Lete, *Mitos y leyendas de canaan según la tradición de Ugarit* (Fuentes de la Ciencia Biblica, 1; Madrid: Institución San Jerónimo, 1981), p. 588, etc.

2.2.2. *To Bite // To Sting*. One of the features shared by Prov. 23.29-35 and an Assyrian incantation against *šimmatu*[47] is the word-pair 'to bite' // 'to sting' predicated of animals. In the incantation the disease (some kind of poisoning which results in paralysis)[48] is apostrophized as follows:

> *taššuki ṣirāniš tazquti zuqaqīpāniš*
> You BITE like a serpent, you STING like a scorpion.[49]

In Prov. 23.32 the effects of over-imbibing are described, including:

> *'ḥrytw knḥš yšk kṣp'ny yprš*
> Ultimately, it will BITE like a serpent, it will STING like a snake.

Both sets of paired similes use alliteration, and onomatopoeia.[50] The connection between wine and poison recurs in Deut. 32.32-33.

b. 'throwing' (Š participle of *ndp*)—J.C. de Moor and K. Spronk, 'Problematical Passages in the Legend of Kirtu (I)', *UF* 14 (1982), p. 167.
c. 'raised ready for hurling' (Š of *dp*)—J. Aistleitner, *Wörterbuch der ugaritischen Sprache* (Berlin: Akademie Verlag, 1963), p. 81.
d. 'citadel' or the like—so Gibson, *Canaanite Myths*, p. 152 (he cites Arabic *sadafu*, 'object seen from afar').
e. 'burnt' (root *šdp*)—M. Dahood, 'Honey that Drips: Notes on Proverbs 5, 2-3', *Bib* 54 (1973), pp. 382-83, but cf. his *Ugaritic–Hebrew Philology* (Rome: Biblical Institute Press, 1965), p. 73. (Cf. del Olmo Lete, *Mitos y leyendas*, p. 628.)

Of these, the best is b; de Moor and Spronk comment, 'We regard *mšdpt* as a feminine Š, complementing *yd* "the stones of your throwing-hand", i.e. your sling-stones' ('Problematical Passages', p. 167). A completely different analysis is provided by Loewenstamm, 'Ugarit and the Bible', pp. 112-13; according to him, the *yd* of *abn yd* does not mean 'hand' but derives from *ydy*, 'to throw'. (He cites Num. 35.18.) However, as de Moor and Spronk point out ('Problematical Passages', p. 167 n. 117) this leaves *mšdpt* unexplained.

47. O.R. Gurney and P. Hulin, *The Sultantepe Tablets II* (London: British Institute of Archaeology at Ankara, 1964), pl. 148 and parallels, as presented by W. von Soden, 'Duplikate aus Ninive', *JNES* 33 (1974), pp. 341-43.

48. 'Eine auch Lähmungen auslösende innere Vergiftung' according to von Soden, 'Duplikate', p. 341; cf. 'Lähmung, Paralyse' in *AHw*, p. 1238a.

49. Gurney and Hulin, *Sultantepe Tablets*, 136:33-34 (and parallels).

50. See my comments (on Prov. 23.32) in *Classical Hebrew Poetry*, p. 27.

2.2.3. *Bone // Flesh*. The collocation *'ṣm wbśr*, 'bone and flesh'—always with a pronominal suffix—occurs in Gen. 29.14, Judg. 9.2, 2 Sam. 5.1, 19.13, 14, Ps. 102.6 and 1 Chron. 11.1. The 'normal' word-pair, *'ṣm // b śr*, is used in Gen. 2.23, Ezek. 24.4 (cf. 10), Job 2.5, 4.14-15 and Sir. 30.14.[51] The inverted sequence (*bśr // 'ṣm*) appears in Exod. 12.46, Mic. 3.2-3, Ps. 38.4, Job 19.20, 33.21, Prov. 14.30 (cf. 3.8) and Lam. 3.4.[52] These texts show that the expression (or word-pair) can have one of three meanings.[53]

1. *Kinship*, in the form 'my/your/his bone and my/your/his flesh' wherever it occurs (except for Ps. 102.6 discussed below), including Gen. 2.23:

> *z't hp'm 'ṣm m'ṣmy wbśr mbśry*
> Now this one, at last is BONE from my BONES and FLESH from my FLESH.

2. *Food*, as in the overt references of Ezek. 24.4, 10,[54] Mic. 3.2-3 and in particular, Exod. 12.46. This last passage is the passover injunction which stipulates that the lamb has to be eaten within a single house and also *l'-twṣy' mn-hbyt mn-hbśr ḥwṣh w'ṣm l' tšbrw-bw*, 'Do not take any of the FLESH outside the house and do not break a BONE of (in?) it'.

3. *One's physical body*, always as a word-pair (Ps. 38.4; Job 2.5; 4.14-15; 19.20;[55] 33.21; Lam. 3.4 and Sir. 30.14). Note, for example, Job 33.21:

ykl bśrw mr'y	Consumed is his FLESH from sight,
wšpy 'ṣmtyw l' r'w	and his unseen BONES are laid bare.[56]

The same semantic word-pair is also used in Akkadian incantations against 'fire', probably some sort of fever. One passage runs:

51. Distant parallelism is in Isa. 66.14b and 17b; Ps. 109.18b and 24b.

52. For distant parallelism, see Isa. 58.7d, 11c; Job 21.6b, 24b.

53. For the second term, see A.F.L. Beeston, 'One Flesh', *VT* 36 (1986), pp. 115-17, and S. Abir, 'Was kann die anthropologische בשׂר-Konzeption zur Deutung der Urgeschichte beitragen?', *ZAW* 98 (1986), pp. 179-86.

54. The usage here is allegorical.

55. For the problems of this text, cf. M. Pope, *Job* (AB, 15; Garden City, NY: Doubleday, 1965), p. 133.

56. Following Pope, *Job*, pp. 215 and 219.

Fire! Fire, fire [of...], fire of [...],
that eats FLESH (*šīrî*), that consumes BONE (*eṣemta*),
whose environs(?) are sinews:
Instead of eating FLESH (*šīrî*),
instead of consuming BONE (*eṣemta*),
[(...)] and having sinews for your environs(?)...[57]

All the more curious, then, is the presence of the word-pair with pronominal suffixes in Ps. 102.6 ('my BONE sticks to my FLESH')[58] where the meaning is the physical body of the psalmist (meaning 3 above) but the form used fits meaning 1 above (i.e. kinship).

2.2.4. *Death (To Die) // Destiny*.[59] Although the similarity between *KTU* 1.17 vi 35-36 and Num. 23.10 has been remarked on[60] the use of a word-pair common to both texts has not. In Num. 23.10

tmt npšy mwt yšry-m	May I myself die the DEATH of an upright man,
wthy 'ḥryty kmhw	May my DESTINY be like his.[61]

the word-pair is *mwt // 'ḥryty* (strictly speaking, *mwt yšry-m // 'ḥryty*). This word-pair, reversed, occurs in *KTU* 1.17 vi 35-38 not in

57. Text and translation: W.G. Lambert, 'Fire Incantations', *AfO* 23 (1970), p. 42; on p. 44 he cites the similar passage (J. Nougayrol *et al.*, *Ugaritica V* [BAH, 80; MRS, 16; Paris: Imprimerie Nationale/Librairie Orientaliste Paul Geuthner, 1968], 17 rev. 24' [pp. 32 and 34]; cf. *CAD*, K, p. 243a). Note the same pair in R.C. Thompson, *Assyrian Medical Texts* (London: Reprint from Proceedings of the Royal Society of Medicine, 1924–26), p. 28, 1 iv 3 (etc.): *daltu šīru sikkūru eṣemtu*, 'the FLESH is the door, the BONE is the bolt'. In the light of the first two texts the restoration proposed for 1QH 8.30-31 looks very probable: 'My wound breaks out like burning fire... [my BON]ES'.

58. The text is difficult; see M.C. Dahood, *Psalms* (AB, 17A; Garden City, NY: Doubleday, 1970), III, pp. 12-13 for a possible solution.

59. Ugaritic *uḫryt*, Hebrew *'aḥ^arît* and Akkadian *aḫrâtu* mean both 'future' and 'progeny'. (For the Akkadian word, see *CAD*, A/1, pp. 193b-94 and texts cited there.) See, in addition, S.D. Sperling, 'A šu-íl-lá to Ishtar', *WO* 12 (1981), pp. 16-17 on *šimtu* and related terms for 'fate, destiny'.

60. For example, Gibson, *Canaanite Myths*, p. 109 n. 9.

61. For the enclitic (emphatic) *-m* on *yšr-m*, see, conveniently, M. O'Connor, *Hebrew Verse Structure* (Winona Lake, IN: Eisenbrauns, 1980), pp. 186-67 (with references).

consecutive lines but in the form of distant parallelism[62] over a stanza of six lines:

a	*mt. uḫryt.mh yqḥ*	A man as (his) DESTINY what does he achieve?
	mh.yqḥ.mt.aṯryt	What does a man get in the end?
b	*spsg.ysk [l]riš.*	Glaze(?) will be poured on my head,
	ḥrṣ lẓr.qdqdy	Lime(?) on top of my skull.
a'	*[w]mt.kl.amt.*	And the DEATH of everyone shall I die;
	wan.mtm.amt	Yes, I will certainly die.[63]

The six-line stanza comprises three couplets, marked a, b and a', where the first matches the last (chiasmus). The term *uḫryt* of couplet a and the first *mt* of the corresponding couplet a' form a word-pair in distant parallelism.

It is no great surprise that cognate terms co-occur in both the Aramaic grave inscriptions from Nerab.[64] The final curse of *Nerab* ii concludes, 'May Sahar, Nikkal and Nusk

yhb'šw mmtth w'ḥrth t'bd
make his DYING odious and may his POSTERITY perish.'

Here the word-pair is *mmtt- // 'ḥrt-*. Identical terms recur in lines 4 and 8 of the same inscription. This corresponds to *Nerab* i 2 (*mt*) and 13 (*'ḥrh*).

62. On this form of parallelism, see D. Pardee, 'Ugaritic and Hebrew Poetry: Parallelism', in *Studies in the History and Archaeology of Palestine: Proceedings of the First International Synopsium on Palestine Antiquities* (Aleppo: Aleppo University Press, 1988), pp. 55-82.

63. This is not the place to discuss difficult *spsg* and *ḥrṣ*. For the problems of the passage, see most recently K. Spronk, *Beatific Afterlife in Ancient Israel and in the Ancient Near East* (AOAT, 219; Neukirchen–Vluyn: Neukirchener Verlag, 1986), p. 152. Unlike Spronk, who, following Healey, translates *mh yqḥ*, 'what takes (it [= Death]) away?', I prefer to translate 'what does he (= a man) achieve?' The expression *minâ ilqe*, 'what did he achieve?', used in Akkadian wisdom texts (W.G. Lambert, *Babylonian Wisdom Literature* [Oxford: Clarendon Press, 1960], p. 240: ii 22-23 and Sargon Legend ii 5-6 [both cited by J. Westenholz, review of B. Lewis, *The Sargon Legend: A Study of the Akkadian Text and the Tale of the Hero who was Exposed at Birth*, *JNES* 43 (1984), p. 77] seems to support this). (Note, in addition, *balāṭa ša lā namāri ana mūti* [variant *mitī*] *mina utter*, 'What profit has life without light over death?' [RS 25.130 = Nougayrol *et al.*, *Ugaritica V*, 164:13'//14' (bilingual) on which cf. *Ugaritica V*, p. 293 and *CAD*, N/1, p. 210a.])

64. See conveniently J.C.L. Gibson, *Syrian Semitic Inscriptions*. II. *Aramaic Inscriptions* (Oxford: Clarendon Press, 1975), pp. 93-98.

2.2.5. *Far // Near*. Del Olmo Lete has discussed occurrences of this pair (*rḥq // qrb*) in Ugaritic and Hebrew.[65] In addition the same semantic pair is used in Babylonian incantation prayers as part of a formula which has two forms, as Mayer has shown:[66]

a	*rūqiš alsika qerbiš šimanni*	from FAR OFF I call to you, hear me CLOSE to;
b	*alsika rūqiš šimanni qerbiš*	I call to you from AFAR, hear me CLOSE to.

2.2.6. *Fat // Blood*. Whenever it occurs in Hebrew in collocation or as a word-pair, the set *dm* + *ḥlb* has a sacrificial connotation. This is evident in texts such as Lev. 3.4, 17, 7.22-27, 33, Exod. 29.12, 13, 20-22, as well as in the P passages Ezek. 44.7, 15 and so on. All these (as well as 2 Chron. 35.10, 14—Passover regulations) use 'fat' and 'blood' in juxtaposition and are intended to be understood literally. Of the passages where these two terms comprise a word-pair, only Exod. 23.18 is a ritual regulation (and cf. Lev. 3.17 cited above). Elsewhere, in Isa. 1.11, 34.6-7 and Ezek. 39.19, the aspect of sacrifice is figurative only. In Isa. 34.6-7 the word-pair recurs three times:

Yahweh has a sword coated with BLOOD,
made greasy with FAT,

with the BLOOD of lambs and goats,
with the FAT of rams' kidneys,

for it is Yahweh's sacrifice in Bozrah,
and a great slaughter in the land of Edom.

Wild oxen shall go down with them,
and steers with the mighty bulls.

Their land shall drink deep of BLOOD,
and their dust shall be greasy with FAT.[67]

The imagery is clear: the officials and nobles of Edom will be put to the sword just like animals slaughtered for sacrifice.[68]

65. G. del Olmo Lete, 'Algunos pares ugarítico-hébreos preteridos', *AuOr* 2 (1984), p. 19 §65.

66. W. Mayer, *Untersuchungen zur Formensprache der babylonischen 'Gebetsbeschwörungen'* (Studia Pohl, Series Maior, 5; Rome: Pontifical Biblical Institute, 1976), p. 130 (Type 3).

67. These data should be added to M. Pope's detailed study 'Isaiah 34 in Relation to Isaiah 35, 40-66', *JBL* 71 (1952), pp. 235-43.

68. On the metaphorical use of animal names, cf. P.D. Miller, 'Animal Names as

Again in Ezek. 39.19 the context is one of sacrifice, this time a macabre sacrificial feast, to which the birds and the beasts are invited.

> You shall eat FAT to satiety,
> you shall drink BLOOD to a stupor
> at my sacrifice which I have sacrificed for you.

Accordingly, sacrificial connotations may have determined the choice of this word-pair in 2 Sam. 1.21a-22:

> For there was defiled
> the Heroes' Shield, Saul's Shield
> —not by anointing with oil (but)—
> by the BLOOD of the slain, by the FAT of Heroes.[69]

2.2.7. *Gather // Seal*. This word-pair appears to have been identified by Cohen as common to Deut. 32.34 and a passage from the Assyrian folktale 'The Poor Man of Nippur'.[70]

hl'-hw' kms 'mdy ḥtwm b'wṣrwt	See, I have GATHERED it with me(?), SEALED in my storehouses.
G-N šitta eṣṣūrāti ibāramma	G-N caught two birds,
ikmis ana quppima iktanak kišippiš	GATHERED into a cage, SEALED with a seal.[71]

In both examples, incidentally, the word-pair occurs in a line with inner (half-line) parallelism.

Designations in Ugaritic and Hebrew', *UF* 2 (1970), pp. 177-86. Also, S. Gevirtz, 'Simeon and Levi in the "Blessing of Jacob" (Gen. 49:5-7)', *HUCA* 52 (1981), p.96.

69. Similar use of *min* occurs in Cant. 1.2. The interpretation proposed here is given below in Chapter 7, 'Chiastic Patterns in Biblical Hebrew Poetry' and, independently, by J. Wansbrough, 'Hebrew Verse: Scansion and Parallax', *BSO(A)S* 45 (1982), p. 10. It is not discussed by P. Kyle McCarter, *II Samuel* (AB, 9; Garden City, NY: Doubleday, 1984), pp. 66-79, esp. 76.

70. H.R. (Chaim) Cohen, *Biblical Hapax Legomena in the Light of Akkadian and Ugaritic* (SBLDS, 37; Missoula, MT: Scholars Press, 1978), p. 39.

71. O.R. Gurney and J.J. Finkelstein, *The Sultantepe Tablets I* (London: The British Institute of Archaeology at Ankara, 1957), p. 38 lines 85-86, with the reading proposed by E. Reiner, 'Another Volume of Sultantepe Tablets', *JNES* 26 (1967), p. 183 n. 7, and *CAD*, K, pp. 115, 451 (as noted by Cohen, *Hapax Legomena*, p. 63 n. 90).

2.2.8. *Heavens // Earth*. This lexical word-pair has been very fully documented for several languages by Avishur[72] but two additional observations can be made. One is that the Ugaritic expression *tant šmm 'm arṣ*, 'heavens' groaning with the earth' (*KTU* 1.3 iii 24, etc.) is like a line from the *Epic of Gilgamesh*:

> *ilsu šamê qaqqaru īpul*
> The HEAVENS shouted, respond did the EARTH.[73]

Also, the same word-pair in the form *šamāmu // erṣetu*, is significant in the *Great Hymn to Shamash*, lines 1-33[74] where it is used in combination with *eliš u šapliš*, 'above and below'.[75]

2.2.9. *Heir // Name*. The epilogue to the Code of Hammurabi includes among its final curses called down on anyone replacing the lawgiver's name with his own:

> May Nintu, eminent Lady of the lands, the mother who created me, deprive him of an HEIR (*aplu*) and not allow him to obtain a NAME (*šumu*); may she not create a child (literally, human seed) in the womb of his people.[76]

It is not accidental, therefore, that Isaiah 14, which has overt references to Babylon and to Assyria, includes a slightly expanded version of the pair 'heir // name' in v. 22:

> I will rise up against them
> (oracle of Yahweh sebaoth)
> and cut off from Babylon
> NAME and remnant, OFFSPRING and posterity.

72. Avishur, *Word-Pairs*, indices. Note also Craigie's comments in 'Word Pairs in the Song of Deborah', pp. 18-19 on this word pair in Hebrew, Ugaritic, Akkadian, Arabic and Egyptian.

73. *Gilg*. VII iv 15. Text: J.H. Tigay, *The Evolution of the Gilgamesh Epic* (Philadelphia: University of Pennsylvania, 1982), p. 285, who follows B. Landsberger, 'Zur vierten und siebten Tafel des Gilgamesch-Epos', *RA* 62 (1968), pp. 129-30 and cites the slight variant in Gilg. Ur 61. Translation: Tigay, *Gilgamesh Epic*, p. 124.

74. Lambert, *Babylonian Wisdom Literature*, pp. 126-29.

75. Another occurrence is W. Farber, *Beschwörungsrituale an Ishtar und Dumuzi: attī Ištar ša ḫarmaša Dumuzi* (Wiesbaden: Steiner, 1977), pp. 240-41 (B 40').

76. Code of Hammurab/pi, Epilogue (col. 51 [Rev. 28] 40-49); cf. A. Finet, *Le Code de Hammurapi* (Paris: Cerf, 1973), pp. 145-46 for a recent translation.

The stock alliterative expression of the last line (*šm wš'r* // *nyn wnkd*; Gen. 21.23; Sir. 47.22b) has itself been productive of other word-pairs.[77]

2.2.10. *Hem // Fringe*. In Mesopotamian texts the normal word-pair or collocation is 'hem and hair' as symbols of a person.[78] The following word-pair, therefore, is unusual:

> *aṣbat qannakama ukīl sissiktaka*
> I hereby grasp your HEM and hold back your FRINGE.[79]

It occurs in Ugaritic, too, and as in the Babylonian passage, the context is one of pleading:

tiḫd.mt bsin.lpš	She seized Mot by the HEM of the robe,
tšṣqn[h] bqṣ.all	She grasped him by the FRINGE of (his) garment.[80]

More accurately, both word-pairs are compound and comprise the two elements 'TO HOLD (verb)' + 'EDGE OF APPAREL (noun)'.

2.2.11. *Horns // Tail*. In the Ugaritic text *KTU* 1.114 the god El is portrayed as drunk enough to soil himself and in that state he meets the *b'l qrnm wḏnb*, 'the creature with two horns and a tail' (line 20).[81] This description is very like two lines from an incantation against *šimmatu* (see above under 'To Bite // To Sting'):

77. Note the break-up of *nyn wnkd* in Job 18.19 and Sir. 41.5 both times connected by distant parallelism with *šm* (Job 18.17 and Sir. 41.14). In Zeph. 1.4 *šm wš'r* is broken up and inverted.

78. See *CAD*, S, pp. 323-25 for occurrences and discussion.

79. *Dumuzi* 3:13; text and translation in Mayer, *Untersuchungen*, pp. 258-59. He also explains the meaning of this formula (pp. 128, 143-44, 147-49). For the terms *qarru* and *sissiktu*, see now M. Malul, '"*Sissiktu*" and "*sikku*"—Their Meaning and Function', *BO* 43 (1986), pp. 20-36.

80. *KTU* 1.6 ii 9-11. Cf. E. Greenstein, '"To Grasp the Hem" in Ugaritic Literature', *VT* 32 (1982), pp. 217-18. Also, especially for the meaning of *all*, S. Ribichini and P. Xella, *La terminologia dei tessili nei testi di Ugarit* (Collezione di Studi fenici, 20; Rome: Consiglio Nazionale delle Ricerche, 1985), pp. 28-29 where this passage is discussed. (Cf. also P.S. Kruger, 'The Hem of the Garment in Marriage. The Meaning of the Symbolic Gesture in Ruth 3:9 and Ezek 16:8', *JNSL* 12 [1984], pp. 79-86.)

81. See Cathcart and Watson, 'Weathering a Wake', p. 46 for brief discussion.

tamḫaṣi ina qarniki	you strike with your HORNS,
tušardi ina zibbatiki	you spray (dung) with your TAIL.[82]

It would seem that Prov. 23.29-35, *KTU* 1.114 and the incantation against *šimmatu* have several elements in common. In view of the scarcity of comparative material[83] further study should take this into account (see further under Conclusions).

2.2.12. *Kingdom // Dominion.* In Ugaritic:

tqḥ.mlk.ʿlmk.	Take your everlasting KINGDOM,
drkt.dt.drdrk.	your eternal DOMINION.[84]

In an Assyrian prophecy:

šarru lā tapallaḫ	King, do not worry!
šarruttu ikkû	Yours is the KINGDOM,
danānu ikkûma	yours is the DOMINION.[85]

2.2.13. *Knee // Mouth.* In 1 Kgs 19.18 Elijah is told there is to be wholesale slaughter of the Israelites, but the oracle closes with a note of mercy:

> Yet I will leave seven thousand in Israel:
> every pair of KNEES (*kl-hbrkym*) which have not bent to Baal,
> and every MOUTH (*kl-hph*) which has not kissed him.[86]

The curious word-pair can be explained as a form of merismus.[87]

82. Text: von Soden, 'Duplikate', pp. 342-43, lines 34-35.

83. See the final comment of von Soden, 'Duplikate', p. 344.

84. *KTU* 1.2 iv 10.

85. Text: K 4310 V 21-23, discussed (without reference to Ugaritic) by M. Weippert, 'Assyrische Prophetien', in F.M. Fales (ed.), *Assyrian Royal Inscriptions: New Horizons in Literary, Ideological and Historical Analysis* (Orientis Antiqui Collectio, 17; Rome: Istituto per l'Oriente, 1981), p. 96. See also Ps. 145.13 and Dan. 3.33.

86. Note the semantic pairs *krʿ*, 'to bend' // *nšq*, 'to kiss' (used in 1 Kgs 19.18) and *našāqu*, 'to kiss' // *kamāsu*, 'to kneel' (*Ee* III 69-70).

87. Unrelated is the same pair ('mouth' // 'knees') in G. Meier, *Die assyrische Beschwörungssammlung Maqlû* (AfO Beiheft, 2; Graz: Ernst Weidner, 1937), III 50-51 (p. 23). Another example of the same word-pair occurs in J. Nougayrol, 'Un chef-d'oeuvre inédit de la littérature babylonienne', *RA* 45 (1951), p. 172 line 6.

2.2.14. *Lion // Sea-Monster (Dragon).* Elsewhere I have commented on the possible similarity between *Aḥiqar* 34 and *KTU* 1.5 i 14-16.[88] Some additional texts can be discussed here. The first comes in an oracle against Egypt (Ezek. 32.2):

> Like a young LION (*kpyr*) among nations have you become;
> and like a DRAGON (*tnym*) in the seas you burst out in your streams (etc.).[89]

The parallelism in some lines from the Hodayoth (1QH 5.9-10) is not so clear:

> You have closed the mouth(s) of young LIONS (*kpyrym*)
> whose teeth are like a sword, whose jaws are like a sharp spear;
> Poison of DRAGONS (*tnynym*) are all their plottings (etc.).[90]

Two Mesopotamian passages may also be significant:

> You become a raging LION (*nešimmî*):
> your mouth is a horned SNAKE (*bašmummî*),
> your nails are (those of) the Anzu-bird.[91]

> ... the DRAGON which turns on itself,
> strength of a LION, which sticks out its tongue towards a serpent.[92]

2.2.15. *Ruin // Heap.* Undeniably, the first part of Mic. 1.6 is difficult:

> *wśmty šmrwn l'y hśdh lmṭ'y krm*

88. See Chapter 2,'The Aḥiqar Sayings: Some Marginal Comments', p. 256. Unfortunately, *KTU* 1.19 iv 60-61 is too broken to be evaluated.

89. Following J. Day, *God's Conflict with the Dragon and the Sea: Echoes of a Canaanite Myth in the Old Testament* (Cambridge: Cambridge University Press, 1985), p. 94 and n. 24.

90. Following B. Kittel, *The Hymns of Qumran* (SBLDS, 50; Chico, CA: Scholars Press, 1981), pp. 83, 85, 91. Also, cf. Sir. 25.16 (Greek text only): *leonti kai drakonti.*

91. E.F. Weidner, 'Das Alter der mittelassyrischen Gesetzestexte. Studien im Anschluss an Driver und Miles, *The Assyrian Laws*', *AfO* 13 (1939), p. 46 rev. ii 2-3, quoted by J.G. Westenholz, 'Heroes of Akkad', *JAOS* 103 (1983), p. 332. The parallelism is not strict.

92. Part of a description of Ninurta. Text and translation (above): J. van Dijk, LUGAL UD ME-LÁM-bi NIR-GÁL. *Le récit épique et didactique des travaux de Ninurta, du déluge et de la nouvelle création, texte, traduction et introduction.* I. *Introduction texte composite. Traduction* (Leiden: Brill 1983), p. 52, lines 10-11.

Although a translation such as 'So I will make Samaria a heap of ruins in open country, a place for planting vines' (NEB) is feasible, problems remain[93] and it is possible instead that the phraseology here evokes various stock expressions used by Assyrian and Babylonian kings in their accounts of conquest. For example,

> *ālānišunu ana tīlim u karmim utêr*
> I turned their cities into HEAPS and RUINS.

The expression follows the pattern 'to turn into' (*ewû/emû*, *šūmû*, *târu/turru*, *šakānu*, *šapāku*) + 'heaps of ruins' (literally, 'heaps and ruins': *tīli u karmi*—with some variations).[94] This is indicative that in Mic. 1.6 *'y* corresponds to *tīlu*, '(ruin-)heap' and *krm*, like Akkadian *karmu* does not mean 'vineyard' but 'heap of ruins'. A probable translation of Mic. 1.6 then, is

> I will turn Samaria into a RUIN,
> the field(s) into plantations that are RUIN-HEAPS.[95]

This is confirmed by a line from the *Epic of Erra* where the pair *alu*, 'city' (here plural) // *šadû*, 'open country' (here collective singular) occurs:

> *ālānišu ana karme ušadâšu tašakkan ana namê*
> Turn their cities into a RUIN, and their pastures into a waste.[96]

93. J.M.P. Smith, W.H. Ward and J.A. Brewer, *Micah, Zephaniah, Habakkuk, Obadiah and Joel* (ICC; New York: Charles Scribner's Sons, 1911): 'Therefore I will turn Samaria into a field, into a planted vineyard', reading *l^{e}śādeh* and omitting *'y* as a gloss (p. 34, with reference to the versions plus other possible corrections). R. Vuilleumier in R. Vuilleumier and C.-A. Keller, *Michée, Nahoum, Habacuc, Sophonie* (CAT, 11b; Neuchâtel: Delachaux et Niestlé, 1971) translates 'Je vais transformer Samarie en ruine/Ses environs, en terre à vigne' (p. 15) noting the correction to *ly'r* (as in Ezek. 21.2) is unnecessary and that *hśdh*, which belongs to the next line, means 'surrounding country' as in Ps. 78.12; Neh. 11.30 etc. (p. 17 n. 7). W. Rudolph, *Micha—Nahum—Habakuk—Zephanja* (KAT, 13/3; Gütersloh: Mohr, 1975), p. 33: 'So mache ich Samaria zu einem Trümmerhaufen "und seine Flur" zu Rebengelände'; *'y* is explained by Arabic *ġajaya*, 'giving shade from above' and the reading followed in the second line is *w^{e}śādeh*.

94. Cf. *CAD*, K, p. 218, and *AHw*, p. 1359b.

95. Note, incidentally, the break-up of *'y hśdh* (Mic. 1.6) in Mic. 3.12/Jer. 26.18.

96. *Erra* V 29; text and translation: W.G. Lambert, 'The Fifth Tablet of the Era Epic', *Iraq* 24 (1962), pp. 122-23. For the meaning of *šadû(m)* cf. A. Heidel, 'A Special Use of the Akkadian Term *Šadû*', *JNES* 8 (1949), pp. 233-35; *AHw*, p. 1125a meaning 10; contrast L. Cagni, *L'epopea di Erra* (Rome: Istituto di Studi

2.2.16. *To Weep // To Bury*. This word-pair has been well documented[97] and on the surface does not appear to be significant since the association of mourning and internment is so commonplace. Despite this, two interesting points emerge with respect to the word-pair. In adoption contracts from Nuzi (in Akkadian) clauses of the following type are used:

> *enūma ᴵpa-i-te-šup imâta uᴵki-in-ni ibakkišu uqabbar*[*šu*]
> when PN 1 dies PN 2 shall weep for him and bury [him].[98]

PN 2 (here Kinni) is the adopted son of PN 1 (Paiteshup) and in this part of the document he undertakes to bury his adopted father. Evidently, then, burial of one's father was an obligation serious enough to require mention in a legal contract.[99]

Secondly, it is usually the son who survives to bury his father (or adopted father). The inversion of roles is particularly highlighted in the *Aqhat Tale* since Dnil has to bury the very son whose filial duties included burial of his father, observance of the funeral rites and care of his tomb (cf. *KTU* 1.17 i 26-33, etc.).

2.2.17. *Voice // Speech*. The Ugaritic word-pair *rgm // hwt* occurs several times as one of two sets:

del Vicino Oriente dell'Università, 1969), p. 125: 'le sue regioni montane'; see his comment (p. 251) as well as A. Faber, 'Semitic Sibilants in an Afro-Asian Context', *JSS* 29 (1984), p. 208 entry 41.

97. Avishur, *Word-Pairs*, p. 558. Note, in addition, *bakû // qebēru* of *Gilg*. M ii 5-6 and *Gilg*. X v 14-15.

98. E.R. Lacheman, *Excavations at Nuzi*. VIII. *Family and Law Documents* (HSS, 19; Cambridge, MA: Harvard University Press, 1962), p. 39 lines 9-11; on this text and related passages, see P. Skaist, 'The Ancestor Cult and Succession in Mesopotamia', in B. Alster (ed.), *Death in Mesopotamia* (Mesopotamia, 8; Copenhagen: Akademisk, 1980), pp. 123-28, esp. 124-25 and 128 n. 14. Note also R.F. Harper, *Assyrian and Babylonian Letters* (Chicago: The University of Chicago Press, 1896), II, p. 437 line 15. Another text (Joint Expedition with the Iraq Museum at Nuzi, 59:22 [from *CAD*, B, p. 37]) is quoted by Avishur (*Word-Pairs*) but he does not comment on the context (burial obligation in an adoption contract). Relevant, too, are J.C. Greenfield's comments on burial in his paper 'Ahiqar in the Book of Tobit', in J. Doré *et al.* (eds.), *De la torah au messie: Mélanges Henri Cazelles* (Paris: Desclée 1980), pp. 329-36, esp. 335.

99. Of course it is normally the son who survives to bury his father. Reversal of this natural order is common to *KTU* 1.19 iii 39-41 (burial of Aqhat's remains) and *Erra* IV 97-98.

a	*bph rgm lyṣa*	Scarce had a VOICE left his mouth,
	bšpt hwt	a WORD his lips.
b	*dm.rgm.iṯ. ly.wargmk*	For I have a 'VOCIFERATION' and I'll VOICE it to you
	hwt. waṯnyk	a WORD and I'll repeat it to you...

The first set is really a formula which uses a word-pair;[100] the second set opens a 'tour'.[101]

A semantically comparable word-pair, *rigmu // atmu*, appears in the Babylonian Theodicy:

rigmu ul iššapu iššapil atmua
My VOICE was not raised, my SPEECH was kept low.[102]

2.3. *Conclusions*

Some passages can be better understood through recognition of word-pairs (e.g. 2 Sam. 1.21; Mic. 1.6) and the meanings of some difficult words can also be established (e.g. Ugaritic *ql'*; Hebrew *kerem*). In addition, there are evidently more pairs common to two or more ancient Semitic languages than those so far collected. However, the differences as well as the similarities among the various traditions are important, too. While sharing common features each tradition had a character of its own, an aspect which tends to be overlooked (see word-pair 13). Finally, some of the accepted word-pairs may need correction (e.g. word-pair 1).

Since word association is a strong element in the formation of word-pairs it follows that pairs common to two (or more) languages are likely to share similar contexts. The brief survey provided here shows, in fact, that such is often the case (see word-pairs 2, 3, 4, 6, 10, 11, 15 and 16). It is not a matter of determining dependence or borrowing between the different traditions, though both did occur. Of more significance is the light which a word-pair plus context in one tradition may throw on the context in another tradition where the

100. For references, cf. Chapter 9 below, 'Introduction to Discourse in Ugaritic Narrative Verse'.

101. On tours, cf. Watson, *Classical Hebrew Poetry*, pp. 349-50. Text: *KTU* 1.3 iii 20-28. The tour comprises *rgm, hwt, rgm, lḫšt, rgm*. A related word-pair is *ṯḥm*, 'message' // *hwt* in *KTU* 1.3 iii 13-14; vi 24-25; 1.4 viii 32-34; 1.5 ii 10-11, 17-18; 1.14 vi 40-41, etc.

102. Texts and translation: Lambert, *Babylonian Wisdom Literature*, pp. 88-89, 292; see notes on pp. 285 and 310.

same pair, or a comparable word-pair, occurs.[103] Nor is etymology so important since word-pairs common to two or more languages tend to be semantically similar.

3. *The Unnoticed Word-Pair 'Eye(s)' // 'Heart'*[104]

In spite of several recent collections of parallel word-pairs,[105] the word-pair 'eye(s)' // 'heart' common to several ancient Near Eastern languages including Hebrew has virtually escaped attention.[106] Perhaps one reasons for such neglect is the complete absence of the word-pair

103. In illustration, some elements (chiefly word-pairs) common to three texts in Hebrew, Ugaritic and Akkadian which have already been touched on above under the headings '*To Bite // To Sting*' and '*Horns // Tail*' can be set out as follows:

a. you (= *šimmatu*) have darkened (*tuṭṭî*) his (facial) features
šimmatu: 24 (cf. 27)
Who gets shadowy (*ḥkllwt*) eyes?
Prov. 23.29

b. but he who does not know him (*wdlyd'nn*) he hits on the snout under the table . . .
KTU 1.114:8
They hit me (*hlmwny*): I did not know (*yd'ty*)
Prov. 23.25b

c. you spray (dung) with your tail
šimmatu: 35
he (= El) floundered in his own excrement and urine
KTU 1.114:21

Once the shared elements have been pointed out it may be possible to progress to better explanations of the texts.

104. First published in *ZAW* 101 (1989), pp. 398-408.

105. S. Rummel (ed.), *Ras Shamra Parallels: The Texts from Ugarit and the Bible* (AnOr 51; Rome: Biblical Institute Press, 1981), III, the continuation of *RSP* I and II. Also, Avishur, *Stylistic Studies of Word-Pairs*, with extensive bibliography. For a discussion of word pairs in terms of linguistic theory, cf. Berlin, 'Word Pairs', pp. 7-16 = *Dynamics*, pp. 64-72.

106. W.R. Watters, *Formula Criticism and the Poetry of the Old Testament* (BZAW, 138; Berlin: de Gruyter, 1976), pp. 160 (entry No. 134), 196 (entry No. 183) and 212 (entry No. 49) simply lists most occurrences of the word-pair. Avishur, *Word-Pairs*, p. 279 mentions this word-pair and refers there to further discussion in Part II, chapter 4 (pp. 497-522) though there is no other reference to the word-pair anywhere else in the book. The reference in the index, p. 761 to p. 655 is incorrect.

from Ugaritic.[107] In the present note all the passages where this word-pair occurs are listed and some are discussed.[108]

We can begin with biblical Hebrew since most of the occurrences are registered in that language. Although both *lb* (or *lbb*), 'heart', and *'yn*, 'eye', are usually A-words,[109] I have chosen to begin with the sequence 'eye(s)' // 'heart' since that is the principal sequence in extra-biblical texts (see below).[110]

3.1. *The Word-Pair as Synonymous*

The first group comprises passages where *'yn* and *lb(b)* are in synonymous parallelism and have practically the same meaning.

3.1.1. *'yn(ym) // lb(b)*. Isa. 44.18; Ps. 73.7; 101.5; Prov. 4.21; 21.4; 23.33; Qoh. 2.10; Sir. 43.18.[111]

Isa. 44.18 They do not know or understand
for too blinded are their EYES to see,
their HEARTS (*lbtm*) to perceive.

This is part of a description of idol-makers and evokes Deut. 28.28.

Ps. 101.5 Haughty of EYES and proud at HEART,
such I cannot endure.

107. But cf. T. Collins, 'The Physiology of Tears in the Old Testament: Part II', *CBQ* 33 (1971), pp. 185-97, who compares *KTU* 1.19 i 34-35 (weeping from the heart) with 1.16 i 25-28 (tears from the eyes), p. 197. The word-pair does not occur in Phoenician or Punic.

108. An earlier and shorter form of this article was included in my paper on word-pairs given in May 1987 at the Altorientalisches Seminar, Tübingen (by invitation of Professor W. Röllig) and in July of the same year to the Society for Old Testament Study. See below, 'The Hebrew Word-pair *'sp // qbṣ*'.

109. *'yn // 'zn*, *'p'pym*, *r'š*, *rgl*; with *'yn* as B-word: *grwn* (Isa. 3.16); *lb(b) // 'zn*, *bśr*, *ḥkm(h)*, *drk*, *zrw'*, *yd*, *kbd*, *kwḥ*, *klywt*, *kp*, *lšwn*, *m'd*, *npš*, *'ṣmwt*, *ph*, *pnym*, *qrb*, *r'š*, *rwḥ*, *śptym*. With some *lb(b)* occurs also as a B-word, and with *'ṣb't* (Prov. 7.3) and *m'yym* (Jer. 4.19; Lam. 1.20) only as a B-word.

110. I have not included Cant. 4.9, 'You have roused me (*lbbtny*), my sister-bride, you have roused me with one of your EYES, with a single gem of your neck-lace' with its unique use of the denominative verb *lbb* (elsewhere only Job 11.12) in parallel with the noun *'yn*. For discussion, see M.H. Pope, *Song of Songs* (AB, 15; Garden City, NY: Doubleday, 2nd edn, 1977), pp. 478-83.

111. Cf. Deut. 4.9; 2 Kgs 10.30. Also Sir. 22.19 (Greek text): 'Hurt the EYE and tears will flow. Hurt the mind (lit. HEART) and you will find it sensitive' (NEB).

The word-pair occurs in a line with internal (half-line) parallelism and the formulaic phrases *gbh-'ynym // wrḥb lbb* correspond to *rwm-'ynym // rhb lbb* in Prov. 21.4.[112]

Prov. 4.21 — Do not let them (my words) deviate from your EYES,
keep them within your HEART (*lbbk*).[113]

Qoh. 2.10 — Everything my EYES demanded I did not refuse them,
I did not deny my HEART any pleasure.

See below on Ezek. 6.9 and so on.

3.1.2. *lb(b) // 'yn(ym)*. Deut. 28.67; Isa. 10.12b; Ezek. 6.9; Pss. 19.9 (cited in section 3.5); 36.2; 131.1; Job 15.12; 17.4-5; Prov. 23.26; Qoh. 11.9; Lam. 5.17 (cf. Num. 15.39; Deut. 15.9).

Ezek. 6.9 — How I was grieved at their lusting HEART that turned away from me;
and at their EYES that lusted after their idols.

This passage, of course, echoes

Num. 15.39 — ... not to follow after your own HEART and after your own EYES which you lust after.[114]

In addition, Sir. 5.2 can be cited:

Do not follow your HEART and your EYES to pursue wicked inclinations.[115]

112. Cf. 2 Chron. 17.6, etc. Note the positive use in Isa. 60.5.

113. The verb *lûz* here in 4.21 and elsewhere is problematic; cf. L. Koehler and W. Baumgartner, *Hebräisches und aramäisches Lexikon zum Alten Testament* (Leiden: Brill, 1967–), pp. 496a-97b. The pair is part of a longer list and recurs in vv. 23 and 25.

114. 'In Ezekiel's new combination, the heart and eye become the agents of sin, endowed with the autonomous impulse later ascribed to them in a midrash to the cited Numbers passage [i.e. 15.39]: "The heart and the eyes are the two brokers of sin" (Numbers Rabba 10.6)', M. Greenberg, *Ezekiel 1–20* (AB, 22; Garden City, NY: Doubleday, 1983), p. 134.

115. For the text, cf. F. Vattioni, *Ecclesiastico* (Pubblicazioni del Seminario di Semitistica, 1; Naples: Istituto Orientale di Napoli, 1968), p. 25.

116. P.C. Craigie, *Psalms 1–50* (WBC, 19; Waco, TX: Word Books, 1983), p. 290 reads *n'm*, 'an oracle' 'as a word standing independently, describing the entire first part of the Psalm (vv. 2-5)'; see also p. 291. On a possible northern origin of *n'm* (and of the whole Psalm), cf. G.A. Rendsburg, 'The Northern Origin of "The Last Words of David" (2 Sam 23,1-7)', *Bib* 69 (1988), pp. 113-21, esp. 115-16.

Job 31.7b is also in the same vein.

Ps. 36.2 An oracle.[116]
An outlaw's flouting is in his HEART (*lbw*! for MT *lby*)
no fear of God before his EYES:

There is marked assonance here though it does not include *lēb*: *peša'* / *rāšā'*; *'ên* / *'enâw*; *b^eqereb* / *l^eneged*. The second component of the word-pairs recurs in the next line which may explain the sequence adopted here.

Ps. 131.1 Yahweh,
my HEART is not haughty,
my EYES are not raised high.

This is an expansion and negation of the single formulaic expression used in Ps. 101.5 and Prov. 21.4 (see above).[117]

Job 15.12 Why is your HEART enraged,
and why do your EYES blink?[118]

The couplet, introductory to v. 13, is of a piece with the rest of the chapter which uses a series of names for parts of the body.

Lam. 5.17 On this account our HEART (*lbnw*) has become sick,
on account of these things our EYES (*'ynynw*)
are gloomy.[119]

The two-fold singular-plural parallelism ('this'—'heart' // 'these things'—'eyes') is intentional.[120]

117. In his review of W. Beyerlin, *Wider die Hubris des Geistes: Studien zum 131. Psalm* (Stuttgarter Bibelstudien, 108; Stuttgart: Katholisches Bibelwerk, 1982), J.W. Betlyon (*JBL* 104 [1985], p. 315) notes that according to Beyerlin '"Heart" [which represents intellectual, rational functions, not just the bodily organ] is used in parallel with "eyes" and represents the totality of a human's being' and 'this becomes the basis for a revised translation [of the whole psalm]'; Beyerlin's version of our couplet (in Betlyon's translation) is 'Yahweh, Pride does not fill my soul, Nor presumption my eyes'. Beyerlin's book is unavailable to me.

118. E. Dhorme, *Le livre de Job* (Paris: Gabalda, 1926), p. 193 translates: 'Pourquoi ton cœur t'emporte-t-il / Et pourquoi tes yeux clignotent-ils?' (ET: *A Commentary on the Book of Job* [trans. H. Knight; London: Nelson, 1967, p. 212]). Heb. *rzm* corresponds to Aram. *rmz*, 'to blink, wink'.

119. Cf. Prov. 23.29. Collins, 'The Physiology of Tears', pp. 19-38 understands 'darkened' to mean 'weakened by tears' (p. 21 n. 7 and p. 31).

120. Berlin, *Dynamics*, p. 46 comments on the singular-plural parallelism here

3.2. *The Word-Pair as Antonymic*

In the second group the two components of the word-pair are contrasted. There are few occurrences.

3.2.1. *'ynym // lb(b).* 1 Sam. 16.7; Prov. 21.2.[121]

1 Sam. 16.7 For it is not as a man sees that God sees,
for a man looks at the EYES
but God looks at the HEART.

There are textual problems here; of chief concern is that LXX$^{(B)}$ εἰς πρόσωπον indicates the correction of *l'ynym* to *lpnym*, 'at the face', in the third line.[122] In that case this passage would have to be excluded from the survey; however, it is uncannily like the following example.

Prov. 21.2 A man's every action is correct (*yšr*) in his own EYES
but Yahweh weighs HEARTS (*lbwt*).

In 16.2 exactly the same words are used, with the substitution of *zk*, 'pure', for *yšr*, 'correct' in the first line, and of *rwḥwt*, 'spirits', for *lbwt* of the second.[123] Evidently, *lb* and *rwḥ* are used in free variation as parallels to *'yn*.[124]

3.2.2. *lb // 'ynym.* Prov. 24.17-18 only:

When your enemy falls do not cheer,
when he stumbles do not let your HEART rejoice,
or Yahweh will see and it will be evil in his EYES
and will divert his anger from him.

In direct contrast with the texts just cited here the antithesis is between a *man*'s heart (i.e., his inner feelings) and *God*'s eyes. A rather loosely structured quatrain is held together by the contrasting pair *lbk // 'ynyw*.

but fails to notice the match within each line. (Also, the reference to p. 80 in the index [p. 174] should be to p. 46).

121. Also Gen. 6.5-8. These passages should be added to those collected by J. Krašovec, *Antithetic Structure in Biblical Hebrew Poetry* (VTSup, 35; Leiden: Brill, 1984).

122. P. Kyle McCarter, Jr, *1 Samuel* (AB, 8; Garden City, NY: Doubleday, 1980), p. 274.

123. Cf. Avishur, *Word-Pairs*, p. 662.

124. See also Prov. 15.30a; Job 31.7b.

3.3. *The Word-Pair in Distant Parallelism*

The third group consists of passages where the word-pair is used in 'distant parallelism', that is, the components are separated by one or more lines.[125]

3.3.1. *'yn(ym) // lb(b)*. Isa. 33.18-17; Sir. 9.8-9 (cf. Prov. 23.6-8).

Isa. 33.17-18 Your EYES will behold the King in his beauty;
they will see the far distant City.
Your HEART (*lbk*) will contemplate an awesome sight.

Here I follow Irwin who argues that the City (Heb. *'ereṣ* lit. 'land', 'territory') is in fact Jerusalem to which the next couplet also refers:[126]

Where is the tallyman? Where is the surveyor?
Where is there one to tally her towers?

Support for his interpretation may come from the *Epic of Gilgamesh* (I 16-17):[127]

Go up onto the wall of Uruk, and walk about,
inspect the base, examine the brickwork, etc.

These five lines (Isa. 33.17-18) comprise a tricolon followed by a couplet.

3.3.2. *lb(b) // 'yn(ym)*. Ps. 119.36-37; Prov. 4.23-25 (see above); 27.19-20; Lam. 2.18. Also Psalms 13; 101; Sir. 13.23–14.11.

Ps. 119.36-37 Bend my HEART to your stipulations,
and not towards gain (*bṣ'*).
Turn my EYES away from seeing uselessness,
grant me life in (following) your path (*bdrkk*).

125. For this type of parallelism, cf. Watson, *Classical Hebrew Poetry*, p. 366 and in general, Berlin, *Dynamics*, especially pp. 3 and 141 (though she does not use this term). Also, W.H. Irwin, *Isaiah 28–33* (BibOr, 30; Rome: Biblical Institute Press, 1977), pp. 172-73; A.R. Ceresko, *Job 29–31 in the Light of Northwest Semitic* (BibOr, 36; Rome: Biblical Institute Press, 1980), p. 242. In particular, see the discussion in D. Pardee, 'Ugaritic and Hebrew Poetry: Parallelism' (unpublished Communication for the First International Symposium on the Antiquities of Palestine, Aleppo, 1980) who defines it as '(parallelism) of elements of two or more units separated from each other by at least one other poetic unit'.

126. Irwin, *Isaiah 28–33*, p. 153.

127. Translation: Tigay, *Gilgamesh Epic*, p. 141.

The positive-negative parallelism of the first couplet is inverted in the second to form a chiastic pattern. The resulting quatrain is exactly central to the stanza (vv. 33-40). The reading *bdrkk* is assured by

Qoh. 11.9 — Follow the direction of (*bdrky*) your HEART
and the vision of your EYES.

The use of *bṣ'*, 'gain', evokes Jer. 22.17: 'Your EYES and your HEART are only set on gain (*bṣ'*)'; cf. Ezek. 33.21.

Prov. 27.19-20 — As water reflects a face,
so a man's HEART (*lb-hadm*) reflects him.
(As) Sheol and Abaddoh are insatiable,
(so) a man's EYES (*'yny hadm*) are insatiable.

Two isolated sayings are juxtaposed because of the word association between 'heart' and 'eyes'.[128]

Lam. 2.18 — Cry from the HEART (*lb-m*) to the Lord,
from (upon) the wall, Daughter Sion!
Shed tears like a torrent
night and day
Give yourself no rest!
Do not let your EYES be still!

Although there are problems concerning translation[129] there is no doubt that the six-line stanza is held together by *lb* in the initial line and *'ynyk* as the closing word. For the connection between the heart and weeping, see below on Ps. 38.11.

Other passages where distant parallelism occurs are as follows: 2 Kgs 22.19-20 (= 2 Chron. 34.27-28); Isa. 60.4-5; Jer. 13.20-22; Zeph. 3.14-20; Pss. 13.3-6; 15.2-4; 119.145-148; Prov. 3.5-7; 28.26-27; Sir. 13.23–14.11.[130] Psalm 101 comprises three sections: vv. 1-2 (spoken by the king), 3-5 (also by the king) and 6-8 (where

128. See, too, Prov. 20.8-9; 28.26-27. On the terseness of 27.19, cf. R. Alter, *The Art of Biblical Poetry* (New York: Basic Books, 1985), pp. 177-78.

129. For the translation of v. 18, cf. T. Collins, 'The Physiology of Tears', p. 34. He comments, 'In Lam 2:18-19 we have one of the best descriptions of the weeping process, and it leaves us in no doubt that the underlying view is that tears originate in the heart and make their way out through the eyes' (p. 33). A different rendering is proposed by T.F. McDaniel, 'Philological Studies in Lamentations, II', *Bib* 49 (1968), pp. 203-204, followed by D.R. Hillers, *Lamentations* (AB, 7A; Garden City, NY: Doubleday, 1972), pp. 39-40.

130. Cf. Ps. 25.15-17 and Job 17.4-5.

Yahweh speaks).[131] Although the terms *lbb* and *'yn* are repeated in this psalm, the word-pair 'eyes' // 'heart' only occurs in v. 5b and closes the second section. In Psalm 13 the sequence is 'heart' (v. 3), 'eyes' (v. 4), 'heart' (v. 6).[132]

Similarly, in Sir. 13.23–14.11, where the contrast between happiness and miserliness marks off the two sections 13.24–14.4 and 14.5-11, a link is effected by the word-pair *lb* // *'yn* in 14.3. Aside from this couplet the term *lb* only occurs in the first section while *'yn* is found only in the second. The key terms *ṭb* and *r'* occur in both sections.

Occurrences of *lb* and *'yn* in Sir. 13.23–14.11

I (13.23–14.4)		II (14.5-11)	
13.24a	*lb*	14.9a	*'yn*
13.25a	*lb*	14.10a	*'yn*, *'yn*
14.2a	*lb*	14.11a	*'yn*
14.3a	*lb*	14.11b	*'yn*
14.3b	*'yn*		

3.4. *Triple Sets*

The word-pair in question sometimes occurs as part of a triple set. In Deut. 28.25

> Yahweh will give you there
> a trembling HEART and failing EYES and a languishing soul,

the sequence is *lb* // *'ynym* // *npš*. In Deut. 29.3 (EV 29.4)

> but Yahweh did not give you
> a HEART for knowing, EYES for seeing or ears for hearing,

the order is *lb* // *'ynym* // *'znym*. In Isa. 6.10 both *lb* // *'zn* // *'yn* and its chiastic inversion *'yn* // *'zn* // *lb* are used. In Jer. 5.21, Ezek. 40.4 and 44.5, though, the component *lb* stands outside the common word-pair *'yn* // *'zn*. Only the two passages from Deuteronomy, then, can be said to incorporate the *lb* // *'yn* word-pair within a triple set. This appears to be confirmed by Deut. 28.67

131. J.S. Kselman, 'Psalm 101: Royal Confession and Divine Oracle', *JSOT* 33 (1985), pp. 45-62.

132. The first occurrence, *lbby*, is considered by O. Loretz and I. Kottsieper, *Colometry in Ugaritic and Biblical Poetry* (Ugaritisch-Biblische Literatur, 5; Altenberge: CIS-Verlag, 1987), p. 46 to be a gloss on *npšy*.

because of your HEART's dread that you dread,
and because of your EYES' vision which you see,

where only the first two components of v. 65 are reiterated. Another triple set occurs in Ps. 38.11:

My HEART is churning, my strength (*kḥy*) has left me,
and the light of my EYE, it too is no longer with me.

Collins (whose translation is reproduced here) comments

> the third line of the tercet [i.e. vv. 9-11] gives us a compact description of the whole process of weeping:
>
> 1. disturbance of the innards—*lby sḥrḥr*
> 2. flowing out of vital *npš*—*'zbny kḥy*
> 3. eyes weakened by tears—*w'wr 'yny gm h-m 'yn 'ty.*[133]

A set of four is 'eye' // 'ear' // 'heart' // 'tongue' (Isa. 32.3-4). In Prov. 6.17-19 'eyes' and 'heart' come within a list of five parts of the body.

3.5. *Ancient Near Eastern Texts*

We can turn now to some ancient Near Eastern texts. A drinking song from Mesopotamia includes the couplet

Let the EYE of the gakkul vat be our EYE,
let the HEART of the gakkul vat be our HEART.[134]

A Babylonian prayer to Marduk also uses this word-pair:

Set your gracious EYES upon [him].
May he himself... [... in] your HEART to grace.

133. Collins, 'The Physiology of Tears', p. 191. Contrast Sir. 22.19 (cited above in n. 111).

134. The song was published by M. Civil, 'A Hymn to the Beer Goddess and a Drinking Song', in R.D. Biggs and J.A. Brinkman (eds.), *Studies Presented to A. Leo Oppenheim* (Chicago: University of Chicago Press, 1964), pp. 67-89 and these lines are quoted by M.E. Cohen, *Sumerian Hymnology: The Eršemma* (HUCA Supplement, 2; Cincinnati: Ktav, 1981), pp. 22-23. The couplet comes in the second section of the song, a toast to an unnamed woman, and can be compared with the anti-drinking passage Prov. 23.33: 'Your EYES will see strange things / your mind (lit. HEART) will utter nonsense'.

Although the text is damaged here,[135] clearly the terms *īnu*, 'eye', and *libbu*, 'heart', are used in synonymous parallelism.[136] Such use of 'eyes' and 'heart' with reference to a god is only matched, in the OT, by 1 Kgs 9.3 (// 2 Chron. 7.16) when Yahweh promises Solomon 'my EYES and my HEART will be there (i.e. in the temple) for all time'. The same synonymous pair in EA 142.7-10

> When I heard the words on the tablet of the king, my lord, my HEART rejoiced and my EYES became radiant

has been compared with

> Ps. 19.9 The precepts of Yahweh are just, making the HEART rejoice,
> the directive of Yahweh is pure, enlightening the eyes.[137]

Noteworthy are the similarity of context and the sequence 'heart' 'eyes'.

In Saying 76 from the *Proverbs of Aḥiqar* synonymous parallelism is evident also:

> My EYES which I lifted upon you,
> and my HEART which I gave you in wisdom
> [you have despised, and] have brought my name into disrepute.[138]

There may be a triplet in Etana (MAV I/F, 9):

> *ia imma*[*ar*(*šu*) *īnu*(?)] *ia išme*[(*šu*) *uznu*(?)] *ia iḫ*[*sus*(*su*) *libbu*(?)]
> Let your EYE no longer see it, let your EAR no longer hear it, let your HEART (= mind) not recall it.[139]

The prose triplet 'heart', 'head', 'eyes' is to be found in EA 144:12-15:

135. Text and translation: W.G. Lambert, 'Three Literary Prayers of the Babylonians', *AfO* 19 (1959–60), pp. 47-66, 59:171-72; also, M.-J. Seux, *Hymnes et prières aux dieux de Babylonie et d'Assyrie* (Paris: Cerf, 1976), p. 180.

136. In addition, G. Meier, *Die assyrische Beschwörungsserie Maqlû* (AfO Beiheft, 2; Graz: Ernst Weidner, 1937), p. 13 (= Tablet II lines 31-32) and Lambert, *JNES* 33 (1974) 280/281: pp. 106-108 (but see his comment, p. 304).

137. M.J. Dahood, *Psalms 1–50* (AB, 16; Garden City, NY: Doubleday, 1968), p. 123.

138. Above, p. 84.

139. Text and translation: J.V. Kinnier Wilson, *The Legend of Etana* (Warminster: Aris & Phillips, 1985), pp. 64-65.

u yiḫdi libbiya u yi[šš]aqi rēšiya u ennamrū šittā ēnaya
(because of my lord's letter) by HEART was pleased, my HEAD was raised and my EYES were bright.[140]

Note, too, the list of four body parts:

[īnu] lemuttu pû lemnu lišānu lemuttu libbi lemnu [ ]
The evil EYE, the evil MOUTH, the evil TONGUE, the evil HEART.[141]

Finally, the following lines from an Aramaic Incantation Bowl can be quoted:

may they be mute in their MOUTHS,
blind in their EYES,
deaf in their EARS,
mournful in their HEARTS, etc.[142]

3.6. *Discussion*

In the Hebrew OT the word-pair under discussion occurs chiefly in Proverbs, Psalms, Isaiah and Sirach. It is also found in prose: Num. 15.39; Deut. 4.9; 15.9; 28.65, 67; 29.3; 1 Kgs 9.3 (= 2 Chron. 7.16); 2 Kgs 10.30 (// 22.19-20 = 2 Chron. 34.27-28); Isa. 10.12b; and so on. In ancient near Eastern texts it does not appear

140. See Avishur, *Word-Pairs*, pp. 563-64, who cites U. Cassuto, *Biblical and Oriental Studies*. II. *Bible and Ancient Oriental Texts* (Jerusalem: Magnes, 1975), p. 56.

141. Part of a bilingual text (lines 6-7) cited in E. von Weiher, *Spätbabylonische Texte aus Uruk* (Berlin: Mann, 1983), II, p. 40. For a list of body parts, cf. *Descent of Ištar* 70-75—eyes, sides, heart, feet, head, complete body—and the comments by E. Reiner, *Your Thwarts in Pieces, Your Mooring Rope Cut: Poetry from Babylonia and Assyria* (Michigan: Horace H. Rackham School of Graduate Studies at the University of Michigan, 1985), pp. 41-42.

142. J. Naveh and S. Shaked, *Amulets and Magic Bowls: Aramaic Incantations of Late Antiquity* (Jerusalem: Magnes; Leiden: Brill, 1985), pp. 164-65: line 7 (and the parallels cited, p. 167). Some examples in Egyptian, taken from W.K. Simpson (ed.), *The Literature of Ancient Egypt* (New Haven; Yale University Press, 1972): 'you are my own heart and my eyes watch you' (p. 196: *Teaching of Ammenemes I to Sesostris*); 'her eye is a stormwind when she sees... Soothe her heart with what has accrued to you' (p. 167: *Maxims of Ptahotep*; 'Let the eyes observe that the heart may be informed' (p. 42: *Tale of the Eloquent Peasant*). Also the set 'eyes' // 'arms' // 'legs' // 'heart' in *Sinuhe* B: 169-71, cited by I. Shirun, 'Parallelismus Membrorum und Vers', in J. Assmann, E. Feucht and R. Grieshammer (eds.), *Fragen an die altägyptische Literatur: Studien zum Gedenken an Eberhard Otto* (Wiesbaden-Dolzheim: Reichert, 1977), pp. 463-92 (479).

to be nearly so common and usually comes within a list of parts of the body.[143] The word-pair 'eye(s)' // 'heart', then, seems to have been more acceptable to Hebrew tradition. Yet, even though some forty or fifty occurrences can be registered it was not so very common, probably because it combined two A-words.

Within the pair the terms 'eye(s)' and 'heart' are normally synonymous even in distant parallelism. Rarely, there is antithesis between the components (see under section 3.3, above) and occasionally there is some degree of progression (the heart desires what the eyes see; inner turmoil causes the eyes to weep). It is clear, too, that the word-pair can be used to structure a poem or a segment of a poem. Curiously, although *lb* and *'yn* are respectively masculine and feminine their gender is foregrounded only twice (Ps. 19.9; Prov. 27.19-20).[144]

Though not of great significance, the pair 'eye(s)' // 'heart' should be included in future compilations and the data collected here, it is hoped, will be of some use in further evaluation of parallel word-pairs.

4. *The Word-Pair 'Eye(s)' // 'Heart' Once More*[145]

To the data collected in a recent article on this parallel word-pair[146] can be added several more occurrences in ancient Near Eastern texts.[147]

143. As in Lambert, *Babylonian Wisdom Literature*, pp. 226-27 ii 17-18 (translation, p. 230). According to Avishur, *Word-Pairs*, pp. 521-22, Hebrew and Akkadian share word-pairs denoting parts of the body.

144. See *Classical Hebrew Poetry*, pp. 123-28. For an appraisal of the phenomenon in poetry, particularly in connection with paired words, cf. Berlin, *Dynamics*, pp. 41-44.

145. First published in *SEL* 9 (1992), pp. 27-31.

146. See above, pp. 284-95. For a different interpretation of Sir. 5.2 (cited p. 286), see P.W. Skehan and A.A. di Lella, *The Wisdom of Ben Sira* (AB, 24; Garden City, NY: Doubleday, 1987), p. 181 and note the additional occurrence in Sir. 23.4b-5 (Hebrew original unattested). On Cant. 4.9, see the translation in D. Grossberg, *Centripetal and Centrifugal Structures in Biblical Poetry* (SBLMS, 39; Atlanta: Scholars Press, 1989), pp. 78-79: 'You have taken my heart with one of your eyes'.

147. The significance of such parallel word-pairs is now accepted by scholars; see, for example, A. Niccacci, *Un profeta tra oppressori e oppressi: Analisi esegetica del capitolo 2 di Michea nel piano generale del libro* (Studium Franciscanum Analecta,

The first set comes from the 'Counsels of Wisdom'. In the section dealing with the duties of a royal treasurer comes the couplet

[a]na mimma šuatu īnka ē tašši	To any of this (treasure) do not 'lift your EYES',
[a]ja ubla libbaka epēš puzru	do not 'raise your HEART' to perpetrate fraud.[148]

Both the expressions in quotes are well-known idioms meaning 'to hanker after'.[149] Here they are meristic.

The word-pair is used twice in succession in a Babylonian love incantation. The four lines read as follows:[150]

In which direction is your HEART going?
In which direction are your EYES loo[king]?
To me [should your] H[EART...]!
At me sho[uld your EYES be look]ing![151]

Yet another example, unfortunately in a broken context, comes from the genre of potency incantations:[152]

Why] are your EYES covered?
[Why] is [...] in your HEART, which a woman...[...]

27; Jerusalem: Franciscan Printing Press, 1989), p. 2. In spite of J. Wansbrough's comment in M. Mindlin, M.J. Geller and J.E. Wansbrough (eds.), *Figurative Language in the Ancient Near East* (London: School of African and Oriental Studies, 1987), p. 112 n. 1, Y. Avishur's extensive collection of these word-pairs is by no means exhaustive.

148. Text: Lambert, *Babylonian Wisdom Literature*, p. 102:86-87; his translation (p. 103): 'But do not covet any of this, nor set your mind on double-dealing'. I have used a strictly literal rendering to highlight the components of the word-pair. For the first line, see also Nougayrol *et al.*, *Ugaritica V*, p. 285.

149. See, conveniently, *CAD*, N/2, pp. 104 and 105.

150. IB 1554; text and translation: C. Wilcke, 'Liebesbeschwörungen aus Isin', *ZA* 75 (1985), pp. 188-209, 202-203, lines 62-65. Wilcke makes no comment on these lines.

151. Similar expressions for erotic glances are used in 'The Kubatim Dialogue', lines 7 and 12 as well as the 'Tavern Dialogue', line 4. For these texts, cf. T. Jacobsen, 'Two *bal-bal-e* Dialogues', in J.H. Marks and R.M. Good (eds.), *Love and Death in the Ancient Near East: Essays in Honor of Marvin H. Pope* (Guilford, CT: Four Quarters Publishing Company, 1987), pp. 57-63.

152. Text: 81-7-27, 73 r. 2'-3', R.D. Biggs, ŠÀ.ZI.GA. *Ancient Mesopotamian Potency Incantations* (TCS, 2; Locust Valley, NY: Augustin, 1967), p. 50 (= no. 35).

Note that here the sequence is the reverse of the two other texts.[153] Our word-pair recurs three times in succession in *Gilg*. Y(OB) III ii 26-37:

īnā[šu imla] di[mtam]	[his EYES brimmed with tears,
il[mu/in l]ibbašu[ma]... uštaniḫ	angry was his HEART,
[īnā ša en]kidu imla dimtam	he was [completely?] dejected.
[ilmu/in] libbašuma ... uštaniḫ	Yes, Enkidu's EYES brimmed with tears,
	angry was his HEART,
	he was [completely?] dejected.

[^{d}GIŠ ut]abbil pānišu	Gilgamesh, lowered(?) his face
[izzakaram] ana enkidu	said to Enkidu:
[ammīnim]īnāka [imlā dim]tam	'Why do your EYES brim with tears,
[ilmu/in libbi]ka ... [tuštaniḫ]	is your HEART angry are you [completely?] dejected'.[154]

From the 'Letter of Gilgamesh':

īnāja limurāma libbī liḫmu
If my EYES see it, my HEART will acquire confidence.[155]

Another example occurs, also in prose, on an inscription of Esarhaddon from Niniveh.[156] In spite of a failed attempt by

153. Note, too, the omen CT 51 147 obv. 15': *umma īnāja issanundu libbašu iḫḫeppi*, 'If (he says) "My EYES are swimming": he will have a broken HEART'. Translation: E. Reiner, 'A Manner of Speaking', in G. van Driel *et al.* (eds.), *Zikir umim: Assyriological Studies Presented to F.R. Kraus on the Occasion of his Seventieth Birthday* (Leiden: Brill, 1982), pp. 282-89, 286.

154. For a recent translation, see S. Dalley, *Myths from Mesopotamia: Creation, the Flood, Gilgamesh and others* (Oxford: Oxford University Press, 1989), p. 142; see also *CAD*, A/1, p. 105a. In the corresponding passage in the Standard Babylonian Version (II iv 9-15) there is no reference to 'heart'.

155. STT 40:31 (par. 41:31), edited by O.R. Gurney, 'The Sultantepe Tablets (continued). VI. A Letter of Gilgamesh', *AnSt* 7 (1957), pp. 127-36. The reading DINGIR.MEŠ-*a-a* has been corrected to IGI(!).MEŠ-*a-a* following Gurney ('Sultantepe Tablets', p. 130 n. 7). Gurney ('Sultantepe Tablets', p. 135, note to line 31) is dubious about the verb *liḫmu* but it has been accepted in *AHw*, p. 319a. Gurney's translation is 'and my eyes shall see it and my heart shall become confident'. The slightly different rendering given above follows *CAD*, A/2, p. 8b. In his study F.R. Kraus ('Der Brief des Gilgameš', *AnSt* 30 [1980], pp. 109-21) translates 'dann will ich es mit (eigenen) Augen sehen und vor Bewunderung erstarren!'

156. R. Borger, *Die Inschriften Asarhaddons Königs von Assyrien* (AfO Beiheft, 9; Graz: Ernst Weidner, 1956), p. 42:30.

Esarhaddon's brothers to poison his reputation his father persists in appointing him crown prince:

šaplānu libbašu rēmu rašīšuma	secretly, his HEART was merciful to him
ana epēš šarrūtija šitkuna īnāšu	and he was intent (lit. his EYES were set) on my ruling as king.[157]

In the dingir.šà.dib.ba incantations[158] comes the sequence:

104 The man on whom you look with favour lives.
105 You look with favour, look with steadfast favour on me.
106 At the glance of your EYES that man lives.
107 You look with favour, look with steadfast favour on me.
108 For me may the HEART of my god become as it was.

Line 104 appears to be a variant of line 106 and in the Sumerian tradition the equivalent of line 108 comes within a different set of lines.[159] Although it is difficult to speak of a parallel word-pair here, the passage has been included for the sake of completeness.[160]

As noted previously, the word-pair also occurs in Sumerian texts.[161]

157. Borger, *Asarhaddons*, p. 42, translates: 'doch insgeheim empfand sein Herz Mitleid und blieb sein Augenmerk darauf gerichet, dass ich das Königtum bekleiden solle'. For the idiom *šakānu + inu*, see *CAD*, Š/1, p. 138a and for another translation, see *CAD*, Š/1, p. 464a under *šaplānu*.

158. Edited by W.G. Lambert, 'Dingir.šà.dib.ba Incantations', *JNES* 33 (1974), pp. 267-322; the passage in question is 280-81, lines 104-108, (Section I). Note especially his comments, p. 304.

159. For details cf. Lambert, 'Dingir.šà.dib.ba', p. 304; for the Sumerian see also p. 291:35.

160. Note also Msk 731030 1-3, D. Arnaud, *Recherches au pays d'Atata, Emar VI.1, 2: Textes sumériens et accadiens, planches* (Paris: Editions Recherche sur les Civilisations, 1985), p. 109; *idem, Emar VI/4: textes de la bibliothèque, transcriptions et traductions* (Paris: Editions Recherche sur les Civilisations, 1987), pp. 345-46: *lìb-bu-ú dá-an lìb-bu qar-ra-as a lìb-bi dan-nim* GÍD.D[A *anasa*] *pur-si-it da-mi ī-na-a*[*s-si*], 'The heart is strong, the heart is a hero. The strong heart's [eyes] are long, it ho[ld]s a bowl of blood', as restored (from parallels) and translated by W. Farber, '*Mannam lušpur ana Enkidu:* Some New Thoughts about an Old Motif', *JNES* 49 (1990), p. 310.

161. For references, see above, p. 292. On the quotation from the drinking song quoted there, see M. Civil, 'The Beer Goddess and a Drinking Song', in R.D. Biggs and J.A. Brinkman (eds.), *Studies Presented to A. Leo Oppenheim* (Chicago: University of Chicago Press, 1964), p. 67-89, esp. the comments on gakkul in line 49 (also applicable to lines 59-60 quoted above). The 'eye of the gakkul vat' was a narrow opening in the top or bottom of the clay container. Besides the twofold

A further occurrence is in the Šulgi Hymn:

igi-íl-la-gá ḫé-eb-da-g[in]-en	Wherever my EYES cast—there I go!
šà-ge-guru$_6$-gá an-ta ḫé-eb-ge-en	Wherever my HEART prompts me—there I arrive.[162]

Another example is

igi-mà làl-bi-im šà-mà ḫi-<is>^{sar}-bi-im	For him who is the honey of my EYE, who is the lettuce of my HEART.[163]

Also

GIR$_5$-i-bí-ír-ra-ma-al-la-zu	Your GIR$_5$, (he) of weeping EYES,
GIR$_5$-mu-lu-à-ḫul-ma-al-la-zu	Your GIR$_5$, he of grievous HEART.[164]

Of interest is the use of the very same pair (though not in parallelism, strictly speaking) in the Hittite Myth of Iluyankas:[165]

§21' The ser[pent] defeated the Storm-god and took (his) H[EART and EYES].

(§22': The Storm-god's son marries the serpent's daughter)

§23' The Storm-god instructed (his) son: 'When you go to the house of your wife, then demand from them (my) HEART and EYES!'

mention of 'heart' in line 60 there are eight other references to 'heart' (in lines 58, 61-63, 75-76 and 78-79). For the possible interchange of 'eye of lettuce' and 'heart of lettuce' see Civil's comments, 'The Beer Goddess', p. 84.

162. A. Falkenstein, 'Sumerische religiöse Texte', *ZA* 50 (1952), pp. 70-71 lines 85-86; translation: J. Klein, 'The Royal Hymns of Shulgi King of Ur: Man's Quest for Immortal Fame', *Transactions of the American Philosophical Society* 71/7 (1981), pp. 1-47, 17 n. 68. Falkenstein comments ('Sumerische religiöse Texte', p. 90): 'Wie in SEM (= E. Chiera, *Sumerian Epics and Myths* [Chicago, 1934]) 58 II 11-12 ist hier igi-íl-la parallel zu sà-ge-guru$_{(6)(7)}$'.

163. S.N. Kramer, 'Cuneiform Studies and the History of Literature: The Sumerian Sacred Marriage Texts', *Proceedings of the American Philosophical Society* 107/6 (1963), pp. 485-527, 508: rev. 21(= N[ippur] 3560 and N 4305); see, more generally, S.N. Kramer, 'The Dumuzi-Inanna Sacred Marriage Rite: Origin, Development, Character' in A. Finet (ed.), *Actes de la XVIIe Rencontre Assyriologique Internationale* (Ham-sur-Heure: Comité Belge de Recherches en Mésopotamie, 1970), pp. 135-41; *ANET*Suppl., p. 108 line 644.

164. S.N. Kramer, 'The GIR$_5$ and the ki-sikil: A New Sumerian Elegy', in M. de Jong Ellis (ed.), *Essays on the Ancient Near East in Memory of Jacob Joel Finkelstein* (Memoirs of the Connecticut Academy of Arts and Sciences, 19; Hamden, CT, 1977), pp. 139-46, 140 and 141. Also B. Alster, 'The Manchester Tammuz', *Acta Sumerologica* 14 (1992), p. 20: 70-71, 'Your eye... Your heart'.

165. Text and translation: G. Beckman, 'The Anatolian Myth of Illuyanka', *JANES*, 14 (1982), pp. 11-25, 15 and 19.

§24' When he went, then he demanded from them the HEART, and they gave it to him. Afterwards he demanded from them the EYES, and they gave these to him. And he carried them to the Storm-god, his father, and the Storm-god (thereby) took back his HEART and his EYES.

The stealing of organs is a folk-tale theme, as Kirk has pointed out.[166]

It is clear that although most frequent in Hebrew[167] the word-pair is attested in a wide range of other languages: in Sumerian, Babylonian, Hittite and Aramaic[168] but not in Ugaritic.[169] In the ancient Near Eastern passages cited the sequence used most often is 'eye(s)' // 'heart'. Since reference to parts of the body is generally from the top down,[170] this too must be the standard sequence. The order is reversed in the Babylonian love incantation, Esarhaddon's inscription, the Hittite text (Myth of Iluyanka) and in both EA 142 and EA 144 (these last two cited in the previous article). In Hebrew the same reverse

166. G.S. Kirk, *Myth. Its Meaning and Functions in Ancient and Other Cultures* (Cambridge: Cambridge University Press, 1971), p. 221. He cites a similar episode in a story in Apollodorus (1, 6, 3) where the sinews of Zeus were removed and then restored. D. Irvin, *Mytharion: The Comparison of Tales from the Old Testament and the Ancient Near East* (AOAT, 32; Kevelaer: Butzon & Bercker; Neukirchen–Vluyn: Neukirchener Verlag, 1978), pp. 66-67 discusses the story but makes no reference at all to the theme (loss of vital organs).

167. See also *'ny // lby*, 'I' // 'my heart' (Ps. 13.6; Cant. 5.2) and *'ny // 'yny* 'I' // 'my eye' (Ezek. 9.10; Job 19.27; inverted in Isa. 43.4). Also, 4Q417 Frag. 2 col. ii line 27.

168. *Aḥiqar*, Saying 76. Note, too, Papyrus Harris 500: 'My HEART like yours longs to do for you/ whatever it desires, whenever I am in your arms. My desire is like eyepaint to my eye:/ when I see you, brightness comes to my EYES'. For other Egyptian examples, see above.

169. The pair is found in the Koran: 'Allah has sealed their hearing and their HEARTS, and on their EYES there is a covering, theirs will be an awful doom' (2.7) on which cf. L. Ibrahim, 'The Qur'anic "Sealing of the Heart"', *WO* 16 (1985), pp. 126-27. It even survives in Modern Hebrew, for example, in C.N Bialik's *'m dmdwmy hh'mh* ('At Twilight'), lines 5-7; see conveniently S. Burnshaw *et al.* (eds.), *The Modern Hebrew Poem itself* (New York: Schocken Books, 1965), p. 28.

170. For example, 'head, throat, ear, shoulder, upper arm, hand, fingernail, side, genitals, testicles, penis, sole, foot, toenail...', in M. Hutter, *Behexung, Entsühnung und Heilung: Das Ritual der Tunnawiya für ein Königspaar aus mittelhethitischer Zeit (KBo XXI 1—KUB IX 34—KBo XXI 6)* (Orbis Biblicus et Orientalis, 82; Freiburg: Universitätsverlag; Göttingen: Vandenhoeck & Ruprecht, 1988), pp. 32-33 lines 23-32.

sequence—'heart' // 'eye(s)'—is marginally more frequent than its counterpart. No reason for such inversion is immediately apparent.

There is no obvious common denominator but many of the passages quoted share certain aspects. The motif of desire which features in the Šulgi Hymn, the 'Counsels of Wisdom' and the Babylonian love incantation is also found in Ezek. 6.9 and Qoh. 2.10. The combination of anger and sorrow depicted in the extract from the *Epic of Gilgamesh* is almost exactly matched in Job 15.12 ('Why is your HEART enraged and why do your EYES blink?'). In some passages there was also an element of progression: what the eye sees has an effect on the heart and conversely, a grieving or angry heart results in tears. The terms were interchangeable in many texts and either could be used in idiomatic expressions. It is evident that within each tradition the same word-pair, which most probably derives from formulas and formulaic expressions,[171] could be exploited in a different way by an imaginative poet though the comparative approach does highlight certain shared elements.[172]

5. *The Hebrew Word-Pair 'sp // qbṣ*[173]

The rare parallel word-pair *'sp // qbṣ* apparently is exclusive to classical Hebrew and, with few exceptions, found only in prophetic writings. The present note examines the occurrences and distribution of this formulaic pair, and in passing will look at some difficult texts which feature the word-pair.

Before going on to consider the word-pair in question it is necessary to establish which is the A-word, and that in turn involves setting out the 'family' of word-pairs belonging to the *'sp-qbṣ* group, but featuring only one component of the pair (Table 1).[174]

171. As ably argued by K. Aitken, 'Word Pairs and Tradition in an Ugaritic Tale', *UF* 21 (1989), pp. 17-39.

172. As I have noted above, 'While sharing common features each tradition had a character of its own, an aspect which tends to be overlooked'.

173. First published in *ZAW* 96 (1984), pp. 426-34.

174. Note the 'parallelism' *'sp // zr' // lqš*, etc. in the Gezer Inscription (*KAI*, p. 182). For the possible word-pair *qbṣ // kns* in Ezek. 22.20, see below.

'sp as A-word (*'sp* //)			*qbṣ* as B-word (// *qbṣ*)		
klmh	'insult'	Ezek. 34.29	*bw'*	'come'	Isa. 43.5; (66.18);
kns	'collect'	Qoh. 2.26			Jer. 31.8;
lqṭ	'glean'	Isa. 17.5			Ezek. 36.24; 37.21;
ntn	'give'	Num. 21.16			Zeph. 3.20
'll	'glean'	Mic. 7.1			(cf. Joel 4.11)
'md	'stand'	Num. 11.24	*hwn*	'wealth'	Prov. 13.11
qbr	'bury'	Jer. 8.2; 25.33;	*yṣ'*	'go out'	Ezek. 20.34, 41;
		Ezek. 29.5 (?)			34.13
		(cf. Gen.49.29)	*yrd*	'descend'	Joel 4.2
rbṣ	'crouch'	Ps. 104.22	*yš'*	'save'	Zeph. 3.19
šwb	'return'	Ps. 85.4			Ps. 106.47
		(cf. 104.29)	*lqḥ*	'take'	Ezek. 36.24; 37.21
			ndḥ	'disperse'	Jer. 49.5
			'zb	'abandon'	Isa. 54.7
			'md	'stand'	Isa. 48.14
			swh	'command'	Isa. 34.16
			rbh	'increase'	Prov. 28.8
					(cf. 13.11)
			šwb	'return'	Ezek. 39.27
bw'	'come'	Isa. 60.20	*bw'*	'come'	Isa. 49.18 = 60.4
grh	'wage war'	Dan. 11.10	*'md*	'stand'	Isa. 44.11
hlk	'walk'	Isa. 58.8	*qbr*	'bury'	Hos. 9.6
		(cf. 52.12)	*qwm*	'rise'	Jer. 49.14 (?)
klh	'complete'	Isa. 32.10	*šwb*	'return'	Jer.23.3 (?); 32.37;
npl	'fall'	Isa. 16.9-10;			(cf.Ezek. 29.13-14)
		Jer. 8.12-13;	*šmr*	'guard'	Jer. 31.10
		Ezek. 29.5 (?)	*šrt*	'serve'	Isa. 60.7
		(cf. Jer. 9.21)[175]			
'zb	'abandon'	Ps. 27.10			
		(cf. Isa. 10.14)			
ṣbr	'heap up'	Ps. 39.7			
		(cf. Job 27.16a, 19a)			
šwb	'return'	Isa. 49.5; Job 39.12			

Table 1

175. For collocation of *'sp* and *npl* in *CTA* 14 i 18-21 and pairing in Jer. 8.12-13, Ezek. 29.5, Isa. 16.9-10, Jer. 9.21, 48.32-22, cf. Dahood, *RSP*, III, p. 33 (section I 39).

From Table 1 the following emerges: *'sp* is more often the A-word and *qbṣ* accordingly the B-word, but not by a large margin. A more detailed breakdown is provided in Table 2.

	A-word	B-word
'sp	10 times (9 roots)	10 times (8 roots)
qbṣ	7 times (7 roots)	20 times (12 roots)

Table 2

Furthermore, both elements of the word-pair 'share' a set of common 'partners', as the next table shows (Table 3).

	A—*'sp*—B		B—*qbṣ*—A	
bw'	0	1	4	1
'zb	0	1	1	0
'md	1	0	1	1
qbr	3	0	0	1
šwb	1	2	1	2
	–	–	–	–
	5	4	7	5

Table 3

Again, *'sp* is more frequently the A-word, but not overwhelmingly.[176] The tables do show, though, that *'sp* is used more commonly as the first component in word-pairs, and *qbṣ* as the second, a result even more striking in the next table (Table 4).

	A-B		B-A
'sp // qbṣ	Gen. 49.1-2; Isa. 11.12; 62.9; Ezek. 29.5 (?); Mic. 2.12; 4.6, 11-12; Hab. 2.5; Zeph. 3.8	*qbṣ // 'sp*	Isa. 43.9; Ezek. 11.17; 39.17; Joel 2.16[177]
	A-A		B-B
'sp // 'sp	2 Kgs 22.20; Isa. 10.14; (33.4); 57.1; Ps. 35.15 (cf. Jer. 8.13-14)[178]	*qbṣ // qbṣ*	Isa. 56.8 (cf. Ezek. 16.37;22.19-22)

Table 4

176. With *šwb*, *'sp* occurs twice as a B-word, *qbṣ* once only (with yet two possible examples).

177. Some of these pairs are listed by L. Boadt, *Ezekiel's Oracles against Egypt: A Literary and Philological Study of Ezekiel 29–32* (BibOr, 37; Rome: Biblical Institute Press, 1980), p. 35, with no comment. Note that his error of Jon. 2.16 for

We now come to the word-pair proper (the subject of this paper), and as before its occurrences will be laid out in tabular form, this time in four sets: normal (A-B) and inverted (B-A) sequences, and the repetitive pairs for each component (A-A, B-B).[179]

Before examining briefly each of the texts listed in Table 4, some comments are in order. To begin with, all the passages come from the prophets, the exceptions being Gen. 49.1-2 (see comments below) and Ps. 35.15. Secondly, no less than three occurrences, all in the 'normal' or A-B sequence, are found in Micah, a fact considered later. Finally, although the possible occurrence in Zeph. 1.2-3 is not included, since the verb there means 'to sweep away',[180] it is possible that the poet was playing on the 'prophetic' word-pair by using *qbṣ* in the final verse (Zeph. 3.20) and so creating a form of envelope figure.[181]

One additional observation is necessary. Although the statistics suggest that *'sp* is more commonly the A-word overall, with *qbṣ*, therefore, appearing more frequently as the second element in word-pairs, there are indications that the two words are practically equivalent. Table 4 shows that either component can be used interchangeably in at least *five word-pairs*. Each component can also be used interchangeably in stock expressions, for example:

(1) *w'sp ndḥy yśr'l* (Isa. 11.12) and
mqbṣ ndḥy yśr'l (Isa. 56.8);
(2) *'spw zqnym* (Joel 1.14) and
qbṣw zqnym (Joel 2.16).

These two arguments find confirmation from rhetoric: generally speaking, little if any significance can be derived from sequence

Joel 2.16 stems from BDB. See, too, W.R. Watters, *Formula Criticism and the Poetry of the Old Testament* (BZAW, 138; Berlin: de Gruyter, 1976), p. 164 (entry no. 226).

178. The repetitive pair *'sp // 'sp* occurs several times in Nougayrol *et al.*, *Ugaritica V*, text 8, on which see M.C. Astour, 'Two Ugaritic Serpent Charms', *JNES* 27 (1968), pp. 13-36, esp. 28-32.

179. Triple parallelism as in Isa. 66.18, Hos. 4.3 and Joel 4.11 is not considered here; Jer. 25.33, however, has been included.

180. See M. Deroche, 'Zephaniah I 2-3: the "Sweeping" of Creation', *VT* 30 (1980), pp. 104-109, esp. 108 n. 7; also, 'Contra Creation, Covenant and Conquest (Jer. viii 13)', *VT* 30 (1980), pp. 280-90, esp. 282.

181. The very opening words of the book (excluding the title) are *'sp 'sp* while the last stanza in ch. 3 begins with the word pair *yš' // qbṣ,* echoing Mic. 4.6.

within the word-pair; the order B-A is not very much different in meaning from the standard A-B sequence (but see on Ezek. 29.5, below). We now come to the texts using the word-pair *'sp // qbṣ* and its variants; for ease of reference the presentation adopted will follow the order of texts as given in Table 4.

Gen. 49.1-2 And Jacob called to his sons, saying:
'Muster (*'sp*), and I shall tell you what is in store for you
in time to come.
Assemble (*qbṣ*) and hear, sons of Jacob,
and listen to Israel your father'.

Both of the relevant verbs are in the *niphal* ('be gathered'; 'be assembled'). The first verse is normally deleted as a prose introduction to the poem[182] but the presence of the rare word-pair suggests, instead, a prose expansion of an original introduction in verse. See below on Isa. 43.9 and note, too, Isa. 48.14 *hqbṣw klkm wšm'w*, 'Come together, all of you, and listen'.

Isa. 11.12 And he will raise a standard to the nations,
and gather (*'sp*) the dispersed of Israel,
and the scattered of Judah shall assemble (*qbṣ*)
from the four corners of the earth.

Only the two central lines of this quatrain are parallel, in the pattern ABB'C. The word-pair and gender-matched parallelism in the form m. + m. // m. + m. // f. + f. // f. + f., lend poetic character to an otherwise prosaic strophe.[183]

Isa. 62.9 But those gathering (*m'sp*) it will eat it and praise Yahweh,
and those who collect (*mqbṣ*) it will drink it in
my holy courts.

Evidently the suffixes in the first line refer to grain and bread respectively; those in the second to grapes and to wine.[184] Of all the passages discussed the original meaning of gathering in cereal and vine crops occurs only here.

182. So M. O'Connor, *Hebrew Verse Structure*, pp. 169-70, following E.A. Speiser, *Genesis* (AB, 1; Garden City, NY: Doubleday, 1964), pp. 361 and 370.

183. Note, too, the gender-matched parallelism in v. 13.

184. On the word-pair 'eat–drink', cf. H.-W. Jüngling, *Richter 19: Ein Plädoyer für das Königtum* (AnBib, 84; Rome: Biblical Institute Press, 1981), p. 110 n. 418.

Ezek. 29.5 On the surface of the field shall you fall,
you shall not be gathered up (*t'sp*),
and you shall not be collected (*tqbṣ*).

In view of the word-pair *'sp // qbr* registered in Table 1, Boadt[185] and others would emend the text here to *tqbr*, '(nor) shall you be buried'. Examined more closely, the facts are as follows. Twice the word-pair in normal sequence denotes *non*-burial: Jer. 8.2 and 25.33 (as part of the triple set *spd*, 'mourn' // *'sp // qbr*; Gen. 49.29 is a prose text). However, in Hos. 9.6 the B-word *qbṣ* is in the A position as *qbṣ // qbr*. There it positively denotes burial, a true case of inverted word-pair sequences (B-A) in mimesis of events described. Accordingly, in Ezek. 29.5, where *non*-burial is predicted, the sequence must be *'sp // qbr*, and *qbṣ* is probably a mistake in the text. See, too, on 2 Kgs 22.20 below.

Mic. 2.12 *'sp ''sp y'qb (b)klk*
qbṣ 'qbṣ š'ryt yśr'l yḥd
I will certainly gather Jacob into the storehouse,
I will definitely collect the remnant of Israel together.

In recognition of the difficulties here the text has been set out in full and discussion will be more extensive than for the other passages quoted. A representative rendering of these lines runs 'Yes, I am going to gather all Jacob together, I will gather the remnant of Israel' (JB). Problems include determining what *klk* means and where the second line ends. With regard to *klk*, which only occurs here, Mays considers that 'all of you (sing.)' seems out of place, commenting 'G (i.e. the Septuagint) assumes *kullō*; MT's second singular is curious, and the direct address is not continued'.[186] I propose, therefore, to understand *klk* as equivalent to Akkadian *kalakku*, 'storehouse, room silo'—as in the translation given above—even though this word is a loan from Sumerian.[187] The imagery is of collecting a scattered Israel as one gathers the harvest into a barn. Similar in expression is the apostrophe in the Ugaritic *Aqhat Tale*:[188]

185. Boadt, *Ezekiel's Oracles*, p. 35 n. 52.
186. J.L. Mays, *Micah: A Commentary* (Old Testament Library; London: SCM Press; Philadelphia: Westminster Press, 1976), p. 73 n. a.
187. See *CAD*, K, pp. 62-64 and compare *AHw*, p. 423 ('Aushub, Silo').
188. *CTA* 19 ii 66-67; cf. 73-74.

ur	Plant!
tispk yd aqht ǵzr	May Aqhat's hand gather you,
tštk bqrbm asm	may it place you within the granary.

This leads on to the second problem: does the following line in Mic. 2.12b, end at *yśr'l*, at *yḥd* or even at *'śymnw*? In view of the Ugaritic passage just quoted it is possible that the last word is in fact a form of *'sm*, 'granary', common to biblical Hebrew (Deut. 28.8; Prov. 3.10), extra-biblical Hebrew[189] and Ugaritic. A translation might then run: 'I will definitely gather Jacob into[190] the storehouse, I will definitely collect the remnant of Israel together into their[191] granary'. Unfortunately, the following lines are even more difficult; apparently the imagery changes from one of harvesting to one of sheep[192] and the connection between them is obscure.

Mic. 4.6	On that Day, Yahweh's oracle,
	I will gather (*'sp*) the lame,
	the banished I will assemble (*qbṣ*).

It is probable that the rest of vv. 6-7 is a later addition to this independent saying[193] and the introductory line is, of course, a stereotyped expression. The couplet, in fact, exhibits semantic-sonant chiasmus,[194] a sure indication of its origin as a unity. Curiously, the terms 'lame' and

189. *KAI*, p. 200, lines 5 and 7.

190. Assuming a shared final *b* (of *y'qb*) before *klk*, or haplography of the same letter.

191. Understanding MT *'śymnw* as a misspelling for *'śmm*, with excision of the vowel letter *yod*, and *-nw* as a mistake for final *mem*—on this second aspect, cf. R. Weiss, 'On Ligatures in the Hebrew Bible (*m* = *nw*)', *JBL* 82 (1963), pp. 188-94. He notes, 'a copyist might...easily take a closed *mem* in his archetype for a combination of *nun* and *waw*, or a ligature of *nun* and *waw* for a closed *mem*' (p. 188) and gives Mic. 7.19 as an example (p. 192). For arguments against the solution proposed here, see A. Niccacci, *Un profeta tra oppressori e oppressi: Analisi esegetica del capitolo 2 di Michea nel piano generale del libro* (Jerusalem: Franciscan Printing Press, 1989), p. 24.

192. A possible translation is 'Like sheep in its fold, like a flock in (its) pasture, (their) number(?) shall be great (*wthy mnh m'd*). The ascent (*m'lh*) of the breach they will breach in front of them, and go through the gate and go out of it. Their king will cross in front of them, with Yahweh at their head'; but problems remain. A distant parallel text is *CTA* 14 ii 85-91.

193. Mays, *Micah*, pp. 27-28, 100.

194. For this poetic device, cf. J.S. Kselman, 'Semantic-Sonant Chiasmus in Biblical Poetry', *Bib* 58 (1977), pp. 219-23.

'banished' are in the feminine singular, usually explained as personification. Note the corresponding passage in Zeph. 3.19 (Table 1).

Mic. 4.11-12 And now,
many nations are assembled (*'sp*) against you (saying):
'Let her be desecrated and our eyes gloat over Sion!
But they do not know Yahweh's thoughts,
they do not understand his plan;
for he will gather (*qbṣ*) them like sheaves to the threshing floor.

Although three lines separate the components of the word-pair, each of the lines with *'sp* and *qbṣ* refers to 'the nations' so that here distant parallelism is in force. The use of a 'harvest' simile evokes Mic. 2.12-13 as set out above. See, in similar vein, Mic. 7.1.

Hab. 2.5 Who opens wide his gullet, like Sheol,
and is insatiable, like Death,
and gathers (*wy'sp*) into himself all the nations,
and collects (*wyqbṣ*) into himself all the peoples.

It is not certain whether 'wine' (so MT) or 'wealth' (1QpHab) is the subject here. The imagery is of the Underworld opening wide its maw to engulf hordes of dead people, as in Isa. 5.14 and the Ugaritic texts.[195]

Zeph. 3.8 For it is my intent to gather (*l'sp*) nations,
to assemble (*lqbṣy*) kingdoms to myself.

The word-pair in question is combined with another pair: *gwym* // *mmlkwt*. The suffix on the second infinitive is curious.

In the second set of Table 4 the word-pair sequence is inverted; texts using this variant will now be looked at.

Isa. 43.9a All the nations are assembled (*nqbṣw*) together,
gathered (*wy'spw*) are the races.[196]

As in Gen. 49.1-2, people are mustered to hear (*šm'*) what will be announced (*ngd*) to them. Chiastic patterning in 9a and 9b is used in combination with the word-pair. See, also, Jer. 4.5a.

Ezek. 11.17 I will gather (*qbṣ*) you from the peoples;
I will collect (*'sp*) you from the countries where you have been scattered, and I will give you the land of Israel.

195. Notably, *CTA* 5 i 14-20. Similarly, *Descent of Ishtar*, lines 19-20.

196. Repointing the second verb as a *niphal*, with *BHK* and most commentators.

This strophe corresponds (but not exactly) to v. 16; it comprises a couplet using the word-pair *qbṣ* // *'sp*, combined with the associated pair *'m* // *'rṣ*, and is closed by a single line or monocolon.

Ezek. 39.17 Say to every winged bird,
to every wild animal:
'Assemble (*qbṣ*) and come,
muster (*'sp*) from around to my banquet'.

The verb *qbṣ* is frequently paired with *bw'* (see Table 1); here, as elsewhere the two verbs are consecutive. Use of *msbyb*, 'from the surroundings', also recurs with *qbṣ* in Ezek. 15.37.

Joel 2.16 Gather (*'sp*) the people,
proclaim (*qr'*) a meeting.
Assemble (*qbṣ*) old men,
gather (*'sp*) children,
even suckling babes.

These lines are a variation on Joel 1.14 as has been noted in passing; see, too, Jer. 4.5. Here the reversed word-pair has been used in combination with one component of the word-pair (*'sp*) and another verb (*qr'*) to form a sequence whose initial letters have the chiastic pattern: *'-q- q-'-*.

Set 3 comprises those texts where *'sp* occurs in repetitive parallelism.

2 Kgs 22.20 I will gather (*'sp*) you to your fathers,
and you shall be gathered (*'sp*) to your grave in peace.

This is Huldah's oracular utterance, the subject of a recent short paper.[197] Notable are the collocation of *'sp* with the root *qbr* (the plural form used here, perhaps, for assonance with *'ābôtēkā*), as in Table 1, and the parallelism of *'sp* in two different conjugations.

Isa. 10.14 As one collects (*wk'sp*) abandoned (*'zbwt*) eggs,
all the land I collected (*'spty*)
with not a flutter of wing,
not an open beak,
not a chirrup.

There is both chiasmus and gender-matching here. The verb *'zb*, elsewhere associated with the word-pair (see Table 1) appears, too.

197. J. Priest, 'Huldah's Oracle', *VT* 30 (1980), pp. 366-68; the translation is his.

Isa. 33.4 And spoil is gathered (*'sp*) as the locust gathers (*'sp*).

Again, a simile from nature. The parallelism is within a single line only, but for completeness this example has been included.

Isa. 57.1 The upright man is destroyed (*'bd*) and no man
takes it to heart;
faithful men perish (*'sp*) with no-one understanding;
truly on account of evil does the upright man perish (*'sp*).

There are problems of stichometry (lineation) here: some would combine the last part of v. 1 with v. 2.[198] The verb *'sp* in the *niphal* is elliptical for 'to be gathered to one's ancestors', that is, to die, as in 2 Kgs 22.20 (cited above) and elsewhere.

Ps. 35.15-16a When I stumbled, they assembled (*'sp*) with glee,
smiters assembled (*'sp*) about me.

The couplet is difficult and in the absence of better solutions, I follow Dahood's rendition.[199] If correct, then the strophe exhibits anadiplosis (terrace pattern) in combination with delayed explicitation of subject ('smiters'). The next passage in the list, Jer. 8.13-14, is a poor example of our word-pair.

The final section of Table 4 lists possible cases of repetitive parallelism with the B-word only.

Isa. 56.8 This is the word of Yahweh,
who gathers in (*mqbṣ*) the outcasts of Israel
'I will gather in (*'qbṣ*) yet others to them, (namely)
to those (already) gathered in (*nqbṣ*)'.

An independent oracle where the second line, a direct quotation, is in parallel with a divine epithet. The repetitive word-pair is reinforced by use of *qbṣ* twice in line 2.

Ezek. 16.37 Therefore, see, I am gathering (*mqbṣ*) all your lovers,
in whose presence you have entered (?),
and all those you have loved,
as well as those you hated—
I am gathering (*wqbṣty*) them against you from
round about.

198. For the interpretation followed here, cf. P.-E. Bonnard, *Le second Isaïe, son disciple et leurs éditeurs. Isaïe 40–66* (Paris: Gabalda, 1973), p. 356. Contrast JB.

199. M.J. Dahood, *Psalms I* (AB, 16; Garden City, NY: Doubleday, 1966), p. 209.

The second line is obscure.[200] Lines 1 and 5 comprise another example of distant parallelism (see above on Mic. 4.11-12).

Ezek. 22.19-21 Because you have all become dross,
see, therefore, I will gather (*qbṣ*) you together in
the midst of Jerusalem.
As men gather together (*wqbṣt*!) silver and copper,
and iron and lead and tin in a (smelting) oven
and kindle fire under it in order to smelt it,
so will I gather (you) together (*'qbṣ*) in my anger,
and collect (*wknsty*!) and smelt you.

Since the text is difficult I have followed Zimmerli[201] but set out his translation as verse. Curiously, the emendation he proposed in the last line (reading *wknsty* for *whnḥty*, following the Greek) finds support from Qoh. 2.26 where *'sp* is parallel to *kns* (see Table 1). Our passage, then, would provide an additional word-pair to that table and yet another example of interchange between *'sp* and *qbṣ*.

The passages (of Table 4) just examined can be classified according to overall meaning into four groups. The word-pair is, first, a general expression for 'to muster' in Gen. 49.1-2, Isa. 43.9, Ezek. 16.37, 39.17, Joel 2.16 and Ps. 35.15-16a. The slightly narrower meaning of gathering together dispersed nations or scattered Israelites is evident in Isa. 11.12, 43.9, 56.8, Ezek. 11.17, Mic. 4.6 and Zeph. 3.8. In group three, 2 Kgs 22.10, Isa. 57.1-2 and Hab. 2.5, the connection is with death and/or burial. Last of all, natural imagery dominates in Isa. 10.14, 33.4, Mic. 2.12 and 4.11-12.

The conclusions to be drawn from the present short survey can be set out as a series of statements.

1. Except in the specialized meaning of 'to die' (of *'sp*), there appears to be little or no difference between the two verbs studied here.
2. The word-pair *'sp // qbṣ* is restricted to texts from the prophets, with no fewer than three examples in Micah. Of the two non-prophetic passages, Gen. 49.1-2 may be prose and Ps. 35.15 is uncertain.

200. For details, cf. W. Zimmerli, *Ezekiel 1: A Commentary on the Book of the Prophet Ezekiel. Chapters 1–24* (Philadelphia: Fortress Press, 1979), p. 330.

201. Zimmerli, *Ezekiel 1*, pp. 461-62.

3. As yet there is no corresponding pair in other ancient Semitic languages.
4. Inversion of sequence (B-A for A-B) in the word-pair is not rhetorically significant, except, perhaps, in Isa. 60.20;[202] Ezek. 29.5 has been discussed above.
5. The word-pair is text-critically and philologically significant for Mic. 2.12, Ezek. 22.19-21 and 29.5.
6. The presence of the word-pair may help distinguish poetry from prose (e.g. Gen. 49.1-2; passages from Ezekiel).
7. There seems to be little evidence that alliteration was a factor either in choice of this word-pair[203] or even in which sequence was adopted.[204] Some alliterative elements can be seen in Gen. 49.1-2, Isa. 11.12b, 62.9 and Mic. 4.11-12, none of much significance.

Lastly, and in general, the evidence presented here illustrates the importance of studying word-pairs which are in the mainstream of ancient Hebrew poetic tradition. It is not enough to examine only those common to Ugaritic, Phoenician and so forth. Both approaches are valuable—the one complementing the other—but the comparative field has been worked without enough awareness that an as yet unspecified proportion of word-pairs is unique within classical Hebrew.

202. G. Widengren, 'Yahweh's Gathering of the Dispersed', in W.B. Barrick and J.R. Spencer, *In the Shelter of Elyon: Essays on Ancient Palestinian Life and Literature in Honor of G.W. Ahlström* (JSOTSSup, 31; Sheffield: JSOT Press, 1984), pp. 227-45 provides comparative material from Mesopotamian texts and shows that the theme of gathering scattered peoples originated in Mesopotamia. Other studies: J. Lust, '"Gathering and Return" in Jeremiah and Ezekiel', in P.-M. Bogaert (ed.), *Le livre de Jérémie: Le prophète et son milieu. Les oracles et leur transmission* (Leuven: Uitgeverij Peeters, 1981), pp. 119-42; Niccacci, *Un profeta*, pp. 24-25. See also 4Q509 frags. 1-4 col. i 17-18.

203. See B. Margalit, 'Alliteration in Ugaritic Poetry: Its Role in Composition and Analysis'—Part I: *UF* 11 (1979), pp. 537-57; Part II: *JNSL* 8 (1980), pp. 57-80.

204. In Mic. 2.12 the reverse pair would be expected; in Isa. 10.14 *qbṣ* would be better for alliteration, in Ezek. 22.19-21, *'sp*.

Chapter 7

CHIASMUS

1. *Strophic Chiasmus in Ugaritic Poetry*[1]

1.1. *Introduction*

Although the presence of chiasmus in Ugaritic poetry has long been recognized, there has been no systematic study of *strophic* chiasmus as yet. With due awareness of previous studies[2] this paper will have the following plan. First comes a section on types of strophic chiasmus which in effect will set out the examples so far identified, under sub-headings (the couplet, tricola, quatrains, a peculiar form of chiasmus and then, longer sequences). Section two will attempt to evaluate these data in terms of patterns and distribution, discussing, too the topics control, rhetorical function and relationship to other poetic devices. Lastly, some tentative conclusions will be outlined.

1.2. *Types*

1.2.1. *The Couplet*

Since the couplet is the dominant, though by no means the only strophic form in Ugaritic verse, most of the examples will come

1. First published in *UF* 15 (1983), pp. 259-70.

2. These include J.W. Welch, 'Chiasmus in Ugaritic', *UF* 6 (1974), pp. 421-36; also his chapter with the same title in J.W. Welch (ed.), *Chiasmus in Antiquity* (Hildesheim: Gerstenberg, 1981), pp. 36-49. Principally he studies chiastic patterns beyond the strophe though he does discuss strophic chiasmus. See, besides, *UT*, pp. 113, 117 for examples (5), (5a), (7), (15), (17), (20) and (23); M.J. Dahood, 'Ugaritic-Hebrew Syntax and Style', *UF* 1 (1969), pp. 24-25, and H. Sauren and G. Kestemont, 'Keret, roi de Ḫubur', *UF* 3 (1971), pp. 181-221, 193 on chiasmus in the eighth 'song' of *Krt* (*KTU* 1.16 v 1-58). The present paper takes up the suggestion made by both Welch and Pardee (in D. Young [ed.], *Ugarit in Retrospect* [Eisenbrauns, IN: Winona Lake, 1981], p. 130) that chiasmus in Ugaritic needs further research.

under this head. For convenience they have been classified into fully chiastic, partially chiastic and nominal or verbless. Other classifications could have been used as will be seen later on.[3]

Full Chiasmus

(1) *KTU* 1.2 i 14-15 (par. 30-31)

lp‘n ’il ’al tpl	M - V	At El’s feet you must fall down,
’al tšt̲ḥwy pḫr m‘d	V - M	you must grovel[4] in the full assembly.

See, too, *KTU* 1.3 iii 9-10.

(2) *KTU* 1.4 vi 38-40

‘dbt bht b‘l y‘db	NP_2 - NP_1 V	The arrangements of his mansion did Baal arrange,
hd ‘db ‘dbt hklh	NP_1 V - NP_2	Hadad arranged the arrangements of his palace.

(3) *KTU* 1.3 ii 17-18 (and par.)

whln		Look!
‘nt lbth tmġyn	NP_1 M - V	Anath her house did reach,
tštql ’ilt lhklh	V - NP_1 M	proceed, did the goddess, to her palace.[5]

This is a formulaic couplet recurring in *KTU* 1.17 iii 24-25 and 19 iv 8-9.[6] For the occurrence in non-chiastic form as a control, see below (under 1.3.3).

(4) *KTU* 1.6 vi 51-52

kṯr wḫss yd	NP_1 - V
ytr kṯr wḫss	V - NP_1

3. Layout for the examples, numbered sequentially for reference, will be (a) *text*, ignoring text criticism unless unavoidable; (b) *analysis*, following the pattern set by T. Collins, *Line-forms in Hebrew Poetry* (Studia Pohl, Series Major, 7: Rome: Biblical Institute Press, 1978), and (c) *translation.*

4. On the verb, cf. J.A. Emerton, ‘The Etymology of *hištaḥawāh*’, *OTS* 20 (1977), pp. 41-55.

5. On *hln*, cf. K. Aartun, *Die Partikeln des Ugaritischen* (AOAT, 21/1.2; Kevelaer: Butzon & Bercker; Neukirchen–Vluyn: Neukirchener Verlag, 1974, 1978), pp. 72-73; on *šql*, W.G.E. Watson, ‘Philology, Lexical Notes Cont.’, *NUS* 26 (1981), p. 11.

6. In view of the fixed wording perhaps *dn’il lbth* should be read in *KTU* 1.17 iii 24.

The translation and even the stichometry of this couplet are uncertain and recently Dietrich and Loretz proposed a radically different reading from that generally accepted.[7] If they are correct, then these lines do not even form a couplet; however, see the discussion under 1.2.4.

(5) *KTU* 1.17 v 10-11

hlk kṯr ky'n	NP_2 - V	The coming of Kothar he surely saw,
wy'n trdq ḫss	V - NP_2	he saw the rapid approach of Hasis.[8]

(6) *KTU* 1.17 vi 35-36

mt 'uḫryt mh yqḥ	NP_1 M - NP_2 V	Man as his future, what does he get?
mh yqḥ mt 'aṯryt	NP_2 V - NP_1 M	What does he get, a man, as his fate?

Here the terrace-pattern[9] is combined with chiasmus in almost mirror formation.

(7) *KTU* 1.19 iii 114-115 (and par.)

knp nšrm b'l yṯbr	NP_2 - NP_1 V	The wings of the eagles did Baal break,
b'l ṯbr d'iy hmt	NP_1V - NP_2	Baal broke their pinions.

See the comments on example (6).

(8) *KTU* 1.24 38-39

'ar yrḫ	V - NP_1	Light, may Y. give,
wyrḫ y'ark	NP_1 - V np_2	may Y. give light to you.

Translations vary; del Olmo Lete includes the previous line and renders 'Nikkal-Ibbu to whom I sing is the light of Y. May Y. shine on you!', with the first *'ar* parsed as a noun.[10] Here I follow the alternative suggested by Gibson[11] but uncertainty remains.[12]

7. M. Dietrich and O. Loretz, 'Anats grosse Sprunge', *UF* 12 (1980), pp. 383-404, 399-400.

8. For example (5a) see below p. 325.

9. See R. Austerlitz, *Ob-Ugric Metrics* (Folklore Fellows Communications, 174; Helsinki: Academia Scientiarum Fennica, 1974), p. 38. For the relationship between chiasmus and anadiplosis, cf. Welch (ed.), *Chiasmus in Antiquity*, p. 151.

10. G. del Olmo Lete, *Mitos y leyendas de Canaan según la tradición de Ugarit* (Fuentes de la Ciencia Bíblica, 1; Madrid: Ediciones Cristiandad, 1981), p. 460; also, *KTU* 1.10 ii 20.

11. J.C.L. Gibson, *Canaanite Myths and Legends* (Edinburgh: T. & T. Clark, 1978), p. 129, where he comments 'Note the "dative" suffix and (if *'ar* in l. 38 is a verb) the chiastic arrangement of the couplet'.

12. Both Welch and Gordon cite *KTU* 1.83 5-7 *lšnm tḥlk šmm ṯṯrp* (*KTU*: *t'rp*) *ym ḏnbtm*.

Partial Chiasmus

(9) *KTU* 1.3 iii 19-20 (par. 1.1 iii 10-11, etc.)

'my p'nk tlsmn	M NP_1 - V	Towards me may your feet run,
'my twtḥ 'išdk	M V - NP_1	towards me speed may your legs.

Dahood's correction of *twtḥ* to *tptḥ* to produce the idiom 'open the legs = to hasten'[13] seems generally to have been abandoned in favour of the root *wḥy*.[14]

(10) *KTU* 1.3 v 33-34 (and 1.4 iv 45-46)

klnyy qšh nbln	NP_1 NP_2 - V	Together, his goblet let us carry,
klnyy nbl ksh	NP_1 V - NP_2	together, let us carry his cup.

There is disagreement on the exact analysis of *klnyy* (variant *klnyn*)[15] but chiasmus favours the translation given here; see below under 'function'.

(11) *KTU* 1.4 ii 3-4

'aḫdt. plkh[. *bydh*]	V - NP_2 M	She grasped her spindle in her hand,
plk. t'lt. bymnh	NP_2 - V M	(her) spindle she lifted up in her right hand.

The alternative reading *qlt* for *t'lt*, defended most recently by Margalit,[16] has much in its favour and there would then be no chiasmus here.

(12) *KTU* 1.4 vi 16-17 (and par.)

ḥš bhth tbnn	M NP_1 - V	Hastily his mansion was constructed,
ḥš trmm hklh	M NP_1 - V	hastily erected was his palace.

(13) *KTU* 1.4 vi 34-35

sb ksp lrqm	V - NP_1 M	Turned had the silver into plates,
ḫrṣ nsb llbnt	NP_1 - V M	the gold had been turned into bricks.

13. M. Dahood, 'Hebrew and Ugaritic Equivalents of Accadian *pitu purida*', *Bib* 39 (1958), pp. 67-69. Accepted in A. Caquot, M. Sznycer and A. Herdner, *Textes ougaritiques*. I. *Mythes et légendes* (LAPO, 7; Paris: Cerf, 1974), p. 165 n. i.

14. So Gibson, *Canaanite Myths*, pp. 145-46; del Olmo Lete, *Mitos y leyendas*, pp. 184 and 543 (glossary).

15. Cf. del Olmo Lete, *Mitos y leyendas*, p. 565 (glossary) with references. Add Aartun, *Die Partikeln*, I, pp. 45, 75.

16. B.L. Margalit, *A Matter of 'Life' and 'Death': A Study of the Baal–Mot Epic (CTA 4-5-6)* (AOAT, 206; Kevelaer: Butzon & Bercker; Neukirchen–Vluyn: Neukirchener Verlag, 1980), pp. 28-29.

(14) *KTU* 1.5 vi 20-22 (cf. 1.6 i 4-5)

yḥrṯ kgn 'aplb	V - M NP_2	He ploughed, like a garden his chest,
k'mq ytlṯ bmt	M - V NP_2	like a valley he furrowed his back.

Once again both lineation and translation vary from scholar to scholar; Margalit defends a very much different rendering[17] which has many merits. If he is correct, then example (14) is invalid.

(15) *KTU* 1.6 iii 12-13 (par. 6-7)

šmm šmn tmṭrn	NP_1 M - V	The skies with oil did rain,
nḫlm tlk nbtm	NP_1 V - M	the streams ran with honey.

(16) *KTU* 1.15 iv 17-18

'lh.ṯrh.tš'rb	M NP_2 - V	Into his presence the 'bulls' she introduced,
'lh.tš'rb.ẓbyh	M V - NP_2	into his presence she introduced the 'gazelles'.

Aside from chiasmus and the nominal word-pair these lines are identical. A rare example is in *Krt*; another is (32) under 1.3.3.

(17) *KTU* 1.17 i 3-4 (and par.)

'uzr 'ilm ylḥm	M NP_2 - V	Attired, the gods he fed,
'uzr yšqy bn qdš	M NP_2 - V	attired, he poured drink to the holy ones.

Difficult *'uzr* has provoked much debate but whatever it proves to mean[18] the chiastic pattern is unaffected.

(18) *KTU* 1.17 ii 8-9

bd(!)n 'i[*l*] *pnm. tšmḫ*	M NP_1 - V	On Daniel, his face lit up,
w'l. yṣhl p'it	M V - NP_1	above, shine did his forehead.[19]

(19) *KTU* 1.17 v 31-33

tb' kṯr l'ahlh	V - NP_1 M	Depart did Kothar to his tent,
hyn tb' lmšknth	NP_1 - V M	Hayyan departed to his dwelling.

(20) *KTU* 1.17 vi 28-29

'ašsprk 'm b'l šnt	V - M NP_2	I will enable you to count years on a par with Baal
'm bn 'il tspr yrḫm	M - V NP_2	you will enumerate months on a par with a son of El.

17. Margalit, *'Life' and 'Death'*, pp. 129-32.
18. See, conveniently, del Olmo Lete, *Mitos y leyendas*, p. 524.
19. For a different version, cf. del Olmo Lete, *Mitos y leyendas*, p. 372.

(21) *KTU* 1.18 iv 30-31 (cf. 1.19 i 32-33)

'lh nšrm trḥpn	M NP_1 - V	Above him, eagles hovered;
ybṣr ḥbl d'iym	Ø V - NP_1	watch[20] did a flock of birds.

(22) *KTU* 1.19 iii 53-54

šršk b'arṣ 'al yp'	NP_1 M - V	May your root not grow into the ground.
r'iš gly bd ns'k	NP_1 V - M	May your tip not droop into the hand of one plucking you.

Elsewhere I have defended a different translation based on the 'root-fruit' word-pair.[21]

Nominal Chiasmus. These texts also belong to the category of partial chiasmus, but have no verb.

(23) *KTU* 1.4 iv 10-11 (par. 1.19 ii 4-5)

št gpnm dt ksp	(V) N Rel. pron. N	Place traces of silver
dt yrq nqbnm	Rel. pron. N N	golden straps.

The verb (*št*) stands outside the chiastic pattern.

(24) *KTU* 1.6 vi 45-47

špš rp'im tḥtk	N N Adv. + pron. suffix	Š., the R. are under you.
špš tḥtk 'ilnym	N Adv. + pron. suffix N	Š., under you are the chthonic gods.

If *tḥtk* should mean 'submit to you' or the like, as seems probable[22] then the chiasmus is verbal (but still partial).

(25) *KTU* 1.3 iii 24-25 (and par.)

t'ant šmnn 'm 'arṣ	'high' - 'low'	The groaning[23] of sky with earth,
thmt 'mn kbkbm	'low' - 'high'	deeps with stars.

Essentially, the chiasmus here is *semantic*.

20. Consult my comments in W.G.E. Watson, 'The Falcon Episode in the Aqhat Tale', *JNSL* 5 (1977), p. 73.

21. In W.G.E. Watson, 'Puzzling Passages in the Tale of Aqhat', *UF* 8 (1976), pp. 374-75. Omitted as obscure or unlikely are *KTU* 1.5 ii 3-5, 15 iii 28-29 and 16 iii 9-11. 1.17 vi 22-23 is peculiar.

22. See especially J.F. Healey, 'Ugaritic ḥtk: A Note', *UF* 12 (1980), pp. 408-409, who defends the meaning '(to) care for' here. Also, D. Pardee, 'The New Canaanite Myths and Legends', *BO* 37 (1980), pp. 269-91, 284. In effect *KTU* 1.2 i 37-38 *hw. ybl. 'argmnk. k'ilm* [*hw.*] *ybl. k(!)bn. qdš. mnḥyk* is also nominally chiastic, as is 1.2 i 18.

23. Rather than 'meeting', in line with the series of keywords used here, namely *rgm*, *hwt*, *rgm* again, and *lḫšt*.

1.2.2. *The Tricolon*

(26) *KTU* 1.3 i 18-20

qm. ybd(!). wyšr	(A) verb: *yšr*	He rose, improvised and sang
mṣltm. bd. n‘m	(B)	—cymbals in the minstrel's hands—
yšr. ġzr. ṭb. ql	(A') verb: *yšr*	he sang, did the dulcet-toned lad.

The pattern is based on content more than on structure, though there is an element of both present. An alternative translation of the central line would be: 'To (the accompaniment of) cymbals the lad *sang*'. Strictly speaking, though, a line follows this tricolon (*‘l b‘l ṣrrt ṣpn*) to comprise a four-line stanza.

(27) *KTU* 1.108: 23-26

lrpi' 'arṣ ‘zk	m. + m.	From the Healer of the Underworld is your strength
ḏmrk l'ank ḥtkk		your power, your power, your juridical competence,
nmrtk btk 'ugrt	f. + f.	your awe-inspiring splendour within Ugarit.

Again, the pattern is ABA', reinforced by the gender-matched structure.[24] The translation is based on Dietrich and Loretz's study[25] which strengthens the case for verbal chiasmus in example (24).

1.2.3. *The Quatrain*

Only one clear example stands out, with an ABBA pattern based on nouns:[26]

(28) *KTU* 1.5 iv 15-18 and 1.17 vi 5-6

šty krpnm yn	A (*krpn*)	They drank beakers of wine,
bks hrṣ dm ‘ṣm	B (*ks*)	in cups of gold the blood of trees.
ks ksp yml'un	B (*ks*)	Cups of silver they filled,
krpn ‘l krpn	A (*krpn*)	beaker after beaker.

The text has been reconstructed by Dijkstra and De Moor[27] and is apparently an expansion of the couplet (identical with the first two lines here) found in *KTU* 1.4 iv 36-38.

24. See my comments on this pattern in Chapter 4, 'The Old Testament'.

25. Cf. M. Dietrich and O. Loretz, 'Baal *rpu* in KTU 1.108: 1.113 und nach 1.17 VI 25-33', *UF* 12 (1980), pp. 171-82, 175.

26. Not counting examples (5) and (5a) which, though consecutive in the text, are really couplets.

27. In M. Dijkstra and J.C. De Moor, 'Problematical Passages in the Legend of Aqhâtu', *UF* 7 (1975), pp. 171-215, 183; cf. p. 175.

1.2.4. *Special Pattern*

The pattern to be considered here, identified by Dietrich and Loretz,[28] comprises a couplet whose component lines have been separated for the insertion of another couplet or a tricolon. As such it is akin to the envelope figure of inclusio.[29] An example from many is:

(29) *KTU* 1.4 iv 4-7 (and par.)

mdl 'r ṣmd phl	(saddle animal)	Saddle a he-ass, yoke a donkey,
št gpnm dt ksp	(saddle: described)	place harness of silver,
dt yrq nqbnm	(saddle: described)	straps of gold,
'db gpn 'atnty	(saddle animal)	prepare my she-asses' harness.[30]

Other texts include *KTU* 1.2 i 38-39; 3 iv 49-53, vi 12-18; 4 viii 1-4; 16 i 46-49; 18 i 17-19, 19-22; 19 ii 12-15, 19-22, iii 47-49; iv 5-7, 36-39, 43-46.[31] At least one example of the same pattern may occur in Babylonian; it is *Atr.* II i 11-19.[32]

(30) Adad should withhold his rain—
 and below, the flood should not come up from the abyss.
 Let the wind blow and parch the ground,
 Let the clouds thicken but not release a downpour,
 Let the fields diminish their yields,
Let Nisaba stop up her breast.

1.2.5. *Longer Sequences*

Several long chiastic sequences have already been discussed by Welch.[33] Additional are *KTU* 1.5 vi 17-21 (and par.) which I have discussed elsewhere;[34] it consists of two tricola. Also, *KTU* 1.96 uses chiasmus to great effect.[35]

28. M. Dietrich and O. Loretz, 'Der Prolog des KRT-Epos (*CTA 14 I 1-35)*', in H. Gese and H.-P. Rüger (eds.), *Wort und Geschichte: Festschrift für K. Elliger zum 70. Geburtstag* (AOAT, 18: Kevelaer: Butzon & Bercker; Neukirchen–Vluyn: Neukirchener Verlag, 1973), pp. 35-36 (unavailable to me). Cf. del Olmo Lete, *Mitos y leyendas*, p. 34 and n. 36.

29. See also Dahood, 'Ugaritic-Hebrew', pp. 25-26.

30. Cf. Gibson, *Canaanite Myths*, p. 59 for the rendering. See example (23).

31. So del Olmo Lete, *Mitos y leyendas*, p. 34.

32. Text and translation in W.G. Lambert and A.R. Millard, *Atra-ḫasīs. The Babylonian Story of the Flood* (Oxford: Clarendon Press, 1969), pp. 72-73.

33. See n. 2, above.

34. See Chapter 4, 'Ugaritic Poetry'.

35. As presented and translated by J.C. de Moor, 'Contributions to the Ugaritic Lexicon', *UF* 11 (1979), pp. 639-54, 647-48. Three chiastic strophes occur in

(31) *KTU* 1.96 5-14

tpnn ʿn bṯy *ʿn bṯt*	A	(*bṯy*, *bṯt*)
tpnn ʿn mḫr	B	(*mḫr*)
ʿn pḫr	C	(*pḫr*)
ʿn ṯġr	D	(*ṯġr*)
ʿn ṯġr lṯġr ṯṯb	D	(*ṯġr*)
ʿn pḫr lpḫr ṯṯb	C	(*pḫr*)
ʿn mḫr lmḫr ṯṯb	B	(*mḫr*)
ʿn bṯy lbṯy ṯṯb *ʿn bṯt lbṯt ṯṯb*	A	(*bṯy*, *bṯt*)

As de Moor notes,

> the poem exhibits a striking symmetrical structure in the second and third strophes [i.e. the two stanzas reproduced here]: a distichon followed by a tristichon—a tristichon followed by a distichon. The aptly chosen similes have been arranged in reverse order in the tristicha, but not in the disticha.[36]

In structural terms, there is chiasmus of ‘wizard–witch’, ‘(tax-)collector’, ‘potter’ and ‘gate-keeper’ to produce the sequence ‘gate-keeper’, ‘potter’, ‘(tax-)collector’ and ‘wizard–witch’, as indicated by the letters A to D.

1.3. *Evaluation*

1.3.1. *Patterns*

Using the taxonomy set out for Hebrew poetry by O’Connor,[37] the following patterns occur.

Front Simple Chiastic Order. Examples (11), (13), (14), (19) and (20). In these, the sequence ABC becomes BAC.

Back Simple Chiastic Order. Examples of ABC becoming ACB are (9), (10), (12), (15), (16), (18), (22) and (24).

KTU 1.6 vi 46-53 but no overall pattern emerges.

36. De Moor, ‘Ugaritic Lexicon’, p. 648. See now G. del Olmo Lete, ‘Un conjuro ugarítico contra el “mal ojo”’, *Anuari de Filologia* 15 (1992), pp. 7-16.

37. M. O’Connor, *Hebrew Verse Structure* (Eisenbrauns, IN: Winona Lake, 1980), pp. 393-94. For another taxonomy see chapter 6 of my *Classical Hebrew Poetry*.

Back Flip Chiastic Order. Only two instances, (2) and (7) for the BCA alteration from 123.

Front Flip Chiastic Order. The sequence ABC is changed to CAB in (3), (4), (5) and (32).

Mirror Chiastic Order. As for front flip chiastic order, only two examples where ABC has become CBA: (1) and (8). Achiastic, according to O'Connor, would be (21) and (23). On (33), (35) and (36) see below.

Other Comments. The common pattern in 'partial chiasmus' comprises the use of identical initial words outside the chiastic sequence, as in

ḥš *bhth tbnn*
ḥš *trmm hklh*

in example (12). Similarly, there is repeated initial *'my* in (9), *klnyy* in (10), *'lh* in (16), *'uzr* in (17) and *špš* in (24). The final word is never identical in such couplets, but often final words can be syntactically the same, e.g. example (30). In (31) every line except two begins with *'n*, and in the third stanza every line also ends with *ṯb*, but the chiastic pattern is not strophic.

1.3.2. *Distribution and Occurrence*
Not counting repetition of the same formulaic expressions, the distribution among the literary texts is as follows:

Baal Cycle	19
Aqht Tale	10
Krt Legend	3
Nkl-wib (1.24)	1
Others	4[38]

There are none in 1.23, the prayer in 1.119, the Rp'um text 1.161 and so on. Some instances are common to 'Baal' and 'Aqht', among them examples (23) and (28).

38. These are *KTU* 1.108 (one), 1.114 (two: lines 1-2 and 14-15) and the text cited in n. 46.

1.3.3. *Controls*
Aside from positing different stichometry there can be little doubt that most of the examples set out above are chiastic or quasi-chiastic. In addition, some degree of control is available from comparison with parallel passages within Ugaritic literary texts. The findings will be set out here.[39]

Two series of almost parallel passages provide controls; the first series relates to example (3):

'nt lbth tmġyn
tštql 'ilt lhklh

to which corresponds *KTU* 1.100: 67-68 (cf. 72-73):

mġy ḥrn lbth	Come, did Horon to his house,
wyštql lḥẓrh	proceed to his court.

Similar is *KTU* 1.114:17-18:

'il hlk lbth
yštql lḥẓrh

In neither of these last two passages is there chiasmus (though it must be conceded that in the second text the verbal word-pair is not *mġy* // *šql* but *hlk* // *šql*.[40] The set represented by example (3) uses almost identical wording but within a chiastic arrangement.

The second series is even more striking and brings in examples (16) and (32) (see immediately) as well as a third text. Curiously, all three are found in *Krt*. We can begin with the new example:

(32) *KTU* 1.14 iv 40-42

hm ḥry bty 'iqḥ	NP2 M - V	If Ḥuray in my house I should take,
'aš'rb ġlmt ḥẓry	V - NP2 M	(if) I should introduce the wench into my court.

The clear chiastic ordering contrasts strongly with *KTU* 1.15 ii 21-23:

'aṯt tqḥ ykrt	NP2 V NP1	The wife you take, O Keret,
'aṯt tqḥ btk	NP2 V M	the wife you take into your house,
ġlmt tš'rb bḥẓrk	NP2 V M	the lass you introduce into your courts, (shall bear seven sons, etc.).

39. For discussion of controls cf. Chapter 4, 'The Old Testament'.

40. On Ug. *mġy*, see now A.R. Ceresko, 'The Functions of *Antanaclasis* (*mṣ'* "to find" // *mṣ'* "to reach, overtake, grasp") in Hebrew Poetry. Especially in the Book of Qoheleth', *CBQ* 44 (1982), pp. 551-69.

Example (16) is again chiastic, but there the verbal word-pair is *'rb*(Š) // *'rb*(Š):

'lh trh tš'rb
'lh tš'rb ẓbyh.

Since chiasmus is so rare in *Krt*, why was it used in example (32)—Krt's vow—and not in the text quoted after it (*KTU* 1.15 ii 21-23), which is a blessing? No convincing explanation presents itself as yet.[41]

1.3.4. *Functions*

As has been noted elsewhere, it is only half a description if a poetic device or technique is identified or even classified unless its rhetorical function can be pin-pointed.[42] Here, some possible rhetorical functions of (mainly) strophic chiasmus will be considered largely as a preliminary to further research.

To Express Merismus. By using a chiastic arrangement poets could express merismus, as in examples (2), (16), (23), (27) and (28). Of these the most convincing are (16) (everyone came in), and (27) (all-powerful god).

For Parallelism. In oral poetry mere parallelism is occasionally chiastic as examples (6), (7) and (9) show.

Formulaic. Examples (1), (3), (12) and (17) are mere stereotyped expressions which use chiasmus and may be related to the foregoing function considered under parallelism above.

Segmentation. Closure is marked by examples (4), (13) and (14) whereas (18) opens a section.

To Express Concerted Action. A novelty in the rhetorical functions of chiasmus is of interest both for itself and its implications. Examples are (4), (10), (19) and (21), but the principal texts are (5) and (5a). In (5) the composite deity Kṯr-w-Ḫss is seen approaching by Danel:

41. Yet another set comprises the examples (5), (5a) and non-chiastic *KTU* 1.17 v 17-19.23-28.

42. On (rhetorical) function consult A.R. Ceresko, 'The Function of Chiasmus in Hebrew Poetry', *CBQ* 40 (1978), pp. 1-10.

(5) The coming of Kothar he certainly saw,
he saw the rapid approach of Hasis.

By using chiasmus the poet counters the effect of splitting up the components of the divine name[43] and conveys the impression of a single entity on the move. The god then gives Danel the composite bow—an action described in the immediately following lines:

(5a) *KTU* 1.17 v 12-13

hlk qšt ybln	(-) NP2 - V	See,[44] the bow he bears,
hl yšrb' qṣ't	(-) V - NP2	look, he has many arrows.[45]

Once again the poet uses a chiastic couplet to the same effect: a manifold deity acting in unison (so to speak). In both (5) and (5a) the syntactic pattern is the same, except for the twofold anaphoric interjection in (5a).

In example (10) all present are expected to 'raise their glasses' in unison, and in (21), the birds are depicted hovering over Aqhat at table as a single flock. All these texts suggest that in example (4), too, the deity Kṯr-w-Ḫss is acting *as a single unit*:

(4) *kṯr wḫss yd*
ytr kṯr wḫss

though here the components of the multiple name have not been separated. Slightly more subtle is example (19) where *kṯr* (minus *ḫss*; cf. line 26) is chiastically paired with *hyn*. Rather than joint departure the insistence here, perhaps, is on *identity* : *kṯr* (*w ḫss*) = 'Hayyan, the skilled craftsman'.

Other Functions. Mimesis of the marriage contract is evident in example (8); example (22) suggests negation of fertility and (25), the contrast between sky and land. Change is the reason for chiasmus in (3), (18), (20) and (31); see also *KTU* 1.5 vi 17-21. In (15) the core of the sequence is chiastic. Why chiasmus is used in (11), (24), (26) and (27) is not clear.

43. Now studied by L. Viganò, 'Il fenomeno stilistico di Break-up di nomi divini nei testi di Ras Shamra–Ugarit', *RBI* 24 (1976), pp. 225-42.

44. For *hlk*, cf. Aartun, *Die Partikeln*, pp. 72-73.

45. Whether *'ašrb'* is an elative plus *ayin* formation of *rb(b)* is uncertain; for the principles involved (but not this example), cf. S. Gevirtz, 'Formative ע in Biblical Hebrew', *EI* 16 (1982), pp. 57-66.

A new example to be looked at is interesting because it suspends identification for dramatic effect; it comes from *Krt*.

(33) *KTU* 1.14 iii 38-39

pd. 'in. bbty. ttn	NP2 - V	Rather, what is not in my house give me:
tn. ly. mṯt. ḥry	V - NP2	give to me the woman 'Blanche'.

The delay is only brief but serves to increase tension and shows that though chiasmus is not used very often in *Krt* the bard could employ it with skill when he wished to.[46]

1.3.5. *Relationship to Other Poetic Devices*

Without going deeply into the topic, which involves rank, the following observations seem valid.

Chiasmus and the Quasi-Acrostic. By using partial chiasmus in examples (9), (10), (12), (16) and (24) the poet maintains identical initial words for both lines in these couplets. However, examples (6) and (25) use full chiasmus and yet the quasi-acrostic sequence persists. Example (31) also manages to combine chiasmus and the quasi-acrostic indicating they are equivalent in rank. Cf. (35) below.

Chiasmus and Oral Poetry. As already mentioned above (under *For Parallelism*) chiastic patterning assisted the bard in improvising poetry with little effort.

Chiasmus and Gender-Matched Parallelism. Congruent parallelism is evident in examples (14),[47] (22) and (25)—this last with the pattern m. + f. // f. + m. Example (27), if correctly interpreted, provides the best occurrence of gender-matched and chiastic parallelism coinciding.[48]

Chiasmus and the Terrace-Pattern. There is some overlap between these two structural devices, as illustrated by

46. On delayed reference, cf. Welch, *Chiasmus in Antiquity*, pp. 40-41. Another formulaic chiastic couplet may be *KTU* 1.100 4.9-10. 15-16 etc.: *mnt nṯk nḥš / šmrr nḥš ḥmt*.

47. See Chapter 4, 'Ugaritic Poetry'.

48. See, too, Chapter 4, 'The Old Testament'.

(34) *KTU* 1.2 i 36-37

‘bdk. b‘l. yymm		Your minion is Baal, O Yamm,
‘bdk. b‘l [nhr]m.		your minion is Baal, O Nahar,
bn. dgn. ’asrkm		Dagan’s son, your captive.

which uses incomplete nominal chiasmus in lines 2 and 3.

Similarly,

(35) *KTU* 1.2 iv 8-9

ht ’ibk b‘lm		Now, your enemy, O Baal,
ht ’ibk tmḫṣ	NP2 - V	now your enemy you must strike,
ht tṣmt ṣrtk	V - NP2	now you must vanquish you foe.

though here the quasi-acrostic element (*ht*) is maintained throughout. The terrace-pattern (anadiplosis) rather than chiasmus is paramount in

(36) *KTU* 1.3 v 19-21

bnt bhtk y’ilm		In the construction of your mansion, O El,
bnt bhtk ’al tšmḫ	M - V	in the construction of your mansion do not rejoice,
’al tšmḫ brm hklk	V - M	do not rejoice in the erection of your palace

since Ugaritic poetry attests precisely this combination elsewhere.[49] It would seem, then, that chiastic forms are a subsidiary feature in staircase parallelism, probably to enhance the step-like pattern.

Discussion. Chiasmus is adopted to achieve a variety of poetic effects: delayed explicitation, quasi-acrostic sequences, parallelism generally and merismus. It can also be pressed into service to counteract the effect of ‘breaking up’ a composite name, as we have seen. In rank, therefore, it must be below these devices, to be called into play only when needed.

1.4. *Conclusions*

Our survey of strophic chiasmus in Ugaritic poetry has reached its end but I will not say it is complete. Additional examples will certainly be identified, while those set out here are liable to be contested. In addition, with the publication of new texts from Ugarit, Ras Ibn Hani and elsewhere the last word has yet to be written.

Within the limits of this essay it is apparent that chiasmus does

49. E.g *KTU* 1.3 v 19-21; 10 ii 13-15, 21-23; 161: 20-22.

occur with a certain degree of frequency in Ugarit, though very much less often in the Krt text.[50] Why this should be the case is a mystery. Is it a mark of earlier date—earlier, perhaps than the Baal and Aqht texts—or a late date? Does it bespeak a different poetic tradition within Ugarit or was it a matter of personal style? As yet we do not know.

Of special interest is the novel rhetorical function described above: chiasmus used to express two or more agents acting as a unit. If correct there may be implications for understanding other Ugaritic texts and the principle may apply to other (ancient) poetic traditions.

2. *Chiastic Patterns in Biblical Hebrew Poetry*[51]

2.1. *Introduction*

2.1.1. *Scope and Aims*

A full-scale study of chiasmus in ancient Hebrew poetry[52] would require more time and more space than is available. Nor could it be the work of a single person, even dependent (as he must be) on the work of others.[53] Accordingly, in the pages which follow the emphasis will not be on exhaustiveness but, rather, on systematic presentation. An attempt is made to order the results achieved so far in the hope of providing a solid foundation for future research.

Another aim is to remove existing confusion. The envelope figure, to take only one example, is related to chiasmus, but the two cannot be simply equated. This explains the need for a section on terminology

50. To some extent this accords with the conclusions drawn by G.H. Wilson in his study 'Ugaritic Word Order and Sentence Structure in the Krt Text', *JSS* 27 (1982), pp. 17-32. Although chiasmus is a technique of oral poetry it does not necessarily follow that verse using chiasmus has been orally composed. This distinction is the subject of R. Finnegan's evaluative work *Oral Poetry: Its Nature, Significance and Social Context* (Cambridge: Cambridge University Press, 1973). On chiastic parallelism see her remarks, p. 101.

51. First published in J.W. Welch (ed.), *Chiasmus in Antiquity* (Hildesheim: Gerstenberg, 1981), pp. 118-68.

52. Here 'ancient Hebrew poetry' means, in effect, the OT with its extra-canonical books (in some traditions), such as Sirach, since no other extra-biblical Hebrew poetry has survived. The Qumran material has not been included.

53. I am particularly indebted to Robert Smith, who provided a long list of texts exhibiting chiasmus, which formed the nucleus of this section, as well as helpful criticism of the first draft.

and the many tables. It must not be forgotten that chiasmus is only one of the many structural devices available to the poet and that chiastic patterns mean little unless incorporated into a larger system of poetic theory. Also, sequences within the strophe differ from chiastic patterns spread over longer segments of text. Clarification of this kind is necessary at the outset.

Generally speaking, the concept of function within poetry has been neglected by commentators.[54] Some work has been done with respect to chiasmus,[55] but the topic has not been adequately covered and is so important that a complete section has been given over to it here.

Finally, this study makes some deliberate omissions. Non-poetic texts, even if they were very probably first composed in verse, have not been considered to avoid introducing methodologically extraneous problems. Generally speaking, extreme novelty has been avoided here, since the primary purpose of the present chapter is to describe the state of the art.[56] Also the relationship between chiasmus and literary form, interesting as it is,[57] has been left for study elsewhere.

2.1.2. *Dating*

No attempt has been made in these pages to correlate chiastic patterns with the dates of poetic texts for several reasons. First, there is no unanimity among scholars regarding the detailed chronology of biblical texts.[58] Secondly, many 'late' books preserve archaic material or

54. On function in poetry, see G.N. Leech, *A Linguistic Guide to English Poetry* (London: Longmans, 1969), p. 4.

55. F.I. Andersen, *The Sentence in Biblical Hebrew* (Janua Linguarum, Series Practica, 231; The Hague: Mouton, 1974), pp. 121-24; A.R. Ceresko, 'The Function of Chiasmus in Hebrew Poetry', *CBQ* 40 (1978), pp. 1-10.

56. By novelty of this order is meant, chiefly, solutions to philological problems. See, however, section 3b.

57. W.L. Holladay ('The Recovery of Poetic Passages of Jeremiah', *JBL* 85 [1966], pp. 401-35, 434) asks, 'To what degree does chiasmus depend on the *Gattung* of a passage?' and 'Does the *Gattung* suggest chiasmus, or is there no close relation between them?' The study of literary forms requires more refinement before it can be related to the presence of chiasmus. For a brief survey of chiasmus, cf. J.H. Stek, 'The Stylistics of Hebrew Poetry. A (Re)New(ed) Focus of Study', *Calvin Theological Journal* 9 (1974), pp. 15-30, 24-25.

58. Systematic proposals are not lacking, e.g. S. Segert, 'Versbau und Sprachbau in der althebräischen Poesie', *MIO* 15 (1969), pp. 312-21; J. Kuryłowicz, *Studies in Semitic Grammar and Metrics* (Prace Jezykoznawe, 67;

deliberately use archaisms. Also, much of the OT has undergone at least one editorial re-working and the difficulties of assigning levels of text to different hands still occupy scholars.

2.1.3. *Metrical Problems*

Although the problem of Hebrew metre is still unsolved, there does seem to be a consensus that it is accentual in character, that is to say, based on stress.[59] The *accentual* theory finds additional support from the following points. First is the fact that in Hebrew stress is phonemic, indicating it to be metrically significant as well.[60] To this argument from phonology can be added two others regarding poetic devices. One is the broken construct chain[61] by means of which an additional stress can be created. In Isa. 19.8, for example, *kol mašlîkê bay*^{e}*'* or *ḥakkâ)* ('All those casting hook into the Nile'), there are 3 stresses, balancing 3 stresses in the first colon. If the word sequence had been, as it normally would be, *kol mašlîkê-ḥakkâ bay*^{e}*'or*, there would have been only 2 stresses.[62] The other is the pivot-patterned bicolon in which the crucial element is silent stress, by which is meant the absence of an expected (final) stress-word. So, in Ps. 59.2:

haṣṣîlēnî mē'oy^{e}*bay '*^{e}*lohîm*	Rescue me from my foes, God,
mitt^{e}*qom*^{e}*may t*^{e}*sagg*^{e}*bēnî*	Against my attackers be my bulwark.

If this example (which was chosen because it also exhibits chiasmus) has been correctly analysed as a pivot pattern,[63] it shows stress to be metrically significant.

Warsaw: Polska Akademia Nauk, 1972), p. 67 n. 2; B. Margalit, 'Introduction to Ugaritic Prosody', *UF* 7 (1975), pp. 289-313, 298 n. 15 and 300 n. 16—but none is convincing. The early Hebrew inscriptions provide a growing body of comparative material by which biblical texts can be dated (a suggestion I owe to Dr John C.L. Gibson of Edinburgh).

59. By far the most readable survey, and still valid today, is W.H. Cobb, *A Criticism of Systems of Hebrew Metre* (Oxford: Clarendon Press, 1905).

60. As Dr John C.L. Gibson pointed out to me, 'Syllable counting may be a viable undertaking for Ugaritic where differences in vowel quantity are phonologically relevant, but is hardly meaningful in the case of a stress-oriented language like Hebrew', Gibson, *Canaanite Myths*, p. 140.

61. Discussed below, 'Other Devices', section 5.

62. See also Isa. 10.5; Pss. 16.11; 71.7; Prov. 17.6.

63. Considered in more detail in section 5 under 'Chiasmus and the Pivot Pattern'.

Of the other theories put forward to explain Hebrew metre, none is convincing.[64] Some seem rather to belong to the level of stichometry and as such are useful, to a limited degree, to determine the length of cola.[65] These problems do not impinge directly on the present study since chiasmus seems to function independently of metre. They have been considered briefly because some scholars maintain there is a relationship between syllable-counting (which they equate with metre) and chiasmus.

2.1.4. *Terminology*

Basic to the ensuing considerations is clarity of terminology. Scholars use different terms for the same component, calling a colon a hemistich, for instance, or employing the words 'stanza' and 'strophe' indiscriminately. This can lead to confusion even though a particular writer may employ his terms consistently.[66] Here, therefore, to avoid all ambiguity, a table of terms will be set out. It must be stressed, though, that more than mere nomenclature is in question, since the terms used imply a certain underlying theory concerning the structure of poetry. Broadly speaking it is as follows: the larger units, whether whole poems or stanzas, are composed of strophes, each strophe comprising one or more cola. These cola, in their turn are made up of still smaller units. Accordingly, a poem can be considered as a set of components (in loose terms, word-units) forming larger and larger complexes which ultimately combine into a single unified structure.[67]

64. Among them can be mentioned the word-unit (Ley, Robinson, Kosmala), the thought-unit, syllable-counting, vowel-counting (Freedman) and letter-counting (Loretz).

65. Syllable-counting is no longer the system of metre most in vogue; a convenient survey with lengthy examples is provided by D.K. Stuart, *Studies in Early Hebrew Meter* (Missoula, MT: Scholars Press, 1976).

66. The problems of terminology are discussed by C.F. Kraft, *The Strophic Structure of Hebrew Poetry (As Illustrated in the First Book of the Psalter)* (Chicago: University of Chicago Press, 1938), pp. 4 n. 5 and 32 n. 1; J. Lotz, 'Notes on Structural Analysis in Metrics', *Helicon* 4 (1943), pp. 119-46, 132; W.F. Albright, *Yahweh and the Gods of Canaan* (London: Athlone Press, 1968), p. 5 n. 15; R. Fowler, 'What is Metrical Analysis?', *Anglia* 86 (1968), pp. 280-320; L. Boadt, 'Isaiah 41:8-13: Notes on Poetic Structure and Style', *CBQ* 35 (1978), pp. 20-34, 24 n. 14.

67. Not only was this the technique of oral (improvised) composition, it also reflects the manner in which written works were compiled.

In accordance with the method of analysis adopted,[68] the definitions will proceed from the smallest units to the largest. Correct analysis can only begin once such terms have been defined with precision.[69] (See Table 1.)

COLON (monocolon)	hemistich	hemistich
BICOLON (strophe)	colon colon	
TRICOLON (strophe)	colon colon colon	
TETRACOLON (strophe)	colon colon colon colon	
PENTACOLON (strophe)	colon colon colon colon colon	
STANZA	strophe 1 strophe 2 strophe 3	
POEM	STANZA STANZA STANZA	

Table 1. *Terminology*[70]

Syllable, *Word*. Since not even linguists can agree on defining these two basic terms, only their generally accepted meanings will be implied here.[71]

68. Small is sure; it is easier to detect patterns within lesser complexes, although, of course, the whole context must never be lost sight of.

69. Note that the term 'verse' has generally been avoided to prevent confusion with the verse-numbering of MT.

70. For chiasmus on a larger scale see section 2.3.2, below.

71. Cf. J. Krámsky, *The Word as a Linguistic Unit* (The Hague: Mouton, 1969).

Hemistich. A subdivision of the colon comprising one or more words.

Colon. A single line of poetry; also called 'stichos', 'stich' and even 'hemistich'. Holladay defines the colon as a group of words in parallelism with another colon[72] but this does not allow for monocola.

Monocolon. A colon standing on its own (within a stanza or poem). It can be defined as a single colon which does not cohere closely with another colon, although in a wide sense no element of a poem stands in total isolation.[73]

Bicolon. Two lines of verse, generally in parallelism; a couplet formed of two (parallel) cola. The bicolon is the standard unit of verse in Hebrew poetry, and is also referred to as 'distich', 'couplet' and 'line'.

Tricolon. A set of three cola forming a single whole or strophe, e.g. Exod. 32.8.

Tetracolon. A unit of verse made up of four cola, sometimes called a 'quatrain', e.g. Jer. 2.13.

Pentacolon, Hexacolon etc. Combinations of five, six (etc.) cola respectively, each set making up a strophe (e.g. 1 Sam. 18.7b).

Strophe. A strophe is a verse-unit made up of one or more cola, and is a general term for monocola, bicolon, tricolon and so forth. Many authors call the stanza a strophe, perhaps because there are occasions when a stanza may contain only one strophe.

72. W.L. Holladay, 'Recovery', p. 403.

73. 'Orphan lines in poetry of pervasive parallels are a contradiction in terms, since whatever the status of a line, all its structure and functions are indissolubly interlaced with the near and distant verbal environment, and the task of linguistic analysis is to disclose the levers of this coaction. When seen from the inside of the parallelistic system, the supposed orphanhood, like any other componential status, turns into a network of multifarious compelling affinities': R. Jakobson, 'Grammatical Parallelism and its Russian Facet', *Language* 42 (1966), pp. 399-429.

Stanza. A combination of one or more strophes. Generally speaking, a complete poem is composed of several stanzas. Some poems, though, comprise only a single stanza (e.g. Psalm 117) just as some stanzas contain only one strophe.

The following symbols will be used:

a, b, c	to denote elements (generally, words) of a colon
A, B, C	to denote complete cola
p	to denote the pivotal element in a pivot-patterned bicolon
R	to denote refrain
x	to denote (extra-chiastic) anacrusis
I, II, III	to denote stanzas

Subscripts and superscripts will be used sparingly, either to press a point home or to avoid confusion. Words in CAPITALS are keywords or significant words within a poem; italicized words are significant for a particular pattern.

2.1.5. *Chiasmus, the Strophe and the Stanza*

A recurrent topic in the analysis of Hebrew poetry is how to divide a poem into strophes and stanzas, but in spite of many sporadic attempts no overall solution has yet been reached. In part this is due to some confusion over the meaning of the terms 'strophe' and 'stanza'. Definitions have already been given, some justification for which must now be provided. According to the terminology adopted here, a stanza is a large unit of poetry which can be subdivided into strophes. So, in Judg. 5.25,

I		Water he requested
II	A	*Milk* she gave
	B	in a lordly bowl
	A	she proffered *curds*

the stanza is made up of two strophes (I, II), a monocolon and an ABA' (chiastic) tricolon.[74] Similarly, a four-line stanza such as Job 21.39 consists of two bicola, and so on with varying combinations of monocolon, bicola, tricola and so on. It can also happen that a stanza cannot be further subdivided into smaller strophes, as when a four-line stanza is a tetracolon.

A poem is generally subdivided into stanzas (e.g. Ps. 119, with 22 stanzas), but some poems comprise only a single stanza, examples

74. However, cf. A. Berlin, *The Dynamics of Biblical Parallellism* (Bloomington: Indiana University Press, 1985), pp. 12 and 95.

being Psalm 117, 2 Sam. 3.33b-34 (see below). To add to the possible confusion, a poem may consist of one stanza and that stanza be made up of only one strophe, for example 1 Sam. 18.7b.

One of the first scholars to realize that by identifying chiastic patterns, stanzas and strophes could then be distinguished, was Möller. This aspect will be considered below, in section 2.6.

2.1.6. *Classifying Chiasmus*

With these distinctions in mind, the classification and typology of chiastic patterns can now be approached. In the main, the 'Types of Chiastic Pattern' (Table 2) follows the layout of 'Terminology' (Table 1). Three broad subdivisions of chiasmus emerge: strophic chiasmus, chiasmus in the stanza, and chiastic poems. First, and possibly most important, is strophic chiasmus, which forms the subject of the whole of section 2.2. Its fundamental component is the chiastic bicolon, which is basic because the bicolon in direct (synonymous) parallelism is the building-block of Hebrew poetry. There follows paragraphs on chiastic forms of the monocolon, tricolon, tetracolon and so on. Other types of chiasmus, including gender chiasmus, are discussed next and, finally, patterns related to chiasmus.

a b a	chiastic monocolon (2.2.2)
A B A	chiastic tricolon (2.2.3)
A B B A	chiastic (ABBA) tetracolon (2.2.4, 2.2.5)
A B C B A	concentric pentacolon (2.2.6)
A B C C B A	chiastic hexacolon (2.2.7)

Table 2. *Types of Chiastic Pattern*

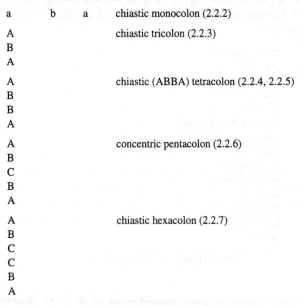

Chiasmus in longer passages (section 2.3) deals with chiastic poems and with segments of poems written in chiastic form. Strict classification is not possible since the subject matter is too varied in form. The topic of chiasmus in the stanza is covered in part by section 2.2 and in part by section 2.3. While not completely satisfactory, this has proved the easiest way of presenting the material and has therefore been adopted here.

The detailed classification, or rather, sub-classification of 2.2.1 has not been carried over into the other types of chiasmus because there the unit is the colon itself or a multiple of the colon.

2.2. *Strophic Chiasmus*

2.2.1. *Chiastic Bicola*

It is not always possible to make a clear distinction between different chiastic patterns. For example, is the standard abc // cba type, with its central, unchanged element (b), complete chiasmus or only partial? Nor can the typology be totally rigid, because some strophes seem to fit none of the categories mentioned here, for example Pss. 72.9, 74.19. The typology adopted here, then, is provisional and further study will reveal a more precise way of differentiating the various patterns.[75] For convenience, a table of chiastic bicola will be set out first (Table 3).

1	*Mirror chiasmus*
	abc // cba
2	*Complete chiasmus*
	ab // ba
	abc // cba
3	*Split-member chiasmus*
	a-bc // bc-a
	ab-c // c-ab
	ab-cd // cd-ab
4	*Partial chiasmus*
	abc // cb
	ab-c // ba-c
	a-bc // a-cb
	abc // ba

Table 3. *Typology of Chiastic Bicola*

75. Strophic chiasmus can also be analysed grammatically and syntactically, for which see Andersen, *Sentence*, pp. 127-40.

Pure or Mirror Chiasmus. The second colon, in this pattern, repeats exactly the same words used in the first colon, but in reverse order; schematically: abc // cba. Since the resulting two lines are mirror images, the term 'mirror' chiasmus seems suitable. In fact, it is simply a form of repetition.

Isa. 22.22[76]	He shall open, and no one will shut; He shall shut, and no one will open

Also 9.2.[77]

Complete Chiasmus. The sequence followed in the second, parallel colon is the reverse of that used in the first, the description 'complete' referring to the fact that none of the components is omitted. Two subtypes belong under this heading:

ab // ba

Jer. 2.19a	You will be punished by your wickedness, Your defections will convict you

And Deut. 32.16; Isa. 3.8; 5.21; 6.7b; 32.6; 42.15a; 54.2; Ezek. 19.7; Hos. 2.2; 4.13; Mic. 4.6; 7.16b; Zeph. 3.19; Pss. 38.11a; 46.10b; 49.7; 78.58; 119.15; 126.5; 139.1; Job 7.14; 36.3; 37.3; Lam. 5.21; Sir. 12.18.

abc // cba. Or, strictly, abc // c'b'a', since it is not mirror chiasmus.[78]

Ps. 81.7	I removed the burden on his shoulder, His hands from the basket were freed

Also, Gen. 9.6; Isa. 14.30; 29.17; 40.12a, 26, 27b; 42.4; 51.4; 62.1b; Pss. 3.8-9; 7.17; 81.7; 142.3; 147.4; Job 17.1; 20.6; 32.14; Prov. 3.10; 8.21; 13.6.

Split-Member Chiasmus. First identified by Möller, this subdivision is basically a variant of complete chiasmus, the a and b components each (either separately or together) split into two further elements. A chart will make this clear (Table 4):

76. Ceresko, 'Function of Chiasmus', p. 9.
77. See also Ezek. 17.24, Mal. 3.24a, Cant. 6.3 and Qoh. 7.1a.
78. 'A rather infrequent sequence' according to M.J. Dahood, *Psalms*, III (Garden City, NY: Doubleday, 1968), p. 345.

complete chiasmus: (ab // b'a')	a	b	b'	a'
split-member chiasmus: (a-bc // bc-a)	a	bc	bc	a
(ab-c // c-ab)	ab	c	c	ab
(ab-cd // cd-ab)	ab	cd	cd	ab

Table 4

a-bc // bc-a. The second component in the chiasmus is made up of two elements (bc), but the chiasmus does not affect their sequence.

Prov. 7.21 *She led him on* with her many persuasions,
By her smooth talk *she pressed him*

And Gen. 32.29b; Isa. 11.1; 29.14b; 32.3, 6c; 48.1; 60.13b, 16; Pss. 6.10; 7.16; 22.13; 35.18; 40.14; 59.3; 69.34; 72.11; 81.17; 105.44; 107.11; 109.16; 116.3; 147.16; Job 13.12; 28.2; Prov. 2.8; 10.10; Lam. 3.22.

ab-c // c-ab. In this pattern both the first and last components of the bicolon are split

Hos. 4.9 *I will punish him* for his conduct
And for his deeds *I will repay him*

Further: Judg. 1.15; Isa. 13.21b; 27.11b; 43.15; 60.2b, 20; 64.1a; Hab. 2.1; Pss. 7.16; 15.3b; Job 10.5; 19.9.
ab-cd // cd-ab. All the components have been further subdivided, the sequence of the subsections being preserved in an overall chiastic arrangement.

Prov. 25.6 Do not claim honour in the king's presence,
And in high positions do not set yourself

Also, Isa. 33.4; Ezek. 11.19; 32.13; Pss. 9.16; 36.12; 78.24; 89.7; Job 3.6; 31.16; Prov. 4.14, 24.

Partial Chiasmus. A set of patterns in which the position of one element remains unchanged and can be considered as standing outside the chiasmus. They are abc // cb, ab-c // ba-c and a-bc // a-cb. (The pattern abc // cba has already been considered.)

abc // cb. The unchanged element is at the beginning, and the pattern itself is a variation of the stereotype abc // bc formation frequent in Hebrew (e.g. Hos. 5.8, 7.1) and in Ugaritic poetry.

Deut. 33.26b Who rides through the heavens to your aid,
and in his majesty, the skies

Also, Isa. 48.18-19; 49.18; Nah. 3.8; Hab. 1.3, 15; Pss. 35.17; 78.33; 80.11; 92.3; 103.7; 105.45; 126.2; 132.4; Job 6.15; 8.5, 18; 27.7; 39.6; Cant. 1.4.

ab-c // ba-c. The c-element is outside the pattern:

Ps. 113.7 Lifting from the dust the feeble,
From the midden, raising the poor

Similarly, Isa. 27.5; 49.22; Pss. 21.9; 143.1.

a-bc // a-cb

Prov. 2.2 Making attentive to wisdom, your ear,
Bending your mind to understanding

And Num. 24.18; Isa. 59.3b; Pss. 85.14; 139.7; Job 3.12; Prov. 2.2.

For the abc // ba pattern see below ('Chiasmus and the Pivot Pattern'). Patterns such as abc // ca (Isa. 45.1; 49.13b) and abc // ba (Jer. 4.2; Mic. 1.4a) probably are not really chiastic, but have been mentioned for the sake of completeness. There is no agreement among scholars concerning the typology given above, since what is an ab // ba sequence for one writer may be considered as abcd // cdab by another. This amounts to lack of agreement on what constitutes metre and how a word-unit is to be defined. A correct and exact typology may go some way, therefore, towards resolving the problem of Hebrew metre (touched on in section 2.1.3) and further refinement is evidently needed.

2.2.2. *The aba (Chiastic) Monocolon*

Akin as it is to the pivot pattern,[79] the aba monocolon[80] differs on two counts. Firstly it is a single line of poetry, not a bicolon; and secondly, it is complete, with no ellipsis of a final stress.[81] For example,

79. And to incremental repetition (expanded colon); on the pivot pattern see sections 1c and 5. It must not be confused with the ABA tricolon.

80. A single colon can be of the following types: aa'a" (three-synonym colon, not a tricolon as in W.G.E. Watson, 'Verse-Patterns in Ugaritic, Akkadian, and Hebrew', *UF* 7 [1975], pp. 483-84); aab, abb and aba (chiastic).

81. The peculiar characteristic of the pivot-patterned bicolon is silent stress, on

Ps. 123.3a Mercy on us. Yahweh, mercy on us

is a chiastic monocolon with the pattern aba.[82] Its function is to open a stanza or poem, as in David's lament for his child:

2 Sam. 19.1b My son, Absalom, my son

or the first line of Psalm 115. Characteristic is the central vocative.[83]

2.2.3. *The ABA (Chiastic) Tricolon*

The ABA (or ABA') three-line strophe is a tricolon which can be described as two parallel cola separated by an isolated line,[84] and forming a close-knit unit. With identical outer cola:

Ps. 27.14	A	Wait for Yahweh
	B	Be strong and stout of heart
	A	Wait for Yahweh

Normally, though, the outermost lines are in parallelism:

Prov. 17.25	A	A worry to his father
	B	(is) a foolish son
	A'	And bitterness to her-who-bore-him

Here the A-colon corresponds to the A'-colon, the central B-colon referring to both of them. The son, of course, comes from both his parents, so that the layout is an appropriate way of expressing their mutual relationship. See, too, Gen. 27.39; 49.8; 1 Sam. 2.2; Isa. 5.25; 14.8; 16.11; 30.31; 51.3; 56.9; Amos 1.3; Nah. 2.4; 3.17; Pss. 9.15; 32.8; 64.11; 86.12; 104.15; Job 3.1-2; 24.14; 34.37; Cant. 1.11; 2.12; 4.12.

Being a chiastic tricolon the ABA-patterned strophe combines the

which see D. Abercrombie, 'A Phonetician's View of Verse Structure', *Linguistics* 6 (1964), pp. 5-13, and N. Frye, *Anatomy of Criticism* (New York: Atheneum, 1965 [1957]), p. 251.

82. It could also be termed a telescoped form of mirror chiasmus (see above, on typology).

83. On Ps. 57.2, 8, 9, see P. Auffret, 'Note sur la structure littéraire du *Psaume* LVII', *Semitica* 27 (1977), pp. 59-73, who notes the stanza-opening function too. For Ps. 67.7b-8a, see section 2.5.3, below; Cant. 1.15 (= 4.1) is a marginal case, Ps. 47.7, exceptionally, forms a bicolon from two successive and identical aba monocola.

84. So R. Austerlitz, *Ob-Ugric Metrics* (Folklore Fellows Communications, 174; Helsinki: Academia Scientiarum Fennica, 1974), p. 47.

functions both of the tricolon and of chiasmus: to open or close a poem or stanza, and to express merismus. These functions will now be illustrated.

To Open a Stanza (or Poem)

Gen. 27.39[85]	A	See, of the fat of the land
	B	will your home be
	A'	and from the dew of heaven above

Also 49.8; Isa. 56.9 (cited below); Amos 1.3; Hab. 2.6; Pss. 4.2; 32.8; Job 3.1-2; 10.1.

To Close a Stanza (or Poem)

		So that
Ps. 9.15	A	I may recount all your praise
	B	in the gates of Daughter Zion
	A'	I may rejoice in your history

The next verse begins a series of curses on the wicked, while *lᵉma'an*, 'so that', alludes to what has gone before; accordingly, v. 15 closes the short stanza, vv. 14-15. Similarly, Isa. 51.3; Ezek. 34.6; Pss. 6.11; 27.14 (cited above); Job 10.22; 34.37; Prov. 5.22.

To Express Merismus

Isa. 56.9	A	All (you) beasts of the field
	B	come to eat
	A'	All (you) beasts of the forest

The clue here, as is often the case, is the word *kol*, 'all, every'. Likewise: Isa. 25.7; Pss. 9.15; 89.17; 109.14; 121.6, 7; Job 10.22; 34.37; Prov. 17.25.

2.2.4. *The ABBA Tetracolon*

The pattern in question is found in tetracola where the first and final cola match (A, A) just as the two central cola correspond (B, B).

Jer. 2.13	A	The fountain of living WATER
	B	To hew themselves CISTERNS
	B	CISTERNS that cannot crack
	A	And cannot hold WATER

85. Although the actual poetic section is very short (vv. 39-40) it is opened by an ABA tricolon.

This type of ABBA-pattern is the most frequent, where the chiastically arranged elements are two words (or words based on two roots), here 'water' and 'cistern'. A related type is where the AA cola are semantically similar (parallel), as are the BB cola. Finally, the pattern can involve other poetic devices or be interlocked with other chiastic sequences, as will be set out below.[86]

Sub-Types of the ABBA Tetracolon. Chiastic word repetition, on the lines of Jer. 2.13 cited above, forms the basis of the following tetracola (with repeated words in parentheses): 2 Sam. 1.24 (clothing jewels ornaments clothing), Isa. 49.24-25 (prey captive captive prey), Jer. 9.3 (friend brother brother friend), Ezek. 19.2b-3a (lion cub cub lion), Nah. 2.12b-13a (lioness cub cub lioness), Pss. 12.4-5 (lips tongue tongue lips), 47.7-8 (gods king king gods), Job 6.25-26 (words argue argue words), 27.10-11 (Shaddai Eloah El Shaddai), Prov. 18.6-7 (lips mouth mouth lips), 31.19-20 (hand palm palm hand),[87] Cant. 2.14 (face voice voice face). Also, Deut. 32.43, Pss. 78.29-30, 113.2-3, Job 21.31-32 and 27.16-17.

In *semantic chiasmus* the repeated words are not in identical pairs but semantically parallel, or else the whole colon is 'repeated' by using a parallel phrase.

2 Sam. 3.33b-4 Must Abner die so base a death?
Your hands were *not* bound
Your feet *not* thrust in fetters
Like one falling at a ruffian's hands you fell

The two central cola are parallel: 'your hands unbound // your feet unbound' (paraphrasing) and the outer cola are related by wordplay (see below). Other examples: Gen. 16.11; Isa. 5.7; Ps. 48.11-12; Prov. 11.18-19; 30.4.

Occasionally the ABBA-pattern *interlocks*[88] with other patterns to

86. A.R. Ceresko, 'The Chiastic Word Pattern in Biblical Hebrew', *CBQ* 38 (1976), pp. 303-11, 305-306 and 'Functions', pp. 9-10 are useful for the lists of ABBA patterns, but unfortunately no distinction is made between occurrence over 4 cola (ABBA tetracola) and distribution over greater or lesser segments.

87. As pointed out to me by Smith, this tetracolon is at the very centre of the acrostic passage Prov. 31.10-31.

88. Termed 'intercalation' by E. Schüssler Fiorenza, 'Composition and Structure of the Book of Revelation', *CBQ* 39 (1977), pp. 344-66, 360-63 (citing R.J. Loenertz), this kind of multistructural overlap (as Smith reminded me) is a

form a more complex arrangement of cola. So, in Ezek. 32.7-8a the sequence

A	and I WILL DARKEN their stars
	...
B	Nor the moon SHALL BEAM OUT ITS LIGHT
B	All the BEAMING LIGHTS in the heaven
A	I WILL DARKEN on your account

interlocks with the sequence (also chiastic):

C	I WILL COVER, when you are blotted out, the heavens
A	And I WILL DARKEN their stars
C	The sun with a cloud I WILL COVER

to form the pattern CACBBA

C	I WILL COVER, when you are blotted out, the heavens
A	And I WILL DARKEN their stars
C	The sun with a cloud WILL I COVER
B	Nor the moon SHALL BEAM OUT ITS LIGHT
B	All the BEAMING LIGHTS in the heavens
A	I WILL DARKEN on your account.

A similar pattern can be identified in Ezek. 21.8b-10[89] and Ps. 72.1-4.[90] Also, Prov. 1.26-27 (chiastic tetracolon in climactic pentacolon), and texts such as Isa. 49.24-25 and Mal. 3.19.

Several other patterns and devices can be combined with the ABBA tetracolon. So, in Prov. 18.6-7, the arrangement of repeated roots coincides with a pattern of gender-reversal which runs:

f. + m.	A	(lips—contention
m. + f.	B	mouth—blows
m. + f.	B	mouth—undoing
f. + m.	A	lips—trap)

both being chiastic. Double wordplay binds the components of 2 Sam. 3.33b-4 (cited above): *nābāl*, 'fool',[91] of the first colon and the verb

feature of Songs (cf. J.C. Exum, 'A Literary and Structural Analysis of the Song of Songs', *ZAW* 85 [1973], pp. 47-79).

89. L. Boadt, 'The A : B : : B : A Chiasm of Identical Roots in Ezekiel', *VT* 25 (1975), pp. 693-99, 697.

90. ABBA—A'B'CCB'A'; cf. J.S. Kselman, 'Psalm 72: Some Observations on Structure', *BASOR* 220 (1975), pp. 77-81.

91. For the meaning of this term, see J.D. Levenson, '1 Samuel 25 as Literature and as History', *CBQ* 40 (1978), pp. 11-28, 13.

nāpal, 'to fall', used (twice) in the last colon; and the PN Abner (cf. *nir*, 'yoke'[92]) exploited by the middle couplet dealing with binding both hands and feet. A phonetic component amounting to end-rhyme is the basis of chiasmus in Gen. 49.11:

He tethers to the vine his ass (*'irô*)
And to the red vine, the colt of his she-ass (*'atonô*)
He washes in wine his cloak (*lebušô*)
And in grape-blood his robes (*sutô*)

the pattern being formed by the pronominal suffixes: *-ô*, *-ô*, *-ô*, *-ô*. See also Prov. 30.4. The break-up of an expression is found in Job 27.10-11, combined with chiasmus:

Will he delight in SHADDAI?
And call on ELOAH at all times?
I will teach you EL's power
What SHADDAI has I'll not conceal

the expression being El-Shadday (see also v. 13). The ABBA pattern also acts as a link here, connecting the series of rhetorical questions (vv. 8-10) with v. 11.

No one single function can be assigned to the ABBA pattern: each case must be inspected in turn. The usual functions of chiasmus are: to express merismus (Gen. 16.11; Jer. 9.3), or antithesis (Jer. 2.13; 9.3; Job 6.25-26; 27.16-17; Prov. 18.6-7); to link components of a poem (Gen. 49.11; Job 27.10-11; Prov. 11.18-19); and to express the reversal of events (Ps. 12.4-5). Noteworthy are Cant. 2.14 which is a refrain and Prov. 31.19-20 which forms the centre of an alphabetic acrostic.

Although the ABBA tetracolon has been considered here under the heading 'strophic chiasmus', there are examples which amount to four-line stanzas formed from two strophes, each a bicolon, the only common element being the repeated keywords:

Jer. 9.3 (a) Each against his FRIEND be on guard
And in every BROTHER put no trust,
(b) For every BROTHER only supplants
And each FRIEND peddles slander

Couplet (a) is a complete unit, as is couplet (b), the link formed by the keyword pattern *rēa'*, *'aḥ*, *'aḥ*, *rēa'*.

92. See P.D. Hanson, 'The Song of Heshbon and David's *NIR*', *HTR* 61 (1968), pp. 297-320.

Similarly, Isa. 44.21; 49.24-25; Hos. 13.14; Ps. 124.4-5; Job 21.31-32; Prov. 3.11-12.[93] Evidently the ABBA sequence serves as a link at stanza level, binding the two component strophes together.

2.2.5. *Other Chiastic Tetracola*

Some tetracola are chiastic without exhibiting the ABBA pattern. For instance

Job 34.2-3 Listen, WISE ONES to my words,
Knowledgeable one, GIVE EAR to me,
For the EAR, words does test,
As the PALATE tastes by eating

where the chiasmus is based on sound: *ḥkm*, *ḥk* (first and last cola), *h'zn*, *'zn* (central cola), the stanza forming an introduction to the block of poetry which follows. Other texts include Isa. 1.18bc, 14.30, 18.6b, 48.18-19, 58.7, Ezek. 11.19[94] and Ps. 3.8-9.[95]

2.2.6. *Chiastic Pentacola*

As with tetracola, it is difficult to differentiate five-line strophes from five-line stanzas. Accordingly, some illustrative examples will be set out and examined. The clearest chiastic structure is ABCBA, as in the first set of texts.

Isa. 28.12 A Who has said to them
B 'This is your resting place.
C Give rest to the weary!
B Yes, this is your place of repose'.
A But they would not listen

'The verse is built concentrically, and the sound effects correspond to the structure',[96] the main thrust of the pentacolon lying in the central colon (C; cf. Isa. 57.21).

93. Following the version by P. Wernberg-Møller, '"Pleonastic" *Waw* in Classical Hebrew', *JSS* 3 (1958), pp. 321-26, 323; the ellipsis of a verb in the last colon is usual in similes—its presence would have ruined the chiastic pattern.

94. As reconstructed by W.H. Brownlee, 'The Aftermath of Judah's Fall According to Ezekiel', *JBL* 89 (1970), pp. 393-404, 396-99.

95. P. Auffret, 'Note sur la structure littéraire du Psaume 3', *ZAW* 91 (1979), pp. 385-402; 'Notes complémentaires sur la structure littéraire des Psaumes 3 et 29', *ZAW* 99 (1987), pp. 90-93.

96. W.H Irwin, *Isaiah 28–33: Translation with Philological Notes* (BibOr, 30; Rome: Biblical Institute Press, 1977), pp. 23-24; his translation is adopted here.

Jer. 2.27c-28	A	And in the period of their disorder they say:
	B	'Up, and save us!'
	C	But where are the gods you fabricated for yourselves?
	B	Let them up and even save you
	A	In the period of your disaster

The central line of this pentacolon[97] is again the most significant as is evident both from the chiastic structure and the allusion to *iy aliyn b'l*, 'Wherever is Mightiest Baal?' of the Ugaritic texts.[98]

Similarly patterned are: Isa. 42.2-4, 55.8-9, Jer. 30.16, Ps. 104.29-30, and finally

Prov. 23.13-14	A	Do not withhold discipline from a lad.
	B	If you beat him with a cane
	C	he'll not die;
	B	Beat him yourself with a cane
	A	And you'll save from Sheol his very self

which is not a simple ABBA-pattern[99] but a five-line stanza centring on 'He will not die' meaning both 'a good hiding will do him no lasting harm' and 'by discipline he will be saved from a worse fate'.

Another chiastic sequence is AABCC, as in Hos. 14.10.[100] More frequent is the ABBA tetracolon with an additional colon, either before it or as the final line. Examples are Isa. 14.19, 56.5.[101] Other patterns occur too.[102]

2.2.7. *Chiastic Hexacola, and Longer Chiastic Sequences*

The more lines there are in a chiastic unit, whether strophe or stanza, the fewer the examples, so that exact typology is difficult. This paragraph will deal with chiastic units of six lines (hexacola) and more.

97. Contrast Ceresko, 'Chiastic Word Pattern', p. 305.

98. *CTA* 7 iv 28 (*UT* 49:iv:28) etc.

99. So Dahood, apud Ceresko, 'The A:B:B:A Word Pattern in Hebrew and Northwest Semitic with Special Reference to the Book of Job', *UF* 7 (1975), p. 81.

100. 'The odd line (B) forms a sort of middle term, or connective link between two couplets': J. Forbes, *Symmetrical Structure of Scripture* (Edinburgh: T. & T. Clark, 1854), p. 26. It is no accident that it is the last stanza in the book (even though NEB sets it out as prose) for which it is a fitting close.

101. Cf. Ceresko, 'Functions', p. 10.

102. Gen. 3.17-18 (Andersen, *Sentence*, p. 99), Jer. 22.30 (ABBCC) and Zeph. 1.17 (ABCA'A").

There are enough instances of chiastic hexacola for a broad grouping into three types: ABCCBA (pure chiasmus), AABBA'A' (an expanded ABA sequence), and lastly, miscellaneous sequences. The classic example of ABCCBA (as part of a nine-colon stanza) is Isa. 6.10:

	A	Be-lard the HEART of this people
	B	Their EARS deaden
	C	Their EYES close fast
	C	To avoid them seeing with their EYES,
	B	Or, with their EARS, hearing,
	A	Or, with their HEART, understanding.

Also, Isa. 65.18, Zech. 2.12-13,[103] Job 33.20-22[104] and perhaps Amos 5.4-5. A variant form of the pattern is ABCCBD in Jer. 4.29. The second type is made up of three bicola:

Isa. 43.19-20	A	I will even make in the desert a path, in the wilderness, streams
	B	I am honoured by the wild beasts, jackals and ostriches,
	A	For I can provide, in the desert, water, streams in the wilderness

Also, Jer. 4.11-12a[105] and Lam. 2.4.

Finally, sets of six cola such as Isa. 5.20 (a chiastic series or list), and Amos 2.11-12 (ABCBAA').

Chiastic heptacola are Amos 5.4-5 (unless a hexacolon) and Ps. 12.4-5:

Ps. 12.4-5	A	Amputate[106] may *Yahweh*
	B	all smooth LIPS,
	C	every TONGUE speaking big;
	D	those who say
	C	'By our TONGUE are we great,
	B	Our LIPS: are with us
	A	Who more *master* than us!'

103. Cf. Ceresko, 'Functions', p. 10.

104. A difficult task to translate, but any attempt must take into account the pattern of repeated words (identified by Ceresko, 'The A:B:B:A Word Pattern', p. 86) 'life, soul (appetite), sight, sight, soul, life'.

105. W.L. Holladay, 'Structure, Syntax and Meaning in Jeremiah IV 11-12A', *VT* 26 (1976), pp. 28-37, 34-37.

106. In Mesopotamia, cutting off the tongue was prescribed punishment for falsehood; see texts in *CAD*, L, pp. 210-11.

The words 'Yahweh' and 'master' (*'ādôn*) are in italics and not in upper case since they do not correspond exactly; there is additional synonymy in the C cola: 'big' and 'great'.

Octocola are Num. 12.6-8[107] and Jer. 4.14-16:

A Wash your heart of wickedness, O JERUSALEM
that you might be saved.
B How long shall they lodge within you,
your EVIL thoughts?
B For a voice is announcing from Dan,
and divulging the EVIL from Mount Ephraim.
A Mention these things, O nations,
divulge them against JERUSALEM.

Further passages are considered in section 2.3 (Chiasmus in Longer Passages).

2.2.8. *Other Types of Chiasmus*

In addition to the various kinds of straightforward structural chiasmus already considered, there are other forms of chiasmus based on different principles. These are skewed chiasmus, assonantal chiasmus, semantic-sonant chiasmus and gender chiasmus.

Skewed Chiasmus. In Holladay's words,

> a chiasmus which, after the midpoint, begins its way back, only to plunge forward briefly once more, and then, in the last line, offers a set of simultaneous balances in several media which psychologically brings us all the way home.

He terms it 'a striking compromise between the chiastic pattern and sequentiality'.[108] His examples are Jer. 16.1-9, 23.1-4 and 23.25-32. The chiastic pattern of Jer. 23.1-4, for instance, is ABCB'D and then D'C'B"A'.

Assonantal Chiasmus. Here belong not only texts which simply exhibit or exploit both chiasmus and assonance (see below, section 2.5.2) but also those with a chiastic pattern of root consonants. Such are Jer. 5.25 and 16.6.[109] There is some overlap with the next category.

107. J.S. Kselman, 'A Note on Numbers XII 6-8', *VT* 26 (1976), pp. 500-504.
108. Holladay, 'Recovery', pp. 432-33.
109. Holladay, 'Recovery', pp. 408 and 418.

Semi-sonant Chiasmus. A combination of chiasmus and assonance 'in which one leg of the chiasmus is formed by a pair of words of similar meaning (the semantic pair), and the other leg is produced by a pair of words of similar sound (the sonant pair)'.[110] So, in Qoh. 7.1a

ṭôb šem	Good repute
miššemen ṭôb	beats good perfume

the four components are chiastically arranged and the similarity of *šēm*, 'name, repute', and *šemen*, 'oil, perfume', is exploited in word-play. Also, Gen. 37.36, 2 Sam. 1.21b and Ezek. 22.2, where the semantic element consists of the same word, repeated, and Jer. 2.7b, where a word-pair is used, and Ps. 147.15 and Lam. 3.22. A subset of this group comprises couplets where the consonants of a word in the first colon have been inverted in the second, as

Prov. 14.4	Without oxen, the manger is CLEAN (*br*)
	But MANY (*rb*) crops result from a bull's strength

Similarly, Ps. 51.19 (*zbhy–tbzh*) and 78.33 (*bhbl–bbhlh*). To these examples of Kselman can be added Isa. 40.4 (*h'qb–lbq'*), Jer. 4.27b-28a (*šmmh–šmym*), Hos. 7.7 (*w'lkw–mlkyhm)* and Ps. 20.5 (*lk–kl*).

Gender Chiasmus. The term 'gender chiasmus' is used as a convenient abbreviation for a complex poetic pattern which involves matching nouns and genders. The basic form (not involving chiasmus at all) is simply a rather sophisticated form of synonymous (or direct) parallelism:

Joel 2.16	Out must go the *groom* (m.) from his chamber (m.)
	and the *bride* (f.) from her bower (f.)

Here, the word for a room is masculine with reference to the bridegroom and feminine with respect to his future wife. The device occurs quite frequently in Hebrew poetry.[111] The chiastic patterns to be considered below are variations of such gender-matched parallelism. Of additional interest is that they share some of the general functions of chiasmus as well as having functions of their own.

110. J.S. Kselman, 'Semantic-Sonant Chiasmus in Biblical Poetry', *Bib* 58, pp. 219-23; cf. Kselman, 'A Note on Gen 7:11', *CBQ* 35 (1973), pp. 491-93 on Gen. 7.11, J.S. Kselman, 'Psalm 72: Some Observations on Structure', *BASOR* 220 (1975), p. 79 on Ps. 72.7 and Ceresko, 'Chiastic Word Pattern', pp. 303-11

111. See above, pp. 201-18.

The sub-sets to be discussed can be grouped into four blocks: strophes where gender-matching obtains, with the additional use of chiasmus; strophes where only cross-matching of genders is apparent; a very small sub-set where chiasmus of both gender and noun occurs, and fourthly, segments of poetry longer than a bicolon. (A complete poem based on gender-chiasmus is set out in section 2.3.)

Chiastically-patterned bicola (with gender-matched synonyms) are best explained by a close look at one clear example.

Job 18.10 Hidden in the *ground* (f.) is a *rope* (m.) for him,
And a *trap* (f.) for him upon the *path* (m.).

The matching of genders is here reversed: in the first colon a masculine noun ('rope') is coupled with a feminine noun ('ground'); in the second, the word 'path' is masculine and its connected noun ('trap') is feminine. The chiastic pattern is based on synonyms:

PLACE — SNARE
SNARE — PLACE

while the resulting pattern of genders is *not* chiastic:

f. m.
f. m.

the function of the two patterns combining to express surprise. Another example is Hab. 3.3

Does cover the *heavens* (m.) his *radiance* (m.)
And his *splendour* (f.) fills the *earth* (f.)

the chiastic arrangement, which expresses merismus[112] being

PLACE ('heavens') — APPEARANCE ('radiance')
APPEARANCE ('splendour') — PLACE ('earth')

again the corresponding genders are not chiastic. Other instances: Isa. 11.4; 28.15; 42.4; 62.1b; Nah. 2.13; Pss. 57.6; 12 (// 108.6); 76.3; 92.3; 147.15; Job 28.2. (For Isa. 28.15 and 18 see below, section 2.4). The function of this pattern is to express merismus (Isa. 42.4; Hab. 3.3; Ps. 57.6 [and par.]; cf. Nah. 2.13), reversal of existing state (Ps. 76.3; Job 28.2), a surprise event (Job 18.10) and harmony (Isa. 11.4; 62.1b).

112. Note the polar word-pair 'heavens' // 'earth' and the verb 'to fill'.

Strict gender chiasmus is obtained not from the cross-arrangement of nouns but by the layout of their genders. So in Prov. 20.9

Young men's *glory* (f.) is their *strength* (m.)
But old men's *splendour* (m.) their *grey hair* (f.)

the antithesis is brought out by the gender pattern

m.	f.
f.	m.

although otherwise the sequence of words in both cola is identical. Similarly, in Isa. 60.17c the elliptic word sequence (abc // b'c') is in effect synonymous, the only contrast being the non-alignment of genders which expresses the change that is to take place:[113]

And I will transform your *overseers* (f.) into *peace* (m.)
your *taskmasters* (m.) to *fairness* (f.)

One last example will show how gender chiasmus can transform plain prose into expressive poetry:

Joel 4.3 They bartered a *lad* for a *lay* (f.)
And a *wench* they sold for *wine* (m.) and drank it

The m. + f. // f. + m. pattern, instead of an expected m. + m. // f. + f. sequence, expresses how utterly beyond the normal people were acting. Further examples: Gen. 49.15 (f.m.m.f.),[114] Deut. 32.14 (f.m.m.f.), Isa. 3.1 (f.m.m.f.), 29.4 (f.m.m.f.), 60.17b (m.f.f.m.), Ps. 25.13 (f.m.m.f.), Prov. 8.20 (m.f.f.m.), 10.15 (m.f.f.m.), 30.19b (f.m.m.f.), Cant. 7.7 (f.m.m.f.); also, Job 29.13 (f.m.m.f.) and Joel 4.10. No single overriding function is evident, so that each text has to be looked at individually. Expressed are antithesis (Prov. 10.15; 20.29), abnormal event (Deut. 32.14; Isa. 29.4; 60.17bc), and paradox (Gen. 49.15; Prov. 30.19b; Cant. 7.7).

Chiasmus and gender chiasmus in combination is found in only two texts, Prov. 10.11 and

Job 31.10 May she grind for *another* (m.), my *wife*
And over *her* may there kneel *others* (m.)

113. It is worth noting how a feminine noun, *p^{e}quddâ* (literally, 'surveillance'), here an abstract noun with concrete meaning, is used to denote men.

114. Recognized by S. Gevirtz, 'The Issachar Oracle in the Testament of Jacob', *EI* 12 (1975), pp. 104-12, 111.

where the pattern is

(V: f.)—(prep. + N: m.)	—	(N: f.)	ab–c
(prep. + suff.: f.)—(V: m.)	—	(N: m.)	c–ab

The function of both types of chiasmus is to express the reversal of existing conditions.

The fourth subset comprises texts longer than the customary bicolon discussed so far. They are Jer. 16.3, Mic. 7.6, Prov. 18.6-7 as well as Gen. 12.6 and 49.3 (for Prov. 18.6-7, see above, section 2.2.3).

Jer. 16.3	For this is what Yahweh says	
	Against the sons	m.
	And against the daughters born in this place	f. + m.
	And against the mothers who bear them	f.
	And against their fathers who sire them in this land	m. + f.

Discussing whether Jer. 16.1-9 is prose, or poetry or something in between, Holladay comments, 'Is it significant that *bmqwm hzh* ("in this place") is masculine and *b'rṣ hz't* is feminine, or is this only coincidence?'.[115] In view of the numerous examples discussed already (especially Jer. 16.9), it would seem that design rather than accident is at work here. The antithesis of death coming to destroy parents and children alike (v. 4) is heightened by the intricate pattern of genders, the line-by-line sequence m.f.f.m. acting in counterpoint with the inversions of the second (f. + m.) and last (m. + f.) cola.

Mic. 7.6	For sons treat like fools (their) fathers	m. + m.
	Daughters rebel against their mothers	f. + f.
	Daughter-in-law against mother-in-law	f. + f.
	A man's enemies are the people in his house	m.m.m.m.

This, the final strophe of Mic. 7.1-6, is a tetracolon with the basic structure m.f.f.m., exactly as in Jer. 16.3, though here all the genders in any one colon match. Again, as in the passage from Jeremiah, the resulting arrangement expresses the reversal of normal events

Gen. 49.3[116]	Reuben, my first-born	
	You are my *strength*	m.
	and the *start* of my vigour,	f. (+ m.)
	pre-eminent in *authority*	f.
	and pre-eminent in *power*	m.

115. Holladay, 'Recovery', p. 417.

116. For translation, see S. Gevirtz, 'The Reprimand of Reuben', *JNES* 30 (1971), pp. 87-98.

The five-line stanza is made up of an introductory monocolon and two bicola which the chiastic gender pattern binds together into a unit. Finally, while not strictly poetry, perhaps the list in Gen. 12.16 also displays the pattern under examination:

Flocks and cattle	f. + m.
and asses and slaves	m. + m.
and maids and she-asses	f. + f.
and camels	c.

The chiastic structure, already recognized by Lund,[117] makes nonsense of Speiser's comment, 'The list of Abraham's acquisitions appears to have been subjected to some reshuffling in the course of transmission, as is indicated by the separation of he-asses and she-asses'.[118] Instead of applying modern occidental reasoning it makes more sense to realize that in the ancient Near East slaves and animals were lumped together as chattels.

2.2.9. *Patterns Related to Chiasmus*

The patterns in question are alternating chiasmus, inclusio and chiastic inclusio, and the chiastic gather-line. To some degree they could be classed as chiastic, but in order to avoid confusion they will be discussed separately.

Alternating Chiasmus. Used by some scholars[119] to describe patterns such as ABA'B' (e.g. Pss. 8.3, 4; 51.7), the term is misleading. It assumes that an ABB'A' pattern has become ABA'B' which is a form of direct parallelism. However, it may be significant in considering the development of chiasmus and so has been mentioned here.

Inclusio. Inclusio or envelope figure is the repetition of the same words at the beginning and end of a section of poetry.[120] It is a form

117. N.W. Lund, *Chiasmus in the New Testament* (Chapel Hill: University of North Carolina Press, 1972), p. 43.

118. E.A. Speiser, *Genesis* (AB, 1; Garden City, NY: Doubleday, 1964), p. 90.

119. E.g. N.W. Lund, 'Chiasmus in the Psalms', *AJSL* 49 (1933), pp. 281-312, 283.

120. See particularly L.J. Liebreich, 'Psalms 34 and 145 in the Light of their Key Words', *HUCA* 27 (1956), pp. 181-92, and N.H. Ridderbos, *Die Psalmen: Stilistische Verfarhen und Aufbau mit besonderer Berücksichtigung von Ps. 1-41* (BZAW, 117; Berlin: De Gruyter, 1972), pp. 35-37.

of distant parallelism, a description more applicable when the repetition is not verbatim, but cannot be confused with chiasmus.

Chiastic Inclusio. Some examples of phonological inclusio are chiastic (see above) such as

Job 26.13 By his wind (*brḥ*) the heavens were made fair
Pierced did his hand the serpent who flees (*brḥ*)

and Job 12.10. Of a different order is

Isa. 37.33-34 He shall not come within this city
Nor shoot an arrow at it,
Nor approach it with a shield;
By the way he came he'll return.
Within this city he shall not come

where the components of two lines in distant parallelism are chiastically arranged (a—b and b—a). Also, Qoh. 8.5b-6c.

Chiastic Gather-Line. A gather-line is the final line of poem which mentions all or most of the elements of the poem,[121] so that a chiastic gather-line is one which reiterates in chiastic order the components of the preceding lines. Examples are Jer. 23.4 and 23.32.[122]

2.3. *Chiasmus in Longer Passages*

2.3.1. *Introductory*

While it is relatively easy to determine the presence of chiasmus in short stretches of text, from the monocolon to the stanza of eight lines, it is considerably more difficult to establish the same pattern for longer sections of poetry.[123] Among the early scholars to consider such extended chiasmus can be numbered Boys[124] and Lund.[125] Lund,

121. 'One line weaves together several words, one word out of each of two, three, or four consecutive lines, either preceding or following the gather-line', B. Thiering, 'The Poetic Forms of the Hodayot', *JSS* 8 (1963), p. 191 (who coined the term).

122. For these poems cf. Holladay, 'Recovery', pp. 424-25.

123. Reflecting the very process by which poetry was composed: the smaller units first, the larger later because they themselves were made up of these lesser units.

124. T. Boys in E.W. Bullinger (ed.), *A Key to the Psalms* (London: L.B. Seeley, 1890); see also J. Forbes, *Symmetrical Structure of Scripture* (Edinburgh: T. & T. Clark, 1854).

125. N.W. Lund, *Chiasmus in the New Testament* (Chapel Hill: University of North Carolina Press, 1972), pp. 64-136

who was rightly critical of Boys's efforts,[126] attempted to be more scientific in method. However, his set of seven 'laws'[127] were deduced from the examples he had collected and could not be applied as controls. Even so, Lund was a careful scholar, and, as in other disciplines, later scholars will remain indebted to these pioneer studies. However, some of Lund's examples do not stand closer scrutiny[128] and many more instances have since been recognized. While not pretending to be exhaustive, the present section will discuss the problem of extended chiasmus, set out a representative selection of chiastic poetical texts and mention other texts for reference.[129]

Certain controls are particularly relevant here to help assess which poetical texts are truly chiastic in structure. Such controls include the following points:[130]

1. First, such chiasmus must be *strict*. There are cases where a poet has applied chiasmus loosely, or where variants of a standard form are used. (Deviation is often the mark of a good poet.) Cases of this nature, though, can only be judged against an established norm.[131]
2. Next, the *whole stretch of text* must be involved, not simply certain select parts. So, for example, omitting vv. 7-8 of Psalm 30 or v. 10 of Psalm 58 (unless this verse can be considered a ballast variant) in order to establish chiasmus—so Lund—is to beg the question.[132]

126. Lund, *Chiasmus in the New Testament*, p. 40.

127. Lund, *Chiasmus in the New Testament*, pp. 40-41 and 95-96.

128. Notably Ps. 101 on which cf. H.L. Kenik, 'Code of Conduct for a King', *JBL* 95 (1976), pp. 391-403.

129. See, R.L. Alden, 'Chiastic Psalms (I): A Study in the Mechanics of Semitic Poetry in Psalms 1–50', *JETS* 17 (1974), pp. 11-28; 'Chiastic Psalms (II): A Study in the Mechanics of Semitic Poetry in Psalms 51–100', *JETS* 19 (1976), pp. 191-200; Ceresko, 'Function', pp. 1-10.

130. For two controls (word-pairs and wordplay based on consonantal assonance) in determining semantic-sonant chiasmus, cf. Kselman, 'Semantic-Sonant', p. 220. A further control, not listed above since it only applies to very few long passages, is comparison with a parallel text (e.g. Ps. 18 // 2 Sam. 22).

131. See Y. Radday, 'Chiasmus in Biblical Hebrew Narrative', in Welch (ed.), *Chiasmus in Antiquity*, pp. 50-117.

132. Analysis into prelude + chiastic passage (e.g. Ps. 30—Lund, *Chiasmus in the New Testament*, pp. 119-20) or the reverse (see 2 Sam. 1.19-27, below) is not, therefore, discounted.

3. *Repetition* of single words (or their synonyms) is of more value than labelling of the order 'God's judgment' or 'Futility of idols'.[133] Traditional word-pairs[134] are also significant.
4. The *basis* on which the chiastic structure is posited *must be stated*, whether it is change of speaker, alteration of gender or content.

2.3.2. *Examples of Large-Scale Chiasmus*

The examples considered to exhibit chiasmus, discussed below, are Judg. 9.8-15, 2 Sam. 1.19-25a (+ 25a-27), Isa. 1.21-26, 28.15-18, Jer. 2.5-9, Hos. 12.3-6, Amos 9.1-4, Ps. 136.10-15, Job 32.6-10 and Qoh. 3.2-8. Mostly they have been culled from the work of other scholars (with some modifications) and not all are of equal merit. Some have been included to make the range as wide as possible, so that both Judges and Qoheleth are represented. Space forbids completeness (many more Psalms could have been analysed).

Jotham's Fable: Judges 9.8-15. This four-stanza poem[135] illustrates how gender chiasmus[136] can be combined with a refrain-like structure. The chiastic pattern is based on the genders of the trees named: the olive (m.), the fig (f.), the vine (also f.) and finally, the boxthorn (m.), in tandem with repetition of 'to anoint a king' in the opening and closing strophes (inclusio).

preamble

One day the trees went 9.8
to ANOINT A KING over themselves.

I

A (m.) They said to the OLIVE TREE
'Be KING over us'.
And the OLIVE TREE said to them 9
'Should I abandon my rich oil
by which both gods and men are honoured
to go and hold sway over the trees?'

133. On Chiasmus and Keywords, see section 5.

134. Useful are *RSP* I and II, supplemented by the corrective book reviews of J.C. de Moor and P. van der Lugt, 'The Spectre of Pan-Ugaritism', *BO* 31 (1974), pp. 3-26; S.E. Loewenstamm, 'Ugarit and the Bible. I', *Bib* 56 (1975), pp. 103-19.

135. See R.G. Boling, *Judges* (AB, 6A: Garden City, NY: Doubleday, 1975), p. 166.

136. Discussed above, section 2.2.8.

II
B (f.) And the trees said to the FIG-TREE 10
'You come and be QUEEN over us'.
But the FIG-TREE said to them 11
'Should I abandon my sweetness
and my lovely fruit
to go and hold sway over the trees?'

III
B' (f.) So the trees said to the VINE 12
'You come and be QUEEN over us'.
But the VINE said to them 13
'Should I leave my wine
which gives cheer to gods and men
to go and hold sway over the trees?'

IV
A' (m.) Then ALL the trees said to the BOXTHORN 14
'You come and be KING over us'.
And the BOXTHORN said to the trees 15
'If you really are going to ANOINT me KING
over you come for refuge under my shade;
but if not,
may fire proceed from the BOXTHORN
and consume the (very) cedars of Lebanon'.[137]

David's Lament: 2 Sam. 1.19-25a (+ 25b-7). The refrain was first recognized by Moulton,[138] the chiastic structure of the first part

137. Philological notes: 'One day the trees went', lit. 'the trees certainly walked'; 'come for refuge', lit 'come, shelter' (hendiadys); 'boxthorn', cf. Akk. *eddetu*, 'boxthorn', *CAD*, E, p. 23 (with discussion) and *atutu*, 'a thorny plant', *CAD*, A/II, p. 522. Not even the close study of this passage, R. Crüsemann, *Der Widerstand gegen das Königtum: Die antiköniglichen Texte des Alten Testaments und der Kampf um den frühenisraelitischen Staat* (WMANT, 49: Neukirchen–Vluyn: Neukirchener Verlag, 1978), pp. 19-32, has taken the differences of gender into account. Note that Crüsemann (*Der Widerstand*, p. 20 n. 9) rejects the meaning 'to hold sway over' in preference for 'to reel around' (*herumzutorkeln*).

138. R.G. Moulton, *The Literary Study of the Bible* (London, 1896; Boston: D.C. Heath, 1899), p. 158. See D.N. Freedman, 'The Refrain in David's Lament over Saul and Jonathan', in J. Bergman, K. Drynjeff, H. Ringgren (eds.), *Ex orbe religionum: Studia Geo Widengren... oblata...* (Studies in the History of Religions, 21; Leiden: Brill, 1972), I, pp. 115-26; reprinted in D.N. Freedman, *Pottery, Poetry and Prophecy: Studies in Early Hebrew Poetry* (Winona Lake, IN: Eisenbrauns, 1980), pp. 263-74.

(vv. 19-25a) by Shea[139] and the ABBA patterns in stanzas II and IV by Ceresko.[140] My translation is based on these and other studies,[141] with some divergences and slightly differing stichometry (especially in v. 22a, considered part of stanza II).

Refrain

The Gazelle of Israel 1.19
upon your hill-flanks slain:
truly the heroes have fallen

I

Give it not out in Gath, 20
proclaim it not in Ashkelon's streets,
in case the Philistine daughters should rejoice
in case the Uncircumcized's daughters should exult.

II

O mountains in Gilboa: 21
no dew
nor rain upon you
fields of the heights,
for there was defiled
the shield of heroes,
the shield of Saul—
anointed though he was with oil—

Refrain by the blood of the slain, 22
by the fat of heroes.

III

Jonathan's bow never turned back—
Saul's sword never returned empty!
Saul-and-Jonathan, 23
beloved-and-graceful
neither in their lives nor in their deaths
were they apart.
Swifter than eagles,
stronger than lions.

IV

Daughters of Israel 24
weep for Saul
who dressed you
in scarlet bejewelled,
who put gold ornaments
on your dresses.

139. W.H. Shea, 'David's Lament', *BASOR* 221 (1976), pp. 141-44.
140. Ceresko, 'Functions', pp. 4-5.

Refrain

Truly the heroes have fallen 25
in the thick of battle(-slaughter)
Jonathan
upon your hill-flanks slain.

V

Grievous 'tis to me on your account, 26
my brother Jonathan,
delightful were you to me greatly,
marvellous you were;
to me, loving you was
more than love for women.

Refrain

Truly, fallen have the heroes 27a
(their) war weapons destroyed.[142]

The main chiastic pattern affects the first four stanzas and the refrains: (R stands for refrain)

R				
I	—	A:	Foreign women	(f.)
II	—	B:	Death of Saul and his men	(m.)
R				
III	—	B:	Jonathan and Saul	(m.)
IV	—	A:	Israelite women	(f.)
R				

It is based on gender (f.m.m.f.) and contrasts negative (I and II) with positive (III and IV, expressed negatively). No strophic chiasmus is present but there are chiastic patterns in II and IV. II is a double ABBA tetracolon followed by a mini-refrain (v. 22a, echoing elements from the main refrains, chiefly the word-pair 'slain // heroes') which is the very centre of the main poem. The pattern is ABBAA'B'B'A'R. And, this very stanza (II) forms the core of the

141. S. Gevirtz, *Patterns in the Early Poetry of Israel* (SAOC, 32: Chicago: University of Chicago Press, 1963), pp. 77-82; W.L. Holladay, 'Form and Word-Play in David's Lament over Saul and Jonathan', *VT* 20 (1970), pp. 153-89.

142. The repeated word-pair *ḥll // gbr* ('slain // heroes') which occurs throughout the poem, always refers to Saul, Jonathan and their fellow soldiers. Accordingly, it cannot denote the enemy in v. 22a—as commonly if not universally accepted—but refers instead to the land being ritually defiled by the shedding of Israelite blood. Neither rain nor dew is to wash it away since it has not yet been avenged.

whole lament. In IV the chiastic sequence (again ABBA) brings the main part of the poem to a close.[143]

The Faithful City: Isaiah 1.21-26. The chiastic arrangement adopted here was proposed by Lack[144] and, while the overall pattern is evident, it is not exact in a mathematical way, being based on content. The turning-point of the poem comes at E and in the lines which follow the reversal of the city's present condition is described, expressed neatly by the inverted sequence DCBA. Inclusio, too, is present.

A How she has become a whore, 1.21
the *faithful city*.
B Replete with justice,
right lodged in her;
but now, murderers!
C Your silver has turned base, 22
your liquor, cut with water.
D Your rulers, rebels, 23
thick with thieves.
Each a lover of bribes,
running after gifts.
No orphan they judge,
the widow's case never comes up before them.
E Accordingly, 24
—utterance of the Lord, General Yahweh, Bull of Israel
D I'll certainly gain respite from my foes,
take vengeance on my enemies.
C Again will my hand be upon you 25
I will refine, like potash, your base-metal
and I'll purge away all your impurities.
B I will restore your judges as before,
and your counsellors as of yore. 26
A Only then will you be called
'Right(-living) town,
faithful city'.

143. For the interlocking refrains, see Freedman, 'The Refrain', p. 120.

144. R. Lack, *La symbolisme du livre d'Isaïe: Essai sur l'image littéraire comme élément de structuration* (AnBib, 59; Rome: Pontifical Biblical Institute, 1973), pp. 164-71.

Undoing the Deal with Death: Isaiah 28.15-18. The chiastic pattern, already known to Lund,[145] is evident as is its function: to express the reversal of existing conditions. The people of Yahweh are to trust in him, not in death. As with the previous poem the chiasmus is based on content, but there is a certain amount of repetition too (italicized). It is difficult to determine whether v. 19 belongs to the passage; it seems to form a connecting link with vv. 20-22.

(For you say)
A We cut a *covenant with Death*, 28.15
and with *Sheol* we made a *pact*.[146]
The flood-lash, when it passes,
will not reach us.[147]
B For we have made *Lie* our *refuge*,
and in Deceit we are *concealed*.
(Accordingly, this is what Yahweh says) 16
C See, I have laid a foundation-stone in Zion,
a granite stone,
a weighty corner-foundation,
laid by the Expert who does not rush.[148]
C And I will set Rectitude the line, 17
and Justice the plummet.[149]
B Away will hail sweep *Lie's refuge*,
Concealment, waters will flood.
A And annulled will be your *covenant with Death*,[150] 18
and your *agreement* with *Sheol* will not stand.
The flood-lash, when it passes,
you will be its base.

145. Lund, *Chiasmus in the New Testament*, p. 45; see, too, Irwin, *Isaiah 28–33*, pp. 26-33.

146. Lit. 'we pressed the breast', an idiom used in Akkadian to mean 'to make an agreement'; for details, see above, p. 212.

147. See Irwin, *Isaiah 28–33*, pp. 27-28 (following Gese).

148. A different analysis is proposed by Irwin, *Isaiah 28–33*, pp. 30-32.

149. S. Gevirtz, 'The Issachar Oracle in the Testament of Jacob', *EI* 12 (1975), p. 111* noted the matching of genders in v. 17a.

150. For *ḥāzût*, 'covenant', see M. Weinfeld, 'Covenant Terminology in the Ancient Near East and its Influences on the West', *JAOS* 93 (1973), pp. 190-99, 197 n. 101. In v. 15 the chiastic pattern 'covenant Death Sheol treaty' is combined with the gender pattern f. + m. // f. + m. In v. 18, however, both these patterns are flouted which expresses how Israel's pact with Hell is to be annulled.

Yahweh Spurned: Jeremiah 2.5-9. The overall pattern results both from content and from repeated keywords and catchphrases.[151] 'Never saying "Where is Yahweh"' recurs in C and C'; 'land' (repeated four times in D) is the keyword of the central section (D, E, D') and 'fathers' (A) corresponds to 'grandchildren' (A'). Finally, in both B and B' there is wordplay on the name 'Baal', in the expressions *lo' yô'ilû*, 'non-profitmaking' and *b^{e}lo' yô'il*, 'for what makes no profit'.[152]

This Yahweh has said: 2.5
A What did your FATHERS find wrong with me,
to keep their distance from me?
B Chasing 'Delusion' and being deluded.
C *Never saying:* 6
'Where is Yahweh'[153]
D who brought us from the LAND, Egypt
steered us through the desert 7
through the LAND of steppe and chasm,
through the LAND both hot and dark,
through the LAND no-one crosses,
where no man lives.
E I BROUGHT YOU TO AN ORCHARD LAND, TO EAT ITS LOVELY FRUIT
D' But, on arrival you fouled my LAND.
my bequest you made disgusting.
C' The priests *never said*: 8
'Where is Yahweh?'
Law-experts did not know me,
pastors rebelled against me;
B' prophets prophesied by Baal,
and after 'no go(o)ds' ran.
A' So, my case against you rests, 9
Yahweh's word,
against your GRANDCHILDREN is my case.

151. See, too, J.R. Lundbom, *Jeremiah: A Study in Ancient Hebrew Rhetoric* (SBLDS, 18; Missoula, MT: Scholars Press, 1975), pp. 70-74 who bases his division on the speakers A(5), Yahweh; B(6-7a), fathers; C(7b), Yahweh; B'(8), priests (fathers) and A'(9), Yahweh.

152. Following J. Bright, *Jeremiah* (AB, 21; Garden City, NY: Doubleday, 1965), p. 15.

153. Again an allusion to 'Where is Mightiest Baal?' of the Ugaritic texts; see above section 2.2.6.

The central line, probably a monocolon, is both the main thrust of the poem and its turning-point.

Yahweh's Lawsuit: Hosea 12.3-6. Holladay has shown, by reference to Gen. 32.20, 35.15 and especially 33.4 (which explains Hos. 12.4-5, Jacob's rivalry with Esau) that this poem is a unit, concentric in pattern.[154] The eleven-line stanza[155] can be set out as follows:

A	A lawsuit: Yahweh's with Israel	12.3
B	Truly he punishes Jacob for his ways,	
C	according to his actions, he repays him.	
D	In the womb he 'jackbooted' his brother (= Esau),	4
E	and in manhood he 'struggled-with-God',	
E	he 'struggled-with(-God)' and won,	5
D	weeping he found favour with him (= Esau).	
C	At Beth-El, He finds him (= Jacob),	
B	and there he spoke with him	
A	Yahweh, God of the Armies	6
	Yahweh is his Name	

Strictly speaking, only the central portion (DEED) is totally concentric; the general scheme is chiastic in a broad sense. The second two lines of v. 3 show inner chiasmus, the central cola (EE) are connected by anadiplosis and the final couplet exhibits incremental repetition.[156] But Coote rejects Holladay's analysis as 'implausibly neat' and also because 'it neglects the significance of Bethel and other wordplays in the chapter'.[157] This example has been included to show that the issue can be controversial and that there is room for scepticism.

154. W.L. Holladay, 'Chiasmus. The Key to Hosea XII 3-6', *VT* 16 (1966), pp. 53-64; cf. H.L. Ginsberg, 'Hosea's Ephraim More Fool than Knave. A New interpretation of Hosea 12:1-14', *JBL* 80 (1961), pp. 339-47; R.B. Coote, 'Hosea XII', *VT* 21 (1971), pp. 389-402; P. Ackroyd, 'Hosea and Jacob', *VT* 13 (1963), pp. 245-59; E.M. Good, 'Hosea and the Jacob Tradition', *VT* 16 (1966), pp. 137-51; M. Gertner, 'The Masorah and the Levites. An Essay in the History of a Concept', *VT* 10 (1960), pp. 241-84.

155. On the significance of the 11-line 'semi-acrostic' stanza, cf. D.L. Christensen, 'The Acrostic of Nahum Reconsidered', *ZAW* 87 (1975), pp. 17-30, 24; P. Auffret, 'Note sur la structure littéraire du Psaume CXXXVI', *VT* 27 (1977), pp. 1-12, 11-12.

156. The translations 'jackbooted' and 'struggled-with-God' are attempts at mirroring the wordplays on 'Jacob' (cf. *'āqēb*, 'heel') and 'Israel'.

157. R.B. Coote, 'Hosea XII', *VT* 21 (1971), pp. 389-402, p. 393 n. 2.

No Escape: Amos 9.1-4. Originally identified by Lund,[158] the pattern suggested by him has here been modified.

A Smite the capital, 9.1b
make the door-post vibrate
in pieces on top of them all.
B Their posterity *by the sword I'll kill*:
no fugitive shall flee,
no survivor survive.
C If they dig down to Sheol 2
there my hand will seize them.
D And if they rise to the sky,
from there I'll bring them down.
D' And if they hide atop (Mt) Carmel, 3
from there, having searched, I'll seize them.
C' And if they hide from my EYES in the sea-deep,
there will I COMMAND the sea-snake to bite them.
A'B' And if their enemies march them into captivity 4
there will I COMMAND *the sword to kill them*,
and I'll fix my EYES on them
with evil, not good intent

The central section (vv. 2-3) is pure chiasmus with the CDD'C'-pattern (depths, heights, heights, depths) forming the nucleus for the rest of the poem. It interlocks with the closing stanza by use of the repeated words: EYES, COMMAND, COMMAND, EYES, and combines with the opening lines to form an inclusio (words in italics). The final four lines deviate slightly from a consistent chiastic pattern.

A Litany: Psalm 136.10-15. A significant study of this psalm appeared recently and is followed here.[159] The repeated refrain makes this six-line stanza (in reality 3 + 3, see presently) into a unit twice that length,

A To the smiter, in Egypt, of their firstborn 136.10
Truly eternal is his kindness
B Bringing Israel from their midst, 11
Truly eternal is his kindness,
A' With powerful hand and extended arm 12
Truly eternal is his kindness,

158. Lund, *Chiasmus in the New Testament*, pp. 86-87.

159. P. Auffret, 'Note sur la structure littéraire du Psaume CXXXVI', *VT* 27 (1977), pp. 1-12, esp. 4; see also the diagram p. 6 and the overall plan of the psalm, p. 9.

A'	To the parter of the Red Sea into two parts, Truly eternal is his kindness,	13
B	Helper-across of Israel through its midst, Truly eternal is his kindness	14
A	Shaking off Pharaoh and his army in the Reed Sea Truly eternal is his kindness.	15

Both groupings (vv. 10-12 and 13-15) are chiastic, and at the same time, the two halves belong together. A, *Egypt smitten*, corresponds to A (v. 15), pursuing *Pharaoh drowned*. Both the B couplets describe Israel's deliverance, while A'A' form the centre: Yahweh exerting his power over the elements. Not only does the vocabulary match ('Egypt and firstborn'—'Egypt and army'; 'Israel'—'Israel'; 'midst'—'midst') but the constructions too:

10	'to' + participle...	('Egypt, firstborn')
11	'and' + causative	('Israel, midst')
12		
13	'to' + participle...	
14	'and' + causative	('Israel, midst')
15		('Pharaoh, army')[160]

The pattern is varied by v. 12 which, though not mathematically central, functions as a hinge, and by the double envelope structure in vv. 13 and 15 ('parter'—'Reed Sea'—'parts'—'Reed Sea').

Elihu's Disclaimer: Job 32.6-10. First noticed by Ceresko on the basis of repeated words,[161] these chiastic lines form Elihu's own preamble to his speech. Considering the length of Elihu's contribution to the debate (32.11–37.24) it is not surprising that he used chiasmus to solicit his listener's attention.[162]

Young am I in days 32.6b
but you are aged[163]
so I was terribly afraid[164]
of DECLARING my INSIGHT to you.

160. Structural studies of this kind provide a good control for the presence of chiasmus.

161. Ceresko, 'A : B : : B : A Word Pattern', p. 85: 'an interesting variant on the A : B : B : A pattern. Its configuration can be represented as A : B : C-D-E : : C-D-E : B : A'.

162. Note the prose introduction, 32.1-5.

163. As is often the case, the opening bicolon is pivot-patterned.

164. Hendiadys, lit. 'I recoiled and was afraid'.

I SAID:[165] Let days speak out, 7
MANY years teach WISDOM;
but it is the spirit in a man,
the breath of Shadday giving them UNDERSTANDING. 8
It is not the MANY(-yeared)[166] who are WISE, 9
or elders who UNDERSTAND correctly.
So I SAY: Listen to me, 10
DECLARE my INSIGHT can I, too.

In Season: Qoheleth 3.2-8. The merit for seeing the complex chiastic arrangement in these seventeen lines is Loader's.[167] He set out its components as either 'favorable' or 'unfavorable' and his analysis is followed here in the main, the symbols (+) and (–) being used instead. Apart from v. 5 the translation presents no obstacles.

To everything, a season, 3.1
and a time for every matter
under the sun.
A time for birth and a time for death + – A 2
A time to plant and a time to uproot plants + –

A time to kill and a time to heal – + B 3
A time to demolish and a time to rebuild – +
A time for weeping and a time for laughing – + 4
A time for mourning and a time for dancing – +

A time for throwing stones away and
  a time for gathering stones 5
A time for embracing and a time to leave off embracing + – B'
A time for seeking and a time for losing + – 6
A time for keeping and a time for rejecting + –

A time for ripping and a time for sewing up – + A' 7
A time for whispering and a time for speaking (up) – +

A time for loving and a time for hating + – C 8
A time for war and a time for peace – +

165. Better 'I thought', but the translation 'I said' preserves the repetition of the verb *'āmar*.

166. On *rabbîm* 'aged', see Dahood, *Psalms*, III, p. 110 and Pope, *Job*, pp. 212-13.

167. J.A. Loader, 'Qohelet 3 2-8—A "Sonnet" in the Old Testament', *ZAW* 81 (1969), pp. 240-42.

The patterns of (+) and (–) suggest an overall chiastic pattern as set out in the second column: A (+ – twice), B (– + four times), B' (+ – four times) A' (– + twice) and a closing chiastic bicolon (C).[168]

2.3.3. *Evaluation*

The examples set out above showing chiasmus over longer passages make it clear that a great deal of variety is possible and that the term 'chiastic' can be interpreted in quite different ways. This does not rule out strictly chiastic passages, listed in the index already referred to. From that list an almost random selection of texts can be mentioned: Isa. 2.6-22; 16.6-12; 29.1-3; 51.1-11;[169] Jer. 5.1-8; 50.2-46;[170] Hos. 8.9-13; Pss. 7.13-17; 15; 29;[171] 30; 51.1-11,[172] 58; 59; 72;[173] 95.1-7c;[174] 105.1-11;[175] 137;[176] 139;[177] Prov. 30.1-4, and Lam. 2.1-22. Most of these texts have been studied very recently. Certain passages, notably Psalm 68,[178] are too uncertain for inclusion; others

168. Positive and negative components are also operative in 2 Sam. 1.19-27 (see above). The chiastic pattern suggests (+ –) for v. 5. Loader considers v. 5 to refer to sexual intercourse and v. 7 to silence during mourning, the thought of the whole 'sonnet' being 'life—death—end—beginning'. Alternatively, v. 5 could denote preparing a field for planting ('to throw stones away', cf. Isa. 5.2) and the building of a cairn for burial ('to collect stones') but until the allusion is known, no certainty is possible.

169. F. Holmgren, 'Chiastic Structure in Isaiah LI, 1-11', *VT* 19 (1969), pp. 196-201. However, there is some doubt about the meaning of *'argi*[a]*'* in v. 5 and with the overall stanza-division.

170. M. Kessler, 'Rhetoric in Jeremiah 50 and 51', *Semitics* 3 (1973), pp. 18-35, 31-35.

171. D.N. Freedman and C.F. Hyland, 'Psalm 29: A Structural Analysis', *HTR* 66 (1975), pp. 237-56.

172. Ceresko, 'Function', p. 6; but he ignores repetition of the root *ḥṭ'* in vv. 4b, 7b, 9a and 11a.

173. Kselman, 'Psalm 72', pp. 77-81.

174. C.B. Riding, 'Psalm 95 1-7c as a Large Chiasm', *ZAW* 88 (1976), p. 418.

175. Ceresko, 'Function', pp. 2-3.

176. D.N. Freedman, 'The Structure of Psalm 137', in H. Goedicke (ed.), *Near Eastern Studies in Honor of William Foxwell Albright* (Baltimore: The Johns Hopkins University Press, 1971), pp. 188, 203-204. But see now C. Kellerman, 'Psalm 137', *ZAW* 90 (1978), pp. 43-58, and P. Auffret, 'Essai sur la structure littéraire du Psaume 137', *ZAW* 92 (1980), pp. 346-77.

177. J. Holman, 'The Structure of Psalm CXXXIX', *VT* 21 (1971), pp. 298-310.

178. For the latest attempt at translation of this difficult Psalm, see J. Gray, 'A

have been analysed along structural lines and are definitely not chiastic;[179] Psalm 67 and Prov. 1.20-33 have been set out below.

2.3.4. *Editorial Chiasmus*

Editors have also used chiastic patterning when compiling books (and portions of books) of the OT. Walker and Lund showed this to be the case in Habbakuk,[180] and Lack has examined Isaiah along similar lines.[181] For example, according to Lack, Isaiah 56–66 has the following pattern: A (56–58), B (59.1-14), C (59.15-21), D (60–62), C' (63.7–64.11), A' (65–66).[182]

Again some books have an overall ABA' pattern, for example Job.

A:	prose	1–2
B:	poetry	3.1–42.6
A:	prose	42.7-17[183]

As already stated, chiasmus at this level has not been discussed and has been mentioned here only for the sake of completeness of treatment.

2.4. *The Functions of Chiasmus in Poetry*

To isolate a particular chiastic pattern in a particular poem is largely a preliminary. The next step is to see how the element in question articulates with the rest of the poem (or structures the whole poem, or even set of poems) and especially to determine what function it fulfils. Here the term 'function' is being used rather broadly to mean the purpose the poet had in mind. Why did he employ a chiastic pattern at this point in the poem? What effect is it intended to have? This section, accordingly, is an attempt at answering such questions, hoping to

Cantata of the Autumn Festival: Psalm lxviii', *JSS* 22 (1977), pp. 2-26. Cf. M.H. Lichtenstein, 'Psalm 68:7 Revisited', *JANESCU* 4 (1972), pp. 97-112, and J.C. de Moor, *The Rise of Yahwism: The Roots of Israelite Monotheism* (BETL, 91: Leuven: Leuven University Press/Uitgeverij Peeters, 1990), pp. 118-28.

179. For instance, see Auffret, *The Literary Structure of Psalm 2.*

180. A. Walker and N. Lund, 'The Literary Structure of the Book of Habakkuk', *JBL* 53 (1934), pp. 355-70. The three sections comprise I: A (1.1-4), B (1.5-11), C (1.5-11), C (1.12-13) B' (1.14-17), A' (2.1-5)—II: K (2.6-8), L (2.9-13), K' (2.14-17), L' (2.15-20)—I': A (3.2), B (3.3-7), C (3.8-10a), B' (3.10b-15), A' (3.16-19).

181. Lack, *La symbolique du livre d'Isaïe, passim.*

182. Lack, *La symbolique du livre d'Isaïe*, p. 125 and the table, p. 128.

183. See Welch, 'Chiasmus in Ugaritic', p. 427 (citing Gordon).

encourage both student and scholar in the quest for better answers.[184]

Broadly speaking, the general function of chiasmus is to break the monotony of persistent direct parallelism.[185] More specifically, chiastic patterns fall into two main classes: *structural* and *expressive*. Structural chiastic patterns contribute to the overall form of a poem (see section 2.3), often providing a key to the poet's plan. 'Expressive chiasmus' is a rather vague term adopted to cover what is in effect non-structural chiasmus, where the device has been used to achieve a certain effect or to heighten an effect already present in the meaning of the words. The table set out here (Table 5) shows the subdivisions within these two broad categories and is at the same time an outline of the ensuing paragraphs.

1. *STRUCTURAL FUNCTIONS* (2.4.1)	
(a)	to open a stanza or poem
(b)	to close a stanza or poem
(c)	to link components of a poem
(d)	to indicate the midpoint of a poem
2. *EXPRESSIVE FUNCTIONS* (2.4.2)	
To express	
(a)	merismus
(b)	reversal of existing state
(c)	emphatic negation or prohibition
(d)	strong contrast or antithesis
(e)	other functions

Table 5. *Functions of Chiasmus*

2.4.1. *Structural Functions*

a. *To Open a Stanza or Poem*. The first of the structural functions is quite straightforward: a chiastically-patterned strophe often serves to begin a stretch of poetry:

Num. 23.7[186] *From Aram* I was fetched by Balaq
(By) the King of Moab *from the Eastern Ridges*

184. See the works by Andersen and Ceresko referred to on p. 329 n. 55.

185. According to Holladay, 'Recovery', p. 409 chiasmus is 'used to vary the steady drumbeat of the normal pattern'.

186. In translation the passive has been used (rather than 'he brought me') in order to bring out the pattern. Balaam seems to be putting the responsibility for his utterances on the Moabite king whose name and title form the central part of this introductory bicolon.

Also: Isa. 32.3; Jer. 14.2; 20.14; Nah. 1.2; 3.1; Hab. 2.1; Pss. 5.2; 19.2; 34.2; 51.3; 92.2; 138.1; 139.1; Job 4.17; 26.5; 29.2.

b. *To Close a Stanza or Poem*. Akin to function (a) is the use of chiasmus to bring a section of poetry to a neat end (see function d).

Job 30.31 Turned to mourning has my lyre,
and my flute to weepers' voices

And Isa. 5.11; 14.20-21; 30.2; 32.6c; 51.11b; Jer. 8.8-9; Amos 5.14-15a; Pss. 1.6; 29.11; 105.45; Cant. 1.11; Lam. 1.22; Qoh. 12.18.[187]

c. *To Link Components of a Poem*. At the level of a complete poem, chiasmus acts as a structuring link throughout (see section 2.3 for examples). Even at the level of the strophe it is evident that a chiastic arrangement welds its components together:

Nah. 1.2[188] A jealous god and an avenger is Yahweh,
An avenger is Yahweh and a wrathful Lord

d. *To Indicate the Midpoint of a Poem*. The midpoint is either the hinge or turning-point in a poem, or its climax. The central strophe may be chiastic, as for example Jer. 2.27b-28a[189] or it may be non-chiastic, but come at the very centre of a chiastic pattern, for example Prov. 1.26-27 (see below).[190]

2.4.2. *Expressive Functions*

a. *To Express Merismus*. Merismus is the expression of totality by the mention of representative parts of that totality. A very common way of expressing merismus is to use a polar word-pair[191] but it is by no

187. See section 2.3.4 for poetry as opening and closing complete books.

188. Present, too, is the terrace pattern; see below, section 2.5.1.

189. Centre of Jer. 2.2-3, 24; cf. W.L. Holladay, *The Architecture of Jeremiah 1–20* (Lewisburg: Bucknell University Press, 1976), p. 32 (courtesy of Smith who also lists Ps. 141.5, Lam. 1.11-12, Prov. 31.19-20 etc.). For Ps. 29.6 see D.N. Freedman and C.F. Hyland, 'Psalm 29: A Structural Analysis', *HTR* 99 (1975), p. 242; Ps. 72.9-11, Kselman, 'Psalm 72', pp. 77-81; Ps. 137.4-6, Freedman, 'Structure', pp. 193-96.

190. Smith lists 1 Sam. 2.1-10, 2 Sam. 22.1-51 // Ps. 18, Lam. 2, 3, 4, 5, as well as Isa. 2.6a-22, 60.1-3 etc.

191. See J. Krašovec, *Der Merismus im Biblisch-Hebräisch und Nordwestsemitischen* (BibOr, 33; Rome: Pontifical Biblical Institute, 1977).

means the only way, as will be shown. In Ezek. 32.13 God has threatened to wipe out all the cattle of Egypt, and adds (with reference to its rivers):

> No longer shall they be churned up by *human feet*,
> *Cattle-hooves* shall not churn them up

Or, with reference to the stars:

> Isa. 40.26b He who led out by numbers *their host*,
> *All of them* called by name

the clue being the use of *kol*, 'all' (as is often the case). Also, Isa. 10.4a; 11.4b; 13.16; 18.6b; 30.14; 42.4; Jer. 2.9; 6.7; Ezek. 17.23; Nah. 1.8; 3.1; Hab. 3.3; Pss. 12.9; 19.2; 20.5; 22.13; 34.2; 38.10; 57.6; 72.11; 83.12; 92.3; 105.44; 145.2, 10, 20; 147.4; Job 7.18; 12.10, 14; 31.4; 37.3; 39.8; Prov. 21.7; Qoh. 2.10; 3.1.

b. *To Express Reversal of Existing State*. Under this heading comes a comparatively large number of examples which perhaps indicates that further subdivisions of function is necessary. The chiastic pattern is used to emphasize the meaning of the words: that a drastic change is either imminent or has already taken place. So, in Zeph. 3.19 Yahweh promises that times will change for the better:

> I will rescue *the lost*
> And *the dispersed* I will gather.

As part of a theophany Mic. 1.4a describes how nature will be affected by Yahweh's appearance:

> Dissolve will the mountains beneath him,
> The valleys will be torn apart.

See Isa. 1.18bc; 5.20-21; 6.7b; 11.1, 4b, 6, 8, 13; 13.10b, 16, 21b; 14.25, 30; 26.19a; 29.17; 30.22; 32.6c; 40.3; 42.4, 12, 15a; 43.18; 48.21b; 49.13b, 14, 18; 59.3; 60.13b; Ezek. 17.4b; Mic. 4.6, 7, 16b; Mal. 3.24a; Pss. 38.8; 46.10b; 76.3; 81.7; 145.2; 147.4; Job 11.4; 17.7; 19.9, 14; 28.2; 34.6; 36.12; 39.6; Prov. 2.2; 3.10; Cant. 1.6.

c. *For Emphatic Negation or Prohibition*. This heading covers negation of three kinds: simple negation, denial and prohibition. The particles *lo'* or *'al* (as expected) are usually present. Simple negation is evident in the following:

Isa. 27.11b[192] Therefore, *no* mercy will be shown them by their Maker,
Their Moulder will show them *no* favour

An example of denial is

Ps. 101.7 *Never* shall dwell within my house an agent of deceit,
A liar shall *never* remain before my eyes

Similarly, v. 3 and Pss. 9.19; 26.4-5; 37.19; 132.4 (= oath), Job 20.9, 20; 21.9; 32.14; Lam. 3.22. Chiasmus is more commonly used for straightforward prohibitions, mostly in wisdom literature, for example

Prov. 25.6 *Do not* put yourself forward in the king's presence
And, in high places, *do not* take your seat

Also Jer. 6.25; Ps. 74.19; Job 3.6; Prov. 23.10; Qoh. 7.5, 10; 11.8.[193]

d. *To Heighten Antithesis or Contrast*. A chiastic pattern helps emphasize antithesis[194] and is particularly frequent in Proverbs, for example

Prov. 13.25 The just man eats to sate his appetite,
But the belly of the wicked is empty

and 10.3, 4, 12; 12.20; 13.24; 14.4 and so on. Also, Pss. 37.19; 38.8; 78.33; 89.7; 145.20; Job 10.5; 11.14; 13.12; 34.6; Qoh. 10.10.

e. *Other Functions*. Finally, a group of rather mixed functions for which perhaps only one representative text can be provided.

To express reciprocity: Ps. 25.3, Zech. 13.9b and Cant. 6.3:

I am my beloved's
and my beloved is mine.

To express 'poetic justice':[195] Jer. 2.19a, 27b-28a, Pss. 9.16, 18.21, 25, 25.3 and 7.16-17:[196]

192. Also Pss. 71.9, 89.34.

193. See, too, Andersen, *Sentence*, p. 135 on Gen. 37.22.

194. Accordingly, Andersen's claim (brought to my notice by Smith) that antithesis is lessened by chiasmus does not apply to poetry; for details, see Andersen, *Sentence*, pp. 73, 121-22, 159-60.

195. M. Lichtenstein, 'The Poetry of Poetic Justice', *JANESCU* 5 (1973), pp. 255-65.

196. Translation: Dahood, *Psalms*, I, pp. 41 and 47.

A pit he dug, but it pitted him,
and he fell into the hole he made;
his mischief recoiled upon his head,
and upon his skull his malice redounded.

As mere emphasis: Jer. 1.4-19, 4.5a, 6.1-7, Ps. 89.3-5[197] and Cant. 1.2-3:

Truly, *sweeter* is your love than wine,
than perfume is your fragrance *sweeter*.

To express a surprise event: Ps. 78.24 and Job 18.10:

Hidden in the ground is a rope for him,
and a trap for him on the path.

To express harmony: Isa. 11.4, Jer. 30.18b, Zeph. 3.19, Pss. 25.3, 72.7 and Isa. 62.1b:

Until out shines, like a light, her justice,
and her deliverance like a torch blazes.

To denote impossibility:[198] Isa. 40.12a, Jer. 5.12b, Job 4.17 and Isa. 40.27a:

Hidden is my way from Yahweh,
and by my God my rights are disregarded.

To express paradox: Qoh. 4.14:[199]

For from the womb even the *king* issued,
For, in spite of his *kingship*, he was born poor.

To express simultaneity: Job 17.7, 19.9, 26.5, 38.38 and Isa. 3.8:

For
stumble did Jerusalem,
and Judah fall.

197. Ceresko, 'Functions', pp. 6-9.

198. See below on rhetorical questions, section 2.5.2.

199. Translation: M.J. Dahood, 'Qoheleth and Northwest Semitic Philology', *Bib* 43 (1962), pp. 349-65, 356-57.

2.5. *Chiasmus and Other Poetic Devices*

Chiasmus is not always used in isolation and is often combined with other poetic devices,[200] an interrelationship which will be explored here. The devices in question can, broadly speaking, be divided into structural and non-structural.

2.5.1. *Chiasmus and Other Structural Devices*

The devices to be considered are anacrusis, ballast variant, the terrace pattern (anadiplosis), word-pairs, the list, the pivot pattern and key-words. Incremental repetition and the acrostic will be treated only briefly. The accompanying chart (Table 6) will help both for comparative purposes and as a convenient summary.

a	b	a		chiastic monocolon
x				anacrusis (2.5.1)
a	b	c		
c	b	a		
a	b	c		ballast variant (2.5.2)
c'	b'	d'		
a	b			terrace pattern (2.5.3)
	b	a		
		c	d	
a	b	p		pivot pattern
b'	a'			(bicolon with silent stress) (2.5.6)
a	b			incremental repetition
a	c			

Table 6. *Chiasmus and Related Patterns*

Chiasmus and Anacrusis. Anacrusis is the presence of an extra-metrical word (or words), generally at the beginning of a line.[201] Similarly, a word (or words) can stand outside the chiastic pattern:

Prov. 6.23 *For,*
a lamp is a command,
teaching is a light

200. I still prefer 'poetic devices' to 'rhetorical devices' because the term 'rhetorical' has negative overtones and because 'poetic' is a better description.

201. T.H. Robinson, 'Anacrusis in Hebrew Poetry', in P. Volz and F. Stummer (eds.), *Werden und Wesen des Alten Testaments* (BZAW, 66; Berlin: de Gruyter, 1936), pp. 37-40.

the pattern being x-ab // ba, x representing the extra-chiastic word *kî*. Also, with both chiasmus and anacrusis: Isa. 17.10; Amos 5.4-6; Pss. 67.5; 107.9, 11; Isa. 5.20, 21 (*hôy*, 'woe'); Hos. 4.4 (*'ak*, 'surely'); Ps. 9.19 (*kî lō'*, 'for not').

Chiasmus and Ballast Variant. In a parallel couplet or bicolon, an equivalent to a word in the first line is sometimes missing from the second. In compensation, the balance is maintained by a lengthening of one of the elements in the second colon. The longer element, called 'ballast variant' is also termed 'expletive' or 'filler' and is characteristic of oral poetry.[202] So in Prov. 5.16

> Should your springs overflow outside?
> In the square your *water-runnels*?

the lack of a verb in the second colon (i.e. *yapûṣû*) is balanced by the long expression *palgê-māyîm*, ballast variant to *ma'ynōtêkā*.[203] Similarly Judg. 5.19 ('kings // kings of Canaan'), Isa. 14.15 ('from upon them // from upon his shoulder'),[204] Ezek. 17.23 ('beneath it // in the shade of its boughs'), 32.4 ('on land // upon the surface of the ground'), Pss. 22.23 ('to my brothers // within the assembly'), 103.7 ('Moses // sons of Israel'), 145.2 ('I will bless you // I will praise your name'), Job 28.26 ('rain // thunderstorm'), 30.31 ('dirge // voice of weepers').[205]

Chiasmus and Terrace Pattern. In the terrace pattern the terminal part of one colon is repeated in the immediately following colon[206] and its use is perhaps one of the easiest ways of producing chiastic verse:

> Nah. 1.2 A jealous god *an avenger is Yahweh*,
> *An avenger is Yahweh* and a wrathful Lord

See too (repeated elements in parentheses): Isa. 29.17 ('Carmel'); Ezek. 22.2 ('you will judge'); Amos 4.7b ('upon one city').[207]

202. For the term 'expletive' and 'filler', see Austerlitz, *Ob-Ugric Metrics*, pp. 64-65, 101-103. See, too, *UT*, pp. 135-37.

203. Noted by W.A. van der Weiden, *Le livre des Proverbes: Notes philologiques* (BibOr, 23; Rome, Pontifical Biblical Institute, 1970), pp. 26, 56 n. 137.

204. Ceresko, 'Chiastic Word Pattern', p. 305.

205. The ballast variant can also be used to balance larger chiastic texts such as Jer. 5.1-8, Ps. 72.9-11 (courtesy Smith).

206. See Austerlitz, *Ob-Ugric Metrics*, p. 38.

207. Also Ps. 37.40, Job 17.15.

Chiasmus and Word-Pairs. Since chiasmus is a variation of parallelism[208] it is not surprising that word-pairs can belong to its structure. Without digressing into the topic of parallel pairs it is enough to point out that chiasmus exploits this device in characteristic ways. The most common is to *invert* the standard (AB) sequence,[209] a good example being Prov. 18.6-7 where the sequence of the word-pair 'mouth // lips' (first bicolon) is reversed in the second ('lips // mouth') resulting in an ABBA tetracolon:[210]

The LIPS of a fool lead to strife,
and his MOUTH for a beating cries out:
a fool's MOUTH is his ruin,
and his LIPS his own snare.

Chiasmus and the List. Although there are only a few examples of chiastically patterned lists, they deserve mention, since the list is a very elementary but effective literary form made even more striking when combined with chiasmus. By employing chiasmus in its central cola the catalogue of Gen. 8.22 becomes poetry:

While the earth lasts,
seedtime and harvest,
  cold and *heat*
  summer and *winter*,
day and night
shall never cease.

Also, Gen. 12.16 (cited above, 2.2.8); Isa. 5.20; Ezek. 34.4; Cant. 4.14[211] and Qoh. 3.2-8 (see section 2.3).

Chiasmus and the Pivot Pattern. As first recognized by Möller[212] some chiastic bicola have the form

208. Welch, 'Chiasmus in Ugaritic', p. 425.

209. The AB sequence is discussed by Boling, '"Synonymous" Parallelism in the Psalms', *JSS* 5 (1960), pp. 221-25.

210. For other examples, see above, section 2.2.3, also section 2.5.8 below.

211. J.C. Exum, 'A Literary and Structural Analysis of the Song of Songs', *ZAW* 85 (1973), p. 64; also, Jer. 51.20-23 (Smith).

212. H. Möller, 'Strophenbau der Psalmen', *ZAW* 50 (1932), pp. 240-56, 248-49; his example is Ps. 5.2. See, in general, Watson, *Classical Hebrew Poetry*, pp. 214-21.

a	b	p
b'	a'	

with the components of the first colon (a, b) repeated and reversed in the second (b', a'), the central element (p) appearing only once. For example Job 18.11

> Around (do) frighten him terrors,
> (Do) harry him at every step.

Also: Isa. 30.8a;[213] 33.17; 59.2; Jer. 4.2b; Ezek. 32.13b; Mic. 1.4a; Nah. 2.5; Pss. 67.7-8; 72.1-2; 75.3; 102.20; 119.149, 166, 174; Job 21.30; 32.6; 38.38, Prov. 15.25.

Chiasmus and Keywords. A keyword is one which occurs several times in a passage and contributes to its meaning.[214] To determine which are the keywords in a text the first step is to tabulate all the repeated words.[215] From such tables it is possible to see whether the words have been arranged chiastically, bearing in mind that synonyms or antonyms can be significant as well. An example of this last point is Ps. 12.4-5 where the synonyms 'Yahweh' and 'Master' amount to variants of the same keyword since they are equivalent in function (see above, section 2.2.6.). One of the first passages to be successfully examined in this way was Lamentations 1,[216] but as a concrete illustration of a rather neglected aspect of chiasmus Prov. 1.20-33 has been chosen.[217] It will be examined in detail.

The chiastic arrangement of the poem was clearly demonstrated by Trible.[218] The tabulation of keywords drawn up here provides

213. W.G.E. Watson, review of W.H. Irwin, *Isaiah 28–33: Translation with Philological Notes*, *Bib* 56 (1975), pp. 275-76.

214. J. Liebreich, 'Psalms 34 and 145', pp. 181-92. Also, R.I. Alden, 'Chiastic Psalms (II): A Study of the Mechanics of Semitic Poetry in Psalms 51–100', *JETS* 19, (1976), pp. 191-200; Ceresko, 'Functions', pp. 1-10.

215. As explained by J. Magne, 'Répétition de mots et exégèse dans quelques Psaumes et le Pater', *Bib* 39 (1958), pp. 177-97.

216. A. Condamin, 'Symmetrical Repetitions in *Lamentations* Chapters I and II', *JTS* 7 (1906), pp. 137-40.

217. On Ps. 139, see Holman, 'The Structure of Psalm CXXXIX', p. 308; on Jer. 2.5-9, 2.33-37, 5.1-8, 8.13-17, 8.18-21 etc., cf. Lundbom, *Jeremiah*, pp. 70-96.

218. P. Trible, 'Wisdom Builds a Poem. The Architecture of Proverbs 1:20-33', *JBL* 94 (1975), pp. 509-18.

A	20a									*(b)*				
	b									*(b)*				
	21a	*(qr')*								*(b)*				
	b									*(b)*				
	c									*(b)*				
B	22a		*pty*											
	b													
	c			*ksl*										
	23a				*šûb*	*(ykḥ)*								
C	23b													
	c													
	d													
D	24a	*qr'*												
	b													
	25a					*'śh*		*kl*						
	b				*ykḥ*		*'bh*		*l'*					
E	26a									*b*	*'êd*			
	b									*b*		*bô'*	*pḥd*	
	27a									*b*		*bô'*	*pḥd*	*k*
	b										*'êd*			*k*
	c									*b*		*bô'*		
D	28a	*qr'*							*l'*					
	b								*l'*					
	29a													
	b								*l'*					
	30a					*'śh*	*'bh*		*l'*					
	b				*ykḥ*			*kl*						
C'	31a													
	b													
B'	32a		*pty*		*šûb*									
	b			*ksl*										
A'	33a													
	b													
	c												*(pḥd)*	

Table 7. *Chiastic Keywords in Prov. 1.20-33*

independent confirmation of Trible's findings, since she made no mention at all of keywords. The overall pattern can be seen at a glance and the heavy clustering in E (vv. 26-27) shows it to be the most important section, as Trible had already proved. In addition, the keyword table provides certain refinements of analysis, notably the stanza-division between v. 23a and 23b (contrast Trible) since the verb *šûb* obviously belongs to both B and B'. Also, prepositions and particles form part of the chiastic pattern;[219] examples are *kol*, 'all', in D, D' and *lo'*, 'not' (also D, D'), repeated four times for emphasis. Finally, there is a tendency for such keywords to be echoed (denoted by parentheses), for example *qārā'*, 'to cry, call' (v. 21a), the preposition *b^{e}*, 'in', used five times in section A (see E) and the nouns 'reproof' (v. 23a) and 'dread' (v. 33c).

Proverbs 1.20-33[220]

A	20a	Wisdom, in the street, bawls,	
	b	In the squares she gives out her voice,	
	21a	From the top of the walls she CRIES,	P
	b	In the entrances to the gates,	Q
	c	In the city she says her say.	P'
B	22a	How long, FOOLS, will you love FOOLISHNESS?	
	b	Scoffers, in scoffing be pleased with yourselves?	
	c	SIMPLETONS, hate knowledge?	
	23a	(How long) will you TURN from my REPROOF?	
C	23b	See!	
	c	I will our out on you my spirit,	
	d	I will make known my words to you.	
D	24a	Because I CRIED (out), but you refused,	
	b	Stretched out my hand, but no one noticed.	
	25a	You have ignored ALL my COUNSEL,	
	b	And my REPROOF you did not WANT,	
E	26a	Aloud will I, at your CALAMITY, laugh,	S
	b	I will mock WHEN PANIC COMES TO YOU,	T
	27a	WHEN TO YOU, LIKE a storm, PANIC COMES	T'
	b	And your CALAMITY, LIKE a whirlwind arrives,	S'
	c	When to you come distress and anguish.	
D'	28a	Then will they CRY to me, but I'll not answer,	
	b	They'll look for me but will NOT find me,	
	29a	Since they hated knowledge,	
	b	But respect for Yahweh did NOT choose.	
	30a	They did NOT WANT my COUNSEL,	
	b	Despised ALL my REPROOF.	
C'	31a	They'll eat the fruit of their wages,	
	b	And with their own counsels be satisfied.	

219. As Magne had already demonstrated—see n. 215.

220. The keywords significant for the pattern are in capitals: two subsets of chiasmus have been marked: PQP' (v. 21) and STT'S' (vv. 26-27). The translation is a little stilted since the emphasis is on mirroring the word-order of the Hebrew.

B'	32a	For, by TURNING away the FOOLS are killed,
	b	And the complacence of SIMPLETONS destroys them.
A'	33a	Who listens to me
	b	Lives securely,
	c	At ease, not dreading evil.

Chiasmus also interacts with other structural devices such as the acrostic,[221] incremental repetition[222] and the refrain.[223]

2.5.2. *Chiasmus and Non-Structural Devices*

The topics to be examined here in connection with chiasmus are the 'break-up' of a standard phase, wordplay in its various forms, the simile, rhetorical questions, sound patterns, the broken construct chain and several minor devices.

Chiasmus and 'Break-up'. Related to the word-pair (perhaps as its origin) is the device now known as the break-up of a stereotype phrase.[224] In essence it involves splitting up the components of a set phrase and distributing them over parallel cola;[225] for example:

Ps. 80.16 Treat kindly[226] what your right hand (*y^{e}mînekā*) planted,
And the son (*ben*) you strengthened for yourself[227]

Here the stock expression 'Benjamin' (*binyāmîn*) which actually occurs in v. 3[228] has been split up, its constituents inverted and from

221. E.g. Nah. 1.4b, Ps. 38.3, 8, 10, 11, 13, 19, 20, 22 (non-alphabetic acrostic) and Ps. 145.

222. As in Ps. 29.8.

223. 2 Sam. 1.19-27; Pss. 76.4, 6; 80.4, 8, 15, 20; Cant. 2.14; 6.3.

224. As explained by E.Z. Melamed, 'Break-Up of Stereotype Phrases as an Artistic Device in Biblical Poetry', *Scripta Hierosolymitana* 8 (1961), pp. 115-53; G. Braulik, 'Aufbrechen von geprägten Wortverbindungen und Zusammenfassen von stereotypen Ausdrücken in der alttestamentliche Kunstprosa', *Semitics* 1 (1970), pp. 1-11; L. Viganò, 'Il fenomeno stilistico di Break-up di nomi divini nei testi di Ras Shamra-Ugarit', *RBI* 24 (1976), pp. 225-242; but contrast C.F. Whitley, 'Some Aspects of Hebrew Poetic Diction', *UF* 7 (1975), pp. 493-502, 493-99.

225. Possibly, therefore, the device belongs under the heading 'structural'.

226. Cognate with Akk. *kunnu*, 'to treat a person kindly' (*CAD*, K, pp. 540-42).

227. The construction with *'al* is difficult; for the last three words, see Dahood, *Psalms*, II, p. 260 who cites Ps. 89.22.

228. Recognition of the break-up precludes deletion of 'Benjamin' in v. 3.

them a chiastic bicolon constructed. Other examples: Isa. 48.7;[229] Pss. 69.34; 78.56;[230] Job 36.3.[231]

Chiasmus and Wordplay. Chiasmus also interacts with or exploits wordplay, mostly in the guise of paronomasia and rootplay.[232] There is chiastic paronomasia in

Gen. 49.4[233] When you ascended (*'ālîtā*) your father's bed,
Then you fouled the suckler's (*'ôlā*) couch

and in Jer. 30.16, Pss. 106.23-24 (*ḥᵃmātô*, 'his anger', and *ḥāmad*, 'to please'), 107.11 and Prov. 24.21-22. Occasionally the consonants of a word in the first colon are inverted to form another word in the second (rootplay) as in

Prov. 7.21 She led him by plenty of smooth-talk (*leqaḥ*)
By the smoothness (*ḥeleq*) of her lips she urged him

both words also being used chiastically. (See section 2.2.8. for other examples.) Syllepsis is used in combination with chiasmus in Isa. 58.10.

Chiasmus and Simile. Chiastic components sometimes comprise similes as in Hos. 4.16

For, *like a heifer*, wildly has Israel run:
Now pasture them, Yahweh, *like lambs in the wide meadow*

Also: 2 Sam. 23.4;[234] Mic. 1.4; Ps. 133.2-3;[235] Qoh. 15.2.

229. M.J. Dahood, 'The Chiastic Breakup in Isaiah 58,7', *Bib* 57 (1976), p. 105.

230. See Dahood, *Psalms*, II, pp. 165, 246.

231. M.J. Dahood, 'Chiasmus in Job: A Text-Critical and Philological Criterion', in H.N. Bream *et al.* (eds.), *A Light unto my Path: Old Testament Studies in Honor of Jacob M. Myers* (Philadelphia: Temple University Press, 1974), p. 126.

232. *Wordplay* and *pun* are generic terms. More specifically, *paronomasia* plays on similar-sounding words (e.g. Mic. 1.10), *rootplay* uses the etymological root of a noun or verb, and *syllepsis* is double meaning.

233. As translated by S. Gevirtz, 'The Reprimand of Reuben', *JBL* 30 (1971), pp. 97-98, who failed to notice the wordplay.

234. Three consecutive, chiastically arranged similes: T.D. Mettinger, 'Structure and Meaning in 2 Sam. 21:1-7', *SEÅ* 41-42 (1976–77), pp. 152-53.

235. See Chapter 8 below.

Chiasmus and Rhetorical Questions. Curiously, chiasmus is frequent in rhetorical questions, examples being Job 6.12, 38.16-17, 25, Prov. 30.4. Its function is to emphasize the inherent contradiction of such questions:

Job 10.5 Like a human's days: *your days*?
Your years like an adult's?

Note, too the chiastic arrangement of interrogative particles in

Jer. 23.23-4[236] (*ha-*) Am I a God at hand, says Yahweh,
and not a God far off?
(*'im*) Can a man hide himself in secret places
where I cannot see him? says Yahweh
(h^a-) The sky and the earth:
Do I not fill them? says Yahweh

Chiasmus and Sound Patterns. The sound patterns to be discussed are assonance, alliteration and rhyme. Of course the three components cannot be clinically isolated, but one or the other does tend to be predominant in a particular verse. To begin with assonance: it can be heard strongly in the central chiastic cola of Hos. 7.7

All of them (*kullām*) are hot as an oven,
they consume (*w^e'āk^elû*) their rulers,
all their kings (*kol-malkêhem*) have fallen,
None among them calls to me,

with echo-assonance in the first line. Further: Jer. 5.25; 30.16; Pss. 20.5; 72.11; Job 21.9; Prov. 2.2, 8; 21.17. Chiastic alliteration, instead, is present in both Cant. 1.6(*s*) and Job 31.16:[237]

If I refused (*'im 'emna'*) any want of the needy,
Or the eyes of the widow made pine (*'almānâ'^a kallê*)

Rhyme with chiasmus is very rare, sample texts being Isa. 3.8a (*kaš^elâ—y^ehûdâ*), 51.7 (*'al-tîr'û—'al-tēḥattû*) and 48.4-5 (see next paragraph).

236. W. Brueggemann, 'Jeremiah's Use of Rhetorical Questions', *JBL* 92 (1973), pp. 358-74 (on 368-69); also, M. Held, 'Rhetorical Questions in Ugaritic and Biblical Hebrew', *EI* 9 (1969), pp. 71-79.

237. Pope, *Job*, p. 198; note the rootplay between *'emna'* and *'ênê*.

Other Devices. Both chiasmus and hendiadys[238] are operative in Ps. 55.6:

> *Terrible fear* comes upon me,
> I am overwhelmed by *shuddering*

the expression 'terrible fear' consisting of two words joined by a copula (*yir'â wāra'-ad*).[239] Also, Isa. 51.3b;[240] Job 17.15; Lam. 2.21. Chiasmus heightens the effect of hyperbole in Job 20.6[241]

> If his statue should rise to heaven,
> or its head to the clouds reach up.

A last device to be considered is the broken construct chain used with a view to producing chiastic word-order:

Isa. 48.4[242]	The sinew (*gîd*) of your neck is iron	a b c
	Your forehead, brass	c' b'

or in Prov. 17.6 where chiasmus results from interposing the word 'sons' between two nouns in the construct.[243]

2.5.3. *The Interrelationship of Chiasmus and Other Poetic Devices*
The survey provided by subsections 2.5.1 and 2.5.2 has been brief and incomplete, but it has shown the extent to which chiasmus and other poetic devices available to the Hebrew bards intermeshed. At times the function of chiasmus is subordinate, in other texts it dominates and occasionally it coincides with functions of other poetic devices. Further research is required to determine the underlying rules of poetic technique.

In order to show, in a practical way, how such structural and non-structural devices interrelate with chiasmus, a single poem will be analysed in detail, the example chosen being Psalm 67, already

238. See H.A. Brongers, 'Merismus, Synekdoche und Hendiadys in der Bibel-Hebräischen Sprache', *OTS* 14 (1965), pp. 100-14.

239. The verb in the singular shows hendiadys to be present.

240. Contrast the plural verb in v. 11.

241. Chiasmus but not hyperbole was noticed by Dahood, in Bream (ed.), *Light*, p. 124 (his translation).

242. Note the rhyme with *'aggîd* ('I shall declare') in v. 5.

243. The bibliography on the broken construct chain is large; see D.N. Freedman, 'The Broken Construct Chain', *Bib* 53 (1972), pp. 534-36 and Gevirtz, *Patterns*, p. 80 n. 31.

examined by Lund.[244] Although some uncertainties of translation remain, they do not obscure the intricacy of the poem.[245] Analysis and discussion will be provided after the translation.

I May God show us mercy and bless us; 67.2
May he look favourably on our plough,[246]
To proclaim[247] on *earth* (f.) your power (m.?),[248] 3
Among all the nations (m.) your deliverance (f.).

R Praise you, will the peoples, O God, 4
Praise you, will the peoples, all of them.

II May the folk be happily rejoicing 5
For you judge the nations with rectitude,
And the folk of the *earth* you care for.[249]

R Praise you, will the peoples, O God, 6
Praise you, will the peoples, all of them.

III *Earth* yielded her produce— 7
Blessed us has God, our own God,
Blessed us has God— 8
Respected his sign[250] have all earth's ends.

244. Lund, *Chiasmus in the New Testament*, pp. 97-98; also T. Boys, *Key to the Book of the Psalms* (London: L.B. Seeley, 1825), p. 60.

245. Some recent studies taken into account include S. Mowinckel, '"Psalm Criticism between 1900 and 1935", (Ugarit and Psalm Exegesis)', *VT* 15 (1955), pp. 13-33, 29; H. Jefferson, 'The Date of Psalm lxvii', *VT* 12 (1962), pp. 201-205; O. Loretz, 'Die Psalmen 8 und 67. Psalmenstudien V', *UF* 9 (1976), pp. 117-22 and H.-J. Kraus, *Psalmen* (BKAT, XV/1; Neukirchen Kreis Moers: Neukirchener Verlag, 1960), pp. 461-63. There is no agreement on either literary form or date. Of course the psalm develops the blessing of Num. 6.24-25, but it has been styled a prayer for rain (Dahood), a hymn of public thanksgiving (Mowinckel) and a harvest song for the Feast of Tabernacles (Kraus). If my translation of v. 2b is correct it may comprise a blessing for the plough at seedtime.

246. Dahood, *Psalms*, II, p. 127 follows Rosenmueller in rejecting the construction *yā'ēr 'ittānû* as anomalous and repoints the second word *'atanu*, 'may he come to us'. My translation presupposes the word *'et*, 'ploughshare', with suffix. For the meaning of *yā'ēr pānâyw*, see Dahood, *Psalms*, I, p. 26.

247. Lit. 'so that known will be' or the like; Dahood prefers 'If... is known'.

248. Assuming Heb. *derek* = Ug. *drkt* (so Dahood, *Psalms*, II, p. 128); see n. 262.

249. For nuances of the final verb, see H. Van Dyke Parunak, 'A Semantic Survey of *NḤM*', *Bib* 56 (1975), pp. 512-43.

250. Repointing MT *'et* to *'ot*, 'sign' since the accusative particle is redundant in poetry.

Overall Chiastic Pattern. Quite clearly, stanzas I and III correspond as regards content. There is also a degree of common vocabulary: 'God', 'bless', 'earth'. They are also related by wordplay: 'plough' (*'ēt*) and 'sign' (*'ōt*); 'may he look' (*yā'ēr*) and '(they) have respected' (*w^{e}yîr^e'û*). The central stanza, unfortunately difficult to translate, links the outer stanzas and uses words from both: 'earth' and 'nations'.

Refrain and Stanza-Structure. The refrain (R: vv. 4 and 6) sections off the poem into stanzas of 4, 3 and again 4 lines, resulting in a pleasing balance. The refrain itself is formed by the use of incremental repetition (staircase parallelism or expanded colon).

Keywords. As already noted certain words are repeated, notably 'peoples' (6×; cf. 'folk' 2× and 'nations' 1×), 'God' (also 6×), 'earth' (meaning both *soil* and the *world* generally) 'all' and 'praise' (each 4×). These words not only contribute to the structure of the poem but also spell out its main theme: by blessing Israel God will induce the whole world to acknowledge his power. (See the next paragraph on repetition of the suffix.)

Structural Patterns. The envelope figure (inclusio) appears three times: the main words of v. 2 are resumed in vv. 7-8, the third stanza opens and closes with the word 'earth' and, thirdly, in the double wordplay of vv. 2 and 8. The suffix *-nû* (first person plural) is used seven times. The two central lines of the last stanza (itself chiastic, of ABBA pattern) comprise a pivot pattern.

Other Devices. Apart from paronomasia, the following devices are present: hendiadys (v. 5 'happily rejoicing' and possibly v. 2 'mercifully bless us'), ballast variant (v. 5 'folk' // 'folk of the earth'; v. 7 'earth' // 'all the ends of the earth'; also in the refrain and in v. 3 'On earth' // 'among all the nations').[251]

Conclusions. By its larger chiastic structure the diverse elements making up the poem are given unity. Even though there is a refrain, repetition and a rigid arrangement of line, there is no sense of monotony and the whole tenor of the psalm is optimistic.[252]

251. If *drk* does mean 'power, dominion', in v. 3 and if it is m., then the bicolon exhibits the chiastic gender pattern f.m.m.f.

252. See now H.-M. Wahl, 'Psalm 67. Erwägungen zu Aufbau, Gattung und

2.6. *The Value of Recognizing Chiasmus*

Apart from the general aspect of increasing one's appreciation of Hebrew poetry (and in addition to what has already been set out regarding function), recognition of chiastic patterns can be valuable in several specific ways.

2.6.1. *Chiasmus, Textual Criticism and Philology*

If it can be established that chiasmus obtains in a particular passage, then it can be better understood at the philological level, which in turn may obviate a textual emendation. Since chiasmus operates at a different level, there is no danger of circular reasoning. Dahood has already examined several texts from Job in this way.[253] Such texts are: Isa. 2.2;[254] 32.1 (asseverative *lamed*);[255] 32.6 (*dbr 'śh 'śh dbr* pattern 'argues in favor of the received text against the Qumran Isaiah Scroll's *ḥwšb* for *ya'aseh*');[256] Jer. 4.14-16;[257] Pss. 10.11-12 (*'ēl* need not be deleted);[258] 78.33 (*b* = 'than'); 138.1 (insertion of *yhwh* in the first colon not required);[259] Prov. 23.10.[260]

2.6.2. *Chiasmus, Poetry and Prose*

The texts examined in this chapter are mainly in verse, but there is a 'grey' area, not quite prose and yet not quiet good poetry, which has not been looked at. While by no means exclusive to verse,[261] chiasmus does seem to indicate (in combination with other factors) that a

Datierung', *Bib* 73 (1992), pp. 240-47.

253. M.J. Dahood, 'Chiasmus in Job: A Text-Critical and Philological Criterion', in Bream (ed.), *Light*, pp. 119-30; he discusses Job 6.15, 8.5, 11.14, 12.10, 13.12, 15.18, 17.7, 19.14, 21.8, 9, 26.5, 28.2, 31.16, 32.14, 34.6, 36.3, 12, 37.3, 39.6, 8 and 41.7.

254. J.S. Kselman, 'A Note on Isaiah II 2', *VT* 25 (1975), pp. 225-27.

255. W.G.E. Watson, review of W.H. Irwin, *Isaiah 28–33. Translation with Philological Notes*, *Bib* 59 (1978), p. 133.

256. Ceresko, 'Chiastic Word Pattern', p. 306.

257. M.J. Dahood, 'Jeremiah 5,31 and *UT* 127: 32', *Bib* 57 (1976), pp. 106-108.

258. Dahood, *Psalms*, I, p. 64.

259. Dahood, *Psalms*, III, p. 276.

260. W.A. van der Weiden, *Le livre des Proverbes: Notes philologiques* (BibOr, 23; Rome: Pontificial Biblical Institute, 1970), pp. 139-40 and Dahood, *Psalms*, II, p. 318.

261. For chiasmus in prose, see Andersen, *Sentence*, pp. 119-40.

particular passage is poetic in character. Many examples could be given[262] (see above on Judg. 9.8-15) but one will suffice here. In critical editions of the Hebrew Bible Mal. 3.19 is printed out as prose, but it exhibits chiastic structure:

For see, *the day is coming*,
    glowing like an oven;
Turned will be *all* the arrogant,
and *all* evildoers to chaff,
Setting them ablaze, *the day that comes*,

that is an ABBA tetracolon with an intrusive second colon. See, too, 1 Sam. 3.17.

This suggests that other passages need to be looked at with a critical eye, to determine whether they are prose or poetry.

2.6.3. *Chiasmus, the Strophe and the Stanza*

Although these topics have already been touched on, in view of their importance and of a certain degree of confusion among scholars, a final example will be given here. It is Isa. 54.2:[263]

(A)	strophe I	Enlarge the site of your tent,	a-bc
		and let the curtains of your home be stretched out.	bc-a
(B)	strophe II	Do not hold back.	
(A')	strophe III	Lengthen your cords,	a'b'
		and your stakes make fast.	b'a'

Chiasmus shows that strophe I is a unit, a chiastically-patterned bicolon. The same applies to strophe III, so that the central strophe II can only be a monocolon. However, the three strophes form a chiastic stanza (symbolized by the letters A, B, A' in parentheses), a unit of a higher order. Chiasmus, then, is a key factor in differentiating such

262. A.R. Ceresko, 'The A : B : : B : A Word Pattern in Hebrew and Northwest Semitic with Special Reference to the Book of Job', *UF* 7 (1975), p. 88 cites Gen. 4.4-5, 12.19, 45.23, Exod. 9.31-2, 33.13, Num. 15.35-36, Deut. 5.8 and 2 Sam. 18.20 as passages now considered verse due to recognition of chiasmus; Ceresko, 'Chiastic Word Pattern', p. 309 cites Gen. 1.5, 2.5-9, 2 Sam. 19.7, Jer. 7.16, 11.7, 16.11 and Ezek. 14.9. See also Isa. 44.11 (M. Dahood, 'Ugaritic-Hebrew Parallel Pairs', in *RSP* I, p. 139), Jer. 44.21 and Obad. 1–2. On Gen. 6.10–9.19 and 6.8-9, cf. G. Wenham, 'The Coherence of the Flood Narrative', *VT* 28 (1978), pp. 336-48.

263. Note, too, the gender-matching in the first bicolon (m. + m. // f. + f.).

self-contained units within a larger pattern, although not many texts are as crystal-clear as this one.

2.6.4. *Other Points*

In passages where there is some doubt about stichometry, chiasmus (if present) can be a useful criterion, for example Ps. 67.5 where the xabc // bca pattern determines the stichometry:[264]

> For you judge the nations justly;
> and the peoples on earth you guide.

Chiasmus, too, indicates the climactic centre (e.g. Ps. 12) and explains why a poem such as Lamentations 3 ends on a dismal note: the real climax lies in vv. 31-33:

> For the Lord is not always angry:
> Even if he punishes cruelly, he'll show compassion,
> in line with his abundant love,
> For he does not mindlessly hurt
> or punish mortal men.

2.6.5. *Chiasmus and the Oral Poet*

The claim that a large part of the OT was orally composed is generally accepted, even though it is not always possible to establish how much derives directly from oral composition. Certainly it is safe to assume that much of the poetry was improvised in front of an attentive audience and that poets employed certain techniques to assist smoothness of delivery. To the question 'Did the use of chiasmus belong to such techniques?', the answer appears to be in the affirmative. To take the simplest case first: having delivered a single line of poetry, the easiest way to produce a second automatically parallel colon would be to repeat the components (perhaps with slight variations) in reverse sequence. In fact, it would seem that students were schooled in precisely this manner. They would be given the first line of a saying and asked to provide a second line to cap it; for example,

> A wise son makes a glad father,

264. Contrast Dahood, *Psalms*, II, p. 126, 'You will lead the nations into the plain // and peoples into the land'.

which has different second lines in Prov. 10.1 and 15.20. Or, a second line was given, the exercise being to provide a suitable first line:[265]

Prov. 10.6	Blessings are on a just man's head, *But the wicked man's mouth hides violence*
Prov. 10.11	A fount of life is a just man's mouth, *But the wicked man's mouth hides violence*

Both are chiastic but the quality of the second 'answer' is higher. Even slight variations resulted in effective couplets. From these it was but a series of steps to more and more elaborate sequences, though it is debatable whether complete texts in chiastic form could have been produced orally. More probably such poems, once committed to writing, were later re-worked (much as were alphabetical acrostics) in order to complete or even create wholesale chiastic patterns.

2.6.7. *Closing Remarks*

Many more topics could have been dealt with, for instance, dating,[266] but conclusions concerning them must be reserved for another occasion, since the extent of the material involved is so large. As stated in the introduction, the main emphasis in the present section has been on terminology and classification. Once these have been surely established (and there is certainly room for further correction and refinement) then a good basis for further research will have been provided.

3. *Further Examples of Semantic-Sonant Chiasmus*[267]

The present short note sets out additional examples of semantic-sonant chiasmus, with a brief comment on theory. The poetic device of

265. For this technique, cf. B. Gemser, *Die Sprüche Salomos* (HAT, 16; Tübingen: Mohr, 1937), p. 45; also J.P. Olivier, 'Schools and Wisdom Literature', *JNSL* 4 (1976), pp. 49-60.

266. A study along the lines of D.N. Freedman, 'Divine Names and Titles in Early Hebrew Poetry', in F.M. Cross, Jr, W.E. Lemke, P.D. Miller (eds.), *Magnalia Dei: The Mighty Acts of God: Essays on the Bible and Archaeology in Memory of Ernest G. Wright* (Garden City, NY: Doubleday, 1976), pp. 55-107 is needed; see especially the chronological tables, pp. 105-107. Another topic is the relationship between chiasmus and enjambment, on which see Andersen, *Sentence*, p. 123, who cites Isa. 60.20, and Dahood, *IDBSup*, p. 671 who mentions Isa. 11.9b, Zeph. 3.19 and the ABBA pattern generally.

267. First published in *CBQ* 46 (1984), pp. 31-32.

semantic-sonant chiasmus was first identified by John S. Kselman who defined it as a combination of assonance and chiasmus 'in which one leg of the chiasmus is formed by a pair of words of similar meaning (the semantic pair), and the other leg is produced by a pair of words of similar sound (the sonant pair)'.[268] In the texts discussed here an even stricter definition applies since in each, both 'legs' combine assonantal and semantic features. The first passage is Mic. 4.6ab:

'ōs^{e}pâ haṣṣolē'â	I'll gather the crippled,
w^{e}hanniddāḥâ '^{a}qabbēṣâ	the cast-out I'll collect.

The Hebrew corresponding to 'I'll gather/collect', a word-pair,[269] begins with and ends in the sound *-â* both times. Similarly, the words for 'crippled' and 'cast-out'[270] begin with *ha-* and also end in *-â*. This couplet is the core of an expanded oracle, and the pattern recognizable here is not present in Zeph. 3.19, its counterpart. A curious form of the same device occurs in Isa. 51.11 as the last two lines of a five-line strophe:

śāśôn w^{e}śimḥâ yaśśîgûn	Joy and gladness they'll 'see',
nāsû yāgôn w^{a}'^{a}nāḥâ	flee shall woe and sadness.

The Hebrew equivalents for 'joy and gladness' and 'woe and sadness' balance chiastically. So, too, do the verbs 'see' (literally, 'obtain') and 'flee'. However, though matching in sound, the second line is exactly opposite in content to the first (antithetic parallelism) resulting in a sophisticated form of partially inverted semantic-sonant chiasmus.

Turning to Akkadian poetry, two or three passages come into the category under discussion. The first comes from the Agušaya Hymn, version A.[271] It closes col. 5 and is written after two ruled lines:

268. 'Semantic-Sonant Chiasmus in Biblical Poetry', *Bib* 58 (1977), pp. 219-23; his examples are Gen. 27.36; 2 Sam. 1.21b; Jer. 2.7b; Ezek. 22.2; Pss. 37.6; 51.19; 78.33; 147.15; Prov. 14.4; Qoh. 7.1a; Lam. 3.22; also Gen. 7.11 and Ps. 72.7.

269. See my paper, 'The Hebrew Word-pair *'sp // qbṣ*', Chapter 6.

270. Literally, 'the lame' and 'the banished'; my rendering is an attempt at reflecting the sound pattern of the original.

271. I follow B. Groneberg, 'Philologische Bearbeitung des Agušayahymnus', *RA* 75 (1981), pp. 107-34; the passage in question is Agušaya A (or I), col. 5, lines 43-44, on which see Groneberg's study, p. 110. Also, cf. *CAD*, Ṣ, p. 89a, and *AHw*, p. 1071. See already B.R. Foster, 'Ea and Ṣaltu', in M. de Jong Ellis (ed.), *Ancient Near Eastern Studies in Memory of J.J. Finkelstein* (Hamden: Connecticut Academy of Arts and Sciences, 1977), p. 80 n. 15. A less certain example, within a

šīruša ṣabā'u	Her flesh is campaigning
ṣelû šarassa	battle her hair.

The first and fourth words correspond in meaning and also in sound: words two and three are also semantically equivalent but are less close in sound, though they both begin with *ṣ* and end in *-u*. The function of this couplet may have been to close a section of the hymn but we do now know enough about chiastic patterns in Assyrian and Babylonian verse to make such a statement with confidence.[272] Another example also comes from a hymn, though only as part of a couplet; the lines in question are 6-7:[273]

Mention of me is sweet—sound health (*šulum balāṭu*)
and the healing touch (*liptu šulmu*) men discourse on.

The closing two words of line 6 match the opening words of the next line in sound and meaning.

The pattern does not seem to occur in Ugaritic poetry, for which two reasons can be proposed. First, in Ugaritic tradition the quasi-acrostic component (two or more lines with the same initial letter)[274] would tend to rule out semantic-sonant chiasmus of the narrowly-defined type under examination here. Second, two-word lines are rare in Ugaritic poetry. Chiastic patterning within a (four-word) line, however, is not completely improbable and may yet be identified.

line, may be *bītbītiš luterruba lunē' bubūti*, 'I will go from house to house to ward off hunger'; text and translation in W.G. Lambert, *Babylonian Wisdom Literature* (Oxford: Clarendon Press, 1960), pp. 78-79, line 140.

272. On chiasmus in Akkadian, see R. Borger, *Babylonisch-assyrische Lesestücke* (Rome: Biblical Institute Press, 1963), I, pp. xxvii-xxviii; W. von Soden, *Grundriss der akkadischen Grammatik* (AnOr, 33; Rome: Biblical Institute Press, 1952), §§130b, 186e; and R.F. Smith, 'Chiasmus in Sumero-Akkadian', in Welch (ed.), *Chiasmus in Antiquity*, pp. 17-35.

273. Text and translation: W.G. Lambert, 'The Gula Hymn of Bulluṭsa-rabi', *Or* 36 (1967), pp. 105-32, esp. pp. 116-17. Note the variants *balāṭi* and *lipitti*; *liptu*, incidentally, normally has a negative connotation; hence the translation, 'mention of me is sweet, (meaning) well-being and health, people discuss it (i.e. Gula's name) (whether in) sickness (or) good health', set out in *CAD*, L, p. 201.

274. See below, pp. 438-41.

Chapter 8

FIGURATIVE LANGUAGE

1. *Tribute to Tyre (Isaiah 23.7)*[1]

The improved understanding of Isa. 23.7 proposed here hinges on recognizing the metaphor of paying tribute, in combination with assigning two or three words their correct roots. A single, recent translation (NEB) will serve to represent current renderings of the verse:

> Is this your busy city, ancient in story,
> on whose voyages you were carried to settle far away?

This is usually explained as a reference to Phoenician colonization[2] which, of course, is quite plausible. However, at least one scholar has taken exception to prevailing opinion,[3] showing it to be open to question, even if the solution he put forward (as will be seen) is not convincing.

The simplest procedure is to present text, translation and notes in that order, the notes helping to offset the unliteral smoothness of the translation.

h^azo't lākem 'allîzâ	Can this be your joyful city,
mîmê-qedem	To whom, since ancient times,
qadmātâ yobilûhā raglêhā	Her tribute they brought to her at her feet,
mērāḥôq lāgûr	Obliged to reverence at a respectful distance?

Part of a taunt-song by Egypt, contrasting Tyre in its heyday when it was prosperous and powerful with its present reduced status, the verse

1. First published in *VT* 26 (1976), pp. 371-74.

2. For example, G.B. Gray, *The Book of Isaiah* (ICC; Edinburgh: T. & T. Clark, 1912), I, p. 390.

3. E. Lipiński, 'Trois hébraismes oubliés ou méconnus', *RSO* 44 (1969), pp. 83-101, esp. 83-86.

is addressed to the inhabitants of the city. The term *'allîzâ* is elliptical for 'joyful city', as is evident from Isa. 22.2, 32.13 and Zeph. 2.15. In Akkadian texts 'joy' and 'town' are similarly connected,[4] and there may be the additional nuance of 'welcoming'[5] the foreign emissaries. Before considering *qadmātāh* the expression *yobilûha raglêha* must first be inspected. The usual translation is 'whose feet carry her', but such a meaning for the *hiphil* of *ybl* would be unique. Generally it means 'to lead' or 'to bear along (offerings)',[6] and in the second meaning is twice attested with the preposition *l* (Pss. 48.30; 76.12). Accordingly, the verbal suffix *-hā* must be dative: 'they bring to her'.[7] The words 'her feet' (*raglêhā*), then, do not form the subject of the verb as is commonly accepted. A rendering more suitable to the context is 'at her feet'. The expression is used in Phoenician, for example *tḥt p'm 'dny b'l šmm*, 'at the feet of my lord, Baal Shamem' (*KAI* 18.7), and in the letter-formula frequent in Ugaritic: *lp'n* X *šb'd wšb'id mrḥqtm qlt*, 'at the feet of X seven times (on my belly) and seven times (on my back) at a respectful distance I fall'.[8] Instead of a preposition, though, the Hebrew here adopts the accusative of place.[9] Lipiński renders *mērāḥôq lāgûr* 'de-ci de-là', a merismus he compares with Akkadian *anniš u ulleš*, 'to and fro'. He cites Theodotion: πορρώθεν εἰς παροικίαν, and translates *gûr* 'voisinage' as in 2 Chron. 26.7.[10] The merits of this solution are outweighed once *mērāḥôq* is seen as belonging to the letter-formula just cited. Loewenstamm has shown that the phrase means 'at a respectful

4. In expressions such as *āl rišāti*, 'jubilant city'; *irâš ālu*, 'the city rejoices'; cf. *AHw*, pp. 980 and 989 for references.

5. As in *ana pān rubê terrumma ḫādika*, 'when you come into the presence of the prince he will welcome you' (so *CAD*, Ḫ, p. 27).

6. 'To lead (a person)', Jer. 31.9; Pss. 60.11; 108.11; 'to bring (tribute)', Zeph. 3.10; 'to bring (offerings)', Pss. 68.30; 76.12.

7. See, in general, M. Bogaert, 'Les suffixes verbaux non accusatifs dans le sémitique nord-occidental et particulièrement en hébreu', *Bib* 45 (1964), pp. 220-47, and note the Ugaritic text cited at the end of the present paper.

8. For details, cf. S.E. Loewenstamm, 'Prostration from Afar in Ugaritic, Accadian and Hebrew', *BASOR* 188 (1967), pp. 41-43.

9. Another example is Isa. 49.23: 'Nostrils to the ground they grovel for you and lick the dust at your feet (*raglêkā*)'.

10. His translation in full runs, 'Est-ce là votre cité joyeuse, dont l'origine remontait aux jours d'antan, et que ses pas portaient de-ci de-là?', Lipiński, 'Trois hébraismes', p. 86.

distance', with the equivalents *mrḥq(t)m* in Ugaritic and *ištu ruqiš* in Akkadian.[11] To the same setting belongs *gûr*, 'to fear, reverence', here preceded by *l* with the nuance of obligation.[12] Finally, a look at difficult *qadmātâ* which in Ezek. 16.55 and 36.11 (plural) means 'former state'. As in Zeph. 3.10, Pss. 68.30 and 76.12 the verb *ybl* (*hiphil* here, as noted above) requires an object with the meaning 'tribute, gift'. It seems likely that *qadmâ* (here suffixed) supplies the missing word; a meaning such as 'presentation' seems indicated by *qedem*[13] which also occurs in the verse, both words having been deliberately chosen by the poet.

Tyre is depicted as a haughty queen with a respectable ancestry welcoming her subject kings who, after grovelling as prescribed (forehead to ground at a distance from the throne), approach and kneel to lay tribute at her feet. Adequate illustration of the two-stage ritual comes from the Ugaritic texts:

lpnnh. ydd. wyqm	In front of her he bows, then rises;
lp'nh. ykr'. wyql	At her feet he kneels, then falls[14]

11. See n. 7.

12. On *lamedh* followed by the infinitive construct to express obligation, cf. P. Joüon, *Grammaire de l'hébreu biblique* (Rome: Pontifical Biblical Institute, 2nd edn, 1947), p. 362, and R.J. Williams, *Hebrew Syntax: An Outline* (Toronto: University of Toronto, 1967), p. 53. Alternatively, the construction *yblw... lgwr* can be compared to *wyškm... lqwm*, 'And he got up early' (2 Kgs 6.15), on which see R. Meyer, *Hebräische Grammatik* (Sammlung Göschen; Berlin: de Gruyter, 1972), III, p. 59. An adequate translation, though, would be difficult to provide.

13. Compare Akk. *meḫertu* and *namḫartu* from *maḫāru*, 'to face, confront'; Heb. *minḥâ* from *naḥâ*, 'to lead'.

14. *KTU* 1.10 ii 17-18; similarly, *KTU* 1.4 iv 25-26. A slightly different sequence is attested elsewhere in the Ugaritic texts, probably due to Babylonian influence; cf. J.C. de Moor, *The Seasonal Pattern in the Ugaritic Myth of Ba'lu* (AOAT, 16; Kevelaer: Butzon & Bercker; Neukirchen–Vluyn: Neukirchener Verlag, 1971), p. 129. A plausible etymology for Ug. *ndd*, which appears to be the root of *ydd*, is adduced by M.J. Dahood, *Psalms I* (AB, 16; Garden City, NY: Doubleday, 1968), p. 257, and *Psalms II* (AB, 17; Garden City, NY: Doubleday, 1968), p. 107. However, A. Caquot, M. Sznycer and A. Herdner (*Textes ougaritiques*. I. *Mythes et légendes* [LAPO, 7; Paris: Cerf, 1974], p. 284), prefer 'Il court (*ydd*) à sa rencontre et s'arrête. Il s'incline et tombe à ses pieds'; cf. p. 154 n. i. Yet a further possibility is championed by J.C. de Moor, 'Ugaritic Lexicography', in P. Fronzaroli (ed.), *Studies on Semitic Lexicography* (Quaderni di Semitistica, 2; Florence: Dipartimento di Linguistica, Università di Firenze, 1973), p. 67 n. 4. See

where even the gods show submission by presenting tribute:

hw ybl. argmnk. kilm	He (Baal), too, will bring you levies, like the gods,
hw ybl. kbn. qdš. mnḥyk	He, too, will bring you, like the holy ones, tribute.[15]

2. *The Imagery in Jeremiah 17.1*

The metaphor of writing on a heart as on a tablet occurs several times in Hebrew.[16] Couroyer has suggested that the origin of the expression is not metaphorical but literal and in fact the reference is to an amulet or inscribed pendant. Even in the one passage from Jeremiah where the reference is to sin, he argues, the writing must have been visible to others, not merely 'internal'.[17] Documentation is now available from Mesopotamia and elsewhere which calls for a re-examination of these lines in Jeremiah.[18]

The text in question is Jer. 17.1:[19]

now J. Tropper, 'Ugaritisch *ndy*, *ydy*, *Ldy gnd* und *d(wd)*', *UF* 20 (1978), pp. 339-50.

15. *CTA* 2 I/ *UT* 137 37-38; for the problems of translation, cf. de Moor, *Seasonal Pattern*, pp. 131-32. Akkadian texts with the same motif can be found in *CAD*, A/2, p. 253, under *argamannu*, and in *CAD*, B, pp. 234-36, under *biltu*.

16. Listed, with discussion, by B. Couroyer, 'La tablette du coeur', *RB* 90 (1983), pp. 416-34; to his examples add 1QH xxi 12.

17. Couroyer, 'La tablette du coeur', pp. 429-31, with reference to Jer. 17.1. Couroyer refers to actual amulets found in excavations (p. 433 n. 39) and concludes, 'L'emploi métaphorique d'écriture sur le coeur lui-même, si c'est de cela qu'il s'agit, n'a pu naître qu'après un usage non métaphorique, car une expression, comme un mot, se réfère d'abord à une réalité concrète avant d'être transposée... Peut-être de nouvelles données permettront-elles de résoudre un jour ce délicat problème' (p. 434).

18. Note that although there is a reference to Jer. 7.1-5 in K. van der Toorn, *Sin and Sanction in Israel and Mesopotamia: A Comparative Study* (Studia Semitica Neerlandica, 22; Assen: Van Gorcum, 1985), p. 165 n. 169, our text is not otherwise discussed and nor is there any reference to the 'tablet(s) of sins' of Mesopotamia.

19. These words seem to be missing from the parallel Jer. 15.12-14 where the text is far from straightforward; see the commentaries and the following note.

a. *Jeremiah 17.1*

ḥṭ't yhwdh ktwbh b'ṭ brzl	The sin of Judah is written with an iron pen,
bṣprn šmyr ḥrwšwh	with a sharp stylus[20] is it engraved
'l-lwḥ lbm...	upon the tablet of their heart...[21]

The evidence from Mesopotamia comprises four references to the 'Tablet(s) of Sins' in Babylonian texts which can be set out as follows.

b. *In a Royal Prayer as Part of a Ritual*[22]

lu hepû ṭuppu arni[*ya*...]	May the tablet of my sins be broken; [...]
lemnetua lu parsa [...]	May my evil deeds be stopped; [...]
saklatua u [...	May my follies (?) and [my... be...]

c. *In a Passage Parallel to the Foregoing Royal Ritual*[23]

lu ḫepû ṭuppi arniya lu puṭṭuru lumniya
May the tablets of my sins be broken, may my misdeed be cancelled.[24]

Farber comments, 'the king then figuratively speaks of breaking the tablets of his sins, with the resulting disappearance of his wrongdoings

20. Heb. *ṣipporen*, 'fingernail' (Deut. 21.12), is here used in a transferred meaning to denote 'stylus' (so BDB, p. 862). It can be noted that in Mesopotamian texts *ṣupru*, '(human) nail', also refers to a nail-impression made on a clay tablet in lieu of a seal (cf. *CAD*, Ṣ, pp. 251-52).

21. The text continues, 'and on the horns of your altars'. For textual criticism, see W. McKane, *Jeremiah*. I. *Introduction and Commentary on Jeremiah I–XXV* (ICC; Edinburgh: T. & T. Clark, 1986), pp. 384-87. J. Bright, *Jeremiah* (AB, 21; Garden City, NY: Doubleday, 1965), p. 117: 'One wonders if vv. 1-4 may not have been the original conclusion of the poem and liturgy in time of drought in xiv 1-10, 19-22'.

22. H. Zimmern, *Beiträge zur Kenntnis der babylonischen Religion* (Assyriologische Bibliothek, 12; Leipzig: 1901), no. 26 (line 5), as translated by I.L. Finkel, 'The Dream of Kurigalzu and the Tablet of Sins', *AnSt* 33 (1983), pp. 75-80. Note that the translation in *CAD*, S, p. 80 is slightly different: 'let the tablets of my sins be broken, let my evil deeds be removed, my acts of ignorance (?) and [...]' ('tablets', in the plural).

23. E. von Weiher, *Spätbabylonische Texte aus Uruk* (Ausgrabungen der Deutschen Forschungsgemeinschaft in Uruk Warka, 11; Berlin: Mann, 1983), II, no. 11, obv. II 11.

24. J.A. Scurlock, 'Was there a "Love-Hungry" *Entu*-priestess Named Eṭirtum?', *AfO* 36/37 (1989/90), pp. 107-12, 110 n. 32 translates, 'May the tablet of my sins be broken'.

from the mind of his people'.[25] The breaking of a tablet, as in (b), (c) and (d), made it null.[26]

d. *In the Long Ritual Known as Šurpu*[27]

> *ṭuppi arnišu ḫītātišu gillatišu māmātišu tumāmātišu ana mê innaddâ*
> May the tablet of his wrongdoing, his sins, his crimes, his oaths, (all) that is sworn by him, be thrown into water!

The text continues, 'may his errors be wiped out, his crimes removed, his oaths undone, etc. Through the invocation of your pure name may be removed, driven away, expelled the sin and the oath which are there to torment men'.[28]

e. *In the Report of a Dream*[29]

mūša anna rabûtu ᵈbel atamar ḫad[iš]	This night, O courtiers, I joyfully beheld Bel!
ᵈnabû ina pānišu izzazzu ṭuppi ḫītātu ana ᵈbel uki[n...]	Nabû, who was standing before him, set up(?) the Tablet of Sins [...]

Finkel considers that, although passages (b) and (d) 'reflect through metaphor the belief in a Tablet of Sins held by the gods', (e) is 'straightforward in its depiction of a literal tablet in divine hands in which a man's sins were recorded'. Passage (c) is similar to (b). Finkel proceeds to wonder whether everyone had his own tablet and whether it was up to one's personal god to keep the record up to date, adding that more frequent reference to tablets of sins would then be expected in the religious texts.[30]

25. W. Farber, 'Associative Magic: Some Rituals, Word Plays, and Philology', *JAOS* 106 (1986), pp. 447-49, 448.

26. Commenting on the breaking and burying of a tablet on which a spell was written Scurlock says ('A "Love-Hungry" *Entu*-priestess', p. 110 n. 32), 'Breaking the tablet should in some sense have cancelled it. This was, of course, the standard method of invalidating written contracts'.

27. Šurpu IV 79-80; text and translation: E. Reiner, *Šurpu: A Collection of Sumerian and Akkadian Incantations* (AfO Beiheft, 11; Graz: E. Weidner, 1958; repr. Osnabrück: Biblio Verlag, 1970), p. 27 (with the change of 'record' to 'tablet').

28. Reiner, *Šurpu*, p. 28 (lines 81-88).

29. Finkel, 'Dream', pp. 75-80. According to Finkel the composition is to be dated to a time after 1126 BC.

30. Finkel, 'Dream', p. 77.

Belief in a tablet preserved in heaven on which misdeeds were recorded is also found in an apocalyptic work, in a passage from Euripides and in the texts from Qumran. These will be considered in turn.

f. *From the Apocalypse of Zephaniah (3.15–4.13)*

> I am wont, however, to take them away and to bring them before the Lord Almighty, in order that He may inscribe their names in the book of the living. Also the angels of the accuser—who is upon the earth they also in turn write according to all the sins of man upon their scrolls; also they sit at the gate of Heaven; they announce to the accuser that he is to inscribe them upon his scroll in order that he may accuse them when they come hither out of the world below.[31]

g. *Also from the Apocalypse of Zephaniah (10.20–12.11)*

The passage is too long to quote but it describes how Zephaniah was brought before the accusing angel who had a scroll in his hand which he opened. The text continues:

> But when he had spread it out, I read it in my own language; I discovered all my sins which I had committed, how they had been written down by him, those which I had committed from my childhood even up to the present day, while they had all been written down on that written-scroll of mine.

There follows a list of sins of omission. Zephaniah then begs God to erase ('wipe away') the scroll.[32]

h. *A Passage from Euripides*

> Do you believe that the sins are written in a book before Zeus, and Zeus reads it and judges men accordingly. The heavens are not large enough to write down the sins.[33]

31. H.P. Houghton, 'The Coptic Apocalypse', *Aegyptus* 39 (1959), pp. 40-91, text on p. 78; quoted (with slightly different wording) by S.M. Paul, 'Heavenly Tablets and the Book of Life', *JANESCU* 5 (1973) [= *The Gaster Festschrift*], pp. 345-53, 349. To his references add 4Q180 3-4; 4QEn^c frag. 5 col. ii 27.

32. Houghton, 'The Coptic Apocalypse', pp. 82-83. The phrase 'written down' occurs five times in the passage and in 12.18-20 there is a reference to another written scroll, though its contents remain unknown.

33. Quoted by Paul, 'Heavenly Tablets', p. 352 n. 46 (see there for references).

i. *4QEnoch^c (4Q204 [4QEn^c]) Frag 5. col. ii 26-27*

For I know the mysteries [of the Lord which] the Holy Ones have told me and have shown me [and which] I read in [the tablets] of heaven. In them I saw written that generation after generation will perpetrate evil in this way...[34]

j. *1QM xii 2-3*

The [bo]ok of the names of all their armies
is with you in your holy dwelling,
[...] in the dwelling of your glory.
And the rewards of your blessings
[...] the covenant of your peace
you engraved for them
with the chisel of life...[35]

k. *1QH ix 24-26*

Everything has been engraved in your presence
with the recording stylus
for all the incessant periods
in the eras of the number of everlasting years
in all their predetermined times.
How will a man recount his sin?
How will he defend his infringements?
How will he answer every just judgment?[36]

l. *1QS x 11*

my sins are before my eyes like graven laws.[37]

Conclusion

The imagery of a tablet on which a person's sins were recorded and which was stored in heaven is first attested in Mesopotamian texts and persisted to the period of the Dead Sea Scrolls and beyond. It occurs here (Jer. 17.1) and elsewhere in the Hebrew Bible (Exod. 32.32-33).[38]

34. F. García Martínez, *Textos de Qumrán* (Madrid: Editorial Trotta, 1992), p. 305.

35. García Martínez, *Textos de Qumrán*, p. 156.

36. García Martínez, *Textos de Qumrán*, p. 365.

37. García Martínez, *Textos de Qumrán*, p. 6.

38. For a possible oblique allusion, see Jer. 31.33.

In passage (f) there is also reference to the 'book of the living',[39] probably an echo of the 'tablet of life' which also occurs in texts from Mesopotamia.[40]

On Jer. 17.1-4 Carroll comments, 'Judah's sin (unspecified) is so deep that it is engraven on the nation's heart and altars' and he is probably right in agreeing with Thiel that 'the original form of the statement [about idolatrous practices] may have been only v. 1, with the fertility rites of v. 2 a later addition in MT'.[41] It would seem, then, that the author (or later editor) of these words has combined two traditional images: the heavenly tablet of sin and the tablet of the heart. The resulting metaphor is decidedly mixed. It is probable, therefore, that the original text ended with *lûaḥ* and the result is a well-formed couplet which conveys an obvious image:

> The sin of Judah is written with an iron pen,
> with a sharp stylus is it engraved upon a tablet.

If so, *libbām* is a later addition (derived from the stock expression 'tablet of the heart') which in turn led to further explanatory glosses. The issue is not clear-cut but it is evident that future explanations of this difficult passage cannot ignore the extra-biblical references to the 'tablet(s) of sin(s)', understood in later tradition as a scroll on which sins were recorded.

3. *Splitting Hairs in Babylon and Israel (Ezekiel 5.1-5)*[42]

According to Zimmerli[43] the shaving, weighing and disposal of hair described in Ezek. 5.1-5 belong to a set of three symbolic actions described in 3.25–5.4a, the original text of which ran as follows:[44]

39. Or 'book of life'; also 4Q380 frag. 31.8; see García Martínez, *Textos de Qumrán*, p. 353.

40. For references to the 'tablet of life' see *CAD*, L, p. 159 (usage b 4').

41. R.P. Carroll, *Jeremiah: A Commentary* (Old Testament Library; London: SCM Press, 1986), p. 349; similarly, McKane, *Jeremiah*, p. 387.

42. First published in *IBS* 4 (1982), pp. 193-97.

43. W. Zimmerli, *Ezekiel 1: A Commentary on the Book of the Prophet Ezekiel. Chs. 1–24* (ET; Philadelphia: Fortress Press 1979 [1969]), pp. 155-56.

44. The text reproduced here is Zimmerli's; the complete text is set out (in translation, with notes) in *Ezekiel 1*, pp. 148-51. The full text of Ezek. 5.1-5 runs, 'And you, son of man, take a sharp sword; use a razor and pass it over your head and beard. And take a balance and divide it (i.e. the hair). One third you shall burn in the

I And you, son of man, take a brick
and lay it before you
and draw upon it a city
and lay siege to it
and build siegeworks against it
and set up a siege wall against it
and establish battering rams round about.

II And you—take wheat and barley
and beans and lentils and millet and spelt
and put them in the same pot
and make bread of them for yourself
and your food shall be 20 shekels a day:
at regular times shall you eat it.
And water you shall drink by measure, a sixth of a hin:
at regular times shall you drink.

III And you, son of man—take a sharp sword
and pass it over your head and beard:
and take a balance
and divide it (the hair).
One third you shall burn with fire,
and one third you shall cut up with the sword
and one third you shall scatter to the wind.

The Babylonian background to stanza I (or Symbolic Action 1) is transparent: clay tablets comprised the commonest medium for writing and for drawing city plans and the like, and the evidence is conveniently presented by Zimmerli.[45] As for stanza II, the cereals listed there point to no specific local background. However, the reference to the loaf per day (4.9—omitted by Zimmerli) echoes the same time-counting device in the *Epic of Gilgamesh*. Also, for Hebrew 'round-cake' (4.12, also omitted in Zimmerli's reconstructed text) LXX has ἐγκρυφίας 'ash-baked bread', the exact equivalent of *kaman tumri* as used in the roof-ritual of a Babylonian text (see presently). Quite

city with fire when the days of the siege are completed; and one third you shall take and cut up with the sword around it, and one third you shall scatter to the wind. And I will draw the sword after them. And you shall take from there a small number and bind them in the skirt of your garment. And you shall take (some) of them and throw them into the fire and burn them with fire. And you shall say to the whole house of Israel: Thus has the Lord Yahweh said: This is Jerusalem! I have set it in the midst of the nations with the lands round about it'.

45. Zimmerli, *Ezekiel 1*, pp. 161-62. Clay tablets were also used for Ugaritic, Hittite, Elamite, Linear B, etc., but only rarely in Palestine.

possibly, then, Zimmerli's excisions cannot be justified by the neatness claimed for the 'original' text (as above).

Having established the Babylonian background to stanzas I and II, we now come to the main subject of this brief note, namely, stanza III (or Symbolic Action 3). Up till now no parallel could be cited for this stanza. Related texts such as Isa. 5.12, Jer. 41.5, 48.37 and passages from the Ugaritic Baal Cycle[46] refer to acts of mourning and therefore are not relevant. However, a recently edited set of Babylonian texts[47] does now provide the background (Babylonian, of course) for this third symbolic action, even if some problems remain unsolved. In this set of Babylonian texts there is a passage which comes in part of a complex ritual designed to cure someone suffering from a whole range of symptoms, including epilepsy, shivering, total indecision and the like.[48] The ritual goes as follows. In a sheep pen everything is made ready. An unmated kid bought for a loaf of ash-baked bread is fed on tamarisk for a day. At night the roof is swept and sprinkled and an altar set up to Ishtar. Offerings of food and drink are provided and Gula, the goddess of healing, is offered loaves of bread. Incense and beer are also offered. The rubric continues, 'You hold a balance high, place the hair of his (the patient's) head and the hem of his garment and weigh them'.

A special song is sung. Next, the kid is slaughtered, its heart roasted and its hide placed near the paraphernalia. The sick man then raises his hand and recites an incantation three times, the text of which includes a reference to the balance prepared by the officiant for the weighing of hair and hem.[49]

46. See, conveniently, J.C.L. Gibson, *Canaanite Myths and Legends* (Edinburgh: T. & T. Clark, 1978), pp. 73 (vi 17-19) and 74 (i 2-3).

47. W. Farber, *Beschwörungsrituale an Ištar und Dumuzi* (Wiesbaden: Steiner, 1977).

48. The complete set of symptoms, which includes dumbness, could easily apply to Ezekiel himself.

49. See Farber, *Beschwörungsrituale*, pp. 64-67 (A Ia 14-21, esp. lines 18-19, and 32). The act of tearing hair from the sick man's forehead and ripping away of his hem (pp. 154, lines 203-204) in what is essentially a mourning ritual arose from confusion with the ritual just described (see Farber's comment, p. 106). Similar confusion may have occurred in our Ezekiel passage which mentions binding a small number of hairs in the hem of his garment (Ezek. 5.3).

Both texts (Ezek. 5.1-5 and the Babylonian ritual) share the following features:

1. removal of hair (by implication in the Babylonian text, but see n. 49);
2. weighing of hair on a balance;
3. reference to the hem of a garment.[50]

There are also differences. In the Babylonian text no explanation is given for weighing hair and hem and the ritual is magic and complex. The passage from Ezekiel, on the other hand, is very clearly a symbolic and not a magical act and its explanation is provided in Ezek. 5.12 (cf. also 5.17). With due allowance for later elaboration[51] it can be schematized as follows:

action	*symbolizing*
one third burnt in the city	pestilence and famine
one third cut up by sword	death by the sword
one third scattered to the wind	dispersion[52]

Beneath the superficial features shared by both traditions lie deeper common concepts. In both it would seem that the hair *represents* the person involved (Ezekiel, the prophet, represented Israel, so his hair was equivalent to the whole nation).[53] Also, actions are not empty gestures but *betoken* events: in Babylonia at the level of (sympathetic) magic, in Israel as prophecy.[54]

50. As mentioned (n. 49) this element may be an interpolation in both texts. See, too, the last part of n. 55.

51. See Zimmerli, *Ezekiel 1*, pp. 152 and 176.

52. There are Ugaritic parallels to these actions, namely, two descriptions of how Mot ('Death') was destroyed. They run, 'She ('Anath) seized divine Mot, with a sword she split him, with a sieve she winnowed him, with fire she burnt him, with millstones she ground him, in a field she scattered him' and, 'Because of you, Ba'al, I have suffered abasement, splitting with the sword, burning with fire, grinding with millstones, winnowing with the riddle, scattering in the sea' (Translation Gibson, *Canaanite Myths*, pp. 77 and 79 [with some abridgment]).

53. Goat's hair, for example, was used to represent a person in Babylonian *namburbi* or apotropaic rituals.

54. Ezek. 5.1-5 is not discussed by M.I. Gruber, *Aspects of Nonverbal Communication in the Ancient Near East* (Studia Pohl, 12; Rome: Biblical Institute Press, 1980). It would be interesting to determine whether the hem connotes an element of supplication as established for other texts by E. Greenstein, '"To Grasp the Hem" in Ugaritic Literature', *VT* 32 (1982), pp. 217-18.

Finally, although the Babylonian text discussed provides an undeniable Babylonian setting for Ezek. 5.1-5, in line with the other two symbolic actions, Ezekiel need not necessarily have depended on that particular Babylonian text.[55]

4. *Reflexes of Akkadian Incantations in Hosea*[56]

Here I wish to develop more fully some points of comparison between the book of Hosea and certain Akkadian texts which I touched on briefly in a recent book review.[57]

Comparison of this type is not new, yet in spite of at least two articles which appeared lately on the same topic[58] there is evidently still much that can be gained from further study on such lines. My article will run as follows: after looking in more detail at certain similarities between Hosea and texts in Akkadian, one difficult verse in Hosea will be examined and a possible solution proposed.

The first point of comparison concerns a general similarity between certain Akkadian incantations plus their rituals, and the book of Hosea. The similarity is threefold: both traditions use a high number of similes, many of these similes are alike if not identical, and there is a tendency to cluster similes together. These aspects will be illustrated in turn.

The high number of similes in Hosea has been remarked on by commentators[59] but it is worth mentioning again here as part of the argument. A rough count gives over fifty in the short compass of thirteen brief chapters; an exact count would have to distinguish more precisely between comparison, metaphor and simile, an unnecessary

55. See now M. Greenberg, *Ezekiel, 1–20* (AB, 22; Garden City, NY: Doubleday, 1983), p. 99 and the commentary, pp. 103-110, with ample reference to elements borrowed from Mesopotamia.

56. First published in *VT* 34 (1984), pp. 242-47.

57. See my review of F.I. Andersen and D.N. Freedman, *Hosea*, *IBS* 3 (1981), pp. 168-70.

58. K.J. Cathcart, 'Micah 5, 4-5 and Semitic Incantations', *Bib* 59 (1978), pp. 38-48; M.J. Geller, 'The Šurpu Incantations and Lev. V. 1-5', *JSS* 25 (1980), pp. 181-92.

59. For example, H.W. Wolff, *Hosea* (trans. G. Stansell; Hermeneia; Philadelphia: Fortress Press, 1974), p. xxiv.

exercise in the present context. When we turn to selected Akkadian incantations, the data are as follows. The *Lipšur* litanies[60] yield some seventeen different similes, the *Šurpu* collection[61] also seventeen, and the dingir.šà.dib.ba series,[62] eleven.[63]

Some of the similes used by Hosea can be matched with figurative speech in the sets of incantations just mentioned. 'Like smoke (from a window)', Hos. 13.3, appears, too, in *Lipšur* II 1 23' (parallel, 7'):

> *māmīt kīma qutri* [*šamê*]
> May the curse rise [skyward] like smoke.

Next, 'like morning cloud' (Hos. 13.3; cf. 6.4, 14.6) is akin to *Lipšur* II 1 25' (parallel, 9'):

> *māmīt kīma erpeti muqqalpītu ina ugāri šanîmma lišaznin*
> May the curse, like drifting cloud, rain down into another field.[64]

Yet another simile in Hos. 13.3, 'like the chaff which swirls from the threshing floor', echoes line 57' of the same text:

> *annū'a ḫitātū'a gillatū'a ša kīma ḫāmī tabkūma elišunu ukabbis*
> My sins, my errors, my crimes that are heaped up like litter;
> on them do I tread

The same wording is used in another (Akkadian) incantation,

60. E. Reiner, '*Lipšur* litanies', *JNES* 15 (1956), pp. 129-49.

61. E. Reiner, *Šurpu: A Collection of Sumerian and Akkadian Incantations* (AfO Beiheft, 11; Graz: E. Weidner, 1958; repr. Osnabrück; Biblio Verlag, 1970). The Alexander von Humboldt Stiftung, Bonn–Bad Godesberg, kindly made a copy of this book available to me.

62. W.G. Lambert, 'DINGIR.ŠÀ.DIB.BA Incantations', *JNES* 33 (1974), pp. 267-322. See, too, G. Meier, *Die assyrische Beschwörungssammlung Maqlû* (AfO Beiheft, 2; Berlin, 1937).

63. On Akkadian similes, cf. G. Buccellati, 'Towards a Formal Typology of Akkadian Similes', in B.L. Eichler (ed.), *Kramer Anniversary Volume: Cuneiform Studies in Honor of Samuel Noah Kramer* (AOAT, 25; Kevelaer: Butzon & Bercker; Neukirchen–Vluyn: Neukirchener Verlag, 1976), pp. 59-70. The use of similes in series is not restricted to incantations. For a set of five in a row outside the *genre*, cf. W.G. Lambert, 'The Converse Tablet: A Litany with Musical Instructions', in H. Goedicke (ed.), *Near Eastern Studies in Honor of W.F. Albright* (Baltimore: The Johns Hopkins University Press, 1971), pp. 335-53, text, p. 345 = rev., lines 1-5.

64. Following *CAD*, M/2, p. 213, which translates: 'let the curse rain down on another field like (rain from) a drifting cloud'.

suggesting it to be formulaic.[65] There are one or two other common similes.[66]

The tendency for clustering of similes is apparent from Hos. 2.5, 6.3 and 14.6 (all sets of three); 13.3 (set of four); 13.7-8 (five in a row) and the group of eight in 14.6-8. The *Lipšur* litanies use sequences of fifteen (II 1 7'-21') and even seventeen similes (II 1 23'-37').[67] Sets elsewhere are shorter, but it can be noted that the sequence 'like fog, like dew, like smoke' in the 'Fire Incantations'[68] corresponds to the same set in Hos. 13.3. Such clustering, not unknown in Hebrew poetry,[69] may have been a stylistic trait within Mesopotamian tradition.

The second point of comparison concerns other similarities between Hebrew and Mesopotamian traditions as represented by the works in question. The sequence 'swearing, lying, killing, stealing, adultery and murder' of Hos. 4.2 is matched by an almost identical list in *Šurpu* II: 33-49. Lines 33-36 deal with scorning gods and goddesses and with having contempt for close relatives. Then comes a section on cheating and lying (lines 37-42):

> He gave with small (measure) but received with large.
> He said 'There is' when there was not.
> He said 'There is not' when there was.
> He used an untrue balance (but) did not use the true balance.

Theft is mentioned next (lines 43-46):

> He took money that was not due to him
> (but) did not take money due to him.

65. In DINGIR.ŠÀ.DIB.BA II: 7 which Lambert, 'Incantations', pp. 284-85, translates: 'I have trodden on my iniquities, sins and transgressions, which were heaped up like leaves'. For a slightly different version, cf. *CAD*, Ḫ, p. 73, where it is pointed out that *ḫamû*, 'litter of leaves, reed, etc.', is clearly differentiated from *tibnu*, 'straw', and *pû*, 'chaff'.

66. The long oven simile of Hos. 7.4-7 may correspond to *Lipšur* I 1 104-13, 114-21, and to *Šurpu* III: 145. Comparable, too, are the 'useless vessel' and 'broken pot' similes of Hos. 8.8, and *Lipšur* II 1 15'-16' (and 31'-32') respectively.

67. See Reiner's edition, 'Litanies', pp. 140-43, lines 7'-21' and 23'-36'.

68. W.G. Lambert, 'Fire Incantations', *AfO* 33 (1970), pp. 39-45, section II: 14-15: 'Scatter like fog, rise like dew, like smoke ascend to the heaven of Anu' (p. 40).

69. See my remarks below, 'The Hidden Simile in Psalm 133'.

He disinherited the legitimated son (and)
did not establish (in his rights) the legitimated son.
He set up an untrue boundary (but) did not set up the true boundary.
He removed mark, frontier and boundary.

This is followed by adultery (lines 47-48):

He entered his neighbour's house,
had intercourse with his neighbour's wife;

and murder (line 49):

He shed his neighbour's blood.[70]

There are certain differences, of course, and the list in *Šurpu* is longer and more complete, but there appears to be a similar (though not necessarily a related) tradition here.[71] Note, too, that the alteration of boundaries referred to here (line 45) and in *Šurpu* III: 54 and 60[72] recalls Hos. 5.10: 'The princes of Judah have become like those who remove the landmark'.[73]

Lastly, the word-pair 'root'–'fruit' of Hos. 9.16 and 14.6-7 has a counterpart in the parallel pair 'root'–'shoot' of *Šurpu* V/VI: 64-65, 133-37 and IX: 1-16, as shown in more detail elsewhere.[74]

We now come to the difficult passage referred to right at the beginning of this article. It is Hos. 13.12:

ṣārûr ʿawōn ʾeprāyim	Bound up is Ephraim's guilt;
ṣᵉpûnâ ḥaṭṭāʾtô	hidden, his sin.

There is no problem regarding translation, but as yet no-one has explained what is meant. Andersen and Freedman see no connection with the immediate context and are probably correct in labelling this couplet 'a completely self-contained oracle'.[75] Vuilleumier-Bessard understands the imagery in terms of wrapping up (*ṣrr*) precious manuscripts and the hiding (*ṣpn*) them away in a safe place such as a

70. Translation as in Reiner, *Šurpu*, p. 14.

71. Since both lists involve common crimes and failings, the similarity cannot be pressed too hard.

72. '(The oath): to fix a boundary but change it, to mark frontier or boundary.'

73. See, too, Deut. 9.14, 27.17, Job 24.2 and Prov. 23.10. As an additional parallel A.D.H. Mayes, *Deuteronomy* (NCB; London: Oliphants, 1979), p. 289, cites ch. 6 of the Egyptian Instruction of Amen-em-opet.

74. See Chapter 2, 'Trends in the Development of Classical Hebrew Poetry'.

75. *Hosea*, p. 637.

cave.[76] Some support for this explanation comes from Jer. 32.14 and the way manuscripts were stored in the Qumran caves.[77] Developing Vuilleumier-Bessard's interpretation, Andersen and Freedman consider 'iniquity' and 'sin' to denote idols (as abstract for concrete) which were hidden away for safekeeping.[78] Other explanations have also been put forward, none convincing.[79]

In view of the similarities between Hosea and the Akkadian texts mentioned, a similarity particularly strong, as it happens, in Hosea 13, another explanation seems preferable. As noted by Geller, one important aspect of the Akkadian incantations is the fact that 'patients' can be unaware of the sin (or sins) they have committed, which in turn accounts for the exhaustive lists provided in such rituals, intended to cover all possible misdemeanours.[80] When the term 'hidden' is found in Hos. 13.12, it is immediately obvious that it refers to unknown offences. There remains the first half of the context-free couplet to consider: why should Ephraim's iniquity be 'bound up'? Again, the answer lies in the different kinds of Akkadian incantation texts already referred to, notably the *Lipšur* litanies, the *Šurpu* texts, the dingir.šà.dib.ba incantations and *Maqlû*. To begin with, both the *Lipšur* litanies and *Šurpu* stress the 'undoing' or 'releasing' of sin.[81] For example, *Šurpu* VIII: 43-47:

> May your sin, your oath, your error, your crime,
> your invocation, your disease, your weariness,
> sorcery, spittle, dirt... be released for you, be
> absolved for you, be wiped off for you.

Similarly elsewhere.[82] Further, the essential component of the litanies, namely, *lipšur*, 'may (So-and-So) absolve', is used in at least

76. R. Vuilleumier-Bessard, 'Osée 13; 12 et les manuscripts', *RevQ* 1 (1958), pp. 281-82. J.L. Mays (*Hosea: A Commentary* [OTL; Philadelphia: Westminster Press, 1969]), p. 180) also takes this view: 'The language comes from the practice of tying together papyrus and parchment documents and putting them in a depository for safe-keeping'.

77. However, see the objections of Andersen and Freedman, *Hosea*, p. 637.

78. *Hosea*, p. 638.

79. E.g. by Wolff, *Hosea*, pp. 221, 227.

80. Geller, 'Šurpu Incantations', p. 185; he refers to 'unawareness of the patient's exact transgression'.

81. See, again, Geller, 'Šurpu Incantations', p. 185.

82. *Šurpu* II: 1.82.129; III (refrain); IV: 60-67, with *lipṭur* in each line; VIII (also a litany); for details, cf. Reiner, 'Litanies', pp. 129-30.

sixty-three consecutive lines (Type I 1 0-62). In *Lipšur* Type II, the recurrent phrase is either *lu paṭranni lu pašranni*, 'let it be released for me, let it be absolved for me', or, *lippaṭrunikku lippašrunikku*, 'let it be released for you, let it be absolved for you'.[83] Related expressions occur in the dingir.šà.dib.ba series (texts I: 16, 112, 113, 120). All these pleas imply bondage of some sort and many texts, in fact, explicitly mention binding. An example is *Šurpu* IV: 70

> *kasīta lirammû*
> May they (the gods) undo the magic bond.

Such passages could be multiplied.[84] Accordingly, in the Hosea passage 'bound up' can only mean 'unabsolved', that is, the adverse effect of the sin remains. The likelihood of this explanation is increased once it is realized that two key concepts of Mesopotamian incantation texts—unknown crime and unabsolved sin—occur together in a single couplet in Hosea. What is more, Hosea 13 exhibits elements akin to these incantations and, as has been seen, there are yet other similarities between other parts of Hosea and the incantation texts discussed. Hos. 12.12, then, is yet another Hebrew passage which can be explained in the light of Mesopotamian belief and ritual practice as attested in the clay tablets of that civilization.[85]

5. *The Hidden Simile in Psalm 133*[86]

The second half of v. 2 in Psalm 133 has always been troublesome to translators and writers of commentaries. Of course a simple solution is to delete these words as an explanatory gloss,[87] but a closer look at

83. Reiner, *Litanies*, pp. 129-30.

84. See *CAD*, K, p. 243, under *kasītu*, 'binding magic', and *AHw*, pp. 453b-54a. Also, the references under *abāru* III, as *ubburu*, 'to clasp', in *AHw*, p. 4b (e.g. *Maqlû* VII: 71). Likewise, the passages cited under *rakāsu*, 'to bind', and *riksu*, 'Hexerei', in *AHw*, pp. 946b and 985a (e.g. *Maqlû* V 55), etc.

85. In addition to the passages discussed by Geller, 'Šurpu Incantations', pp. 181-92 (notably, Lev. 5.1-5), and by Reiner, 'Litanies', p. 149 (Ps. 40.13), others can be listed. They are Hos. 4.3b and *Lipšur* II 22', 37'; the *šā'il* litany of *Šurpu* II: 104-128 and Isa. 7.10; the list of musical instruments in *Šurpu* III: 88-91 and Ps. 150.3-5. see, too, my note 'Splitting Hairs in Israel and Babylon', below.

86. First published in *Bib* 60 (1979), pp. 108-109.

87. So, for instance, H.-J. Kraus, *Psalmen* (BKAT, 15; Neukirchen–Vluyn: Neukirchener Verlag, 1972), p. 889, and O. Loretz, 'Psalmenstudien', *UF* 4 (1972), pp. 101-16. A.R. Ceresko, 'The A : B :: B : A Word Pattern in Hebrew and

the structure of vv. 2-3a points to an alternative answer. The lines in question, which form a tricolon, can be set out as follows:

kaššemen haṭṭôb 'al-hārō'š *šeyyōrēd 'al-hazzāqān*
z^e qan-'ah^a rōn *šeyyōrēd 'al-pî middôtāyw*
k^e ṭal-ḥermôn *šeyyōred 'al-har^e rê ṣiyyôn*

The skeletal structure for each colon is *k^e…šeyyōrēd 'al-…*,[88] recognition of which leads to two essential observations. The first is that the expression *'al-hārō'š*, 'upon the head', does not belong to the underlying pattern but forms part of the unit preceding *šeyyōrēd*. In other words, 'like the sweet oil upon the head' is the equivalent of 'like the dew of Hermon'. The second observation is now obvious: 'Aaron's beard' is also a simile corresponding to the other two similes, differing only in ellipsis of the comparative particle *k^e*. The tristich can now be translated:

Like sweet oil on one's head,[89] flowing down[90] over one's beard,
Like Aaron's beard, flowing down over the collar[91] of his robes;
(And) like the dew of Hermon, flowing down over Zion's mountains.

Ellipsis, common enough in poetry, is particularly a feature of simile.[92] Clustering of similes is frequent, too, in Hebrew as well as in Ugaritic and Akkadian.[93] Much rarer, however, is the triple simile.

Northwest Semitic with Special Reference to the Book of Job', *UF* 7 (1975), pp. 73-88, 81-82 retains the phrase, but for the wrong reason. As will be seen, his identification of an ABBA word pattern is incorrect.

88. The presence of a shared *š* was established by M.J. Dahood, *Psalms* III (AB, 17A; Garden City, NY: Doubleday, 1968), p. 251. My thanks are due to him for an exchange of letters concerning this verse.

89. Literally 'like the sweet (or precious: cf. Dahood's translation) oil on the head'.

90. For the nuance 'to flow' of this verb, cf. Jer. 9.17, Ps. 119.137 and Akk. *arādu*, 'to flow' as well as 'to descend'.

91. So Dahood, *Psalms* III, p. 252.

92. See A. Schott, *Die Vergleiche in den akkadischen Königsinschriften* (MVAG, 30/2; Leipzig: Hinrichs, 1926), pp. 3-8.

93. For Akkadian, cf. G. Buccellati, 'Towards a Formal Typology of Akkadian Similes', in Eichler (ed.), *Kramer Anniversary Volume*, pp. 59-70, esp. 65-66. For Ugaritic, U. Cassuto, *The Goddess Anath: Canaanite Epics of the Patriarchal Age. Texts. Hebrew Translation, Commentary and Introduction* (ET; Jerusalem: Magnes, 1971 [1951]), pp. 24-25, and J. Gray, *The Legacy of Canaan: The Ras Shamra Texts and their Relevance to the Old Testament* (VTSup, 9; Leiden: Brill, 1965),

Other examples in Hebrew are 2 Sam. 23.4[94] and Job 7.1b-2. Its function in the present psalm is a double one, apparently. It sustains the listener's interest, and it connects the opening and closing lines of the poem.[95]

6. *The Metaphor in Job 10.17*[96]

This note attempts to determine the meaning of a difficult strophe in the book of Job by applying the principle of congruity of metaphor[97] and by comparison with extra-biblical passages.[98] The text in question, Job 10.17, has provoked a variety of explanations and since they have been surveyed recently by Grabbe[99] there is no need for more than summary reference here. The Hebrew text runs:

(a) *tḥdš 'dyk ngdy*
(b) *wtrb k'sk 'mdy*
(c) *ḥlypwt wṣb' 'my*

The main obstacle to intelligibility is the second word in line (a), *'dyk*. Traditionally it is taken to mean 'witnesses' (so MT and ancient versions, including LXX, Aq., Theod., Vg. and the Targums)[100] even

pp. 298-99. Note the sequence of 5 similes in Hos. 13.7-8 and 11 in Sir. 50.6-10.

94. Recognized by T.N.D. Mettinger, 'Structure and Meaning in 2 Sam. 23:1-7', *SEÅ* 41-42 (1976–77), pp. 152-53; there is ellipsis of k^e in two consecutive cola.

95. On functions of the simile, see A. Preminger (ed.), *Princeton Encyclopedia of Poetry and Poetics* (London: MacMillan Press, 1975), p. 767. For a different solution, see now D.T. Tsumura, 'Sorites in Psalm 133.2-3a', *Bib* 61 (1980), pp. 416-17. See also O. Loretz, 'Marziḫu im ugaritischen und biblischen Ahnenkult. Zu Ps 23; 133; Am 1,6-7 und Jer 16,5.8', in M. Dietrich and O. Loretz (eds.), *Mesopotamica—Ugaritica—Biblica: Festschrift für Kurt Bergerhof zur Vollendung seines 70. Lebensjahres am 7. Mai 1992* (AOAT, 232; Kevelaer: Butzon & Bercker; Neukirchen–Vluyn: Neukirchener Verlag, 1993), pp. 93-144.

96. First published in *Bib* 63 (1982), pp. 255-57.

97. M.J. Dahood, 'Congruity of Metaphors', in *Hebräische Wortforschung: Festschrift zum 80. Geburtstag von Walter Baumgartner* (VTSup, 16; Leiden: Brill, 1967), pp. 40-49.

98. I am grateful to Professor B. Margalit of Haifa for his detailed critique of a previous draft. The views expressed here, of course, are my own.

99. L.L. Grabbe, *Comparative Philology and the Text of Job: A Study in Methodology* (SBLDS, 34; Missoula, MT: Scholars Press, 1977), pp. 63-66.

100. The versional evidence is surveyed by Grabbe, *Comparative Philology*, p. 63. He points out, too, that form criticism favours the meaning 'witness' (p. 65)

though semantic parallelism with either line (b) or line (c) would then be totally lacking. An alternative is to assign the word a meaning related to combat (so Symm., Syr.) and many scholars prefer this solution. Yet another possibility, first proposed by Dahood,[101] is to compare Ugaritic *ǵdd*, 'to swell', and translate 'vexation' or the like, but there are objections to such a view.[102] Ultimately, the problem is not one of parallelism, but of *metaphor* and the solution lies not in pitting versional evidence against modern philological proposals (based on ancient languages) but in determining which metaphor the poet is using here. If the underlying figure is forensic, then *'dyk* means 'your witnesses'. If, on the other hand, these lines speak of combat, as the context in v. 16 seems to indicate, then this particular word must have an appropriate meaning.

The expression *ḥ^{a}lîpôt w^{e}ṣābā'* is a key component in our text: if we can pinpoint its meaning we can decide on the nature of the metaphor here. A pointer in the right direction is provided by a neo-Babylonian text which uses almost identical terms: *ḫantiš* ^{LÚ}*ḫalpi šuprānu ṣābē pitinūtu* ^{LÚ}*kidinniya u nēpišu*, 'Quickly, do send replacements, strong men, troops under my protection and equipment'.[103] Not only does this indicate a military meaning for the Hebrew expression; it also suggests hendiadys.[104] Accordingly, 'fresh troops' is correct, as several commentators have long assumed.[105]

The metaphor in Job 10.17, therefore, is probably military in character: God is depicted as a general sending out successive waves of

but this can be countered by arguments mustered in the present note.

101. Dahood, *Psalms I*, p. 197, followed by A.C.M. Blommerde, *Northwest Semitic Grammar and Job* (BibOr, 22; Rome: Pontifical Biblical Institute, 1969), p. 60.

102. See Grabbe, *Comparative Philology*, p. 64, who argues that the Arabic cognate primarily concerns glandular swelling and that in any case this word is poorly attested (if at all) elsewhere in Ugaritic.

103. A.T. Clay, *Yale Oriental Studies* 3, p. 188: 8-10, cited in *CAD*, Ḫ, p. 49. See also *AHw*, p. 313a.

104. So already M.H. Pope, *Job* (Garden City, NY: Doubleday, 1965), p. 79, though he opts for the forensic interpretation. On hendiadys, cf. G.T. Wright, 'Hendiadys and *Hamlet*', *Proceedings of the Modern Language Association* 96 (1981), pp. 168-93.

105. For discussion of *ḥlp* / *ḫlp* in Hebrew, Ugaritic, Akkadian (and Aramaic), see the survey by O. Loretz, *Die Psalmen* (AOAT, 207/2; Neukirchen–Vluyn: Neukirchener Verlag, 1979), II, pp. 417-19.

troops against his enemy, Job. If such is the case, then *'dyk* must also denote 'troops'. A much-discussed passage in Ugaritic also suggests as much, though unfortunately scholars do not agree on its meaning. It is *CTA* 14 ii 85-87 / *UT Krt* 85-87 (repeated verbatim in 176-78):[106]

'dn ngb wyṣi	The assembled *troop* must sally out
ṣbu ṣbi ngb	—the vast assembled army—
wyṣi 'dn m'	sally out must the combined *forces*.

Here, too, the root and meaning of *'dn* are a matter of dispute. If *-n* is an afformative, any of the following Arabic roots (and their derivatives) may be cognate: *'adā* (*'dw*), 'to run, speed, gallop; engage in hostile action'; *'adda*, 'to count, number', hence *'idda*, 'numerous army'; *'dy*, 'to pass by', hence 'seasonal labourers'.[107] If the final consonant is part of the root, then the cognate would be *'adanatu*, 'company of men, multitude' (from *'dn*, 'to remain, stay').[108] The strophe in Ugaritic and the verse from Job share many common features, notably the common semantic field 'army' which already suggests a meaning for *'dn // 'dy(k)*. Of particular significance is the compound word-pair in the Keret text: *'dn // ṣbu ṣbi* of the first two lines and *ṣbu ṣbi // 'dn* of lines two and three. It is arguable that a corresponding parallel pair is used in the Hebrew passage (*'dyk // ṣb'*) and that the meaning of the first element is 'your troops', parallel to 'army'. The Arabic cognate would be *'dw*, 'to engage in hostile action' (see above) and the final letter of Ugaritic *'dn*, also 'troops', in afformative. Accordingly, Job 10.17 can be rendered:

You renew your combatants opposite me,
—and increase your irritation with me—
with relief-troops against me.

106. Discussed by F.C. Fensham, 'Notes on Keret 79(b)-89 (CTA 14: 79(b)-89)', *JNSL* 7 (1979), pp. 17-25. With most scholars I now take *ngb* as a passive form of *gbb* ('to gather'). See now F. Renfroe, 'The Transition from "Army" to "Enemy"', *UF* 19 (1987), pp. 231-33.

107. The solution mentioned last is by Fensham, 'Notes', pp. 21-23, and is novel if unconvincing. He equates *'dn* with the same word used in non-literary Ugaritic texts to denote seasonal labourers on a lower social scale than *bnšm*—as proposed by M. Dietrich, O. Loretz and J. Sanmartín, 'Zur ugaritischen Lexikographie (xi): Lexikographische Einzelbemerkungen', *UF* 6 (1974), p. 33—the root being *'dy*, 'to pass by'.

108. For a convenient list of opinions, cf. J. Gray, *The Krt Text in the Literature of Ras Shamra* (Leiden: Brill, 2nd edn, 1964), p. 39.

Chapter 9

Preludes to Speech

1. *Introductions to Discourse in Ugaritic Narrative Verse*[1]

1.1. *Introduction*

This note examines expressions used to introduce speech in the Ugaritic literary texts[2] tracing their development from the single line, through the couplet, to the tricolon and the rare quatrain. Similar studies have been carried out by Loewenstamm and de Moor.[3] First will come a section setting out the formulae and their variants. Then expansions of these formulae will be examined. After discussion of the prosodic and rhetorical functions of such expressions in both simple and extended forms comes a final paragraph on a post-speech formula. Of course, speeches (and messages) are not always introduced by a formula[4] but when present the prelude to speech is rarely less than a line in length.[5] The reverse is a description of 'speaking' with no

1. First published in *AuOr* 1 (1983), pp. 253-61.

2. See G. del Olmo Lete, *Mitos y leyendas de Canaan según la tradición de Ugarit* (Fuentes de la Ciencia Bíblica, 1; Madrid: Ediciones Cristiandad, 1981), pp. 52-60 and his bibliography, l. 55 n. 78. Unfortunately the preliminary study on this topic in R. Whitaker, 'A Formulaic Analysis of Ugaritic Poetry' (unpublished dissertation, Harvard University, 1969), is unavailable to me.

3. S.E. Loewenstamm, 'The Address "Listen" in the Ugaritic Epic and the Bible', in G. Rendsburg *et al.* (eds.), *The Bible World: Essays in Honor of Cyrus H. Gordon* (New York; Ktav and The Institute of Hebrew Culture and Education of New York University, 1980), pp. 123-31, J.C. de Moor, 'The Art of Versification in Ugarit and Israel-I', in Y. Avishur and J. Blau (eds.), *Studies in the Bible and the Ancient Near East Presented to S.E. Loewenstamm on his Seventieth Birthday* (Jerusalem; E. Rubinstein's Publishing House, 1978), pp. 119-39; II, *UF* 10 (1978), pp. 187-217; III, *UF* 12 (1980), pp. 311-15.

4. As in *KTU* 1.2 i 40; 1.6 i 5-6; 1.13:21; 1.14 iii 21.33; 1.19 ii 15-16, 22-23; 1.23:71, etc.

5. E.g. *KTU* 1.1 iv 16 in broken context; cf. J.C.L. Gibson, *Canaanite Myths*

actual speech as in *KTU* 1.4 vii 29-37, which has no actual bearing on our discussion.

1.2. *The Formulae*

Here are listed one-line formulae used to introduce speech in Ugaritic verse. The first half-dozen are the commonest and, as will be seen, they are also those which can occur in expanded form. For ease of reference the formulae have been identified by letters; a number after a slash denotes a variant (e.g. F/2 = second variant of formula F).

A	*wy'n lṭpn 'il dp'id*	Answer did Lutpan, kindly god.

By far the commonest formula[6] this expression can be set out schematically as (*w*) + *'ny* (usually *yqtl*) + geographical/personal name. The meaning 'to reply' is normally present only in a weak sense though the formula occurs often in speeches of dialogue. Note the anomalous variant A/1 *y'n ǵlmm y'nyn* which is used before a negation and is difficult to translate.[7]

B	*yš'u gh wyṣḥ*	He raised his voice and shouted.

Again a frequently used formula[8] which follows the pattern *nš'* (*yqtl*) + *g* + suffix + *w* + *ṣ*(*y*)*ḥ* (*yqtl*). There appear to be no variants.

C	*gm lǵlmh b'l kyṣḥ*	Aloud to his youths did Baal shout.

Though superficially resembling B, formula C[9] is better treated as independent. The variant C/1 *gm yṣḥ 'il lrbt 'aṯrt ym*—also as *gm yṣḥ 'il lbtlt 'nt*—is not significant.[10] It is not clear whether *špš tṣḥ lmt*[11] belongs here as a variant or not.

D	*wrgm l'aḫtk ṯṯmnt*	And say to your sister Octavia.

and Legends (Edinburgh: T. & T. Clark, 1978), p. 39; del Olmo Lete, *Mitos y leyendas*, p. 159.

6. *KTU* 1.1 iv 13 (quoted), pp. 17, 25-26, etc.

7. *KTU* 1.3 iv 5; del Olmo Lete, *Mitos y leyendas*, p. 186, opts for 'Respondiéronle los macebos esta respuesta'.

8. *KTU* 1.1 ii 17; 1.2 iii 15; 1.3 iii 35-36; 1.5 ii 16-17 and elsewhere.

9. *KTU* 1.4 vii 52-53 (cited).

10. Texts: *KTU* 1.6 i 43-44 and 1.6 iii 22. Both are single lines of verse.

11. *KTU* 1.6 vi 22-23; cf. 1.161:19.

Essentially a messenger formula, D[12] has a variant, D/1 *lyrgm l'al'iyn b'l*[13] and a corresponding form in the passive, formula G, discussed below.

E	*w[yṯ]b ṯr 'abh 'il*	Respond did Bull El, his father.

Although the formula here is based on a restoration,[14] I have included it because it also occurs in expanded form (see below).

F	*ql lb'l ttnn*	Loudly they spoke to Baal.

This formula is followed by a couplet announcing good news.[15] A variant, F/1, inserts a divine name into the same formula: *[ql] lb'l 'nt ttnn*.[16]

G	*rgm l'il ybl*	Word was brought to El.[17]
H	*wywsrnn ggnh*	His inner self instructed him.

Strictly speaking this line is the second half of a 'structurally' parallel couplet.[18]

I	*wyqrb bš'al krt*	He (= El) approached, asking Krt.[19]
J	*ṯm ydr krt ṯ'*	There did Noble Krt make a vow.[20]
K	*bšm tg'rm 'ṯtrt*	Athtart rebuked him by name.

A variant of K[21] is K/1: *bhm tg'r ṯǵr bt 'il*, 'The doorman of El's house reproves them'.[22]

12. *KTU* 1.16 i 38-39; cf. 1.14 v 32 (and 1.2 i 33).
13. *KTU* 1.4 v 12.
14. Following *KTU* 1.14 ii 6; cf. Gibson, *Canaanite Myths* , p. 165.
15. *KTU* 1.10 iii 32.
16. *KTU* 1.10 ii 32. For the prosodic implications, see my discussion in a review of J. Kugel, *The Idea of Biblical Poetry, Parallelism and its History* (New Haven; Yale University Press, 1981), above, pp. 51-53. Altogether different is the formula *wtn qlh b'rpt, KTU* 1.4 v 8.
17. *KTU* 1.23: 52, 59; also, *rgm lyt[pn] ybl* in 1.19 iv 50-51.
18. *KTU* 1.16 vi 26.
19. *KTU* 1.14 i 37-38; cf. *tqrb qḫ[h wtš'al/tṣḥ]*, 1.16 ii 17, and, more remotely *[w/k]yqrb b'l bḥnth*, 1.17 i 16.
20. *KTU* 1.14 iv 36-37.
21. *KTU* 1.2 iv 28, on which cf. D. Pardee, 'The New Canaanite Myths and Legends', *BO* 37 (1980), pp. 269-91, 274.
22. *KTU* 1.114:12; the line *b'il 'abh g'r* (same text, line 14) is not followed by direct speech. For translation of 1.114, cf. K.J. Cathcart and W.G.E. Watson,

L	*wyp'r šmthm*	He proclaimed their (joint) name.[23]
M	*yṣly 'rpt bḥm 'un*	He abjured the clouds in the terrible drought.[24]
N	*hm 'aṯtm tṣḥn*	If both women should shout.

This formula[25] introduces a speech within a speech. Related (or variant, N/1) is *wṣḥ hm 'm nǵr mdr'*, 'They shouted to the guardian of the sown'.[26]

O	*ṣḥ lqṣ 'ilm*	He invited the gods to the carving.

Though superficially similar to N, the meaning in O[27] is totally different.[28]

1.3. *Expansions of the Formulae*

Here, expansions of the formulae just listed will be set out (following the same sequence) and discussed briefly.

1.3.1. *Expansions of A*

A-1	*y'n 'il bšb't ḥdrm* *bṯmnt 'ap sgrt*	El spoke from seven rooms, from eight antechambers.

The couplet occurs twice,[29] though no reason for its use is immediately apparent.

A-2	*wt'n btlt 'nt* *ṯṯb ybmt l'imm*	Virgin Anath replied, the 'sister-in-law' of the peoples made response.

'Weathering a Wake a Cure for a Carousal', *PIBA* 4 (1980), pp. 35-58

23. *KTU* 1.2 iv 11.18 where Kothar is naming a double-headed axe; cf. del Olmo Lete, *Mitos y leyendas*, p. 614. Also, 1.13:32.

24. *KTU* 1.19 i 38-40, following del Olmo Lete, *Mitos y leyendas*, p. 389. Note the preceding 'filler' line *'apnk dn'il mt rp'i*. Related, perhaps, is *qr my*[*m*] *mlk yṣm* in 1.19 iii 45-46.

25. *KTU* 1.23:3.42-43.46.

26. 1.23:69.

27. *KTU* 1.114:2; see n. 22.

28. Other possible formulae include *KTU* 1.17 i 34-36 (blessing) and the series of questions in 1.16 v 10-22.

29. *KTU* 1.3 v 10-12 // 25-27.

Twice this introduction is followed by a lengthy speech[30] while in another text it forms part of a tricolon which also comes before a long speech.[31]

A-3	*wy‘n dn’il mt rp’i*	Danel, R.-man, replied,
	yṯb ġzr mt hrnmy	the adult, H.-man, responded.
	yš’u gh wyṣḥ	He raised his voice and shouted.

In effect this climactic strophe[32] comprises a couplet (= A-2) plus a standard speech-introduction formula (= B). It closes the period of mourning for Aqhat and marks a transition to normal life.

1.3.2. *Expansion of B*

B-1	*wypqd krt ṯ‘*	Noble Krt gave orders,
	yš’u gh wyṣḥ	raised his voice and shouted.

The B-formula here[33] comes in the second line. Krt has just been cured; he is ordering preparations for a celebration sacrifice and this couplet marks a transition to normal life once more (see above on A-3). For the set of expressions involving the verb *ṣḥq*, see below.

1.3.3. *Expansion of C*

C-1	*’any lyṣḥ ṯr ’il ’abh*	Sighing, Bull El his father exclaimed,
	’il mlk dyknnh	El, the king who established him,
	yṣḥ ’aṯrt wbnh	Athirat and her sons exclaimed,
	’ilt wṣbrt ’aryh	the goddess and her band of relatives.

Here I follow del Olmo Lete.[34] Gibson[35] considers these words to belong to Anath's description of Baal ('[Yet] groaning he indeed cries out to the bull El his father, etc.') which obviates the difficulty of parsing *yṣḥ* (third line) with *’aṯrt bnh* as subject, though this problem is not insurmountable. Each time it is used this introduction is followed by eight lines stating that Baal has no palace. It belongs, therefore, to formulaic language.

30. *KTU* 1.3 iv 21-22; 1.19 i 5-6.
31. *KTU* 1.4 v 49-50; see 1.20 i 7-8.
32. *KTU* 1.19 iv 18-20, followed by a tricolon.
33. *KTU* 1.16 vi 14-16.
34. Del Olmo Lete, *Mitos y leyendas*, p. 191; the texts are *KTU* 1.3 v 35-37 // 1.4 i 4-8 // 1.4 iv 47-50.
35. Gibson, *Canaanite Myths*, p. 54.

1.3.4. *Expansions of B and C*

We come now to expansions of B and C which include the aspect of happiness and rejoicing and seem to comprise an independent semantic set.[36]

C-2	*šmḫ rbt 'aṯrt ym*	Lady Asherah of the Sea rejoiced,
	gm lǵlmh ktṣḥ	aloud did she call to her page.

Asherah is reacting to the sight of silver and gold.[37]

B-2	*ṣḥq btlt 'nt*	Virgin Anath laughed;
	tš'u gh wtṣḥ	she raised her voice and exclaimed.

The couplet introduces the announcement of good news to Baal: his palace is to be built.[38] In the Aqhat text the same couplet precedes Anath's offer of marriage.[39] Kothar-and-Hasis also use this introduction for the 'I told you so' speech concerning the windows:[40]

B-3	*ṣḥq kṯr wḫss*	Kothar-and-Hasis laughed,
	yš'u gh wyṣḥ	raised his voice and exclaimed:
	lrgmt lk 'al'iyn b'l	'Did I not tell you, O Mightiest Baal,
	ṯṯbn b'l lhwty	that you would come back to my word?'

Here, too, belong two texts which insert a couplet or tricolon between the B-2 couplet.[41]

B-4[1]	*šmḫ lṭpn 'il dp'id*	Latipan, kindly god, rejoiced;
	p'nh lhdm yṯpd	his feet he placed on the footstool,
	wyprq lṣb wyṣḥq	he uncreased his forehead and laughed,
	yš'u gh wyṣḥ	raised his voice and shouted.

Here[42] El announces his joy at knowing Baal to be alive.

36. See the preliminary study by del Olmo Lete, 'Notas de semántica ugarítica', *AF* 2 (1976), pp. 233-36.

37. *KTU* 1.4 ii 28-29, plus 10-line speech. Note that in 1.4 v 35-36 an introductory formula appears to be missing.

38. *KTU* 1.4 v 25-26.

39. *KTU* 1.18 i 22-23.

40. *KTU* 1.4 vii 21-22; the second couplet appears to play on the introductory formula under discussion; *ṯ(w)b*, 'to return' evokes the meaning 'to reply'.

41. See n. 34. *KTU* 1.4 iv 27-30 simply joins the 'action' tricolon to our formula; accordingly, it is not discussed as an expansion here.

42. *KTU* 1.6 iii 14-17.

In the variant a line parallel to the first is inserted and, as del Olmo Lete noted, the line sequence within the following couplet is inverted:

B-4²	*bdn'il pnm tšmḫ*	Danel's face gleamed joyfully,
	w'l yṣḥl p'it	above, his brow shone, etc.
	yprq lṣb wyṣḥq	
	p'n lhdm yṯpd	
	yš'u gh wyṣḥ	

The strophe is followed by a quatrain (Danel can relax now) and then come the lines (six couplets) listing stock characteristics of the ideal son.[43] There is, incidentally, a near-parallel to examples from this set in the Babylonian *Epic of Erra*:[44]

išmes[um] Erra immerā pānūšu	Erra listened to him; his face shone;
kī ūme n[aparde]e uḫtambisu zīmūšu	like a shining bright day his looks were exuberant.
īrumma [ana] Emeslam irtami šubassu	He entered Emeslam and took his seat.

These three lines, which mark an important moment in the poem[45] are followed by a couplet introducing Erra's instructions to Išum.

1.3.5. *Expansions of D*

D-1	*wrgm lbn 'ilm mt*	And tell divine Mot,
	ṯny lydd 'il ǵzr	repeat to the hero, El's favourite.

43. *KTU* 1.17 ii 8-12. Del Olmo Lete, 'Notas', p. 234 n. 17 comments: 'En todo caso la formula de discurso directo debe considerarse *como elemento aparte e independiente*' (emphasis mine). Here, too, can be included the formula

'il yẓḥq bm lb	El laughed inside himself
wygmḏ bm kbd	and rejoiced inwardly.

(*KTU* 1.12 i 12-13) which is followed by direct speech without the act of speaking mentioned (= Ø prelude).

44. For text and translations, cf. W.G. Lambert, 'The Fifth Tablet of the Era Epic', *Iraq* 24 (1962), pp. 120-21; L. Cagni, *L'epopea di Erra* (Studi Semitici, 34; Rome: Institutio di Studi del Vicino Oriente, 1969), pp. 124-25 and L. Cagni, *The Poem of Erra* (Sources and Monographs Sources from the Ancient Near East, 1/3; Malibu: Undena Publications, 1977), p. 58.

45. So Cagni, *Poem*, p. 59 n. 160.

Here[46] and in two other passages the injunction precedes a message.[47] The fourth occurrence is before the 'told you so' speech.[48]

D-2	*lk l'abk yṣb*	Go to your father, Yassub,
	lk l'abk wrgm	go to your father and say,
	ṯny l[krt ṯ' / 'adnk]	repeat to [Krt the Noble (or) your master]

As with D-1 the 'messenger formula' comes after a command ordering movement to the addressee. Here[49] the repetitive pattern is followed by staircase parallelism.

D-3	*qmm 'aṯr 'amr*	Standing, advance and speak,
	ṯny d'tkm	repeat your communication,
	wrgm lṯr 'aby 'il	and say to my father, Bull El,
	ṯny lpẖr m'd	repeat to the full assembly.

The execution of this command differs slightly:[50]

D-4	*qmm 'aṯr 'amr*	Standing, they advanced and spoke,
	ṯny d'thm	repeated their communication.
	'išt 'ištm yi'tmr	They appeared like a fire, two fires
	ḥrb lṭšt lšnhm	their tongue a sharpened sword.
	rgm lṯr 'abh 'il	They spoke to the Bull, his father Ilu.

A figurative couplet is inserted after the first two lines ('[Like] a fire, two fires they appeared/ [like] a sharpened sword, their tongue')[51] while the final line is omitted.

1.3.6. *Expansion of E*

E-1	*yṯb 'al'iyn b'l*	Reply did Mightiest Baal
	yt'dd rkb 'rpt	respond did the Cloudrider.

A long, important complaint follows;[52] the initial word is based on restoration.[53] There appear to be no other expansions of E.

46. *KTU* 1.4 viii 29-31.
47. *KTU* 1.3 iii 11-12, 21-23.
48. *KTU* 1.3 iv 7-8.
49. *KTU* 1.16 vi 27-29.
50. Command: *KTU* 1.2 i 15-17, restored from execution, lines 31-33.
51. Following J.C. de Moor, *The Seasonal Pattern in the Ugaritic Myth of Ba'lu* (AOAT, 16; Kevelaer: Butzon & Bercker; Neukirchen–Vluyn; Neukirchener Verlag, 1971), p. 129.
52. *KTU* 1.4 iii 10-11.
53. Strictly, *y[ṯ]b*; see, conveniently, del Olmo Lete, *Mitos y leyendas*, p. 197.

1.3.7. *Expansions of *X*

*X is the unattested formula *ytn gh bky* of which two examples appear to be expansions:[54]

X-1	*ybky wyšnn*	He wept, gnashing his teeth;
	ytn gh bky	he gave vent to weeping.

Both lines use hendiadys. The couplet belongs to a tricolon with the opening line *'l 'abh y'rb*, 'He entered his father's presence', which is a prelude to Elhu's speech of concern for Krt's approaching demise. The same couplet (in the feminine) introduces the same speech from Elhu's sister, Octavia.

1.4. *Discussion*

Having examined the prelude-to-speech formulae with their variants and expansions, we now have to consider the occurrence, distribution, development and purpose of the collected data. To begin with, variants of the standard formulae are few; they include A/1, C/1, D/1, F/1, K/1 and perhaps N/1. Expansions of the formulae are never based on these variant forms. As for occurrence, A and B are the most frequently used, followed by C and D. The expansions (including variants) have corresponding ratios of occurrence.[55] No hard and fast conclusions can be drawn concerning development, but there are indications that single-line formulae were expanded rather than the other way about. Three factors point towards development in this direction. (1) Single-line formulae outnumber attested expansions (in the ratio of approximately 15:6). (2) Expansions are never based on variants of such formulae (as already mentioned). (3) The expansions tend to have several variants, while maintaining the standard formulae unchanged whereas these standard formulae have few variants (hardly more than one per formula in about six cases). Such considerations, in fact, suggest the following line of development: single word, single line, couplet, tricolon, quatrain. It can even be argued that the initial stage is Ø, that is absence of any speech-introducing element, but this would only apply to the evolution of this particular kind of formula

54. *KTU* 1.16 i 13-14 and ii 35-36 (f.). For the idiom *ytn g(h)*, cf. 1.2 iv 6 and 1.16 i 55.

55. A: very frequent—A-1, 2, 3: six times; B: frequent—B-1, 2, 3, 4: seven times; C: three times—C-1, 2: four times; D: four times—D-1, 2, 3, 4: seven times; E: once—E-1: once.

and could not have validity for the general development of verse units.[56]

With regard to the expansions, no hard and fast rules emerge concerning their purpose. They can introduce lengthy speeches, they can mark a climax or important moment in a poem and they can be used simply as messenger formulae. A table will show the distribution.

a	introducing long speech C-1 (formulaic); C-2; B-2; B-4²; E-1; X-1.
b	marking key passage A-2; A-3; B-3; B-4¹; X-1.
c	messenger formula D-1; D-2; D-3; D-4.

It can be noted that X-1 combines both structural (a) and rhetorical (b) functions, an anomaly which may suggest it is a pseudo-expansion. Also, inner-variants of B-4 have different functions, which is curious. A-1 is unassigned (see above) and set (c) comprises variants of the expanded messenger formula.

1.5. *Speech-Closing Formula*

Unnoticed has gone the peculiar use of a formula which comes *after* a speech in Ugaritic narrative verse, as a form of closural device,[57] though in effect it tends to open a stanza.

bph rgm lyṣ'a	Barely had the word left his mouth,
bšptn hwth	the speech (left) his lips

The couplet is used four times in *Aqhat*, in three of which Danel is asking Baal to break the wings of birds suspected of concealing his son's remains.[58] The formula is not used when the same deity is requested to heal these creatures. The fifth occurrence is more problematic[59]—we cannot even be sure whether the suffix *-h* is masculine or feminine—and it may be followed by a further reference to speech,

56. For a discussion of expansion and contraction, see de Moor 'Versification'.

57. On this feature of poetry, cf. B.H. Smith, *Poetic Closure: A Study of how Poems End* (Chicago: University of Chicago Press, 1968), and E. Häublein, *The Stanza* (London: Methuen, 1978), pp. 53-71.

58. Texts: *KTU* 1.19 ii 26; iii 7.21-22.35-36.

59. *KTU* 2 iv 6 is discussed in detail by D. Pardee, review of Gibson, *Canaanite Myths*, *BO* 37 (1980), p. 273.

though no speech is quoted.[60] The only certainty is that, as in the *Aqhat* text, the connotations are entirely negative.

1.6. *Closing Remarks*

The present study is very much in the nature of a beginning.[61] Better evaluation of the data collected here is required and the material presented needs further sifting. Examples not discussed or referred to only in passing require closer analysis. In addition, the study of comparative material will provide a wider frame of reference than has been adopted here.[62]

60. For references to preceding speech in Babylonian literature, cf. *Atr.* I iii 166-167; vii 385; viii 403-404 (and par.); II iii 29, etc. and *Erra* I 92-93, 163, 179, 190-91; V 20-21 (cited above), etc. For immediate action after discourse, cf. *Erra* IV 139-150.

61. The stanza division in del Olmo Lete, *Mitos y leyendas*, was very helpful for this particular study.

62. I have in mind the literature from Mesopotamia. F. Sonnek, 'Die Einführung der direkten Rede in den epischen Texten', *ZA* 46 (1940), pp. 225-35 is very much out of date. A survey of some easily available material yields the following partial picture. *Erra*: near-equal number of monocola (I 31, 94, 126, 164; IIb 15; IIIc 57; IIId 2; IV 130, 137; V 4, 48) and couplets (I 104-105, 129-130, 168-169, 179-180; IIc 2-3; IIIc 28-29, 34-35, 38-39; V 16AB; cf. IV 37-38) with some partial lines. *Atraḫasis*: chiefly couplets; note the 6-line introduction in II 364-369. In some contest literature the characters are distinguished by different introductory couplets, e.g. Ox and Horse (W.G. Lambert, *Babylon Wisdom Literature* [Oxford: Clarendon Press, 1960], p. 177 line 24, etc. and p. 178 line 19, etc.); Tamarisk and Palm (*Babylonian Wisdom Literature*, p. 156 line 2 and 7-8, note p. 158 line 7 for a variant). Unusual couplets occur in *Babylonian Wisdom Literature*, p. 165 lines 14-15 and p. 171 lines 25-26. The 'Dog' tricolon is noteworthy (p. 192 lines 14-15 = p. 194 lines 24-25 = p. 207 lines 1-2) as is the quatrain on p. 210 lines 6-9. Other texts include p. 190 lines 6 and 9 (Fox); p. 194 lines 12-13, etc. (answer + weeping); p. 196 lines 17-18; p. 204 line 17 and p. 208 lines 18-19. For the Gilgamesh Epic, cf. J.H. Tigay, *The Evolution of the Gilgamesh Epic* (Philadelphia: University of Pennsylvania Press, 1982), pp. 60-61, 136, 233, including comparison with *Atraḫasis*. (Note that Tigay spells 'Sonnek' 'Sonneck' throughout.) See now K. Hecker, *Untersuchungen zur akkadischen Epik* (AOAT, 8; Kevelaer: Butzon & Bercker; Neukirchen–Vluyn: Neukirchener Verlag, 1974), pp. 174-80. For Egyptian verse, cf. J.L. Foster, 'The Ancient Egyptian Genre of Narrative Verse', *JNES* 39 (1980), p. 109 n. 17.

2. *Abrupt Speech in Ugaritic Narrative Verse*[63]

Almost invariably passages of speech in Ugaritic literary texts are provided with an introduction comprising one or more lines.[64] There are occasional exceptions, though, where the expected introduction is missing. One passage, *KTU* 1.12 i 12-13, has already been mentioned. De Moor has commented on three more examples[65] but there are others; all these form the subject of the present note. First they will be listed and then some attempts at explanation will be made. After the conclusions additional examples of passages introducing discourse will be given in a short appendix.

2.1. *Occurrences*

a. *KTU 1.2 i 13-19.*

tbʿ. ġlm[*m* etc.,	Depart, boy[s etc.

Unfortunately the preceding line—[*u*]*ṭ. ṯbr. aphm*—is difficult to translate. Del Olmo Lete suggests 'breathing satisfaction(?)'.[66] The alternative rendering 'the bills of their beaks (open) to a span',[67] if correct, would of course, comprise a type of introduction; however, the speaker appears to be Yammu (line 11).

b. *KTU 1.2 i 38-40.*

ap. anš. zbl. bʿl	However, Prince Baal became angry,
[*yuḫ*]*d. byd. mšḫṭ.*	[he gras]ped the attacking-weapon in his hand,
bm. ymn. mḫṣ.	the smiting-weapon in his right
ġlmm. yš[ ]	in order to strike(?) the two lads.
[*ymnhʿ*]*nt. tuḫd.*	[His right hand A]nat grasped,
šmalh. tuḫd. ʿṯtrt.	Athtartu grasped his left.[68]

63. First published in *UF* 22 (1990), pp. 415-23.

64. See 'Introductions to Discourse in Ugaritic Narrative Verse', above.

65. 'Unintroduced direct oration' is referred to three times by J.C. de Moor, *An Anthology of Religious Texts from Ugarit* (Nisaba, 16; Leiden: Brill, 1987), p. 64 n. 291 (on *KTU* 1.4 vii 43); p. 72 n. 337 (on *KTU* 1.5 ii 8); and p. 82 n. 399 (on *KTU* 1.6 i 6).

66. Del Olmo Lete, *Mitos y leyendas*, p. 169; literally, 'con rotura de sus fosas nasales' (p. 524).

67. De Moor, *Anthology*, p. 31.

68. For possible restorations see del Olmo Lete, *Mitos y leyendas*, p. 172.

With no other warning the words of one goddess (or perhaps of both) follow: (end of line 40)

ik. mḫ[*ṣt mlak. ym*] etc.	How could you hi[t Yammu's messenger?], etc.

c. *KTU 1.3 i 25*
The lines beginning *pdr. yd‘* [(or *pdr<y>. yd‘*) may open a speech;[69] if so, there is no prelude.

d. *KTU 1.4 vii 42-43*

bkm. yṯb. b‘l. lbhth	Instantly Baal returned to his villa.
u mlk. u bl mlk	'Should a monarch or a commoner etc.'

e. *KTU 1.5 ii 6-7*

yraun. aliyn. b‘l	Mightiest Baal feared him,
ṯt‘. nn. rkb. ‘rpt	the Cloud-rider dreaded him.

This preamble is followed by the abrupt imperative *tb‘* etc., 'Leave! etc.' Note that in the corresponding passage (1.6 vi 30ff.) there is the additional line *y‘r. mt. bqlh.*, 'Mot was troubled at her speech' and some scholars restore a speech introduction in line 32.[70]

f. *KTU 1.6 i 6-8.*
Here Anath performs a rite of mourning (described in lines 2-6) and then exclaims *b‘l. mt...* 'Baal is dead...' Curiously, when in *KTU* 1.5 vi 11-22 Ilu is described as performing the same rite (preceded by other acts of mourning) these very words are prefaced by the line *yšu. gh*[.] *wyṣḥ*, 'He raised his voice and shouted'.[71]

g. *KTU 1.12 i 12-13*

il. yẓḥq. bm lb.	Ilu laughed deep inside,
wygmḏ. bm kbd	and rejoiced to the core.

Ilu's words begin in the next line (14).[72]

69. So de Moor, *Anthology*, p. 4 and n. 19; contrast del Olmo Lete, *Mitos y leyendas*, p. 180.

70. For example, *y*[*šu. gh. wyṣḥ*], de Moor, *Seasonal Pattern*, pp. 230-31; J.C. de Moor and K. Spronk, *A Cuneiform Anthology of Religious Texts from Ugarit* (Semitic Study Series, 6; Leiden: Brill, 1987), p. 43; for other possibilities see del Olmo Lete, *Mitos y leyendas*, p. 234, textual notes.

71. As explicitly noticed by de Moor, *Anthology*, p. 82 n. 399.

72. The speech in lines 9b-11 does not seem to be preceded by an

h. *KTU 1.16 i 55*

Although the immediate context is broken it looks as if Pughatu's words are simply preceded by *tbky*, 'she wept'.

i. *KTU 1.16 v 41*

Ilu is described raising his cup. His words follow unannounced:

at. š[*'tqt* etc.	'You, Š. etc.'

j. *KTU 1.17 vi 41-42*

g]*m. tṣḥq. 'nt*	Al]oud laughed Anath,
wblb. tqny...	while in her mind she was plotting...[73]

followed by

ṯb. ly. laqht. ġzr. etc.	'Return to me, O manly Aqhat, etc.'

This contrasts strongly with *KTU* 1.18 iv 16 where virtually the same words are preceded by *wt'n. btlt. 'nt.*, 'And Virgin Anatu replied'.

k. *KTU 1.18 iv 39-40*

The beginning of both lines in the couplet (lines 37b-39) are broken but it seems that Anat's statement of regret concerning Aqhat's death is preceded simply by *wtbk*, 'and she wept'.

l. *KTU 1.19 ii 14-15*

Having noticed the new growth in the desolate land, Dnil

bṣql. yḥbq wynšq	embraces and kisses the b.

He then breaks into prayer: *aḥl. an.*, 'Would that...'[74]

m. *KTU 1.23:64-65*

y. aṯt. itrḫ	O wives I married!
ybn. ašld...	O sons I sired!...'

Only the context (lines 59-64) shows that the speaker is Ilu.

introduction either, but the context is broken.

73. For the syntax, cf. E. Verreet, *Modi ugaritici: Eine morpho-syntaktische Abhandlung über das Modalsystem im Ugaritischen* (Orientalia Lovaniensia Analecta, 27; Leuven: Uitgeeverij Peeters, 1988), p. 240.

74. De Moor, *Anthology*, p. 252: 'I beseech (you gods)'; cf. p. 252 n. 190.

n. *KTU 1.100:71b-76*

The exchange of words here is devoid of any reference to the speakers, but it is generally agreed that they are Horon, the Mare and again Horon.

ptḥ. bt. mnt	Open the Chamber of Incantation!
ptḥ. bt. wuba.	Open the Chamber so that I may enter!
hkl. wištql.	The Palace, that I may proceed!
tn. km. <mhry> nḥšm.	Provide as my <bridal payment> snakes!
yḥr. tn. km mhry.	Lizards provide as my bridal payment,
wbn. bṯn. itnny	and young serpents [as] my price?
ytt. nšm. mhrk.	I grant snakes as your bridal payment;
bn. bṯn itnnk	young serpents [as] your price![75]

2.2. *Functions*

Throughout Ugaritic narrative verse, including the 'para-mythological texts',[76] speech-passages are preceded by various equivalents of 'he/she/they said/answered', and so on. Even in a text such as *KTU* 1.23, which appears to be some type of ritual, the same rule applies. As demonstrated above, though, there are exceptions and these require explanation. Some may be cases of scribal omission. In other passages the writer is probably trying to express an emotional event, a recognized device in Akkadian narrative verse. Commenting on a passage from the *Epic of Gilgamesh* (*Gilg*. I iv 16-21) Foster states, 'the poet conveys excitement by dropping the conventional poetic formulae introducing direct speech'.[77] Occasionally the word used is tantamount to a verb denoting speech (*bky*, 'to weep'; *ṣḥq*, 'to laugh'). The

75. The translation follows B.A. Levine and J.-M. de Tarragon, '"Shapshu Cries out in Heaven": Dealing with Snake-Bites at Ugarit (*KTU* 1.100, 1.107)', *RB* 95 (1988), pp. 481-518, esp. 492 (with a minor change). For another version, cf. D. Pardee, *Les textes para-mythologiques* (Ras Shamra-Ougarit IV; Mémoire no. 77; Paris: Editions Recherche sur les Civilisations, 1988), pp. 203-204, 221-23. For the meaning and Hurrian origin of *itnn*, see now W. von Soden, 'Hurritisch *uatnannu* > mittelassyrischen *utnannu* und < ugaritisch *itnn* > hebräisch *'ätnan* "ein Geschenk, Dirnenlohn"', *UF* 20 (1988), pp. 309-311.

76. To use the term coined by Pardee, *Les textes*, p. 261.

77. B. Foster, 'Gilgamesh: Sex, Love and the Ascent of Knowledge', in J.H. Marks and R.M. Good, *Love and Death in the Ancient Near East: Essays in Honor of Marvin H. Pope* (Guilford, CT: Four Quarters Publishing Company, 1987), pp. 21-42; his comment is on p. 24 and additional examples are listed in n. 20.

passages set out above can be allocated to one or more of the following headings:

1. *Expression of emotion*: (b) Baal is angry; (e) Baal is afraid; (f) mourning; (g) rejoicing; (h) mourning; (j) Anath's reaction to Aqhat's rebuff; (k) mourning; (l) Danel is overcome at seeing the new growth; (m) Ilu has to abandon his wives and sons; (n) climax of the serpent text.
2. *'To weep/laugh' equivalent to verb of speaking*: (g), (h), (j), (k).
3. *Scribal omission*: (f)?, (j)?
4. *Unexplained*: (a), (c), (d), (i).

Of course, set 2 (use of *bky*, *ṣḥq*) overlaps set 1 (to convey emotion) and the use of such 'weak' verbs for ensuing speech indicates that in all probability only one set is involved. In set 3 the parallel passages suggest that a speech-prefatory line was left out by mistake, though there is no iron-clad certainty. No explanation is readily to hand for set 4, although example d apparently depicts suddenness of action.

2.3. *Conclusions*

Generally, an introduction to speech was omitted in order to express an emotional reaction. Evidently, too, Ugaritic narrative verse was exactly that: narrative. There can be no question of any dramatic presentation involving different speakers or actors, otherwise there would be no need for the introductions marking dialogue. Where there is no introduction, the identity of the speaker is clearly shown, usually by a description of an action (or series of actions) performed by the speaker of the words which immediately follow.[78] In fact, it is almost a rule that the last person mentioned is the next to speak. If the Ugaritic literary texts were recited orally, and the indications are that such was the case, then they must have been declaimed by a single person.

78. In *KTU* 1.119 (for which I follow G. del Olmo Lete, 'Liturgia sacrificial y salmodia en Ugarit', *AuOr* 7 [1989], pp. 27-35) the words to be recited (line 25) are prefaced by the verb *tdn*, '(they) shall proclaim' in line 23. However, the prayer in lines 28-34a is not preceded by any reference to use of the voice, though there is the rubric 'raise your eyes to Baal' and in line 34b there is the assurance that 'Baal will certainly hear your plea'.

2.4. *Appendix*

To complement the present note several preludes to speech, unnoticed in my earlier article[79] are appended here. They are: *qrit. lšpš. umh*, '(She) called out to Shapshu, her mother' (*KTU* 1.100:4); *tqru lšpš umh*, 'She called out to Shapshu, her mother' (*KTU* 1.100:8, 14, 19, 25, 35, 40, 45, 51, 57) and *špš bšmm tqru*, 'Shapshu calls out in the heavens' (*KTU* 1.107:9and 44). In *KTU* 1.16 v 9-22. Ilu is portrayed repeatedly asking the gods which of them is going to heal Krt's illness. The preliminary phrase used, which is a startling innovation, has three variants, the most complete in lines 19-20: *yṯdṯ yšb'. rgm*, 'He repeated the question six or seven times'.[80] The couplet in *KTU* 1.23:12 is a rubric and not, strictly speaking, an introduction to speech.[81]

The expansion of *wy'ny. bn ilm. mt*, 'And divine Mot replied' (*KTU* 1.133:1-2) to *wy'n gpn. wugr. / tḥm. bn. ilm. mt. / hwt. ydd. {bn.} il. ġzr*, 'And Gapnu-wa-Ugaru replied: "Message of divine Mot, word of Ilu's favourite, the warrior"' (*KTU* 1.5 i 11-14) is also significant.[82]

79. See pp. 414-24. Examples also in Verreet, *Modi ugaritici*, pp. 99-103.

80. It is clear that in *KTU* 1.16 v 13-14 and 16-17 the corresponding preliminary lines are respectively 'He repeated the question three or four times' and 'four or five times' though the text is incomplete.

81. See also *td rgm* in *KTU* 1.93: 1. Note that in spite of the introduction in *KTU* 1.3 i 18-21, which includes the expression 'the dulcet-toned lad sang' (*yšr. ġzr. ṭb. ql*) his actual words remain unknown. The same applies to *KTU* 1.4 vii 29-31. as mentioned in the previous article.

82. Pardee, *Les textes*, p. 160, suggests *KTU* 1.133 is a simplified version of *KTU* 1.5 i 11-22; he comments, 'Cette facilité relative fait penser à une composition orale, exécutée peut-être par un débutant; ou bien à un texte rendu plus facile, par rapport à un original, et inscrit au programme d'une école'.

Chapter 10

PATTERNS AND RHETORICAL DEVICES

1. *Anaphoric Alliteration in Ugaritic Verse*[1]

Although no actual alphabetic acrostics have yet been found, it is remarkable how often consecutive lines in the Ugaritic text tend to begin with the same letter or group of letters. This is achieved either by repeating the same word (anaphora), or by using an identical initial letter. A few examples of each type will be examined here and then the implications of such quasi-acrostics will be briefly evaluated.

The commonest way of achieving groups of lines with identical opening letters is by *repetition*.[2] The most frequent unit is, as would be expected, the couplet, for example *KTU* 1.6 iv 15-16:

iy aliyn b'l	*Where is* Mightiest Baal?
iy zbl b'l arṣ	*Where is* the Prince, Earth-Lord?[3]

Tricola also occur, for example *KTU* 1.6 vi 27-29:

lys' alt ṯbtk	*Indeed* he will pull up the support of your seat.
lyhpk ksa mlkk	*Indeed* he will overturn the throne of your kingdom.
lyṯbr ḫṭ mṯpṭk	*Indeed* he will break the sceptre of your rule.[4]

1. First published as 'Quasi-Acrostics in Ugaritic Poetry', *UF* 12 (1980), pp. 445-47.

2. On anaphora, the repetition of the same word at the beginning of each line, cf. G.N. Leech, *A Linguistic Guide to English Poetry* (London: Longmans, 1969), pp. 80-81, 85; J. Dubois *et al.*, *Dictionnaire de linguistique* (Paris: Larousse, 1973), p. 33; *Allgemeine Rhetorik* (Munich: W. Fink, 1974), pp. 127-29.

3. Also *KTU* 1.4 i 30-31 (*kt.il*); ii 21-24 (*ik*); iv 45-46 (*klynyn*); 59-60 (*p'bd*), viii 18-19 (*k*); 5 vi 23-24 (*my*); 6 ii 17-19 (*npš*) 14 iv 19-20 (*aṯr*) etc.

4. As translated by J.C.L. Gibson, *Canaanite Myths and Legends* (Edinburgh: T. & T. Clark, 1978), p. 81. Also *KTU* 1.4 viii 2-4 (*'m*); 16 iii 13-16 (*kly*); 100:70-71 (*b'dh*) etc.

Quatrains include *KTU* 1.4 v 51-54 (and par.): four lines each beginning *ḥš* ('Quickly'); *KTU* 1.23:32-33 with initial *hlh* ('See, she') four times consecutively. Longer sequences are comparatively rare. Six lines beginning *tld* ('She shall bear') in *KTU* 1.15 ii 7-12; seven with initial *'lk* ('on your account') in *KTU* 1.6 v 11-19—of which six have the sequence *'lk pht* ('on your account I experienced'). In *KTU* 1.4 vi 47-54 no less than eight lines start with *špq* ('she supplied') but this enumeration is not surprising in a ritual section of the text.[5]

More significant are sequences where the same consonant is used to open each line *without word repetition*, which requires more skill on the part of the poet. Strophic units include couplets such as *KTU* 1.17 i 16-18:

abynt dnil mt rpi	*M*isery of Danel, Rapiu-man
anḫ ǵzr mt hrnmy	*M*oaning of the adult, Hrnmy-man.

and *KTU* 1.14 iii 55-57 (*lqḥ*- and *lla*-), as well as tricola (for example, *KTU* 1.17 ii 27-30). *Mixed* forms also occur with combinations of word repetition and identical initial consonant, as in *KTU* 1.14 iv 19-22:

aṯr ṯn ṯn hlk	*A*fter two, two went,
aṯr ṯlṯ klhm	*a*fter three, all of them.
aḥd bth ysgr	*A* bachelor closed up his house.
almnt škr tškr	*A* widow became a mercenary.

The first two lines both begin with *aṯr* and the *a*-initial sequence is carried on by completely different words (*aḥd*, *almnt*—contrast the use of *yḥd* in the parallel text *KTU* 1.14 ii 43). Another mixed set is *KTU* 1.16 with three line-initial negative particles in the form of *l*- followed immediately by *lpnk* ('in front of you': vi 45-49). Examples could be multiplied, but we will now turn to the implications of this procedure.[6]

Recognition of the quasi-acrostic in Ugaritic has implications for

5. See also *KTU* 1.161 which has no less than eleven consecutive lines beginning with *q*; also *a* (3), *k* (5) and *š* (6). W.T. Pitard, 'The Ugaritic Funerary Texts RS 34.126', *BASOR* 232 (1978), pp. 65-75 makes no reference to this aspect of the text. See J. Healey, 'Ritual Text *KTU* 1.161. Translation and Notes', *UF* 10 (1978), pp. 83-88, 85 n. 10.

6. For such quasi-acrostics in Hebrew, cf. P.W. Skehan, 'Strophic Patterns in the Book of Job', *CBQ* 23 (1960), pp. 125-42, 127.

stichometry; for example *KTU* 1.3 vi 7-9 which is a tricolon:[7]

[‘b]r gbl	*Cross* over Byblos.
‘br q‘l	*Cross* over Qeilah.
‘br iht np šmm	*Cross* over the islands of Memphis.

Anacrusis can be established in *KTU* 1.19 ii 17-18:

ur	Plant!
tispk yd aqht ǵzr	*M*ay Aqhat the adult’s hand gather you,
tštk bqrbm asm	*m*ay it place you inside the barn.

and again, a few lines further on (22-23):

aḥl an	Oh if only
šblt tp‘ baklt	the ear of corn would sprout in the dry land,
šblt tp‘ bḫmdrt	the ear of corn would sprout in the withered crop!

Similarly, *hn* (‘See!’) in *KTU* 1.24: 45-47 and *bn* (‘Son!’) in *KTU* 1.16 i 25-27. From the point of view of style it is interesting that often the quasi-acrostic series is broken in the last line, for instance *KTU* 1.3 ii 36-37:

[ṯ]‘r ksat lksat	*T*idily she put chairs with chairs,
ṯlḥnt [l]ṯlḥn<t>	*t*ables with tables,
hdmm tṯar lhdmm	*f*ootstools she put with footstools.

where the last line begins with *h* instead of *ṯ*, as expected.[8] The presence of this device can sometimes help in restoration or reconstruction of missing words and letters (as in the text just cited). It can also mark off stanzas; for example, *KTU* 1.3 iv 22-36 is a speech by Anath comprising four *a*-initial lines (*an*, *ašt*, *ask*, *ar*), a *y*-couplet (*yšt*, *yb‘r*), again four *a*-lines (*aqry*, *ašt*, *ask*, *ar*) a mixed sequence and then two closing lines beginning with *ṯ*. Though not totally consistent, there is an evident pattern here marred only by the line *lk lk ‘nn ilm*, ‘Get moving, attendants of the gods!’ which is the main content of her message and therefore the focus of interest. That such segments of poetry are not accidental is shown even better by *KTU* 1.4 iv 50-55 where two *w* lines, followed by a regular sequence of line-initial words beginning with *m* mark off reported speech (Anath quoting

7. Contrast Gibson, *Canaanite Myths*, p. 54 for whom this strophe is a couplet. On *iht* cf. M.J. Dahood, ‘Egyptian *’iw*, “island” in Jeremiah 10,9 and Daniel 10,5’, *Quaderni di Semitistica* 5 (1978), pp. 101-103 esp. 103 n. 9.

8. Also *KTU* 1.6 iv 1-3, 11-14, 14 iii 16-19; 16 i 25-27.

Baal's words to El) as a distinct unit. Clearly the poets chose their words to fit these formal constraints, a case in point being *KTU* 1.3 i 13-15, where instead of the expected *qb't*, 'goblet' as part of a word-pair with *ks*, *krpn* is used:

ks qdš ltpnh aṯt	*A* holy cup which woman should not see,
krpn lt'n aṯrt	*a* vessel no goddess should eye.[9]

Finally, these considerations may have some relevance for the relationship between written and oral poetry in Ugaritic tradition. It is probable that the quasi-acrostic, which is basically an extension of initial alliteration, was originally just a by-product of pervasive parallelism and that it was only made overt when the oral poetry of ancient times was committed to writing.[10]

2. *Delaying Devices in Ugaritic Verse*[11]

The contribution of Professor Oswald Loretz to the study of Ugaritic and Hebrew verse is well known. Here, in his honour, I have chosen a

9. For similar considerations on alliteration in general, cf. B. Margalit, 'Alliteration in Ugaritic Poetry: Its Rôle in Composition and Analysis', *UF* 11 (1979), pp. 537-57.

10. J.J.A. Mooij, 'On the "Foregrounding" of Graphic Elements in Poetry', in D.W. Fokkema, E. Kunne-Ibsch and A.J.A. van Zoest (eds.), *Comparative Poetics in Honour of Jan Kamerbeek Jr* (Amsterdam n.d.), pp. 89-102 notes that 'written poetry allows for devices of foregrounding not available to oral poetry' (p. 94). On acrostics, see Lambert, *Babylonian Wisdom Literature*, p. 67; M.-J. Seux, *Hymnes et prières aux dieux de Babylonie et d'Assyrie* (LAPO, 8; Paris: Cerf, 1976), pp. 115-28; S. Bergler, 'Threni V. Nur ein alphabetisierende Lied? Versuch einer Deutung', *VT* 27 (1977), pp 304-20; D.N. Freedman, 'Acrostics and Metrics in Hebrew Poetry', *HTR* 65 (1972), pp. 366-92; D.N. Freedman, 'Acrostic Poems in the Hebrew Bible, Alphabetic and Otherwise', *CBQ* 48 (1986), pp. 408-31; M. Löhr, 'Alphabetische und alphabetisierende Lieder im Alten Testament', *ZAW* 25 (1905), pp. 173-98. P.A. Munch, 'Die alphabetische Akrostichie in der jüdischen Psalmendichtung', *ZDMG* 90 (1936), pp. 703-10; S. Paul, 'Mnemonic Devices', *IDBSup*, pp. 600-602; T. Piatti, 'I carmi alfabetici della bibbia: chiave della metrical ebraica?', *Bib* 31 (1950), pp. 281-315, 427-58. See now W.M. Soll, 'Babylonian and Biblical Acrostics', *Bib* 69 (1988), pp. 305-23. Practice alphabets have been found in Ugaritic on what must have been exercise tablets (*KTU* 5.1–5.22). Note 5.1 with fifteen words beginning with *y* and 5.8, a list of five personal names beginning with *il*-.

11. First published in *SEL* 5 (1988), pp. 207-18.

non-controversial topic which will, I hope, lead to a better understanding of these ever-fascinating verse traditions.

2.1. *Introduction*

In my book on Hebrew poetry I treated 'Delayed Identification' rather briefly.[12] Here I will expand on the same topic, chiefly with reference to Ugaritic, taking into account also recent work by Alster,[13] Berlin[14] and Clines.[15] In order to broaden the base of comparison I have also included examples in Akkadian tablets as well as some additional examples in Hebrew.

Since there is a certain amount of confusion in terminology, with descriptions such as 'particularizing parallelism', 'the parallelism of greater precision' and 'delayed identification' used almost interchangeably, it seems methodologically sound to begin by setting out passages in Ugaritic verse where some degree of delay is evident and then proceed to finer definitions. For ease of reference these texts are given in the sequence of *KTU*, tagged by identifying letters.

12. W.G.E. Watson, *Classical Hebrew Poetry: A Guide to its Techniques* (JSOTSup, 26; Sheffield: JSOT Press, 2nd edn, 1986), pp. 11, 16, 338-39, also 25 and 34.

13. B. Alster, *Studies in Sumerian Proverbs* (Mesopotamia, Copenhagen Studies in Assyriology, 3; Copenhagen: Akademisk Forlag, 1975), p. 55. He notes, 'The origin of Sumerian parallelism is obviously the oral technique of composing. Therefore the most common type is the "adding" parallelism which makes it easy to expand an idea into two or more lines, while at the same time keeping the listener in suspense about the issue. This is the reason why the persons are usually not introduced by name in the first phrase in a group or are introduced first by an epithet'. But see n. 44 below.

14. A. Berlin, 'Shared Rhetorical Features in Biblical and Sumerian Literature', *JANESCU* 10 (1978), pp. 35-42, esp. 35-37. See also her *Enmerkar and Ensuḫkešdanna: A Sumerian Narrative Poem* (Occasional Publications of the Babylonian Fund, 2; Philadelphia: University of Pennsylvania, University Museum, 1979), p. 15 n. 24.

15. D.J.A. Clines, 'The Parallelism of Greater Precision. Notes from Isaiah 40 for a Theory of Hebrew Poetry', in E.R. Follis (ed.), *Directions in Biblical Hebrew Poetry* (JSOTSup, 40; Sheffield: JSOT Press, 1987), pp. 77-100.

2.2.2. *Passages in Ugaritic with Delay*

a. *KTU 1.2 i 34-35*

tn. ilm. dtqh.	Hand over, O Gods, the one to whom you render homage,
dtqynh [*hml*]*t.*	the one to whom the crowd renders homage.
tn. b'l. w'nnh.	Give up Baal and his attendants,
bn. dgn. arṯm. pḏh	Dagan's son so I may possess his gold.[16]

Baal's identity is not revealed until the third line but the real purpose of this demand only emerges right at the end, in the last two words ('so I may possess his gold').

The reply (lines 36-38) echoes the demand by mentioning the tribute in the last two lines after three set in partially repetitive parallelism.

b. *KTU 1.3 i 22-24*

ytmr. b'l. bnth.	Baal saw his daughters.
y'n. pdry bt. ar.	He spied Pdry, daughter of light,
...	...

The names of daughters, already specified as Baal's, are held over to the second and consecutive lines.

c. *KTU 1.3 ii 32-35*

trḥṣ. ydh. bt[*l*]*t. 'nt*	Virgin Anath washed her hands,
uṣb'th. ybmt. limm.	the sister-in-law of the peoples, her fingers
[*t*]*rḥṣ. ydh. bdm. ḏmr*	she washed off her hands warriors' blood,
[*u*]*ṣb'th. bmm'. mhrm*	off her fingers soldiers' gore.

Although there is some anticipation in lines 30-31 (*ymḥ bb*[!]*t. dm. ḏmr*, 'Warrior's blood was wiped from the house'), the complete action is not described until the third line.[17] To some degree this corresponds to lines 23-28 where Anath exults and the reason given for her glee is that she is knee-deep in blood.

16. Translation: G. del Olmo Lete, *Mitos y leyendas de Canaan según la tradición de Ugarit* (Fuentes de la Ciencia Bíblica, 1; Madrid: Ediciones Cristiandad, 1981), p. 172; cf. glossary, p. 561, under *yqy*. To his cognates add Akk. *(w)aqû*, 'to wait for, await', *AHw*, pp. 1461-62 (where Ethiopic *wqī*, 'keep, preserve', is also cited). Does this explain the proper noun Aqht?

17. It looks as if an underlying example of staircase parallelism (*trḥṣ ydh btlt 'nh* // *trḥṣ ydh bdm ḏmr*) has been expanded by an inserted couplet.

d. *KTU 1.6 i 39-43*

tšmḫ ht aṯrt. w.bnh.	Athirat and her sons may celebrate now,
ilt. wṣbrt. aryh.	(as can) the goddess and her kinsmen's clan,
kmt. aliyn b'l	for Almighty Baal is dead,
kḫlq. zbl. b'l. arṣ	the Prince, the Earthlord has perished!

e. *KTU 1.6 iii 18-21*

aṯbn. ank. wanḫn.	I myself can sit and relax,
wtnḫ. birty. npš	my feelings can relax within me, too,
kḥy. aliyn. b'l	for Almighty Baal is alive,
kiṯ. zbl.b'l. arṣ	the Prince, the Earthlord exists!

Evidently these two passages correspond and in both cases the second line is expletive in function, providing a brief postponement of the significant third line (echoed in the fourth).

f. *KTU 1.6 i 43-55*. Now that Baal is dead El demands a successor but we do not know who this is to be until the twelfth line of the section (= line 54) when *'ṯtr* is named.[18] Within this dialogue comes an additional delay (lines 50-52).

g. *KTU 1.14 ii 9-26 (// iii 52–iv 6)*. Kirta is told by El to make preparation for sacrifice, but the god to whom these actions are directed is not named until the fifteenth line[19] (lines 23-24). It is, of course, El himself.

h. *KTU 1.14 iii 22-32 (and par.)*

qḥ. ksp. wyrq. ḫrṣ	Take silver and yellow gold,
yd. mqmh. w'bd. 'lm.	etc. (translation difficult)
ṯlṯ sswm.mrkbt	
btrbṣ. bn. amt	
qḥ. krt. šlmm šlmm	Take many peace-offerings, Kirta,
wng. mlk. lbty.	AND MOVE AWAY, O KING, FROM MY HOUSE,
rḥq. krt. lḥẓry.	be far, Kirta, from my courts.
al. tṣr. udm. rbt. etc.	Do not besiege Great(er) Udum etc.

The crucial part of king Pbl's message only comes in the sixth line; it is then reinforced (in the next line) by synonymous parallelism.

18. See the comment in del Olmo Lete, *Mitos y leyendas*, p. 137.
19. Omitting line 20 as dittographical.

i. *KTU 1.14 iii 33-49*. Kirta's reply also has this delaying component:

lm. ank ksp. wyrq. ḫrṣ	What use to me are silver and yellow gold (etc.)?
yd. mqmh. wʿbd ʿlm.	
ṯlṯ. sswm. mrkbt	
btrbṣt. bn. amt.	
pd. in. bbty. ttn	Rather, give me what is not in my house,
tn. ly. mṯt. ḥry etc.	give me the lady Hry, etc.

Once again the core of the message comes in the sixth line (and even then it is additionally delayed by the extra line 'Rather, give me what is not in my house'). But this is not all. After a poetic description of his wife, Kirta proceeds to explain *why* he needs her back:

wld. špḥ. lkrt	(so) shall she bear progeny to Kirta,
wġlm. lʿbd. il	a prince to El's servant.[20]

j. *KTU 1.13 iv 40-43*

hm. ḥry. bty iqḥ.	If I should take H. to my house,
ašʿrb. ġlmt ḥẓry	introduce the girl into my residence,
ṯnh. k(!)spm atn	(then) twice her (weight) in silver shall I donate,
w.ṯlṯth. ḫrṣm	thrice her (weight) in gold.

The vow, introduced by the solemn formulae of lines 38-39, is expressed in the third and fourth line here.

k. *KTU 1.15 ii 21-25*

aṯt [.tq]ḥ. ykrt.	The wife you take, O Kirta,
aṯt tqḥ. btk[.]	the wife you take into your house,
[ġ]lmt. tšʿrb ḥẓrk.	the girl you introduce into your residence,
tld.šbʿ. bnm lk	shall bear you seven boys,
wṯmn. tṯmnm lk.	eight, even, shall she produce for you.
tld. yṣb[.]ġlm etc.	She shall bear the boy Yaṣṣubu etc.

This segment begins with staircase parallelism, used here to delay the nature of the action predicted of Kirta's wife ('[she] will bear seven sons/children for you'). This is only a partial climax; the real climax comes two lines later when the birth of Yṣb (Yaṣṣubu) is foretold.[21]

20. Here I follow del Olmo Lete, *Mitos y leyendas*, p. 296; contrast Gibson, *Canaanite Myths*, p. 86. The effect is the same in either version.

21. For the overall meaning here, cf. D.T. Tsumura, 'The Problem of Childlessness in the Royal Epic of Ugarit', in T. Mikasa (ed.), *Monarchies and Socio-Religious Traditions in the Ancient Near East* (Bulletin of the Middle Eastern

l. *KTU 1.15 iii 17-19*

tbrk. ilm. tity	The gods gave blessing and went,
tity. ilm lahlhm	the gods went to their tents,
dr.il. lmšknthm	El's family (went) to their dwellings.

The destination of the gods is not made clear until the second line. At the same time, generic 'the gods' is specified as 'the generation of El'.

m. *KTU 1.17 v 9-13 (and par.)*

bnši 'nh. wyphn.	On raising his eyes he did see him,
balp šd. rbt. kmn.	a thousand acres away, ten thousand hectares
hlk. kṯr ky'n etc.	Kothar's gait he perceived etc.[22]

It is not immediately clear who it is that Danel has seen since the reference for the pronominal suffix in the first line does not transpire till line 3. Evidently, too, *blp šd rbt kmn* is used as a filler in order to sustain the (mild) suspense.

n. *KTU 1.17 vi 20-25*

adr. ṯqbm blbnn.	The finest ash-trees from Lebanon,
adr. gdm. brumm	the finest sinews from wild oxen,
adr. qrnt. by'lm.	the finest horns from mountain-goats,
mtnm b'qbt. ṯr.	(the finest) tendons from a bull's hocks,
adr bġl il. qnm	the finest reeds from vast cane-brakes,
tn. lkṯr.wḫss.	give to Kothar-and-Hasis;
yb'l. qšt. l'nt	he'll make a bow for Anath,
qṣ't. lybmt. limm.	arrows for the sister-in-law of the peoples.

Five lines are devoted to listing the components to be collected, in the sixth Anath is told whom to give them to and only then is the end-product (i.e. the composite bow) actually mentioned.[23]

Culture Center in Japan, 1; Wiesbaden: Otto Harrassowitz, 1984), pp. 11-20.

22. T. Muraoka, *Emphatic Words and Structures in Biblical Hebrew* (Jerusalem: Magnes; Leiden: Brill, 1985), pp. 158-64 discusses Ug. *k* but he remains sceptical that 'the alleged emphatic *k* in Ugaritic is a case of genuinely analogous use (i.e. to emphatic *kî* in Hebrew)'. See, too, A. Aejmelaeus, 'Function and Interpretation of כִּי in Biblical Hebrew', *JBL* 105 (1986), pp. 193-209, esp. 208.

23. For possible corrections to these lines, cf. J. Sanmartín, 'Zu ug. *adr* in *KTU* 1.17 VI 20-23', *UF* 9 (1977), pp. 371-73. For *adr* he prefers the meaning '(the) strongest' but it may mean 'cut'. On composite bows, cf. B. Margalit, *The Ugaritic Poem of AQHT: Analysis and Interpretation, Seminar Papers SBL Annual Meeting*

o. *KTU 1.18 i 12-14*

w[qra] aqht. wyplṭk	And call Aqht so he may deliver you,
bn [dnil] wy'd̮rk.	Dnil's son and he'll free you
byd. btlt. ['*nt*]	from the hand of Virgin Anath.[24]

The completion of the verbal action (line one, parallel to line two) comes in line three.

p. *KTU 1.19 iv 51-52*

agrtn. bat. bd̮dk.	Our employer has come into your pavilion,
[ ] *bat. bhlm.*	[PN] has come into your tent.

The identity of the newcomer, announced to Yatpan, is first given as 'she who hired us' and then, presumably, as her name. Whether this is [*pǵt*] (as in lines 48, 50, 55) or ['*nt*] because she looks like that goddess is still uncertain.

q. *KTU 1.23:50 (// 55)*

hn.	See!
špthm. mtqtm.	Their lips are sweet,
mtqtm. klrmn[*m*]	sweet as pomegranates.

The simile is delayed slightly.

2.3. *Classification*

Before considering these seventeen examples in Ugaritic it is necessary to clarify the terminology by setting out some definitions, illustrated by passages from other ancient Near Eastern traditions.

In 'particularizing parallelism' an indeterminate or common noun mentioned in one line of verse is more narrowly defined in a later line. For example, Ezek. 30.13a:

wh'bdty glwlym	I will destroy idols[25]
whšbty 'lylym mnp	I will wipe out 'gods' from Noph (= Memphis).

1986 (Missoula, MT: Scholars Press, 1986), pp. 246-61, esp. 250, 259-60. Also R. Miller, E. McEwen and C. Bergman, 'Experimental Approaches to Ancient Near Eastern Archery', *World Archaeology* 18 (1986), pp. 178-95.

24. Other restorations: *w*[*tšal*]; *w*[*yba*]; *w*[*ṣḥ.'m*]; see del Olmo Lete, *Mitos y leyendas*, p. 381.

25. It is possible that *glwl* means 'stela'; see M. Greenberg, *Ezechiel 1–20* (AB, 22; Garden City, NY: Doubleday, 1983), p. 132 for discussion and bibliography. In support of this meaning, cf. *gll.* 'stone' in the phrase *tynr' rbh dygll*, 'a large flint

The generic term 'idols', which could denote any kind of cult objects is here specified as the gods of Memphis. Another designation for this type is 'delayed identification'. A good example is Sir. 48.1-11 where Elijah's name is held over until v. 4.[26]

Other examples are of the type 'epithet' // 'PN' (personal name) as in Sir. 47.12-13:

[w]b'bwrw 'md 'ḥryw	And because of him (i.e. David) as his successor came
bn mśkyl šwkn lbtḥ	a shrewd son who lived in security.
šlmh mlk bymy šlwh	SOLOMON was king in times of peace
w'l hnyḥ lw msbyb	and God gave him tranquillity all around.

Here the vague epithet *bn mśkyl* is parallel to the personal name *šlmh*.[27] To this category also belong Isa. 22.15b (*hskn hzh* // *šbn'*) and Isa. 22.20.[28] Similarly, the 'city' of Lam. 1.1 is not named until 1.4 (as Zion) and is referred to as 'Jerusalem' only in 1.7.

This type of delay is taken to extremes in Akkadian (Assyro-Babylonian) poetry. For example, in a neo-Babylonian lament which runs to 23 lines the blame for depriving Ištar 'of her spouse' (line 5), 'her beloved spouse' (lines 13, 23) is assigned to Bel (= Marduk) only in the final line. In fact, as Lambert comments, 'the most striking thing about this Akkadian text comes like a hammer-blow at the end, in the very last word'.[29] Similarly, the hero of the *Epic of Gilgamesh* is not actually named until line 26 of the first tablet (col. i).[30] By

rock of unhewn stone' in line 14 of Bowl 13, edited by J. Naveh and S. Shaked, *Amulets and Magic Bowls: Aramaic Incantations of Late Antiquity* (Jerusalem: Magnes; Leiden: Brill, 1985), pp. 200-201 (though they do not make the connection with Heb. *glwl*).

26. Contrast the Greek text with Ελιας in the first line.

27. This reverses the standard PN_1 // *bn* PN_2 sequence; see my *Classical Hebrew Poetry*, p. 133. It is here that Mesopotamian verse diverges from West Semitic tradition. In Sumerian and Akkadian verse a generic epithet (or occasionally no epithet, i.e. 0) is matched by the name of a god or person in the corresponding slot of the parallel line in what has been termed 'substitution parallelism'. In Ugaritic and Hebrew the personal or proper name comes first, with an epithet as its equivalent in the next line. In effect, these are forms of antonomasia.

28. Berlin, *Shared Rhetorical Features*, p. 37 cites Deut. 32.9, Pss. 29.5 and 89.4.

29. Text and translation: W.G. Lambert, 'A Neo-Babylonian Tammuz Lament', *JAOS* 103 (1983), pp. 211-15; his comment is on p. 214.

30. Text and translation: D.J. Wiseman, 'A Gilgamesh Fragment from Nimrud',

contrast, Erra of the *Epic of Erra* is named in line 5 of tablet I, though even there the focus is on Išum, his opposite number.[31] The name Nabu in a prayer to that god occurs first in line 7;[32] in a hymn to Marduk the god is first named in line 8;[33] Ninurta's name is delayed to line 15 in a prayer to him[34] and so on.

In the 'parallelism of greater precision' a rather vague expression in the first line is made clearer, more explicit in the second. One of the examples provided by Clines is Isa. 40.22:

hnwṭh kdq šmym	who stretches out the heavens like a thin thing,
wymtḥm k'hl lšbt	and spreads them out like a tent to dwell in.

As he notes, 'the blurred and indefinite image of line A [i.e. *dq*, 'something thin'] is brought into focus in line B'.[35] See also Jer. 5.15 and Ps. 59.4.

A third kind of delaying device is more dramatic in character and does not seem to have been recognized. In such cases the beginning of an action is described but only later is the reason (or the effect) of the action (or sequence of actions) made clear. For want of a better term I have used the descriptive label 'dramatic delay'.

For example, in the Babylonian Theodicy seven and a half lines intervene between 'I will ask you a question' (line 25) and the question itself 'Can a life of bliss be assured?' (line 33).[36]

hylylw	Wail:
hh lywm ky-qrwb ywm	'What a day!' for the day is near,
wqrwb ywm lyhwh	and the day of Yahweh is near,
ywm 'nn 't gwym yhyh	a day of clouds, disaster-time for the nations
etc.	will it be.[37] (Ezek. 30.2-3)

Iraq 37 (1975), pp. 157-63 on 160-61. This would correspond to the second line of the *narû* tablet presumed to begin in line 25. According to J.H. Tigay, *The Evolution of the Gilgamesh Epic* (Philadelphia: University of Pennsylvania Press, 1982), pp. 140-44, this is a later addition.

31. Cf. P. Machinist, 'Rest and Violence in the Poem of Erra', *JAOS* 103 (1983), pp. 221-26, 223 n. 15.

32. Seux, *Hymnes et prières*, pp. 265-66.

33. Seux, *Hymnes et prières*, pp. 128-31.

34. Seux, *Hymnes et prières*, pp. 314-16.

35. Clines, *Parallelism of Greater Precision*, p. 79.

36. Lambert, *Babylonian Wisdom Literature*, pp. 72-73. Also, Ee IV 123-26 (cited by Lambert, 'Tammuz Lament', p. 214 n. 4) and add IV 119-22.

37. W. Zimmerli, *Ezechiel* (BKAT, 13/2; Neukirchen–Vluyn: Neukirchener Verlag, 1969), p. 723 translates: '[Heulet:] Ha, der Tag! Ja, nahe ist ein Tag, "nahe"

Other examples: Gen. 49.5-7b, 14-15; Ezek. 12.1-6; 27.3b-26 (ignoring prose insert: 10-25; contrast 26.17-21); 28.2b-7; 30.2b-4; Isa. 40.9-10; Mic. 1.2-5; Nah. 2.1; Prov. 1.11-15, 20-26; 2.1-5; 9.1-6; Job 4.12-17; 27.2-4; 28.1-12; 31.5-6, 7-8, 9-12, 13-15, 16-22, 24-26 (climax); 32.6–33.3 (long introduction)[38]. An example in prose is 1 Sam. 3.15b.

Once these definitions have been applied to Ugaritic the examples of delay in various guises and degrees can be assigned to the following slots, though the lines of demarcation are not always clear.

DELAYED IDENTIFICATION	a, b, i, m, p
PARALLELISM OF GREATER PRECISION	c, l, o, q
DRAMATIC DELAY	d, e, f, g, h, i, j, k, n

The table shows that most of the examples can be assigned to 'dramatic delay'. What is not shown is that in many of the examples there is a partial climax followed by a full dénouement, a double delay as it were. This applies to a, f, i, k and n. There are also some mixtures. It can be noted, too, that examples b and q are relatively weak.

As Clines has remarked, in Hebrew the parallelism of greater precision is related to staircase parallelism, number parallelism, automatism, word-pairs and ballast-variants.[39] This applies to Ugaritic, too, of course. Additional types of delay are introduction to speech,[40] riddles,[41] rhetorical questions[42] and distant parallelism.[43] Here, too, can be mentioned the cumulative simile found in both Hebrew and Ugaritic.[44]

ist der Tag Jahwes, ein Tag des Gewölks, (Gerichts-)Zeit der Völker wird er sein'.

38. See also Deut. 32.9 (courtesy of Paul Sanders).

39. Clines, *Parallelism of Greater Precision*, pp. 87-93. On climax in number parallelism, cf. G. del Olmo Lete, 'Nota sobre Prov 30.19 (*w^{e}derek geber b^{e}'almah*)', *Bib* 67 (1986), pp. 68-74, esp. 70 where he remarks 'el último [miembro de la serie] es siempre climático'.

40. See Chapter 9, 'Introductions to Discourse in Ugaritic Narrative Verse'. Note, in Hebrew, Deut. 32.1-3 (8 lines); Joel 1.2-3, 5, 8, 11, 13; 2.1; 3.9.

41. E.g. Prov. 23.29(-30).

42. E.g. Isa. 60.9; Mic. 6.6-7; see my *Classical Hebrew Poetry*, pp. 338-42.

43. An example is *Ee* IV 138 (and V 62), which describes what happened to the two halves of Tiamat's body.

44. Examples in *Classical Hebrew Poetry*, p. 259 and add Prov. 26.2. An example of delay in a prose text (*KTU* 5.9) is discussed by D. Pardee and R.M. Whiting, 'Aspects of epistolary verbal usage in Ugaritic and Akkadian', *BSO(A)S* 50 (1987), pp. 10-11.

The function of these different kinds of delay is not suspense[45] so much as the carrying forward of the narrative by impelling the reader/listener to pay attention. Significant, too, is the subordinate role played by parallelism to the need for sustaining the attention of the audience/reader.[46]

A final example, once again from Akkadian (the Story of Adapa),[47] will show how there can be a succession of different delaying devices in a single passage:

eṭlu ana manni kâ emâta	Young man, for whom have you become like this?
ladapa ana manni karra lubšata	Adapa, for whom are you garbed in mourning?

(First delay: generic *eṭlu* // PN; repeated question.)

45. Berlin, *Shared Rhetorical Features*, p. 36 n. 6 denies there is an element of suspense in the particularizing stanza as Alster proposed (see above n. 13). On delay and suspense, cf. S. Ullmann, *Language and Style: Collected Papers* (Oxford: Basil Blackwell, 1966), pp. 105, 106 and 188. Also, W. Weaver, 'Probability, Rarity, Interest and Surprise', *Scientific Monthly* 67 (1948), pp. 290-92 and the remarks by C. Osgood, 'Comments to Part Three', and G.A. Miller, 'Closing Statement', both in T.A. Sebeok (ed.), *Style in Language* (Cambridge, MA: MIT Press, 1960), pp. 100 and 394-95 respectively.

46. If delay is the superordinate then the feature 'parallelism' shared by the different types of parallelism in general may only superficially be a common component.

47. Text and translation: S.A. Picchioni, *Il poemetto di Adapa* (Budapest: G. Komoroczy, 1981), pp. 116-17 and 118-19 (= Frammento B 26-31 // rev. 51-56). Cf. E. Reiner, *Your Thwarts in Pieces Your Mooring Rope Cut: Poetry from Babylonia and Assyria* (Michigan: Horace B. Rackham School of Graduate Studies at the University of Michigan, 1985), p. 51: 'Only then, about 65 lines in the poem [Nergal and Ereškigal], does Ereškigal instruct her attendant Namtar to go up to heaven for her portion of the banquet'. Similarly, in the Ugaritic prayer *KTU* 1.65:1-19, it would seem that the climax comes right at the end:

In the divine lance,
in the divine axe,
in the divine mace,
in the fat-offering to Ilu,
in the burnt-offering to Ilu,
in the regular oblation to Ilu,
in the satisfaction of Ilu
[we trust].

cf. G. del Olmo Lete, *La religión cananea según la litúrgia de Ugarit: Estudio textual* (Aula Orientalis Supplementa, 3; Sabadell: Editorial Ausa, 1992), pp. 228-29.

ina mātini ilū šina ḫalqūma	From our land two gods have disappeared
anāku akana epšeku	and (therefore) I still act in this manner

(Second delay: identity of gods withheld, forcing the next question.)

mannu ilū šena ša ina māti' ḫalqū	Who are the two gods who have disappeared from the land?

(Third delay: Adapa's words repeated in the form of a question.)

ᵈdumuzi u ᵈgizzida šūnu	They are Dumuzi and Gizzida!

(At last, the answer to the initial question.)

There is no real 'suspense' since the gods are named in line 24 (// 39) and these are the very gods who are asking the questions, but the fact remains that this six-line exchange assists the thrust of the narrative. Paradoxically, therefore, delaying devices, if skilfully used, do not slow up the linear reading of a text but function instead as part of its dynamic forward impulse.

3. *The Structure of 1 Samuel 3*[48]

The analysis of 1 Samuel 3 presented here is intended principally to lay bare the bones of narrative structure with apposite comment of a restricted nature. The underlying pattern of this section is quite simple, as will be seen. Initially, I worked with MT largely as it stands, in class lectures, but out of interest I tried the same procedure using McCarter's reconstructed text[49] and to my surprise reached much the same results. The implication is that narrative patterns were not linked rigidly to set texts. Rather, different oral traditions could make use of identical plots and end up with different versions of the same story. It is only an accident of history that the frozen form represented by MT has come to be accepted as the standard text.

The first stage in our examination of 1 Samuel 3 (including 1 Sam. 4.1a) is to set out the complete chapter in translation using a sequence of letters to mark off the principal sections.

A 1 The lad Samuel was serving Yahweh under Eli's control,
and Yahweh's word was rare in those days;
there was (however) no false vision.[50]

48. First published in *BZ* 28 (1984), pp. 90-93.

49. P. Kyle McCarter, *I Samuel* (AB, 8; Garden City, NY: Doubleday, 1980), pp. 94-97.

50. For obscure *niprāṣ* P. Kyle McCarter (*I Samuel*, p. 95) accepts the meaning

B 2 It happened (when)
Eli was lying in his own place,
his eyes were becoming so dim
he wasn't able to see;
3 the sacred lamp had not yet been doused
and Samuel was sleeping in the temple.

C C_1 a 4 Yahweh called: Samuel, Samuel,
b He said: Here I am.
c 5 He ran to Eli
d and said: Here I am because you called me.
e But he said: Lie down again.
f So he went and lay down.

C_2 a 6 Yahweh called once again: Samuel, Samuel.
b (absent)
c Samuel went to Eli
d and said: Here I am because you called me.
e But he said: I did not call you;
lie down again
f (absent)

7 Samuel did not know Yahweh yet,
nor had Yahweh's word been revealed to him.

C_3 a 8 Yahweh called Samuel a third time.
b (absent)
c He got up and went to Eli
d and said: Here I am because you called me.

Eli then understood that Yahweh was calling the lad.
e 9 He said: Go and lie down.
If anyone calls you
say: 'Speak, for your servant is listening'.
f Then Samuel went
and lay down in his own place.

C_4 a 10 Then Yahweh came and stood
and called as at the other times.

'widespread' but he also suggests *ḥazôn niprāṣ* (or *pōrēṣ* or even *pārūṣ*) 'may be a technical designation of some kind, perhaps referring to a cultic practice whereby visions were regularly obtained'. It is also possible that Heb. *prṣ* here may be cognate with Akk. *parāṣu* in its meaning 'to lie' (*AHw*, p. 832: 'D: lügen') cf., too, the derivatives *piriṣtu*, 'lie; under false pretences', *parriṣu*, 'lying' and *parrāṣu*, 'liar' (*AHw*, pp. 866, 834). Cf. Jer. 14.14, 23.25-26 etc. for the concept of false prophecy.

b Samuel said:
Speak, for your servant is listening.

11 Yahweh said to Samuel:
See, I am going to do something in Israel
which anyone hearing about—both his ears will tingle.

12 On that day
I shall bring about all I said about his family
(from) start to finish.

13 I am letting him know I have passed judgment on his family
for all time,
because he knew his sons were cursing God
but did not restrain them.

14 Therefore, I have made an oath against Eli's family:
'Never, ever, shall the guilt of Eli's family be atoned
for by sacrifice or by offering'.
f And Samuel lay down till morning
and got up early in the morning.

D 16 He opened the temple doors.
Samuel was frightened of reporting the vision to Eli.
a Eli said to Samuel:
b Samuel, my son.
c And he said: Here I am.

17 What were the exact *words* Yahweh *spoke* to you? asked Eli
Don't *hide* (them) *from me*.
May God do this and even more to you
if you *hide* one word *from me*
of all the *words* which he *spoke* to you.

18 So Samuel told him all the words
and hid nothing from him.
He (Eli) said: He is Yahweh.
Let him do what he thinks best.

E 19 Samuel grew up
and Yahweh was with him.
he did not let any of his words 'fall to the ground'.

20 The whole of Israel was aware
—from Dan to Beersheba—
that Samuel was confirmed as a prophet of Yahweh.

21 Yahweh continued appearing at Bethel
when he revealed himself to Samuel
4.1a and the word of Samuel was for the whole of Israel.

The passage given above can be arranged according to the following scheme:

A (3.1)	LACK	no prophecy
B (3.2-3)	SETTING	Eli purblind and asleep (and old); Samuel asleep (and young)
C (3.4-15)	LACK SUPPLIED	prophecy returns
C_1 (4-5)	first false start	first call
C_2 (6-7)	second false start	second call
C_3 (8-9)	third false start	third call
C_4 (10-15a)	real start	fourth call and Yahweh's oracle
D (3.15b-18)	PART REPETITION (of C_4)	Samuel informs Eli
E (3.19–4.1a)	RESUMPTION (of C)	Samuel, a prophet.

The classic 'nuclear two motifeme sequence' of *lack–lack liquidated* (or, as I prefer, lack supplied) described as 'a move from disequilibrium to equilibrium' by Dundes[51] is undoubtedly fundamental here. Israel is without prophecy at the start of ch. 3, but by its end prophecy (through Samuel) has returned. In other words, the lack has been supplied. The same sequence recurs elsewhere in 1 Samuel. In ch. 1 Hannah is barren (lack) but through supernatural agency Samuel is born to her (lack supplied); in 16.14-23 Saul lacks a bard until David the musical poet is found; in ch. 21 the hungry men eat the sacred bread (vv. 2-7) and weaponless David reacquires Goliath's sword (vv. 9-10). To these evident examples, and still restricting ourselves to 1 Samuel, can be added the giving of a monarch (Saul) to kingless Israel (8.1–10.27a) as well as Saul's finding of the she-asses which had been lost (9.1-20).

The characters named right at the start (3.1) had already been introduced (chs. 1–2).[52] The setting (B = 3.2-3) provides unmistakable polarity,[53] not only in presenting Eli as old and Samuel as young and

51. A. Dundes, *The Morphology of North American Indian Folktales* (Folklore Fellows Communications, 195.81.3; Helsinki: Academia Scientiarum Fennica, 1964). Cf. V. Propp, *Morphology of the Folktale* (trans. L. Scott, 2nd edn by L.A. Wagner; Austin: University of Texas Press, 1968), p. 119.

52. For story, characters, setting and interpretation as the building blocks of narrative structure, cf. L. Doležel, 'From Motifemes to Motifs', *Poetics* 4 (1972), pp. 55-90.

53. For the binary principle, see, of course, the writings of C. Lévi-Strauss and the comments of A. Dundes in his preface to Propp, *Morphology*, pp. xi -xiii.

inexperienced (see v. 7), but by contrasting their capacities for vision. Eli was blind in every way whereas Samuel was to be the new seer. The series of false starts (C_{1-3} = 3.4-9) increases the tension and also serves to fill out the narrative by repetition. This corresponds in pattern if not in content to the threefold tasks set for seeker-heroes in folktales. Each call, false or not, is based on a common schema (indicated by the marginal letters a-f) and it is notable that whereas not all six elements recur every time (see the comment 'absent', above in C_2 and C_3) additional elements can also be inserted (e.g. 'Eli then realized that Yahweh was calling the lad' in C_3). Truncated forms of the oral schema occur, too, in 3.10 and 3.16 (D). Noteworthy, besides, is the chiastic patterning in 3.17, based on keywords:

(a) *dbr dbr*
(b) *kḥd* (+ *mn*)
(c) (central oath)
(b') *kḥd* (+ *mn*)
(a') *dbr dbr*

In D, under pressure, Samuel makes his (abbreviated) report to Eli—again, repetition in disguised form. Finally, E reiterates that the lack of prophet and prophecy has been adequately supplied. As regards plot, both these sections (D, E) are inessential.

As mentioned at the beginning, the material presented here is ripe for deeper analysis which will surely refine many of the points made only in passing. Meanwhile it is interesting to observe that whether MT or a reconstructed text (based on the Dead Sea Scrolls and the versions) is adopted there is considerable variation even between repeated patterns within this chapter (I am thinking, in particular, of the call schema) which too severe ancient editing might otherwise have obliterated. The fluctuations of oral narrative persist, in some degree, in the texts handed down to us and remain to be detected by the observant reader.

Also significant are the following lines in the *Epic of Gilgamesh*:

> Sleep, which is poured on mankind, fell upon him (= Gilgamesh). In the middle watch he ended his sleep. He arose and said to his friend (= Enkidu): 'My friend, did you not call me? Why am I awake? Did you not touch me? Why am I startled? Did not some god pass by? Why is my flesh numb? My friend, I saw a third dream.'[54]

54. Text and translation as in J.H. Tigay, *The Evolution of the Gilgamesh Epic*

4. *Symmetry of Stanza in Jeremiah 2.2b-3*[55]

Framed by introductory[56] and closing formulae,[57] Jer. 2.2b-3 ('the seed oracle') emerges as a self-contained unit or poem, as most commentators are agreed.[58] Yet, in spite of intense discussion of this passage[59] no one has noticed the symmetrical gender patterning it exhibits. Once the text and translation are set out with grammatical gender made explicit, the pattern becomes apparent.

(v. 2b)	I	a	*zkrty lk*	*ḥsd n'wryk*
		b		*'hbt klwltyk*
		c		*lktk 'ḥry bmdbr*
		d		*b'rṣ l' zrw'h*
(v. 3)	II	a	*qdš yśr'l lyhwh*	
		b	*r'šyt tbw'th*	
		c	*kl 'klyw y'šmw*	
		d	*r'h tb' 'lyhm*	

(Philadelphia: University of Pennsylvania Press, 1982), pp. 284 and 121-22. This lends confirmation to the conclusion reached by R. Gnuse ('A Reconsideration of the Form-Critical Structure in 1 Samuel 3: An Ancient Near Eastern Dream Theophany', *ZAW* 94 [1982], pp. 379-90), that this chapter is not a prophetic call narrative but 'an auditory message dream' with Mesopotamian parallels. See now D.W. Wicke, 'The Structure of 1 Sam 3: Another View', *BZ* 30 (1986), pp. 256-58.

55. First published in *JSOT* 19 (1981), pp. 107-10.

56. 'The word of Yahweh came to me as follows: "Go and shout into the ears of Jerusalem as follows".' The Greek translators abbreviated this editorial formula to 'And he said'; cf. J.G. Janzen, *Studies in the Text of Jeremiah* (HSM, 6; Cambridge, MA: Harvard University Press, 1973), p. 111. For the Greek version of 2.2b-3 see p. 26.

57. 'Yahweh's oracle' (end of v. 3).

58. Following T.J. Meek, 'The Poetry of Jeremiah', *JQR* 14 (1923–24), pp. 281-91, esp. 281-82. For example E.W. Nicholson, *The Book of Jeremiah: Chapters 1–25* (Cambridge Bible Commentary on the NEB; Cambridge: Cambridge University Press, 1973), pp. 28-30; J. Bright, *Jeremiah* (AB, 21; Garden City, NY: Doubleday, 1965), pp. 9, 14.

59. Notably O. Loretz, 'Die Sprüche Jeremias in Jer. 1,17–9,25', *UF* 2 (1970), pp. 109-30, esp. 114. For discussion of the relationship of our text to larger complexes within Jeremiah, cf. J.R. Lundbom, *Jeremiah: A Study in Ancient Hebrew Rhetoric* (SBLDS, 18; Missoula, MT: Scholars Press, 1975), p. 74, and particularly W.L. Holladay, *The Architecture of Jeremiah 1–20* (Lewisburg: Bucknell University Press, 1976), pp. 30-34.

(v. 2b)	I	a	I remember[60]	the devotion (m.) of your youth (m.),
		b		the love (f.) of your nuptials (f.),
		c		your coming after me through the desert (m.),
		d		through unseeded land (f.).
(v. 3)	II	a	Holy (m.) was Israel (m.) to Yahweh,	
		b	the first (f.) of his yield (f.).	
		c	All consuming it were at fault (m.),	
		d	evil (f.) came to them.	

Note that the translation is somewhat stilted since it attempts to reproduce the word order and wording of the original.

Two stanzas make up the poem; the first is a quatrain (v. 2b); the second (v. 3) comprises two strophes, each a couplet. Stanza II is marked off from stanza I both by content and by its opening 'pivot pattern' bicolon.[61] Grammatical gender seems to be distributed over each stanza in the following manner:[62]

I	a	m. – m.	II	a	m. + m.
	b	f. – f.		b	f. – f.
	c	m.		c	m.
	d	f.		d	f.

Evidently the poet has not applied a format automatically; instead, as can be seen, he has varied some of the components. In IIa 'holy was Israel' is a verbless clause consisting of two masculine nouns while its counterpart (Ia) comprises two nouns in bound form ('your youthful devotion'). Further, in IIc ('all eating it were guilty') the gender, which is masculine, is implicit. In spite of these deviations it would appear that the gender pattern was intended and is virtually the same for each stanza. It can be added to those collected and examined elsewhere.[63]

60. On the construction used here, cf. T. Muraoka, 'On the So-called *Dativus Ethicus* in Hebrew', *JTS* 29 (1978), pp. 495-98, who comments, 'The preposition Lamedh followed by the matching pronominal suffix seems to have the effect of creating a self-contained little cosmos around the subject' (p. 497).

61. See Watson, 'The Pivot Pattern in Hebrew, Ugaritic and Akkadian', *ZAW* 88 (1976), pp. 239-53. I now consider such verses to be couplets (or bicola) and not tricola. Common to couplets of this type is the element of silent stress in the second line which balances the 'pivotal' word.

62. The – sign denotes a construct state relationship; + denotes predication.

63. See above; also A. Berlin, 'Grammatical Aspects of Biblical Parallelism',

It is one thing to point out an objective arrangement in a text, as here; it is rather more difficult to determine reasons for its presence. At the outset it can be conjectured that Jeremiah used a set pattern as a framework for his oracle. At a deeper level, it would seem that he adopted the polarity of gender here since he was using a male–female metaphor to portray the relationship between Yahweh and Israel. In stanza I the metaphor is particularized as the bond between groom and bride; in stanza II less clearly as the attitude of a landowner to his crops (combining the figurative use of 'jealousy' with the transparent metaphor of 'ploughing'). In addition, the play on gender heightens the contrast between Yahweh and his people.

How alert, though, can Jeremiah's listeners have been to the patterning described here? On reflection, the answer is that they were more alert than we might at first imagine in view of the following. Texts such as 'Those saying to a tree: "You're my father" / and to a stone: "You're my birth-giver"' (Jer. 2.27) show both prophet and people adverted to gender since the couplet loses its thrust if *'ēṣ* ('tree') is not recognized as masculine or *'eben* ('stone') as feminine.[64] In our text the underlying structure is simple and occurs twice; since Jeremiah was addressing some of the most learned men of his time, it is not too much to assume that they at least could appreciate his poetic technique. Lastly, even if neither speaker nor listener noticed the gender pattern, it remains the only element common to both stanzas[65] and may perhaps have been borrowed from an earlier poetic tradition.

5. *An Unrecognized Hyperbole in Krt*[66]

5.1. *Introduction: The Problem*

With the exception of one difficult line, which forms the subject of this section, scholars agree, in the main, on how to translate the

HUCA 50 (1979), pp. 17-43 (esp. 27-30).

64. See, too, Jer. 2.25a, 3.24, 4.10, 13, 19b, 6.7, 18.13-17, 31.8 and the texts listed in the article mentioned in the previous footnote.

65. Line-form analysis, for example, does not uncover the symmetry under discussion; cf. T. Collins, *Line-forms in Hebrew Poetry: A Grammatical Approach to the Stylistic Study of the Hebrew Prophets* (Studia Pohl; Series Major, 7; Rome: Pontifical Biblical Institute, 1978), p. 134 for analysis of Jer. 2.3. Nor does metrical analysis, in spite of Meek's assertion in 'The Poetry of Jeremiah', p. 282.

66. First published in *Or* 48 (Rome: Pontifical Biblical Institute, 1979), pp. 112-17.

passage describing how Keret's army was mustered.[67] There is also consensus that the passage employs hyperbole and so is not to be taken at face value. The disagreement concerns the words *'wr mzl ymzl*, and to be more precise centres on the meaning of *mzl*. So far solutions have been attempted by the philological approach[68] and have not proved convincing. It will be argued in the present section that the meaning of the line in question can be inferred by adducing a parallel from Akkadian literature which shows the problematic sentence to be hyperbole, in line with the rest of the passage. The presentation will be as follows. First, the complete passage will be set out, with my own translation and minimal philological notes. Next, the Akkadian parallel will be given and then the translation I propose for *'wr mzl ymzl*. The section will close with some general remarks on hyperbole.

5.2. *The Mustering of Keret's Troops*[69]

I MOBILIZATION

'dn ngb wyṣi	The whole troop must go out,
ṣbu ṣbi ngb	The whole army must take the field,
wyṣi 'dn m'	And out must go the troop en masse.

67. Text: *KTU* 1.14 ii 32–iii 1 and 1.14 iv 13-31. The *CTA* numbering is 14 ii 85–iii 105 and 14 iv 176-194, corresponding to *UT* Krt 85-105 and 176-194. Translations consulted include H.L. Ginsberg, *The Legend of King Keret: A Canaanite Epic of the Bronze Age* (BASORSup, 2-3; New Haven: ASOR, 1946); J. Gray, *The Krt Text in the Literature of Ras Shamra: A Social Myth of Ancient Canaan* (Documenta et Monumenta Orientis Antiqui, 5; Leiden: Brill, 2nd edn, 1964); C.H. Gordon, *Ugarit and Minoan Crete: The Bearing of their Texts on the Origins of Western Culture* (New York: Norton, 1966), pp. 103-104 and 106-107; H. Sauren and G. Kestemont, 'Keret, roi de Ḫubur', *UF* 3 (1971), pp. 181-221, and A. Caquot, M. Sznycer and A. Herdner, *Textes ougaritiques*. I. *Mythes et légendes* (LAPO, 7; Paris: Cerf, 1974), pp. 516-19 and 528-29. Also, the draft of the revised edition of *Canaanite Myths and Legends* a copy of which Dr John C.L. Gibson kindly sent me. See now *Canaanite Myths*, pp. 84 and 87.

68. Notably J.A. Emerton, 'The Meaning of the Root *mzl* in Ugaritic', *JSS* 14 (1969), pp. 22-33. The author lists nine solutions and adds a further two of his own. Also, G. del Olmo Lete, 'Notes on Ugaritic Semantics I', *UF* 7 (1975), pp. 89-102, 91-93.

69. The text and translation follow the 'command' version (*KTU* 1.14 ii 32–iii 1) as it is the more complete. Apart from slight variations in tense and vocabulary the corresponding account of the 'performance' (*KTU* 1.14 iv 13-31) is essentially identical.

II A NUMBERLESS HOST

ṣbuk ul mad	Your army is a huge force:
ṯlt mat rbt	Three hundred times ten thousand;
hpṯ dbl spr	Freemen without number;
ṯnn dbl hg	Archers without count.
hlk lalpm ḫḏḏ	And by the myriad like rain.[70]
aṯr ṯn ṯn hlk	After two, two march,
aṯr ṯlṯ klhm	After three, all of them.[71]

III EVEN EXEMPT CLASSES CONSCRIPTED

yḥd bth sgr	Let the solitary man shut up his house,
almnt škr tškr	The widow become a mercenary.
zbl ʿršm yšu	Let the laid up lay hold of his bed,
ʿwr mzl ymzl	The blind man...
wyṣi trḫ ḥdṯ	Even the newly-wed is to go:
ybʿr lṯn aṯt	He will forsake his wife on another's account,
lm nkr mddth	On the enemy's account, his beloved.[72]

IV CLOSING SIMILE

kirby tškn šd	Like locusts they shall occupy the field,
km ḥsn pat mdbr	Like grasshoppers, the desert fringe.

Notes to the Translation

ʿdn ngb wyṣi etc. The parallelism between *ʿdn ngb wyṣi* and *wyṣi ʿdn mʿ* shows that *ʿdn ngb* corresponds to *ʿdn mʿ*. In both expressions *ʿdn* is a noun ('troop')[73] qualified by a word indicating totality (*ngb*, 'all' and *mʿ*, 'together').[74] This interpretation is confirmed by the Akkadian expression *napḫaršunu*, 'all of them' used in the equivalent

70. This translation of the couplet is defended in *Or* NS 45 (1976), pp. 440-41.

71. In the second half of the stanza the sequences *ṯlṯ*, *ṯnn*, and *hlk* are repeated in reverse order: *ṯn*, *hlk*, *ṯlṯ*. In fact, the whole stanza is marked by repetition (*rbt*, *dbl*, *aṯr*) and assonance (*mad / mat*; *hlk / klhm*; *dbl / alpm*) their function being to convey the impression of a massed army on the march.

72. This tricolon is fully dealt with in W.G.E. Watson, 'Ugaritic and Mesopotamian Literary Texts', *UF* 9 (1977), pp. 277-79. Briefly, *ṯn // nkr* denotes the enemy on whose account (causal *l*) the newly-wed (normally exempt) has to leave behind (*bʿr*) his wife.

73. Following Ginsberg, *Legend*, p. 37.

74. For *mʿ*, 'all together', see Gray, *Krt Text*, p. 39. The word *ngb*, here considered equivalent to Akk. *nagbu*, 'totality', may also mean 'provisions' (see next note) but the topic of provisioning (if such it is) ended in the previous section. Essentially, the whole of the passage is a list or catalogue, with the 'total' as its head.

text from the *Epic of Erra* (cited below, section 5.3). In the second line *ṣbu* is a verb, 'to muster'.[75]

ṣbuk (par. *ṣbuh*) *ul mad*. Compare *mādu ṣābūka*, 'your numerous soldiers' (EA 38.5) and *ṣābum mādumma*, 'a numerous army' (ARM III 18.10).[76]

t̲lt̲ mat rbt. This can only mean 3,000,000 (men).[77]

yḥd (par. *aḥd*) *bth sgr* (par. *ysgr*). Two texts from Nuzi listing personnel released (*muššuru*) from military service to return home (and *bītišunu*) include entries of the form PN *ēdēnu*, 'PN, solo'.[78] It can be

75. In view of the Mari parallel usually cited (*ṣābūšu ṣidītam nagib*, ARM XV 229) it is perhaps possible to read *ṣbu ṣd*(!)*i ngb*, 'the army is furnished with provisions', but the variant *ṣba* discounts such an emendation.

76. On *ul*, 'force', cf. Ginsberg, *Legend*, p. 37.

77. Clearly an exaggeration. 'In the earliest periods, the average size of most cities in Palestine, Syria, Anatolia, and Mesopotamia ranged from 5 to 10 acres. There were also a number of principal cities covering an area of hundreds of acres. On the reasonable assumption that there were roughly 240 inhabitants to an urban acre, the population figures of most of the cities of the ancient Middle East ranged from 1,000 to 3,000 with some cities boasting a population of between 5,000 and 10,000. There were a few exceptions where the population reached scores of thousands. The proportion of fighters among the inhabitants averaged 25 per cent. So that the small cities had about 300 fighting men, the medium-sized cities about 1,000 to 2,000, and the large cities several thousand.' Y. Yadin, *The Art of Warfare in Biblical Lands in the Light of Archaeological Discovery* (trans. M. Pearlman; London: Weidenfeld and Nicolson; New York: McGraw-Hill, 1963), p. 19. For sizes of actual armies, cf. pp. 294, 112, and note the ideal figure of 288,000 in 1 Chron. 27. Even the rendering 'Captains, a hundred myriads'—so F. Renfroe, 'The Transition from "Army" to "Enemy"', *UF* 19 (1987), p. 231—implies an exaggeration.

78. Or 'PN—individual/single man (from a family group)'. For the texts, cf. G. Contenau, 'Textes et monuments', *RA* 28 (1931), p. 30 no. 4 and pp. 31-32 no. 7. It seems that *ēdēnu* is a numerical adjective used after proper names to distinguish them from entries in the form PN$_1$, PN$_2$ *šinamunu*, 'PN$_1$, PN$_3$: a group of two'; and PN$_1$, PN$_2$, PN$_3$ *kikamunu* (or *kukamunu*), 'PN$_1$, PN$_2$, PN$_3$: a group of three' as in E.R. Lacheman, *Excavations at Nuzi Vol. VI: The Administrative Archives* (HSS, 15; Cambridge, MA: Harvard University Press, 1955), p. 52 lines 6', 8', 13', 15', p. 57 lines 1-5, p. 71 lines 8-17. PN *ēdēnu* also contrasts with PN *ù* 1 ŠEŠ/DUMU—*šu*, 'PN and his brother/son' in HSS 15,66. For the information concerning Nuzi I am indebted to Professor Dr Walter Mayer of the Altorientalisches

conjectured that at Ugarit such a person was possibly an old campaigner who was granted a house in return for his war service.[79]

almnt škr tškr. As Ginsberg proposed long ago, even women were called up.[80] Note that in Hebrew *śākar* refers to the hiring of mercenaries.[81]

zbl 'ršm yšu. Not 'Let the sick man be carried in his bed'[82] but 'Let the invalid carry his own bed', the whole point of the hyperbole being the implied absurdity of such an act. The translation 'Let the laid up lay hold of his bed' is an attempt at reproducing the wordplay (strictly speaking, *talḥin*)[83] of the original. Like Akkadian *zabālu*, Ugaritic *zbl* very probably means both 'to carry, transport' and 'to linger' (said of sick person or disease).[84]

5.3. *The Parallel in Akkadian*

The key to understanding the passage from *Krt* just quoted is supplied by a short section from the *Epic of Erra*. After a few opening lines tablet IV begins with a description of an army formed from civilians who are normally non-combatant. The text and translation are as follows:[85]

Seminar, Westfälische Wilhelms-Universität Münster who kindly supplied me with transcripts of all the relevant texts as well as detailed philological comment. The opinions expressed (slightly at variance with *CAD*, E, p. 27a and *AHw*, pp. 186a, 474a, 1241) are therefore his.

79. As is suggested by CH̬ para. 26 and 31.

80. Ginsberg, *Legend*, p. 38.

81. 2 Sam. 10.6; 1 Chron. 19.6-7; 2 Chron. 25.6; see also Judg. 9.4.

82. As in most translations; exceptions are H. Sauren and G. Kestemont, 'Keret, roi de Ḫubur', *UF* 3 (1971), p. 197: 'Que l'aveugle fasse son lit' and Gordon, *Ugarit and Minoan Crete*, p. 104 (and p. 107): '(Let) the invalid carry the bed'.

83. The Arabic technical term for syllepsis or double entendre. Another example in Ug. is ***nšu riš*** *ḥrṯm*, 'the ploughmen lifted their heads' (*KTU* 1.16 iii 12) where the expression 'to lift one's head' is meant both in its literal sense and as an idiom for 'to rejoice'.

84. See *CAD*, Z, pp. 1-5. This point seems to have escaped M. Held, 'The Root *ZBL/SBL* in Akkadian, Ugaritic and Biblical Hebrew', *JAOS* 88 (1968), pp. 90-96.

85. Text: L. Cagni, *L'epopea di Erra* (Rome: Istituto di Studi del Vicino Oriente dell'Università, 1969), p. 104 lines 6-11; translation p. 105 nn. 225-26. A slightly different version is given by T. Jacobsen, *The Treasures of Darkness* (New Haven: Yale University Press, 1975), pp. 227-28. Note that in Cagni's transliteration line

mārū bābili	The Babylonians,
ša kīma qanê api pāqida lā išû	who like reeds of a canebrake had no patron,
napḫaršunu elīka iptaḫrū	all assembled round you:
ša kakku lā idû šalip pataršu	The unskilled at arms—his dagger was drawn;
ša tilpānu lā idû malât qašassu	The unskilled with arrows—his bow was at the ready;
ša ṣalta lā idû ippuša tāḫāza	The unskilled in war engaged in combat;
ša abara(?) *lā idû iṣṣūriš išu'u*	The unskilled with wings(?)[86] flew like a bird.
ḫašḫašu pētân birki iba'a	The cripple overtakes the swift-footed;[87]
akû bēl emūqi ikattam	The weakling overcomes the strong man.

The significance of this parallel for understanding the Ugaritic text will be discussed in the next section.

5.4. *The Meaning of 'wr mzl ymzl*

As has already been pointed out, the whole of the passage describing the drafting of Keret's army (section 5.2, above) is hyperbole. The same applies to the segment cited in section 5.3 from the *Epic of Erra*. Both texts imply that every available person irrespective of age, sex or physical fitness formed part of the motley army. There were to be no exemptions.[88] Of course in neither case is the description meant to be understood literally: we are in the realm of overstatement. But it is significant that in both passages specific mention is made of persons

10b should come after line 11—see L. Cagni, *Das Erra-Epos: Keilschrifttext* (Rome: Biblical Institute Press, 1970), pp. 24 and 75.

86. For this difficult line, cf. Cagni, *L'epopea*, p. 226; M. Tsevat, 'Erra IV: (7-)10', *RA* 81 (1977), p. 184.

87. In a different context (wisdom sayings) the Mesopotamian texts from Ras Shamra provide an interesting parallel: dumu lú.ad$_4$.ad$_4$ (ZA-*tēnu*).ke$_x$ (KID) dumu.lu.kaš$_4$ dab.da: *mār* (DUMU) *ḫu-um-mu-ri mār* (DUMU) *la-si-mu i-ba-'a*, 'The son of the cripple overtakes the son of the runner' (J. Nougayrol *et al.*, *Ugaritica* V [BAH, 80; MRS, 16; Paris: Imprimerie Nationale/Librairie Orientaliste Paul Geuthner, 1968], text 164:34'-35', p. 294). See also Isa. 35.6.

88. As already recognized by Ginsberg, *Legend*, p. 38: 'There are no exemptions from this draft!' Exemption from military service was in any case a privilege, well-attested in Mesopotamia; cf. A.L. Oppenheim, *Ancient Mesopotamia: Portrait of a Dead Civilization* (Chicago: University of Chicago Press, 1964), pp. 120-21. In Ugarit itself exemptions from active duty were occasionally granted; cf. A.F. Rainey, 'The Military Personnel of Ugarit', *JNES* 24 (1965), pp. 17-27 who cites *PRU* III 80 (RS 16.239) 14-15 and 140 (RS 16.132) 17 (p. 17 and n. 7). And, as Rainey mentions (p. 20 n. 66), citing CḪ para 10:5 and 11:45, the penalties for even hiring a substitute were severe.

with a physical disability behaving like (or even better than) able-bodied people. This indicates that stanza III of the *Krt* text describes those normally exempt from military service not as left behind, but as conscripted along with the others.

What is required, then, to suit the context of *Krt* which is in line with the Akkadian parallel and at the same time comprises a hyperbole is a translation implying that the blind man acts in an extraordinary way. Versions such as 'the blind man will be left behind'[89] or 'will grope his way'[90] do not satisfy these conditions. They would merely describe what a blind person usually does. A more suitable translation is, therefore '(Let) the blind man overtake the runner'.

A sightless person is generally hesitant in walking and would only run in exceptional circumstances (e.g. over very familiar terrain or in a specially organized race); normally he would proceed with extreme caution.[91] In other words, the sentence comprises a hyperbole, corresponding to 'Let the laid up lay hold of his bed', in the first half of the couplet.

As everyone recognizes, the difficult verb is *mzl*. Here it is taken to be akin (as is often the case in Semitic) to other roots beginning with the two consonants *mz-*.[92] If this is the case, then *mzl* would be cognate with Arabic *mazana*, 'to go away, fly away'[93] and *maza'a*, 'to run, gallop, bound along'.[94] The first word in the expression *mzl ymzl*

89. Or alternatively 'will surely lament': Emerton, 'Meaning', pp. 22-23.

90. E.g. Caquot, Sznycer and Herdner, *Textes ougaritiques*, I, p. 518; see n. f.

91. Cf. Isa. 59.9-10 where 'groping like blind men' is the punishment for 'rushing headlong into crime'.

92. On this phenomenon in Semitic, cf. S. Moscati, 'Il biconsonantismo nelle lingue semitiche', *Bib* 28 (1947), pp. 113-35; G.J. Botterweck, *Der Triliterismus im Semitischen* (BBB, 3; Bonn: Peter Hanstein, 1952); J. Heller, 'Neuere Literatur zur Biliterismus-Frage', *ArOr* 27 (1959), pp. 678-82; S. Moscati, A. Spitaler, E. Ullendorff and W. von Soden, *An Introduction to the Comparative Grammar of the Semitic Languages: Phonology and Morphology* (Porta Linguarum Orientalium NS, 6; Wiesbaden: Otto Harrassowitz, 1964), pp. 72-75 and 129. For strictures against invoking the principle of biliteral bases to resolve philological problems, see J. Barr, *Comparative Philology and the Text of the Old Testament* (Oxford: Oxford University Press, 1968), pp. 166-70. His reservations do not apply here since the meaning of *mzl* has been established by the context.

93. Already suggested by I. Al-Yasin, *The Lexical Relation between Arabic and Ugaritic* (Shelton Semitic Series, 1; New York: Shelton College, 1952), p. 72.

94. See also, perhaps, Akk. *maziānu*, 'racetrack for horses(?)' (*AHw*, p. 637). See now F.M. Fales, 'La radice **MZL* nei testi di Ebla', *SEL* 1 (1984), pp. 23-26.

is not an infinitive absolute,[95] but either a participle (**māzilu*) or a *qattal* form (**mazzāl*) meaning 'runner'.[96] The verb *ymzl* (with *'wr* as subject) is a D stem used in its comparative sense.[97]

5.5. *Hyperbole*

Hyperbole is very common in texts from the ancient Near East, and yet has not been much commented on.[98] To remedy this, and because of its importance to a correct understanding of a long-standing crux in *Krt* (if what has been set out above is valid), some remarks on the subject will be appended here. The Ugaritic texts exhibit their own fair share of hyperbole[99] and, in general, it is true that the device occurs more often in descriptions of military exploits.[100] It is also a fact that in such martial contexts hyperboles tend to occur in clusters, as witness the two texts discussed in this section as well as the account of Anath's attempt at annihilating Mot, where no fewer than five consecutive hyperboles are used.[101]

95. Although the translation 'he surely runs' cannot be entirely excluded.

96. Note that *mzl ymzl* and *zbl* alliterate.

97. For the comparative *piel*, see E. Jenni, *Das hebräische Pi'el: Syntaktisch-semasiologische Untersuchung einer Verbalform im Alten Testament* (Zürich: EVZ-Verlag, 1968), pp. 72-74. Especially relevant is the use in Ps. 105.22 of *ḥkm* in the *piel*: 'to instruct his princes in person, and make the elders even wiser'. As Jenni remarks (p. 75) 'the elders are already wise', which shows the verb to have a comparative sense'.

98. See I.H. Eybers, 'Some Examples of Hyperbole in Biblical Hebrew', *Semitics* 1 (1970), pp. 38-49, and the remarks of J.C. de Moor, 'Rāpi'ūma-Rephaim', *ZAW* 88 (1976), p. 330.

99. Examples: hyperbole is used to express exaggerations of a numerical nature such as 'seventy // eighty' (*KTU* 1.5 v 19-20, of Baal copulating), 'thousands // tens of thousands' (*KTU* 1.4 i 26-28 etc.) and the stock formula *balp šd rbt kmn* (*KTU* 1.3 iv 38 etc.) as well as Yaṭpanu's boast: 'The hand that felled Aqhat will strike down enemies by the thousands' (*KTU* 1.19 iv 58-59). Other examples are the greed of the newly-born gods ('a lip to heaven, a lip to earth etc.' *KTU* 1.23:61-64), the seven years' mourning in place of the customary seven days (*KTU* 1.19 iv 15-16 for Aqhat; *KTU* 1.6 v 8-9 for Baal), and the enormous stature of Baal (implied by the description of Athtar as inadequate for his throne: *KTU* 1.6 i 59-61).

100. See especially D. Stuart, 'The Sovereign's Day of Conquest', *BASOR* 221 (1976), pp. 159-64, where he discusses the tradition of a true sovereign being able to win a war in a single day. Also, in general, cf. the exaggerated statistics common to all accounts of military victory.

101. *KTU* 1.6 ii 31-37; cf. v 11-19.

It seems to me that the function of hyperbole (or at least one of its functions)[102] is to denote extravagance of size, numbers, proportions, quality and so on without having to resort to extravagant language. Hence its appeal. To say, for instance, 'The skies will rain down oil, the wadies will run with honey' (*KTU* 1.6 iii 12-13) is to employ common, everyday language to express the unusual. And it is expressing the fantastic in terms of the mundane which makes hyperbole so effective. In sum, hyperbole belongs to economy of expression which then, as now, is a mark of good poetry.[103]

6. *Apostrophe in the Aqhat Poem*[104]

There is a difference between personification and apostrophe. Both presume or imagine that inanimate objects can act as animate and even sentient beings, but in apostrophe the personified object is addressed directly. One definition for apostrophe is 'a figure of speech in which a thing, a place, an abstract quality, an idea, a dead or absent person, is addressed as if present and capable of understanding'.[105] An example of personification in Ugaritic verse is the well known passage *CTA* 3C 19-22:

(1)	*rgm ʿṣ*	A word from wood,
	wlḫšt abn	a rustle from rock,
	tant šmm ʿm arṣ	sighing of sky to land,
	thmt ʿm kbkbm	deeps to stars.

Here, trees, stones, sky, stars, ocean and land are represented as conveying a message one to another. There are other examples.[106] By

102. It is not enough simply to identify and label various poetic devices taken out of context. Each time the particular function of a device must be ascertained. Consult Leech, *A Linguistic Guide*, p. 4.

103. For the principle of thrift in oral poetic technique, cf. A.B. Lord, *The Singer of Tales* (Harvard Studies in Comparative Literature, 24; Cambridge, MA: Harvard University Press; London: Oxford University Press, 1960), pp. 50-53.

104. First published in *UF* 16 (1984), pp. 323-26.

105. J.A. Cuddon, *A Dictionary of Literary Terms* (London: André Deutsch, 1977), pp. 51-52.

106. *CTA* 3B ii 40-41 (sky, stars); 3C iii 23 (sky, again); 16 i 6-7 and ii 106-108 (rocks etc. weep); 16 vi 35-36. 50-52 (sickness as bedmate). Cf. 17 ii 13-14 (soul at ease). A sampling of Lambert, *Babylonian Wisdom Literature*, results in examples on p.60 line 96, p. 100 line 39 and especially pp. 150-212 and 216-220 (fables and contest literature, and popular sayings respectively).

contrast, apostrophe implies the *vocative* as in the equally much quoted episode where Kothar(-and-Hasis) names the magic clubs. It is *CTA* 2 iv 11-15:

(2) *šmk at ygrš*	Your very name is 'Yagrush';
ygrš grš ym	Yagrush! Drive Yamm,
grš ym lksih	drive Yamm from his throne,
nhr lkḥṯ drkth	Nahar from his sovereign seat.
trtqṣ bd b'l	Twirl in Baal's hand,
km nšr buṣb'th	in his fingers like an eagle.
hlm ktp zbl ym	Hit Prince Yamm's shoulder
bn ydm ṯpṭnhr	'Judge' Nahar's torso.[107]

Here, as in the near-parallel passage (lines 19-23) the club is told its name and its task. With the giving of a name the apostrophe is made even more apparent. Not only is each club provided with a name, but both times the name is foregrounded by the use of wordplay (*ygrš–grš*; *aymr–mr ym*) which in turn focuses attention on the apostrophe. Again, there are additional examples of the device[108] but we will concentrate on only two sets in the Aqhat poem. The first text is *CTA* 19 ii 61-74:

(3) *ydn <dn> il ysb palth*	Daniel approached and toured his dry land;
bṣql yph bpalt	he noticed a shoot in the dry land,
bṣql yp byǵlm	he noticed a shoot on the wasteland.
bṣql yḥbq wynšq	He hugged and kissed the shoot.
aḥl an	Oh if only
bṣql ynp' bpalt	the shoot would sprout in the dry land,
bṣql yp' byǵlm	the shoot would sprout in the wasteland!
	(Refrain:)
ur	Plant!
tispk yd aqht ǵzr	May adult Aqhat's hand gather you,
tštk bqrbm asm	may it place you inside the barn.

107. For 'twirl' (lines 13 and 21), see D. Pardee, 'The New Canaanite Myths and Legends', *BO* 37 (1980), pp. 269-91, 274, especially his comment: 'The option should... certainly be considered that Baal not only held the weapon in his hands but that he struck with the weapon retained in his grasp rather than throwing it'. On the last couplet, see Y. Avishur, 'Expressions of the Type *byn ydym* in the Bible and Semitic languages', *UF* 12 (1980), pp. 125-34.

108. In Ugaritic: *CTA* 16 vi 1-2; in Akkadian, the famous passages in *Atraḫasis* and *Gilgamesh* where the reed-wall and the hut are spoken to directly.

ydnh ysb aklth	He approached and toured his exhausted land;
yph šblt baklt	he noticed an ear of corn in the exhausted land,
šblt yph bḥmdrt	an ear of corn he noticed in the parched land.
šblt yḥbq wynšq	He hugged and kissed the ear of corn.
aḥl an	Oh if only
šblt tpʻ baklt	the ear of corn would sprout in the exhausted land,
šblt tpʻ bḥmdrt	the ear of corn would sprout in the parched land!
	(Refrain:)
ur	Plant!
tispk yd aqht ġzr	May adult Aqhat's hand gather you,
tštk bqrbm asm	may it place you inside the barn![109]

In each half of example (3) there are three actions. First, Dnil sees and greets a shoot just beginning to grow in poor agricultural land; then he expresses a wish, and finally he addresses the plant itself. This action sequence occurs twice. Already, after catching sight of the green sprout (or the ear of corn) Dnil treats it as animate by kissing and even embracing it. This personification sets the scene for the following apostrophe, when Dnil speaks twice to the young growth (employing identical words both times—perhaps a refrain) using the generic term *ur*[110] and expressing the wish that it will become a crop to be harvested by his son. What has now to be examined is the reason for the use of apostrophe here.[111]

At the superficial level apostrophe occurs here as an indicator of

109. In the main this version follows Gibson, *Canaanite Myths*, for differing translations see Caquot, Sznycer and Herdner, *Textes ougaritiques*, I, pp. 446-47, and the comments in Pardee, 'New Canaanite Myths', p. 289, with bibliography. On *šblt*, cf. P. Swiggers, 'The Word *šibbolet* in Jud. XII.6', *JSS* 26 (1981), pp. 205-207; also, D. Marcus, 'Ridiculing the Ephraimites: The Shibboleth Incident (Judg. 12:6)', *Maarav* 8 (1992), pp. 95-105. The quasi-acrostic component of this passage has been commented on elsewhere above, p. 433; here can be noted the long sequence of couplets with identical initial letters broken only by the anacrusis of *aḥl an* (but note the alliteration even here) and of *ur*. Also noteworthy is the word order *bṣql yph bpalt* (line 62) instead of expected **yph bṣql bpalt*, to match the word sequence in the second segment.

110. Compare now Akk. *urû*, *AHw*, p. 1436. But see n. 119, below.

111. Much of what follows, and indeed the impetus for this short note derive from 'Apostrophe', ch. 7 of J. Culler, *The Pursuit of Signs: Semiotics, Literature, Deconstruction* (London: Routledge & Kegan Paul, 1981), pp. 133-54 and nn. 233-34.

deep feeling; Dnil is deeply worried at the blighted crops.[112] There is another level also. Apostrophe acts with indifference to the sequence of time in narrated events[113] a viewpoint evident in example (3). The sprouting grain is addressed as if it were already a full field of standing corn ready for the reaper, whereas at this point in the narrative it only comprises one or two isolated and straggling shoots. As noted by Gibson[114] the irony (the *dramatic* irony, I may add) is precisely Dnil's hope that Aqhat will gather in the ripened corn, a hope he pronounces unaware that all along his son is dead. Once informed of Aqhat's demise he proceeds to hunt for and find his remains, and then bury them. After which he curses the localities he thinks could be responsible, speaking to each of the three directly by name: *Qr-mym*, *Mrrt-tǵll-bnr*[115] and *Qrt-ablm*.[116] This, example (4), is the second instance of apostrophe, namely *CTA* 19 iii 151–iv 169. Here, Dnil, in cursing three localities, is using poetry in the true sense of that term, making events happen on a scale which is timeless (see *'nt…p'lmh*, 'now and for ever').[117]

How far, then, are we dealing with poetry and how much is magic? Are the magic words in verse because they are then considered to be more effective[118] or are we in the realm of poetry, of a narrative poem, where events are created by words? In example (2) the magic maces perform exactly as they are told to, striking Yam-Nahar and felling him. The apostrophe would appear to 'work'. Yet, unlike Dnil (as in examples [3] and [4]) the speaker is a god. Even when Dnil's

112. In poems, apostrophes 'serve as intensifiers, as images of invested passion', Culler, *The Pursuit of Signs*, p. 138.

113. 'A poem may invoke objects, people, a detemporalized space with forms and forces which have pasts and futures but which are addressed as potential presences', Culler, *The Pursuit of Signs*, p. 149.

114. Gibson, *Canaanite Myths*, p. 26.

115. For the meaning of this name cf. Watson, *UF* 8 (1976), p. 374 n. 20.

116. See E.C.B. MacLaurin, 'qrt-'Ablm', *PEQ* 110 (1978), pp. 113-14.

117. See Culler, *The Pursuit of Signs*, pp. 142-43 and 150.

118. See the following lines in a prose ritual, written on the left hip of a figurine (text: W.G. Lambert, 'An Address of Marduk to the Demons', *AfO* 19 [1959–60], pp. 114-19, 119, lines 27 and 33): *ṣī lumun šunāti lemnūti / erba dumuq ekalli* and *ṣī lumun ekalli / erba ḫiṣib šadî u mātāti*, 'Go out, Evil of bad dreams! Come in palace God!'; 'Go out, palace Evil! Come in, rich yield of mountain and plain!' Also the address to goat's milk in W. Farber, *Beschwörungsrituale an Ištar und Dumuzi* (Wiesbaden: Steiner, 1977), p. 68 lines 55-56.

words do prove efficacious (notably in the passage where he invokes Baal to break and mend the wings of birds) the effect is attributable to a deity. I would argue, instead, that magic and poetry are inextricably interconnected. For the audience of ancient times magic was often poetry; for us today poetry can be magic. Apostrophe highlights the poet's skill with words and is a measure of his audience's sophistication.[119]

7. *Allusion, Irony and Wordplay in Micah 1.7*[120]

In the second part of an oracle against Samaria, which may or may not be authentic,[121] comes the following two-strophe stanza:

wkl-pslyh yktw	All her statues shall be shattered;
wkl-'tnnyh yśrpw b'š	all her [?] shall be burnt by fire;
wkl-'ṣbyh 'śym šmmh	all her idols shall I reduce to ruin.
ky m'tnn zwnh qbṣh	For, from a whore's hire did she gather(?),
w'd-'tnn zwnh yšwbw	and back to a whore's hire will they go.

In the first three-line strophe the only problem is presented by the word *'tnnyh* since the ostensible meaning 'her (whore's) hire' does not fit the pattern of each line.[122] The pattern is the nominal phrase 'all her *idols*' followed by a verbal clause denoting *destruction*. Accordingly, the whole of the second line is usually omitted as a later gloss by translators because it lacks any reference to idols.[123] If this

119. For other studies of Ugaritic poetic technique, see my 'An Example of Multiple Wordplay in Ugaritic', *UF* 12 (1980), pp. 443-44; Chapter 10 §1; Chapter 4 §1; Chapter 6 §1 and elsewhere. G. del Olmo Lete's scholarly and comprehensive work *Mitos y leyendas* reached me once this note was complete. His rendition of my example (3), pp. 390-91, differs in two respects. After *aḥl an* ('¡Ojalá!') in lines 15 and 22 he interprets *bṣql* (and *šblt*) as apostrophe: '¡oh tallo...!' (and '¡oh espiga...!'). The word *ur*, instead, he connects with *byǵlm* (and *bḥmdrt*) as 'ardiente' (see, too, his glossary, p. 525), though this would go against the word-pairs *palt // yǵlm* and *aklt // ḥmdrt*. Whoever is correct, there is no denying the presence of apostrophe here. On magic expressed by words, cf. D.R. Hillers, 'The Effective Simile in Biblical Literature', *JAOS* 103 (1983), pp. 181-85. On apostrophe, see J. Wansbrough, 'Hebrew Verse: Apostrophe and Epanalepsis', *BSOAS* 45 (1982), pp. 425-33.

120. First published in *Bib* 65 (1984), pp. 103-105.

121. See the commentaries; the same sentiments recur in Mic. 5.12-13.

122. Although AV, RV, JB and TEV all translate 'earnings' or the like.

123. For example, W. Rudolph, *Micha—Nahum—Habakuk—Zephanja* (KAT,

line is not to be deleted then the noun *'tnn* (here plural) must refer to an object of (pagan) worship condemned by the prophet-poet. To determine what it might be we have to turn to the literary texts from Ugarit.

In the Ugaritic Serpent Incantation[124] which has spawned quite a number of philological studies, most of which I have tried to consult,[125] the following passage occurs (lines 73-76).

tn km <mhry> }{ yḥr	'Give as my bride-price, O Serpent, (or: O Horon),
tn km mhry <nḥšm>	give as my bride-price snakes,
wbn bṯn 'itnny	(give) serpent-sons (as) my payment'.[126]
ytt nḥšm mhrk	'I herewith give snakes as your bride-price,
bn bṯn 'itnnk	serpent-sons as your payment'.[127]

Pardee comments that *mhr* means 'bride-price' in Hebrew, Ugaritic, Arabic and Aramaic, and adds,

> Considering the established usage for *mhr*, it must be assumed that *'itnn* is a generic word for gift (cf. Hebrew *mtn*), a more specific word for gift given by a man to a woman, or more specifically yet, a gift given by the groom to the bride at marriage.[128]

13/3; Gütersloh: Mohr, 1975), p. 33; R. Vuilleumier, in R. Vuilleumier and C.-A. Keller, *Michée, Nahoum, Habacuc, Sophonie* (CAT, 11b: Neuchâtel: Delachaux et Niestlé, 1971), p. 18 n. 2.

124. Nougayrol *et al.*, *Ugaritica V*, text 7, pp. 564-74 = *KTU* 1.100 = *UT* 607.

125. See D. Pardee, 'A Philological and Prosodic Analysis of the Ugaritic Serpent Incantation *UT* 607', *JANESCU* 10 (1978), pp. 73-108, with bibliography. Also C.H. Bowman and R.B. Coote, 'A Narrative Incantation for Snake Bite', *UF* 12 (1980), pp. 135-40; M. Dietrich and O. Loretz, 'Die Bannung von Schlangengift (KTU 1.100 and KTU 1.107:7b-13a. 19b-20)', *UF* 12 (1980), pp. 171-82.

126. This is my own reconstruction of the text as 'staircase parallelism' based on suggestions by Y. Avishur, 'Addenda to the Expanded Colon in Ugaritic and Biblical Verse', *UF* 4 (1972), p. 4, and Pardee, 'Analysis', pp. 99-100, and n. 99. The text on the tablet runs: *tn. km. nḥšm. yḥr. tn. km / mhry. wbn. bṯn. 'itnny / ytt. nḥšm. mhrk. bn bṯn / 'itnnk /* (with / marking line-end). The copyist omitted the first occurrence of *mhry* transposing in its place *nḥšm* from the second line of the tricolon. He had previously left out *nḥš* from line 6, several letters here and there and possibly a complete stanza after line 34 (on which see Pardee, 'Analysis', p. 87).

127. The use in both Mic. 1.7 and the Ugaritic text of a stanza comprising a three-line and a two-line strophe is one of many pointers to a common poetic tradition, no more.

128. Pardee, 'Analysis', p. 101. On Ug. *itnn*, see W. von Soden, 'Hurritisch *uatnannu* > Mittelassyrisch *utnannu* und > ugaritisch *itnn* > hebräisch *'ätnan* "Ein Geschenk, Dirnenlohn"', *UF* 20 (1988), pp. 309-11.

The corresponding term in Hebrew is obviously much narrower referring as it does to a commercial transaction at a much lower level.[129] Various explanations have been put forward for this Ugaritic text as a whole, but however it is interpreted in the lines quoted above snakes are equated with payment made for a wife, a key factor in the argument presented here.

The Hebrew word *'tnn* occurs three times in our Micah passage. In the final couplet it undeniably means '(prostitute's) price' as elsewhere in Hebrew. In the preceding tricolon, however, as already noted, it cannot possibly have the same meaning, parallel, as it is, to the two words *psl* and *'ṣb*. Instead, I suggest it to be a variant of the noun *tannîn*, 'sea-serpent, dragon' (Ug. *tnn*) here spelt with prosthetic *aleph*.[130] It is noteworthy that the plural of *'tnn* is found only here. Whether the reference is to an actual reptile as an object of worship or whether *'tnn*, 'serpent', is used only for the sake of parallelism[131] is not clear.

The significance of the last couplet is obscure: why should idols and so forth have been 'gathered' from a prostitute's fee and how could they subsequently return to this payment? It is possible that *qbṣh* is not a verb (whether 'she gathered', or with emendation, 'were gathered')[132] but a suffixed noun. The meaning of Hebrew *qbṣ* (perhaps as *qibbûṣ*) would then match Ugaritic *qbṣ* as in *pḫr qbṣ dtn*, 'the gathering of the Ditan clan'[133] in the extended meaning of 'pantheon'.[134] I would accordingly translate:

> For from a hussy's hire is her pantheon,
> and back to a hussy's hire will they go.

129. See Deut. 23.19; Isa. 23.17-18; Ezek. 16.31, 34, 41 and Hos. 9.1.

130. Consult GKC, §19m and P. Joüon and T. Muraoka, *A Grammar of Biblical Hebrew. Part One: Orthography and Phonetics* (Rome: Editrice Pontifico Istituto Biblico, 1993), §§17a and 88 L a. Examples are *tmwl* and *'tmwl*, 'yesterday' (with prosthetic *aleph* followed by *t*) and *zrw'* or *'zrw'*, 'arm'.

131. Comparable is the triple set *psl // 'lylym // kl-'lhym* in Ps. 97.7. For the (inverted) pair *'ṣb // psl* (+ *nsk*) see Isa. 48.5.

132. See apparatus in *BHK*.

133. *CTA* 14 iii 4 and 15. On Ug. *qbṣ*, 'clan', see J. Macdonald, 'An Assembly at Ugarit?', *UF* 11 (1979), p. 523.

134. This meaning has already been proposed by M.J. Dahood, 'Hebrew-Ugaritic Lexicography IX', *Bib* 52 (1971), pp. 343-45 for Isa. 57.12-13a.

Without pressing the logical argument too closely,[135] I understand this to mean that Samaria used her ill-gotten gains to provide statues of gods for worship (including, perhaps, images of snakes) much as in Judg. 17.1-5, and that once shattered, burnt and melted down these same idols will once again become mere money. The *'tnn zwnh*, converted into a *qbṣ* of *psl*, *'tnn* and *'ṣb*, will be turned back into *'tnn zwnh*.[136]

The text linking 'serpent(-idols)' in Mic. 1.7b with '(prostitute's) fee' used twice in 1.7a is the Ugaritic passage already quoted. Without this 'intertext'[137] the two strophes in Micah would be unintelligible. The poet is alluding to the tradition recorded in the Ugaritic 'Snake' tablet and at the same time playing on twin meanings of *'tnn*. It is a measure of his skill that he could provide an alternative pronunciation of *tannîn* to achieve the desired effect which, with its obligatory element of irony, belongs fully to a long tradition of idol-polemic.[138]

135. A similar solution, along different lines, is set out by Smith in the ICC commentary, J.M.P. Smith, W.H. Ward and J.A. Brewer, *A Critical and Exegetical Commentary on Micah, Zephaniah, Nahum, Habakkuk, Obadiah and Joel* (Edinburgh: T. & T. Clark, 1912), p. 40 based on the hypothetical root *tnn*, 'to resemble, be equal'.

136. Note, incidentally, that the parallelism of *qbṣ* with *šwb* occurs in Jer. 23.3. For the motif of idols consumed by fire, cf. Deut. 7.5, 25. For this practice in Mesopotamia, cf. N. Na'man, 'The Recycling of a Silver Statue', *JNES* 40 (1981), pp. 47-48.

137. A convenient discussion of intertextuality is available in M. Riffaterre, *Semiotics of Poetry* (London: Methuen, 1978). 'A major point on which there would be agreement [in semiotics]...is that literary works are to be considered not as autonomous entities, "organic wholes", but as intertextual constructs: sequences which have meaning in relation to other texts which they take up, cite, parody, refute, or generally transform', J. Culler, *The Pursuit of Signs: Semiotics, Literature, Deconstruction* (London: Routledge & Kegan Paul, 1981), p. 38; see, also pp. 100-18. For the function of allusion, cf. C. Schaar, 'Vertical Context Systems', in H. Ringbom *et al.* (eds.), *Style and Text: Studies Presented to Nils Erik Enkvist* (Stockholm: Sprakforlaget Skriptor, 1975), pp. 146-57.

138. E.g. Isa. 45.20-21; 48.14-20.

8. *Antithesis in Ugaritic Verse*[139]

In a review of Krašovec's book on antithesis[140] I touched on some aspects of theory.[141] Without going into too much detail, I will here provide further comments, supplementing the definitions and discussion already given by Krašovec[142] and also provide illustration, using examples from the Ugaritic texts.

Antithesis has been defined as:

> a stylistic device based on opposition of terms, statements, motifs, or themes.[143]

Another definition:

> Antithesis is a form of expression which consists of opposing two words or groups of words of opposite meaning within the same statement.[144]

Antithesis, therefore, implies the concept of opposition, or more accurately, of antonymy. Antonymy, in turn, is defined as:

> A term used in semantics as part of the study of oppositeness of meaning. 'Antonymy' is one of a set of sense relations recognised in some analyses of meaning, along with synonymy, hyponymy, incompatibility and others. In its most general sense, it refers collectively to all types of semantic oppositeness.[145]

139. First published in *UF* 18 (1986), pp. 413-19.

140. J. Krašovec, *Antithetic Structure in Biblical Hebrew Poetry* (VTSup, 35; Leiden: Brill, 1984).

141. The review appeared in *AuOr* 5 (1987), pp. 171-72.

142. Krašovec, *Antithetic Structure*, pp. 1-7.

143. S. Elkhadem, *The York Dictionary of English—French—German Spanish Literary Terms and their Origin* (Fredericton, N.B.: York Press, 1976), p. 11.

144. J. Dubois *et al.*, *Dictionnaire de linguistique* (Paris: Larousse, 1973), p. 37. Another definition: 'A contrasting of ideas made sharp by the use of words of opposite or conspicuously different meaning in contiguous clauses or phrases', A. Preminger (ed.), *Princeton Encyclopedia of Poetry and Poetics* (London: Macmillan Press, 1975), p. 40. See, further, A. Rodway, 'By Algebra to Augustanism', in R. Fowler (ed.), *Essays on Language and Style* (New York: Humanities Press; London: Routledge & Kegan Paul, 1966), pp. 53-67. He shows that antithesis can be intermeshed with 'linguistic devices of all kinds' (p. 52), sometimes at the expense of 'correct' grammar. See, too, B.H. Smith, *Poetic Closure: A Study of how Poems End* (Chicago: University of Chicago Press, 1968), pp. 168-71.

145. D. Crystal, *A First Dictionary of Linguistics and Phonetics* (London: André

The sub-types of antonymy have been grouped into two different sets of three by some linguists.[146] Lyons proposes (1) *complementary antonyms* (e.g. father–mother), (2) *antonyms proper*, or gradable antonyms (e.g. fast–slow), and (3) *antonyms by converseness* (e.g. give–take). For his part, Katz prefers (1) *contradictories* (e.g. dead–alive) with no intermediate stage, (2) *contraries* (e.g. wet–dry) where intermediate stages (in our example, damp) are possible, and (3) *converse* (e.g. teach–learn) 'which, like the converses of Lyons, imply syntactic transformations and entail an inferential relation of the type "if...then"'.[147] Eco comments, 'Even a superficial glance at some pairs of antonyms reveals that (1) The same term can entertain different relationships provided that it is inserted into different axes' (e.g. *work* is the contrary of *play* but also of *unemployment*—my example). Further, Eco states, 'The same term can entertain a contradictory or converse or contrary antonymous relation depending on the rhetorical...way in which these relations are viewed'.[148] Eco explains this lack of precision by invoking Lakoff's 'fuzzy concepts'.[149] Our labelling, therefore, depends on our point of view in a particular case; once the terms of reference are provided, ambiguity will be reduced.[150]

Antonymy has been examined most recently by Warczyk[151] who distinguishes five types of semantic antonymy. They are as follows. (I use his terminology, in translation, and his examples.) (1) *begin–end* (e.g. inflate–deflate), (2) *an act and its eliminant* (e.g. attach–detach), (3) *P–non-P* (e.g. present–absent), (4) *more–less*, involving adjectives of degree (e.g. big–little), and (5) *terms for spatial orientation* (e.g.

Deutsch, 1980), p. 27. For the terms 'synonymy', 'hyponymy' and 'incompatibility', see pp. 344-45, 176-77 and 182 respectively.

146. J. Lyons, *Introduction to Theoretical Linguistics* (Cambridge: Cambridge University Press, 1971), pp. 460-70, esp. 463-64; J.J. Katz, *Semantic Theory* (New York: Harper & Row, 1972), p. 159. Cf. U. Eco, *A Theory of Semiotics* (London: Macmillan Press, 1971), p. 81 for a succinct description.

147. Eco, *Theory*, p. 81.

148. Eco, *Theory*, p. 81.

149. Eco, *Theory*, p. 82. Lyons, *Introduction*, p. 469, also points out that the difference between antonyms and complementaries 'is not always clear-cut in the "logic" of everyday discourse'.

150. See, further, Eco, *Theory*, pp. 125-29, no. 2.13.

151. R. Warczyk, 'Antonymie, négation ou opposition?', *Orbis* 31 (1982 [1985]), pp. 30-58.

East–West), *colour*, *sensations of taste*, *kinship* and *emotions* or intellectual qualities. He concludes,

> the unvarying element of antonymic relations, the 'antonymic operator', is the difference between the expressions which is reduced to *negation* for types 1, 2 and 3 or to *inversion* larger–smaller, more–less for type 4.[152]

Whichever sub-system of antonymy is adopted (and it is evident that the different classifications overlap), Warczyk touches on the heart of the matter when he writes,

> Antonymy is a general term which denotes the phenomenon of opposition in meaning based on negation or inversion. Opposition in meaning presupposes not only details by which the terms of the opposition are distinguished from each other but also the *details which are common* to the two terms of the opposition. These details comprise the basis for the opposition in question.[153]

In other words, the antonymy of two terms is based on a common element which they share.

These theoretical considerations can now be tested against the results of a field study conducted a few years ago in Australia among the Walbiri.[154] Hale, who carried out the survey, describes *tjiliwiri*, a way of speaking used by initiated Walbiri men in association with their rituals. 'In very general terms, the rule for speaking tjiliwiri is as follows: replace each noun, verb and pronoun of ordinary Walbiri by an "antonym"'.[155] For example, *njuntu A-npa kiriḍi* (you stative—you tall) in ordinary Walbiri becomes *n̯atju A-ṇa ḍan̯kaḷpa* (I stative—I short) in *tjiliwiri*, both meaning 'You are tall'.[156] The basic principle followed is that of minimal opposition involving polarity (good–bad) and taxonomy (kite–grey falcon) and reflecting both polysemy and synonymy. Some antonyms are determined by Walbiri culture, which includes an element of taboo. Of significance is the author's conclusion that the principle of antonymy applied in speaking *tjiliwiri* is semantically based, in other words

152. Warczyk, 'Antonymie', p. 43.
153. Warczyk, 'Antonymie', p. 57 (emphasis mine).
154. K. Hale, 'A Note on a Walbiri Tradition of Antonymy', in D.D. Steinberg and L.A. Jakobovits, *Semantics: An Interdisciplinary Reader in Philosophy, Linguistics and Psychology* (Cambridge: Cambridge University Press, 1971), pp. 472-82.
155. Hale, 'A Note', p. 473.
156. Hale, 'A Note', p. 473, with further examples.

> the process of turning Walbiri 'up-side-down' [as the speakers themselves describe it] is fundamentally a process of opposing abstract semantic objects rather than a process of opposing lexical items in the grossest and most superficial sense.[157]

This is confirmed by the rapid learning process (two to four weeks). Non-speakers listen to dialogues between guardians, where one speaks *tjiliwiri* and the other 'translates' into Walbiri, and in this way determine the principle involved by intuition. In addition it can be noted that antonyms cannot be formed by using the negative; if necessary, a suitable word has to be coined.[158]

We can turn now to passages in Ugaritic where antithesis is used. The first text where antithesis is found is

(1) *KTU* 1.16 vi 1-2[159]

[m]t. dm. ḫt	May Motu surely be shattered!
š'tqt dm(!) li.	May Š. surely overcome!

This is echoed in the near-repetition of the couplet (as envelope figure) at the end of 'Kirta's Cure':

(2) *KTU* 1.16 vi 13-14.[160]

mt. dm. ḫt.	Motu surely was shattered.
š'tqt dm. lan	Š. surely overcame.

In each case, the second line appears to be a classic 'tjiliwiri' version of a 'Walbiri' original (or vice versa, of course), with *Š'tqt* as a culturally determined antonym to *Mt* ('She who expels'–'Death') reinforced by female–male polarity—and *l'y* the converse of *ḫtt*.

Another example of antithesis, where the man–woman contrast is even stronger, is

(3) *KTU* 1.17 vi 39-40.[161]

qštm [nṯq.(?)] mhrm	The Bow is a warriors' [weapon],
ht. tṣdn. tinṯt	Does womankind go hunting now?

157. Hale, 'A Note', p. 477.

158. Hale, 'A Note', pp. 478-79 ('the negative may not be used to create *tjiliwiri* opposites', by general convention).

159. For textual problems see, conveniently, del Olmo Lete, *Mitos y leyendas*, p. 319.

160. For the text, again see *Mitos y leyendas*, p. 320. Note that S. Gevirtz ('Formative ע in Biblical Hebrew', *EI* 16 [1982], pp. 57-66, 63) translates *š'tqt* 'the surpassing one' (*š* elative).

161. The restorations are largely guesswork and would need to be corroborated by

For discussion, see below.

Again, the male–female opposition—with stronger elements of taboo than in (3)—is used antithetically:

(4) *KTU* 1.3 i 12-15

bk rb. 'ẓm.	A huge beaker, enormous,
ridn. mt. šmm	a vat for giants (lit. men of the sky);
ks. qdš ltphnh aṯt	a holy cup no woman should see,
krpn lt'. aṯrt	a goblet no goddess (even) should eye.

Although negatives are involved, the overall antithesis with its taboo component, combined with the oppositions *huge vessel–small vessel* and *man–woman* indicate that these lines should not be relegated to positive–negative parallelism (on which see below).

The next example is textually uncertain[162] but its tenor argues for inclusion here:

(5) *KTU* 1.17 vi 41-42

[g]m. tṣḥq. 'nt.	Anath laughed [al]oud,
wblb. tqny [—?]	but in her mind she hatched [a plot(?)]

Whichever restorations are adopted, the contrast between Anath's public demeanour (outward laughter) and her private thoughts (inwardly plotting) emerges as a clear case of antithesis.[163] Before examining antithesis on a scale beyond the strophe and stanza (i.e. antithesis proper not just antithetic parallelism) examples of antithetic parallelism within a line will be listed. They include:

(6) *KTU* 1.3 iv 33[164]

atm. bštm. wan. šnt	You (plur.)... but ... I

collation. Meanwhile, B. Margalit, 'Restorations and Reconstructions in the Epic of Aqhat', *JNSL* 9 (1981), pp. 92-94 merits attention. This example of antithetic parallelism was cited by S. Segert, 'Parallelism in Ugaritic Poetry', *JAOS* 103 (1983), p. 300. He comments, 'The semantic contrast between strong men and weak women is expressed within a relaxed parallelism; a negative answer is expected for the rhetorical question in the second colon'.

162. The restorations are uncertain and collation is required. Margalit ('Restorations and Reconstructions', pp. 92-95) prefers to restore [*bpn*]*m* at the beginning of the couplet, on alliterative grounds. He also judges the couplet to end with *tqny*, arguing, too that the following strophe begins with a particle such as *wn*. However, can *qny* used absolutely mean 'to forge a plot'? For the verb *qny*, 'to acquire, etc.' or 'to make', cf. del Olmo Lete, *Mitos y leyendas*, glossary, p. 619.

163. Cf. Ps. 55.20.

164. For a possible translation see above, p. 70. Segert ('Parallelism in Ugaritic

(7) *KTU* 1.23:32[165]

hlh. tšpl. hlh. trm.	See her, she goes down; see her, she goes up

At the macrostructural level, antithesis is evidently fundamental to the *Kirta Tale*. Childless Kirta gains children (not wives) as Tsumura has shown;[166] a similar loss and gain motif, again of children, recurs in *KTU* 1.23, while in *Aqḥat* the sequence would appear to be loss (strictly speaking, no children), gain and finally loss.[167]

In *KTU* 1.23 there is antithesis, too, between *Mt.wŠr* who sits enthroned

bdh. ḫṭ. ṯkl	in his hand the staff of sterility,
bdh ḫṭ. ulmn.	in his hand the staff of widowhood

(lines 8-9) and *Il* who also has *mṭ. ydh*, but uses it in a scene of sexual potency (lines 37-44).[168]

Another scene exhibiting antithesis, this time of a complex order, is

Poetry', p. 300) also mentions this as 'a probable antithetic parallelism... perhaps within one colon' (under 4.1.4).

165. Unless this is simply contrastive parallelism; so Segert, 'Parallelism in Ugaritic Poetry', p. 299; he also cites lines 61-62 of the same text and *KTU* 1.12:58-61 as contrastive.

166. D.T. Tsumura, 'The Problem of Childlessness in the Royal Epic of Ugarit. An Analysis of KRT [*KTU* 1.14:1]:1-25', in T. Mikasa (ed.), *Monarchies and Socio-Religious Traditions in the Ancient Near East*: *Papers read at the 31st International Congress of Human Sciences in Asia and North Africa* (Bulletin of the Middle Eastern Culture Center in Japan, 1; Wiesbaden: Otto Harrassowitz, 1984), pp. 11-20. The author kindly sent me an offprint. To his examples, p. 11 n. 2, should be added the Story of Ahiqar.

167. For an example of the move from 'lack' to 'lack supplied' in Hebrew narrative cf. above, section 3.

168. For the contrast between our 'Western' view of fertility and the corresponding concept in the ancient Near East, cf. W.G. Lambert, 'Trees, Snakes and Gods in Ancient Syria and Anatolia', *BSO(A)S* 48 (1985), p. 436 and n. 8. The wordplay between *ḫṭ*, 'staff' and *mṭ* (*ydh*), 'staff (in his hand)' is quite complex in view of the equivalent *šbṭ. zy. nrgl*, 'the plague of Nerigal' for *šibṭu*, 'plague' in line 38 of the Assyro-Aramaic bilingual from Tel Fekherye. In 'Notes on the Akkadian-Aramaic Bilingual Statue from Tel Fekherye', *Iraq* 45 (1983), pp. 109-14, 116, J.C. Greenfield and A. Shaffer comment, 'The gloss *šbt zy nrgl* seems to be a word play on *šbṭ*, "plague, disease", Akkadian *šibṭu*, and *šbṭ*, "staff", alluding to the lion-headed staff, the symbol of Nergal, cf. *RIA* II, 488b. Akkadian *ḫaṭṭu* has a similar semantic range, from "staff" to "illness", cf. *CAD* Ḫ, 155a.' Is it possible that similar wordplay lies behind difficult *'db uḫry mṭ ydh* (*KTU* 1.19 iii 56 etc.)?

KTU 1.17 vi 16-45, parts of which have been discussed briefly (examples [3] and [5], above). With speech introductions[169] omitted and some condensation, the passage can be set out as follows:

PROMISE (1)	*'nt*	*irš ksp watnk*
		ḫrṣ wašlḥk
		wtn qštk 'm btlt 'nt
		qṣ'tk ybmt limm
REJECTION (1)	*aqht*	*adr ṯqbm blbnn*
		...
		tn lkṯr wḫss
		yb'l qšt l'nt
		qṣ't lybmt limm
PROMISE (2)	*'nt*	*irš ḥym watnk*
		blmt wašlḥk
		...
		ap ank aḥwy aqht ġzr
TRANSITION	*aqht*	*al tšrgn ybtltm*
		...
REJECTION (2)		*wan mtm amt*
REJECTION (3)		*qštm... mhrm*
		ht tṣdn tintṯ
TRANSITION		*gm tṣḥq 'nt*
		wblb tqny
THREAT	*'nt*	...
		ašqlk tḥt p'ny
		...

Here there is a series of interwoven antitheses. Overall, the opposition is between promise (twofold) and threat—both on the lips of Anath. Within this frame comes the antithesis between Anath's promise and Aqhat's rejection (threefold).[170] Subordinate again are the following sets:

(a)	price for bow (silver, gold)	bow priceless
(b)	bow for women	bow for men
(c)	immortality	mortality.

169. See Chapter 9, 'Introductions to Discourse in Ugaritic Narrative Verse'.

170. Del Olmo Lete (*Mitos y leyendas*, p. 340) considers the dialogue here to be based on a pattern of offer-refusal, but the polarities are rather more interwoven.

In (a) the antithesis emphasizes that skill and natural materials cannot be bought, in (b) that cultural taboo cannot be broken, in (c) that man is mortal. In addition, the transition from promise to threat is marked by the speech-introductory antithesis 'Aloud(?) laughed Anat etc.'

Since antithesis is relatively rare (as, too, is antithetic parallelism) in Ugaritic verse, when it does occur it is obviously of significance. As has been said, antithesis can characterize whole narratives or parts of narrative. At the microstructural level it can be rhetorically important as well. In the example just given (from *Aqhat* the second traditional passage (also example [5]) marks off threat from promise.

It would seem, too, that antithesis heightens, or rather exaggerates, the contrast between two terms, emphasizing their difference and so belongs, in effect to hyperbole.[171] This is apparent in examples (1), (2), (5), (6) and elsewhere. In (3) there is also an element of underlying irony. In (7), however, the antithesis is weak and simply helps describe the presence of two women in the scene. For this confirmation comes from the immediately following couplet in which one woman is said to cry *ad ad*, 'Father, father', and the other, *um um*, 'Mother, mother', although both are addressing El. The sequence *um um* is therefore semantically zero and appears simply to create a parallel for *ad ad*.

Antithesis is distinct from positive–negative parallelism. We have already seen this to be true of the antonymic *tjilibri* 'dialect' of Walbiri (see above), where simply negating a noun, verb or pronoun to form its antonym is disallowed, by convention. Berlin, too, describing the positive–negative form of syntactic parallelism ('In this type of parallelism a statement phrased in the positive is paired with one phrased in the negative') remarks, 'This is not to be confused with Lowth's "antithetic parallelism", which need not involve a negative transformation'.[172] Positive–negative parallelism occurs in Ugaritic as

171. 'Das einfache Nebeneinander hat die Wirkung, die beiden in Opposition stehenden Terme gleichzeitig zu verstärken. Man sieht daraus, daß die Antithese, wenn sie auch nicht notwendigerweise auf die Kombination von zwei Hyperbeln gründet, trotzdem von sich aus hyperbolischen Charakter hat', J. Dubois *et al.*, *Allgemeine Rhetorik* (Munich: W. Fink, 1974), p. 226; cf. pp. 224-25.

172. A. Berlin, *The Dynamics of Biblical Parallelism* (Bloomington: Indiana University Press, 1985), p. 56. To supplement her comments (pp. 56-57) I would add the following. Whereas positive-negative parallelism is, in essence, synonymous—for example, 'Swim, do not sink!' can be analysed as [+ SWIM] // neg

well as in Hebrew, of course, and some examples will show how this kind of parallelism differs from antithesis and antithetic parallelism. It is really a form of synonymous parallelism.

(8) *KTU* 1.2 i 19
tb‘. ǵlmm. lyṯb Depart did the lads; they did not stay.

With parallels in *KTU* 1.2 i 13 and 1.5 i 9 = ii 13.

(9) *KTU* 1.2 iv 17.[173]
‘z. ym. lymk. Strong was Yammu; he did not collapse.

(10) *KTU* 1.18 iv 12-13 (// 40-41).[174]
at. ‘[l. qšth] tmḫṣh. Are you really going to hit him for his bow?
qṣ‘th. hwt. lt[ḥwy] Are you really not allowing him to live (just) for his arrows?

Another example is *KTU* 6:30, in broken context.[175] More intriguing is the combination of positive–negative parallelism (*il. dyd‘nn // wdlyd‘nn*) and antithetic parallelism (*y‘db. lḥm. dmṣd. lh // ylmn. ḫṭm. tḥt. ṯlḥn*) in *KTU* 1.114:7-8.[176]

I will close by commenting briefly on two ‘devices’ which are related to antithesis, namely, euphemism and oxymoron. Euphemism is ‘the substitution of an agreeable or inoffensive word or term for one that is indelicate, blasphemous or taboo’.[177] Examples in Ugaritic

[– SWIM]—antithetic parallelism is antonymic and usually contrasts two sets. For example, ‘Grow vegetables, eradicate weeds’ may be set out as [+ PLANT (verb)] [+ FOOD] // [– PLANT (verb)] [– FOOD]. Note that Warczyk (see above) considers antonymy by negation as entirely possible.

173. See my comments above, p. 114. G. del Olmo Lete, ‘Notas de semántica ugarítica II’, *AF* 2 (1976), pp. 227-51, 233-36.

174. Also, *KTU* 1.19 i 14-16.

175. It runs *yḥ. wlymt* (cited by P. Xella, *I Testi rituali di Ugarit*. I. *Testi* [Pubblicazioni del Centro di Studio per la civiltà fenicia e punica, 21; Studi Semitici, 54; Rome: Consiglio Nazionale delle Ricerche, 1981], p. 6).

176. Contrast Segert, ‘Parallelism in Ugaritic Poetry’, p. 300. For a translation of these lines, cf. K.J. Cathcart and W.G.E. Watson, ‘Weathering a Wake a Cure for a Carousal’, *PIBA* (1980), pp. 35-58.

177. S.M. Paul, ‘Euphemism and Dysphemism’, *EncJud*, pp. 959-62, on p. 959. See, in addition, D. Marcus, ‘Some Antiphrastic Euphemisms for a Blind Person in Akkadian and Other Semitic Languages’, *JAOS* 100 (1980), pp. 307-10. Also D. Marcus, ‘The Barren Woman of Psalms 113:9 and the Housewife: An Antiphrastic Dysphemism’, *JANESCU* 11 (1979), pp. 81-84. A new example may be Isa. 33.15 (cf. Deut. 32.11).

are the term *bt ḫpṯt*, 'House of Freedom' to designate the underworld (in *KTU* 1.4 viii 8 and 1.5 v 15)[178] and the terms *n'my* // *ysmt*, 'Pleasure' // 'Paradise' (*KTU* 1.5 v 28-30) which also denote the realm of the dead.[179] Oxymoron, which also involves antonymous relationships, has yet to be identified in Ugaritic but does occur in other ancient Semitic languages.[180]

178. Del Olmo Lete, *Mitos y leyendas*, p. 553, comments, 'por antítesis, "casa de (la pérdida de) libertad" '—but the words in brackets are unnecessary. On *bt ḫpṯt*, cf. O. Loretz, *Ḫabiru-Hebräer: Eine sozio-linguistische Studie über die Herkunft des Gentiliziums* 'ibri' *vom Appellativum* ḫabiru (BZAW, 160; Berlin: de Gruyter, 1984), pp. 252-63, esp. 262 and n. 60.

179. Cited in *Classical Hebrew Poetry*, p. 309, under 'irony'.

180. To the bibliography and discussion in *Classical Hebrew Poetry*, pp. 312-13 add. M.K.L. Ching, 'A Literary and Linguistic Analysis of Compact Verbal Paradox', in M.K.L. Ching, M.C. Haley and R.F. Lunsford (eds.), *Linguistic Perspectives on Literature* (London: Routledge & Kegan Paul, 1980), pp. 175-81 (first published in *College Compositions and Communications* 26 [1975], pp. 384-88). A new example of oxymoron in Hebrew is Ps. 38.12.

I will add here examples of antithesis not discussed by Krašovec, who also failed to mention J.A. Loader, *Polar Structures in the Book of Qohelet* (BZAW, 152; Berlin: de Gruyter, 1979). They are 1 Sam. 2.1-10 (cf. T.J. Lewis, 'The Songs of Hannah and Deborah: *ḥdl*-II ["growing plump"]', *JBL* 104 [1985], pp. 105-14), Isa. 52.1-2 (cf. 51.17-23); Prov. 12.28 (cf. E. Puech, *RB* 92 [1985], pp. 435-36; Sir. 1.25; 3.9; 4.29-31; 5.11-12; 6.8-12, 24-31; 10.3, 14-15, 19, 31; 11.5-6, 10-13, 14, 25; 12.8, 9, 16-17; 13.9-11, 17-20, 21-23; 16.3b-4, 12a; 17.28, 31; 18.1-14, 17a; 19.24; 20.1-8; 30.14, 17; 31.1-4, 20; 32.15, 18; 33.2, 7-15 (on antithesis itself!); 34.4; 37.4, 18, 19, 25; 39, 11, 24, 25-27; 40.12; 41.1-2, 15, 16, 24; 42.1-8, 14a. P. van der Lugt, *Strofische structuren in de bijbels-hebreeuwse poezie* (Dissertationes Neerlandicae Series Theologica; Kampen: Kok, 1980), p. 188, briefly discusses 'Antithetisch parallellisme in distichische versregels', with examples. See, too, R. Gordis, *Poets, Prophets, and Sages: Essays in Biblical Interpretation* (Bloomington: Indiana University Press, 1971), pp. 72-74 on Ps. 20.6, Prov. 10.7 and Qoh. 10.6. J.P. Boons, 'Synonymie, antonymie et facteurs stylistiques', *Communications* 10 (1967), pp. 167-88 is unavailable to me.

Indexes

Index of Old Testament Texts

Index of Ancient Texts

Ugaritic

ARAMAIC

AKKADIAN

INDEX OF SUBJECTS

INDEX OF AUTHORS

ADDITIONS AND CORRECTIONS TO *CLASSICAL HEBREW POETRY* (SECOND EDITION)

Bibliographical Details Missing from pp. xvii-xviii

Alonso Schökel, L., *Estudios de poética hebrea* (Barcelona: Juan Flors, 1963).

Andersen, F.I., and D.N. Freedman, *Hosea* (AB, 24; Garden City, NY: Doubleday, 1980).

Bühlmann, W., and K. Scherer, *Stilfiguren der Bibel: Ein kleines Nachschlagewerk* (Biblische Beiträge, 10; Fribourg: Schweizerishes Katholisches Bibelwerk, 1973).

Cassuto, U., *The Goddess Anath: Canaanite Epics of the Patriarchal Age. Texts, Hebrew Translation, Commentary and Introduction* (ET; Jerusalem: Magnes, 1971 [1951]).

Collins, T., *Line-Forms in Hebrew Poetry: A Grammatical Approach to the Stylistic Study of the Hebrew Prophets* (Studia Pohl, Series Major, 7; Rome: Pontifical Biblical Institute, 1978).

Culler, J., *Structuralist Poetics: Structuralism, Linguistics and the Study of Literature* (London: Routledge & Kegan Paul, 1975).

Culley, R.G., *Oral Formulaic Language in the Biblical Psalms* (Near and Middle East Series, 4; Toronto: University of Toronto Press, 1967).

Dahood, M.J., *Psalms*. I. *1–50* (AB, 16; Garden City, NY: Doubleday, 1965).

—*Psalms*. II. *51–100* (AB, 17A; Garden City, NY: Doubleday, 1968).

—*Psalms*. III. *101–150* (AB, 17B; Garden City, NY: Doubleday, 1970).

Driver, G.R., *Semitic Writing from Pictograph to Alphabet* (Schweich Lectures 1944; ed. S.A. Hopkins; London: Oxford University Press, rev. edn, 1976).

Dubois, J., *et al.*, *Dictionnaire de linguistique* (Paris: Larousse, 1973).

Elkhadem, S., *The York Dictionary of English–French–German–Spanish Literary Terms and their Origin* (Fredericton: York Press, 1976).

Fowler, R. (ed.), *Essays on Language and Style* (New York: Humanities Press; London: Routledge & Kegan Paul, 1966).

Geller, S.A., *Parallelism in Early Hebrew Poetry* (HSM, 20; Missoula, MT: Scholars Press, 1979).

Gevirtz, S., *Patterns in the Early Poetry of Israel* (Chicago: Oriental Institute, 1963).

Gray, G.B., *The Forms of Hebrew Poetry* (New York: Ktav, 1972 [1915]).

Gray, J., *The Legacy of Canaan: The Ras Shamra Texts and their Relevance to the Old Testament* (VTSup, 9; Leiden: Brill, 1965).

Häublein, E., *The Stanza* (London: Methuen, 1978).
Hecker, K., *Untersuchungen zur akkadischen Epik* (AOATS, 8; Kevelaer: Butzon & Bercker; Neukirchen–Vluyn: Neukirchener Verlag, 1974).
Irwin, W., *Isaiah 8–33: Translated with Philological Notes* (BibOr, 30; Rome: Biblical Institute Press, 1977).
Kugel, J., *The Idea of Biblical Poetry: Parallelism and its History* (New Haven: Yale University Press, 1981).
Leech, G.N., *A Linguistic Guide to English Poetry* (London: Longmans, 1969).
Loretz, O., *Die Psalmen. Teil II. Beitrag der Ugarit-Texte zum Verständnis von Kolometrie und Textologie der Psalmen. Psalm 90–150* (AOAT, 207/2; Kevelaer: Butzon & Bercker; Neukirchen–Vluyn: Neukirchener Verlag, 1979).
Lugt, P. van der, *Strofische structuren in de bijbels-hebreeuwse poëzie* (Dissertationes Neerlandicae, Series Theologica; Kampen: Kok, 1980).
Nowottny, W., *The Language Poets Use* (London: Athlone Press 1962).
Pope, M.H., *Job* (AB, 15; Garden City, NY: Doubleday, 1965).
—*Song* (AB, 7C; Garden City, NY: Doubleday, 1977).
Riffaterre, M., *Semiotics of Poetry* (London: Methuen, 1978).
Sebeok, T.A. (ed.), *Style in Language* (Cambridge, MA: MIT Press, 1960).
Seux, M.-J., *Hymnes et prières aux dieux de Babylonie et d'Assyrie* (Paris: Cerf, 1976).
Smith, B.H., *Poetic Closure: A Study of how Poems End* (Chicago: University of Chicago Press, 1968).
Speiser, E.A., *Genesis* (AB, 1; Garden City, NY: Doubleday, 1964).
Ullmann, S., *Principles of Semantics* (repr.; Oxford: Basil Blackwell, 2nd edn, 1959).
—*Language and Style: Collected Papers* (Oxford: Basil Blackwell, 1966).
Watters, W.R., *Formula Criticism and the Poetry of the Old Testament* (BZAW, 138; Berlin: de Gruyter, 1976).
Welch, J.W. (ed.), *Chiasmus in Antiquity* (Hildesheim: Gerstenberg, 1981).
Wimsatt, W.K. (ed.), *Versification: Major Language Types* (New York: Modern Language Association and New York University Press, 1972).

Supplementary Bibliography

As before the items are listed according to topic followed by unclassified entries:

§3.6 Authorship
Foster, B.R., 'On Authorship in Akkadian Literature', *AIUON* 51 (1991), pp. 17-32.

§3.7 Prose or verse
In general, see J.C. de Moor and W.G.E Watson (eds.), *Verse in Ancient Near Eastern Prose* (AOAT, 42; Kevelaer: Butzon & Bercker; Neukirchen–Vluyn: Neukircher Verlag, 1993).

Farber, W., *Schlaf, Kindchen, Schlaf! Mesopotamische Baby-Beschwörungen und Rituale* (Winona Lake, IN: Eisenbrauns, 1989), pp. 148-70.
Lichtenstein, M.H., 'Idiom, Rhetoric and the Text of Genesis 41:16', *JANESCU* 19 (1989), pp. 85-94.
Pardee, D., 'Structure and Meaning in Hebrew Poetry: The Example of Psalm 23', *Maarav* 5–6 (1990), pp. 239-80.
Renger, J., ' "Versstrukturen" als Stilmittel in den Inschriften Sargons II von Assyrien', in T. Abusch, J. Huehnergard and P. Steinkeller (eds.), *Lingering Over Words: Studies in Ancient Near Eastern Literature in Honor of William L. Moran* (HSS, 37; Atlanta: Scholars Press, 1990), pp. 425-37.

§3.8 Closure:
Meier, S.A., *Speaking of Speaking: Marking Direct Discourse in the Hebrew Bible* (VTSup, 46; Leiden: Brill, 1992), p. 235.

§§4.1-4.3
Lord, A.B., *Epic Singers and Oral Tradition* (Ithaca, NY: Cornell University Press, 1991).

§6.1 Parallelism: introduction
Berlin, A., 'Parallelism', in D.N. Freedman (ed.), *Anchor Bible Dictionary* (Garden City, NY: Doubleday, 1992), V, pp. 155-62.
Landy, F., 'In Defense of Jakobson', *JBL* 111 (1992), pp. 105-13.
Lieberman, S.J., 'Are Biblical Parallels Euclidean?', *Maarav* 8 (1992), pp. 81-94.
Zevit, Z., 'Roman Jakobson, Psycholinguistics and Biblical Poetry', *JBL* 109 (1990), pp. 385-401.

§6.6 Janus parallelism
Noegel, S.B., 'A Janus Parallelism in the Gilgamesh Flood Story', *Acta Sumerologica* 13 (1991), pp. 419-21 [on Gilg. XI 25-27].

§7.8 Hexacola
Loretz, O., 'Hexakola im Ugaritischen und Hebräischen. Zu KTU 1.3 IV 50-53 *et par.*', *UF* 21 (1989), pp. 238-40 [he rejects hexacola in Hebrew verse].

§8.2 Chiasmus and chiastic patterns
Example in Sumerian: 'Like her mouth her vulva [is sweet], Like her [vulva] her mouth [is sweet]'—Text: B. Alster, 'Sumerian Love Songs', *RA* 79 (1985), pp. 127-59, 131 rev. i lines 12-13. A significant example in Akkadian is presented by M. Dietrich, '"Ein Leben ohne Freude..." Studie über eine Weisheitskomposition aus den Gelehrtenbibliotheken von Emar und Ugarit', *UF* 24 (1992), pp. 9-29, esp. 22.

Chiasmus and sound patterns: T.P. McCreesh, *Biblical Sound and Sense: Poetic Sound Patterns in Proverbs 10–29* (JSOTSup, 128; Sheffield: JSOT Press, 1991) [mirror chiasmus: cf. Prov. 15.12 (p. 46); phonic chiasmus: Prov. 26.14 (p. 118); chiasmus: Prov. 10.12 (p. 31); 13.7 (p. 33 = root chiasmus); 18.13 (p. 32); 27.14 (p. 45); chiasmus and textual criticism: on Prov. 25.13 (pp. 71-72); on Prov. 22.7 (pp. 68-71); on Prov. 22.10 (pp. 61-63)]. Also, E. P. Sanders, 'Chiasmus and the Translation of *1Q Hodayot* VII, 26-27', *RevQ* 6 (1968), pp. 427-31.

§9.2 Assonance

Segert, S., 'Assonance and Rhyme in Hebrew Poetry', *Maarav* 8 (1992), pp. 171-79.

§9.4 Rhyme

Segert, S., 'Assonance and Rhyme in Hebrew Poetry', *Maarav* 8 (1992), pp. 171-79.

§9.6 Wordplay

P.R. Raabe, 'Deliberate Ambiguity in the Psalter', *JBL* 110 (1991), pp. 213-27. [He discusses three types: phonetic (Pss. 16.4; 59.16), lexical (Pss. 4.5; 30.13; 49.13, 21; 110.19b; Song 2.12) and grammatical. This last category is subdivided into (1) ambiguous antecedent (Pss. 12.8a; 16.4), (2) unspecified subject or object (Ps. 49.9 [subject]; 57.4 [object]), (3) portmanteau phrase (Pss. 23.6; 49.12), (4) ambiguous word order (Pss. 4.9; 11.5a) and (5) ambiguous phrase positioning (Pss. 59.14; 110.6). As examples of sustained ambiguity he discusses Pss. 7 and 110.4-7. Finally, he proposes three controls for determining the presence of ambiguity: inner-Hebrew usage, context and significance].

§10.1 Imagery

Geller, S.A., 'The Language of Imagery in Psalm 114', in T. Abusch, J. Huehnergard and P. Steinkeller (eds.), *Lingering Over Words: Studies in Ancient Near Eastern Literature in Honor of William L. Moran* (HSS, 37; Atlanta: Scholars Press, 1990), pp. 179-94.

Waldman, N.H., 'The Imagery of Clothing, Covering, and Overpowering', *JANESCU* 19 (1989), pp. 161-88.

§10.3 Metaphor

Weisberg, D.B., 'Loyalty and Death: Some Ancient Near Eastern Metaphors', *Maarav* 7 (1991), pp. 253-67.

§11.01 Repetition

Zurro, E., *Procedimientos iterativos en la poesía ugarítica y hebrea* (BibOr, 43; Rome: Biblical Institute Press; Fuentes de la ciencia biblica, 4; Valencia: Institución San Jeronimo, 1987).

—p. 278 n. 21: As E. Reiner (*Your Thwarts in Pieces, Your Mooring Rope Cut: Poetry from Babylonian and Assyria* ([Michigan: Horace H. Rackham School of Graduate Studies at the University of Michigan, 1985], p. 42) explains, the sequence 'eyes, arms, feet, heart, head, all' (*Descent of Ishtar* 69-75) is because the stripped Ishtar is 'no longer protected by crown, breastplate, bracelets, or anklets'.

§11.03 Envelope figure

Frymer-Krensky, T., '*Inclusio* in Sumerian', *RA* 79 (1985), pp. 93-94.

§11.04 (pp. 290-93)

See now M. Dietrich and O. Loretz, *'Jahwe und seine Aschera': Anthropomorphes Kultbild in Mesopotamien, Ugarit und Israel. Das biblische Bildverbot* (UBL, 9; Münster: Ugarit-Verlag, 1992), pp. 134-53, with an extensive bibliography on Psalm 82 (pp. 149-53).

§11.07 Ellipsis (gapping)

Greenstein, E.L., 'How does Parallelism Mean?', in *A Sense of Text: The Art of Language in the Study of Biblical Literature* (JQRSupplement 1982; Winona Lake, IN: Eisenbrauns, 1983), pp. 41-70.

Moor, J.C. de, 'Syntax Peculiar to Ugaritic Poetry', in de Moor and Watson (eds.), *Verse in Ancient Near Eastern Prose*, pp. 191-205, esp. 200-205.

§11.08 Irony

O'Connell, R.H., 'Isaiah XIV 4b-23: Ironic Reversal through Concentric Structure and Mythic Allusion', *VT* 38 (1988), pp. 407-18.

Unclassified

Auffret, P., '"Pourquoi dors-tu, Seigneur?" Etude structurelle du psaume 44', *JANESCU* 21 (1992), pp. 13-34.

Berlin, A., *Biblical Poetry through Medieval Jewish Eyes* (Bloomington: Indiana University Press, 1991).

—'Motif and Creativity in Biblical Poetry', *Prooftexts* 3 (1983), pp. 231-41.

Boyce, J., 'The Poetry of the Damascus Document and its Bearing on the Origin of the Qumran Sect', *RevQ* 14/4 56 (1990), pp. 615-28.

Cloete, W.T.W., 'A Guide to the Techniques of Hebrew Verse', *JNSL* 16 (1990), pp. 223-28.

Dion, P.E., *Hebrew Poetics: A Student's Guide* (Mississauga, Ont.: Benben Publications, 1988).

Dorsey, D.A., 'Literary Architecture and Aural Structuring Techniques in Amos', *Bib* 73 (1992), pp. 305-30.

Eksell, K., 'Remarks on Poetical Functions of the Genitive in some Northwestern Semitic Poetry', *Orientalia Suecana* 38–39 (1989–90), pp. 21-30.

Elman, Y., 'Authoritative Oral Tradition in Neo-Assyrian Scribal Circles', *JANESCU* 7 (1975), pp. 19-32.

Giese, R.L., 'Strophic Hebrew Verse as Free Verse', *JSOT* 61 (1994), pp. 29-38.

Greenstein, E.L., 'Aspects of Biblical Poetry', *Jewish Book Annual* 44 (1986–87), pp. 33-42.

—'How does Parallelism Mean?', in *A Sense of Text: The Art of Language in the*

Study of Biblical Literature (JQRSupplement 1982; Winona Lake, IN: Eisenbrauns 1983), pp. 41-70.

Hens-Piazza, G, 'Repetition and Rhetoric in Canaanite Epic. A Close Reading of KTU 1.14 III 20-49', *UF* 24 (1992), pp. 103-12.

Kuntz, J.K., 'Recent Perspectives on Biblical Poetry', *Religious Studies Review* 19 (1993), pp. 321-27.

Lescow, T., *Das Stufenschema: Untersuchungen zur Struktur alttestamentlicher Texte* (BZAW, 211; Berlin: de Gruyter, 1992).

Niehoff, M., 'Did Biblical Characters Talk to Themselves? Narrative Modes of Representing Inner Speech in Early Biblical Fiction', *JBL* 111 (1992), pp. 577-95.

O'Connor, M., '"Unanswerable the Knack of Tongues": The Linguistic Study of Verse', in L.K. Obler and L. Menn (eds.), *Exceptional Language and Linguistics* (New York: Academic Press, 1982), pp. 143-68.

—'The Pseudo-Sorites in Hebrew Verse', in E.W. Conrad and E.G. Newing (eds.), *Perspectives on Language and Text: Essays and Poems in Honor of Francis I. Andersen's Sixtieth Birthday July 28, 1985* (Winona Lake: Eisenbrauns, 1987), pp. 239-53.

Parunak, H. Van Dyke, 'Transitional Techniques in the Bible', *JBL* 102 (1983), pp. 525-48.

Petersen, D.L., and K.H. Richards, *Interpreting Hebrew Poetry* (Minneapolis: Fortress Press, 1992).

Schiffrin, D., 'Tense Variation in Narrative', *Language* 57 (1981), pp. 45-62.

Skehan, P.W., and A.A. Di Lella, *The Wisdom of Ben Sira* (AB, 39; Garden City, NY: Doubleday, 1987), pp. 63-74 ['The Poetry of Ben Sira': several MSS written stichometrically; assonance, alliteration and rhyme; chiastic patterns; inclusio; twenty-two- and twenty-three-line poems].

Snyman, S.D., 'Antitheses in the Book of Malachi', *JNSL* 16 (1990), pp. 179-97.

Tournay, R.J., *Quand Dieu parle aux hommes le langage de l'amour: Etudes sur le Cantique des Cantiques* (Paris: Gabalda, 1982).

Tsumura, D.T., 'Literary Insertion (AXB) Pattern in Biblical Hebrew', in *Proceedings of the Eighth World Congress Jewish Studies, Jerusalem, August 16-21, 1981 Division A: The Period of the Bible* (Jerusalem: Magnes, 1982), pp. 1-6.

—'Hab 2 2 in the Light of Akkadian Legal Practice', *ZAW* 94 (1982), pp. 294-95.

Wahl, H.-M., 'Psalm 67. Erwägungen zu Aufbau, Gattung und Datierung', *Bib* 73 (1992), pp. 240-47.

Watson, W.G.E., 'Introduction to Speech in Ugaritic and Hebrew', in G.J. Brooke, A.H.W. Curtis and J.F. Healey (eds.), *Ugarit and the Bible: Proceedings of the International Symposium on Ugarit and the Bible Manchester, September 1992* (Ugaritisch-Biblische Literatur, 11; Münster: Ugarit-Verlag, 1994), pp. 383-93.

Williams, G.R., 'Parallelism in the Hodayot from Qumran' (Annenberg Research Institute, formerly Dropsie College 1990/1991; Ann Arbor: UMI, 1992).

Zevit, Z., 'Cognitive Theory and the Memorability of Hebrew Poetry', *Maarav* 8 (1992), pp. 199-212.

Corrections

In addition to remarks made by reviewers, the following corrections are required:

p. 51 line 15 Exod. 14.3 (not 14.8); line 33 Jer. 11.21 Job 3.1ff.
p. 53 line 32 Gen. 1.5 (not 5.1) 1 Kgs 5.11.
p. 109 line 8 metre is unpredictable in Hebrew poetry—Revell, *VT* 31 (1981), p. 186 n. 1.
p. 142 n. 82 cf. Deut. 25.18.
p. 156 line 11 additional examples of staircase parallelism: Ezek. 2.6 and 1 Chron. 17.16 (// 2 Sam. 7.18).
p. 158 line 26. Add Jer. 2.19 and Job 1.18.
p. 278 line 15 on 1.96: See now G. del Olmo Lete, 'Un conjuro ugarítico contra el "mal ojo" (KTU 1.96)', *Anuari de filologia* 15 (1992), pp. 7-16.
p. 294 (table): *'sp* occurs six times (not five), *p* five times (not four), *'r* eight times (not five) [G.J. Norton, 'The Day of Yahweh in the Book of Zephaniah' (dissertation, University College, Dublin 1986), p. 144 n. 14; reference courtesy John Healey].
p. 313 line 26 (Oxymoron) Add Prov. 15.32; 27.14.
p. 331 line 29: additional examples of the break-up of a phrase: Ps. 39.13 (cf. Gen. 23.4); Isa. 40.28-31 (cf. Deut. 25.18).
p. 384 n. 2: the numbers are cardinal not ordinal:

'ONE	may release, Shamash the Warrior;
TWO	may release, Sin and Nergal;
THREE	may release, Ishtar, Ba'u and Anunitum;
FOUR	may release, Anum, Enlil, Ea and Nintu;
FIVE	may release, Adad, Ninurta, Zababa, Tishpak and Ningirsu;
SIX	may release, Urash, Marduk, Asari, Asalluhi, GAL and Tutu;
SEVEN	may release, the Seven (= Sebetti), the great gods;'

Corrections to Index
p. 401 col. 2 line 18 reflexive congruence (not congrvence).
p. 403 last line under 'staircase parallelism'—add 150-156.
p. 443 col. 2 line 2 *sb // nsb*: p. 280 n. 30
p. 456 line 12 for *JSNL* read *JNSL*

JOURNAL FOR THE STUDY OF THE OLD TESTAMENT

Supplement Series

8 GENESIS 1–11:
STUDIES IN STRUCTURE AND THEME
P.D. Miller
9 YAHWEH AS PROSECUTOR AND JUDGE:
AN INVESTIGATION OF THE PROPHETIC LAWSUIT (*RIB* PATTERN)
K. Nielsen
10 THE THEME OF THE PENTATEUCH
David J.A. Clines
11 STUDIA BIBLICA 1978 I:
PAPERS ON OLD TESTAMENT AND RELATED THEMES
Edited by E.A. Livingstone
13 ISAIAH AND THE DELIVERANCE OF JERUSALEM:
A STUDY OF THE INTERPRETATION OF PROPHECY
IN THE OLD TESTAMENT
R.E. Clements
14 THE FATE OF KING SAUL:
AN INTERPRETATION OF A BIBLICAL STORY
D.M. Gunn
15 THE DEUTERONOMISTIC HISTORY
Martin Noth
16 PROPHECY AND ETHICS:
ISAIAH AND THE ETHICAL TRADITION OF ISRAEL
Eryl W. Davies
17 THE ROLES OF ISRAEL'S PROPHETS
David L. Petersen
18 THE DOUBLE REDACTION OF THE DEUTERONOMISTIC HISTORY
Richard D. Nelson
19 ART AND MEANING:
RHETORIC IN BIBLICAL LITERATURE
Edited by David J.A. Clines, David M. Gunn & Alan J. Hauser
20 THE PSALMS OF THE SONS OF KORAH
Michael D. Goulder
21 COLOUR TERMS IN THE OLD TESTAMENT
Athalya Brenner
22 AT THE MOUNTAIN OF GOD:
STORY AND THEOLOGY IN EXODUS 32–34
R.W.L. Moberly
23 THE GLORY OF ISRAEL:
THE THEOLOGY AND PROVENIENCE OF THE ISAIAH TARGUM
Bruce D. Chilton

24 MIDIAN, MOAB AND EDOM:
THE HISTORY AND ARCHAEOLOGY OF LATE BRONZE AND IRON AGE JORDAN AND NORTH-WEST ARABIA
Edited by John F.A. Sawyer & David J.A. Clines

25 THE DAMASCUS COVENANT:
AN INTERPRETATION OF THE 'DAMASCUS DOCUMENT'
Philip R. Davies

26 CLASSICAL HEBREW POETRY:
A GUIDE TO ITS TECHNIQUES
Wilfred G.E. Watson

27 PSALMODY AND PROPHECY
W.H. Bellinger, Jr

28 HOSEA:
AN ISRAELITE PROPHET IN JUDEAN PERSPECTIVE
Grace I. Emmerson

29 EXEGESIS AT QUMRAN:
4QFLORILEGIUM IN ITS JEWISH CONTEXT
George J. Brooke

30 THE ESTHER SCROLL:
THE STORY OF THE STORY
David J.A. Clines

31 IN THE SHELTER OF ELYON:
ESSAYS IN HONOR OF G.W. AHLSTRÖM
Edited by W. Boyd Barrick & John R. Spencer

32 THE PROPHETIC PERSONA:
JEREMIAH AND THE LANGUAGE OF THE SELF
Timothy Polk

33 LAW AND THEOLOGY IN DEUTERONOMY
J.G. McConville

34 THE TEMPLE SCROLL:
AN INTRODUCTION, TRANSLATION & COMMENTARY
Johann Maier

35 SAGA, LEGEND, TALE, NOVELLA, FABLE:
NARRATIVE FORMS IN OLD TESTAMENT LITERATURE
Edited by George W. Coats

36 THE SONG OF FOURTEEN SONGS
Michael D. Goulder

37 UNDERSTANDING THE WORD:
ESSAYS IN HONOR OF BERNHARD W. ANDERSON
Edited by James T. Butler, Edgar W. Conrad & Ben C. Ollenburger

38 SLEEP, DIVINE AND HUMAN, IN THE OLD TESTAMENT
Thomas H. McAlpine

39 THE SENSE OF BIBLICAL NARRATIVE II:
STRUCTURAL ANALYSES IN THE HEBREW BIBLE
David Jobling

40 DIRECTIONS IN BIBLICAL HEBREW POETRY
Edited by Elaine R. Follis

41 ZION, THE CITY OF THE GREAT KING:
A THEOLOGICAL SYMBOL OF THE JERUSALEM CULT
Ben C. Ollenburger

42 A WORD IN SEASON:
ESSAYS IN HONOUR OF WILLIAM MCKANE
Edited by James D. Martin & Philip R. Davies

43 THE CULT OF MOLEK:
A REASSESSMENT
G.C. Heider

44 THE IDENTITY OF THE INDIVIDUAL IN THE PSALMS
Steven J.L. Croft

45 THE CONFESSIONS OF JEREMIAH IN CONTEXT:
SCENES OF PROPHETIC DRAMA
A.R. Diamond

46 THE BOOK OF JUDGES:
AN INTEGRATED READING
Barry G. Webb

47 THE GREEK TEXT OF JEREMIAH:
A REVISED HYPOTHESIS
Sven Soderlund

48 TEXT AND CONTEXT:
OLD TESTAMENT AND SEMITIC STUDIES FOR F.C. FENSHAM
Edited by W. Claassen

49 THEOPHORIC PERSONAL NAMES IN ANCIENT HEBREW:
A COMPARATIVE STUDY
Jeaneane D. Fowler

50 THE CHRONICLER'S HISTORY
Martin Noth
Translated by H.G.M. Williamson with an Introduction

51 DIVINE INITIATIVE AND HUMAN RESPONSE IN EZEKIEL
Paul Joyce

52 THE CONFLICT OF FAITH AND EXPERIENCE IN THE PSALMS:
A FORM-CRITICAL AND THEOLOGICAL STUDY
Craig C. Broyles

53 THE MAKING OF THE PENTATEUCH:
A METHODOLOGICAL STUDY
R.N. Whybray

54 FROM REPENTANCE TO REDEMPTION:
JEREMIAH'S THOUGHT IN TRANSITION
Jeremiah Unterman

55 THE ORIGIN TRADITION OF ANCIENT ISRAEL:
1. THE LITERARY FORMATION OF GENESIS AND EXODUS 1–23
T.L. Thompson

56 THE PURIFICATION OFFERING IN THE PRIESTLY LITERATURE: ITS MEANING AND FUNCTION
N. Kiuchi
57 MOSES: HEROIC MAN, MAN OF GOD
George W. Coats
58 THE LISTENING HEART: ESSAYS IN WISDOM AND THE PSALMS IN HONOR OF ROLAND E. MURPHY, O. CARM.
Edited by Kenneth G. Hoglund, Elizabeth F. Huwiler, Jonathan T. Glass & Roger W. Lee
59 CREATIVE BIBLICAL EXEGESIS: CHRISTIAN AND JEWISH HERMENEUTICS THROUGH THE CENTURIES
Edited by Benjamin Uffenheimer & Henning Graf Reventlow
60 HER PRICE IS BEYOND RUBIES: THE JEWISH WOMAN IN GRAECO-ROMAN PALESTINE
Léonie J. Archer
61 FROM CHAOS TO RESTORATION: AN INTEGRATIVE READING OF ISAIAH 24–27
Dan G. Johnson
62 THE OLD TESTAMENT AND FOLKLORE STUDY
Patricia G. Kirkpatrick
63 SHILOH: A BIBLICAL CITY IN TRADITION AND HISTORY
Donald G. Schley
64 TO SEE AND NOT PERCEIVE: ISAIAH 6.9-10 IN EARLY JEWISH AND CHRISTIAN INTERPRETATION
Craig A. Evans
65 THERE IS HOPE FOR A TREE: THE TREE AS METAPHOR IN ISAIAH
Kirsten Nielsen
66 SECRETS OF THE TIMES: MYTH AND HISTORY IN BIBLICAL CHRONOLOGY
Jeremy Hughes
67 ASCRIBE TO THE LORD: BIBLICAL AND OTHER STUDIES IN MEMORY OF PETER C. CRAIGIE
Edited by Lyle Eslinger & Glen Taylor
68 THE TRIUMPH OF IRONY IN THE BOOK OF JUDGES
Lillian R. Klein
69 ZEPHANIAH, A PROPHETIC DRAMA
Paul R. House
70 NARRATIVE ART IN THE BIBLE
Shimon Bar-Efrat
71 QOHELET AND HIS CONTRADICTIONS
Michael V. Fox

88 THE PERSUASIVE APPEAL OF THE CHRONICLER: A RHETORICAL ANALYSIS
Rodney K. Duke

89 THE PROBLEM OF THE PROCESS OF TRANSMISSION IN THE PENTATEUCH
Rolf Rendtorff
Translated by John J. Scullion

90 BIBLICAL HEBREW IN TRANSITION: THE LANGUAGE OF THE BOOK OF EZEKIEL
Mark F. Rooker

91 THE IDEOLOGY OF RITUAL: SPACE, TIME AND STATUS IN THE PRIESTLY THEOLOGY
Frank H. Gorman, Jr

92 ON HUMOUR AND THE COMIC IN THE HEBREW BIBLE
Edited by Yehuda T. Radday & Athalya Brenner

93 JOSHUA 24 AS POETIC NARRATIVE
William T. Koopmans

94 WHAT DOES EVE DO TO HELP? AND OTHER READERLY QUESTIONS TO THE OLD TESTAMENT
David J.A. Clines

95 GOD SAVES: LESSONS FROM THE ELISHA STORIES
Rick Dale Moore

96 ANNOUNCEMENTS OF PLOT IN GENESIS
Laurence A. Turner

97 THE UNITY OF THE TWELVE
Paul R. House

98 ANCIENT CONQUEST ACCOUNTS: A STUDY IN ANCIENT NEAR EASTERN AND BIBLICAL HISTORY WRITING
K. Lawson Younger, Jr

99 WEALTH AND POVERTY IN THE BOOK OF PROVERBS
R.N. Whybray

100 A TRIBUTE TO GEZA VERMES: ESSAYS ON JEWISH AND CHRISTIAN LITERATURE AND HISTORY
Edited by Philip R. Davies & Richard T. White

101 THE CHRONICLER IN HIS AGE
Peter R. Ackroyd

102 THE PRAYERS OF DAVID (PSALMS 51–72): STUDIES IN THE PSALTER, II
Michael Goulder

103 THE SOCIOLOGY OF POTTERY IN ANCIENT PALESTINE: THE CERAMIC INDUSTRY AND THE DIFFUSION OF CERAMIC STYLE IN THE BRONZE AND IRON AGES
Bryant G. Wood

104 PSALM STRUCTURES:
A STUDY OF PSALMS WITH REFRAINS
Paul R. Raabe

105 RE-ESTABLISHING JUSTICE
Pietro Bovati

106 GRADED HOLINESS:
A KEY TO THE PRIESTLY CONCEPTION OF THE WORLD
Philip Jenson

107 THE ALIEN IN ISRAELITE LAW
Christiana van Houten

108 THE FORGING OF ISRAEL:
IRON TECHNOLOGY, SYMBOLISM AND TRADITION IN ANCIENT SOCIETY
Paula M. McNutt

109 SCRIBES AND SCHOOLS IN MONARCHIC JUDAH:
A SOCIO-ARCHAEOLOGICAL APPROACH
David Jamieson-Drake

110 THE CANAANITES AND THEIR LAND:
THE TRADITION OF THE CANAANITES
Niels Peter Lemche

111 YAHWEH AND THE SUN:
THE BIBLICAL AND ARCHAEOLOGICAL EVIDENCE
J. Glen Taylor

112 WISDOM IN REVOLT:
METAPHORICAL THEOLOGY IN THE BOOK OF JOB
Leo G. Perdue

113 PROPERTY AND THE FAMILY IN BIBLICAL LAW
Raymond Westbrook

114 A TRADITIONAL QUEST:
ESSAYS IN HONOUR OF LOUIS JACOBS
Edited by Dan Cohn-Sherbok

115 I HAVE BUILT YOU AN EXALTED HOUSE:
TEMPLE BUILDING IN THE BIBLE IN LIGHT OF MESOPOTAMIAN AND NORTHWEST SEMITIC WRITINGS
Victor Hurowitz

116 NARRATIVE AND NOVELLA IN SAMUEL:
STUDIES BY HUGO GRESSMANN AND OTHER SCHOLARS 1906–1923
Translated by David E. Orton
Edited by David M. Gunn

117 SECOND TEMPLE STUDIES:
1. PERSIAN PERIOD
Edited by Philip R. Davies

118 SEEING AND HEARING GOD WITH THE PSALMS:
THE PROPHETIC LITURGY FROM THE SECOND TEMPLE IN JERUSALEM
Raymond Jacques Tournay
Translated by J. Edward Crowley

119 TELLING QUEEN MICHAL'S STORY:
AN EXPERIMENT IN COMPARATIVE INTERPRETATION
Edited by David J.A. Clines & Tamara C. Eskenazi

120 THE REFORMING KINGS:
CULT AND SOCIETY IN FIRST TEMPLE JUDAH
Richard H. Lowery

121 KING SAUL IN THE HISTORIOGRAPHY OF JUDAH
Diana Vikander Edelman

122 IMAGES OF EMPIRE
Edited by Loveday Alexander

123 JUDAHITE BURIAL PRACTICES AND BELIEFS ABOUT THE DEAD
Elizabeth Bloch-Smith

124 LAW AND IDEOLOGY IN MONARCHIC ISRAEL
Edited by Baruch Halpern & Deborah W. Hobson

125 PRIESTHOOD AND CULT IN ANCIENT ISRAEL
Edited by Gary A. Anderson & Saul M. Olyan

126 W.M.L.DE WETTE, FOUNDER OF MODERN BIBLICAL CRITICISM:
AN INTELLECTUAL BIOGRAPHY
John W. Rogerson

127 THE FABRIC OF HISTORY:
TEXT, ARTIFACT AND ISRAEL'S PAST
Edited by Diana Vikander Edelman

128 BIBLICAL SOUND AND SENSE:
POETIC SOUND PATTERNS IN PROVERBS 10–29
Thomas P. McCreesh

129 THE ARAMAIC OF DANIEL IN THE LIGHT OF OLD ARAMAIC
Zdravko Stefanovic

130 STRUCTURE AND THE BOOK OF ZECHARIAH
Michael Butterworth

131 FORMS OF DEFORMITY:
A MOTIF-INDEX OF ABNORMALITIES, DEFORMITIES AND DISABILITIES
IN TRADITIONAL JEWISH LITERATURE
Lynn Holden

132 CONTEXTS FOR AMOS:
PROPHETIC POETICS IN LATIN AMERICAN PERSPECTIVE
Mark Daniel Carroll R.

133 THE FORSAKEN FIRSTBORN:
A STUDY OF A RECURRENT MOTIF IN THE PATRIARCHAL NARRATIVES
Roger Syrén

135 ISRAEL IN EGYPT:
A READING OF EXODUS 1–2
G.F. Davies

136 A WALK THROUGH THE GARDEN:
BIBLICAL, ICONOGRAPHICAL AND LITERARY IMAGES OF EDEN
Edited by P. Morris & D. Sawyer

137 JUSTICE AND RIGHTEOUSNESS:
BIBLICAL THEMES AND THEIR INFLUENCE
Edited by H. Graf Reventlow & Y. Hoffman

138 TEXT AS PRETEXT:
ESSAYS IN HONOUR OF ROBERT DAVIDSON
Edited by R.P. Carroll

139 PSALM AND STORY:
INSET HYMNS IN HEBREW NARRATIVE
J.W. Watts

140 PURITY AND MONOTHEISM:
CLEAN AND UNCLEAN ANIMALS IN BIBLICAL LAW
Walter Houston

141 DEBT SLAVERY IN ISRAEL AND THE ANCIENT NEAR EAST
Gregory C. Chirichigno

142 DIVINATION IN ANCIENT ISRAEL AND ITS NEAR EASTERN ENVIRONMENT:
A SOCIO-HISTORICAL INVESTIGATION
Frederick H. Cryer

143 THE NEW LITERARY CRITICISM AND THE HEBREW BIBLE
David J.A. Clines & J. Cheryl Exum

144 LANGUAGE, IMAGERY AND STRUCTURE IN THE PROPHETIC WRITINGS
Philip R. Davies & David J.A. Clines

145 THE SPEECHES OF MICAH:
A RHETORICAL-HISTORICAL ANALYSIS
Charles S. Shaw

146 THE HISTORY OF ANCIENT PALESTINE FROM THE PALAEOLITHIC PERIOD
TO ALEXANDER'S CONQUEST
Gösta W. Ahlström

147 VOWS IN THE HEBREW BIBLE AND THE ANCIENT NEAR EAST
Tony W. Cartledge

148 IN SEARCH OF 'ANCIENT ISRAEL'
Philip R. Davies

149 PRIESTS, PROPHETS AND SCRIBES: ESSAYS ON THE FORMATION
AND HERITAGE OF SECOND TEMPLE JUDAISM IN HONOUR OF
JOSEPH BLENKINSOPP
Eugene Ulrich, John W. Wright, Robert P. Carroll & Philip R. Davies (eds)

150 TRADITION AND INNOVATION IN HAGGAI AND ZECHARIAH 1–8
Janet A. Tollington

151 THE CITIZEN-TEMPLE COMMUNITY
J.P. Weinberg

152 UNDERSTANDING POETS AND PROPHETS: ESSAYS IN HONOUR OF
GEORGE WISHART ANDERSON
A.G. Auld

153 THE PSALMS AND THEIR READERS: INTERPRETIVE STRATEGIES
FOR PSALM 18
D.K. Berry

154 MINḤAH LE-NAḤUM: BIBLICAL AND OTHER STUDIES PRESENTED TO NAHUM M. SARNA IN HONOUR OF HIS 70TH BIRTHDAY
M. Brettler and M. Fishbane (eds)

155 LAND TENURE AND THE BIBLICAL JUBILEE: DISCOVERING A MORAL WORLD-VIEW THROUGH THE SOCIOLOGY OF KNOWLEDGE
Jeffrey A. Fager

156 THE LORD'S SONG: THE BASIS, FUNCTION AND SIGNIFICANCE OF CHORAL MUSIC IN CHRONICLES
J.E. Kleinig

157 THE WORD *HESED* IN THE HEBREW BIBLE
G.R. Clark

158 IN THE WILDERNESS
Mary Douglas

159 THE SHAPE AND SHAPING OF THE PSALTER
J. Clinton McCann

160 KING AND CULTUS IN CHRONICLES: WORSHIP AND THE REINTERPRETATION OF HISTORY
William Riley

161 THE MOSES TRADITION
George W. Coats

162 OF PROPHET'S VISIONS AND THE WISDOM OF SAGES: ESSAYS IN HONOUR OF R. NORMAN WHYBRAY ON HIS SEVENTIETH BIRTHDAY
Heather A. McKay and David J.A. Clines

163 FRAGMENTED WOMEN: FEMINIST (SUB)VERSIONS OF BIBLICAL NARRATIVES
J. Cheryl Exum

164 HOUSE OF GOD OR HOUSE OF DAVID: THE RHETORIC OF 2 SAMUEL 7
Lyle Eslinger

166 THE ARAMAIC BIBLE: TARGUMS IN THEIR HISTORICAL CONTEXT
Edited by D.R.G. Beattie & M.J. McNamara

167 SECOND ZECHARIAH AND THE DEUTERONOMIC SCHOOL
Raymond F. Person

168 THE COMPOSITION OF THE BOOK OF PROVERBS
R.N. Whybray

169 EDOM, ISRAEL'S BROTHER AND ANTAGONIST: THE ROLE OF EDOM IN BIBLICAL PROPHECY AND STORY
Bert Dicou

170 TRADITIONAL TECHNIQUES IN CLASSICAL HEBREW VERSE
Wilfred G.E. Watson